"A monumental achievement!
*The Story of Christian Theology* is eminently readable,
a welcome and helpful guide to the history
of Christian theology."

**DONALD G. BLOESCH,**
*Professor of Theology Emeritus,*
*Dubuque Theological Seminary*

"Roger Olson's *The Story of Christian Theology*
is a real page-turner. Here is no bloodless
and passionless history of ideas.
Olson's *Story* pulsates with real people
living in real time who pray, study, argue, struggle and even
occasionally beat each other up over what and how to believe.
Olson is convinced that beliefs matter and that the story
of Christian theology is not yet finished.
Without much effort readers can find
themselves in this story too."

**TIMOTHY WEBER,**
*Dean and Professor of Church History,*
*Northern Baptist Theological Seminary*

"A lucid and fair-minded account of highlights
in the history of Christian thought. . . .
An adventure in theological ideas."

**GABRIEL FACKRE,**
*author of* The Christian Story *and* The Doctrine of Revelation

"Historical theology has never been known for winning
popularity contests in Christian classrooms.
It is too dated and too abstract. But Roger Olson is
out to change that common perception.
He has taken this aging beauty, dressed her up in
a stylish story-telling outfit and trained her
to speak to a contemporary audience.
For my students Olson's *The Story of Christian Theology*
has just moved to the top of my
you've-got-to-meet-her list."

**BRUCE L. SHELLEY,**
*Professor of Church History,*
*Denver Seminary*

"An ideal history of Christian theology lies beyond the realm of human possibility, but all church members, along with pastors and students, will surely profit from Professor Olson's new presentation. In reasonably concise form, it uses judiciously selected incidents and movements to tell the story as a vast array of theologians, monks, ecclesiastics and teachers wrestled with the divine truths revealed in the life, death and resurrection of Jesus Christ. This historical survey offers a good foundation, not only for Christian scholarship but also for authentic Christian witness and ministry."

**GEOFFREY W. BROMILEY,**
*author of* Historical Theology

"In this clear and eminently readable text, Roger Olson not only tells the story of Christian theology in all its richness and diversity but also shows why the questions faced were important then and remain so for us today. Theology is shown to be about salvation and hence an ultimately practical endeavor. This is a book that deserves a wide readership in both the classroom and the church."

**HENRY H. KNIGHT III,**
*Assistant Professor of Evangelism, Saint Paul School of Theology*

"Congratulations to Roger Olson for giving us a masterful survey of the main contours of Christian theology from the second century to the present day. This work is written with admirable clarity, capturing the major figures and movements with accurate descriptions as well as with an eye toward the effects of their views for later periods and contemporary times.

Beginning as well as more advanced students can turn here with confidence to gain a sure sense of how the story of Christian theology has developed, what its primary issues have been and how the whole Christian church has been affected by what its theologians have believed, argued about and—unfortunately—at times have literally fought over. This is a fine achievement, a superb resource grounded in solid scholarship. Here is a volume that will be eminently useful for many years to come."

**DONALD K. MCKIM,**
*Academic Dean and Professor of Theology, Memphis Theological Seminary*

# The STORY *of* CHRISTIAN THEOLOGY

## *Twenty Centuries of Tradition & Reform*

ROGER E. OLSON

An imprint of InterVarsity Press
Downers Grove, Illinois

*InterVarsity Press*
*P.O. Box 1400, Downers Grove, IL 60515-1426*
*World Wide Web: www.ivpress.com*
*E-mail: email@ivpress.com*



*InterVarsity Press® is the book-publishing division of InterVarsity Christian Fellowship/USA®, a movement of students and faculty active on campus at hundreds of universities, colleges and schools of nursing in the United States of America, and a member movement of the International Fellowship of Evangelical Students. For information about local and regional activities, write Public Relations Dept., InterVarsity Christian Fellowship/USA, 6400 Schroeder Rd., P.O. Box 7895, Madison, WI 53707-7895, or visit the IVCF website at <www.intervarsity.org>.*



*Cover photograph: Stock Photos, Albrecht Dürer, Alte Pinakothek, Munich. Oil on wood Renaissance/Glow Images.*

*ISBN 978-0-8308-1505-0*

*Printed in the United States of America* ♾

*As a member of the Green Press Initiative, InterVarsity Press is committed to protecting the environment and to the responsible use of natural resources. To learn more, visit greenpressinitiative.org.*

**Library of Congress Cataloging-in-Publication Data**

*Olson, Roger E.*
*The story of Christian theology : twenty centuries of tradition & reform / Roger E. Olson.*
*p. cm.*
*Includes bibliographical references and index.*
*ISBN 0-8308-1505-8 (pbk. : alk. paper)*
*1. Theology, Doctrinal—History. I. Title.*
*BT21.2.057 1999*
*230'.09—dc21* *99-18734*
*CIP*

**P** 27 26 25 24 23 22 21 20 19 18 17
**Y** 25 24 23 22 21 20 19 18 17 16

*Dedicated to*
*Niels C. Nielsen,*
*my* Doktorvater
*and friend*

# ABBREVIATIONS
# & GENERAL INFORMATION FOR READERS

In the early chapters of this book frequent use is made of writings of the early church fathers as contained in the multi-volume sets *The Ante-Nicene Fathers: Translations of the Writings of the Fathers Down to A.D. 325*, ed. Alexander Roberts and James Donaldson. 10 vols. Grand Rapids, Mich.: Eerdmans, 1988; *A Select Library of the Nicene and Post-Nicene Fathers of the Christian Church*, ed., Philip Schaff. 14 vols. Grand Rapids, Mich.: Eerdmans, 1984; and *A Select Library of Nicene and Post-Nicene Fathers of the Christian Church*, second series, ed., Philip Schaff and Henry Wace. 14 vols. Grand Rapids, Mich.: Eerdmans, 1984. (Identical multi-volume sets are also published by Hendrickson Publishing of Peabody, Mass.) These sets are generally available in seminary and university libraries.

Endnote documentation in this volume will refer to these sets using initials and volume numbers. *ANF* refers to the *Ante-Nicene Fathers* series, *NPNF* refers to the *Nicene and Post-Nicene Fathers of the Christian Church* series, and the *Nicene and Post-Nicene Fathers of the Christian Church*, second series will be designated by *NPNF2*. These abbreviations will be followed by the volume number.

All dates throughout this book are A.D. unless designated otherwise by use of B.C. In most cases a person's years of birth and death are shown in parentheses immediately after *the first mention* of his or her name and not again. The years shown in parentheses after the names of rulers and popes indicate their reigns rather than their lifetimes. Technical theological and philosophical terms are usually defined in the context where they first appear. Use the index to find that first use and definition of a seemingly obscure term.

# PREFACE

People live from the stories that shape their identities. Those of us who call ourselves Christians are shaped by the Christian story. The Christian story, however, includes more than just the biblical narrative. That narrative and the individual stories, psalms, letters and other pieces of literature that go together to communicate it have a certain primacy for most Christians. It is our metanarrative—the overarching story of God's path with his people in creation and redemption. Christians are people who find their identities in that story and seek to live by the vision of reality it expresses. Unfortunately, too many Christians are almost completely ignorant of the continuing secondary narrative of God's work with his people—the body of Christ—after the biblical narrative ends. This book is an attempt to fill in the gap that exists in many Christians' awareness of that story. That gap begins with the end of the New Testament and the conclusion of the lives and ministries of the apostles and goes up to contemporary Christianity. What has God been doing for two thousand years to lead his people into understanding of the truth? Theology is just that—faith seeking understanding of God's truth.

Faith seeking understanding: for two thousand years Christians have been wrestling with that task and seeking to fulfill it. The narrative of that search for the truth within the church is virtually unknown to many contemporary Christians even though their own personal stories as believers in Jesus Christ are deeply affected by it. Our situation is like that of people who do not know their ancestry—where their family came from or who they were. Only the situation is more serious than that. It is more like the situation of people who wish to be a good citizens of a nation but know little or nothing of its history, including its founding, its wars, its heroes, its principles and its leaders.

Living as fulfilled and functioning followers of Jesus Christ is similar to being good citizens of a nation. It requires knowing the stories of the people who have sought to follow Christ and be his disciples through many different cultures and epochs of history. By filling in at least one part of that story for readers—the story of Christian beliefs—I hope this book will contribute to their Christian discipleship as well as to their self-understanding. I also hope and pray that it will strengthen the universal church of Jesus Christ, which so desperately needs to recover its sense of belonging to the great story of God's work with his people over hundreds of years.

The idea of this book grew out of the course "Church Fathers and Reformers: The Story of Christian Theology," which I have taught at Bethel College (St. Paul, Minnesota) for fifteen years. I found many excellent books about the history of Christian thought, but none quite suited me or my students. We made do with what we could find, but we always felt the need for something different. In conversations with friends, colleagues and Rodney Clapp, then senior editor of InterVarsity Press, the general idea and outline for this book developed and eventually came to fruition.

To a large extent, the chapters are based on lectures I have given many times, but I added a great deal of research to them before and during my sabbatical in the fall of 1997, so graciously provided by the trustees of Bethel College. I would like to thank my friend and coauthor Stanley J. Grenz for his encouragement and advice as I conceived the book and began working on it. I also offer my heartfelt appreciation to my editor, Rodney Clapp, who gave me great freedom as well as support and advice as I began writing. The Bethel College Alumni Association provided a generous grant for purchase of the entire set of writings of the church fathers that was invaluable in my research for and writing of the first several chapters. I thank the association for its support. My dear wife, Becky, and daughters, Amanda and Sonja, offered me their love and understanding throughout the months that I almost literally chained myself to my home office desk and worked at my word processor. They gave me space when I needed it and encouragement to keep going when I needed that.

Above all I would like to thank the man who nurtured me through my years of doctoral study at Rice University in Houston, Texas: my adviser and the chairman of the Religious Studies Department, Dr. Niels C. Nielsen. Even after my graduation and his retirement, he has remained my mentor, model and friend, and I look up to him as to a father. He is without question the dearest and most important man in my life, and he is largely responsible for whatever I have accomplished that is good and positive as a Christian scholar.

# INTRODUCTION
# Christian Theology as Story

While a history is perceived to be as dry as dust by many modern readers, a story is always eagerly welcomed and greeted with interest. And yet history is made up of stories. *Story* in this sense does not mean fiction or fable but "narrative." The telling of history is the retelling of stories—narratives that recount (hopefully, as accurately as possible) the events, movements, ideas and lives of people who have shaped cultures, religions and nations.

The history of Christian theology can and should be told as a story. It is full of complex plots, exciting events, interesting people and fascinating ideas. This book is an attempt to tell that story well, doing justice to each of its subplots.

One thread runs throughout the story of Christian theology and holds the many stories together as a single great narrative of the development of Christian thought. That thread is the common concern all Christian theologians (whether professional or lay) have had with salvation—God's redemptive activity in forgiving and transforming sinful humans. Certainly other concerns come into play throughout the story, but the concern for understanding and properly explaining salvation seems to underlie most others. A modern historian of theology has rightly noted that "in the case of a theologian the problems of soteriology [doctrine of salvation] are usually found to be the basis from which he built up his other doctrinal views."[1] Thus the story of Christian theology is the story of Christian reflection on salvation. Inevitably it also involves reflection on the nature of God and God's self-revelation, on the person of Jesus Christ, and on many, many other beliefs connected with salvation. But at bottom it is all about salvation—what it is, how it happens and the roles God and humans play in bringing it about.

This concern with salvation was especially evident in the formative and reformative stages of Christian doctrinal development. The great debates over proper Christian belief about God, Jesus Christ and sin and grace that consumed the attention of the early church fathers from approximately 300 to 500 were largely about guarding and protecting the gospel of salvation. The divisions that took place within Christendom and its theology during the sixteenth century and that led to both Protestant and Catholic reformations in Europe were also largely due to differing interpretations of the gospel. At other times the issue of salvation, what it entails and how best to guard and protect it faded into the background as church leaders and theologians debated other matters and struggled to find answers to other questions. Even at these times, however, one can detect the echo of concern with salvation reverberating through the theological reflections and controversies. It would not be fair to impose a rigid theme of "concern with salvation" on every theologian and epoch of the story of theology, so at times that theme will be a prominent feature of this narrative and at other times it will be virtually invisible.

But what about theology? As with history, many modern readers are conditioned to assume that it also must be dry, dull, impractical and far removed from normal, everyday living—even from Christian living. Stanley J. Grenz and I have tried in an earlier book to correct this mistaken impression. Theology is inevitable insofar as a Christian (or anyone) seeks to think coherently and intelligently about God. Not only is theology inevitable and universal; it is also valuable and necessary. Without the formal reflection on the meaning of the gospel of salvation that constitutes theology, that gospel would quickly devolve into mere folk religion and lose all conviction as truth and influence on the church or society. For readers unconvinced of the importance and value of theology, I recommend my earlier volume *Who Needs Theology? An Invitation to the Study of God* (Downers Grove, Ill.: InterVarsity Press, 1996).

One can find many volumes on the history of Christian thought and theology written on many different levels. Histories of Christianity are also numerous and readily available. The present volume is certainly not intended to replace any of them but only to make a new contribution to the collection. Without any claim to uniqueness for this volume, I would merely say that few books on these subjects are readily available to common Christian folks—those with little or no previous acquaintance with the history and development of Christian theology. This book is intended for the untutored Christian layperson or student as well as for the interested Christian pastor who wants a "refresher course" in historical theology. It makes no pretense of being scholarly in the sense of offering fresh insights based on original research or new proposals for academic debate. It is a modest survey of the main highlights of Christian historical theology for readers without even a modicum of previous knowledge or understanding of that fascinating story.

Insofar as possible with a book about historical theology, then, I intend this volume to be user-friendly. It is written with a bare minimum of technical theological jargon, and where some of that is unavoidable it is clearly defined in the context where it is used. Although the main subject matter of the book is ideas (beliefs, doctrines, theories), it seeks to connect them with concrete events and real persons and to explain as clearly as possible why the ideas mattered and why they were developed. Often that is because of controversies and conflicts over proper Christian beliefs and spirituality. No doctrine of Christianity ever developed out of thin air. Every belief—whether considered "orthodox" (theologically correct) or "heretical" (theologically incorrect)—arose because of a challenge. That challenge may have been a distortion of the gospel in a message that claimed to be Christian, or it may have been a popular belief or spiritual practice that was considered unbiblical or antithetical to authentic Christian faith. It may have been a non-Christian philosophy or cultural belief that challenged Christian thinkers to respond by developing a better alternative from Christian sources.

In any case, the story of Christian theology is not a story of ivory-tower professional thinkers dreaming up obscure and speculative doctrines to confuse simple Christian believers. Without denying that something like that may have happened from time to time in Christian history, I wish to counter that popular image by showing here that every major Christian belief arose for pressing, practical reasons. Even such a seemingly obscure question as "How many angels can dance on the head of a pin?" was not debated by Christian thinkers of the past merely to wile away time or make themselves seem erudite. The point was to explore the nature of nonhuman spiritual beings such as angels and counter an idea that they are material beings that occupy spaces. One famous (or infamous) legend of the story of Christian theology is that bishops and theologians of the Eastern Orthodox tradition were debating that very question about angels in the great cathedral of Constantinople (Byzantium) while the Muslim Saracen invaders were breaking through the gates of the city and destroying the last vestiges of the once powerful Christian empire. Whether that is true or not is irrelevant to my point, which is simply that all questions debated and beliefs developed have been for some reason—never for no reason.

Admittedly, some reasons for theological debate and development are better than others, but please do not assume that just because an idea in this story seems at first speculative or impractical, it was pulled out of thin air. Much of the story recounted here will consist of explaining the tensions, conflicts and controversies that lay in the backgrounds of such seemingly speculative ideas as the triunity of God (Trinity) and hypostatic union (humanity and deity) of Christ. Neither belief is clearly articulated in the Bible. Furthermore, when they were being developed by the leading thinkers of the early church (fourth and fifth centuries), the canon of Christian Scripture was just being identified and formalized.[2]

Why were these seemingly technical but absolutely crucial Christian doctrines developed? Certainly not because the bishops and other leaders of early Christendom had nothing better to do. The reason is simply that ideas about God and Jesus Christ that undermined the gospel were quickly arising and gaining popularity, and if widely accepted, they would lead to a "different gospel" and a different religion than that taught by the apostles and handed down through the early centuries of the church. In almost every case doctrines were proposed and developed because someone perceived the gospel to be at stake.

Today we have the doctrines of the Trinity and of the two natures of Jesus Christ, and most branches of divided Christianity accept them without much debate. In fact, they are widely taken for granted even if poorly understood. And yet most of the false beliefs that arose in the early church that caused these doctrines to be developed are still alive and well today—sometimes within branches of Christianity that officially confess belief in the doctrines of the Trinity and of the humanity and divinity of Jesus Christ, and sometimes in so-called cults and among liberals and free thinkers on the fringes of Christianity. Understanding how and why these and other crucial beliefs of Christianity were developed and so precisely defined helps avoid their present neglect and possible eventual loss.

Readers will be helped by knowing several basic presuppositions of this book. First, I assume that beliefs matter. That should be clear by now. What people believe affects how they live. There can be no vital, dynamic, faithful Christian discipleship completely devoid of doctrinal understanding. There never has been and there never will be. A person cannot serve God faithfully without knowing something about God's nature and will.

Throughout much of the history of Christianity beliefs mattered much more than they do to many contemporary Christians. Reading and understanding the story of Christian theology requires a prior awareness that the Christians of past ages who wrestled with doctrinal issues really cared about believing the right things about God. That was true not only of bishops and professional theologians but also of ordinary laypeople in the churches.

In the fourth century the great Cappadocian church father Gregory of Nyssa complained that he could not go anywhere or do anything in Constantinople—the new capital of the Roman Empire—without being engaged by tradespeople in debates over the Trinity. In his seminal work on the Trinity, *On the Deity of the Son and of the Holy Spirit,* he wrote, "If you ask for change, someone philosophizes to you on the Begotten and the Unbegotten. If you ask the price of bread, you are told, 'The Father is Greater, and the Son is inferior.' If you ask 'Is the bath ready?' someone answers, 'The Son was created from nothing.' "[3]

Gregory of Nyssa was certainly not complaining about the involvement of ordinary Christians in theological disputes. If his comment has something of the ring of complaint, it is because the majority of the laypeople at that time seemed to sympathize with his opposition—the Arian or semi-Arian heresy that rejected the full equality of Jesus the Son with God the Father. Like many other doctrinal controversies before and after that one, laypeople as well as professional church leaders and theologians have often been actively involved in debating proper Christian beliefs. Beliefs mattered then and they should matter now.

A second assumption is that sometimes beliefs matter too much. Few will disagree with that! Throughout two thousand years of Christian theology there have been many completely unnecessary debates, conflicts and even deaths over fairly minor points of Christian doctrine. Without in any way denigrating the Protestant Reformers and their great reforming work of the sixteenth century, I would argue that their failure to unite due largely to disagreements about interpretations of Christ's presence in the Lord's Supper is a scandal and a blot on the history of Protestant theology. Of course Luther, Zwingli, Calvin and other Reformers disagreed about other things as well, but that doctrinal issue seems to have been the all-consuming point of division that prevented Protestant unity. And there is no excuse for the burnings, drownings and beheadings of people judged to be heretics.

Sometimes doctrinal and theological correctness has mattered too much. But if anything, the pendulum has swung to the opposite extreme in our day so that many Christians know little or nothing about Christian doctrines or how they developed or why. Christianity is in danger of becoming little more than a folk religion of therapeutic worship and individual feelings.

Third, valid Christian beliefs—those that are considered true—are not all on the same level of importance. Some are dogmas and are worth serious and even heated defense. I consider the Trinity and incarnation to belong in that category. For that reason I look on and treat the fourth-century Egyptian bishop and theologian Athanasius as a great hero. He suffered exile from his home city and diocese of Alexandria five times due to his intransigence regarding those beliefs. (His story is told in chapter eleven.)

Other beliefs that are true are not as crucial to the gospel or to the identity of Christianity and its message, but they are nevertheless important. These I call doctrines, as distinct from dogmas.[4] These are beliefs that few, if any, major groups of Christians have or would consider essential to believe in order to count as a Christian but that at least some groups of Christians consider tests of fellowship.

That is, in order to belong to their particular tradition, denomination or church, a person must confess them or at least not deny them. For example, Baptists—those of my own tradition, which dates back to the seventeenth century—insist that believers' baptism (so-called adult baptism), normally by immersion in water, is the normative mode of baptism. But Baptists do not deny the authentic Christianity of persons who believe in and practice infant baptism. For Baptists, then, believers' baptism by immersion is a doctrine but not a dogma.

Finally, there is a third category of beliefs that I call theological opinions or individual interpretations. During the Reformation some Protestant leaders labeled this category *adiaphora,* from a Latin term for "things that don't matter very much," or "matters of indifference." From my own perspective an example of this would be details of beliefs about the exact nature of angels and about the details of events surrounding the second coming of Christ. Throughout most of church history these and other fairly minor matters have been discussed but not often hotly debated.

While I do not condone persecution of anyone because of their beliefs (as a Baptist, I believe strongly in freedom of conscience), I do think that genuine dogmas were rightly defended—sometimes even to death—by church fathers and Reformers. This is a story few Christians know about, and telling it is one of the purposes of this book. Were it not for dear Athanasius—the fourth-century "saint of stubbornness"—the dogmas of Christ's full and true deity and God's triunity would probably have been swamped in a morass of political compromise within the empire and the church. While the great chronicler of the fall of Rome, Edward Gibbon, may have thought that the unity of the Roman Empire was wrongly destroyed by such stubborn refusal to compromise, I judge that what was at stake was the integrity of the gospel itself.

A fourth important assumption of this book is that there does exist a line of influential Christian thinkers and ideas between the New Testament and today, and that even though this line is open to debate, correction and revision, it is not merely a collection of "dead white males" identified by a powerful elite within the church to support the dominance of a certain group of leaders. This point may seem obscure to some readers. Teachers and scholars of religion and theology will know what I mean. A growing tendency in academic circles is to reject the idea of a definite collection of classics in any area of study in favor of greater inclusiveness and representation of minorities and women. There is something right about that movement. Certainly the traditional canon of cultural classics, heroes and icons ought to be expanded. But that is not to say that genuine influence is unimportant in determining what writers and thinkers of the past should be studied. I would dearly love to find records of influential women theologians of the early church, the medieval age, and the Reformation. But while women certainly were present and influential in the spiritual life of Christianity throughout its entire history, until modern times none were able to greatly influence the course and direction of the church's theology.

To some critics the dearth of church mothers[5] is evidence either of bias on the part of male theologians or of the hopelessly patriarchal nature of Christianity itself. I believe it is evidence of the patriarchal nature of Western culture in general (of which Christianity is an integral part) and of cultural accommodation by the Christian church and its institutions. There ought to have been church mothers parallel with church fathers. The fact there were not is a scandal for the church but not justification for revisionist histories that invent them.

What people in North America today call ethnic minorities were well represented in the early church and its theology. The previously mentioned hero Athanasius, for example, was known to contemporaries without insult as "the black dwarf" due to his stature and skin color. He was African, as were many other great thinkers of the early church. Many others were Semitic—of Arabic or Jewish ancestry and ethnic identity. In fact, a strong case could be made that the most formative and influential thinkers of early Christianity—both heretical and orthodox—lived and worked in Egypt and other parts of North Africa. They certainly could not rightly be considered "dead white males"!

Throughout much of the 1980s a movement to deny the existence of any kind of main line of influential thinkers and ideas rose to popularity amid great controversy. Without rejecting a certain validity in calls for greater expansion and inclusion in the lists of influential thinkers, I believe that an objectively identifiable list of influential Christian thinkers exists, and in this book I have concentrated on that in order to provide readers with a kind of base line for understanding the story of Christian theology. If a person wishes to understand how Christians came to believe in the dogma of the Trinity, for example, it is simply dishonest to pretend that someone other than Origen, Athanasius and the three Cappadocian fathers played the leading roles in that drama. Others may have played minor roles, but these men unquestionably were the leading actors.

Some readers may wonder about this main line of most influential Christian thinkers from a quite different perspective: "Why know about these people when I've never heard of them? How can they be so important when my pastor never mentioned them?"

To answer this I appeal to my own "trickle-down theory."[6] Even people who have never heard of Athanasius, for example, are greatly influenced by him. Among other things, Athanasius wrote a treatise on the deity of Jesus Christ titled *De Incarnatione,* or *The Incarnation of the Word.* In that slim volume he presented a strong case for the deity of Jesus Christ as equal with the Father's own deity and thus helped establish the dogma of the Trinity against a growing tide of sympathy for a kind of Jehovah's Witness-like belief in Christ as a great creature of God. A long line of Christian thinkers, including the Protestant Reformers, considered Athanasius's work conclusive and definitive. Athanasius also compiled the first authoritative list of sixty-six inspired books of the Christian Bible in his Easter letter circulated to Christian bishops in 367. He identified a list of secondary books that would later emerge in the Western church (Latin, Roman Catholic) as the inspired Apocrypha. Finally, Athanasius also visited Christian hermits living in desert caves in Egypt and wrote a hagiography (biography of a saint) about one of them—Anthony of the Desert. *The Life of St. Anthony* made its way into Europe via Athanasius's exile and became an important basis for the rise of monasticism and monasteries, which in turn greatly influenced Western Christianity for many centuries.

All in all, then, Athanasius serves as a good example of my trickle-down theory that explains why modern Christians should study and understand Christian thinkers of long ago whose names they have never heard. Even though they have never heard their names, those theologians have influenced the Christianity that has nurtured them spiritually and shaped their identity. They are part of all Christians' "great cloud of witnesses" (Heb 12:1). They are our spiritual and theological ancestors. Learning their stories and the roles they played in the great story of Christian theology is an exercise in self-understanding. It is like learning about your own family roots.

But why study heretics—those like Arius whose ideas were judged to be serious distortions of the gospel and rejected by great thinkers such as Athanasius? Wouldn't it be better to concentrate only on the truth tellers, the cloud of witnesses? This story of Christian theology will include much discussion of those naysayers to orthodoxy, the theologically incorrect teachers of the church who often promoted false gospels or distorted versions of the gospel of Jesus Christ. What is the value of such study?

A popular misconception—perhaps a Christian urban legend—is that the United States Secret Service never shows bank tellers counterfeit money when teaching them to identify it. The agents who do the training, so the legend goes, show bank tellers only examples of genuine money so that when the phony money appears before them they will know it by its difference from the real thing. The story is supposed to make the point that Christians ought only to study truth and never heresy.

The first time I heard the tale as a sermon illustration I intuited its falseness. On checking with the Treasury Department's Minneapolis Secret Service agent in charge of training bank tellers to identify counterfeit money, my suspicion was confirmed. He laughed at the story and wondered aloud who would start it and who would believe it. At my request he sent me a letter confirming that the Secret Service does show examples of counterfeit money to bank tellers.

I believe it is important and valuable for Christians to know not only theological correctness (orthodoxy) but also the ideas of those judged as heretics within the church's story. One reason is that it is almost impossible to appreciate the meaning of orthodoxy without understanding the heresies that forced its development. What we now know as orthodoxy (not "Eastern Orthodoxy" but orthodoxy as "theological correctness") did not pop out of the church like Athena out of Zeus's head in Greek mythology. It grew through challenges from heresy. In order to understand the orthodox dogma of the Trinity properly, it is necessary to understand the teachings of Arius of Alexandria, who seriously challenged belief in God's eternal threeness in the early fourth century.

Another good reason for studying heresies and heretics is that one never knows when God might strike a heavy blow with a crooked stick. Luther's colorful imagery in that phrase drives home the point that even a heretic might have something to contribute to a proper Christian understanding of truth. Almost all traditional Christian thinkers since the sixteenth century agree with John Calvin and the city council of Geneva that Michael Servetus was a heretic by orthodox Protestant standards. He denied the deity of Christ and the Trinity (like Arius in the fourth century) as well as many other points of traditional Christian belief. But his prophetic challenge to the overbearing dominance of the city by Reformer John Calvin would gain strong agreement from most lovers of freedom of conscience today.

Many of those who were considered heretics in Luther's and Calvin's time advocated soul liberty and freedom of religion. In fact, between the time of the first Christian Roman emperor, Constantine, in the fourth century and the eighteenth-century movements for toleration of all religions in Britain and America, so-called heretics were almost the only ones arguing for religious freedom.

A fifth and final assumption underlying this account of Christian theology's story is that God works in mysterious ways to establish his people in truth and to reform theology when needed. I make no pretense of historicism—the methodological assumption that all ideas are reducible to and explainable by historical-cultural contexts. As a convinced and committed Christian I believe in God's providential guidance (not necessarily control) of all events. The story of Christian theology, I believe, is more than a human story. It is part of the story of God's interaction with his people the body of Christ. With contemporary theologian Hans Küng, I believe that God maintains the church in truth—but not in a smooth evolution of its progressive discovery. God works through human agents who are sinfully clouded in mind and heart. There have been periods in the history of the church and its theology when seeing the hand of God maintaining it in truth is a sheer act of faith. There are other periods or chapters of the story when it takes little faith to see God at work restoring truth.

The point here is simply that this volume should not be read as a neutral, scientific-historical description of the evolution of Christian theology. Neither should it be read as the kind of highly biased account typical of some of the most famous or infamous church histories. The very first book-length church history was penned by Bishop Eusebius in the fourth century, and it was clearly intended to demonstrate the hand of God behind the rise to power of Emperor Constantine—the first Roman emperor to embrace Christianity. Every attempt is made here to be factually correct and to present the story of Christian theology with as little distortion as possible. At the same time, I cannot hide the fact that I believe God has never been absent from the church, even in the dark eras when truth's light shown dimly. If there is any "hero" of this story, it is not Constantine or Athanasius—as great and influential as they were—but God himself, to whom belongs all glory and honor.

The story of Christian theology inevitably involves some discussion of philosophy and philosophical influences. Since the second century—where our story begins—philosophy has been theology's main conversation partner. At times it seems to have been more than a junior partner. That is part of the story—philosophy's role in the development of formal Christian beliefs. Third-century North African Christian theologian Tertullian asked rhetorically, "What has Athens to do with Jerusalem?" He meant to protest the growing use of Greek philosophy (Athens) by Christian thinkers who ought to have been relying solely on Scripture and Christian sources (Jerusalem). Second-century church father and apologist (defender of the faith) Justin Martyr referred to Christianity as the "true philosophy," while third-century Christian teacher Clement of Alexandria identified Greek thinker Socrates as a "Christian before Christ." The greatest of all medieval Catholic thinkers, Thomas Aquinas (thirteenth century), often appealed to "the Philosopher"—by which he meant pre-Christian philosopher Aristotle—alongside of or even in place of church fathers in settling disputed questions. Later Catholic thinker Blaise Pascal (seventeenth century) asserted that "the god of the philosophers is not the God of Abraham, Isaac and Jacob!"

The relationship between philosophy and Christian reflection forms a very important part of the story of Christian theology. It provides some of the juiciest tension in that story. But at times it can seem fairly technical and abstruse. I will attempt to simplify it here without skipping over it. I ask for patience from both beginning students and general readers and from fellow teachers and scholars. The former may find that aspect of the narrative bewildering at times, while the latter may find it horrifyingly simplistic.

The story of Christian theology begins in the second century—about one hundred years after Christ's death and resurrection—with the rise of confusion among Christians in the Roman Empire due to challenges to Christian belief both within the church and from outside of it. The main internal challenges were similar to the cacophony of voices many present-day Christians would call "the cults," while the external challenges were similar to those voices many today would call "skeptics." From these challenging voices arose the need for and beginnings of orthodoxy—a definitive statement of Christian theological correctness. The only alternative was total confusion.

Let the story begin . . .

# PART I

# The Opening Act

## *Conflicting Christian Visions in the Second Century*

*The story of Christian theology does not begin at the beginning. That is, Christian* theology began well after Jesus Christ walked the earth with his disciples and even after the last disciple and apostle died. Theology is the church's reflection on the salvation brought by Christ and on the gospel of that salvation proclaimed and explained by the first-century apostles.[1]

The last disciple of Jesus to die was John "the Beloved"—Jesus' youngest disciple—who died in about 90, although the exact date is uncertain. Reliable tradition—left by John's own disciples in the second century—says that he died in Ephesus and was the bishop (*episkopos,* "overseer") of all the Christians and Christian churches in that region of Asia Minor (modern Turkey). John is a pivotal figure in the story of Christian theology because his death marked an important turning point. So far was we know, no recognized or widely acknowledged apostle survived John. With his death Christianity entered into a new era for which it was not entirely prepared. No longer would it be possible to settle doctrinal or other disputes by turning to an apostle.

The apostles were men and women of early Christianity with tremendous prestige and authority. They were eyewitnesses of Jesus or at least persons closely connected with his ministry or the ministries of his disciples.[2] While they were alive, there was no need for theology in the same sense as afterward. Theology was born as the heirs of the apostles began to reflect on Jesus' and the apostles' teachings to explain it in new contexts and situations and to settle controversies about Christian belief and conduct.

Of course the apostles left behind writings. John, for example, left a Gospel of Jesus Christ, some letters and the vision he received while in exile on the island of Patmos.[3] These apostolic writings were not bound together between leather covers with "Holy Bible" stamped on the front, however, and in 100 the idea of a "New Testament" as a canon of Christian Scriptures was yet undeveloped. That is not to say that no Christians thought of the apostles' writings as Scripture. Most Christians around that time probably did consider authentic writings of apostles very special in some sense, and occasionally second-century Christian church fathers did quote them as Scripture. The problem was that no single church or even region of Christianity—such as Rome or Ephesus or Egypt—had a complete collection of the apostolic writings, and there was widespread disagreement about which books and letters were genuinely written by apostles.

Eventually the need for a written record and interpretation of the teachings of Jesus and the apostles became so pressing that individual churches, groups of churches and eventually all Christian leaders collected, limited and defined the writings of apostles and people closely connected with them. Thus the Christian Bible, or canon of Scripture, evolved slowly and painfully with much controversy. During the second century, however, that process was only beginning.

The first Christian theologians were bishops and other ministers and leaders of Christian congregations in the Roman Empire. They have come to be known as the apostolic fathers because they are assumed to have been men who knew one or more of the apostles but who were not apostles themselves. Their part of the story of Christian theology will be told in this section. The section will end with a discussion of Irenaeus, the late-second-century bishop who was perhaps the first Christian to attempt to set forth a complete account of Christian theology. Some have called him the first Christian systematic theologian. Between discussions of the apostolic fathers and Irenaeus will appear treatment of a group of Christian thinkers of the second century generally lumped together as the apologists. They were men who attempted to defend Christianity in its infancy against misunderstanding and persecution and in the process often integrated it with a Greek philosophical perspective.

Theology itself—as the search for orthodoxy (theological correctness)—began with the challenges posed to Christian teachings by cultists who presented themselves within the church and to the pagan world as truer or higher Christians than the leading heirs of the apostles. These challenges to the apostolic message and to the authority of the apostles' appointed successors were so successful in creating chaos and confusion that the rise of formal theological reflection to answer them became necessary. The bishops—who in second-century Christianity simply were overseers of a group of churches in a city or territory—responded to critics and cultists by remembering what the apostles had taught, gathering, preserving and interpreting their written legacies and writing letters and booklets to be circulated among churches. In that process Christian theology was born. With the apostolic fathers theology remained in its infancy and only later began to grow toward maturity with Irenaeus and church fathers after the second century.

# CHAPTER 1

# Critics & Cultists Cause Confusion

*The main troublers of apostolic Christianity in the second century were the* Gnostics, Montanus and the Montanists, and the anti-Christian orator Celsus. Others challenged the stream of teaching and practice flowing from the apostles through their appointed bishops, but in the bishops' eyes these were the primary opponents to be answered and overcome.

Gnosticism is a generic label given to a wide variety of Christian teachers and schools that existed on the fringes of the early church and became a major problem for Christian leaders in the second century. It comes from the Greek word *gnosis,* which means "knowledge" or "wisdom."

**Gnosticism**

One second-century tradition tells of the disciple John's encounter with a leading Gnostic teacher in Ephesus around 90. Cerinthus may have been one of the earliest Gnostic teachers and troublers of Christianity in the late first century. According to the tradition, John was going into the public bath in Ephesus with some of his disciples when he perceived Cerinthus there. He rushed out of the bathhouse without bathing, exclaiming, "Let us fly, lest even the bathhouse fall down because Cerinthus, the enemy of the truth, is within."[1]

John's antipathy to the Gnostic teacher Cerinthus was continued by later Christian leaders into the second and third centuries. Why? Who were the Gnostics and why were they considered the main "enemies of the truth" by John and the

apostles' successors in the early church? I will give a brief description of second-century Gnosticism and some of its modern heirs and then return to a more detailed discussion of Gnosticism's teachings at the end of this chapter.

The Gnostics did not have a unified organization, and they disagreed among themselves over many matters, but they all believed that they possessed a special, higher spiritual knowledge or wisdom than that possessed and taught by the bishops and other church leaders of the second century. In a nutshell, they believed that matter, including the body, is an inherently limiting prison or even evil drag on the good soul or spirit of the human person and that the spirit is essentially divine—a "spark of God" dwelling in the tomb of the body. For all of the Gnostics, salvation meant achieving a special kind of knowledge not generally known or even available to ordinary Christians. That *gnosis,* or knowledge, involved awareness of the true heavenly origin of the spirit within, its essential divine nature as an offshoot of God's own being, and Christ as an immaterial, spiritual messenger sent down from the unknown and unknowable God to rescue and bring home the stray sparks of his own being that had become trapped in material bodies. They all agreed that Christ did not actually become incarnate as Jesus but only appeared to be human.

This is only a thumbnail sketch of second-century Gnosticism. It will be filled in with more details later. For the moment, suffice it to say that this esoteric form of Christianity presented itself to early Christians as a special message for elite persons and as the truer and higher but hidden gospel handed down orally from Jesus by an inner group of his disciples. Christians certainly could find faint echoes and hints of the Gnostic message in what they heard about the apostolic teachings from their bishops and pastors and in the apostolic epistles that circulated among them. But the Gnostic gospel went far beyond the apostles' teaching about war between "flesh" and "spirit."

Many second-century Christians were attracted to this as a special form of Christian truth—higher and better and more spiritual than that taught by the bishops to the unwashed and uneducated masses. Gnosticism appealed to and fostered spiritual elitism, secrecy and division within the budding young Christian church.

In the twentieth century numerous individuals and groups proclaiming themselves "New Age Christians" resurrected the second-century Gnostic message. In fact, echoes of Gnosticism have remained within Christian churches over the centuries, but were muted by official suppression by the Christian emperors and state churches. With modern pluralism and tolerance of dissenting views, as well as separation of church and state, gnosticism has once again reared its head to challenge the apostolic gospel of salvation. Seldom does it identify itself as "gnosticism." Often it is presented by self-styled esoteric Christians as a purer form of Christianity for genuinely spiritual people who cannot abide the smothering dogma and institutionalism of officially orthodox churches.

As the so-called New Age movement gained momentum in Britain and the United States throughout the 1970s and 1980s, two persons appeared within it to merge New Age thinking with gnostic Christianity: George Trevelyan and Elizabeth Clare Prophet.

Sir George Trevelyan, often known as "the father of the British New Age movement," wrote popular books such as *A Vision of the Aquarian Age: An Emerging Spiritual World View* to promote a revival and renewal of gnosticism. He wrote,

> A remarkable change is taking place in the intellectual climate of our time. The holistic world view is penetrating our consciousness and superseding the rational materialism which is surely proving inadequate to explain our fantastic universe. Really we are recovering what was called the Ageless Wisdom of the Ancient Mysteries, which knew that the Universe is Mind and not mechanism, that the Earth is a sentient creature and not just dead mineral, that the human being is in essence spiritual, a droplet of Divinity housed in the temple of the body. This vision, once apprehended, lifts the basic fear of death in our death-ridden culture. The body may be destroyed, but the soul/spirit in each of us is deathless and immortal.[2]

Like second-century Gnostics, Trevelyan did not found a denomination or church but settled for being a teacher of this higher wisdom of the divinity of the human soul.

Elizabeth Clare Prophet, known to her followers as "Guru Ma," has founded her own distinct religious movement known as The Church Universal and Triumphant. Her message of New Age Christianity almost exactly parallels early Christian Gnosticism. She has plumbed the Gnostic writings known as the Nag Hammadi library found in the Egyptian desert in 1945 and found within them the same basic message as that allegedly revealed to her by "ascended masters" such as Jesus and Saint Germain. In *Reincarnation: The Missing Link in Christianity* Prophet argues that the Gnostics were the true Christians who inherited and passed on to their followers the higher and more spiritual teachings of Jesus and his apostles such as reincarnation and the identity of the soul with God.[3] Prophet's account of early Christianity is the reverse of that told by most church historians and historical theologians. For her the true heroes and martyrs of the early church were Gnostics like Cerinthus, Valentinus and Basilides, while the heretical villains were the church bishops and fathers who argued against them and eventually contributed to their suppression.[4]

Trevelyan and Prophet and many others who espouse various forms of esoteric Christianity—often linked somehow with the so-called New Age movement—are showing that gnosticism is alive and well in modern-day Christianity. But it also appears in less blatant manifestations. Wherever people denigrate material, physical existence in the name of "spirituality" or for the same reason elevate the human soul or spirit to the status of divinity, the heresy of gnosticism is encroaching once again on the apostolic message and infecting Christianity.

**Montanism**

While the second-century church leaders—the heirs and successors of the apostles—saw the greatest danger in Gnosticism, they were confronted as well by a fanatical movement among their followers that seemed to explode out of nowhere. It was known to its adherents as the New Revelation and the New Prophecy and known to its opponents as Montanism after the name of its founder and chief prophet: Montanus.

Montanus was a pagan priest in the region of Asia Minor known as Phrygia who converted to Christianity in the middle of the second-century. No library of his writings like the Gnostics' has been found. Most of what we know about his movement and its teachings comes down to us from second-century church fathers who wrote against them and from Eusebius, who wrote a history of the Christian church in the fourth century. Montanus rejected the growing belief in special authority for bishops (as heirs of the apostles) and for apostolic writings. He considered the churches and their leaders spiritually dead and called for a "new prophecy" with all the signs and wonders of the halcyon days of the early church of Pentecost.

The problem for the bishops and leaders of the churches was not so much Montanus's critique of spiritual deadness or calls for revival as his self-identification as God's spokesman without equal. He referred to himself as "the Mouthpiece of the Holy Spirit" and accused the standard church leaders of chasing the Holy Spirit into a book by trying to limit divine inspiration to apostolic writings. He strenuously opposed any such limitation or restriction and seemed to emphasize the continuous power and reality of inspired utterances such as his own.

Montanus gathered a group of followers around himself at Papuza, a town in Phrygia, and built a commune there. Two women named Prisca and Maximilla joined him, and the trio proceeded to prophesy the soon return of Christ to their commune and condemn the bishops and other leaders of the major metropolitan sees (areas with bishops over them) as dead, corrupt and even apostate. Montanus and the two women prophets fell into trances and spiritual frenzies, speaking in the first-person voice as if God the Holy Spirit were speaking directly through them. In one instance the Spirit supposedly spoke through Montanus about himself: “Behold the man [Montanus] is like a lyre, and I strike the strings like a plectrum. The man sleeps and I wake. Behold! It is the Lord who moves the heart of [the] man.” In speeches Montanus—or the Spirit in him—said to his followers, “I am the Lord God, born among men. I am neither an angel nor a priest. I am God the Father, come to you.”[5]

For a few decades the church had become increasingly nervous about self-appointed prophets, fearing that they may be attempting to replace the apostles as special authorities raised up by God apart from the structures of the church. The main churches of the Roman Empire and their bishops had come to assume something like the later concept of “apostolic succession” in order to preserve unity in visible structure and teaching. If a bishop could trace his ordination pedigree (so to speak) back to one of the apostles of the first century, he was a worthy and valid bishop. If he could not, he was not.

But there were still roving and stationary charismatic prophets among Christians in the middle of the second century. At times they could be very troublesome, as one of the earliest postapostolic writings, the *Didache,* shows. That anonymous text from the early second century offers conflicting advice to Christians about how best to handle these entrepreneurial prophets who came speaking words from God.

The church leaders’ harsh response to Montanus was not so much because he and his female companions proclaimed words from God or advocated strict asceticism (no marriage, no sex, severe fasting) as that they rejected the apostles’ heirs and claimed special inspiration and authority for their own messages. When Montanus’s followers began founding separate congregations rivaling the bishops throughout the Roman Empire, the latter reacted swiftly and severely. Perhaps too severely.

Some would say it was a classic case of throwing the baby out with the bath water. Since they did not have the support of the state (Roman Empire) and were in danger of persecution themselves, a group of bishops from around the area where Montanus lived met privately and wrote up a document excommunicating him and the two women and all their followers.

Perhaps this was the first true schism, or organizational split, within Christianity. In many cities of the Roman Empire there were, from about 160 on, two distinct Christian congregations—one adhering to the leadership of a bishop in apostolic succession and one adhering to the New Prophecy of Montanus.

In reaction to the excesses and exclusive claims of Montanus and his followers, the church's leaders leaned further and further away from supernatural utterances such as tongues and prophecies and other miraculous gifts and signs and wonders of the Spirit. Eventually such charismatic manifestations wrongly became so identified with Montanus and the Montanist schism that they almost died out altogether under pressure from fearful bishops and later Christian emperors.

Is Montanism—or something like it—still alive and well in the modern era? The August 14, 1991, *Christianity Today* magazine featured a cover story on a Montanist-like movement called the Kansas City Fellowship.[6] This particular movement, led by a charismatic group of self-styled prophets, had many of the marks of early Christian Montanism but without some of the excesses. The centerpiece of the movement—as in many other similar charismatic sects—was personal prophecy delivered by special prophets to guide individuals' lives and predict the course of the world's future. Without rejecting the Bible, the prophets considered themselves able to speak words from God of equal weight and importance. One labeled himself "Paul's successor" (referring to the apostle Paul).

Other recent charismatic movements have emphasized an alleged difference between *logos* and *rhema*—two Greek words for "word"—such that modern-day messages from God through prophecies *(rhema)* may supersede and even correct apostolic writings that were true and relevant for the first century *(logos)*. Wherever and whenever prophesy is elevated in theory or practice alongside or higher than Scripture, Montanism rears its head. Like Gnosticism, Montanism challenged the early church and challenges the church in modern times to think and respond theologically in order that Christianity may not become anything and everything and thus nothing in particular.

**Celsus**

Gnosticism and Montanism constituted the two main internal threats to the church and its apostolic message, that is, to unity and integrity within early Christianity. A major external challenge arose from Jewish and pagan writers and speakers such as Fronto, Tacitus, Lucian, Porphyry and especially Celsus.

The best-known of such polemical opponents of Christianity was the pagan philosopher Celsus, who wrote a book against it known as *The True Doctrine: A Discourse Against the Christians* in about 175 or 180. The entire content of the book has been preserved for posterity by third-century Christian philosopher and theologian Origen of Alexandria, who responded to it in *Contra Celsum (Against Celsus)*.[7]

Little is known about Celsus. From what little information scholars can piece together, he was an educated Roman citizen and self-styled philosophical orator who may have been raised in a Christian home and who turned in adulthood toward Greek philosophy. What's important is Celsus's challenge to the church of the second century. At a time when rumors and false accusations about Christians were rampant and Christians were widely persecuted and considered ignorant and superstitious if not disloyal by emperors and commoners alike, Celsus offered a stunningly brilliant and articulate critique of Christian belief. He did not engage in rumor mongering, but simply pointed out what appeared to be inconsistencies and superstitious elements of Christian doctrine from the viewpoint of someone committed to an eclectic blend of Greek philosophy, "the true doctrine."

It was one thing for Christians to refute blatantly false rumors such as bloody rituals where they baked and ate infants (a popular rumor among Romans about Christian "sacrifices," which were really innocent but private eucharistic ceremonies). It was another thing entirely to respond intellectually and even philosophically to an educated and articulate Roman orator. But it needed to be done because Celsus probably had the emperor's ear. Marcus Aurelius, Roman emperor in the late second century, was a philosopher and opponent of Christianity. Refuting Celsus was a way of calming down the imperial wrath against Christianity, which was largely based on the supposition—possibly fueled by Celsus—that Christians were ignorant riffraff who believed stupid and superstitious things and were even a danger to the empire.

Celsus's attack on Christianity offers a wealth of information about second-century Christian life and belief. In spite of obvious distortions and misrepresentations, *On the True Doctrine* helps church historians understand what Christians believed and how that was seen by non-Christians. For example, Celsus made absolutely clear that Christians of his time believed in and worshiped Jesus Christ—a man—as God:

> Now, if the Christians worshiped only one God they might have reason on their side. But as a matter of fact they worship a man who appeared only recently. They do not consider what they are doing a breach of monotheism; rather they think it perfectly consistent to worship the great God and to worship his servant as God. And their worship of this Jesus is the more outrageous because they refuse to listen to any talk about God, the father of all, unless it includes some reference to Jesus: Tell them that Jesus, the author of the Christian insurrection, was not his son, and they will not listen to you. And when they call him Son of God, they are not really paying homage to God, rather, they are attempting to exalt Jesus to the height.[8]

In response to the Christians' worship of Jesus, Celsus wrote that "it cannot be the case that God came down to earth, since in so doing he would have undergone an alteration of his nature.[9] There was the challenge Celsus presented. And thus the heart of Celsus's "contribution" to Christianity was this challenge to think through and somehow make coherent two seemingly conflicting claims. Christians claimed to be monotheists—believers in one God—together with Jews and most educated Roman citizens. Celsus was a monotheist, although his notion of God was far different from Jews' or Christians' and was based more on Plato's "form of the good." Christians also claimed that Jesus was God—or at least God's *Logos* (Word, Wisdom)—equal with the heavenly Father and Creator of all things. In this double claim Celsus could see only blatant contradiction and an insult to the perfection of God's nature as immutable (unchanging).

Celsus hammered this and other apparent contradictions and inconsistencies against Christian teaching. He attempted to show that their worldview was silly and vastly inferior to the generic, eclectic spiritual philosophy of one God over all taught by Platonic philosophers. Christians were faced with a choice: either ignore Celsus and critics like him and retreat into a folk religion without intellectual defense or rise to the challenge and develop cogent doctrines that would reconcile seemingly contradictory beliefs such as monotheism and the deity of Jesus Christ.

The same challenge and choices face modern Christians. One twentieth-century "Celsus" was British philosopher Bertrand Russell (1872-1970), who criticized Christianity from the standpoint of his own philosophy, which may best be described as a form of secular humanism. Like his second-century counterpart Celsus, Russell wrote a book—*Why I Am Not a Christian*—that attempted to expose Christianity as unsophisticated and superstitious. Whereas Celsus considered a general Platonic philosophy to be "the true doctrine" compared to which Christianity was superstition, Russell assumed the truth of secular humanism as the true doctrine for educated twentieth-century people. Perhaps no other single anti-Christian polemic has been as influential as Russell's, and numerous Christian apologists have attempted to refute it. In doing so they follow in the footsteps of the second-century Christian writers known as the apologists.

Christians rose to the challenge presented by Celsus. Their response to pagan opponents such as Celsus as well as to fanatics such as Montanus and heretics such as Gnostics gave birth to Christian theology. But why? Why did second-century Christian leaders (such as you will read more about in the rest of this chapter) choose to develop theological responses to cultists and critics? The answer is simple: for the sake of salvation. Not out of pride or power or some impulse toward speculation but for the sake of preserving the integrity of the gospel and for the sake of evangelism, they responded theologically. Theology was born in order to answer questions, to satisfy the needs of inquiring minds both within and outside the church. The only alternatives were complete disunity of faith (schisms brought on by heresies) and sheer fideism—which is what Celsus accused Christians of—refusing to answer and relying on blind faith without reason. Christians set out to conquer the cultists and critics through reasonable persuasion by showing the inner logic and coherence of the message handed down from the apostles.

Montanus and his New Prophecy posed a serious threat to church unity, and the church responded harshly—perhaps too harshly in the light of the sudden demise of spiritual gifts and signs and wonders in Christianity. Celsus and his skeptical, philosophical attacks posed a serious threat to Christianity's credibility at a time when the emperor, who was an intellectual, often judged individuals and groups in his empire by their intellectual acumen and beliefs. The church eventually responded by developing a coherent worldview every bit as intellectually powerful as Celsus's or the emperor's. In the process, as we will see, the church may have absorbed too much of the spirit of Greek philosophy into its worldview in order to make it respectable to educated Romans. But the greatest threat of all was Gnosticism, and it is now time to end this chapter with a more detailed and in-depth treatment of it and the church's theological response to it.

### Gnostic Theology

One contemporary scholar of Gnosticism has declared that it was "the first and most dangerous heresy among the early Christians."[10] Second-century Christian leaders and thinkers expended enormous energies examining and refuting it, and in the process began developing orthodox Christian doctrines that would be the counterparts and alternatives to Gnostic teachings. In other words, what we call "orthodoxy" was born out of conflict between the appointed heirs of the apostles and the Gnostics who claimed to carry forward a secret tradition of teaching from those same apostles. A later chapter will deal with Irenaeus of Lyons, who presented in print the first full-fledged refutation of Gnosticism from an orthodox Christian perspective. Here our focus will be on what Gnosticism was and why it was considered so serious a threat by bishops and other leaders of the Christians in the second century throughout the Roman Empire.

The basic belief of all Gnostics was that "this cosmos is incurable and must be rejected."[11] Gnosticism offered not only an account of this inherent evil of creation; it also offered a spiritual solution for the individual—a method of salvation from that incurably evil environment (including the body) back to the soul's true home. Second-century Gnostics differed a great deal among themselves about the details, but all of them shared five major family resemblances that make them Gnostics in spite of disagreement.[12]

First, they believed in one God who is wholly transcendent, spiritual and far removed from the fallen, material universe, which he did not create. The physical universe was created by an evil or demented lesser god (a "demiurge").

Second, human beings are sparks (or droplets) of the same spiritual substance that God is and have somehow become trapped in physical bodies, which are like tombs to be escaped.

Third, Gnostics all agreed that the "fall" that led to sin and evil is identical to the fall into matter. Creation and fall coincide. As long as spirits are trapped in physical bodies and materiality, they will be subject to sin, which is caused by ignorance of their true nature and home.

The fourth common feature of Gnostic belief was their vision of salvation. All Gnostics agreed that salvation is to escape from the bondage of material existence and travel back to the home from which souls/spirits have fallen. The possibility is initiated by the great Spirit, God, who wishes to draw back into itself all the stray bits and pieces. God sends forth an emanation of himself—a spiritual redeemer—who descends through layers and layers of reality from pure spirit to dense matter and attempts to teach some of the divine sparks of Spirit their true identity and home. Once awakened, they are able to begin the journey back. Salvation is by knowledge—self-knowledge.

Finally, all of the Gnostics (so far as anyone knows) considered themselves Christians and regarded Jesus as the human vehicle for this heavenly messenger, "Christ." All rejected the idea of God becoming incarnate, dying and rising bodily. Such beliefs were considered unspiritual and against true wisdom because they entangled spirit with matter. However, most Gnostics in the second century did see Jesus as special in that he was the vehicle taken over by and used by the Christ-being sent from God. But for most Gnostics, at least, that heavenly redeemer who entered Jesus at his baptism by John in the river Jordan left him before he died on the cross.

Second-century Gnostics were divided into numerous "schools" (movements) following different teachers. Irenaeus studied twenty of them and set forth in great detail their similarities and differences. Many of their main differences had to do with details of mythology about how the good spirits (sparks of the divine) fell and became entrapped in material bodies. Throughout the century these tales became more and more elaborate with widely varying accounts of different emanations from and splits within the *plerōma* (divine fullness) that led eventually to this evil, fallen world and the spirits' entrapment in it. Other variety within Gnosticism arose

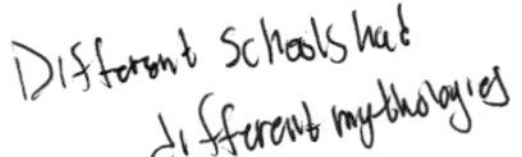

due to different interpretations of the soul's journey back through the levels of reality between the physical and the spiritual. Some Gnostics attempted to name scores of beings supposedly guarding various levels the souls must pass through. Knowing the names of these "aeons" and "archons" (like good and evil angels and demons) was seen by some Gnostics as part of the *gnosis*. Other Gnostics kept things simpler and merely emphasized meditation and asceticism to prepare for release from the body at death.

Another point of disagreement among Gnostics was Christology—belief about Christ. All agreed that Christ is a heavenly, spiritual redeemer who neither became flesh and blood nor rose bodily from death.

Some taught that this Christ appeared as Jesus, but that Jesus was never really a physical human. This Christology is known as docetism—from the Greek word *dokeō*, which means "to appear" or "to seem." Thus for these Gnostics Jesus only seemed to be human. His entire earthly existence was a charade in which he pretended to be flesh and blood for his disciples' sakes.

Other Gnostics taught a dualistic Christology in which "Christ" entered into Jesus at the baptism and left him just before he died. He used Jesus' vocal chords, for instance, to teach the disciples but never actually experienced being human.

Gnosticism was a different gospel of salvation—a different idea of the human condition to which salvation is the solution and a different idea of the solution itself. How far back this alternative gospel goes in history is much debated. Some scholars believe it may have predated Christianity among Jews in Egypt, for instance. However, no records of non-Christian Gnosticism have been found, whereas many documents of second-century Gnosticism have been discovered, including entire Gnostic Gospels such as the *Gospel of Thomas*.[13]

Most probably Gnosticism arose among Christians in Egypt in the late first century and early second centuries, but Gnosticism certainly had precursors. Hints and echoes of Gnosticism may easily be detected in some of the apostles' writings. John's epistles, for instance, stress that Christ has come in the flesh: "Many deceivers have gone out into the world, those who do not confess that Jesus Christ has come in the flesh; any such person is the deceiver and the antichrist!" (2 Jn 7 NRSV). In all likelihood John was already combating proto-Gnosticism in first-century Christian congregations.

Why and how Gnosticism arose among Christians are hotly debated questions. There are no firm answers. Some scholars suggest the influences of religions of India on Egyptian Christians. Others stress syncretism of Christianity with various mystery religions of the Roman Empire. Some simply see in Gnosticism an intense form of tendencies latent within Greek philosophy and culture generally insofar as they denigrated material existence and elevated spiritual reality. There may never be definite answers to questions such as these.

### The Early Christian Response to Gnosticism

Second-century Christian leaders and writers responded vigorously to Gnosticism. As it grew in places like Rome—probably through importation from Egypt—Christian teachers like Justin Martyr wrote refutations of its gospel. Although lost, Justin's book *Syntagma,* or *Compendium Against All Heresies,* was probably written in Rome around 150. That was probably the first major anti-Gnostic polemic by an orthodox, catholic Christian.[14] Other second-century church fathers wrote against Gnostics as well as against other heretics such as Marcion of Rome (who had strong similarities to Gnosticism) and Montanus and various minor false teachers. But Gnosticism formed the main foil to orthodox, apostolic, catholic Christianity throughout the second century, and "the history of the early church was profoundly influenced . . . by the struggle against the gnostics."[15]

Out of conflicts with these and other heresies and critics, second-century Christianity began to formalize and institutionalize its faith and life. It is easy to decry some aspects of that formalization process. Some would say that with it a lot of the life went out of Christianity. That may be true. However, once the threat to the gospel constituted by Gnosticism, Celsus and Montanus is fully understood, it is more difficult to criticize the responses of the church fathers. If they went too far in standardizing Christian belief, life and worship, it was for a good cause. The only alternative was confusion and chaos within a folk religion without any definite structure.

The first group of church fathers that began responding to heretics within the church were the apostolic fathers. Some of them knew apostles personally. Others simply lived a part of their life at the same time as apostles. They formed important links back to the apostles in that transitional period at the end of the first century and beginning of the second century when Christians found themselves without apostles and with Christ not yet returned. We now turn to their common and individual stories.

# CHAPTER 2

# The Apostolic Fathers Explain the Way

A *person like Polycarp was very important to second-century Christians.* He was bishop of the Christians in Smyrna on Asia Minor's western coast near Ephesus when he was arrested by Roman authorities and publicly executed in about 155. What made him so important, however, was his connection with one of the Lord's disciples—John.

As already noted, John was the last of Jesus' disciples to die, and with him died the class of early Christian leaders known as apostles. Polycarp had been tutored in the faith by John and therefore was considered a living link with the disciples of Jesus and the apostles. In the absence of a Christian Bible (other than the Hebrew Bible, which Christians would come to call the Old Testament) men like Polycarp were considered the best and most authoritative sources of information about what the apostles taught and how they led the churches.

Polycarp's aura of special authority fell upon his own disciples—men like Irenaeus who were trained in Christian faith by him. He passed on to them the traditions of the apostles, and until the New Testament was identified and agreed upon by Christians in the fourth century, this oral tradition and the authority of apostolic succession proved invaluable in the Christian struggle against heresies and schisms within the church. At times, however, this special aura of authority could present problems for Christianity as some of the apostles' successors introduced their own ideas into the stream of early theology. As we will see, occasionally these fathers of the generation after the apostles gave the gospel their own unique interpretations that began to turn it away from the great themes of grace and faith so strongly emphasized by Paul and other apostles and more toward the gospel as a "new law" of God-pleasing conduct and behavior.

Justo González takes nothing from the apostolic fathers' importance or value when he rightly notes that "not only in their understanding of baptism, but also in their total theological outlook, one senses a distance between the Christianity of the New Testament—especially that of Paul—and that of the apostolic fathers. References to Paul and the other apostles are frequent; but in spite of this the new faith becomes more and more a new law, and the doctrine of God's gracious justification becomes a doctrine of grace that helps us act justly."[1]

Of course this shift was subtle and not absolute. It was a barely but definitely perceptible turn in these second-century Christian writings toward legalism, or what may be better termed "Christian moralism." Although the apostolic fathers such as Ignatius and Polycarp quoted Paul more than James, it was the latter's spirit that breathed through them. Perhaps due to a perceived moral and spiritual laziness and decline among Christians, they emphasized the need to avoid sinning, obey leaders and work hard to please God more than the need for liberation from bondage to the law.

In spite of this subtle shift, which especially Protestants tend to point out and lament, the apostolic fathers are to be admired and lauded for their stalwart defense of the incarnation of God in Jesus Christ against the Gnostics' denials. Some of them died martyrs' deaths at the hands of Roman authorities and therefore are much to be respected for their death-defying confession of Christ and his gospel under persecution. Their main significance here, of course, is as Christianity's first theologians. The category "apostolic fathers" consists of persons and documents that interpreted and applied the apostolic message in the first apostleless generation, which was besieged by false gospels and attacks from pagan skeptics.

Who were these apostolic fathers? Since the sixteenth century, church historians have listed anywhere from eight to ten authors and anonymous documents in this category. (Historians traditionally refer to certain anonymous documents as "apostolic fathers.") Agreed on by all are Clement, Ignatius, Polycarp, the *Didache (Teaching of the Twelve Apostles), Epistle of Barnabas* and *Shepherd of Hermas.* Others commonly listed and described as apostolic fathers are the so-called *Second Letter of Clement,* whose real author is unknown, the *Martyrdom of Polycarp,* the *Epistle to Diognetus,* and fragments of writings by Papias. Our focus here will be only on those that virtually all scholars agree upon as belonging to the writings of Christians in the first generation after the demise of apostleship.

Before proceeding to individual discussions of the apostolic fathers, it will be helpful to note that some of these writings' authors are unknown. Immediately on hearing the label "apostolic father," it is natural to assume a person is meant. Of course each of these documents had at least one author, but in some cases scholars have no idea who that author is. A document such as the *Didache* is described as one of the apostolic fathers because even though its author is unknown it displays marks of very early postapostolic Christian life and thought and was preserved by the churches because of its early date and importance in instructing churches in a time when no apostles were available. Scholars agree unanimously that the apostle Barnabas—Paul's companion on his journeys—did not pen the *Epistle of Barnabas.* It was almost certainly written by an early-second-century Christian who wished his writing to have apostolic authority. While attaching someone else's name to a document is considered a form of lying today, it was not looked on that way in ancient times. The *Epistle of Barnabas* was preserved not because it was written by an apostle and in spite of the fact that no one was sure who wrote it. The advice and instruction found in it was judged valuable by second-century Christians, and in it they found echoes of the teachings of apostles.

One more point of interest to note before proceeding to discuss individual apostolic fathers is that many, if not most, of the writings in this category were treated as Scripture alongside the Gospels and apostles' epistles by some Christian churches in the second century. In fact, one way of understanding this category is as the books that came to be judged orthodox but barely missed being judged canonical, inspired Scripture when the Christian canon was being determined. In other words, these writings were hardly distinguished from the writings of apostles by some Christians in the Roman Empire but were ultimately excluded because they received no universal agreement as Scripture and were judged not to be of apostles or even closely connected with apostles in the same way that Luke's Gospel and the book of Acts and the epistle to the Hebrews were.

### Clement of Rome

Fortunately we do know the identities of some of the apostolic fathers. Clement was bishop of Rome—overseer of the house churches in Rome—in the last decade of the first century. His letter to the Corinthian church from the church at Rome—known commonly as *1 Clement* (to distinguish it from the *Second Letter of Clement)* is probably the first preserved Christian writing outside of what we now call the New Testament. It was written in about 95. Some second-century Christians in Egypt considered it Scripture, as they did many of the apostolic fathers. Indeed, it reads very much like Paul's own letters to the Corinthians. Some scholars believe, based on internal evidence in this letter, that Clement must have known Paul personally and imitated his style and message.

Clement wrote to the quarreling Christians in Corinth for many of the same reasons that Paul wrote to them. Besides urging them to remain strong and true to their faith under persecution, he commanded them to reject division and strife and unify as one body of believers in Christ. Apparently the church was just as full of dissension as it was in the middle of the first century when Paul intervened with his letters. But Clement's solution to their schismatic attitudes and actions was stronger than Paul's. Whereas Paul had pointed to their union in one Spirit and one baptism through faith in Christ, Clement ordered them to obey the bishop God had appointed to be over them. This same solution to dissent and division within churches appears in other apostolic fathers such as Ignatius.

Apparently open rebellion against leadership had broken out in the Corinthian Christian congregations. It is clear that by the time Clement wrote to them from Rome there was more than one meeting of Christians and a single leader had emerged to be over all of them—a kind of "super pastor" known as the "bishop." Some of the younger Christians of the city had rejected the bishop's authority and even tried to depose him. Clement began by appealing to their sense of respect and honor: "Let us respect our leaders; let us honor our elders; let us instruct our young with instruction that leads to the fear of God."[2] Later, however, he berated them for their disobedience to the bishop and other leaders whose ministry, he said, "had been held in honor by them blamelessly."[3] Finally, Clement laid down a principle of Christian leadership and discipleship: "Therefore it is right for us, having studied so many and such great examples, to bow the neck and, adopting the attitude of obedience, to submit to those who are the leaders of our souls, so that by ceasing from this futile dissension we may attain the goal that is truly set before us, free from all blame."[4]

There is nothing particularly new or noteworthy for Christian theology in *1 Clement*. Much of it echoes apostolic writings such as Paul's epistles in the New Testament. Certainly it contributed, however, to the overall subtle shift toward Christian moralism in second-century Christianity by linking discipleship closely with obedience to duly appointed leaders and with living a moral life.

One interesting aspect of the epistle is Clement's odd appeal to the myth of the phoenix to support belief in the resurrection. Apparently some in the church at Corinth were still not fully accepting belief in bodily resurrection—a problem Paul had addressed in 1 Corinthians 15. Clement argued that the resurrection of the bird known as the phoenix was a sign of hope and promise of the bodily resurrection.[5] His wording of this argument makes clear that he took the myth of the phoenix literally and thought it a sign given by God pointing toward believers'

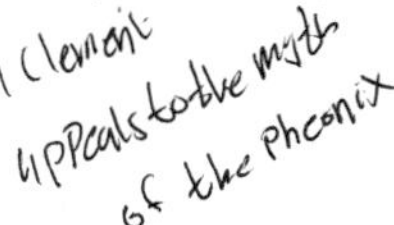

future resurrection. If this letter had been included in the New Testament, modern Christians would certainly be embarrassed by that superstitious aspect of it.

Why did Clement write so authoritatively to the Corinthian Christians when he was himself only the bishop of Rome? He seems to have had a consciousness of special responsibility and authority that may have stemmed from the idea of apostolic succession. He heard about continuing division and even open rebellion among Christians in Corinth. Who better to order them to settle down and obey their leaders than the bishop of Rome—the successor of Peter and Paul, who both died martyrs' deaths in that city a few decades earlier?

Later developers and defenders of the theory of papal supremacy would use Clement's presumption as evidence to support it. The epistle itself, however, indicates no such belief on Clement's part. Just because he felt duty-bound to intervene because he saw himself as in some sense Paul's successor is no indication that he or any other early Christian bishop of Rome believed in their spiritual supremacy over all Christians everywhere.

### The Didache

The *Didache,* also known as *The Teaching of the Twelve Apostles,* is hardly comparable with *1 Clement* even though it was written about the same time. Scholars knew of this document's existence from allusions to it in early Christian writings long before it was discovered in 1873. Nothing is known of its author, but most scholars conclude from internal evidence that it was written as a circular letter to Christian churches in the Roman province of Syria (which included Palestine) around the turn of the century (101). A few scholars suggest an earlier date that would make it the very first extant Christian writing outside the New Testament.

The *Didache* seems to have been written to shore up Christian morality and to instruct Christians in how to treat prophets who come to them claiming to speak words of the Lord. It also contains detailed advice and instructions for daily Christian living, spirituality and worship. The book opens with a dualistic vision of "two ways" followed by humans—the way of life and the way of death. The way of life is clearly the way of love for God and neighbor and strict moral law keeping. Much of its descriptions of these two ways of living are taken directly from the Gospels and Old Testament writings. As in the case of other apostolic fathers, the *Didache* hardly mentions grace, faith, forgiveness, justification or any of the other distinctive notes of Paul's letters and his gospel of salvation. The way of salvation described in it is a certain lifestyle of faithfulness and obedience to God's commandments and to Christian ministers.

Specifically, the *Didache* admonishes its Christian readers to be humble, accept as good whatever happens, "knowing that nothing transpires apart from God," remember and honor the one who preaches God's Word "as though he were the Lord," and "keep strictly away from meat sacrificed to idols."[6] Interesting to note is the difference between that last piece of terse advice and Paul's own conditional approval of Christian eating of meat sacrificed to idols in 1 Corinthians. The *Didache,* like other apostolic fathers, presents Christians with a strict morality and somewhat legalistic vision of Christian living more than with a gospel of Christian liberty and freedom from the law.

Included in the *Didache* are fairly detailed instructions on baptism and the Lord's Supper. A significant section of this relatively brief document consists of interesting and somewhat strange instruction regarding how to receive, test and treat self-proclaimed prophets of God. They are to be welcomed so long as they teach the things contained in the *Didache.*

Surely its readers must have felt somewhat confused by the conflicting advice. On the one hand, prophets were not to be tested or evaluated, and on the other hand, their conduct was to be examined and judged:

> Do not test or evaluate any prophet who speaks in the spirit, for every sin will be forgiven, but this sin will not be forgiven. However, not everyone who speaks in the spirit is a prophet, but only if he exhibits the Lord's ways. By this conduct, therefore, will the false prophet and the [true] prophet be recognized. . . . Everyone who comes in the name of the Lord is to be welcomed. But then examine him, and you will find out—for you will have insight—what is true and what is false.[7]

Among other signs of false prophets were that they stay more than two or three days, ask for money and order meals "in the spirit," which probably means demanding food in exchange for prophecies. On the other hand, the *Didache* commands Christians to give their prophets the firstfruits of their produce, "for they are your high priests"! It would be most difficult to deduce a coherent way of testing and treating self-proclaimed Christian prophets from this little booklet.

Toward its end the *Didache* tells its readers to "appoint for yourselves bishops and deacons worthy of the Lord, men who are humble and not avaricious and true and approved, for they too carry out for you the ministry of the prophets and teachers. You must not, therefore, despise them, for they are your honored men, along with the prophets and teachers"[8] Apparently, then, wandering charismatic prophets and teachers were scarce and perhaps often considered more trouble than they were worth. While the author of the *Didache* did not want to reject their ministry entirely and even wanted to preserve honor and respect for the best of them, he also wanted the Christians not to rely on them too much. His advice was to put in their place more permanent ministers to oversee the congregation.

**Ignatius of Antioch**

While the *Didache* is full of fascinating and confusing information about the life of Christian congregations in Syria around the end of the first century, it offers little in the way of theology. Much more coherent and theological are the letters of a third apostolic father—Ignatius of Antioch, who wrote seven letters to Christian congregations while on his way to Rome to be killed. Ignatius was bishop of the Christians in Antioch—a very important city of the Roman Empire in Syria as well as an important city for Christians. It was there that they were first called Christians, and from there Paul launched his missionary journeys. Ignatius was martyred in Rome around 110 or 115 and therefore almost certainly knew some of the apostles or at least their immediate successors. He was highly revered and respected by early-second-century Christians, which is perhaps why the Roman authorities arrested and publicly executed him.

Ignatius wrote letters to Christians in Ephesus, Magnesia, Trallia, Rome, Philadelphia and Smyrna. He also wrote a letter to Polycarp, who would follow in his footsteps of martyrdom a few decades later. While journeying to Rome under guard, Ignatius heard of a conspiracy by certain Christians to rescue him. In his letter he urged them not to rescue him: "I implore you: do not be 'unseasonably kind' to me. Let me be food for the wild beasts, through whom I can reach God. I am God's wheat, and I am being ground by the teeth of the wild beasts, that I might prove to be pure bread."[9] Just before writing this, Ignatius also wrote that "Christianity is greatest when it is hated by the world."

While some critics have accused Ignatius and other early Christians of being masochistic in their desire to be martyred, it seems that he considered his impending martyrdom a gift and a sign. Other Christians held similar attitudes. About one hundred years later, North African Christian theologian Tertullian wrote that "the blood of the martyrs is the seed [of the church]." In other words, the more the Romans persecuted and killed Christians, the more the church grew. Ignatius must have felt the same way.

Ignatius dealt with all kinds of issues in his letters, and it may be fair to say that these letters contain the first real theology in Christianity. The definitions, explanations and interpretations contained in them go far beyond what is to be found in the apostles' own writings. However, there is no reason to think that Ignatius believed himself to be on the same level as the original apostles, receiving new revelations from God. Rather, he believed that he was simply interpreting and applying apostolic Christianity to the needs of his readers in their unique situations.

Ignatius strongly emphasized Christian obedience to bishops. His letters frequently drive home this command: Do nothing without the bishop and regard him as the Lord himself because "the bishop is nothing less than God's representative to the congregation."[10] To the Magnesian Christians, Ignatius wrote: "As the Lord did nothing without the Father, either by himself or through the apostles (for he was united with him), so you must not do anything without the bishop and the presbyters [elders]."[11] To the Ephesians, he wrote, "It is obvious, therefore, that we must regard the bishop as the Lord himself."[12] Some commentators see in such statements the beginnings of what has been called the "monarchical episcopacy"—the tendency in later Christianity to elevate the bishop *(episkopos)* to a special spiritual status of power and authority. Certainly Ignatius's sentiment about bishops is a quantum leap beyond what can be found in the apostles' own writings and no doubt arose from a pressing need to keep order in an increasingly diverse and unruly Christianity.

Ignatius also condemned the docetic Christology of Gnosticism without taking on Gnosticism as a whole. He affirmed most strongly the true deity and humanity of Jesus Christ as God appearing in human form. Of Jesus' true physical humanity, he wrote to the Trallians, "But if, as some atheists (that is, unbelievers) say, he suffered in appearance only (while they exist in appearance only!), why am I in chains? And why do I want to fight with wild beasts? If that is the case, I die for no reason; what is more, I am telling lies about the Lord."[13] By affirming the genuine suffering of Jesus, Ignatius countered the Gnostics' Christology, especially the docetic version of it. But some early Christians questioned the genuine deity—equality with God—of Jesus Christ.

Occasionally critics of orthodox doctrines have questioned whether belief in Jesus' true deity and humanity existed among Christians before the fourth-century councils and creeds. Ignatius settles that question. While he affirmed Jesus Christ's genuine humanity to the Trallians, he unequivocally affirmed his genuine deity to the Ephesians when he wrote that "God appeared in human form to bring the newness of eternal life."[14] Without spelling out in technical detail the full-blown dogma of Christ's person, Ignatius clearly anticipates it with these twin affirmations. There can be no serious doubt that Christians immediately after the apostolic age believed in Jesus Christ as both truly God and truly human.

Finally, Ignatius seems to have invented a theologically pregnant term for the Lord's Supper—the Eucharist or Communion ceremony. For him, partaking of the eucharistic meal constituted a major aspect of the process of salvation. How does a person become saved and live forever with Jesus Christ? By "breaking one bread, which is *the medicine of immortality*."[15] Ignatius clearly conceived of the Eucharist (Communion meal) as a sacrament—a means of grace that creates a transformation of the person participating in it. He did not elaborate a theory of this, but he meant to emphasize that by partaking of the bread and wine of the Lord's meal, a person is gaining a participation in divine immortality that overcomes the curse of death brought about by sin. Later Christians of both Eastern Orthodox and Roman Catholic persuasions used Ignatius's description of the Eucharist as "medicine of immortality" to justify belief in salvation as a sacramental process of *theosis*—"divinization" or "deification." Through the sacraments Christians gradually receive a limited share of the divine nature and become more than merely human.

Ignatius, like other apostolic fathers, left behind a helpful and troubling legacy for Christianity to wrestle with. For those Christians who value hierarchy of church leadership and a high sacramental view of salvation—grace transforming persons through sacramental rites—Ignatius is a hero and proof that this interpretation of the church and the gospel is early and authentic. Low-church Protestants who value simple, congregational church government and who consider baptism and the Lord's Supper "ordinances" rather than sacraments are not as enthusiastic about Ignatius's legacy. However, all Christians can agree that Ignatius passed on authoritatively an incarnational Christology that affirmed Jesus Christ as truly God and truly human and thus helped pave the way for full affirmation of the dogma of the Trinity. He also contributed to Christian unity and the fight against heresies, especially Gnosticism, and died a courageous death for the cause of Christ.

## Polycarp

Ignatius wrote most of his letters to churches, but one he wrote to his junior colleague Polycarp of Smyrna. He advised Polycarp, "If you love good disciples, it is no credit to you; rather with gentleness bring the more troublesome ones into submission."[16] Polycarp died a death similar to Ignatius's in his own city of Smyrna around 155. Sometimes the document known as the *Martyrdom of Polycarp*—a gruesomely detailed eyewitness report of his death—is included among the apostolic fathers. Other than its possible influence on the growing "cult of martyrs" among Christians (that is, the tendency to venerate martyrs as "saints"), this document has no theological significance. Polycarp himself, however, wrote at least one letter—to the Christians at Philippi. It is known, therefore, as the *Letter of Polycarp to the Philippians* and is usually included among the apostolic fathers. However, it also lacks great theological sophistication or significance for the story of theology.

### The Epistle of Barnabas

The *Epistle of Barnabas* was probably written in Alexandria, Egypt, between 70 and 135. The latter date is more likely than the former one. Nothing is known of its author except that he was almost certainly acquainted with one or more apostles such as Apollos (who is mentioned in the New Testament book of Acts) in his youth. Why he chose to represent his epistle as written by the apostle Barnabas is unknown. The epistle contains allegorical interpretations of Old Testament texts and attempts to show that the Christian church supersedes the Hebrews as God's people.

Before the *Epistle of Barnabas* was written, Jewish scholars in Alexandria, Egypt, had already interpreted the Hebrew Bible allegorically. Philo of Alexandria was a contemporary of Jesus' who was probably the most influential Jewish biblical scholar and theologian of the ancient Jewish diaspora. He attempted to show the harmony between Moses' teaching and the Old Testament generally and Greek philosophy, especially that of Plato and his followers. Christians in and around Alexandria were deeply influenced by Philo's method of interpreting the Old Testament nonliterally. The *Epistle of Barnabas* is a notable example. *Barnabas* says that when Moses forbade eating swine, he really meant, "You must not associate . . . with men who are like swine."[17]

It is tempting now to ridicule such allegorical interpretations as ludicrous, but modern readers should know that they were extremely common in the ancient world, especially in cultures profoundly influenced by Greek philosophy. In general, early Christians did not reject the literal or historical meanings of Scriptures, but they often looked for two or three layers of meaning in them. The "spiritual meaning," which is often difficult for modern readers to see in the same way, was considered the truer and deeper meaning than the literal, historical or ethical ones. The *Epistle of Barnabas* is just one example of this method of biblical hermeneutics. Later Christian scholars and theologians in Alexandria especially built on it and took it further.

Like other apostolic fathers, the *Epistle of Barnabas* portrays the way of salvation primarily in moralistic terms. Without denying salvation by grace as a sheer gift, *Barnabas* emphasizes a legalistic life of dos and don'ts as part and parcel of receiving final salvation: "It is good, therefore, after learning all the Lord's commandments which are written here to walk in them. For the one who does these things will be glorified in the kingdom of God; the one who chooses their opposites will perish together with his works. This is why there is a resurrection, this is why there is recompense."[18]

### The Shepherd of Hermas

The final apostolic father to be considered here is a document known as *The*

*Shepherd of Hermas,* whose author may have been the brother of Pius, the bishop of Rome around 140 to 145. *Hermas* is especially important in our story because, of all the Christian writings that came close to being included in the New Testament as the canon of Christian Scriptures was being determined, it came closest without finally being included. Various second- and third-century proposals listed it as either among the inspired books or as one of a secondary group of books to be used as inspirational Christian reading. The great church father Irenaeus of Lyons accepted *Hermas* as Scripture, as did third-century fathers Clement of Alexandria and Origen. Even the great Athanasius in the fourth century at first accepted it, though finally, however, he excluded it from the list in his Easter letter in 367. Without doubt, *The Shepherd of Hermas* had great influence among postapostolic Christians in various portions of the Roman Empire, and yet it is virtually unknown by most Christians today.

*Hermas* contains a series of visions and their explanations given by an angel to Hermas himself. Many of the interpretations are in parable form and are interspersed with commandments, instructions and mandates for Christian living. As one modern commentator says, *Hermas* is "one of the more enigmatic documents to have survived from the postapostolic period. . . . [But] it stands as an important witness to the state of Christianity in Rome in the mid-second century."[19] The angel who appears to Hermas as a shepherd reveals much to him in imagery like the apocalyptic symbolism of the New Testament book of Revelation. Much of it is difficult if not impossible to understand today. The import seems to be warning and preparation for impending persecution and conflict between Christians and opposing forces of darkness.

What catches the reader's attention, however, is *Hermas's* exhortations and commands to Christians and to Christian churches. As with other apostolic fathers, the tone is moralistic if not legalistic. Without denying or completely neglecting the themes of God's gracious forgiveness, *Hermas* seems more concerned to warn Christians about presumptuous sinning. In fact, the book warns that a person will be forgiven only once after baptism.[20]

The message of *Hermas* is that God's mercy is narrowly limited. God will forgive, but not endlessly. Furthermore, forgiveness is conditioned on keeping God's commandments. The Shepherd tells Hermas that "there will be forgiveness for your previous sins if you keep my commandments; in fact, there will be forgiveness for everyone, if they keep my commandments and walk in this purity"[21]

The belief that there could be only one pardon for sin after baptism contributed to a growing custom among converts to Christians to wait to be baptized until death was near. Of course this never became a universal practice, nor was it encouraged by church leaders, but it is easy to see how some "weaker" Christian converts would want to wait as long as possible to be baptized.

*Hermas* also delivers regulations and exhortations about marriage and divorce, wealth and money, citizenship and the testing of prophets as well as many other pressing issues for Christians in the Roman Empire. The book strictly forbids remarriage after divorce for any reason and strongly suggests that it is best for Christians to avoid sex altogether, whether married or otherwise. Overall *Hermas* points toward a strict, puritanical lifestyle bordering on asceticism. The gospel it proclaims is hardly recognizable as Christian insofar as it emphasizes the path to salvation as one of struggle, fear and self-denial. The great prestige of this book probably contributed to a growing moralistic and ascetic ideal for Christian living in the third and fourth centuries.

The clearest and most succinct statement of *Hermas's* version of the gospel appears near its beginning when the Shepherd (angel) first appears to Hermas and commands him to write:

> First of all, believe that God is one, who created all things and set them in order, and made out of what did not exist everything that is, and who contains all things but is himself alone uncontained. Believe in him, therefore, and fear him, and fearing him, be self-controlled. Keep these things, and you will cast off all evil from yourself and will put on every virtue of righteousness and will live to God, if you keep this commandment.[22]

This summary of the gospel speaks not only for *Hermas* but also summarizes nicely the overall sentiment of the apostolic fathers. While all mention God's mercy in response to true repentance and occasionally express the necessity of God's grace through the cross of Christ, they seem more concerned with promoting Christian virtue and obedience by instilling fear of judgment for moral failure. They also stress right belief about God, creation, Christ, the church and other matters.

A final point of the significance of *Hermas* has to do with its implicit Christology. During the second century the church was just beginning to struggle with right understanding of the nature and person of Jesus Christ. While all of the apostolic fathers who touch on the subject rejected docetism and Gnostic dualism, they were not united in their own ways of expressing how deity and humanity are related in Jesus Christ. *Hermas* seems to assume that Jesus was the incarnation of the Holy Spirit—a view known in the history of theology as "Spirit Christology." By later doctrinal standards, this would be considered a heresy, and it may be one reason Athanasius finally rejected *The Shepherd of Hermas* from the canon as he was guiding the church toward a settlement of that thorny issue.

*Hermas* explains that Jesus Christ was God in the flesh because

> the preexistent Holy Spirit, which created the whole creation, God caused to live in the flesh that he wished. This flesh, therefore, in which the Holy Spirit lived, served the Spirit well, living in holiness and purity, without defiling the Spirit in any way. So, because it [the flesh/humanity of Christ] had lived honorably and chastely, and had worked with the Spirit and had cooperated with it in everything, conducting itself with strength and bravery, he chose it as a partner with the Holy Spirit, for the conduct of this flesh pleased the Lord.[23]

Entirely missing, of course, is a full understanding of the Trinity and especially of the concept of the second person of the Trinity, the Son or Word (Logos), who became incarnate as Jesus Christ by taking on a human nature. But to expect the later doctrine (or dogma) of the two natures and one person of Christ or of the Trinity to be spelled out or even understood so early is probably expecting far too much from a second-century church father. Nevertheless, this implicit Spirit Christology seems confused and no doubt contributed to the delay of full agreement and definition of orthodoxy regarding the person of Christ and the Trinity.

### The Significance of the Apostolic Fathers

By this point some readers may be wondering why these apostolic fathers—or at least some of them—are included in the story of Christian theology as heroes of orthodoxy. Why not consider them heretics? Certainly compared to the gospel of grace, their messages seem severely moralistic, focusing on conduct rather than mercy and on salvation as a struggle rather than a gift. But it is important to keep in mind that they were attempting to counter rampant antinomianism (rejection of law and commandments) among Christians. The attitude that pervades them grows out of the same concern as the book of James in the New Testament: "Faith without works is dead." However, their prescribed antidote to the poison of antinomianism seems at times as bad or worse than the poison itself.

It would be wrong to hold the apostolic fathers in contempt or to reject them as implicit heretics merely because they did not fully understand and correctly communicate those dogmas of the church that were carved out only much later. It is to their credit that they stood up against Gnosticism and other perversions of the faith in spite of their own failings at many points.

The role of the apostolic fathers in the story of Christian theology is an ambiguous one. Especially the Protestant Christian's attitude toward that role and contribution will be ambivalent. On the one hand, the apostolic fathers provided a bridge between the apostles and orthodox, catholic Christianity and helped preserve and establish a relatively unified and theologically sound church. On the other hand, to one degree or another, they fell far short of handing on in their traditions the pure gospel of salvation as a gift that is not of works but of grace alone. Paul wrote to the Philippians, "Work out your own salvation with fear and trembling; for it is God who is at work in you, enabling you both to will and to work for his good pleasure" (2:12-13 NRSV). The apostolic fathers emphasized the first part of the message and most often neglected the second.

At about the same time that many of the apostolic fathers were writing to instruct Christians in right belief and conduct, another group of Christians in the Roman Empire were writing letters to pagan critics and Roman authorities defending the integrity of Christianity against misunderstandings and persecution. These writers are known as the apologists, and their part of the story of Christian theology comes next.

# CHAPTER 3

# The Apologists Defend the Faith

T*he story of Christian theology is deeply influenced by philosophy—especially* Greek (Hellenistic) philosophy. That comes as a surprise and often as a shock to Christians who assume that Christianity and philosophy are opposed to one another. That assumption is not at all uncommon and indeed is to be found very early in the story of Christian theology. One of the most influential church fathers, Tertullian, was appalled at the extent to which some of his contemporaries were using Greek philosophies such as Platonism and Stoicism to explain Christian ideas to pagan audiences. As already quoted, Tertullian asked in rhetorical indignation, "What indeed has Athens to do with Jerusalem? What concord is there between the [Platonic] Academy and the Church? What between heretics and Christians?"[1] One rift running right down the middle of Christian theology from very early on has been that between Christian thinkers who wish to meet critics on their own ground and argue the faith reasonably and even philosophically, and Christian thinkers who see that endeavor as a dangerous accommodation to enemies of the faith. Tertullian represents the latter approach.

The apologists were Christian writers of the second century who attempted to defend Christianity against pagan opponents such as Celsus. While a few of them like Tertullian rejected the philosophical approach, most of the apologists attempted to demonstrate similarities between the Christian message and worldview and the best of Greek philosophy. A few even considered Christianity "true philosophy" and attempted to show its superiority as philosophy to Hellenistic thought. In the process, of course, they had to compare and contrast the two in a way that implied their commensurability. That is, they could not be wholly dissimilar as Tertullian thought. While this idea was scandalous to Tertullian and some other early Christian thinkers, it was widely accepted in portions of Christianity, especially Alexandria and Rome, the two most important centers of culture in the Roman Empire.

The apologists' enterprise of examining and defending Christianity in light of Greek philosophy was not entirely new. A century or more earlier the Jewish scholar Philo had attempted to wed Judaism and Greek philosophy in Alexandria, Egypt. His great influence there among both Jews and Gentile God-fearers probably helps to explain why Alexandrian Christians in the second and third centuries were most open to this project of explaining the Bible and Christian beliefs philosophically. Some of the apologists emulated Philo's positive evaluation of Greek philosophers. Philo, for instance, had taught that Plato's philosophy and Moses' teachings were both based on divine revelation and at heart were similar if not identical. In order to make this work he had to interpret the Hebrew Scriptures allegorically. By using that method, he was able to blend Greek and Hebrew ways of thinking about God, creation and humanity. Philo's approach to Jewish thought was already widely accepted (though not without controversy) among Jews of the diaspora, and Christian apologists of the second century built on that foundation in order to show a similar consistency between the best of Hellenistic thought and their own fairly sophisticated versions of the Christian message.

Of course the apologists could also point back to Paul as a precursor and model. Acts 17 recounts the story of Paul's encounter with Greek philosophers in Athens in which he quoted some of their own poets and attempted to find a point of contact for his message in their belief in an "unknown God." Paul's attempt at Athens may be rather slim support for what some of the second-century Christian apologists tried to accomplish, but at least dialogue between an apostle and Greek thinkers in which the former quoted the authorities of the latter lent some credence to what they were trying to do.

## Greek Philosophy

Before discussing who these apologists were and how they contributed to the story of Christian theology, it will be helpful to briefly consider the main contours of the Greek philosophy many of them saw as an ally of Christian theology.

When the second-century Christian defenders of the faith looked around them in the Roman Empire and attempted to discover modes of thought that would help them communicate with thoughtful, reflective pagans such as Roman emperor

Marcus Aurelius, they saw all kinds of possibilities that simply had to be rejected. For example, the empire was rife with mystery religions—secretive initiation cults full of elaborate myths about dying and rising gods and paths to immortality through secret initiation ceremonies involving such things as being baptized in the blood of a slaughtered bull. There were also the occult philosophies of various magicians such as Apollonius of Tyana and Pythagoras, whose followers banded together secretly to put into practice their paranormal powers and study the esoteric meanings of numbers and heavenly bodies. Then there were the various temple ceremonies and myths about the Greek and Roman pantheons of gods and goddesses of Olympus such as Zeus and Apollo and Diana.

The second-century Christian apologists chose instead to defend the truth of Christianity on the basis of the philosophies of Platonism and Stoicism—or an amalgam of the two—that were widely accepted as superior to the other options mentioned above. Celsus, for example, simply assumed that all right-thinking, educated, seriously reflective people of the empire understood and believed in "the true doctrine," by which he meant a hybrid philosophy combining elements of Platonism, Stoicism and Epicureanism. While the Christian apologists found little of value in the Epicurean ingredient of the recipe, they found much common ground between the Christian life and worldview and the generic blend of Platonism and Stoicism that made up the common Greek philosophy of much of the Roman Empire in the second century.[2]

Greek philosophy rejected the polytheism of popular religion as well as the myths and initiation ceremonies of the mystery religions. That is not to say that all educated and reflective Roman citizens who believed in Greek philosophy completely avoided involvement with the temple rituals and initiations of pagan religion. But they tended to demythologize them and look upon these cults as fraternal organizations for fun and fellowship (or sensual satisfaction). Like Celsus, most educated and thoughtful people of the empire considered "true doctrine" to include belief in a single deity whose exact identity is beyond human knowledge but who shaped the universe and rules over it as a kind of benevolent and just despot. Those who leaned more toward Stoicism than Platonism tended to identify the divine with nature and its orderly course. In any case, Greek philosophy was monotheistic rather than polytheistic and contended strongly for the ultimately spiritual nature of the reality behind and beneath the visible things. It also affirmed the immortality of souls and the importance of living a "good life" of ethical behavior that sought the balance between extremes and avoided pure sensuality and selfishness.

The god of Greek philosophy was considered the *arché,* or ultimate source and origin of all things, even though it did not create the universe *ex nihilo* (out of nothing). Rather, it was seen as the source from which all things in the universe flow by emanation like rays from the sun and as the origin of order and design in everything. God is simple substance, completely free of body, parts or passions, immutable (unchangeable) and eternal (timeless). He (or it) is everything that finite creation is not—the epitome of metaphysical and moral perfection untouched by finitude, limitation, dependency, emotion, passion, change or decay.

The influence of such a philosophical theology on Philo in first-century Judaism is clear. He and other "Jewish philosophers [of the Hellenistic world] were eager to explain Old Testament ideas in relation to the highest levels of Greek theology, notably Middle Platonism."[3] Philo saw many similarities between the god of Greek philosophy who was one, metaphysically and morally perfect, and the creator and judge of all souls, and the Yahweh of the Hebrew tradition, who was the Creator, lawgiver and judge of everyone. Moses and Plato fit together nicely in Philo's version of Jewish Middle Platonism. This was the Jewish precedent for the Christian apologists' task of persuasively communicating Christian ideas to educated and reflective Romans. They were simply standing on Philo's shoulders and building a Hellenistic-Christian superstructure on his Hellenistic-Jewish foundation.

## The Category of Apologists

Who were these Christian apologists and exactly what did they contribute to the story of Christian thought? Of what value was that contribution?

As in the case of the apostolic fathers, there is no universal agreement about the category of the apologists. The category itself is, of course, a later invention of church historians and theologians. Lists of the apologists vary, and much of the diversity arises from attempts to include or exclude the author of the anonymously written *Epistle to Diognetus* and Origen and Tertullian.

The latter two lived and worked into the third century and in many ways stand apart from the other apologists as more highly developed and sophisticated in their theological approaches and contributions. Because they mainly wrote speculative and original Christian theologies (especially Origen) and antiheretical works (especially Tertullian) and because of their massive literary productions, they are often categorized more as "teachers of the church" than as apologists. Each one did, however, write apologies (defenses of Christian faith). Origen and Tertullian will be given separate treatment from the apologists in this recounting of the story of Christian theology in spite of the fact that they are often considered to belong in that category.

The *Epistle to Diognetus* is often listed with the apostolic fathers. Due to the fact that its author is completely unknown and to its clearly apologetic purpose and content, here it will be included with the apologists even though it is not highly philosophical in nature.

The apologists were Christian writers of the second century who were trying to influence relatively humane Roman emperors such as Marcus Aurelius and Antoninus Pius to take Christianity seriously if not as true. Most of them wrote open letters to these and other emperors and officials of the Roman Empire in which they attempted to explain the truth about Christian belief and behavior, often in philosophical ways. Church historian Robert Grant explains their purpose and contribution well: "These writers were contemporaries of the gnostics [and apostolic fathers] but took a very different path. Instead of esoteric spiritualism the apologists confidently used philosophical reason, and though they attacked philosophers they used their language whenever they could. They thus created the basic method of traditional Christian theology."[4] Grant's assertion about traditional Christian theology's "basic method" may be controversial. Certainly not all of it has been as heavily philosophical as many of the apologists' writings. Throughout the story of Christian theology, philosophy's use has been hotly debated and many have blamed the apologists for going too far in allowing Greek ideas to shape their own thinking about God. But Grant is right that "the major apologists gave Christianity a theology related to philosophy"—for better or worse.[5]

Besides the *Epistle to Diognetus,* the second-century Christian apologists were Aristides, Justin Martyr, Melito of Sardis, Athenagoras of Athens, Tatian and Theophilus of Antioch. Although their exact dates and other details of their lives are often unknown, all probably lived completely within the second century within the borders of the Roman Empire. Some were bishops and some were laymen. Some became martyrs and some of their deaths are unknown. All of them individually and together shaped the story of Christianity largely by making sure that it did not retreat under withering criticism into an underground existence as just another mystery religion. They helped develop Christian thought into theology proper—intellectual and reasonable examination and defense of the Christian message.

Of all the apologists three stand out as especially major characters in Christian theology's story. That is because of the highly developed nature of their thinking about God and because of their influence on later Christian thinkers such as Irenaeus, Origen and even Athanasius. They are Justin Martyr, Athenagoras and Theophilus.

**Justin Martyr**

Without doubt Justin Martyr deserves his reputation as "the most important second-century apologist"[6] because of his creative ideas about Christ as cosmic Logos and about Christianity as true philosophy. Many later Christian thinkers simply assumed the truth of Justin's suggestions and arguments in these areas and built on them in developing their own theologies. Justin was born into a Greek family in Palestine sometime in the first half of the second century. Very little is known of his pre-Christian life except that he became a philosopher of the Platonic school and then left that in favor of Christianity after a conversation with a mysterious old man. Tradition (from Eusebius) has it that Justin continued to wear his philosophical robe or tunic after converting to Christianity—no doubt a matter of some gossip and controversy among Christians in Rome when Justin arrived there to begin teaching Christianity around 150. It is clear from Justin's writings that he considered himself a Christian philosopher—a philosopher of Christ—just as he had been a philosopher of Plato. Also clear is that he considered the two compatible at many points. He referred to Plato's teacher Socrates as a "Christian before Christ." It may have been against Justin that Tertullian coined his famous rhetorical question "What has Athens to do with Jerusalem?"

Some of Justin's writings have been lost, but extant are three fairly brief but profound apologetic works. The *First Apology of Justin (Apology I)* was probably written in 155 on the occasion of Polycarp's martyrdom. It is a strongly worded and bold address to Emperor Antoninus Pius calling for a more just treatment of Christians. Justin exposed the evil practice of persecuting Christians merely because of their religious affiliation apart from any examination of behavior. He contradicted the prevalent rumors about Christians and argued that Christians are good citizens—although they may find it necessary to practice civil disobedience now and then—who worship God reasonably. Justin called on the emperor to reverse his decrees of persecution against Christians even though, he wrote, "we reckon that no evil can be done us, unless we be convicted as evil-doers, or be proved to be wicked men; and you, you can kill, but not hurt us."[7]

Folded within his pleas for justice were expositions of Christian beliefs and defenses of them. He argued that Plato—almost certainly the emperor's favorite philosopher—was indebted to Moses! He explained Christian worship and sacraments and explained why Christians reject idols.

At the end of his *First Apology* Justin addressed the emperor courageously: "If these things seem to you to be reasonable and true, honour them; but if they seem nonsensical, despise them as nonsense, and do not decree death against those who have done no wrong, as you would against enemies. For we forewarn you, that you shall not escape the coming judgment of God, if you continue in your injustice; and we ourselves will invite you to do that which is pleasing to God."[8]

For reasons unknown, Justin was himself executed in Rome by Roman authorities in 162. His *Apologies* reveal more than a few hints that he foresaw such a fate—at least as a very real possibility. Whether or not emperors actually read his open letters is debatable, but almost without doubt they were read by some Roman officials. While their bold assertiveness may have contributed to Justin's own death, the *Apologies* almost certainly gave Christians greater courage to keep pressing for justice from Roman authorities who claimed to be reasonable and fair.

Justin's *Second Apology (Apology II)* was addressed to the Roman senate around 160. Its tone has a certain desperation as Justin recounts examples of unjust and irrational treatment of Christians by the emperor and other Roman officials. Here the apologist pulled out every stop and argued that Roman treatment of Christians arose out of ignorance and prejudice and that it was only for Christians' sakes that God hesitated to wreak ruin upon the world. He compared Christ favorably with Socrates (a great hero of most Roman senators and other educated, upper-class Romans) and concluded by stating of Christians that "our doctrines are not shameful, according to sober judgment, but are indeed more lofty than all human philosophy," and asking his Roman readers to judge quickly in a manner becoming piety and philosophy "for your own sakes."[9] Justin probably meant that God's judgment was imminent due to their persecution of Christians.

Justin's third and final extant work is the *Dialogue with Trypho the Jew.* It contains Justin's autobiographical reflections about his philosophical journey and conversion to Platonism and then to Christianity and his theological explanations of how Christian belief in the incarnation—which the Jewish philosopher Trypho considered absurd—is consistent with monotheism.

Through his writings Justin explored and explained the concept of Christ as the Logos of God in order to explicate Christian beliefs. For him, this idea—rooted in both Greek and Hebrew thought—was the key to unlocking the mysteries of the Christian gospel. In his account of doctrine, the Logos is God's preexistent Spirit—a second God—who became incarnate in Jesus Christ. Justin was one of the first Christians to explain the Logos and Spirit concept in relation to the Father using the analogy of fire. He told Trypho that the Son's (Logos's) generation from the Father in no way diminishes the Father because, like fire kindled from fire, "that from which many can be kindled is by no means made less, but remains the same."[10] Although Justin did not clearly or completely work out the distinction between the Logos and Spirit as two persons of the Trinity—a task yet to be fulfilled by later Christian theologians—he was beginning the process of trinitarian reflection in response to Trypho's accusation "You endeavor to prove an incredible and well-nigh impossible thing: that God endured to be born and become man."[11]

Justin identified Jesus Christ with the "cosmic Logos," who is God's offshoot and agent in creation. Clearly he was interpreting the opening verses of John's Gospel as well as borrowing from Hellenistic ideas about the Logos. Almost every Greek philosophy—as well as Philo's Hellenistic Jewish theology—had a role for a being known as the Logos. In every case the Logos was thought of as a mediating being between the one God and creation. Justin was saying, "That is who we mean when we Christians speak of Christ—he is the cosmic Logos known to Greeks."

This Logos (Christ) was in the world before Jesus Christ. He spoke through both Jewish prophets and Greek philosophers. Justin called him the *Logos spermatikos*—the "seed of the Logos"—in every human being and the source of all truth whenever it is understood and uttered. One of the most famous passages in early Christian literature appears in Justin's *Apology II* and expresses his view of the universal, cosmic Logos who is Christ:

> I confess that I both boast and with all my strength strive to be found a Christian; not because the teachings of Plato are different from those of Christ, but because they are not in all respects similar, as neither are those of the others, Stoics, and poets, and historians. For each man spoke well in proportion to the share he had in the spermatic word *[logos spermatikos]* seeing what was related to it. . . . Whatever things were rightly said among all men, are the property of us Christians. For next to God, we worship and love the Word who is from the unbegotten and ineffable God, since also he became man for our sakes, that, becoming a partaker of our sufferings, He might also bring us healing.[12]

Thus Justin used the cosmic Logos concept to explain why Christians may embrace all truth as God's truth—whatever its human source may be—and why Christians can believe in and worship Jesus Christ as God (a "second God") without rejecting monotheism. Christ as the universal Logos preexisted Jesus as God's Son as fire taken from fire—somewhat less than God himself but of God's own nature and substance. The same Christ as universal Logos is the source of all truth, beauty and goodness. But Justin argued that only Christians know the Logos fully because he became flesh in Jesus Christ. In this way Justin established a Christian tradition of Logos Christology that replaced Spirit Christology and reached toward the doctrine of the Trinity while at the same time expressing a Christian appreciation of philosophy and culture as rooted in the activity of the Logos before he became incarnate as Jesus Christ.

**Athenagoras of Athens**

Like Justin, Athenagoras the Athenian was both a philosopher and a Christian. Among other documents he wrote *A Plea for the Christians* in the form of an open letter to Emperor Marcus Aurelius when he was about to visit Athens. Like Justin and other apologists, he tried to persuade the emperor to cease persecuting Christians, and one of his main strategies was to refute the most common false accusations and rumors about them. But more pertinent to the story of Christian theology is Athenagoras's reflections on Christian belief about God and his Son, Jesus Christ.

Apparently Athenagoras believed that it would help the emperor to stop persecuting Christians if he understood that Christians believed in a God much like he believed in. Marcus Aurelius was a philosopher most influenced by Stoicism, whose god was virtually equated with the immutable and perfect order of the universe. Certainly the Stoics affirmed one god and rejected polytheism even if they came close to embracing a pantheistic view of god and the world. In any case, the most significant portions of Athenagoras's *Plea* has to do with the Christian doctrine of God.

First, Athenagoras quoted various Greek poets and philosophers in order to remind the emperor that the best of Hellenistic thought was monotheistic. He then proceeded to assure the emperor that Christians were not "atheists" as one popular cavil claimed:

> That we are not atheists, therefore, seeing that we acknowledge one God, uncreated, eternal, invisible, impassible, incomprehensible, illimitable, who is apprehended by the understanding only and the reason who is encompassed by light and beauty, and spirit, and power ineffable, by whom the universe has been created through His Logos, and set in order, and is kept in being—I have sufficiently demonstrated.[13]

Interesting to note is how Athenagoras described the God Christians believe in. While there is no debate about the biblical basis of such divine attributes as "uncreated" and "eternal" and few would question that God is "invisible" (apart from the incarnation in Jesus Christ), many Christian scholars have questioned whether Athenagoras was perhaps unduly influenced by Greek ideas of divinity when he characterized God as "impassible" (incapable of suffering or emotional feeling) and "incomprehensible" (beyond human understanding). Especially when he affirmed that the God Christians believe in is "apprehended by the understanding only and the reason," doubts arise about the relative weight of Hebrew versus Greek thinking in his doctrine of God.

Athenagoras described God primarily with negative attributes. That is, he explained what God is *not* rather than what God *is.* Later Christian theologians labeled this approach "apophatic theology," and it became a major part of the story of Christian theology. Apparently Athenagoras and later apophatic thinkers assumed that God's perfection means being unlike anything created. Thus God can only be truly described by saying what he is *not* rather than what he *is.* He is not imperfect, and to change or suffer or even be comprehensible by the human mind is to be tainted by creaturely imperfection. The result, of course, was a gradual diminishing of the biblical God's personal nature. Of course neither Athenagoras nor any other Christian thinker rejected God's personal being, but some of the ways in which they began to describe God seem to be more like the transcendent origin and ground of all things *(arché)* in Greek philosophy, which is rather abstract, than the very concrete, personal and interactive God of the Hebrew Bible and apostolic writings.

Athenagoras continued his *Plea* to the emperor by answering the charge that it is ridiculous that God should have a Son. This was a common point for ridiculing Christian belief. Christians spoke often and adoringly of God's Son, Jesus Christ. Why would educated, reflective pagans such as Celsus and Marcus Aurelius find this offensive and evidence of ignorance and superstition? For one thing, the full Christian doctrine of the Trinity had not yet been developed. It was only latent or incipient within Christian thought. It seemed to pagans that Christians were simply contradicting themselves by saying that God is one and that God has a Son who is worthy of worship. It also seemed to imply some imperfection in God if he gave birth to a Son. Did he become a father? Can God "become" anything? How can one be a father of a son eternally? These and many other questions were largely unanswered by Christians at the time Athenagoras and other apologists wrote. To many pagan opponents of Christianity, the whole idea of God giving birth or having a Son sounded mythological.

Athenagoras presented one of the first theological explanations of the doctrine of the Trinity in order to clear away the misconceptions and objections against Christian belief: "We acknowledge a God, and a Son his Logos, and a Holy Spirit, united in essence—the Father, the Son, the Spirit, because the Son is the Intelligence, Reason, Wisdom of the Father, and the Spirit an effluence, as light from fire."[14] This is perhaps the earliest relatively clear statement of the doctrine of the Trinity in Christian theology. In that same context Athenagoras also stated that the Logos is God's "first product" even though he was not brought into existence, as he always had existed within God as his Logos. Athenagoras did not delve into the thorny issue of how the Logos (Son of God) is incarnate in Jesus

Christ. He simply assumed that the emperor and other readers knew that this Logos is the very same Christ Christians worship and that he is believed to be eternally in the Father and yet to have "come forth" from the Father. The details are left unresolved.

Both Justin and Athenagoras made use of a well-known Greek idea that is also found in apostolic writings—the Logos—to solve certain problems inherent in Christian belief and worship. Their intentions were good. Some of the unintended consequences are troubling. Later Christian thinkers of the third and fourth centuries wrestled mightily with questions of the Logos's relation to God the Father. However, the apostolic fathers cannot be faulted for using the idea as a bridge between Christian teaching about God and Greek philosophical theology.

### Theophilus of Antioch

The last apologist to be considered here is Theophilus of Antioch, who wrote three books *To Autolycus* around 180. Little is known about Theophilus other than that he was bishop of the Christians in Antioch—one of the most important cities of the empire for pagans and Christians alike. He succeeded as bishop the person who succeeded Ignatius on his martyrdom in 115, probably the year Theophilus was born. Theophilus died of an unknown cause sometime in the 180s.

Autolycus was Theophilus's pagan friend, and the latter wrote his three books to respond to disparaging comments he had made about Christianity. Theophilus's modern translator says of his apologetic books that "the whole treatise is well fitted to lead an intelligent pagan to the cordial acceptance of Christianity."[15] Theophilus's apologetic writings are less philosophical than either Justin's or Athenagoras's. He even criticized Greek literature and philosophy. His own influence seems to have come mainly from Hellenistic Judaism but without the strong allegorizing method of interpreting Scripture. Theophilus well represents the Antiochene approach to biblical interpretation, which tended to be more historical and literal than the Alexandrian allegorical method.

Theophilus is noted in the story of Christian theology for first introducing the concept of *creatio ex nihilo*—creation out of nothing. That is not to say that other and even earlier church fathers did not believe it. But Theophilus explicitly contradicted the Greek tendency to view the universe as eternal. After quoting the opening verses of Genesis, he averred that "this, sacred Scripture teaches at the outset, to show that matter, from which God made and fashioned the world, was in some manner created, being produced by God."[16]

In spite of the influence of Greek thought on the apologists generally, at this one point Theophilus managed to steer Christian thought away from the Greek consensus. How perfect, after all, is a God who has a finite counterpart such as matter to wrestle with from all eternity? Eternal matter would limit God. If God is truly infinite and perfect, then the universe must be created freely and out of absolutely nothing.

Like the other apologists Theophilus used the concept of Logos to explain God's relationship with the world. The Logos is God's agent in creation and in speaking through the prophets. He is eternally within God and is emitted (literally, "belched") into being by the Father so that the perfect Father, God, can relate to the world of time and creation and speak by the Logos through the prophets:

> God, then, having His own Word internal within His own bowels, begat Him, emitting Him along with His own wisdom before all things. He had this Word as a helper in the things that were created by Him, and by Him He made all things. He is called "governing principle" *[arché],* because He rules, and is Lord of all things fashioned by Him. He, then, being Spirit of God, and governing principle, and wisdom, and power of the highest, came down upon the prophets, and through them spake of the creation of the world and of all other things. For the prophets were not when the world came into existence, but the wisdom of God which was in Him, and His holy Word which was always present with Him.[17]

Theophilus's thinking about the Trinity was a bit confused. He failed properly to distinguish between the Word (Logos) of God and the Spirit of God. Other early Christian theologians simply adjusted this so that God's Spirit is his eternal Wisdom and the Son is his eternal Word (Logos). Interesting to note, however, is that Theophilus clearly interpreted the Son of God (Word, Logos) as eternal in God. Later orthodoxy rejected the idea that God "emitted" him just before creation, however, because this implies change in both God the Father and his Word.

Theophilus had little or nothing to say about Jesus Christ. Like other second-century apologists he was more interested in the status of the Logos-being who became incarnate in Jesus Christ than in the historical man Jesus himself. This is understandable in that the apologists were all attempting to answer questions and concerns posed by Greek and Roman pagans, and their most pressing concerns about Christian theology had to do with Christ's status vis-à-vis God. The solution is found in the preexistent, heavenly Logos, not in the historical life of the man Jesus.

### The Apologists' Ambiguous Legacy

What did apologists like Justin, Athenagoras and Theophilus contribute to the story of Christian theology? Much indeed. But like the apostolic fathers, they left an ambiguous legacy. If not for the apologists and their work, Christianity may very well have been reduced to an esoteric mystery religion or else a mere folk religion without any influence in the wider public sphere of culture. The apologists took the Christian message public and defended it vigorously and rigorously against misunderstandings and false accusations. In the process they launched Christian theology beyond the bare, minimal reflections of the apostolic fathers onto a new plane of formal, rational thought about the implications of the apostolic message for Christian belief about God, Christ, salvation and other important beliefs. They also attempted to relate and communicate those ideas to the wider world of pagan culture—much like Paul's endeavor at Athens. From the apologists on, official Christian theology would be public and not just a private belief system for the initiated few.

The apologists also contributed much to the story of Christian theology in the way of initial reflection on the all-important Christian beliefs about God and Jesus Christ, and in the process began laying the foundation for the full-fledged doctrine of the Trinity yet to be constructed. Unfortunately, most of them had little to say about the historical Jesus, whom they all believed to be the incarnation in time and material existence of the eternal Son of God. Their main concern, however, was to explicate the meaning of Christian belief in Jesus Christ as God incarnate. In order to explain this to non-Christian Greeks and Romans, they turned to the well-known concept of the cosmic Logos—a spiritual mediator between the divine world and the material world. Although they often confused the preexistent Logos with the Holy Spirit—or at least failed appropriately to distinguish them—the apologists made clear Christian monotheism as belief in one God, the Father of all; his emanation, the Logos (Son of God), who is eternal in him and comes forth from him into the world; and the Holy Spirit, who is the Father's Wisdom and Power.

The apologists' use of Greek philosophy has been hotly debated among Christians. Seventeenth-century French Christian thinker Blaise Pascal declared, "The God of the philosophers is not the God of Abraham, Isaac and Jacob!" Many critics accuse the apologists of unwittingly creating a hybrid of Hebrew and Christian thought about God with Greek—especially Platonic—notions of deity. The influential Protestant church historian Adolf Harnack called this the "Hellenization of Christianity" and traced its course from the apologists on through later church fathers. Other church historians defend them and their theologies against such accusations. Perhaps Robert Grant is closest to the accurate assessment of the apologists when he writes that "in spite of their inadequate semiphilosophical theology, the apologists did maintain much of the biblical teaching."[18] Their tendency toward an overemphasis on God's infinity and perfection—defined in Greek philosophical terms—contributed to difficulties Christians later experienced in understanding and explaining the incarnation—God in human flesh experiencing human sufferings, limitations and even death. And yet one finds many gems of Christian truth and great insights into Christian living in their writings.

Until the final quarter of the second century, Christianity lacked any single great teacher. No single apostolic father or apologist stands out as head and shoulders above the rest. None were great systematic thinkers who pulled together Christian belief in a coherent whole that was both truly biblical and intelligible to inquiring pagan minds. The first great systematic theologian in the story of Christian theology is Irenaeus, bishop of Lyons. His contribution to that story comes next.

# CHAPTER 4

# Irenaeus Exposes Heresies

C*hristianity's first theologians were the apostolic fathers, and they wrote* primarily to exhort, encourage and instruct Christian churches in the transitional time after the deaths of the apostles. Their letters were brief and directed at specific problems. A few of them such as Ignatius of Antioch began to reflect on the meaning of Christian beliefs and practices and add their own words to those of the apostles. No Christian apostle ever referred to the Lord's Supper as the "medicine of immortality." This was the beginning of Christian theology, but not a very auspicious one. The apologists added their voices to the chorus of Christian theology by writing to non-Christian authorities to explain Christian beliefs and practices. In the process they often interpreted them using non-Christian philosophy. Like the apostolic fathers, however, the apologists barely went beneath the surface in exploring and explaining Christian belief as a whole. The apostolic fathers and apologists laid the foundation of Christian theology but did not build upon it. Irenaeus added at least the first story of a superstructure to that foundation.

### Irenaeus's Life and Ministry

Irenaeus was born in or near Smyrna in Asia Minor in about 120. As a young man he was tutored in Christian faith by the great bishop Polycarp of Smyrna, from whom he learned the traditions of Jesus' disciple the apostle John. Sometime around midcentury Irenaeus was sent to the other end of the Roman Empire to be a presbyter (elder) among Christian emigrants from Asia Minor to Gaul

(France). Irenaeus settled in Lyons on the Rhone River in southern Gaul and quickly rose in the ranks as a noted young leader among the Christians there.

In 177 Emperor Marcus Aurelius unleashed a terrible persecution of Christians in the Rhone Valley. Bishop Pothinus was killed along with hundreds if not thousands of Christian laypeople and presbyters. The accounts of this particular local persecution are terrifying to read. Apparently the local population devised ingenious and cruel methods of killing Christians. One popular method was packing Christians into small rooms without windows and closing the doors so that they slowly suffocated. Another means of execution was to sew them up in fresh animal skins and put them out in the hot sun to die by slow asphyxiation.

Irenaeus escaped death during the anti-Christian pogrom in Gaul because he had been sent to Rome to protest heresies that were being brought to Christians in his home region from there. During several journeys to Rome, he gained a reputation among Christians as a man skilled in diplomacy and mediation. While he was in Rome in the time of great persecution, he encountered a former disciple of Polycarp who had converted from apostolic Christianity to one of the fastest growing Gnostic cults—Valentinus's school of Gnosticism. Irenaeus was dismayed then and was dismayed even more so when he returned to his own Christian community in Gaul and discovered that Valentinus's and other forms of Gnosticism were catching on among Christians there.

Irenaeus became bishop of the Christians in and around Lyons and spent much of his time and energy fighting the growing influence of Gnosticism. He wrote five volumes known as *Adversus haereses*—Latin for *Against Heresies.* Although he wrote in Greek, because he and his fellow Christians in Lyons were mostly from Asia Minor, Irenaeus's writings have survived only in Latin translations. The longer title for *Against Heresies* is *A Refutation and Subversion of Knowledge Falsely So-Called.* It was the first sustained critical examination and refutation of Gnosticism by an influential Christian leader, and because of Irenaeus's link through Polycarp back to John, it was widely accepted as authoritative and contributed significantly to Gnosticism's eventual decline among Christians. In the process of exposing Gnosticism, Irenaeus also developed a Christian interpretation of redemption that profoundly influenced the entire course and direction of Christian theology, especially in the Eastern regions of the Christian church where Greek was the main language. Some Eastern Orthodox theologians aver that all of theology is but a series of footnotes to Irenaeus. In any case, it would be difficult to overestimate his influence.

Irenaeus also wrote a little handbook of Christian doctrine entitled *Proof of the Apostolic Preaching,* also known as *Epideixis,* as a brief summary of his larger and more complex *Against Heresies.* This practice of writing a small introduction to Christian doctrine and theology for laypeople who might have difficulty reading and understanding the weightier books became a common practice for centuries to come. In Latin such a slim volume came to be called an *enchiridion,* a term meaning both "handbook" and "dagger." Such little volumes of Christian teaching were considered weapons of spiritual warfare.

Irenaeus died in Lyons during a massacre of Christians in 202. Nothing is known for certain about the manner of his death, but he was counted a martyr and saint by both Greek-speaking Christians of the East and Latin-speaking Christians of the Western half of the Roman Empire. His greatest impact theologically, however, was in the East where he was born.

Irenaeus is a crucial figure in the story of Christian theology because he was instrumental in defeating Gnosticism and because he was the first Christian thinker to work out comprehensive theories of original sin and redemption. However, he was far from being a speculative thinker. Back in Alexandria, Egypt, some other younger contemporaries of Irenaeus would soon begin to develop speculative theologies that attempted to provide Christian answers to all the mysteries of reality. Irenaeus was not a philosophical theologian even though he went beyond the actual words of the apostles in order to provide a comprehensive and coherent apostolic account of sin and redemption that would be a powerful alternative to Gnosticism. A major modern interpreter of Irenaeus has rightly written that

> no more than other Christian authors of his era does Irenaeus write out of an interest in the problems of theology for their own sake. His work is, in the strictest sense, occasional, motivated by pastoral rather than purely intellectual concerns. In consequence, what he has to say and the way in which he says it are jointly determined by the concrete situation to which he addressed himself.[1]

That "concrete situation" was Gnosticism and its growth among Christians in all parts of the Roman Empire. Irenaeus considered it a genuine threat to the gospel and to the survival of authentic Christianity. But his own explanation of the truth was shaped by his need to counter the false gospel of Gnosticism. That is not to say it was infected or corrupted by it. It is only to note that, as is so often the case, the heresy opposed indirectly shaped at least the form if not the content of the orthodoxy gradually being developed as its alternative. Thus if Irenaeus's theology of redemption seems somewhat speculative at times, it is not because he set out to write an abstract, speculative theology but because he felt the need to provide Christians attracted to Gnosticism with a version of apostolic Christianity that would meet their needs for answers to certain questions about the origin of sin and evil and the hope of redemption.

**Irenaeus's Assault on Gnosticism**

Irenaeus's assault on Gnosticism was anything but the kind of cool, rational approach modern people might expect of a bishop or theologian. He clearly considered it foolish and sinister and wished to expose it once and for all as a complete corruption of the gospel in the guise of "higher wisdom for spiritual people." In order to expose Gnosticism, Irenaeus spent months and years studying at least twenty distinct Gnostic teachers and their schools. He found that the most influential one was the Valentinian Gnosticism that had taken hold among Christians in Rome through the teachings of a Gnostic leader named Ptolemaeus. Therefore, he focused on exposing that one as ridiculous and false with the hope that all the others would be crushed by the weight of its fall.

Irenaeus's approach to the critique of Gnosticism in *Against Heresies* was threefold. First, he attempted to reduce the Gnostic worldview to absurdity by showing that much of it was invented mythology with no foundation on anything other than imagination. This first strategy included exposing Gnosticism's inner contradictions and fundamental incoherence. Its truth claims conflicted with one another. Second, he attempted to show that the Gnostic claim to authority going back to Jesus and the apostles was simply false. Finally, he engaged Gnostic interpretation of Scripture in debate and showed it to be unreasonable and even impossible.

In the background of Irenaeus's polemical exposé of Gnosticism lie several assumptions. He clearly assumed that he had a special role and position as one tutored in Christianity by Polycarp, who in turn was mentored by John. Many of the Gnostics claimed that John was part of an inner group of Jesus' disciples who received from the Savior a "secret teaching" not available to most Christians because they were not spiritually fit to understand it. While they could find hints of their own worldview and gospel in apostolic writings, they had to rely on a secret oral tradition as the main source of their authority. Irenaeus assumed that if such a teaching existed, Polycarp would have known of it and would have told him about it. That none of the bishops of the Christians recognized or acknowledged it seriously undermined the Gnostics' claim.

Another basic assumption underlying Irenaeus's critique of Gnosticism was that the Gnostics were the ones who broke the unity of the church. They were the schismatics. Irenaeus highly valued the church's visible unity that consisted in the fellowship of the bishops appointed by the apostles. The Gnostics stood outside of that and were parasites on it. For Irenaeus and many of his readers this was a major strike against them.

One difficulty often encountered in reading *Against Heresies* is the sheer volume of Irenaeus's recounting of Gnostic beliefs. It is easy to get bogged down in that and give up reading altogether. For example, Irenaeus explained the teaching of Valentinus regarding the origin of the world this way:

> He maintained that there is a certain Dyad (two-fold being), who is inexpressible by any name, of whom one part should be called Arrhetus (unspeakable), and the other Sige (silence). But of this Dyad a second was produced, one part of whom he names Pater, and the other Aletheia. From this Tetrad, again, arose Logos and Zoe, Anthropos and Ecclesia. These constitute the primary Ogdoad. . . . There is another, who is a renowned teacher among them, and who, struggling to reach something more sublime, and to attain to a kind of higher knowledge, has explained the primary Tetrad as follows: There is [he says] a certain Proarche who existed before all things, surpassing all thought, speech, and nomenclature, whom I call Monotes (unity). Together with this Monotes there exists a power, which again I term Henotes (oneness). This Henotes and Monotes, being one, produced, yet not so as to bring forth . . . the beginning of all things, an intelligent, unbegotten, and invisible being, which beginning language terms "Monad." With this Monad there co-exists a power of the same essence, which again I term Hen (One). These powers then—Monotes, and Henotes, and Monas, and Hen—produced the remaining company of Aeon.[2]

Irenaeus stopped his laborious exposition of Gnostic metaphysics at this point and responded passionately with a parody of this so-called Christian view of creation based on allegedly higher knowledge and wisdom:

> Iu, Iu! Pheu, Pheu!—for well may we utter these tragic exclamations at such a pitch of audacity in the coining of names as he has displayed without a blush, in devising a nomenclature for his own system of falsehood. For when he declares: There is a certain Proarche before all things, surpassing all thought, whom I call Monotes; and again, with this Monotes there co-exists a power which I also call Henotes,—it is most manifest that he confesses the things which have been said to be his own invention, and that he himself has given names to this scheme of things, which had never been previously suggested by any other. It is manifest also, that he himself is the one who has had sufficient audacity to coin these names; so that, unless *he* had

> appeared in the world, the truth would still have been destitute of a name. But, in that case, nothing hinders any other, in dealing with the same subject, to affix names after such a fashion as the following: There is a certain Proarche, royal, surpassing all thought, a power existing before every other substance, and extended into space in every direction. But along with it there exists a power which I term a *Gourd;* and along with this Gourd there exists a power which again I term *Utter-Emptiness.* This Gourd and Emptiness, since they are one, produced (and yet did not simply produce, so as to be apart of themselves) a fruit, everywhere visible, eatable, and delicious, which fruit-language calls a *Cucumber.* Along with this Cucumber exists a power of the same essence, which again I call a *Melon.* These powers, the Gourd, Utter-Emptiness, the Cucumber, and the Melon, brought forth the remaining multitude of the delirious melons of Valentinus. . . . If any one may assign names at his pleasure, who shall prevent us from adopting these names, as being much more credible [than the others], as well as in general use, and understood by all?[3]

If Irenaeus's modern reader perseveres through the pages and pages of explanation of Gnostic systems and terminology, the reward is the occasional gem of wry humor and sarcasm that reveals something of Irenaeus's personality and abhorrence of Gnosticism's patently absurd worldview.

All of the major Gnostic sects and schools denigrated the physical creation and denied its origin in the supreme God of goodness and light. Most of them, including Valentinus's school, introduced levels of emanations from God of pure spirit and light who gradually fell away and somehow ended up creating the material universe, including human bodies wherein sparks of the divine (souls, spirits) are imprisoned and entrapped. Against this view of creation Irenaeus affirmed the Christian doctrine of God as both Creator and Redeemer of material as well as spiritual existence. Against the Gnostics he quoted John 1:3 and other Old Testament and apostolic passages (later to be included in the New Testament) that treat God as the Creator of all things through his Word and Spirit, and he discounted their own interpretations of biblical references to angels and spiritual powers and principalities as fabulous and incredible.

**Irenaeus's Theory of Redemption**

While Irenaeus's critique of Gnosticism played a significant role in the story of Christian theology by exposing that belief system as heretical by biblical and apostolic standards, his real contribution to theology's story lies in his own alternative vision to Gnosticism. Historical theologians have labeled that Irenaean contribution the "theory of recapitulation," from the Latin term *capitus,* which means "head." Without doubt Irenaeus himself used the Greek term *anakephalaiosis,* which comes from the root *kephalē,* which means "head." *Anakephalaiosis* and *recapitulatio* literally mean "reheading" or "providing a new head." Of course, Irenaeus was not thinking at all of a literal head, as the top part of a body, but of "head" as the source or origin of something, such as the head of a river or stream. In *Against Heresies* and in *Proof of the Apostolic Preaching,* Irenaeus laid out what he believed to be the apostolic Christian teaching about Christ's work of redemption as providing a new "head" of humanity—recapitulation.

The Gnostics thought of Christ's work as purely spiritual and denied the incarnation. For them Christ—the heavenly redeemer—never did get entangled with flesh-and-blood existence. He came down through the levels of aeons and archons and either appeared as a human being without truly taking on human physical nature or else entered into the body of a human being known as Jesus of Nazareth in order to use it as his instrument for teaching about the spiritual origin of human souls. In either version of Gnostic Christology, Christ's work did not require incarnation. His mission was merely to reveal a message to spirits. The material-physical dimension had nothing to do with it, and when Jesus was crucified, Christ was not in him or with him. The human life and death of the man Jesus, then, played no role in redemption. The Gnostics rejected the historical, physical life and death of Jesus from their soteriology (doctrine of salvation).

Irenaeus sought to show that the gospel of salvation taught by the apostles and handed down from them centered upon the incarnation—the human flesh-and-blood existence of the Word, the Son of God. Therefore he emphasized every point of Jesus' life as necessary for salvation. Christ's work on our behalf went far beyond his teachings and extended to the incarnation itself. For Irenaeus (and most of the church fathers after him) incarnation itself was redemptive, not merely a necessary step toward either Christ's teachings or the cross event. Rather the becoming human of the Son of God—God's eternal Word (Logos) experiencing human existence—was what redeems and restores fallen humanity if they let it. This idea has come to be known as saving incarnation and is absolutely crucial to the entire course of the story of theology from Irenaeus on. That is why whenever a theology arose that somehow seemed to threaten the incarnation of God in Jesus, the church fathers reacted so strongly. Any threat to the incarnation—however subtle—was perceived as a threat to salvation. If Jesus Christ was not both truly human and truly divine, salvation is incomplete and impossible. The entirety of redemption hangs on the reality of Christ's flesh-and-blood birth, life, suffering, death and resurrection as well as on his eternal power and deity.

For Irenaeus, then, the incarnation was the key to the entire history of redemption and to personal salvation. The incarnation itself was transformative. It began a process of reversing the corruption of sin that results in alienation from God and death. *Anakephalaiosis,* or recapitulation, was Irenaeus's theological expression for how the physical incarnation of the Word in Jesus Christ works to transform humanity. In a literal sense the entire human race is "born again" in the incarnation. It receives a new "head"—a new source, origin, ground of being—that is unfallen, pure and healthy, victorious and immortal. It is "fully alive"—both physically and spiritually.

The Gnostics held out no hope for the human race as a whole or even for whole human beings. Only spirits—and only a few of them—had any hope of being transformed and that only through *gnosis* (knowledge). Irenaeus deeply implanted into the Christian consciousness a belief and a hope in Jesus Christ as transformer of the whole human race through his fusion of divinity with humanity in the incarnation.

Exactly how does Irenaeus's anti-Gnostic theory of redemption—recapitulation—work? That is, what is the mechanism by which the incarnation itself transforms and saves humanity? First of all, it must be understood that Irenaeus assumed a solidarity of humanity in both sin and redemption. That assumption is foreign to many modern Christians, who tend to think and live in a much more individualistic—if not atomistic—fashion. Irenaeus and his colleagues in the early church were no "Jesus-and-me" Christians. He believed and taught that what Adam did in the Garden of Eden (Gen 3) and what Jesus Christ did through his entire life (including his death) affected other human beings automatically because Adam and Jesus Christ (the "second Adam") are not merely individuals but fountainheads of humanity.

In the background of this thinking, of course, stands Paul's reflections on Adam and Christ in Romans 5. Without some awareness of that all-important passage, it is impossible to grasp what Irenaeus is teaching. His theory of recapitulation was an extended and sustained interpretation of Romans 5. Christ is very literally the second Adam of the human race, and in him "God recapitulated in Himself the ancient formation of man [Adam], that he might kill sin, deprive death of its power, and vivify man and therefore His works are true."[4]

When Irenaeus wrote that in Jesus Christ God "recapitulated the ancient formation of man," he meant that in the incarnation the Word (Logos) took on the very "protoplast" (physical source) of humanity—the body of Adam—and lived the reverse of Adam's course of life that resulted in corruption. All of humanity is descended from that protoplast—the first Adam. Therefore in order to reverse the Fall and renew the race that fell because of Adam, the Word had to live through it in order to transform both it and its posterity. From Mary, then, the Word took "the very same formation" as Adam—not just one like it. Adam was in some mysterious way reborn of Mary as the humanity of Jesus Christ. For Irenaeus

> if man is to be saved, it is necessary that the first man, Adam, be brought back to life, and not simply that a new and perfect man who bears no relation to Adam should appear on the earth. God, who has life, must permit His life to enter into "Adam" the man who truly hungers and thirsts, eats and drinks, is wearied and needs rest, who knows anxiety, sorrow and joy, and who suffers pain when confronted with the fact of death.[5]

This is Irenaeus's "proof" of the incarnation against the Gnostics who denied it. Without the incarnation Christ could not have reversed the fall of Adam and redemption would not be accomplished. Sin and death would remain forever fundamental aspects of the human condition.

For Irenaeus, Jesus Christ provided redemption by going through the entire scope of human life and at each juncture reversing the disobedience of Adam. Whereas the first Adam disobeyed God and fell, introducing corruption and death into human existence, the second Adam obeyed God and lifted humanity up to a higher state than even Adam experienced before he fell.

The real crux of Christ's accomplishment of redemption came at the event of temptation by Satan in the wilderness. When Satan came to Eve and to Adam, they were conquered and fell. When Satan came to Adam again in Christ, he was conquered and put down, and humanity through its connection with Christ achieved a great victory and regained life.

If the temptation was the crux, the cross and resurrection were the culmination of Christ's work of recapitulation. By dying in obedience to God, Jesus Christ provided the ultimate sacrifice and conquered death. Those who willingly participate in Christ's new humanity by choosing him rather than the first Adam as their "head" through repentance, faith and the sacraments receive the transformation made possible by the incarnation of the Son of God. They enter into a new humanity—a new race—with the hope of sharing in God's own immortal, divine nature.

For Irenaeus, then, redemption was a process of restoring creation rather than one of escaping creation as in the Gnostics' soteriology. It was a process of reversing the corruption that entered into creation through Adam's fall, and "the end of this process is man's entrance upon a life which is no longer subject to the limitations of generate existence; a life in which, in fact, the liabilities of creaturehood are overcome by the grace of God. This life is characterized by that incorruption which both results from and leads to the vision of God and the mirroring of God's glory in man himself."[6] Irenaeus clearly envisioned salvation as transformation of humans into partakers of the divine nature (2 Pet 1:4). This idea of redemption—known to later church fathers as "divinization," or "deification" *(theosis)*—lies in the background of Irenaeus's vision of Christ's work as recapitulation.

God's purpose and goal in redemption is to reverse the sin, corruption and death introduced into humanity by Adam and lift humanity up to life and immortality. The incarnation accomplishes this as a possibility by fusing humanity with divinity. Humans may be "divinized" by solidarity with Christ while remaining humans and not becoming God himself. The basic contours of this vision of salvation are assumed by most later church fathers. During the Reformation of the sixteenth century, however, most Protestant theologians rejected or neglected it in favor of a more forensic (legal) and individualistic view of salvation as personal reconciliation with God.

By the end of the second century the story of Christian theology had progressed quite a way from its beginning and yet had far to go. Irenaeus's theory of redemption as recapitulation represented a quantum leap of intellectual reflection beyond the simple moralism of some of the apostolic fathers. And yet it left much unanswered regarding the relationship between the Word and God the Father and regarding the Holy Spirit and the unity of all three. It also left unanswered questions about how redemption is applied to individuals and why some are included in Christ's new humanity and some are not. These and many more questions come to the fore and provided grist for the mill of later theological debate and controversy.

At the end of the second century and opening of the third (200/201), Gnosticism and Montanism were waning in importance and influence. Other heresies were arising and would be dealt with by Tertullian and Cyprian and other third-century church fathers. The bishops in apostolic succession were gaining a monopoly on authority in the churches so that more and more people within the churches and outside of them recognized one relatively united orthodox and catholic church of Christ represented by the bishops. This made it much easier to defeat the various heresies that arose, although, as we shall see, that struggle remained a challenging one. The idea of salvation as primarily received through sacraments, including infant baptism and the Eucharist, was becoming normative, although a few voices rose in protest. The church and its structure and theology were gradually becoming formalized and standardized. A certain line of orthodoxy

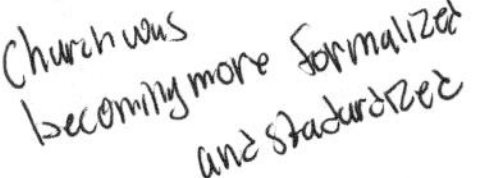

represented especially by Ignatius, Justin Martyr and Irenaeus was widely recognized and acknowledged.

As the second century closed and the third century dawned, one great question stood on the horizon as yet to be resolved: What is the proper relationship between Greek philosophy and Christian thought? The apologists had not solved that complex problem. In fact, they had contributed to its deepening. Toward the beginning of the third century, two great North African church fathers appeared in the story of Christian theology to wrestle with this and related issues. Both of them laid foundations for later theological reflection in their own regions of North Africa. Clement of Alexandria founded the "School of Alexandria" in Greek-speaking Egypt and profoundly influenced the entire Eastern region of Christianity in the Roman Empire. Tertullian in Carthage led the Western, Latin-speaking region of Christianity in a different direction. Their differences help explain why the Great Church, both orthodox and catholic, eventually split up and went separate ways as Eastern Orthodox and Roman Catholic.

# PART II

# The Plot Thickens

## *Third-Century Tensions & Transformations*

*The second century witnessed many changes in Christian thinking about God and* salvation. These may be viewed either as a diversion and digression from the message of Jesus and the apostles or as an unfolding and development of that message's meaning in new contexts. Perhaps the best way to regard the overall trend of Christian theology throughout the century is as a mixture of both digression and development. The first Christian theologians were the apostolic fathers, and while they sought to keep some semblance of order and unity in the church and began the fight against heresies such as Gnosticism, they also tended to present the Christian gospel as a message about morality. Some of them introduced ideas about bishops and sacraments that have seemed to many Christians quite foreign to the spirit of the New Testament.

The second group of Christian theologians were the apologists. These writers turned their faces toward the hostile world outside the church and attempted to explain the Christian worldview and lifestyle to sophisticated, powerful leaders of the Roman Empire in an intelligible and appealing way. In the process they prevented Christianity from becoming just one more secretive mystery religion of the empire, carved out a niche for Christian thought quite distinct from Jewish theology and worship, and related Christian belief to the wider world of Greek philosophy. Some of them began to speculate about the mysterious Christian belief in the triunity of God and how that is compatible with the monotheism of Judaism and Platonism. They built on and developed the concept of the Logos to do this, and while answering some questions about the relationship of Jesus Christ the Savior to God, they left many questions unanswered and left a legacy of some confusion. The apologists also tended to adopt Greek ways of thinking and speaking about God and God's relationship with the world that seemed to them to fit quite nicely with the biblical and apostolic teachings. Some Christian thinkers of the third century and afterward, however, would protest this amalgam of biblical and Greek thought and accuse it of illegitimate syncretism—the mixing of foreign elements into an unstable compound.

Finally, the end of the second century witnessed the rise of true constructive theology with the great Irenaeus. He forged the first system of Christian doctrinal teaching out of the fires of controversy with heresies, especially the various Gnostic schools. His concept of salvation as recapitulation stepped beyond anything clearly delineated in Scripture or in the apostles' writings, and yet it was intended as nothing more than their interpretation. Irenaeus's ideas about the saving incarnation, the solidarity of humanity in Adam and in Christ, and Christ's work as reversing the disobedience of Adam became standard in Christian thinking, preaching and teaching in both the Eastern and Western Christian churches for ages to come. In many ways Irenaeus's basic interpretation of the gospel formed a kind of base line for orthodox theology. Only during the Protestant Reformation of the sixteenth century would Irenaeus's thought become somewhat controversial as the Reformers and their heirs scoured the history of Christian theology for deviations from what they considered the true base line and final authority: the Holy Bible. Some of Irenaeus's concepts seemed alien to Scripture, and some Protestant thinkers accused his theory of recapitulation of being a "grossly physical" notion of salvation that deviated from Paul's emphasis on salvation as forgiveness and reconciliation.

As the second century drew to a close, a new epoch of the story of theology was opening. The geographical and cultural locus of the story shifted to North Africa. Greek philosophy and its relation to the Christian gospel and apostolic teachings became a point of major contention among North African Christian thinkers. Out of North African cities such as Alexandria and Carthage (in what is now Tunisia) came the great third-century defenders, interpreters and organizers of Christian thought and life. In many ways the third century was the North African century of Christian theology.

Many modern Western Christians are surprised to find that Africa rather than Europe produced many of the greatest Christian thinkers and leaders of the early centuries. A little knowledge of the Roman Empire, however, would explain why this was true and natural. The city of Alexandria, Egypt, was the second largest city of the empire and was in many ways its cultural and intellectual center. The city named after Alexander the Great was a melting pot of philosophies, religions and ethnic traditions that all contributed to its cosmopolitan flavor. The great Jewish philosopher and biblical commentator Philo had lived and worked there in the time of Jesus and left his stamp upon Hellenistic Judaism, which in turn influenced Christian thought in that city. A rich tradition of Platonism was flourishing in Alexandria during the early centuries of Christianity and inevitably influenced the ways in which Christians thought and taught about God and spirituality, as we will see in the cases especially of Clement and Origen, the two greatest Alexandrian Christian thinkers of the third century. Gnosticism exhibited a powerful presence in and around Alexandria, as did the various mystery religions. Finally, emissaries from Eastern religions and spiritualities, such as various forms of Hinduism, were active in Alexandria. Gnosticism and some Eastern religions tended to emphasize the spiritual over the physical and viewed bodily existence as prisonlike. They also tended to emphasize the eternal (nontemporal) over the historical and viewed time and history as limiting if not illusory. Some critics would say that they were "so heavenly minded they were no earthly good," although that may be going too far. In any case, this influential presence of Gnostics and missionaries of Eastern religions in Alexandria helps explain the special flavor of Alexandrian Christian thought with its emphasis on spiritual meanings hidden within the Hebrew Scriptures and apostolic writings and speculation about the nature of the soul and afterlife and spiritual world. It also helps explain why the Christian ascetic tradition of spirituality through denial of bodily comforts, needs and pleasures arose in that cultural milieu.

By the end of the second century and beginning of the third-century, Christianity was flourishing in Alexandria and the surrounding region. One of the first Christian catechetical schools (similar to a seminary) was founded there about that time, and out of it came a series of great Christian speculative thinkers and theologians who were influenced by, and in turn attempted to influence, the culture of that city and religion. As early-church historian H. Kraft notes in his study of the Christian school of Alexandria, "In Alexandria the different religions and philosophies were willing to enter into contact with one another to learn from one another and to exercise a mutual influence. But alongside such syncretism, we find also mission and apologetic; this means that one set of convictions tried to establish itself as superior to all the rest."[1] That was the double mission of the great Alexandrian Christian teachers Clement and Origen—to demonstrate the basic compatibility of the best of Greek thought with Christian beliefs and to demonstrate Christianity's superiority as the pinnacle of truth over Greek thought and all other alternative philosophies and worldviews. Their task was much like that of the earlier apologists, and they are sometimes considered among the apologists in the lists of early-church theologians. A major difference, however, lies in the fact that for the most part they wrote for and to other Christians rather than to Greek philosophers and leaders of the empire.

An entirely different approach to Christian thought and life developed several hundred miles away in North Africa in the city of Carthage and its environment. Carthage lay across the Mediterranean Sea from Rome and engaged in lively commercial and cultural exchange with the capital city of the empire. Although philosophy was hardly absent from its milieu, the cultural atmosphere of Carthage and that part of North Africa was much more pragmatic than speculative. Carthage had a rich tradition of law and civic virtue and commerce. Platonism and other speculative, spiritual philosophies were not unknown, but Stoicism—a Greek philosophy that emphasized morality and justice—tended to capture the interest and imagination of Carthaginians. Christians in Carthage were interested in developing a sound system of church life that could weather the coming storms of the empire and that provided a basis for Christian community and moral living. Certainly they were also interested in doctrinal issues and delved deeply into controversies that arose among the various Christian teachers in Rome, for example, but overall their attention was more on the practical and judicial life of the church than on speculation about spiritual and invisible realities beyond the day-to-day life of ordinary people.

Although it is admittedly a generalization, it would not be too far off the mark to say that Alexandrian culture and Christianity tended to be otherworldly in interest, while Carthaginian culture and Christianity tended to be more this worldly in interest. These are difficult points to explain and defend, but a careful study of the leading thinkers of both North African regions reveals the subtle difference of emphasis and attention. For the most part the Christians of Carthage were deeply suspicious of the speculative mindset of the Alexandrians. The Alexandrians, insofar as they paid any attention at all to their Carthaginian brothers in the faith, no doubt returned the favor by being distrustful of their lack of interest in philosophical speculation as manifesting a Christian anti-intellectualism.

The leading Christian thinkers of western North Africa (the region with Carthage as the center) were Tertullian and Cyprian. No single Christian leader or thinker of Rome or any other part of Europe stands out as their equal in profound thought and influence during this transitional and transformative period of early Christian theology. Both were widely read and discussed in Rome and other parts of the empire, and their impact was felt everywhere among Christians, especially in the Latin-speaking Western half of the empire.

During the third-century, Christian theology took giant leaps forward and suffered severe setbacks. Persecution on an empirewide scale held back Christian reflection and interaction for decades. Christian thinkers and leaders had to flee for their lives, and their books were collected and burned. This was true especially in the century's second half when emperors Decius and Diocletian instituted empirewide persecutions of Christians that drove them underground and silenced many of the leading Christian voices. Various heresies arose that were challenged by Christians leaders but managed to hang on tenaciously. Several major schisms continued into the third century or arose during it. Montanism flourished in Carthage—far from its birthplace in Asia Minor. Leading Christians, including Tertullian himself, defected to it at times. Other Christian sects arose during the third century. In Rome the Novatian schism ripped the church apart, and in North Africa the Donatists became more numerous for a time than the adherents of the Great Church[2] (catholic and orthodox) itself. In spite of severe persecutions and martyrdoms of great Christian leaders such as Cyprian, the church grew and flourished. Tertullian wrote harshly against the persecutions by the emperors and yet egged them on with the claim that "the blood of the martyrs is the seed [of the church]." This seemed to be true. The more the Roman leaders attempted to stamp out the "cult" of Christianity, the more it grew both in numbers and in determination.

During the third century the first church buildings—known as "basilicas"—were constructed for Christian worship. The canon of Christian Scriptures was virtually solidified, even if its official recognition and universal acknowledgment waited almost a hundred more years. The institutional organization of Christianity developed along the lines of the imperial order of Rome, with bishops gradually becoming archbishops over metropolitan "sees"—the great urban centers that formed hubs of commerce and culture. Without complete freedom of travel and communication, all of this development took place in fits and starts and suffered severe setbacks at times during the century. Nevertheless, by century's end (300) the orthodox and catholic Christian church of the Roman Empire—the only Christian church we know much of anything about from that time—was firmly entrenched in nearly every city and region and was prepared to become the dominant religious force within the next hundred years. This is largely due to the efforts of men like Clement and Origen in the East and Tertullian and Cyprian in the West.

# CHAPTER 5

# North African Thinkers Examine Philosophy

T*he relationship between philosophy and Christian theology has been a major* point of controversy within Christian thought throughout its history. Clement of Alexandria and Tertullian of Carthage represent opposite ends of the Christian spectrum of thought about that issue. While many later Christian thinkers have attempted to mediate between these two poles, there have always been those who lined up with one or the other. Clement followed in the footsteps of the great second-century apologist and martyr Justin and regarded Christianity as the true philosophy that does not contradict and cancel out Greek philosophy but fulfills it. He saw the best of Greek thought, such as the philosophies of Socrates and Plato, as preparation for the gospel and as a useful tool in the hands of skillful Christian thinkers. Because of this high estimation and positive use of non-Christian thought, Clement has been labeled by some "almost the prototype of a liberal theologian."[1]

Tertullian (roughly contemporary with Clement) took the opposite attitude toward pagan philosophy and its relationship with Christian thought. While it is uncertain whether he had Clement's theology in mind, he almost certainly was thinking of that approach to philosophy and theology when he asked in exasperation, "What has Athens to do with Jerusalem?" And yet the truth of the matter is that neither Clement nor Tertullian was as extreme on this issue as many have suggested.

Clement certainly did *not* attempt to reduce Christianity to a generic Greek philosophy with a veneer of the gospel thrown over it in order to make it palatable and acceptable to sophisticated Alexandrian minds. He did *not* attempt to resolve all conflicts between them by smoothing them out into a synthesis. This is apparent in his rejection of the Greek ideas that the universe is eternal and that its creation was merely the shaping and molding of matter by a demiurge or demigod. He insisted on the doctrine of *creatio ex nihilo* (creation out of nothing) as the Christian view of God and the world even if it flew in the face of every major Greek thinker and system of thought. Nevertheless, Clement did tend to bend over backward to discover and display every possible point of similarity between Plato's philosophy (for example) and the apostles' teachings.

Tertullian did not entirely avoid the influence of Greek philosophy in his own theology. While attempting to present a purely biblical, apostolic set of doctrines, he allowed certain Stoic ideas, such as the essentially material nature of all being, to creep in unrecognized. For Tertullian as for the Stoics, even "spirit" was but a refined form of matter.

It is traditional to emphasize the extreme polarity between Clement and Tertullian at this point, however, and readers should know that they did indeed set in place opposite trajectories for Christian thinking that still exist today. Clement is the prototype of the broad, liberally minded, intellectual and philosophical Christian theologian who seeks to synthesize Christian belief with culture as much as possible. A twentieth-century "Clement" would be Paul Tillich (1886-1965), a German philosophical theologian who attempted to create a harmony of various philosophies and divine revelation using a "method of correlation." A twentieth-century "Tertullian" would be the Swiss theologian Karl Barth (1886-1968), who failed in spite of himself to entirely avoid every hint of philosophy even in his mature theology. Barth, like Tertullian, sought to produce a purely Christian system of belief untainted by pagan or secular modes of thinking. Down through the centuries of Christian theology, the role of philosophy in Christian thinking has been a major bone of contention and remains so today.

**Clement's Life and Career**

The details of Clement of Alexandria's life are shrouded in mystery. All that is known is that he became the head of Alexandria's Christian catechetical school upon the death of its founder, Pantaenus, around 200 and that he fled Alexandria to avoid persecution and possible martyrdom in 202. He died sometime between 211 and 216. His connection with the formal hierarchy of the Alexandrian church is obscure. He does not seem to have been ordained as a minister or a priest, and his writings notoriously neglect discussion of the community of Christians, focusing instead on the individual believer's spirituality and thought life. Without doubt he was steeped in the Middle Platonism that formed the generic philosophy of most educated Alexandrians, and he may have been involved in the emergence of a new type of Platonic philosophy known as Neo-Platonism. Not very much is certain about Clement's life or education or contribution other than the few writings that survive from his pen. But that he was strongly influenced by Justin Martyr is a valid guess. In many ways his Christian philosophy seems to be an extension of Justin's.

Five books by Clement are extant today. They are *Exhortation to the Heathen, The Instructor,* the *Stromata, Who Is the Rich Man That Shall Be Saved?* and *Excerpts from Theodotus.* Most likely all were written while he was principal of the Christian school in Alexandria and were for the instruction of young men (and perhaps some women) aspiring to become Christian leaders.

The *Exhortation to the Heathen* is a polemic against paganism, especially what Clement considered superstitious and idolatrous belief and worship. The book presents a more positive picture of Greek philosophy, especially that which was considered consistent with Christian truth. Even then, however, Clement strongly suggested that whatever truth there was in Greek philosophy—and he found much—was borrowed by the Greeks from other cultures and religions such as Egypt, Babylon and the Hebrew people. That which Greeks such as Socrates and Plato spoke truly they either borrowed from divinely inspired sources such as Moses or they received directly by inspiration from God and his Word (Logos).

*The Instructor,* also known by its Greek title *Paedagogus,* refers to the divine Word of God, the Logos. In this little book Clement discussed Jesus Christ as the cosmic Word and Wisdom of God whose main role in salvation was to teach by exhortation how to overcome the unnatural passions and live a purely spiritual life of obedience, contemplation and rational action. Above all Clement stressed that the Christian life of obedience is a life according to (consistent with) reason: "For the life of Christians, in which we are now trained, is a system of reasonable actions—that is, of those things taught by the Word—an unfailing energy which we have called faith."[2]

The *Stromata,* also known as *Miscellanies,* constitutes Clement's attempt to create a comprehensive Christian philosophy. In it one finds an unsystematic and eclectic philosophy in which Clement blended various sources and drew inspiration from many wells. The author expressed his approach well: "Our book will not shrink from making use of what is best in philosophy and other preparatory instruction."[3]

## Clement and Greek Philosophy

More than any other early Christian writer, Clement of Alexandria valued the integration of Christian faith with the best learning of the day. His motto was "all truth is God's truth wherever it may be found," and he attempted to bring together those stray rays of divine light that he believed were diffused throughout the various philosophical and religious systems while submitting all to the overriding authority of the Hebrew Scriptures (allegorically interpreted, of course) and the apostolic tradition. One modern historical theologian summarizes Clement's overall aim:

> on the basis of the Bible and with the help of scientific methods to erect an edifice of speculative thought which could stand up under criticism, both as interpretation of the Bible and as philosophy. . . . It is no exaggeration to say that Clement was the first who, in reality and not only in intention, brought philosophy and theology into close relationship to one another.[4]

When Clement wrote about and used philosophy, he meant that generic Greek philosophy so pervasive and influential in Alexandria, Athens and throughout the Roman Empire known as Platonism. His thought was on the cutting edge between so-called Middle Platonism and Neo-Platonism and probably leaned toward the latter. Clement specifically addressed the issue of Paul the apostle's negative attitude toward philosophy in his epistles and argued that Paul had in mind only certain specific systems of thought such as Epicureanism and some Stoicism, not philosophy in general. Clement believed that the right kind of philosophy—that exemplified in Socrates and Plato and their heirs in his own time—was in a sense "a work of Divine Providence."[5] He regarded it as God's way of preparing the Greeks for Christ just as the law of Moses was God's way of preparing the Hebrew people for the coming of Christ as the Messiah. He frequently referred in his writings to "the truth-loving Plato" and called him an imitator of Moses.

What about Platonism did Clement find so extraordinarily conducive to understanding and communicating Christian truth? For one thing, it rejected the immoral and capricious pantheon of gods and goddesses of the Greeks and Romans and focused on a single ultimate spiritual reality from which everything else derives its being and goodness. He rejected its idea of creation as an impersonal and eternal process of emanation from that divine source and insisted on the doctrine of a temporal creation "out of nothing" by the personal God of Scripture. Nevertheless, compared to the unethical, immoral and arbitrary gods and goddesses of Greek myths, and compared to the superstitions of the mystery religions, Platonism seemed to him to be a viable ally for Christianity in the pagan world. Furthermore, it held a vision of afterlife and of a spiritual dimension to everything and pointed people away from physical and bodily pleasures toward the higher, spiritual realities. In all this and much more Clement found echoes of and parallels with Christian truth in the best of Greek philosophy.

Clement believed that philosophy could aid in Christianity's fight against heresies. False teachings often arise from mental confusion; philosophy tries to be logical and uses dialectic (critical examination) to test truth claims and beliefs. If God's revelation is intelligible, then using logic and dialectic to study interpretations of it will surely lead to a sounder set of beliefs and morals than ignoring them. On this role of philosophy, Clement wrote, "Perspicuity accordingly aids in the communication of truth, and logic in preventing us from falling under the heresies by which we are assailed."[6] This is ironic in light of Tertullian's denunciation of philosophy as the *cause* of heresies among Christians! For Clement, philosophy could serve as a *curative* of heresies among them.

### "True Gnosticism"

One of the more controversial areas of Clement's theology is his ideal of the Christian as "the true gnostic" or "the perfect gnostic." Because one can find faint echoes of Gnosticism in Clement's writing (as in Neo-Platonism), some have concluded that Clement was an ally of the second-century Gnostics and their remnants in the third century. That is highly unlikely. By "true gnostic," Clement meant a person of wisdom who lives a life of the mind and shuns the lower life of the pursuit of bodily desires and pleasures. Such a person was imaged by Clement as a Christian Socrates or Plato—a person who stands against the general tendency to "go with the flow" of the confused crowd who revel in partying and seeking material gain. Such a person seeks to be conversant with all kinds of wisdom and aims to rise above bodily passions, becoming Godlike in virtue and wisdom. Clement went so far as to state that the true Christian gnostic can "become God" in this life by putting off "desire" and becoming "impassible, free of anger."[7] Of course he made clear that he did *not* mean that the true gnostic actually becomes perfect in the same way God is perfect. Rather, he meant that such a person puts on the image of God and becomes truly good, although only in a created way and dependent upon God. He had in mind the idea of divinization—the idea that the goal of salvation is to share in the divine nature by having the image of God fulfilled and by attaining immortality.

For Clement any achievement of perfection was a work of God that comes about through the human person yielding to God by shunning the lower life of the body and seeking the higher life of the mind through contemplation and study.

The "teacher" throughout this process is Jesus Christ himself—the Word of the Father who "cures the unnatural passions of the soul by means of exhortations."[8] Clement saw Jesus Christ not as just a man who taught good things and died a martyr's death like Socrates but as the embodiment of divine Wisdom and in some sense God himself. Those who would argue that no Christian before the fourth century thought of Jesus Christ as God have not read Clement. When he wrote of Christ as our Instructor, he clearly did not mean only that he was a "great human teacher." No, according to Clement, Jesus Christ was the divine Logos—the cosmic Spirit of Wisdom and Truth who emanated from the Father and came in human form in Jesus Christ. He was the fulfillment of all the previous partial truths that pointed toward him, and he teaches his people through many different means. Clement's high Christology is clearly expressed in *The Instructor:*

> Now, O you, my children, our Instructor is like His father God, whose Son He is, sinless, blameless, and with a soul devoid of passion; God in the form of man, stainless, the minister of his father's will, the Word who is God, who is in the Father, who is at the Father's right hand, and with the form of God is God.[9]

The influence of Greek philosophy on Clement's thought manifested itself in several ways. First of all, he treated the body and matter in general as a "lower nature" and contrasted them sharply with the "higher and better" nature of the soul, which he described as the rational portion of the person. This differs from Gnosticism because Clement expressly denied that matter or the body are evil. They are simply inferior to spirit and soul. This is, of course, a more Platonic view of humanity and creation than a biblical view. Plato and his heirs emphasized the spiritual side of the human person as higher and better than the physical side and equated it with reason. While one may find faint echoes of such a dualism in biblical teachings, nowhere does the Bible teach that the soul or spirit is the rational part of the human person or that the body is "the lower nature." Clement's tendency to equate salvation with Godlike perfection attained through rational contemplation and abandonment of all bodily desires and passions virtually shouts, "Greek philosophy!"

Finally, Clement's views of God and the image of God in the human person reveal his Greek orientation. Over and over again Clement reiterated his view that God is passionless and so should the true gnostic be. "Imitating God" through receiving "instruction from the Word" (Jesus Christ) means striving for a state of perfect passionlessness through self-control. Passions and desires are inherently limiting, and God, according to both Clement and the prevailing Greek philosophy of his time, is inherently free of all creaturely limitations, including passions (desires and emotions). Clement's God was like the God of Greek philosophy—a bare unity without parts or passions that cannot even be described except negatively and who can only relate to the world of nature and history through an intermediate being called the Logos. Clement's ideal person—the true gnostic—is a human as much like God as possible: self-controlled, serene, unmoved and unaffected, rational and calm. One is tempted to think of Plato's "philosopher-kings" as described in his book *The Republic.* Clement's doctrine of God is a third-century echo and elaboration of second-century apologist Athenagoras's teaching. Both belong to that line of Christian thought that subtly shaped the Christian idea of God to fit Greek philosophical speculation.

An obvious question for Clement's interpretation of God's nature is, What about the dark wrath of Yahweh? If God is without parts or passions, why is he described in the Hebrew Scriptures as angry, wrathful and vengeful? Clement answered: "Anthropomorphisms!" That is, he viewed biblical references to God's wrath and anger as mere figures of speech or as ways humans perceived and experienced God. What about the anger of Jesus in the temple when confronted with the thieving money changers? What about his crying out in fear and agony during his "passion"? Clement did not expressly address these challenges to his Greek-inspired view of God and of the perfect person. One can only surmise that he would say these experiences and feelings were all parts of the humanity of the Son of God and not proper to his deity. This is certainly the answer given by later theologians who accepted Clement's picture of God's essential nature. Whatever in the biblical narrative describes God or Jesus Christ in ways unworthy of divine being he interpreted as allegory or anthropomorphic speech or he relegated to the human side of the Son of God in his incarnation as Jesus Christ.

### Tertullian's Life and Career

Tertullian was horrified by Clement's overall approach to Christian theology. He spent much of his energy combating it. That was certainly not his only contribution to Christian theology, however. Tertullian also fought against various heresies about God and Jesus Christ that had little or nothing to do with Greek philosophy even though he thought one could always find that evil influence lurking somewhere as the cause of all heresies.

Tertullian was born in about 150 and probably lived his whole life in Carthage, although he may have visited Rome frequently. Some scholars believe that he lived in Rome for a while. By occupation he was a lawyer. When he converted to Christianity in about 190, he devoted his legal knowledge and skills to explicating and defending the orthodox Christian faith. He was never ordained to the priesthood, nor was he ever elevated to sainthood by the orthodox-catholic church that he left in about 207—a few short years before his death. He may have died of natural causes around 212.

One of the great controversies surrounding Tertullian's life is over his defection—if defection it was—from the Great Church of the bishops in apostolic succession. Tradition says that he joined the Montanist "New Prophecy" church in Carthage due to dissatisfaction with the main church's decline into moral and theological decadence. There is no proof of that, but it is a well-attested tradition and would help explain why this great early Christian writer, who was so orthodox in most ways, was never canonized as a saint.

Tertullian's writings breathe a different spirit than Clement's and those of the entire Christian school of Alexandria. In fact, when comparing and contrasting them, one wonders how both approaches to Christian theology could coexist within one united church. Yet even after Tertullian's lapse into Montanism, his legacy within the catholic church of the West lived on in Christian thinkers who followed his approach of opposing divine revelation to human speculation. Clement and his followers in the East (especially his pupil Origen) tended to look for correlations between revelation and human speculation. Tertullian's theological attitude and mindset may be described as more close-minded toward the possibility of truth genuinely helpful to Christian life and thought found outside divine revelation. While he did not reject the idea of all truth being God's truth, so central to Clement's project, he did find little truth useful to Christianity outside of the biblical revelation God gave to Israel and the apostles, which he considered inspired and unique.

While the terms *liberal* and *conservative* describe modern rather than ancient types of theologies,[10] it may not be too far off the mark to say that Tertullian is the prototype of a conservative—even fundamentalist—Christian thinker, while Clement is the prototype of a liberal Christian thinker. Both would agree that all truth is God's truth wherever it may be found, but Clement was much more optimistic about the human mind's capability of rising above apparently conflicting truth claims and discovering a synthesis of truth transcending traditional biblical and Greek thought. Tertullian was pessimistic about the human mind's ability to avoid idolatry and dangerous syncretism in such an effort and warned Christians to stay away from too much study of philosophy lest they be seduced into heresy.

Tertullian's extant written legacy includes about thirty works. The bulk of them are antiheretical treatises aimed at exposing the errors of various Christian teachers in Rome. His largest and in many ways most important work is the five-volume

*Against Marcion.* Marcion was a second-century teacher among Christians in Rome who attempted to drive a permanent and solid wedge between Christianity and everything Hebrew, including the God of Israel (Yahweh) and the Father of Jesus Christ. Marcion also attempted to define a canon of Christian Scriptures limited to Gentile writings. Some of his thoughts about humanity and creation smacked of Gnosticism, and Tertullian held back nothing in his scathing written attack on Marcion's teachings. In the process Tertullian expounded many key Christian beliefs in new ways, delving deeply into their true meanings and drawing out their implications.

Another object of Tertullian's antiheretical wrath was the Roman Christian teacher Praxeas. Tertullian's massive critique *Against Praxeas* was written after Tertullian had defected to Montanism, but its influence throughout the Western Christian churches was "immediate and permanent."[11]

Praxeas was perhaps the first Christian theologian to attempt to explain the doctrine of the Trinity in systematic detail. In the process, however, he apparently explained away the real ontological threeness of the persons of God. That is, Praxeas denied that Christians believed in three distinct identities or even relations within the one divine being. If Tertullian's account of what Praxeas taught is correct, he reduced the Father, Son and Holy Spirit to three aspects or roles of the one-person God. Praxeas's view later came to be known as modalism and was revived by another later teacher of Christians in Rome named Sabellius. Thus it is also sometimes known as Sabellianism.

Tertullian perceived this modalistic explanation of the triunity of God as a dangerous heresy and declared in typical fashion, "Praxeas did a twofold service for the devil at Rome: he drove away prophecy, and he brought in heresy; he put to flight the Paraclete [Holy Spirit] and crucified the Father."[12] Praxeas was apparently anti-Montanist, and thus Tertullian accused him of driving away prophecy. The heresy Praxeas is accused of bringing in is modalism. If modalism is true, then the Holy Spirit is not a distinct person of God but just another name for or manifestation of the Father and Son, and furthermore not only was the Son of God crucified but so too was the Father.

### Tertullian's Theology

Tertullian worked out minute details of the doctrine of the Trinity in contrast to Praxeas's heresy. Perhaps because he defected to Montanism, Tertullian's contribution in this area was set aside or largely forgotten. Later Eastern Christians had to work their way in the same direction on their own in almost total ignorance of Tertullian's achievement. The ultimate outcome of the formal doctrine of the Trinity at councils and through creeds of the fourth and fifth centuries came very close to Tertullian's formulations about 100 to 150 years earlier. As one historian notes, "Tertullian's treatise *Against Praxeas* is significant because some of its phrases and terminology seem to foreshadow what would become generally accepted formulas centuries later. This is so in trinitarian doctrine as well as in Christology."[13] In some sense then Tertullian was the father of the orthodox doctrines of the Trinity and person of Jesus Christ even though he died outside the catholic and orthodox Great Church.

Besides *Against Marcion* and *Against Praxeas,* Tertullian also wrote an *Apology* around 200 and a systematic treatise on Christian belief entitled *Prescription Against the Heretics* of uncertain date. Tertullian is sometimes listed among the apologists because of his *Apology,* which is addressed to "rulers of the Roman Empire" and contains very lawyerlike arguments against Christianity's persecutors and for Christianity's innocence. Besides pointing out the injustice of Roman officials' treatment of Christians, however, the *Apology* also explains Christian life, worship and belief in ways that sometimes go far beyond what had been written by others and that anticipated later orthodoxy as propounded by the great Christian councils.

Tertullian strove to explain why Christians worship Jesus Christ rather than Caesar or any other so-called god and yet at the same time insist that God is one and heavenly. In order to explain this, he turned to the often-used concept of the Logos of God and appropriated an analogy that would become a favorite one for Christian thinkers wrestling with this issue. The Logos, Tertullian carefully explained, is both God and God's offshoot through which he relates to creation. This Logos is, of course, Christ, the Son of the Father. Tertullian used the sun analogy to explain their relationship: "This ray of God, then, as it was always foretold in ancient times, descending into a certain virgin, and made flesh in her womb, is in his birth God and man united."[14]

It is in *Prescription Against Heretics* that Tertullian's negative attitude toward Greek philosophy primarily appears. His "prescription" against all the various heresies appearing in Rome and elsewhere was that Christians should strictly avoid attempting to rationalize Christian beliefs using Greek philosophical categories and concepts alien to biblical truth. Most scholars agree that he intended to warn against the kind of approach to theology and philosophy taken by Justin Martyr earlier and by Clement of Alexandria in his own time. His famous (or infamous) rhetorical question appears in chapter seven: "What indeed has Athens to do with Jerusalem?"[15] *Athens* refers to the Platonic Academy and by extension to all Greek philosophy. *Jerusalem* refers to the teachings of Jesus and the apostles.

While Tertullian did not disallow questioning and seeking *within* Christian faith and belief—that is, within the bounds of apostolic succession and the "apostolic rule of faith"—he did reject any study of nonbiblical, nonapostolic sources to supplement or even interpret that witness to truth that transcends all human inquiry and investigation.

Some of Tertullian's statements about Christian faith and belief without philosophical support seem fairly extreme. For example, he wrote, "To know nothing in opposition to the rule (of faith) is to know all things."[16] On the surface, at least, this statement makes little or no sense. In the overall context of the *Prescription,* however, Tertullian was using hyperbole to drive home his point that the most important knowledge is that consistent with and in conformity to the apostolic message. More controversial is his remark regarding Christian belief in the incarnation and death of the Son of God. Controverting other theologians' attempts to explain it speculatively and philosophically, Tertullian burst out with "It is by all means to be believed, because it is absurd" and "The fact is certain, because it is impossible."[17]

In spite of these outbursts of fideism (belief by blind faith), Tertullian was no sheer anti-intellectual and certainly did not merely believe things on blind faith without any thought or examination. Historical theologian Justo González is correct when he softens that harsh critique of the North African Latin father:

> But the truth is that Tertullian is not a blind irrationalist. He does believe that there are things that are simply too wonderful to be understood such as the crucifixion or the power of baptism. But this is not a general claim that belief has to be based on rational impossibility. He rather believes that unrestrained speculation can lead far afield, and that the actual revelation of God is what is really important to the Christian.[18]

Nevertheless, Tertullian would heartily reject the ideal of the mature Christian as the "true gnostic" set forth by his contemporary Clement of Alexandria. For Tertullian the mature Christian was a person completely uninterested in mental speculation beyond Scripture and the apostles' teachings and the church's rule of faith (tradition of handing down the apostles' teachings). Such a mature Christian is immune from heresies because they all arise from vain intellectual curiosity beyond what the church teaches and what Christians have always believed. Furthermore, such a mature Christian lives a morally rigorous life.

Tertullian has also been accused of being the first Christian puritan due to his voluminous writings on morality and obedience and strictness of behavior including appropriate dress and appearance. He accepted the idea promulgated by

*The Shepherd of Hermas*—a book he especially loved and was influenced by—that Christians are forgiven for only one serious, intentional sin after baptism. For that reason he argued vehemently that baptism should be delayed until the believer is certain of strength to sin no more.[19]

**Tertullian on the Trinity**

While best known for his rejection of theology informed by philosophy, Tertullian's most important contribution to Christian thought lies in his careful and fairly precise delineation of the doctrine of the Trinity against Praxeas. With a few exceptions, Tertullian's expositions of both the doctrines of the Trinity and the humanity and deity of Christ laid the foundation for later official church orthodoxy in both the East and West. To what extent and how his thought influenced later church leaders and theologians is unclear, but the conceptual parallels are uncanny. It is not too much of an exaggeration to say that Tertullian seems to have already settled these doctrines hundreds of years before the rest of the church settled them, and if later church leaders and theologians had only listened more carefully to Tertullian, many theological disputes and controversies could have been avoided. In the Latin West, Tertullian's formulations may have been neglected because of his defection to Montanism. That the Eastern churches were virtually unaware of Tertullian's writings may have been because he wrote in Latin, a language that increasingly was not studied in the East, and because he was so vehemently antiphilosophical, whereas for the most part the major voices of Eastern theology highly valued philosophy as a conceptual tool for theology.

Tertullian's doctrines of the Trinity and the person of Christ were forged in the fires of controversy with Praxeas, who, according to Tertullian, "maintains that there is only one Lord, the Almighty creator of the world, in order that out of this doctrine of the unity he may fabricate a heresy. He says that the Father Himself came down into the Virgin, was Himself born of her, Himself suffered, indeed was Himself Jesus Christ."[20] Tertullian coined the label *patripassianism* for this heresy. It means "the suffering (and dying) of the Father." This has come to be a theological synonym for Praxeas's and Sabellius's modalist view of the Trinity down through the ages of church history.

Apparently Praxeas taught that there is only one personal identity in God and that this singular identity could be manifested either as the Father or as the Son or as the Holy Spirit. Later modalists would use the imagery and language of the Greek and Roman theater to illustrate their idea of the proper Christian doctrine of the Trinity: a single actor or actress could play three roles in the same production by wearing different masks. The word for such a mask in a play is the same as that often used for "person." Thus the modalists could say, when Christians confessed belief in "one God in three persons" (or similar language), they were not violating Jewish and Greek monotheism because the "three persons" are only masks the one God wears on the "stage" of history.

Tertullian was the first Christian theologian to confront and reject with great intellectual vigor and clarity this seemingly simple vision of God's triunity. If it is true, he declared, then the Father died on the cross, and that is not only improper to the Father but absurd. Clearly the apostolic testimony is that only the Son died on the cross. Against Praxeas's modalism Tertullian developed a somewhat more complex vision of "organic monotheism." That is, God's "oneness" does not rule out or exclude a kind of multiplicity, just as biological organisms can be "one" and yet made up of interconnected and mutual parts.

In *Against Praxeas* Tertullian provided a fairly clear statement of this organic monotheism:

> All [three—Father, Son, and Holy Ghost] are of One, by unity (that is) of substance; while the mystery of the dispensation is still to be guarded, which distributes the Unity into a Trinity, placing in their order the three Persons—the Father, the Son, and the Holy Ghost: three, however, not in condition, but in degree; not in substance, but in form; not in power, but in aspect; yet of one substance, and of one condition, and of one power.[21]

In other words, according to Tertullian the God Christians believe in is *one substance and three persons (una substantia, tres personae),* and by *substance* he meant that fundamental ontological being-ness that makes something what it is, while by *person* he meant that identity of action that provides distinctness. The basic, underlying idea is "distinction without division."

Tertullian went to great lengths to demonstrate the distinctness of the three divine persons from Scripture. In this detailed demonstration it is clear that Tertullian accepted most of the books of what later came to be the Christian New Testament as inspired and authoritative, as did at least some of his opponents.

Tertullian argued that while the Father is in some sense "greater" than the Son and the Spirit, he has never existed without them. The Word and the Spirit existed in God the Father before there ever was a world and "came forth" from him into creation without in any way becoming lost or separated from the source of their own being in God the Father. They are inseparable, undivided yet distinct persons with the Father, who remains the "monarch" over all.

Tertullian, like other early church fathers, loved to use analogies drawn from creation to illustrate abstract theological ideas and principles:

> Now the Spirit indeed is third from God and the Son; just as the fruit of the tree is third from the root, or as the stream out of the river is third from the fountain, or as the apex of the ray is third from the sun. Nothing, however, is alien from that original source whence it derives its own properties. In like manner the Trinity, flowing down from the Father through intertwined and connected steps, does not at all disturb the Monarchy [of the Father], whilst it at the same time guards the state of the Economy [of creation].[22]

By "the state of the Economy" Tertullian meant the threeness of God's activity in salvation history. The Father speaks from heaven; the Son stands in the river being baptized; the Spirit descends in the form of a dove from heaven upon Jesus. Jesus cries out to the Father, "Not my will but thine be done," and later offers up his spirit to his Father in the submission of lonely death. The Spirit is "sent" by the Son into the church as "another comforter (Paraclete)." But contrary to the modalists' claim, this emphasis on the distinctness of persons in no way detracts from the "monarchy" of monotheism in which there is one supreme divine source of all being—God the Father. According to Tertullian, the Father is still that supreme source and ruler over all even though he has always had with him his Word and Spirit and sends them into the world as his agents without losing them through division or separation. They remain of his same divine substance.

When he turned to explaining the humanity and deity of Christ, Tertullian used the same basic concepts of substance and person: Jesus Christ was of both a divine substance and a human substance (which Tertullian sometimes confusingly referred to as "spirit" and "flesh") and yet also only one person, not two persons or two identities. Interesting to note is one of his reasons for emphasizing the distinction between Jesus Christ's two natures or substances. It is improper for God to suffer. God is impassible—incapable of suffering.[23] Thus in order for Jesus Christ both to suffer and to be divine, he had to have two distinct natures or substances and only one of them—the human—could have suffered and died. Tertullian affirmed that the two natures of Christ "acted distinctly" and that while the two natures are "conjoined" in Jesus, they must not be confounded so that both are capable of the same activities and experiences. One gains the picture, then, of a dual being of Christ—something with which later Christian theologians and councils would struggle mightily. The reason for it is to protect the divinity in Jesus Christ from experiencing what is not proper to divine being: limitation, imperfection, suffering.

This is highly ironic, of course. After all his fussing and fuming against philosophical speculation in theology, Tertullian ended up assuming a very Greek philosophical notion of divine being—very much like Clement of Alexandria's! In fact, their basic concepts of God's nature as simple, immutable and impassible are strikingly similar and derived more from Greek culture and philosophical theology than from Hebrew or apostolic teachings about God. The God of Israel was, if anything, passionate. And if God did not somehow or other suffer in Jesus Christ, then the incarnation itself would seem to be a chimera—a mere illusion or charade. That is not to endorse patripassianism but only to note that *some* of Tertullian's assumptions and arguments seem to have been based more on Greek philosophy than on divine revelation.

Neither Clement nor Tertullian focused much attention on salvation. They were more concerned with discovering the proper relationship between philosophy and theology and with delineating the nature of God and his relationship with the world. What can be said with a fair degree of certainty, however, is that they both believed in human free will and its ability to cooperate with God's grace in salvation. Clement's idea of salvation centered on becoming a "true gnostic"—a mature, divinized human person in whom God's image is restored and who lives a life of serenity, morality and rationality.[24] Tertullian's idea of salvation centered on baptism, which he considered a true sacrament without carefully defining its function, and living a life of strict obedience to God's will. Tertullian's vision of salvation picked up where the apostolic fathers left off and extended the influence of their moral rigorism into North African and Latin Christianity centered on Rome. Clement's vision of salvation picked up where the apologists left off and extended their intellectualism into Eastern Greek Christianity.

Clement's greatest claim to fame in the story of Christian theology is his influence upon Origen, the greatest Alexandrian church father and speculative Christian theologian of the early church. Tertullian's claim to fame includes his influence upon Cyprian, the most influential North African bishop of the third century, who indelibly left his mark upon the Latin tradition of Christianity.

# CHAPTER 6

# Origen of Alexandria Leaves a Troubling Legacy

*Origen of Alexandria is the first early Christian father and theologian* whose biography is fairly well known. The details of the lives of earlier fathers and even Origen's contemporaries are shrouded in mystery, whereas Origen's life is almost as controversial as his system of thought. Like his mentor, Clement of Alexandria, he loved speculation and far surpassed Clement in attempting to construct a synthesis of Greek philosophy and biblical wisdom in a grand system of Christian thought. He was a great genius and renowned scholar who produced approximately eight hundred treatises during his career and attracted even pagan aristocrats and would-be pagan philosophers to his Christian catechetical school. Like Tertullian he was a maverick who challenged church leaders and, while exalting the great tradition of prophetic and apostolic teaching as the touchstone of all truth, was himself accused of defecting from the church in Alexandria and of deviating from received orthodox teachings.

Even though he is widely considered one of the most important theologians in the history of Christianity, Origen was never canonized as a saint and his memory in all major branches of Christianity is marred by suspicions of heresy and by his posthumous condemnation by a general council of the church in 553. He was accused of teaching that human souls preexisted their descent into bodies, a charge that is almost certainly true. Modern adherents of the New Age movement and esoteric

Christianity believe that Origen taught reincarnation, but that is almost certainly not true. They are wrongly extrapolating from his teaching about the preexistence of souls. Origen believed in only one mortal bodily existence for each soul and firmly believed in and taught the bodily resurrection of the dead to immortal life. Origen was also accused of teaching the doctrine of *apokatastasis*—ultimate, universal reconciliation of all creation, including Satan, with God. He certainly did hold out a hope for some kind of universal salvation of all creatures, but whether or not he included Satan in that hope is debatable. Finally, he was accused of being the source and fountainhead of all kinds of later heresies. Theologians claiming to be his followers—Origenists—did fall into many heresies after his death and eventually almost every heresy condemned by the orthodox catholic church was blamed on Origen, whether it had any connection with him or not.

What the church forgot when it condemned Origen is that not only heretics but also many of the greatest heroes of orthodoxy were deeply influenced by and indebted to Origen and his teachings. The stalwart defender of the doctrine of the Trinity Athanasius (fourth century) was as much an Origenist as was any heretic. The Cappadocian fathers Basil and the two Gregories (also fourth century) were in many ways Origen's theological heirs, as were numerous other great thinkers in the East. The Western Latin churches, however, were not as impressed with or influenced by Origen for understandable reasons. He wrote only in Greek and was a speculative thinker along the lines of Justin Martyr and Clement of Alexandria. Tertullian was the "Origen for the West," and Origen was the "Tertullian for the East."

### Origen's Life and Career

Origen was born in either 185 or 186 in Alexandria, Egypt. He died in either 254 or 255 in Caesarea, Palestine, where he spent much of his life. His father was martyred by Roman authorities in a pogrom against Christians. Tradition says that when Origen's father was in prison awaiting execution, the son wanted to turn himself over to authorities and die with him. Origen's mother is alleged to have hidden the sixteen-year-old boy's clothes so that he was unable to leave the house and thus saved his life. Origen may have had a desire to die for Christ—what later Christians would call a "gift of martyrdom"—and felt frustrated that he did not die with his father. He read in the Gospels Jesus' words about some men becoming "eunuchs for the kingdom of heaven" and castrated himself at an early age. Such an act was highly controversial even then and was used by Alexandria's Christian bishop as a reason not to ordain Origen to ministry.

Origen was a student at Alexandria's catechetical school and probably was taught there by Clement of Alexandria. There is some speculation to the effect that he may also have studied at the pagan school of Platonic philosophy in that city and rubbed shoulders with key founders of the Neo-Platonic philosophy that was just beginning to become popular at that time. Some scholars have even suggested that Origen himself may have been among the founders of Neo-Platonism. While highly unlikely, it is possible that Origen knew and studied with Ammonius Saccas and Porphyry, who were Plotinus's teachers, Plotinus being the person credited with building Neo-Platonism into a respected and widely influential philosophy of the late Roman Empire.

Origen showed such brilliance even as a youth that when Clement fled Alexandria under persecution and the Christian school needed a new principal, he was asked to take over that important position at the age of eighteen. While leading the school, Origen also began a prolific writing career that encompassed intellectual and scholarly works of all kinds.

He took on the Roman philosopher Celsus, who was attacking Christianity as ignorant and superstitious, in a devastating response to *On the True Doctrine* titled *Contra Celsum*, or *Against Celsus*. More than any other single Christian apology, this book of Origen's defeated a Goliath of opposition to Christianity and ushered the young religion into a new age of respectability in spite of continuing persecution.

Origen's aim in his writing career was "to provide Christians who raise intellectual problems with answers in accordance with Scripture, so that they do not go and seek them in great gnostic sects."[1] He was apparently quite successful. One wealthy convert from Valentinian Gnosticism to orthodox Christianity named Ambrose was so impressed with Origen's work that he provided him with a house and secretary and seven stenographers as well as copyists and calligraphers and paid for the publication of his manuscripts. This patronage made it possible for Origen to author approximately eight hundred manuscripts. According to one historian, Origen may have been the most prolific writer of the ancient world.[2] Eventually he became so well known as a philosopher that Roman emperor Alexander Severus's mother, Julia Mammaea, asked him to tutor her. She was not a Christian, needless to say, but nevertheless sought out the great Origen because she had heard of his intellectual powers and teaching skills.

In spite of, or perhaps partly because of, his great popularity and fame, Origen fell into conflict with his bishop, Demetrius of Alexandria. Origen wanted to be ordained to full priesthood, but Demetrius declined to permit it due to Origen's self-castration. At least that was one excuse given by the bishop. The true reason may have been professional jealousy and fear that if ordained, Origen might rival him for power within the Christian hierarchy in Alexandria. Eventually Origen became impatient and asked the bishop of Caesarea in Palestine to ordain him, and that bishop gladly complied. That caused a rift with the bishop of his home city, and Origen never did return to Alexandria. He moved his teaching and writing headquarters to Caesarea in 233. There Origen turned the catechetical school into a "kind of missionary school aimed at young pagans who were showing an interest in Christianity but who were not yet ready . . . to ask for baptism: Origen was thus introducing these to Christian doctrine through a course in philosophy, mainly inspired by Middle Platonism of which he offered them a Christian version."[3]

Origen finally got his wish to die a martyr's death. During the great Decian persecution of Christians throughout the empire in the middle decade of the third century, Origen was arrested and tortured by Roman authorities. He died as a result of the torture. He left an ambiguous legacy of both intellectual greatness and confusion for later Christian thinkers to wrestle with. On the one hand, his profound arguments and insights helped the educated classes of the Roman Empire take a view of Christianity different from Celsus's. They began to look upon Christianity as a viable philosophical and religious alternative to the numerous competing visions of reality and spiritualities within the empire. On the other hand, Origen's explanations of Christian doctrines such as the Trinity and person of Jesus Christ set the stage for great controversy one hundred years after his death.

Origen's most important theological works were his *Contra Celsum* and *De Principiis,* or *On First Principles.* The latter constitutes Origen's great system of Christian philosophy in which he unfolded theological reflections on the nature of God and his Logos and creation and many other subjects. Of course Origen wrote numerous other treatises, but *On First Principles* is one of the great classics of Christian thought that profoundly affected the course of theology afterward.

It is to Origen that we owe the text of Celsus's polemic against Christianity. In *Contra Celsum* Origen quoted Celsus's book *On the True Doctrine* almost in its entirety and refuted it point by point. Origen called Celsus's objections to Christianity "trifling and altogether contemptible"[4] and attempted to show the superiority of the wisdom of Scripture to that of Greek philosophy. Against Celsus, Origen averred that "to those who have eyes to behold the venerable character of Scripture, the sacred writings of the prophets contain things more worthy of reverence than those sayings of Plato which Celsus admires."[5] Of course, like Clement, Origen found much of value in Greek philosophy and highly regarded Plato's philosophy himself. Nevertheless, especially when arguing against Celsus, Origen chose to emphasize that Greek philosophy and Plato were merely anticipations of the higher and fuller truth to be found in divine revelation.

According to Origen philosophy is incapable of providing a saving knowledge of God, and it has no ability to cure a person of sin because "in it the false is inextricably mingled with the true."[6] Nevertheless, he allowed that Christian theology itself is a kind of "divine philosophy" that surpasses and replaces all other philosophies and may use them as servants in its task of leading persons to a true knowledge of God and to salvation.

Origen used an analogy from the Old Testament to illustrate the proper Christian attitude toward Greek philosophy. Just as the Hebrew people took property of the Egyptians with them in the exodus, so God's people are always allowed to use the "spoils of the Egyptians" in borrowing truth from pagan sources where it may be useful in explicating the meaning of Scripture and communicating the gospel to pagan inquirers. Ever since Origen, "despoiling the Egyptians" has been a cliché in theology for Christian use of pagan or secular ideas.

Against Celsus, then, Origen claimed that Christian truth is not completely in conflict with Greek philosophy at every point but that it rises higher in its concepts and especially in its ability to identify a particular historical manifestation of the divine goodness—Jesus Christ. A typical example of Origen's refutation of Celsus is his response to the latter's claim that Jesus Christ was merely a magician like many others and not God, as Christians claim. To Celsus, Origen replied,

> There would indeed be a resemblance between them, if Jesus, like the dealers in magical arts, had performed His works only for show; but now there is not a single juggler who, by means of his proceedings, invites his spectators to reform their manners, or trains those to the fear of God who are amazed at what they see, nor who tries to persuade them so to live as men who are justified by God.[7]

In the final analysis Origen appealed to the historical fact of Jesus' resurrection, to the lives and deaths of the apostles, and above all to "the manifestation of the Spirit and power" in the entire history of the people of God as proof of the truth of Christianity. It is apparent that for Origen there was no single proof or argument that by itself would sweep away Celsus's objections and skepticism. It was rather a series of ideas and facts that, woven together, constituted a strong case for Christianity's truth and superiority over the Greek and Roman philosophies and mythologies. At the end of *Contra Celsum* one has the sense that Origen has at least raised Christianity to an intellectual level alongside Celsus's "true doctrine" (Greek philosophy) and made it impossible from then on for anyone to declare Christianity a folk religion fit only for the ignorant and superstitious.

**Origen on Faith and Reason**

Origen has often been misinterpreted as a rationalist or intellectual Christian who put reason and philosophy before faith. Hopefully, enough has been written here already to dispel that notion. Origen may have been an intellectual, but when it came to theology he emphasized the roles of divine revelation and faith at least as much as the roles of philosophy and reason. For the Christian, reasoning about God and salvation must take place within a commitment of faith, and that includes an acceptance of the truth of the church's tradition and especially the teachings of the apostles. Like Clement, Origen recognized and acknowledged truth outside of Scripture but rejected the possibility of truth in conflict with divine revelation. Like Tertullian and almost every other theologian of the early church, he ended up unwittingly accepting and teaching some ideas that seem more consistent with pagan philosophy and culture than with the teachings of Moses and other prophets and Paul and other apostles. The church as a whole later judged that this was indeed the case and condemned Origen as a heretic. Nevertheless, in his actual description of the "divine philosophy" of Christian theology, Origen promoted strict adherence to the Scriptures and the apostolic tradition and argued that speculation beyond them is only permitted where it remains consistent with them.

The problem is that Origen was very much enamored with speculation and it sometimes led to conclusions that seem patently unbiblical. For example, Origen wondered why Paul wrote in Romans that God "hated Esau" before he was born or had done anything good or bad. Instead of opting to explain it in terms of divine foreordination and election (Origen believed strongly in free will), he appealed to the Greek idea of the preexistence of souls.[8] According to Origen all souls enter the world from a preexistent spiritual state where they have made free choices of obedience or disobedience to God. Only the human soul of Jesus survived this preexistent probation with innocence, and that is why the human Jesus on earth was sinless—not because he was divine but because he did not sin in the preexistence. Esau must have sinned especially grievously, and that fault before birth is why God "hated" him before he was born or did anything good or bad. The natural corollary, of course, is that Jacob must have lived well and obeyed God before birth. According to Origen, this premortal, spiritual probation explains why humans enter the world in such unequal conditions. It is his own form of what some Eastern religions call "karma." Such speculation seemed innocent and even helpful to Origen, but it goes far to explain why some other Christians regarded him as a heretic.

The same tendency toward extrarevelational speculation appears in Origen's great hope of *apokatastasis* (ultimate reconciliation). As always, he began his explanation and defense of his idea by referring to Scripture. In this case, he was attempting to explore and explain what Paul meant when he wrote in 1 Corinthians that in the end God will be "all in all" (15:28). Under some influence from Greek philosophical ideas of being and unity as belonging together, Origen interpreted this statement as implying an eventual perfection and blessedness of all creation resting in God without any hint of sin or evil or even temptation. While stopping short of eschatological pantheism (creation becoming one with God), Origen did affirm a union of God and all creation at the consummation of God's plan. Whether Satan will be included in that is somewhat unclear. For centuries critics have argued that Origen believed in and taught even Satan's and the demons' salvation and inclusion in the great restoration. However, some scholars have asserted that Origen himself denied holding such a view in some of his letters and that it was a rumor about him spread by his enemies.[9] Whatever may be true of Origen's hope for Satan, it seems that he did believe in and teach a universalism of salvation of human "rational souls" at the end of the world. In a classic statement of this great hope Origen wrote that at the end of history

> God will be "all," for there will no longer be any distinction between good and evil, seeing evil nowhere exists; for God is all things, and to Him no evil is near: nor will there be any longer a desire to eat from the tree of the knowledge of good and evil, on the part of him who is always in the possession of good, and to whom God is all. So then, when the end has been restored to the beginning, and the termination of things compared with their commencement, that condition of things will be re-established in which rational nature was placed, when it had no need to eat of the tree of the knowledge of good and evil; so that when all feeling of wickedness has been removed, and the individual has been purified and cleansed, He who alone is the one good God becomes to him "all," and that not in the case of a few individuals, or of a considerable number, but He Himself is "all in all." And when death shall no longer anywhere exist, nor the sting of death, nor any evil at all, then verily God will be "all in all."[10]

Here as elsewhere Origen based his interpretation as much on speculation drawn from Greek philosophy as on biblical exegesis. Neo-Platonism, for instance, emphasized the oneness of being so that ultimate being—God—would have to be the absolutely undifferentiated One. It seems that Origen believed that in order for God to be God, he must reconcile everything to himself. An ultimate dualism of reality—good and evil—cannot be allowed to exist. It would be forever a challenge to God's being as creator and unifier of everything. This logic would seem to push Origen in the direction of even Satan's salvation, although he may not actually have affirmed that.

Origen's theological reflections began with the proper roles of faith and philosophy, and as already seen, these were brought by Origen into a close relationship, while divine revelation and faith were given the primacy. At least that was Origen's intention and stated method. When he turned to Scripture and its interpretation, Origen showed his true Alexandrian colors by emphasizing the spiritual meaning of much of it and the allegorical method of its interpretation. Without slavishly following Philo or Clement, Origen did build faithfully on their hermeneutical approaches and found little value in the historical-literal meaning of the Old Testament, while discovering there riches of gospel truth hidden within its symbols and allegories.

### Origen's Allegorical Interpretation of Scripture

Like Philo before him, Origen distinguished among three levels of meaning in Scripture, requiring a threefold manner of understanding and interpreting it. The three levels correspond to the three aspects of the human person: corporeal (bodily), soulish (rational and ethical) and spiritual (having to do with salvation in the highest sense).

The bodily meaning of a text is its literal reference, and Origen admitted some things that are useful on that level. For example, some of the legislation given by God through the prophets is instructive and helpful for Christians. An example, of course, would be the Ten Commandments.

The soulish meaning of a text is its moral significance. Origen urged that in many cases a biblical story offers an ethical and moral principle hidden beneath the surface of the literal and historical meaning. Old Testament prohibitions of certain foods really refer to moral practices of not associating with evil people.

Finally, for Origen the most important level of meaning in Scripture is the spiritual one, which is also mystical and almost always refers in cryptic fashion to Christ and the Christian's relationship with God. The spiritual-mystical meaning is always there—even if undiscovered and unrecognized—and it is the Christian exegete's task to strive to uncover it. More often than not it reveals something about the believer's *theosis,* or divinization, as the ultimate goal of salvation and Christian living.

One of Origen's purposes in allegorical interpretation was to relieve the unbearable pressure put on Christians by skeptics like the pagan writer Celsus, who ridiculed many Old Testament stories as absurd and improper to God. God's humanlike qualities and especially God's wrath as portrayed there came in for great criticism and sarcasm. Long before Origen or even Clement, of course, the Jewish scholar Philo had already set the trend in Alexandria for relieving this pressure. Such passages that seem to describe God in ways unworthy of divine being are not to be taken literally. They are, for example, anthropomorphisms in which God is being described in human images as having hands and feet. Or they are allegories in which God is being described in human images as having certain emotions that Greeks would consider absolutely contrary to divine *apatheia* (serenity and self-sufficiency). Origen joined Celsus in ridiculing the literal interpretations of many such passages as absurd and impossible.

One example of Origen's figurative interpretation as it was used to relieve tension related to the Christian doctrine of God lies in his treatment of biblical language about God's wrath. Celsus and other Greek critics of the biblical tradition (Jewish and Christian) argued that wrath is improper to divine being since divinity is absolute and cannot be forced into emotional outbursts by creatures. Such a deity would be too much like the capricious, unpredictable and all-too-human gods of Olympus. Origen agreed. In *Contra Celsum* he wrote, "We speak, indeed, of the 'wrath' of God. We do not, however, assert that it indicates any 'passion' on His part, but that it is something which is assumed *[sic]* in order to discipline by stern means those sinners who have committed many and grievous sins."[11] He went on to compare biblical statements about and narratives depicting God's wrath with biblical language about God sleeping. If one is figurative, why not the other? According to Origen, then, any biblical statements that conflict with what is proper to God must be interpreted figuratively and (if they are narratives) allegorically. Just as God cannot really sleep, neither can God experience passions such as wrath.

This presupposition seemed obvious to Origen, and that can only be because, like most other church fathers and theologians of the Roman Empire, he was unduly influenced by the Greek philosophical theism of the Platonic tradition, which attempted to remove everything considered creaturely or imperfect from divinity. On many things Origen was willing to stand firmly against Greek culture and philosophy,[12] but in the doctrine of God's attributes he seemed to capitulate all too readily to Greek metaphysical assumptions about emotion as evidence of imperfection.

In spite of a method of biblical interpretation that many today would consider playing fast and loose with Scripture, Origen did highly regard the prophetic and apostolic writings. While he almost certainly did not believe in its "inerrancy," and while he did freely interpret it figuratively, he also affirmed unequivocally that God is Scripture's author and even treated the human authors as mouthpieces or secretaries of the Holy Spirit. He considered his own allegorical interpretation of the Old Testament justified by the apostles' uses of the Hebrew Bible. Paul, for example, interpreted the Pentateuch prohibition of muzzling oxen while they are treading corn as referring to his own freedom to receive gifts and offerings to support his ministry. Furthermore, in Galatians Paul interpreted the Old Testament story of Abraham, Sarah and Hagar allegorically. By no means did Origen intend to mistreat Scripture as anything less than fully authoritative. His concern was only to remove by allegorical and figurative interpretation what he saw as a false stumbling block put in the path of educated pagans by literalistic interpretation.

### Origen's Doctrine of God

Origen's doctrine of God is one of the most highly developed and complex in the history of Christian theology. It is both profound and confusing. Like Scripture, God was a flashpoint of controversy between Christian intellectuals like Origen and Greek and Roman intellectuals like Celsus. The latter and most others like him considered Christian teachings about divinity hopelessly primitive and contradictory. They asked how anyone could believe that the one God of the universe, who created and sustains all things, was born as an infant. Who was running the universe during God's infancy? Of course Origen was not the first Christian to attempt an answer. But he was one of the first to provide a sustained account of Christian belief about God and Jesus Christ and their relationship that was aimed at defeating such objections. In the process he both cleared and muddied the waters of Christian teaching so that decades after his death his troubling legacy in this area erupted in the greatest controversy in the history of Christian theology.

Many things seem obvious and settled to Christians sixteen to seventeen centuries after Origen's lifetime. One is tempted to ask how it was possible for so many beacons of light to shine forth from the same mind that also sent out so many confusing signals about God and Jesus Christ. One to two centuries after his death, both arch-heretics and champions of orthodoxy appealed to Origen as their mentor and found supporting statements in his writings. For all his rigorous, systematic treatment of doctrinal themes Origen could at times fall into such frustrating contradiction that shaking one's head in bewilderment is the inevitable response. On the one hand, Origen never tired of affirming and asserting in no uncertain terms the absolute divinity of the Logos who became Jesus Christ as eternal and equal with God the Father. On the other hand, he also fell repeatedly into the trap of subordinationism—the tendency to reduce the Logos to something less than the Father. The Holy Spirit was neglected if not almost totally ignored in Origen's trinitarian musings.

The place to begin any attempt to understand Origen's doctrine of God and why it became a troubling legacy for the church is to examine his view of God's nature and attributes. For him, God is Spirit and Mind, simple (uncompounded), incorporeal, immutable and incomprehensible. God is "simple substance" without body, parts or passions.[13] Of course Origen had much more to say about God, but this is enough to indicate the influence of Middle Platonism if not Neo-Platonism upon his thinking.

One of Celsus's main arguments against Christianity was that the incarnation would necessarily introduce imperfection into God. If God "came down" to humans, he necessarily changed—for the worse! But God cannot change in any way—for better or for worse—according to Celsus and all other Greek (especially Platonic) thinkers. Origen refused to back off from either of the two crucial affirmations of Christian doctrine: that God is one and perfect in every way (and he even strengthened this through the use of Platonic philosophy) and that Jesus Christ is God. Those few untutored interpreters of Origen who claim that he did not teach the full and true deity of the Son, Jesus Christ, are simply wrong. Throughout his works he frequently referred to Jesus Christ as the "Divine Word, who is God." What could be clearer than this statement in *On First Principles:* "What belongs to the nature of deity is common to the Father and the Son."[14] So how did he answer the questions and accusations of Celsus and his ilk?

## Origen's Concept of the Logos

First of all, Origen attempted to solve the riddles of the doctrines of God and the incarnation by exploiting to its fullest the concept of the Logos. Second, Origen rejected any real ontological change in divinity—even in the Logos—in the process of becoming incarnate: "For, continuing unchangeable in His essence, He condescends to human affairs by the economy of His providence."[15] Both affirmations became stock in trade of especially Eastern Christian thought from Origen on. At the same time, however, both were expressed by Origen in ways that led to very differing interpretations and even heresies and schisms.

For Origen the Logos was the key to making intelligible Christian belief in God together with belief in the incarnation of God in human form as Jesus Christ. The Logos is God's "stainless mirror" (perfect image) and "offshoot" (like a ray of the sun) that has always been with the Father and in the Father as his Word (expression). The Logos is eternally generated or eternally begotten by the Father, and according to Origen, there is no dissimilarity whatever between the Father and the Word.

Origen never tired of emphasizing that the Logos/Word is God's very Son and in no way created or begotten in time. This is ironic since Arius, the archenemy of the doctrine of the Trinity in the fourth century, claimed Origen as the source of his subordinationism of the Son in which he declared that "there was when the Son was not." Anyone who reads Origen carefully cannot miss his strong declarations of the eternity of the Logos, the Son, with the Father. Referring to the "generation," or "begetting," of the Son by the Father, he wrote that the Son is equal with God the Father "because this generation is as eternal and everlasting as the brilliancy which is produced from the sun. For it is not by receiving the breath of life that He is made a Son, by any outward act, but by His own nature."[16] And Origen declared of the Logos that "there was not [a time] when He (the Son) was not."[17] With regard to the whole Trinity and all three persons within it, Origen wrote that "nothing in the Trinity can be called greater or less, since the fountain of divinity alone contains all things by His word and reason, and by the Spirit of His mouth sanctifies all things which are worthy of sanctification."[18]

On the other hand, Origen saw a primary purpose in exploiting and explicating the idea of the Logos as lying in its value for demonstrating how the world-transcending God could relate to time and history through incarnation. Thus the Logos, though eternal and equally divine, must be somehow subordinate to God the Father. Origen introduced a strong note of subordination of the second and third persons of the Trinity—even in the "immanent Trinity" before creation—by affirming that the Father is the source of all divinity and they derive their divine being and goodness from him. An excellent example of this eternal subordination of the Logos and Spirit appears when Origen said, "We say that the Savior and the Holy Spirit exceed all creatures without possible comparison, in a wholly transcendent way but that they are exceeded by the Father by as much or even more than they exceed the other beings."[19]

Apparently only the Logos and not the Father could become incarnate because while it is somehow proper for the Logos to enter time and history, it is not proper for the Father to do so. Nevertheless, even the Logos underwent no real change in becoming human in Jesus Christ. Part of Origen's solution to this lies in his speculation about the preexistent human soul of Jesus.

Although he is very difficult to interpret on this point, Origen apparently believed that God prepared a soul-substance between deity and human flesh and attached it to the Logos before the birth of Jesus in Bethlehem so that the "incarnation" actually began in the preexistence. The point and purpose of this speculation is to explain how a divine being—even one somehow subordinate to God—could unite with flesh and blood without being tainted by imperfection. The introduction of preexistent intermediate realities is supposed to help make this intelligible within the framework of Greek thought. The Logos became united with a human soul and the two grew together in the preexistent state, and then this union became the God-man in Jesus Christ through the virgin Mary:

> This substance of a soul, then, being intermediate between God and the flesh—it being impossible for the nature of God to intermingle with a body without an intermediate instrument—the God-man is born, as we have said, that substance being the intermediary to whose nature it was not contrary to assume a body.[20]

The "intermediate instrument" that became incarnate, then, was the composite reality of the divine Logos (something or someone eternal but somehow less than God the Father) and the preexistent rational soul of Jesus. The preexistent soul of Jesus was so united with the Logos that it was like iron filled with fire. It was divinized and yet remained creaturely and thus was the perfect instrument for the Word's descent into human existence without change.

Origen's second point is that even in the incarnation—all throughout the earthly human existence of Jesus Christ—the divine Logos in him never experienced real change. Only the human body and soul of Jesus suffered and died. The divine Logos entered into human existence but was not tainted by creaturely imperfection. Origen said of Jesus Christ, "We consider Him as a man, distinguished beyond all other men by an intimate communion with the Eternal Word."[21]

Many questions arise about Origen's theology. One of the most pressing is, did he truly do justice to the incarnation? Is Jesus Christ treated as "truly God and truly human" in Origen's theology? On the one hand, there is no question that he considered the Logos—God's Son—who became incarnate in Jesus Christ as divine, even if somehow subordinate to the Father from eternity. On the other hand, whether and to what extent Origen truly considered Jesus Christ in his earthly existence "God" is unclear. He was a man in "an intimate communion with the Eternal Word [Logos]," but was he God?

What seemed to hinder Origen from fully and unequivocally affirming the deity of Jesus Christ was his prior commitment to the Greek idea of divine nature as simple, immutable, impassible and unable to be disturbed by time or emotion *(apatheia)*. This idea of God caught on and became virtually synonymous with "Christian theism" in orthodox and catholic Christianity, but Origen's specific solutions to how to make it intelligible together with affirmation of incarnation (Jesus' divinity) were rejected. Something seems unfair about that. A later church father who himself offered little in the way of coherent explanations of Christian beliefs accused Origen of being the fountainhead of virtually every heresy that came along to plague the church in the fourth and fifth centuries. One of Origen's modern defenders remarks that "it is the progress of theology that made Origen look like a heretic," because he was unable to foresee the heresies to come and reply to them in advance and because he naively used some expressions that later theologians would give a heretical sense.[22]

**Origen on Salvation and His Legacy**

Little has been said so far about Origen's doctrine of salvation, and that is because nothing particularly new appears in it. Like other church fathers of his time, Origen emphasized salvation as a process of transformation into the image of God and eventually into partial participation in God's own nature called *theosis,* or divinization. Also like all the other early church fathers and theologians of his time and before, Origen considered this process a synergistic one. That is, he emphasized the free participation of the human person *and* the absolute necessity of God's grace apart from any predestination or determination of persons' free choices.

The entire Eastern branch of Christendom tended to follow Origen's outline of salvation by accepting synergism and divinization as key concepts of its soteriology. In Eastern Orthodox theology God's grace enables human response, but the latter must be free and uncoerced. Also, salvation is seen as a lifelong process of gradual transformation in which human will and energy cooperates freely with divine grace in the hope that eventually the person will reflect God's glory and participate in God's immortal nature.

In the story of Christian theology, is Origen a villain or a hero? Actually, there are very few such stark characters in the story. Most players are some shade of gray, and determining exactly what shade that is often comes down to a matter of perception and relative theological judgment.

Just because Origen was condemned as a heretic by a sixth-century council caught up in all kinds of political-theological wrangling says little or nothing about his true Christian orthodoxy. Protestants especially should avoid rejecting him for that reason alone. Many Protestant heroes were condemned as heretics during and after their lives.

Like so many others in this story, Origen's contribution is a mixture of the positive and the negative. In terms of overall influence he stands alongside Irenaeus before and Augustine afterward. He was in many ways a model of a great Christian intellectual, and he sacrificed his life in service of the faith. On the other hand, his ambiguous teaching about God, the Trinity and Jesus Christ left a troubling legacy that eventually erupted into civil war within the church. While he is not to blame for that, he can be criticized for failing to see the glaring inconsistencies within his system caused largely by uncritical acceptance of Greek notions of divine being and creaturely imperfection.

# CHAPTER 7

# Cyprian of Carthage Promotes Unity

W*ho is Cyprian? Many readers already somewhat familiar with the story* of Christian theology may well wonder why an entire chapter of this version of that story is being devoted to a person usually overlooked or only briefly noted in surveys of church history and historical theology. While Cyprian of Carthage may not have been one of Christian theology's great original thinkers or a genius of speculative or polemical theology—and thus not to be compared with Origen or Tertullian—his role in the development of organized Christianity is paramount.

Cyprian lived, worked and wrote at a turning point in the life of Christianity. His contribution lay not in some completely new idea or synthesis of philosophy and divine revelation. His contribution lay in his ideas about leadership and his actual personal leadership in the church at a time of great persecution, strife, schism and heresy within Christianity. At a time when Christian leaders were generally laying low to avoid persecution and when heretics and schismatics were tearing the church apart, Cyprian stepped forward and both taught and lived a style of Christian leadership that became normative for the catholic and orthodox church for a thousand years. It remains the basic vision of the church's structure and leadership in the Roman Catholic branch of Christianity, although most Protestants reject it.

## Cyprian's Significance

To be specific, Cyprian standardized the role of bishop within the Great Church and made it absolutely central to the ecclesiology (doctrine and life of the church) of catholic and orthodox Christianity. The life and thought of Cyprian is in many ways the answer to the often-asked question "How did the Christian church become Catholic?" That is, Cyprian's ideas about the office of bishop greatly contributed to making Christianity both East and West a highly structured spiritual hierarchy.

Of course, as already noted Cyprian did not invent this Christian ecclesiology (which would better be called episcopal after *episkopos,* the Greek word for "bishop"). It was developing long before Cyprian appeared on the scene. In fact, Cyprian has often been called "the Ignatius of the West" because of his emphasis on bishops and Christian obedience to them. What was relatively new in Cyprian was his virtual equation of the church itself with the community of bishops. For him, anyone who attempted to live, worship or teach as a Christian apart from the sanction of a duly ordained bishop in apostolic succession was inventing his or her own new schism and had left the church of Jesus Christ behind. And for Cyprian and those who agreed with him, this would be serious business, for, as he never tired of saying, "Without the church as mother one cannot have God as father" and "Outside of the church there is no salvation."

Cyprian's significance in the story of theology lies, then, in his innovative linkage between ecclesiology and soteriology—between the doctrine of the church and the doctrine of salvation. This linkage revolved entirely around the office of bishop. Already in the later decades of the second century and early decades of the third century, the office of bishop was crucial to the life of Christian congregations generally throughout the Roman Empire. The earliest Christian bishops had simply been chief pastors of Christian congregations. The term *episkopos,* which is usually translated "bishop," simply means "overseer." The first bishops were men like Timothy who were appointed by apostles or by Christian congregations to provide spiritual leadership. When conflicts broke out in Christian communities in Corinth and other Roman cities, highly regarded bishops like Clement of Rome and Ignatius of Antioch wrote letters urging the lay Christians to respect and obey their bishops. Throughout the second century, however, the office of bishop gradually became an administrative one in which a Christian minister oversaw the spiritual and administrative needs of congregations within a certain rural or metropolitan area. Often these "sees" (or later "dioceses") matched Roman civil territories, and so in each province or city a Christian bishop oversaw the churches just as a Roman governor or proconsul oversaw the secular bureaucracy and enforced peace and order.

Especially during the third century, certain problems arose that needed urgent solutions. What if a bishop fell into heresy? What if a bishop abused his powers?

What if two men claimed to be bishop of the same group of Christian congregations and their ministers? Who would decide who was a true Christian bishop and by what criteria? In the minds of most Christians of the Roman Empire in the third century it was no more feasible to have more than one recognized bishop in a single region over a group of churches than to have two competing Roman governors of the same province. Unity of empire and church seemed to correspond in the minds of many Christian leaders—well before there was any anticipation of a Christian emperor.

Constantine, the first Roman emperor to consider himself a Christian, was not even anticipated in the third century. Rather, by and large, Roman emperors were extremely hostile to Christianity, and two in particular—Decius and Diocletian—hotly persecuted Christians. Nevertheless, unity of the churches was just as much an unquestioned ideal as was unity of the empire. It did not even enter most Christians' minds to suggest that Christian congregations or pastors could "do their own thing."

What made the situation troubling and called for a radical solution was that many Christian leaders and the congregations who looked up to them were beginning to do their own thing. In large part because of the empirewide persecution under Decius in the middle of the third century, some Christians in Rome and North Africa were acting as if bishops were dispensable and as if certain spiritual men and women ("confessors of the faith") who had suffered persecution and even torture without denying Christ could simply declare other Christians' sins forgiven and readmit them to full fellowship without any permission of a bishop. Other Christians were insisting that bishops and priests who had "lapsed" (denied Christ under torture or threat of death) were not valid Christian leaders and that their sacramental rites of ordination and baptism were invalidated. On occasion, priests who had been ordained by a bishop who later lapsed were being rejected by congregations for no other reason. Persecution and confusion resulting from it threatened total chaos in Christianity.

Cyprian stepped into the fray to clear up the confusion and provide a set of guidelines to unify all congregations, ministers and individual Christian believers around bishops. The result was the formation of Catholic ecclesiology. The same ecclesiology is accepted by Eastern Orthodoxy. It is the common, basic ecclesiology of Christendom from the time of Cyprian until the Protestant Reformation of the sixteenth century. Church historian Hans von Campenhausen summarizes Cyprian's significance in this regard: "With Cyprian began the line of 'curial' bishops who attempted to perform their ecclesiastical office in the magisterial style of the consuls and pro-consuls [of the empire], with whom he did not shrink from being directly compared."[1]

### Cyprian's Life and Ministry

Cyprian was born Thascius Cyprian into a wealthy family in Carthage around 200. He received the best education possible and rose in the ranks of North African Roman society. His exact profession before conversion is unknown, but he probably spent much of his time administering his family's vast estates and living a life of upper-class leisure. Under the influence of a Christian presbyter (priest) named Caecilius, Cyprian converted to Christianity from the traditional pagan religious beliefs and practices of his family. His conversion took place at the age of forty-six and Thascius immediately changed his name to Caecilius. However, he has always been known by his family name, Cyprian, in the annals of church history.

Soon after his conversion Cyprian began distributing his wealth to the poor—an act that endeared him to the suffering masses of persecuted Christians in and around Carthage. According to Pontius the Deacon (who wrote a hagiography of Cyprian titled *The Life and Passion of Cyprian* soon after the bishop's death) after Cyprian's conversion

> his house was open to every comer. No widow returned from him with an empty lap; no blind man was unguided by him as a companion; none faltering in step was unsupported by him for a staff; none stripped of help by the hand of the mighty was not protected by him as a defender. Such things ought they to do, he was accustomed to say, who desire to please God. And thus running through the examples of all good men, by always imitating those who were better than others he made himself also worthy of imitation.[2]

Also soon after Cyprian's conversion the Christian people of Carthage called for his ordination to the priesthood and then his elevation to the position of bishop over the regional churches. Cyprian served as bishop of Carthage from 248 until his public execution by Roman authorities in 258.

That was a turbulent decade in the life of the churches throughout the Roman Empire, and nowhere more so than in North Africa and especially around Carthage, where the persecution was intense. Often such persecutions focused on the leaders of Christian communities, and in order to avoid an untimely death and provide leadership from afar, Cyprian fled into the North African desert for a time. While some Christians criticized him for this, others defended his action as a mere "concealment" for a season so that the Christians would not be leaderless after the persecution lifted. During his exile Cyprian stayed in constant communication with his congregations and priests through correspondence smuggled in and out of Carthage by a constant stream of messengers. Also during the exile Cyprian wrote numerous epistles to other bishops throughout the empire and worked tirelessly to hold the churches together and urge faithfulness and endurance under great duress.

When it seemed that the worst of the persecution under Emperor Decius had lifted, Cyprian returned to Carthage and resumed his public role as leader of the Christians in that important city and region. He called other bishops to attend synods (councils) at Carthage to settle important disputes over the confessors' claim to be able to forgive sins and over doctrinal matters about the person of Christ. He engaged in lively correspondence about these and other controversies and gradually took on the role of a major teacher of Christians throughout the empire. So widely honored and respected was Cyprian that the bishops of Rome felt threatened by him and occasionally criticized or even cut off fellowship with him.

A public dispute broke out between Cyprian and Stephen the bishop of Rome, whom many historians consider the first true pope. The argument was over whether one bishop should stand out as supreme over all the rest. Earlier bishops of Rome had hinted at such a primacy for their see, but Stephen asserted it vigorously and threatened to break fellowship with other bishops who would not agree with him. A formal schism between him and Cyprian was impending when another persecution brought the controversy to a standstill. Eventually Stephen and Cyprian both died and the issue had to wait for another day.

Besides Cyprian's numerous epistles, two of his larger works stand out as especially important: *Concerning the Lapsed* and *On the Unity of the Church*. The former deals with the issue of Christians who had denied Christ in some way during persecution and whether they should be admitted back into fellowship with the church, and if so, how. This was a tremendously emotional and complex issue, and Cyprian stood squarely in the center of the swirling controversy. *On the Unity of the Church* deals with Cyprian's passionate belief that visible unity among Christians—especially bishops—and truth and salvation all are inseparable. At a time when the church of Jesus Christ was faced with extinction or at least complete dissolution under persecution and because of disagreements and dissension, Cyprian argued forcefully that without visible unity the church does not exist and salvation is not possible. While his arguments may seem forced and somewhat strange to modern, individualistic minds, they made great sense in his own time and helped establish the attitude that salvation is linked inextricably with the church's unity and that the church's unity is inseparable from the fellowship of bishops.

According to his biographer, Cyprian had a vision of his own death just before he was arrested by Roman authorities. Cyprian's escape was plotted by devoted followers, but like Socrates of ancient Athens and Ignatius on his way to die in Rome, the bishop refused to cooperate and, to all accounts, died at the hand of the swordsman nobly in full view of pagans and Christians alike. He was immediately lauded as a martyr by Christians throughout North Africa and eventually revered as a great saint throughout the churches of the empire.

Of course Cyprian had his critics during his lifetime and after his death as well. Bishop Stephen of Rome, feuded with Cyprian over his refusal to acknowledge Stephen's supremacy. Many of the confessors intensely disliked Cyprian for his harsh criticism of their practice of declaring forgiveness and readmitting lapsed Christians to full fellowship without consulting any bishop or even priest of the church. In the controversy surrounding the issue of the lapsed, some considered Cyprian too lenient and some considered him too rigorous in his demands for penance. Yet, overall, Cyprian's authority and influence was virtually unmatched among Christians throughout the third century.

**Cyprian's Doctrine of Salvation**

One of the most interesting and influential aspects of Cyprian's theology is his doctrine of salvation. Cyprian was not a speculative thinker like Origen. He wrote very little about the immanent Trinity and the relations among the three persons or their unity. His focus was on the practical side of Christian theology, and he worked tirelessly to connect salvation and the church—soteriology and ecclesiology. For him salvation is a process that begins within the bosom of the church with conversion at baptism and continues within the church until death.

Cyprian was one of the first church fathers to clearly and unequivocally affirm baptismal regeneration—the idea that salvation happens at and by water baptism duly administered by an ordained bishop or his authorized agent the priest. His own testimony of conversion makes clear that he considered baptism the act that put off his old life and brought him new life in Christ. While he attributed all the saving energy to the grace of God, he considered the "laver of saving water" the instrument of God that made him "born again" so that he received a new life and put off what he had previously been. The "water of new birth" animated him to new life by the Spirit of holiness working through it.[3]

In an epistle on infant baptism Cyprian strongly affirmed that infants are all born guilty of Adam's sin and that the guilt is only washed away by the water of baptism. He argued against those who in his own time still rejected baptism of infants. Infants, he asserted, have "contracted the contagion of the ancient death at its earliest birth" and by baptism "are remitted not his own sins, but the sins of another [Adam]."[4]

In an epistle discussing baptisms conducted by heretics and schismatics, Cyprian stated that the priest who baptizes ordinarily gives to the person being baptized "remission of sins" and impartation of the Holy Spirit, but that if the baptizing priest is a heretic, the effect of the baptism is spiritually void: "How then can one who is baptized among them [heretics] seem to have obtained remission of sins, and the grace of the divine mercy, by his faith, when he has not the truth of the faith itself?"[5] The rationale for Cyprian's view of baptismal regeneration is provided in a summary form in the same letter:

> But it is manifest where and by whom remission of sins can be given; to wit, that which is given in baptism. For first of all the Lord gave that power to Peter, upon whom He built the Church, and whence He appointed and showed the source of unity—the power, namely, that whatsoever he loosed on earth should be loosed in heaven. And after the resurrection, also, He speaks to the apostles, saying, "As the Father hath sent me, even so I send you. And when He had said this, He breathed on them, and saith unto them, Receive ye the Holy Ghost: whosesoever sins ye remit, they are remitted unto them; and whosesoever sins ye retain, they are retained." Whence we perceive that only they who are set over the Church and established in the Gospel law, and in the ordinance of the Lord, are allowed to baptize and to give remission of sins; but that without, nothing can either be bound or loosed, where there is none who can either bind or loose anything.[6]

Cyprian's further reflections on salvation make clear that he considered it a lifelong process that only begins with baptism. By baptism, sins are forgiven and the Holy Spirit is imparted. From there the regenerated believer is to stay steadily on a course of faithfulness to the one true church and its doctrines and a life of repentance made visible by acts of penance such as giving alms to the poor and fasting. Cyprian's vision of salvation is one of strict obedience to the commands of Christ. Immortality—the ultimate goal of salvation—depends on rigorous moral self-control and self-sacrifice: "How can we possess immortality, unless we keep those commands of Christ whereby death is driven out and overcome, when He Himself warns us, and says 'If thou wilt enter into life, keep the commandments'?"[7]

Especially when a believer lapses into serious sin, Cyprian prescribed harsh penance before restoration to the full fellowship of the church and to the sacraments. Against those who would be too lenient, he advocated periods of fasting and prayer and the giving of possessions to the poor for forgiveness and restoration. Against those who would be too strict, he advocated eventual mercy and renewal of fellowship, but only after the sinner has proven sorrow and a change of heart and life. In Cyprian's theology of salvation we see the beginning of a fully formed "penitential system." Centuries later entire handbooks of penance detailing particular acts of repentance for specific sins would become standard within the Western (Roman Catholic) churches.

Absolutely clear in Cyprian's account of salvation is that when a sinner attains to the heavenly vision and immortality, it is all God's doing and a work of mercy and grace. Humans cannot coerce God or force his grace to work within them or on their behalf. In spite of later Protestant polemics against the penitential system that grew out of Cyprian's theology, Cyprian himself was not guilty of works righteousness or self-salvation. Nowhere did he suggest that a person can earn salvation as a reward for good works; he only emphasized that a truly repentant sinner being saved by God's grace will necessarily demonstrate true repentance by outward acts. Refusal to do them would constitute apostasy—loss of grace. Cooperation with God's grace in the process of salvation is, for Cyprian, simply "practical Christianity" that avoids the heresy of antinomianism, which rejects all law and moral living in favor of license and taking advantage of the liberty of grace.

On the other hand, the suspicion that Cyprian unintentionally contributed to a growing tendency toward moralism and works righteousness within the church is not entirely unjustified. Even though he attributed all the efficacy of salvation to God's mercy and grace, he also made its preservation in one's life completely dependent on faithfulness to the path of perfection: "It is a slight thing to have been able to attain anything; it is more to have been able to keep what you have attained; even as faith itself and saving birth makes alive, not by being received, but by being preserved. Nor is it actually the attainment, but the perfecting, that keeps a man for God."[8]

Whether this view of salvation necessarily implies something less than grace as a sheer gift and righteousness by works is a matter of disagreement between Protestants and the ancient churches of East and West, who tend to follow Cyprian's line to one extent or another. Protestants of the sixteenth century and afterward came to condemn any such synergism (cooperative effort) in salvation and argue that making the preservation of God's declared righteousness dependent upon "keeping the faith" in moralistic terms amounts to legalism and denial of salvation by grace alone. Defenders of Cyprian's theology argue that any other view than his inevitably leads to antinomianism and "cheap grace."

### Cyprian's Vision of Church Unity

As mentioned earlier, one of Cyprian's most notable contributions lies in his unbreakable link between salvation and the unity of the church. Since he saw the church as the "indispensable ark of salvation"[9] and the "womb" apart from which no one can live and breathe spiritually,[10] he tended to establish a unified, visible church as the basis for salvation. Anyone who either leaves the church or divides it cannot be saved, for "he cannot possess the garment of Christ who parts and divides the Church of Christ" and "he can no longer have God for his Father who has not the church for his mother."[11]

For Cyprian the unity of the church, and thus the very possibility of salvation, resides in the office of bishop. Just as Peter received from Christ the power to remit sins and passed it along to his successors through ordination in apostolic succession, so Peter received from Christ the authority to be the first bishop and hold the church together in union, without which there can be no truth or salvation: "Thence, through the changes of times and successions, the ordering of bishops and the plan of the Church flow onwards, so that the church is founded upon the bishops, and every act of the church is controlled by these same rulers."[12]

According to Cyprian, a true bishop is one so recognized by the majority or all the other bishops of Christendom in apostolic succession who also teaches the truth faithfully. There can be no such thing as a self-appointed bishop. Nor can a heretic be a bishop. Anyone who schismatically separates himself from the communion and fellowship of other bishops is a false bishop.

At the same time, however, Cyprian refused to recognize or acknowledge any one bishop as the head over all. Occasionally he acknowledged—as if reluctantly—that the bishop of Rome may be the "first among equals," but for him this was only an honorary title. When Stephen the bishop of Rome attempted to cancel the decisions of a synod of bishops called by Cyprian in Carthage, Cyprian simply refused to recognize his declaration.

Cyprian's own view is what González refers to as a "federated view of the episcopate."[13] That is, each bishop functions in harmony with all the others and there is no one over all. They are interdependent and ought to arrive at every decision by consensus. Of course, while this worked relatively well during Cyprian's own lifetime, eventually in the Latin West the Roman Catholic tradition elevated the bishop of Rome to supreme authority and eventually declared him infallible. The Eastern church, however, adopted the federated episcopacy. González sums up Cyprian's and the Eastern Orthodox churches' view of church order and government well:

> The unity of the church is in its episcopate, of which all bishops share as if it were a common property. This unity is not something to be added to truth, but is rather an essential part of Christian truth, so that where there is no

> unity there is also no truth. Apart from this unity there is no salvation. Apart from it there is no baptism, or Eucharist, or true martyrdom. However, this unity does not consist in being subject to a "bishop of bishops," but in the common faith, love, and communion of all bishops among themselves.[14]

What this meant in practical terms was that under Cyprian's model no person could perform any saving act efficaciously apart from the authority of a true bishop. "Saving acts" include baptism, the Eucharist (Lord's Supper), forgiveness and restoration to the church, and other ceremonies and declarations important to a person's eternal salvation. Anyone who attempts to restore a person to full fellowship in the church without a bishop's sanction (directly or indirectly) is committing an act against the bishop, and it is empty. This was declared by a synod under Cyprian's leadership in Carthage shortly before his death. The confessors could no longer act apart from the bishops. This was a great victory for Cyprian and the hierarchical unity of the visible church and a terrible defeat for the priesthood of all believers.

While Cyprian's ecclesiology and its linkage with salvation has undergone many permutations and modifications in every branch of Christendom—and been entirely rejected by some—it is still alive and well today. As this chapter was being written, the news was reported that Lutheran and Episcopalian Christians in the United States failed to agree on a formula of concord that would have allowed their ministers to serve parishes in the other denomination and would have brought about greater union of many kinds between them. The reason had primarily to do with the Episcopalians' requirement that bishops in apostolic succession be immediately involved in Lutheran ordinations and other important ecclesiastical functions. The majority of Lutherans voting on the concordat rejected that ecclesiology as too Catholic. For them, what is at stake is the Protestant principle of the "priesthood of all believers." While Episcopalians affirm that same principle, Lutherans fear that their actual ecclesiology undermines it. The roots of that ecclesiology go back to Cyprian.

### Cyprian's Legacy

What is Cyprian's significance in the story of Christian theology? Put rather simply, it is that he helped create the orthodox-catholic episcopal ecclesiology that centers around bishops. It is an ecclesiology accepted by the Eastern Orthodox churches and some Protestants as well. It is an ecclesiology that helped unify the church in a time of great trouble and schism, but at the same time it helped undermine the immediacy of the ordinary believer's relationship with God and his or her ability to dissent and speak prophetically to the hierarchy of the church. From Cyprian on, the office of bishop in Christendom would be both a curse and a blessing. The blessing was in its power to unify. The curse was in its power to crush dissent and individual initiative within the church.

Cyprian's legacy is still controversial among Christians. Some modern Christian historians and theologians argue that the kind of hierarchical ecclesiology that he helped bring about and that he justified in his writings was necessary. Without it, Christianity was in danger of dissolving into "conventicles of a more or less syncretistic character."[15] In other words, heresies, schisms, fanaticism and beliefs and practices alien to apostolic Christianity were so prevalent in early Christianity that order needed to be established to avoid complete chaos and confusion. Even some of Cyprian's critics say that it is easier to decry what happened through his influence than explain how it could have been otherwise. Without the dominating authority of bishops and without their synods (official meetings) to settle disputes, the Christian religion would have lost its identity.

Other modern Christian historians and theologians argue that Cyprian's solution to unifying the church was too extreme and that the result was something barely recognizable as apostolic Christianity. One such critic says that "at the heart of this official thinking [Cyprian's ecclesiology] stands the church as a sacro-social totality, a community of Christian ideas and of the Christian way of life, which lays down for its leaders an 'ecclesiastical,' quasi-political pattern of conduct."[16] In other words, the church began to become firmly institutionalized along the lines of the Roman Empire. In the process, as necessary as it may have been, the church changed for the worse. Lost was the idea of the priesthood of believers, the role of prophets and freedom and spontaneity in worship and church life generally. From the true church being *where the Spirit is* it moved to being *where the bishop is.* In the process, however, at least an identifiable body of teachings and practices became inextricably linked with Christianity, and the danger no longer loomed as large that Christianity would become compatible with anything and everything—a result that would have rendered it meaningless.

# CHAPTER 8

# Christianity Gets Its Act Together

A *major episode in the story of Christian theology is the transformation of* the Christian religion from a relatively disunited, spiritual-pneumatic (charismatic), virtually underground sect within the Roman Empire to a highly organized, hierarchical, visible institution that by the end of the third century was a permanent fixture on the landscape of the empire. And it was poised to become that empire's official religion. Most of the transformation happened in the third century, although every part of it can be traced to earlier roots. How and why the transformation took place will be the main focus here.

Three main developments together made up the transformation of early Christianity: the formalization of its hierarchical organizational structure centering on bishops, the formulation of creeds summarizing the essentials of what must be believed in order to be a Christian, and the identification of a canon of Christian Scriptures. None of these developments was completely started or finished in the third century, but it was during that era that their final outcomes became virtually inevitable—not in every detail but in general shape and outline.

The reasons for these three developments and the general transformation of the church have already been touched upon. Here we will examine them in more detail. First, the disappearance of apostles presented the church with a crisis of authority. All Christians agreed that the apostles had special status and authority to teach, correct and settle disputes. Even the Gnostics appealed to a secret tradition handed down from a select group of Jesus' disciples. The church needed a way to govern itself after the apostles. This need was especially felt because of the rise of heresies and schismatic sects within Christianity in the second century. Without some organizational structure, any person could corrupt the teaching of the church by persuasion and charismatic flair. Gnosticism especially posed a threat to the doctrines of Christianity and forced the second-century Christians to look to powerful leaders to squelch it.

Second, persecution forced the church to deal with some issues that required strong leadership. Who would speak for the Christians in a region? Who would attempt to negotiate with the Roman proconsul in a territory? After the persecution died down who would decide which Christians would be allowed back into their leadership roles as ministers and teachers and which ones would be excluded because they had become traitors to the faith by denying Christ or even collaborating with the authorities? Would it be the so-called confessors who had suffered imprisonment and torture? Or would it be a more formal authority—the bishops?

Third and finally, because of the problem of erring bishops the church was forced to develop a strong hierarchy, creeds and confessions of faith, and a canon of Christian Scriptures. If the bishop represents and leads the church and if great spiritual authority resides in that office, what should be done with a bishop who falls into gross sin or heresy or who becomes a traitor during persecution? This problem especially forced the third-century church to strengthen the community of bishops and led to rule of the church by synods or official gatherings of bishops.

For these and other reasons the Christian church of the Roman Empire "got its act together" in the sense of formally organizing itself. The first and in many ways most important step in this process had to do with the emergence of the authority of bishops and the gatherings of bishops called "synods."

**The Role of Bishops**

At the beginning of the Christian story (late first century to early second century), each congregation had an elder or group of elders, and it ran its own affairs under them. Eventually, very early in the church's history, most churches selected one elder to serve as bishop—a kind of "superelder"—to guide and direct the elders under him. Bishops gradually gained more and more authority and control as individual congregations spawned new churches, and in many cases the bishop of the mother congregation remained bishop of those it mothered. By the end of the third century the city of Rome had forty individual congregations divided into parishes and all of them led by a single bishop.[1] We have already seen in Cyprian's theology the theoretical justification of this episcopal ecclesiology and some of its results. Bishops gradually acquired a special spiritual status by which they alone were able to declare who truly belonged to the catholic and orthodox Christian church—the Great Church—and who was a heretic or sinner beyond the pale of forgiveness. This virtually empowered the bishops to excommunicate persons from the church, and the acquisition and monopoly of power by bishops in the third century represented a quantum leap forward in formal, hierarchical ecclesiology.

This development is sometimes called the "clericalization of church life,"[2] and it had far-reaching effects beyond merely the establishment of a flow chart for church administration. At the top of the ladder of hierarchy stood the bishop, and "once elected, his authority was practically unchallengeable. He was the high priest, . . . descendent of the apostles, and endowed with apostolic powers."[3] Beneath the bishop were clergy of various kinds arranged in an elaborate set of relationships of authority and power, all governed by a growing body of "canon law." This was a formal, written body of ecclesiastical rules and regulations. Many bishops had entire bureaucracies working under them overseeing the diocesan affairs. Bishop Cornelius of Rome, self-proclaimed pope of the middle of the third century, had 155 clergy of various ranks working under him in Rome.[4] Some of them were presbyters (the same as elders) and they served as ministers and priests of congregations as well as servants of the bishop in administration. Deacons were also ordained clergy, but rather than serving as sacramental priests they functioned as overseers of charitable work and also performed administrative tasks for the bishop. Some of the clergy were simply administrators who worked under the bishop in correspondence, carrying messages to other bishops and maintaining the organization of the see or diocese.

As the church became clericalized, the role of the laity tended to diminish. At the beginning of the third century lay Christians—ordinary believers who had no official function as ministers—often performed baptisms and led in worship, including the Lord's Supper. Most Christian congregations allowed for some spontaneous lay participation. Lay believers such as those who suffered for Christ during persecution were widely regarded as having the ability to declare others' sins forgiven after proper repentance. All that changed with the clericalization process:

> The liturgy was becoming more formal and the penitential system more exact. The administration of both had become a clerical preserve. At the beginning of the [third] century the laity in the church at Carthage might still expect to take an individual part in the service, to "prophecy," or sing something of one's own composition. The laity could also baptize, and this seems to have been the tradition in Rome also. By mid-century this had

> changed. Cyprian never speaks of baptism by laity in his many references to the subject. The celebration of the mysteries [sacraments] was the prerogative of priests alone.[5]

At the top of the ladder of clericalization stood the bishop—the "superpriest" and chief administrator as well as judge of all Christians in his see. Normally, bishops did not interfere in one another's affairs. Thus at the beginning of the third century Christianity was a patchwork quilt of sees or bishoprics spread out all over the empire with no larger visible organization. Even though one bishop—the bishop of Rome—claimed to have a kind of supremacy over all the rest, no other bishop recognized the legitimacy of that claim until later. Cyprian argued that the unity of the church lay in the fellowship of the bishops. But what should be done when a bishop—the highest officer in church administration—fell into gross sin or heresy or betrayed Christ and his church during persecution? Eventually the need arose for synods of bishops that would make important decisions that affected more than one see and that would examine the credentials of bishops suspected of sin, heresy or betrayal.

The precedent for bishops meddling in others' affairs may be seen in Clement of Rome's letter to the Corinthians. In *1 Clement* the bishop of Rome sternly warned the members of the church at Corinth to cease and desist their rebellion against their appointed leaders. During the second century and into the third century, other bishops wrote letters to bishops and congregations outside their own sees, attempting to set them straight on various issues. Occasionally bishops even appointed other bishops when presbyters of neighboring sees were unable or unwilling to elect their own spiritual leaders. One of the first synods of bishops took place in the middle of the second century to examine the Montanist movement, and the result was the formal expulsion of Montanus and all his followers from the Great Church.

The first instance of a synod of bishops excommunicating a bishop took place in Antioch in 268. It may have taken place in the first Christian church building, or basilica, ever built in a major Roman city. The basilica in Antioch was built in about 256. A group of bishops of surrounding sees gathered there to examine the teachings of a bishop named Paul of Samosata. Apparently Paul taught a version of the doctrine of Christ that has come to be known as adoptionism because it explains Jesus' divinity as his special relationship with God the Father beginning with his baptism in the Jordan River.

According to Paul, Christians are strict monotheists and must never even imply the existence of more than one God. He believed that the developing doctrine of the Trinity, including the eternal deity of the Son, threatened the monotheism of

Christianity. Therefore he said that Jesus Christ was a man adopted by God as his special human son. Jesus entered into a unique position in relation to God without actually becoming God. Paul of Samosata placed Jesus somewhere above other humans due to his elevation to sonship by the Father and somewhere below God due to his humanity and God's absolute oneness. The effect, of course, was a complete denial of the Trinity, and Jesus Christ was reduced to a great prophet. The synod of bishops gathered in Antioch in 268 condemned Paul's teaching and deposed him from his position as bishop of Samosata, a suburb of Antioch.

Of course, the synod of Antioch had no official "teeth" to enforce its decisions. Neither did any other bishop or synod. Christians were still a persecuted minority even if they were thriving and building basilicas and even planning a great cathedral near the emperor's palace. Such synods had only as much authority as they were given by groups of Christians. Occasionally a bishop or synod appealed to the Roman authorities for help in enforcing their decisions. That was a common practice among all kinds of societies, including religious groups. The Roman authorities chose by and large to stay out of religious disputes unless the civil peace was at stake. Nevertheless, for the most part such synods accomplished much in terms of persuading ordinary Christians and their ministers and deacons to go along with their decisions. The unity of the church was at stake and most Christians deferred to the authority of bishops and synods. Paul of Samosata was deposed by his own people due to the declaration of his condemnation by the synod of 268. It was a great victory not only for orthodoxy but also for catholicity. Thankfully, it was also a victory for the gospel.

By the end of the third century the clericalization of Christianity was nearly complete. The church was for all practical purposes identical with the fellowship of bishops in apostolic succession. Although various schismatic groups, such as Montanists and Gnostics and others, still existed, there was emerging clearer than ever the Great Church both orthodox and catholic. All that was needed to solidify its unity and hierarchical power and forever rid it of the pesky heretics and schisms was one supreme bishop with absolute authority over all the others and a Christian emperor who would throw the weight of the "sword" (force, coercion) behind the bishops of the Great Church. Those two steps were taken in the fourth and fifth centuries so that by 455, at the great Council of Chalcedon, the crucial influences in deciding true doctrine and church policy were the emperor and the pope—the bishop of Rome.

### The Rules of Faith

When bishops attempted to judge theological correctness individually or in synods, what standards or criteria did they use? As already noted, there was no unanimously agreed on Christian Bible up until this time. Deciding that Paul of Samosata's teaching regarding Christ was a heresy was not as simple as turning to a few key passages of Scripture and proving that it violated them. That is not to say that bishops of the second and third centuries never appealed to Scripture. Of course they did. They appealed to the Hebrew Bible—usually interpreted somewhat symbolically and allegorically—and to a variety of scrolls and manuscripts considered apostolic in some sense. However, what one bishop considered inspired Scripture was not necessarily the same as that which another bishop considered Scripture. In the absence of a formally recognized canon of Christian Scripture, the bishops appealed to amorphous "tradition." A later theologian defined tradition as "what has been believed everywhere by everyone at all times."[6]

Of course *nothing* has been believed "everywhere by everyone at all times"! The rule itself is meant to apply only to true Christian believers. They are the "everyone." But the rule, or "canon," has several major flaws, including the problem of identifying just who is a "true Christian," which is the very problem it is supposed to help solve. Using it to solve the problem involves a great deal of circularity. Nevertheless, the bishops and other leaders and theologians of Christianity in the third century had a sense of apostolic tradition, and they attempted to identify it and formalize it in a creed that could serve all churches everywhere. The makings for such an authoritative creedal summary of apostolic doctrine were found in an ancient baptismal formula used in the churches of Rome.

Sometime during the late second century or early third century someone formulated out of those Roman Christian sayings what has come to be known as the Apostles' Creed. Earlier it was known as the Old Roman Creed. One version of it reads:

I believe in God, the Father almighty,
*creator* of heaven and earth.
I *believe* in Jesus Christ, his only Son, our Lord.
*He* was conceived by *the power* of the Holy *Spirit.*
and born of the Virgin Mary.
He suffered under Pontius Pilate,
was crucified, died, and was buried.
He descended *to the dead.*
On the third day he rose again.
He ascended into heaven,
and is seated at the right hand of the Father.

He will come again to judge the *living* and the dead.
I believe in the Holy *Spirit,*
the holy catholic Church,
the communion of saints,
the forgiveness of sins,
the resurrection of the body,
and the life everlasting. Amen.[7]

The exact lineage of this creed is unknown. While its roots go back to the Roman church in the second century, its full formulation and official acceptance as *the* unifying "symbol," or "rule of faith" (creed), did not come about until much later. A rudimentary form of it can be found in Tertullian's *On the Veiling of Virgins* around 200, and the Roman church leader and writer Hippolytus included a question-and-answer form of it in *Apostolic Tradition* around the same time. Rufinus, a Latin translator of Origen and theologian in his own right, included a nearly complete text of this creed in about 404. The full form and official acceptance of the creed came about under Emperor Charlemagne of the Holy Roman Empire (or the Frankish Latin Kingdom) around 813. Some scholars place its official status as an authoritative creed for all Christians everywhere as late as 1014.[8]

The history of the official acceptance of a creed, however, should not throw one off. The fact is that some form of the Apostles' Creed or Old Roman Symbol was widely accepted as an authoritative summary of the apostolic tradition in the third century. Its purpose was to provide a criterion for membership in the church catholic and orthodox. Its wording intentionally excluded Gnostics and certain other heretics. In the long run, of course, this creed was too cursory for that purpose. In the fourth century, as we will see, the bishops found it necessary to formulate and promulgate another creed that put flesh on the skeleton of the Apostles' Creed. The Nicene, or Niceno-Constantinopolitan, Creed (325 and 381) made clear the correct interpretations of certain ambiguous passages in the Apostles' Creed and emphasized the trinitarian doctrine implicit there. Together, the Apostles' Creed and the Nicene Creed form the twin unifying authoritative statements of apostolic faith for much of Christendom. Even during the Protestant Reformation of the sixteenth century, most branches of Protestantism and their leaders (Luther, Zwingli, Calvin) embraced them and even considered any Reformers who wouldn't embrace them as heretics.

It is interesting to note that these "rules of faith," or creeds, predate the final and official agreement regarding the canon of Christian Scriptures. In fact, in one sense there never has been a universal agreement on the Christian canon! Nevertheless, the point is that the existence of some form of the Apostles' Creed recognized by most Christian churches of the Roman Empire almost certainly predates the "closure of the canon" in its various forms here and there. The Eastern Orthodox and Roman Catholic churches—both of which claim to be the true modern forms of the undivided Great Church of the Roman Empire—still emphasize the authority of tradition over canon. That is, they believe that the canon of Scripture—its exact identification as a certain set of inspired and holy writings—is a product of the apostolic tradition that earlier gave rise to the episcopal ecclesiology of the church and the rules of faith. That does not mean that they subordinate the truth of Scripture to something else other than God. Rather, in their theologies tradition stemming from the apostles themselves has historical and ecclesiastical priority over canon. It is that living tradition embodied within the fellowship of the bishops and expressed in the rules of faith that eventually gave rise to *recognition* of certain writings as inspired. As we will see in the chapters on the Protestant Reformation, Protestants by and large take a different view of the matter—setting inspired text over unwritten tradition. There is a sense in which both Eastern Orthodoxy and Roman Catholicism do the opposite.

### The Development of the Christian Canon

How then did the Christian canon of Scripture—the Christian Bible—come into existence? The story is extremely complicated and cannot be recounted in great detail here. In fact, it is a debated and debatable story. Any retelling of it is bound to draw fire from people committed to a different version. Nevertheless, the basic outline and contours of that story will constitute the focus of the remainder of this chapter.

The apostles themselves used the Hebrew Bible and clearly considered it authoritative. Although many Jewish writings existed in the time of Jesus and the apostles, the canon of Hebrew Scripture was relatively fixed and clear. The party of the Pharisees dominated the Jewish synagogues, and after the destruction of the temple in Jerusalem in 70 they sought to reform Judaism so that it could exist indefinitely in diaspora (exile from Palestine) without a temple, and one part of that process was the formal definition of the inspired Scriptures of Judaism. Although some debate exists about the Council of Jamnia where Jewish rabbis met in 90, it seems that some important steps toward the official canonization process took place there. The Jewish Bible was defined as twenty-two inspired books: Pentateuch through Lesser Prophets. In later Christian Bibles some of the books of the Jewish canon have been separated so that they make up a total of thirty-nine individual books. The Greek version of the Hebrew Scriptures known as the Septuagint, or LXX, contained all of those as well as some books written after Malachi that are of mainly historical significance. These include the books of Maccabees and other so-called (by Christians) intertestamental or apocryphal books. Most of the early church fathers of the second century used the Septuagint, as did Paul and other apostles. Yet they quoted frequently from a variety of the twenty-two canonical books of the Hebrews and rarely from the later historical and apocryphal books.

By and large, then, it is safe to say that most of the early church fathers of the second and third centuries accepted the Jewish leaders' decision to expand the inspired Scriptures beyond just the Pentateuch (Genesis through Deuteronomy) and to restrict them to the twenty-two (or thirty-nine) books of the Law and Prophets. This then was "the Bible" of the earliest Christian churches after the apostles.[9] Around the time of Clement of Rome and the other apostolic fathers, the apostles' letters and the Gospels that were believed to have been written by apostles or those closely associated with them were collected and referred to as the "Apostles," juxtaposing them with the "Prophets" of the Hebrew Bible. Thus by the year 200 several church fathers and bishops were referring to a collection of inspired, authoritative writings known as "the Prophets and Apostles" and treating this amorphous mass as a criterion and norm of truth for Christian belief and practice. Yet no officially recognized or unanimously agreed upon Christian equivalent to the Hebrew Bible yet existed.

Scholars generally agree that once again the church owes a great debt to a heretic. According to one leading church historian, "the idea and the reality of a Christian Bible were the work of Marcion, and the Church which rejected his work, so far from being ahead of him in this field, from a formal point of view simply followed his example."[10] Marcion was an influential Christian teacher in Rome in the middle of the second century. Although widely separated geographically, Marcion and Montanus were contemporaries and had certain common characteristics. Although Marcion's theology was closer to some forms of Gnosticism, like Montanus he considered the church badly in need of reform, and he set about to reform it by attempting to rediscover and promote what he considered to be the true, original teaching of Jesus. In order to do this Marcion believed it necessary to strip away all vestiges of Judaism from Christianity—including the Hebrew Bible and its God, Yahweh. For him the Old Testament had no validity for Christians whatever, and he considered the God described in it a tribal, bloodthirsty demigod who did not deserve Christian adoration or worship. Marcion's similarities to Gnosticism come out in his idea that the God of the Old Testament wrongly created matter and that matter is the cause of evil. For Marcion the Old Testament Yahweh was more demonic than divine.

Marcion was perhaps the very first Christian to attempt to define a Christian canon of inspired Scriptures, and he wanted to limit it to only those writings by apostles that he considered free of any taint of Judaism. Marcion's Bible contained two parts: an edited version of Luke's Gospel and ten of Paul's epistles. Even the "Apostle" was edited by Marcion so that all "Judaizing elements" were stripped from the ten epistles.

Marcion and his anti-Jewish version of Christian Scripture caught on quickly among some Christians, and Marcionite churches popped up in Rome and Carthage and other cities. The leading church fathers and bishops severely attacked Marcion and his following. Tertullian's *Against Marcion* is an excellent example of Christian anti-Marcionite polemics from around the turn of the century (201). Irenaeus also criticized Marcion and his teaching in *Against Heresies*, as did other second- and third-century church fathers. Some early Christians clearly considered Marcion the arch-heretic and main enemy of orthodox and catholic Christianity. But Marcionite churches survived in cities throughout the empire until they were suppressed by the first Christian emperors.

One response to Marcion's truncated canon of Christian Scriptures was to produce a correct canon, and the first semiofficial attempt was at Rome. Around 170 the Roman Christian church produced the Muratorian Canon to counter Marcion's and provide Christians with a full list of authoritative "Prophets and Apostles." The Muratorian Canon listed all four Gospels, Acts and every other book contained in the New Testament, as it was eventually defined, except Hebrews, James and 1 and 2 Peter. It also included *The Wisdom of Solomon* but significantly excluded the ever-popular and influential *Shepherd of Hermas*. The Muratorian Canon represents a crucial step in the development of the Christian church's official organizational life: it was the first attempt to identify a definitive list of Christian writings on a plane equal to the Hebrew Bible. While its list was not the final accepted version, it did entrench in Christian thinking the idea of a Christian Bible and made clear that it would not exclude the Hebrew Scriptures and would not be open to every new prophecy or writing someone claimed as inspired.

The exact criteria used by the composers of the Muratorian Canon is unclear. In fact, there has always been debate over which criteria were most important in guiding the church to recognize certain writings as authoritative and inspired. Church historian von Campenhausen is most nearly correct when he labels the main criterion the "prophetic-apostolic principle."[11] This is not a rigid rule but a flexible measurement by which writings were judged by early Christians involved in this process. The prophetic-apostolic principle simply means that books and letters had to be widely recognized throughout the Christian churches as reflecting apostolic authority (if not written by an apostle) and as presenting important truth for salvation and Christian living. That is, for any work to make it into the canon, it had to be a product of "primitive Christianity" and be widely used as a helpful guide to teaching and living Christianity.

Church fathers such as Irenaeus, Tertullian and Origen created their own lists of Christian Scriptures, and they varied somewhat from the Muratorian Canon and from each other. Irenaeus listed the four Gospels and most of the later canonized epistles, which he clearly treated as inspired, authoritative Scripture. He rejected the Gnostics' Gospels and Marcion's truncated canon. Shortly after Irenaeus, Tertullian followed the same pattern, as did Origen. Both Tertullian and Origen considered certain Christian writings verbally inspired in the same sense as the Hebrew Scriptures and used them to settle doctrinal controversies. In their writings we see the implicit concept of a New Testament alongside the Hebrew Scriptures as the Old Testament in how they treated the writings they considered prophetic-apostolic and authoritative. A difference remained between them, however, in that Tertullian wished to treat the canon as a black-or-white, either-or category, while Origen acknowledged a set of Christian writings as doubtful and disputed but nevertheless helpful.

According to von Campenhausen, "It is undisputed that both the Old and the New Testaments had in essence already reached their final form and significance around the year 200."[12] That may be a bit optimistic given the discrepancies between the lists of Christian Scriptures provided by Tertullian and Origen, who both wrote around that time and shortly afterward. Nevertheless, there is some truth in von Campenhausen's assertion, especially over against those who would relegate the whole idea of a Christian New Testament and Bible to a much later date. One cannot read Irenaeus, Tertullian or Origen without noting their devotion and submission to those writings they considered especially inspired and authoritative for Christians, and there was significant overlap between their lists in spite of some differences.

The main debates over which writings should be included in a Christian canon of Scriptures surrounded Hebrews, 1 and 2 Peter, Jude, 3 John, Revelation, James, and the *Didache, Shepherd of Hermas* and the *Epistle of Barnabas.* A few early church fathers and churches even treated *1 Clement* as Scripture. Gradually, however, the consensus grew that all in the first list—Hebrews through James—should be included because of their wide use throughout Christian churches (even though some of them were virtually unknown in some churches) and because of their links with apostles. Jude probably was only finally accepted because of the widely believed tradition that its author was Jesus' brother. The works in the second list above

*(Didache* through the *Epistle of Barnabas)* were finally rejected in spite of the fact that some churches and church fathers considered them inspired, because they lacked the crucial prophetic-apostolic quality and links to primitive Christianity.

The final steps in the formal canonization process and creation of the New Testament took place in the later fourth century. The first list containing all twenty-seven books Matthew through Revelation and no others was produced by Athanasius, bishop of Alexandria and leading defender of orthodoxy, in his Easter letter to Christian congregations in Egypt in 367. From Athanasius's wording one does not get the sense that he was introducing an innovation. Instead he seems to have been attempting to nail down an already generally received tradition. Two synods met in North Africa at Hippo and Carthage in 393 and 397 respectively. Both affirmed Athanasius's list as final and authoritative. From then on, the New Testament was settled. In part, of course, that was because these synods received imperial backing and the church of the late fourth century had the emperor's power to stamp out dissent and enforce conformity. Nevertheless, the New Testament as identified and made official at those synods has stood the test of time and been gladly received as final and closed by all major branches of Christianity ever since. The only major dispute has revolved around the Old Testament and whether it should include the Apocrypha, and if so, what authority the books contained in it should have for Christians.

The Christian church "got its act together" by around 300. By that time a Christian cathedral stood within sight of the imperial palace at Nicomedia and the landscape of the empire was dotted with basilicas. Bishops ruled with authority over the churches, Christian liturgy was becoming standardized, a creed was available for testing orthodoxy, and for all practical purposes the church had its authoritative Bible. Synods of bishops met occasionally to settle disputes. A penitential system was developing to determine how repentance of wayward Christians could be evaluated. The Great Church was becoming visible, highly structured and formalized. All it lacked was political power to enforce its orthodoxy against the schismatics who claimed to be Christian but stood apart from catholic and orthodox Christianity. This was soon to arrive in the person of Emperor Constantine the Great, who "converted" to catholic Christianity in Rome sometime between 311 and 313.

However, the greatest threat to Christian unity and perhaps to the gospel itself was to come not from the heretics, schismatic sects and enemies outside the Great Church. It was to come instead from *within* the church itself. Christianity had weathered many storms in the two centuries since the last apostle died, but it was yet to encounter the greatest doctrinal hurricane of all.

# PART III

# A Great Crisis Rocks the Church

## *The Controversy About the Trinity*

*The story of Christian theology took many surprising twists and turns during the fourth* century. Perhaps no event in the history of Christian theology was more surprising and influential than the "conversion" of the Roman Empire to Christianity. Beginning with that momentous event the relationship between Christian theology and secular politics became intimate. The two were inextricably interwoven for at least a thousand years—for better or worse. The story of theology in the fourth century is inseparable from the story of the empire. Just how surprising and significant this fact is will become clearer as the story unfolds.

At the end of the third century and beginning of the fourth—around 301—the persecution of Christians begun on an empirewide scale by Decius in the middle of the third century and continued by Diocletian later had begun to lift. Christianity had survived the massive pogroms and executions and had managed to build church buildings, develop its hierarchical ecclesiology, solidify its beliefs and spread into every major city and town throughout the empire. No one can say just what percentage of the citizens and subjects of the empire were Christians by that time, but a fair estimate would be about 5 percent. That would be true especially in the major cities and surrounding areas. The Christian presence in Rome, Carthage, Alexandria, Antioch and Lyons in Gaul was significant and permanent. Nevertheless, Christians lived under a cloud. Emperor after emperor had tried to eradicate the religion from the empire and especially from the imperial household, court, army and bureaucracies. Around 310 Christianity was strong in spite of persecution, but no one expected what was to happen next, and how the church responded can only be understood in light of the terrible half century and more of bloody persecution it had just endured.

In October 312 a leading general of the Roman army named Constantine attacked Rome to unseat the man who claimed to be emperor—Maxentius—and place himself on the throne of the empire. Constantine had been commanding general of the Roman legions in Britain and parts of Europe north of the Alps for several years and believed that he had a stronger claim to be emperor than any of his rivals. He almost certainly was well acquainted with Christianity, but there is no evidence of any conversion to it or even strong sympathy for it before his siege of Rome in 312. According to his biographer, the Christian bishop Eusebius, Constantine appealed to any god who could help him defeat his rival and saw a vision of a Christian symbol and the words "In this sign conquer." He is supposed to have entered into battle the next day with the symbol of Christ emblazoned on his battle banners and shields, and his enemy Maxentius was thrown over the Milvian Bridge just outside Rome and drowned in the Po River. Eusebius, who saw Constantine as a great hero, compared Maxentius to Pharaoh and Constantine to Moses and declared the victory an act of God.

After becoming emperor, Constantine issued the Edict of Milan, which officially declared imperial toleration of Christianity (313). From then on he promulgated a series of edicts that restored property to Christians and gradually began to favor Christians and Christianity over other religions. He never did make Christianity the official religion of the empire, however, and he remained Pontifex Maximus, or high priest, of the official pagan religion of the empire until his baptism just before his death in 337.

Throughout his reign as emperor, Constantine's relationship with Christian leaders was a stormy one. He came to consider himself the "bishop of all the bishops" and the "thirteenth apostle" even though he was a pagan and refused baptism until he was almost literally on his deathbed. Unifying the church seemed to be one of his obsessions, and dominating its leadership was his way of attaining that goal. The Christian churches of the empire were severely divided at the time of his accession, and he wanted to use Christianity as the "glue" to reunify the empire. In order to do that he had to stamp out schism, heresy and dissent wherever he found it. By the time of his death, Constantine had not entirely succeeded, and many church historians would argue that he in fact sided as often with heresy as with orthodoxy.

During Constantine's reign several important events for Christianity and theology took place. First, as already noted official persecution lifted and being Christian—at least in name—became popular and prudent. Hordes of unconverted pagans flooded into Christian churches merely to gain status in the eyes of the imperial court and the bureaucracy under Constantine.

Second, Constantine left Rome and built a "new Rome" in the East as the new imperial capital of the empire. He chose the city of Byzantium (today's Istanbul in Turkey) and renamed it after himself: Constantinople. Throughout his life one of his main projects was to build the most beautiful city the world had ever seen and place at its center his own great palace and cathedral.

Third, the most divisive schism the Christian church had ever experienced broke out within it during Constantine's reign. It began in Alexandria and spread to the rest of the empire with special impact in the Greek-speaking Eastern half. It became known as the Arian controversy, and it lasted in stages throughout most of the century. Constantine and his heirs became embroiled in the controversy, taking various sides at different times.

Fourth, the church held its first ecumenical (universal) council to settle doctrinal and ecclesiastical conflicts: the Council of Nicaea in 325. Constantine called it and presided over it. The formal and official orthodox doctrine of the Trinity was hammered out at the council and expressed in a creed known generally as the Nicene Creed but officially as the Niceno-Constantinopolitan Creed. (Its final version was written at the Council of Constantinople in 381.) It eventually became the universal statement of faith of Christendom and remains so for most branches of Christianity.

In these chapters we will concentrate on the story of the development of the formal and official Christian dogma of the Trinity throughout the fourth century. The opening scenes of the story take place in Alexandria, Egypt. The backdrop is Origen's troubling legacy, which was discussed in part two. The next scenes take place in Constantinople and the small town of Nicaea next to it, where the emperor lived and worshiped during the construction project of his new capital city. Then the story takes us back to Alexandria and from there into all parts of the empire. An identifiable hero emerges—Athanasius, the young bishop of Alexandria and champion of the orthodox trinitarian doctrine of Nicaea. The final episodes of this portion of the story of Christian theology center in and around Asia Minor (modern Turkey) and especially Constantinople, where three friends (including two brothers) known as the Cappadocian fathers worked hard to explain the Trinity in a way that the majority of Christian leaders could accept and endorse in a final formulation of the great creed of the Great Church at the second ecumenical council. By the end of the century (400), orthodox, Nicene (trinitarian) Christianity had become the official religion of the Roman Empire and had begun to persecute its rivals, especially those who called themselves Christians but who rejected the official theology and ecclesiology of the emperors and bishops of the Great Church.

# CHAPTER 9

# Alexandrians Argue About the Son of God

*Something truly amazing happened in Alexandria in 318. Rioting between* Christians broke out in the streets over a point of theology. It all began with an argument between the bishop, Alexander, and a popular and ambitious presbyter named Arius. The bishops of Alexandria were usually elected by the presbyters of the city, and one way to become bishop was to promote oneself among them as a champion of truth and righteousness. Arius's exact motives for challenging the authority of Bishop Alexander are unclear, but they may have had something to do with Arius's desire to succeed him as bishop upon his death if not before. In any case, Arius led a minirebellion of Christians against the bishop after he heard Alexander preach a sermon that he considered too close to the heresy of Sabellianism. That is, Arius thought he detected in the bishop's theology at least a trace of the old modalistic heresy of Praxeas and Sabellius that reduced the Father, Son and Holy Spirit to mere names or aspects of the one divine person, God. Arius began to preach sermons, deliver lectures and write letters criticizing Alexander's theology and leadership, and gradually the conflict between the two Christian leaders developed into a full-blown theological and ecclesiastical war between their devoted followers.

**Arius of Alexandria**

The details of Arius's life are unknown. Perhaps he was born in what is now Libya in North Africa. He certainly studied theology at the Christian catechetical school in Antioch under the influential theologian Lucian of Antioch (died in 312), who had himself been influenced by the heretic bishop Paul of Samosata. Although none of his writings have survived, many modern scholars consider Lucian a root of numerous heresies in the early church. Like many in Antioch he tended to emphasize the humanity of Jesus Christ rather than his deity and tried to find a way to explain the incarnation of God in Christ without making Jesus himself God or falling back into Paul of Samosata's adoptionist heresy.

While Arius was studying under Lucian in Antioch, he became a close friend of another of Lucian's theological students, a man named Eusebius of Nicomedia, who would later become an important and influential bishop. The two remained friends and colleagues throughout their lives and thought alike about the person of Jesus Christ, salvation and the nature of God. It is almost certain that their beliefs and theological formulations were derived from their common mentor, Lucian. Like him, they both hated and feared the heresy of Sabellianism (modalism) more than the heresy of adoptionism, which may not have seemed dangerous compared to the idea implicit in Sabellianism that God the Father was actually crucified and died on the cross because Jesus Christ (according to the modalist way of thinking) actually *was* the Father incarnate!

Of course, neither Lucian nor Arius nor Eusebius could openly embrace and teach adoptionism. That had been declared heresy by the Synod of Antioch in 268. With the conversion of Constantine such declarations by large groups of bishops had teeth, and anyone who dared to claim that Jesus Christ was not in any sense God but only a human prophet adopted by God into a special relationship would be in danger of losing his position in the church and possibly even being exiled by the emperor. It is unlikely that any of the Antiochenes, including Lucian and his students, even secretly believed in the adoptionist heresy, but it is likely that many of them had come to think of Jesus Christ as the incarnation not of God but of a great creature of God—the Logos, who had a beginning in time and remained forever subordinate to the Father not only in terms of his role but also in terms of his very being.

Also in the background of Arius's teaching stood Origen, who had probably influenced Lucian as well. In the early fourth century Origen was still considered by many Christians to have been the greatest teacher of the church. He was not generally considered a heretic yet. That would happen only in the sixth century and in part because of his alleged role in influencing heretics such as Lucian, Arius and others. As we have seen earlier in the story Origen was of two minds about the being of the Logos, who is the Son of God and became human in Jesus Christ. On the one hand, Origen strongly affirmed an equality of the Logos with

God the Father. Without any doubt Origen believed that the Logos is God's eternal emanation, shooting forth like a ray of the sun from God and sharing eternally in his glorious nature. On the other hand, Origen also affirmed a subordination of the Logos to the Father in order to account for his mediatorship between the immutable divine nature of God and the corrupt world of nature and history. The Logos, according to Origen, is somehow less than the Father, although he never explained exactly what that means.

Christians trained in biblical scholarship and theology at Alexandria tended to stress one side of Origen's Christology—the eternal equality of the Logos with the Father. (Perhaps because of fear of Montanism, the Holy Spirit was neglected in these discussions, although it is clear that all parties believed in the Holy Spirit.) The Alexandrians claimed Origen as one of their own even though he had left Alexandria and taught for the latter portion of his life in Caesarea in Palestine. They claimed to know Origen best, and they were experts at finding in his writings those passages that stressed Jesus as the eternal Son of God. The Antiochenes also studied Origen's theology and found there the emphasis on the "monarchy of the Father" as well as the humanity of Jesus Christ and the Logos as an intermediate being between God and creation. In Origen they saw an emphasis on the Logos's subordination to God and enigmatic phrases that seemed to refer to him as a creature and somehow less than the Father.

In the deep background of the clash between Arius and Alexander over the nature of the Logos lay Greek philosophy. It is something both had in common, even if they interpreted and applied it differently. Both sides of the conflict simply assumed that divinity is ontologically perfect in such a way that any change at all is impossible for it and improper to attribute to it. Thus God, being divine and therefore absolutely perfect, cannot experience change because to change is always to change either for the better or for the worse, and in either case God would not be God if he could change.

Absolute static perfection—including *apatheia,* or impassibility (passionlessness)—is the nature of God according to Greek thought, and nearly all Christian theologians came to agree with this. Of course, they could find in the Scriptures several supporting passages that denied change and variability in God. God's immutability and impassibility, then, became chief attributes of God in Christian theology, and Arius and his followers exploited the argument that if Jesus Christ is the incarnation of the Logos and if the Logos is divine in the same sense that God the Father is divine, then God's nature would be changed by the human life of Jesus in time and God would have suffered in him. But that is impossible. Therefore the Logos who became incarnate in Jesus Christ must not be fully divine but rather must be a great and exalted creature.

Arius's opponents also believed that divine being cannot change in any way and struggled with how to respond to Arius's argument. They held tenaciously to the traditional Christian belief that the Logos is divine and shares in God's very nature from all eternity, but exactly how to explain the incarnation of the Logos in humanity was a task of thought that had not yet been finished. Arius forced the church to complete it as far as humanly possible.

Perhaps conflict between Arius and the Alexandrian bishop Alexander was inevitable since Arius was trained in Antioch before arriving in the Egyptian city to be ordained a priest in 311. One of his duties as presbyter there was to direct the exegetical school, which was a school of biblical interpretation for priests and lay Christians who wanted to teach. Apparently Arius was a charismatic personality who attracted such a strong and devoted following that when he openly challenged Bishop Alexander about his theology of Christ and the Trinity, many Alexandrian Christians rallied to his cause. Arius accused Alexander of denying the true humanity of Jesus Christ and of promoting the Sabellian heresy. Pushing the issue further, he began to teach Alexandrian Christians that the Logos (or Son of God) was a creature and not equal with the Father. He said that a key difference between the Son and the Father was that the latter was eternal and immutable, whereas the former—the Logos—was created before the world and was capable of changing and suffering. He appealed to those Scripture passages in the Prophets and Apostles where the Word of God (Logos) is subject to God and where Jesus Christ is submissive to the Father.

**Alexander of Alexandria**

Bishop Alexander was by all accounts a gentle and tolerant bishop who did not relish conflict, but eventually he decided to respond to Arius's criticism and to his teaching about God and Jesus Christ by correcting him through correspondence and sermons and, when those milder courses failed, by calling a synod of bishops to Alexandria to examine Arius's views and rule on whether they were orthodox or not. Before the synod could meet, however, Arius rallied his Christian followers, and they began marching through the streets of Alexandria past the great church and the bishop's house carrying placards and chanting slogans such as "There was when the Son was not." And as one historian has noted, "The spread of Arius' ideas amongst the working classes [of Alexandria] was stimulated by the composition of popular songs 'for the sea, for the mill, and for the road', suitably set to music."[1] The mob of Arius's followers were energized by the songs and slogans as well as by Arius's personality even if they did not fully understand the theological issues that were at stake. Eventually there was some rioting in the streets of the city when Alexander's supporters marched against Arius and the two groups met in front of the cathedral.

When the synod called by Alexander met in 318, about one hundred bishops from various sees around the Eastern part of the empire met and heard Alexander's critique of Arius's theology. Alexander accused Arius of teaching that the Logos could have fallen like Satan. He accused Arius also of repeating the adoptionist heresy of Paul of Samosata in a slightly more sophisticated form. The reason Paul's Christology had been condemned by a synod in 268 was that it had denied the deity of Jesus Christ and rejected the Trinity. Arius's Christology did the same even if it affirmed a preexistence of the Logos as a great heavenly being—something the bishop of Samosata did not affirm. According to Alexander the difference was slight. In either case God himself has not united with humanity and therefore we are not saved (divinized) by the union. Our very salvation is at stake, Alexander argued.

## Arianism

The irony is that Arius and his followers responded in the same vein, namely, that our very salvation is at stake and that if Alexander's view prevailed, then Jesus Christ could not have been truly human (since humanity and divinity are so separate by nature) and therefore his accomplishment of salvation for us could not be a true victory that we could emulate. For Arius and his followers salvation meant freely following Christ's example of submission to God. If Jesus did not choose to follow God's will in a human way, then his example is of no use to us.

So the difference between Arius and Alexander over the nature of Jesus Christ and the Logos who became incarnate in him had to do with soteriology—the doctrine of salvation. Alexander was assuming the orthodox view of salvation going back to Irenaeus; Arius was assuming a view of salvation that emphasized freely conforming to God's moral standards. Thus an important difference between the two Alexandrians was that "salvation, for orthodoxy, is effected by the Son's essential identity with the Father—that which links God and Christ to creation is the divine nature's assumption of flesh. Salvation for Arianism is effected by the Son's identity with the creatures—that which links Christ and creatures to God is conformity of will."[2]

The one hundred or more bishops gathered at the synod in Alexandria in 318 condemned Arius and his teaching about Christ as heresy and deposed him from his position as presbyter. He was forced to leave the city. Alexander and the traditional view of the Logos as fully divine was vindicated—temporarily. However,

Arius did not let the matter rest. He fled to his old friend Eusebius of Nicomedia, who was by then an important bishop, and was accepted by him. From Nicomedia, Arius and Eusebius began a letter-writing campaign to bishops who had not attended the Alexandrian synod.

Arius's only known written works are these and later letters and one book titled *Thaleia,* which means "banquet." All have been lost, and only fragments of Arius's works are able to be reconstructed from quotations found in his opponents' writings. Typical of his statements about the relationship between the Son and the Father is this one:

> And Christ is not true God, but by participation . . . even he was made God. . . . The Son does not know the Father exactly, nor does the Logos see the Father perfectly, and neither does he perceive nor the Logos understand the Father exactly; for he is not the true and only Logos of the Father, but by a name alone he is called Logos and Sophia and by grace is called Son and Power.[3]

Arius also exploited the apostolic word *begotten* (in Greek, *gennetos*) used to describe Jesus Christ as the Son of God. Thus if the Son of God who became Jesus Christ was "begotten," he must have had a beginning in time, and since it is of the essence of God to be eternal—without beginning or end—then the Son of God must be a great creature and not God himself. It was this distinction—between God as unbegotten *(agennetos)* and the Son of God (Logos, Jesus Christ) as begotten—that Arius emphasized in his profession of faith written in 320 in exile under the protection and patronage of his friend Eusebius of Nicomedia. The letter was signed by two bishops, six priests and six deacons and sent to Alexander as well as to a number of other leading opponents of Arius. In it Arius wrote:

> We acknowledge one God, who alone is unbegotten, who alone is eternal, who alone is without beginning, who alone is true, who alone is immortal, who alone is wise, who alone is good, who alone is full of power; it is he who judges all, who controls all things, who provides all things; and he is subject to no change or alteration; he is just and good; he is the God of the Law and the Prophets and of the New Covenant: This one God, before all time, begot his only-begotten Son, through whom he made the ages and the universe. He begot him not just in appearance, but in fact; by his own will he made his son to subsist and he made him unchangeable and unalterable. God's perfect creature, he is unlike any other creature; begotten, yes, but unique in the manner of his begetting: . . . But we say that he was created by God's

> will, before all ages; from the Father he received being and life, and in creating him the Father conferred his own glory on him. Yet the Father, in giving all things into his possession, did not despoil himself of them: he contains all things in himself in an unbegotten way, for he is the source of all things. Therefore, there are three substances (hypostases).[4]

Thus Arius and his colleagues—the Arians—affirmed a kind of Trinity made up of three "divine" beings (Father, Son and Holy Spirit), only one of whom is truly God. He continued in his profession of faith to affirm unequivocally that only the Father is "without beginning" and that the Son, though a great creature who shares many of God's attributes, did not exist before he was begotten by the Father.

The two key elements of Arius's thought about God and the Logos are these: First, God is by nature removed from creatureliness, and if the Logos became human in Jesus Christ, he must be a creature. Second, salvation is a process of being joined with God by grace and free will, and if Jesus communicates salvation to us, it must be something he accomplished by grace and free will in a manner that we can emulate; and if he was God, then salvation would not be something he could accomplish. Under these two conceptual pressures, Arius and his followers pushed the relationship between God the Father and Jesus Christ further and further apart so that to many of their opponents it appeared that they were denying any genuine sense of Christ's divinity and rejecting the Trinity entirely.

**Alexander's Response to Arianism**

Alexander responded to Arius's letter-writing campaign with a work of his own that he sent to numerous bishops and church leaders. It is the *Deposition of Arius,* and as the title implies it was Alexander's attempt to explain Arius's condemnation and deposition from his position in Alexandria. In this encyclical letter the Alexandrian archbishop set forth a succinct summary of Arius's and the Arians' heresy regarding God and the Son of God and asked that his fellow bishops and ministers of the empire not receive the heretics nor comply with Bishop Eusebius's request to treat them well, "for it becomes us who are Christians to turn away from all who speak or think any thing against Christ, as being enemies of God, and destroyers of souls; and not even to 'bid such God speed,' lest we become partakers of their sins, as the blessed John hath charged us."[5] Alexander's summary of the Arian heresy reads like a description of the main distinctive doctrine of the modern-day Watchtower Bible and Tract Society, which is more popularly known as the Jehovah's Witnesses[6]:

> And the novelties they have invented and put forth contrary to the Scriptures are these following:—God was not always a Father, but there was a time when God was not a Father. The Word of God was not always, but originated from things that were not; for God that is, has made him that was not, of that which was not; wherefore there was a time when He was not; for the Son is a creature and a work. Neither is He like in essence to the Father; neither is He the true and natural Word of the Father; neither is He His true Wisdom; but He is one of the things made and created, and is called the Word and Wisdom by an abuse of terms, since He Himself originated by the proper Word of God, and by the Wisdom that is in God, by which God has made not only all other things but Him also. Wherefore He is by nature subject to change and variation, as are all rational creatures.[7]

Notice Alexander's mode of argument in this summary statement: Although it is presented as a straightforward summary of Arius's teaching, its form contains a subtle polemical argument against it. One of Arius's and his followers' main charges against belief in the equality of the Son with the Father was that it undermines God's immutability. If the Son of God is truly God, then God cannot be immutable as all believe him to be because the Son changed through entering into history and suffering in the flesh of Jesus Christ. Alexander turned the tables on Arius and charged that he in effect denied the immutability of the Father by saying that he was not always Father but only became so by creating a son. From this letter onward, this became one of the main weapons of the orthodox bishops against Arianism in all its forms: if Arianism is true, then the Father has not always been Father but only became Father by begetting (creating) the Word, and that would contradict God's immutability.

Alexander followed his summary statement of Arius's heresy with a brief but fairly detailed exegesis of the first chapter of the Gospel of John, where the Logos is said to have been "in the beginning with God" and the agent of God in all creation. He also mentioned other apostolic passages that refer to the equality of the Son with the Father, but interestingly neglected to mention the all-important statement in John 1:1 that "the Word was God." Alexander closed his encyclical letter by signing it, together with numerous Alexandrian presbyters and deacons, and mentioning that Arius and his teaching had already been condemned by a synod of over one hundred bishops.

Eventually Emperor Constantine heard of the controversy. His personal chaplain, Bishop Hosius, informed him of it and reported that the bishops of the East were being divided by the quarrel between Arius and Alexander. In all probability most bishops of the empire did not understand what the controversy was all about. They received an impressive letter from Arius's supporter Bishop Eusebius of Nicomedia that put the Arian teaching in the best light possible. It is highly probable that nearly all bishops believed in some kind of subordination of the Son to the Father—that is, the monarchy of the Father. On the other hand, they received the official-sounding and impressive encyclical letter from Bishop Alexander. The average bishop was undoubtedly quite confused. A formal schism threatened to break apart the church and few if any wanted that. Least of all did Constantine want it. He had hoped that Christianity would provide the badly needed religious "glue" to hold his shaky empire together, and he was not pleased to hear that its leaders were embroiled in a seemingly esoteric debate over divine metaphysics.

We will see as our story continues that Emperor Constantine took the dramatic step of ordering all Christian bishops from throughout the empire to come to a meeting to settle this doctrinal dispute and decide exactly what it is that Christians must believe in order to be considered authentically Christian. What happened at this first ecumenical council at Nicaea in 325 will be recounted in some detail, but first it will be helpful to stop and briefly discuss how important this controversy between Arius and Alexander really was.

Why did Alexander and his presbyters and others react so vehemently to Arius's teaching? The simple answer is that they perceived it as threatening salvation itself. Modern Christians tend to separate salvation as forgiveness and a "personal relationship with God" from doctrinal belief. That separation was completely foreign to most Christians throughout the history of the church. What one believed mattered very much. *Heresy* was belief and teaching about God, Jesus Christ and salvation that threatened to distort the gospel message and the Christian life so severely that it could become "another gospel" and another religion, not the one taught by the apostles.

The status of Jesus Christ in relation to God had always been assumed by Christian leaders and thinkers. Jesus Christ is in some sense God, and that is what makes Christianity and its gospel unique compared to other monotheistic religions such as Judaism and monotheistic philosophies such as Platonism and Stoicism. Alexander was simply shocked to discover that a leading Christian presbyter and teacher right under his own nose was denying any ontological identity (sameness of being) of Jesus Christ with God. This had already been rejected as rank heresy by the Synod of Antioch when it condemned Paul of Samosata and his teaching—or so thought Alexander. But Arianism was a subtler form of the denial of Jesus' deity than adoptionism. It affirmed a preexistence of the Son of God and ranked him higher than any other creature. Thus Jesus Christ was not a man elevated to

Deity—which is what Paul of Samosata had taught—but a "divine being" incarnated in a human being. Still the "divine being" in Jesus Christ was not equal with God the Father.

Alexander was quite right to be shocked and dismayed, especially since Arius's teaching was made so attractive to the masses of Alexandrian Christians. Although the Jehovah's Witness organization and its teaching did not yet exist in the fourth century, the situation was as if it were about to become the belief of the entire Christian church. The result, Alexander was rightly convinced, would be the end of the gospel as we know and believe it. For only if Jesus Christ is God are we saved. Alexander knew it intuitively. His young assistant Athanasius would be the one to spell it out and convince the entire church—including emperors and leading bishops—that it was true. Even before there was a New Testament to appeal to as the written authority for Christian faith and practice, the implicit apostolic faith of early Christianity revolved around the scandal of the deity of Christ. The reason Christians held on to it tenaciously in the face of pagan ridicule and Roman persecution as well as all kinds of attempts to water it down was that it was the linchpin of the gospel. If it were removed in any way, then the hope for eternal participation in God's own life and for forgiveness and restoration to the image of God would fall apart. The gospel itself would be wrecked.

With Arius and his challenge the church came to a crossroads. There could not be a more important issue for Christian theology to settle. On this issue there could not be tolerance of pluralism. Even today, with the rise of liberal theology and doctrinal pluralism, the World Council of Churches—the ecumenical umbrella organization for Christian cooperation throughout the world—requires of all member denominations that they confess, "Jesus Christ is God and Savior." This was the common belief of early Christians as well. Alexander was right to draw the line in the sand and virtually demand that other bishops deny Arius haven and help.

But how would he enforce that demand? He had no power over other bishops. All he could do was appeal to them by means of letters. Meanwhile other bishops such as Eusebius of Nicomedia were supporting Arius. Only a higher power could intervene to decide which gospel would become official Christian teaching in the empire. Who could settle the controversy but the emperor himself—the mighty Constantine? Yet his intervention in this all-important debate created as many problems as it solved.

# CHAPTER 10

# The Church Responds at the Council of Nicaea

E*mperor Constantine lived and worshiped in various locations while building* his new capital city. One favored site of residence and rule was the little town of Nicaea near Constantinople. There the emperor and his court and chaplain administered the affairs of church and empire in the East. When in the West, Constantine resided at Milan in northern Italy. Rome was all but abandoned by the imperial court from Constantine onward. It was to Nicaea, then, that Constantine called all the bishops of the church to settle the debate over the person of Christ and the Trinity.

The bishop of Nicaea, Theognis, was an Arian in that he sided with Eusebius of Nicomedia and Arius in claiming that Alexander's strong emphasis on the ontological oneness of Father and Son in the Godhead would lead inevitably to Sabellianism. Other bishops agreed. The first ecumenical council was destined from before its official opening to be divisive.

**The Council of Nicaea**

In order to grasp the significance of the Council of Nicaea, one has to stop and recollect the situation of the Christian church only a few years before 325. Bishops and other Christian leaders were fiercely persecuted and sometimes executed by Roman authorities. Church buildings were confiscated and turned into temples to the gods and goddesses or places to worship the emperor. The Christian church was generally looked on as a strange religious sect that was a potential threat to the empire because it was full of subversives who refused to honor the emperor by venerating his "genius." Suddenly everything was changed. The world seemed literally turned upside down. Now a Roman emperor—one of the strongest in many years—was ordering all Christian bishops to come to a meeting where he would preside over their deliberations.

Some Christians perceived the inherent threat of imperial domination in place of imperial persecution. Most did not. The emperor summoned the bishops, promising to pay expenses and provide protection. Most bishops from the East attended. Poor travel conditions and language difficulties prevented many bishops of the West from attending. Nevertheless, both East and West branches of Christianity—Orthodox and Catholic—came to acknowledge this meeting in Nicaea in 325 as the first ecumenical council of the church. Others would follow but none would be as important.

Three hundred and eighteen bishops were present at the opening ceremonies. Unfortunately, no contemporary records of the actual sessions of the council have survived. Constantine's biographer, Bishop Eusebius of Caesarea, wrote an account of the council, but the actual minutes and detailed eyewitness reports are not available. Apparently Constantine placed himself on a throne raised above the meeting hall where the bishops sat. The emperor had at his side his chaplain, Hosius, who frequently whispered in his ear and served as a mediator and messenger between the emperor and leading participants. Some of the gathered bishops attempted to object to this imperial conduct, but they were silenced by the emperor and his guards. Constantine made abundantly clear in his opening remarks that he intended to serve as the "bishop of the bishops" and guide and direct the deliberations to a satisfactory conclusion.

The council lasted two months and covered many issues confronting the church. Approximately twenty distinct "canons," or decrees, were issued by the emperor and bishops about subjects ranging from deposing lapsed bishops to the ordination of eunuchs. With regard to the latter question, incidentally, it was decided that eunuchs could be ordained to the priesthood so long as their castration was not voluntary. Also the bishop of Alexandria was declared to be a "patriarch" over the bishops of surrounding regions of North Africa, and the bishop of Rome was declared the rightful honorary head of the bishops of the West. The council provided opportunity to settle many ancient questions and issues that had plagued the churches, including the exact manner for dating Easter and what to do with bishops who moved from one see to another. But all of these matters were of secondary importance to the main reason for the council. The emperor had called the council to settled the Arian controversy, and that was what most of the bishops wanted to hear about first and foremost.

Of the 318 bishops present at the opening of the council, only 28 were clearly Arians from the outset. Arius himself was not allowed to attend the council as he was not a bishop. He was represented by Eusebius of Nicomedia and Theognis of Nicaea. Alexander of Alexandria led the prosecution against Arius and Arianism and was aided by his young assistant Athanasius, who would succeed him as bishop of Alexandria a few years later. Many—perhaps the majority—of the bishops had little understanding of the issues involved in the controversy. As church historian Justo González notes,

> the vast majority [of the bishops] does not seem to have understood the importance of the matter at hand, and their fear of Sabellianism made them reluctant to condemn subordinationism in very strong terms. Besides, the emperor, whose interest was in the unity of the Empire rather than in the unity of God, was inclined to find a formula that would be acceptable to the greatest number of bishops possible.[1]

Modalism had never been officially condemned and still seemed a great threat to orthodox teaching about the Trinity. It reduced Father, Son and Holy Spirit to three modes or aspects of God and implied patripassianism—the idea that the Father suffered on the cross. To most of the bishops, this popular belief was a live heresy among people and priests and needed strong and careful correction. If Arian subordinationism was a useful antidote to the poison of modalism, then many of them would be loath to condemn it. They would readily condemn adoptionism, but the subtle subordinationism of the Son of God in Arius's teaching was more difficult to portray in black-and-white terms. The twenty-eight Arian bishops believed they had every chance of convincing the majority and perhaps even the emperor of the soundness of their position.

According to one account, soon after the council opened someone called for a reading of the Arian position so that all could know exactly what was to be debated. At that point the Arians—or at least some of them—made a serious strategic error. Alexander and his bishops must have been delighted. Bishop Eusebius of Nicomedia stood before the council and read a clear and blatant denial of the deity of the Son of God, emphasizing that he is a creature and not equal with the Father in any sense. The statement must have read something like Arius's letter excerpted in the previous chapter. Before Eusebius finished reading it, some of the bishops were holding their hands over their ears and shouting for someone to stop the blasphemies. One bishop near Eusebius stepped forward and grabbed the manuscript out of his hands, threw it to the floor and stomped on it. A riot broke out among the bishops and was stopped only by the emperor's command.

Apparently, in spite of circulating letters written by Arius and Alexander before the council, most of the bishops were naive about how clear-cut the issue really was. They had come to the council hoping to hear something moderate—a mediating position between these two opposite views. When one of their own expressed the Arian side in such stark terminology, making clear that they considered the Son of God a mere creature, they were convinced that this was heresy, even if Alexander's strong opposite position was not the only alternative. After the hubbub died down and the emperor restored order, the council turned its attention to finding a solution.

**The Nicene Creed**

Gradually the idea of writing a unifying and compulsory creed summarizing "the ancient faith of the church" in as few words as possible arose and gained popularity. The emperor favored the idea and asked his chaplain, Hosius, to begin working out the details in conferences with various bishops. The Arians and their sympathizers argued strongly for use only of biblical wording. Alexander and his aide Athanasius recognized this as a ploy. The Arians had become adept at "Scripture twisting" so that any biblical terminology could be interpreted in their favor. The only way to bring closure to the debate and make clear once for all that Arian subordinationism was heretical was to use extrabiblical terminology that clearly spelled out the unity of Father and Son as equal within the Godhead.

After some wrangling and little agreement, Constantine himself proposed that the new creed include the affirmation that the Son is *homoousios*—consubstantial—with the Father. It may be that Hosius recommended the wording to him and that Hosius may have been influenced in that direction by Alexander and Athanasius. Another possible source is Bishop Eusebius of Caesarea. In any case, the compound word *homoousios*—made up of the Greek words for "one" and "substance"—was accepted by the majority of bishops to describe the relationship of the Son of God to the Father. They are "one substance," or "one being." The language is reminiscent of Tertullian's earlier Latin phrase *una substantia.*

The Arians were horrified. Some non-Arians were mystified and worried. The anti-Arian trinitarians Alexander and Athanasius and their friends were jubilant.

The Arian bishops and their sympathizers pointed out that since the Greek word *ousia* could mean an individual subsistent thing like a person, saying that Father and Son are *homoousios* could be interpreted as saying that they are identical in every way, including being the very same person in two disguises. That would be modalism and Sabellianism. The more common meaning of *ousia,* however, was "substance" or "being," and affirming that Father and Son are *homoousios* simply meant to most of the bishops that they share all the same essential attributes of deity. If the Father is eternal, so is the Son. If the Son is omnipotent, so is the Father. And so forth. The emperor and most of the bishops were not particularly concerned at this point to define their distinctions.

Later some fence-sitting bishops who were reluctant to condemn Arianism would remember that one of the main proponents of the *homoousios* formula was bishop Marcellus of Ancyra—a noted crypto-Sabellian. That is, he secretly believed in the modalist heresy. Being a modalist was not necessarily "illegal" so long as one was cautious about how it was affirmed. Marcellus's support of the formula later compounded its difficulties. Even before the Council of Nicaea adjourned, many bishops were afraid that it was unwittingly making Sabellianism orthodox and catholic. Marcellus was triumphant. Alexander and his cohorts were unconcerned. To them Sabellianism was a much less dangerous heresy than Arianism. Their attitude was to deal with it later.

Finally the emperor appointed a commission of bishops to write up the creed to be signed by all the bishops, including those who were unable to attend the council. The result was the first Nicene Creed, which did not include the third article on the Holy Spirit and the church. That would be added later by the second ecumenical council at Constantinople in 381. The Nicene Creed (known also simply as "Nicaea") was patterned after the Apostles' Creed, adding wording to make clear that Arianism is wrong:

> We believe in one God, the Father almighty, maker of all things visible and invisible; And in one Lord Jesus Christ, the Son of God, begotten from the Father, only-begotten, that is, from the substance of the Father, God from God, light from light, true God from true God, begotten not made, of one substance *[homoousios]* with the Father, through Whom all things came into being, things in heaven and things on earth, Who because of us humans and because of our salvation came down and became incarnate, becoming human, suffered and rose again on the third day, ascended to the heavens, and will come to judge the living and the dead; And in the Holy Spirit.[2]

The phrase "begotten not made" is an excellent example of the extrabiblical wording that Alexander insisted was necessary to rule out Arianism. *Begotten* is a biblical word for the Son of God. The Gospel of John uses it frequently. But *not made* is never to be found attributed to the Son of God in Scripture. The distinction, however, is all-important. If the Son of God is "made" or "created," then he is not truly God. Scripture affirms that he is divine and salvation requires that he be divine. The bishops gathered at Nicaea recognized that they were affirming a deep mystery, but they were willing to affirm mystery rather than allow heresy. Also found in the middle of the creed is the phrase "of one substance with the Father" to describe the Son of God who became Jesus Christ. That phrase is an English translation of *homoousios,* and is simply an updated version of the older English word *consubstantial,* which is often found in English versions of the creed. All in all, the creed nailed down orthodoxy for the Great Church against Arianism while leaving the door open to Sabellianism.

Attached to the end of the creed itself was an "anathema"—a brief statement of the heresy being denounced: "But as for those who say, There was [a time] when He [the Son of God] was not, and, before being born He was not, and that He came into existence out of nothing, or who assert that the Son of God is of a different hypostasis or substance, or is created, or is subject to alteration or change—these the Catholic Church anathematizes."[3] The emperor made unmistakably clear that this meant Arius was deposed and condemned as a heretic. He was to be exiled together with any bishops who supported him. For the first time a Christian heretic was condemned and punished by a secular ruler for nothing more than believing and teaching the wrong doctrine.

The emperor required all bishops to sign the new creed or be deposed from their sees and sent into exile. Several Arian bishops signed it reluctantly. Only two refused to sign it, Eusebius of Nicomedia and Theognis of Nicaea. Their refusal was a great blow to the emperor and the other bishops as they were considered extremely influential and everyone knew that unless they would sign the creed, the matter could not be ended so easily. As the council closed, the matter remained unresolved. A creed had been written that clearly condemned as heresy a doctrine held by two of the leading bishops of the East. It also left the door open to a different heresy—Sabellianism—and had as one of its champions a bishop who actually held that heresy. A pagan ruler had called, presided over and provided theological wording to Christian bishops and ordered them to sign a highly ambiguous theological document. González is correct that

> there was a great ambiguity in the Nicene formula. The creed, whose main purpose was to affirm the divinity of the Son, could also be interpreted as an affirmation of the divine unity. This, coupled with the fact that the formula of Nicaea remained silent regarding the distinction between the Father, the Son, and the Holy Spirit, soon made it suspect as a concession to Sabellianism. This is why, in spite of the condemnation of Arianism at Nicaea, that condemnation did not prove sufficient to expel it from the church, and for

more than fifty years the controversy raged before the church finally and definitively condemned Arianism.[4]

That final and definitive condemnation of Arianism that truly "stuck" was at the Council of Constantinople in 381. During the intervening half century, various Arian and semi-Arian bishops and emperors helped subordinationism make a comeback, and at times the entire Christian church seemed on the verge of rejecting the Trinity completely and establishing as orthodox doctrine something akin to what modern-day Jehovah's Witnesses believe. The story of how that was prevented and of how the doctrine of the Trinity was finally interpreted and established will occupy the next two chapters.

**Ecumenical Councils**

It will be helpful to discuss briefly the concept and nature of ecumenical councils, of which Nicaea was the first. At the time of the Council of Nicaea the distinction between a local synod of bishops and an ecumenical council was not clear-cut. However, as the Great Church looked back on the council from a later perspective, that distinction stood out in bold relief due to two major factors. First, the Council of Nicaea was called and presided over by an emperor. There was a central presiding authority with real power. Earlier councils (synods) were called by a bishop and the only authority their declarations carried was authority of persuasion. Second, the Council of Nicaea was a universal council in the sense that all the bishops in apostolic succession and in fellowship with the other bishops of the Great Church were invited to participate. That only 318 of approximately 500 bishops attended did not count against the council's universality. All were welcome and guaranteed paid expenses and protection by the emperor. Looking back upon this groundbreaking meeting, then, the major branches of Christendom one hundred, two hundred and thirteen hundred years later all recognized a quantum leap in ecclesiastical authority from a local council or synod of bishops to this universal, ecumenical council.

During the fifty years after the Council of Nicaea several more ecumenical councils were called by emperors, but later these were denounced by emperors and church leaders alike because they were by and large antitrinitarian. In other words, deciding which councils were authentic and authoritative parts of the Great Tradition of the church became a theological problem in its own right. It was not until 451 that a universal council at Chalcedon finally and definitively decided that the Council of Nicaea and the Council of Constantinople (381) had in fact been the first two truly ecumenical councils of the church to the exclusion of several others. It also declared a council of all bishops shortly before itself the "Robber Synod" rather than a true council. The Council of Chalcedon decided that it was the fourth ecumenical council and declared the version of the Nicene Creed written at the second ecumenical council—Constantinople—authoritative and binding on all clergy throughout the empire. Although commonly known as the Nicene Creed, it is more accurately the Niceno-Constantinopolitan Creed. As we will see, the third ecumenical council turned out to be one held in Ephesus in 431. It did not actually promulgate a creed but made some major decisions about heresies regarding the person of Jesus Christ.

The Great Church eventually decided that four ecumenical councils of the early church had been held and that their decisions and actions were to be considered binding on all Christian clergy. Generally, emperors enforced this decision with the advice and guidance of leading bishops of major sees who were known as "patriarchs." This entire process of governing the church doctrinally was, of course, a logical extension of Cyprian's ecclesiology. Cyprian had envisioned synods of bishops ruling the church's affairs, but once a Christian emperor was in place—something Cyprian had not even imagined—it was logical that leading bishops would look to him to enforce decisions made by ecumenical councils. The four ecumenical councils that even Protestants generally regard as having some special authority for Christian doctrine are Nicaea I (325), Constantinople I (381), Ephesus I (431) and Chalcedon (451).

The process of calling ecumenical councils to make important theological decisions continued after Chalcedon, but there is little agreement across the board in Christendom about the later councils. The Eastern Orthodox churches recognize seven ecumenical councils, though there is some debate among its leaders about the exact nature of the seventh. The Roman Catholic Church recognizes twenty-one ecumenical councils, with the most recent one being Vatican II, held from 1962 to 1965. The magisterial Protestant denominations such as major Lutheran, Reformed and Anglican (Church of England, Episcopalian) denominations recognize only the first four as having any special authority, and even they are considered subordinate to Scripture.

Many nonmagisterial Protestant denominations and traditions pay little or no attention at all to the ecumenical councils. Numerous "Bible-only" and non-creedal denominations of Protestantism reject the whole idea of ecumenical councils of bishops called together and presided over by emperors as a symptom of Constantinianism—the disease of allowing secular and pagan rulers to dominate church life and meddle in biblical and theological interpretation. These denominations—including many Baptists, Pentecostals, Mennonites, Churches of

Christ and many more in the so-called free-church tradition—consider the church to have fallen away from its true nature sometime in the first few centuries after the apostles. For them the deference shown to the pagan emperor Constantine by Christian bishops in the fourth century was the final straw in the process of Christendom's devolution from apostolic Christianity to a near-paganized Roman religion. This attitude toward the Great Church under Constantine and afterward comes in many degrees and shades, but by and large, free-church Protestants ignore the councils and creeds of the fourth century and later in favor of a "back-to-the-Bible" principle and separation of church and state.

One could look at Christian attitudes toward the great ecumenical councils as lying along a spectrum with Eastern Orthodoxy at one end and most Pentecostals at the other end. Most Christians' attitudes lie somewhere in between, although Pentecostals are certainly not the only ones who ignore or reject the councils and their decisions as having any special authority. Many Baptists, Churches of Christ, Holiness churches, Anabaptists and others crowd around the same end of the spectrum as Pentecostals. Eastern Orthodox bishops consider their family of churches as the continuation in the modern world of the Great Church of the Roman Empire under Constantine. They also believe that the Great Church under Constantine was the authentic continuation in the fourth century of the apostles' church of the first century. To the Eastern Orthodox bishops, all the other branches of Christianity are schisms. Even the Roman Catholic Church is a schism from Orthodoxy that was made official in 1054. The Orthodox regard the seven ecumenical councils as virtually carrying the same authority as Scripture itself. Both Scripture and the councils are parts of "Tradition," which is God's authoritative revelation to his people in history.

At the other end of the spectrum of attitudes toward the ecumenical councils and creeds, Pentecostals and some other free churches tend to regard the ecumenical councils and creeds as having no authority for Christians because they were so far removed from the New Testament church in both time and ethos. That is not to say that Pentecostals and other free-church Christians reject all the doctrines of the councils and their creeds. Not at all. Many of them agree wholeheartedly with the doctrine of the Trinity but argue that since it can be found in Scripture, it is unnecessary to confess the metaphysical language of the creeds. To those who reject the doctrine of the Trinity, the free churches simply appeal to the New Testament and the experience of Father, Son and Holy Spirit in the Christian life. Of course, most of the free churches (including Pentecostals) have found it necessary to formulate their own statements of faith that summarize the essential doctrines of the New Testament to guard against heresies. Often these contain the teachings of the Nicene Creed within themselves. Nevertheless, free-church Protestants argue that all humanly devised statements of faith are revisable in the light of Scripture and carry no authority in and of themselves apart from Scripture. A few free-church denominations and traditions refuse to have any formal statements of faith. The result, of course, is often doctrinal confusion and chaos.

Between the Eastern Orthodox and free-church Protestant attitudes toward early church councils and creeds lie numerous variations and gradations. Many evangelical Christians of the modern era have come to regard the first four councils and the Nicene (Niceno-Constantinopolitan) Creed as cornerstones of Christian truth to be respected but not venerated as having the same authority at Scripture itself. Even many free-church evangelical theologians express high regard and great respect for the Nicene Creed and the landmark decisions of the first four councils and argue that they are like United States Supreme Court landmark decisions—authoritative interpretations of the constitution. Scripture is like the U.S. constitution in their eyes. The first few councils and especially the Nicene Creed borrow their authority from Scripture. To change analogies, they are like the light of the moon—reflected from the sun and yet helpful in the black night of ignorance and error.

For better or worse, Emperor Constantine presided over an ecumenical council and enforced its doctrinal decisions. But that was just the beginning of the great controversy over the Son of God and the Trinity. It was meant to end the Arian controversy, but instead it really served as a catalyst for it. The explosion took place after the bishops left the council in 325. They began to reflect on what it had accomplished and corresponded among themselves about it. Soon it became clear that the language of the creed it had promulgated was ambiguous and, like Scripture itself, could be interpreted in various ways—some of them heretical. Constantine became convinced that the council had not finished its work and that it had, in fact, written the wrong wording into the creed. He wanted to take it all back and rewrite it. One little man stood in his way. For a time it was Athanasius against the world.

# CHAPTER 11

# Athanasius Stubbornly Keeps the Faith

*When Alexandrian bishop Alexander went to the Council of Nicaea to* argue the trinitarian case against Arius and his followers, he took with him a young assistant named Athanasius, who was only in his twenties and yet showed great promise as a theologian. It is unlikely that Athanasius played any significant role in the council, but afterward he was groomed by Alexander to become his heir as leader of the Alexandrian see. When Alexander died in 328, the thirty-year-old Athanasius succeeded him in that pivotal ecclesiastical position. No doubt many detractors despised his youth and questioned whether the "Black Dwarf"—as he had come to be known—could cut it as a patriarch of the church at such a tender young age. Soon, however, even his enemies had to admire his great acumen, wisdom and courage.

## Athanasius's Life and Career

Athanasius served as archbishop and patriarch of Alexandria for forty-five years until his death in 373. He spent approximately one-third of that time in forced exile due to his steadfast defense of the key terminology of the Nicene Creed in the face of imperial opposition. With good reason he has come to be known as the "saint of stubbornness" because of his uncompromising opposition to anything that smacked of Arianism—even when emperors threatened his life. It may not be much of an exaggeration to say that all Christians have Athanasius to thank that the theology of Jehovah's Witnesses is not the "orthodoxy" of most of Christendom. He is truly one of the great heroes of the faith, and yet, like Origen before him, he left a troubling legacy. Unlike Origen, Athanasius's reputation is unsullied in all major branches of Christendom. Although some of his opinions turned out to be heretical by later standards of orthodoxy, he was never condemned or even harshly criticized. He is considered a saint by the Eastern Orthodox churches as well as by the Roman Catholic tradition. Protestants also generally consider him one of the great teachers of the early church. González expresses the consensus of most Christian theologians when he says that "Athanasius was without doubt the most remarkable bishop ever to occupy the ancient see of Alexandria, and . . . he was as well the greatest theologian of his time."[1]

In his own century and during his own lifetime Athanasius was extremely controversial. He was perceived by many other bishops and by several emperors as an inflexible and single-minded controversialist who refused to compromise theologically for the sake of ecclesiastical unity. A leading modern church historian writes of Athanasius that "throughout his forty-five year episcopate (328-373), he aroused an uncommon degree of opposition from the most varied sources. Worse than that, he seemed to revel in controversy. He seldom spared an opponent. As a pamphleteer, he outdid the emperor Julian himself."[2] Another modern church historian records that Athanasius "was a bit of a tyrant, and violent acts were committed in his name" and yet at the same time places him on a pedestal as "the pillar of the church; he cleansed the temple in imitation of Christ, not with whips but with persuasive arguments."[3]

In order even to begin to understand Athanasius and the controversy surrounding him, one must be acquainted with the context of church and state within which he lived and worked. "During the middle decades of this century, from 340 to 380, the history of doctrine looks more like the history of court and church intrigues and social unrest."[4] Emperor after emperor switched back and forth from Arianism to orthodoxy to semi-Arianism and back to orthodoxy. One emperor, Julian, was a convert to paganism from Christianity and attempted to return the empire to its pagan roots with no success. But to Athanasius, Julian was less a threat to Christian truth than those emperors who waffled on the doctrine of the Trinity and sought compromises with the Arians, whom he regarded as the forces of the antichrist. Athanasius reminds one of an early Martin Luther. Like the sixteenth-century Protestant Reformer, he faced into the wind of social and doctrinal conflict and turmoil and stood his ground for truth. Luther's axiom "Peace if possible, but truth at any cost!" could have been Athanasius's as well.

When Athanasius succeeded Alexander as bishop at the young age of thirty, trouble was brewing in church and empire. After the Council of Nicaea the

Sabellian bishop Marcellus of Ancyra had proclaimed it and its creed a great triumph for modalism. He and his fellow Sabellians declared that the term *homoousios* (consubstantial) had identified the Father and the Son so closely that they are to be considered one and the same subsistence, or personal identity. Their only difference is in appearance or manifestation. The creed and council had failed to explain the correct distinction between Father and Son and had neglected the Holy Spirit almost altogether. This played right into the hands of both the Sabellians and the Arians. The Sabellians could claim the whole event as a victory for their interpretation of the Trinity, and the Arians could agree and use that to condemn it.

Sometime between 325 and 332—just as Athanasius was taking over his duties as bishop of Alexandria—Emperor Constantine began to switch sides under pressure from bishops and advisers who were secret sympathizers with Arius and the two bishops who sided with him and suffered deposition and exile. The fallout from the council had been intense. Argument and turmoil had not ceased. Some who had signed the creed and the anathemas against the Arians were appalled at the Sabellian spin being put on the creed by Marcellus and others. They managed to worm their way into the emperor's confidence, and he gradually began to consider changing the creed and even restoring Arius and the bishops of Nicomedia and Nicaea.

In 332 Constantine declared Arius restored as presbyter in Alexandria and ordered the new bishop to accept him back into communion there. Athanasius refused unless Arius would affirm *homoousios* as describing the relation between Father and Son. Arius would not. Athanasius rejected him and ignored the emperor's pleas and threats. As a result Athanasius was exiled by Constantine to the farthest outpost of the Roman Empire in the West—the German city of Trier. His exile began in November 335 and lasted until Constantine's death in 337. During his time away from his see, however, Athanasius remained the only recognized bishop of Alexandria. The bishops of Egypt and the presbyters and people of Alexandria refused to replace him, and he remained their beloved bishop even in exile.

On his travels to and from Trier, Athanasius made many contacts with Christian leaders in the West who came to sympathize with him. After all, Constantine was not universally considered a hero in the Latin West for moving the imperial seat eastward to Constantinople. Just because Athanasius was being exiled by the emperor was no reason for them to shun him. He was received by many Western bishops with open arms, and his influence among them for trinitarian orthodoxy (the Nicene formula) was profound. He also introduced them to the new phenomenon of Christian hermit monks in the Egyptian deserts. One of Athanasius's personal heroes was Anthony of the Desert—one of the first miracle-working desert ascetics. Athanasius wrote a book titled *The Life of Anthony,* and it became the basis for acceptance of monasticism among Christians throughout the empire.

While Athanasius was in exile in Trier, Arius died—one day before he was to be restored as a Christian presbyter in a special ceremony in Constantinople. Some scholars have speculated that he may have been poisoned by his enemies. In any case, his death in 336 came only months before Constantine's own death on May 22, 337. Constantine lived as a pagan and died as an Arian. Hardly an admirable curriculum vitae for "the first Christian emperor"! Nevertheless, his death brought to an end a great chapter in Christian history. From then on, with one brief exception, Roman emperors would consider themselves Christians in some sense and constantly interfered in ecclesiastical and theological affairs.

Constantine's successor was his son Constantius, and he allowed Athanasius to return to his see in Alexandria. His restoration was not to last, however. Athanasius's relationship with Emperor Constantius was a stormy one. The emperor, who ruled until his death in 362, constantly hounded the bishop, who seemed the last key holdout for trinitarian orthodoxy against Arianism and semi-Arianism.

The emperor wanted peace, and uniformity was its path. He came to believe that the term *homoousios*—ironically, suggested and enforced by his father, Constantine—should be replaced in the Nicene Creed with *homoiousios,* which means "of a similar substance" and would be acceptable to the semi-Arians and even many trinitarians. If accepted, the new terminology would have made orthodox the belief that the Son and the Father share a "similar substance" or a "like being" instead of the belief that they are of the same substance or being.

Those who lobbied for this change are generally considered "semi-Arians," and their star rose high in church and empire around 360 as Constantius sided with them. The change would have ruled out a Sabellian interpretation of the Trinity by making clear that the Father and the Son are not identical. But it would also have opened the door to an Arian subordinationist interpretation by implying that perhaps the Son is not God in the same way that the Father is God.

Athanasius stubbornly resisted the change and even condemned it as rank heresy and equated its supporters with the antichrist. As we will see, his concern was not merely to defend some sacrosanct wording but to defend the gospel itself. For Athanasius and his supporters, salvation itself depends on the Son of God being God and not merely a great creature "like God." For him "the fundamental issue is that only very God can unite a creature to God"[5] and "salvation is not . . . possible through an hierarchical chain, from the Father through an intermediate Son to creatures. For an intermediary separates as much as he unites creatures with the Father."[6] As much as he abhorred Sabellianism, Athanasius abhorred Arian subordinationism even more, and the semi-Arian "compromise" (which did not necessarily state explicitly that "there was when the Son was not") was unacceptable to him because the entire gospel hinged on Jesus Christ being truly God as well as truly human.

One modern critic of early Christian orthodoxy has suggested that Athanasius played a role in the downfall of the Roman Empire because of his obstinacy over one tiny letter that in Greek is only a diacritical mark over a vowel. Edward Gibbon argued that *homoousios* and *homoiousios* are so close in both appearance and meaning that Athanasius should have accepted the latter rather than cause so much strife and dissension over the difference. By way of response, evangelical theologian Millard Erickson recounts the (probably apocryphal) story of a wealthy woman of the Victorian era who traveled to Europe and found an expensive necklace she wished to buy. Wanting her husband's agreement (it was the Victorian era!), she telegraphed back home to tell him the price. The husband's message back to her caused the breakup of their marriage. He had written "No! Price too high," but the telegraph operator had dropped the exclamation mark. The wife spent the money, which caused financial ruin for the family and the end of their marriage.

Although admittedly a parable and not historical fact, the story makes the point that in many cases one tiny letter or punctuation mark can make a great difference in the meaning of a message. Contrary to Gibbon and Emperor Constantius, the difference between *homoousios* and *homoiousios* is the difference between the divine and the creaturely. One says that the Son *is* God. The other says that the Son is *like* God. If a being is God, then saying he is like God is entirely wrong. If a being is only *like* God, then declaring him to *be* God would be heresy if not blasphemy. Athanasius saw this and resisted the seductive compromise.

Because of his opposition to compromise, trumped-up charges were brought against Athanasius in Alexandria and he was forced to flee to Rome in 339. Eventually he was cleared of the charges of financial improprieties and abuse of power and was allowed to return to Alexandria. In another episode of the conflict the emperor came to Alexandria on imperial business and planned to snub Athanasius. The latter is supposed to have walked boldly out of his house and confronted the emperor by grabbing his horse's bridle in the procession and lecturing him on proper theology. That story may be legend. In another well-attested episode, however, Athanasius was publicly attacked by Roman guards while leading worship in the cathedral in Alexandria. When the troops burst into the church with the clear intention of arresting and possibly killing Athanasius, the congregation surged around him and protected him. He was able to slip away from the city and lived with the desert monks for five to six years until things cooled down back in the city.

In all, Athanasius endured five exiles: "Seventeen years, out of forty-six as bishop, Athanasius had spent in exile. Politics and theology had ever intermingled. So Athanasius lived, defending his understanding of the Catholic faith, as declared at Nicaea."[7]

In the middle of it all Athanasius managed to call a council at Alexandria. Not all bishops attended, of course, so it is not considered an ecumenical council. It had the support neither of the emperor nor of many leading bishops of the church. Nevertheless, it prepared the way for the second ecumenical council to come—the Council of Constantinople, which would take place after Athanasius's death and largely because of his work. His own synod in Alexandria met in 362. The bishops gathered there reaffirmed *homoousios* as the only proper description of the relationship of the Son of God to the Father and explicitly rejected both the semi-Arian *homoiousios* and Sabellianism as heresies.

The synod took a new step that would be crucial in the success of the Nicene doctrine of the Trinity at the Council of Constantinople in 381. Aided by his friends the Cappadocian fathers (Basil and the two Gregories), Athanasius proposed and the synod accepted an explanatory statement that declared the Father, Son and Holy Spirit to be three distinct but not separate *hypostases* of the one God. This absolutely crucial conceptual leap can be understood only in the context of the theological contributions of the three Cappadocian fathers, which must await the next chapter. Suffice it to say for now that *hypostasis* (of which *hypostases* is the plural) is a Greek word that could either mean "individual subsistence" (like a person) or else "common substance" (like human nature). In other words, it could be synonymous with ousia (substance) or not. If not, it generally meant the particular thing or individual example (subsistence) of a common substance or species. This was clearly the intended meaning at Athanasius's Alexandrian synod in 362.

The purpose of putting forth this new idea was to contradict Sabellian modalism by making clear that Father, Son and Holy Spirit, though one substance *(homoousios)*, are not the same identical person or subsistence. They are three distinct persons *(hypostases)* and not merely three masks or manifestations or aspects of the one personal God, as Sabellianism averred. It seems that at his synod in Alexandria, Athanasius and the trinitarian bishops gathered there had finally come around to Tertullian's Latin trinitarian formula carved out against Praxeas a century and a half earlier—*una substantia, tres personae*. But in 362 this was far from being universally accepted.

Athanasius's main theological treatises include *De Incarnatione*, translated as *On the Incarnation of the Word*, and *Four Discourses Against the Arians*. Of course he wrote numerous letters and smaller theological tracts, pamphlets and books. But these two are his main works on the subject of the Godhead and salvation. Among his other, less important works are *The Life of Anthony* and *Against the Heathen*.

*On the Incarnation of the Word* is still considered a great Christian classic and is still in print seventeen hundred years later. It is a classic of early Christian constructive theology. Athanasius probably wrote it during his first exile in Trier. It is a book about the necessity of a real incarnation of God in humanity for human salvation and stresses the deity of Jesus Christ. It assumes the traditional deification or divinization model of salvation that goes back at least to Irenaeus and perhaps further back in the history of theology. But the book also contains exegetical reflections on Scripture passages relating to Jesus Christ and his deity and profound wrestling with the relationships among Father, Son and Holy Spirit. One of Athanasius's main aims in the work was to make clear that the Son is begotten but not made. The book's Christology is strongly reminiscent of Origen's, and indeed Athanasius has often been considered a "right-wing Origenist" by scholars of historical theology. That is, his interpretation of Origen is traditional and conservative, whereas the Arians' was radical and "left wing."

*Against the Arians* is Athanasius's more polemical work directed at the heresies of the Arians and semi-Arians. It was written sometime between 356 and 360 when the Arian heresy under the guise of semi-Arianism was about to become the enforced orthodoxy of the entire church. The message is the same as that contained in *On the Incarnation of the Word* but expressed negatively by deconstructing radical subordinationism. The main message is that "the Logos is not a creature but is of one substance with the Father, . . . because only so is our salvation fully realized and guaranteed."[8]

Athanasius died in 373 in Alexandria. He spent the last seven years of his life in his home city as its bishop in relative peace and quiet. The emperor was Valens and he leaned strongly toward Arianism, but after forcing Athanasius into exile once, Valens relented and allowed him to go home. Valens himself died soon afterward and the next emperor, Theodosius, was a strong supporter of the orthodox, trinitarian faith championed by Athanasius and his Cappadocian friends. It was Theodosius who called the second ecumenical council at Constantinople where the Nicene Creed was strengthened and finally adopted as the binding universal creed for all Christians. It was also Theodosius who declared orthodox, catholic Christianity the one and only official religion of the Roman Empire. Athanasius did not live to see the fruit of his life's work.

### Athanasius's Theology

Throughout his main theological works, Athanasius followed three lines of theological reasoning regarding the relationship of the Son of God to the Father. All three are meant to support and even prove the ontological unity of substance *(homoousios)* of Father and Son. On a few occasions Athanasius explicitly included the Holy Spirit in this unity, but his main concern was to counter Arianism and thus he concentrated on the person of Christ and the question of his status vis-à-vis the Father. His Cappadocian friends would take up the cause of the Holy Spirit.

The first line of reasoning Athanasius used to support the equality of Son with Father is metaphysical. The heart of the argument is that if the Father is God, then the Son must be God as well, for otherwise the Father would have changed in becoming Father. If there was a time when the Son was not, then there was a time when the Father was not a father. For him, the Son is part of the definition of God as Father, and "God's offspring is eternal, for His nature is ever perfect. . . . What is to be said but that, in maintaining 'Once the Son was not,' they rob God of His Word, like plunderers, and openly predicate of Him that He was once without His proper Word and Wisdom, and that the Light was once without radiance, and the Fountain was once barren and dry."[9] For Athanasius, denial of the eternal deity of the Son of God was a serious offense against the Father: "This assault upon the Son makes the blasphemy recoil upon the Father."[10]

Athanasius shared with the Arians and almost all who called themselves Christians an intense belief in the immutability of God, and he exploited this against radical subordinationism. If God "became" Father, then he underwent change and alteration. If the Son of God is the express image of the Father and his radiance and light—all of which Scripture clearly teaches—then he has always existed with the Father even if he is "begotten" of him: "But God is not as man, as Scripture has said; but is existing and is ever; therefore also His Word is existing and is everlasting with the Father as radiance of light. . . . Hence He is God also, as being God's Image, for 'the Word was God,' says Scripture."[11]

This metaphysical argument for the equality of God's Son with God himself presented a problem for Athanasius when he turned to describing the nature of the humanity and divinity of Jesus Christ in *On the Incarnation of the Word.* After all, if divinity is strictly immutable, how could it become united with human existence in any real way? The Arian and semi-Arian solution was to say that the Logos, or Son of God, is *not* truly divine. Athanasius would reach back to Origen and other theologians before his own time for a different solution. For him, the Son of God did not change in entering into human existence in Jesus Christ. Just how far this is compatible with real incarnation is debatable, but that was Athanasius's solution.

In fact, Athanasius went very far in this direction. In order to preserve the Son's true deity equal with the Father's, he felt he must rescue him from any taint of creatureliness in his incarnation. He frequently referred to the incarnation as the Logos's *use* of a human body. In *On the Incarnation of the Word* he said that even during the earthly life of Jesus Christ, the Logos (or Son of God) "was not bound to His body, but rather was Himself wielding it, so that he was not only in it, but was actually in everything, and while external to the universe, abode in His Father only."[12] Later christological heretics would appeal to Athanasius's theology at this very point, and the church would have to ignore the fact that the venerable Alexandrian bishop seemed to disconnect the deity and humanity of Christ from one another.

The second line of argument that Athanasius used in defending the Son's full deity was soteriological. For him, the whole point of theology was to preserve and protect the gospel, and the gospel is about salvation. The kernel of his reasoning here is that if the Son of God is not "truly God" in the same sense as the Father, then salvation as re-creation is impossible. Only God can undo sin and bring a creature to share in the divine nature:

> For if, being a creature, He [the Word] had become man, man had remained just what he was, not joined to God; for how had a work been joined to the Creator by a work? or what succour had come from like to like, when one as well as other needed it? And how, were the Word a creature, had He power to undo God's sentence and to remit sin, whereas it is written in the Prophets, that this is God's doing?[13]

In the background of Athanasius's thought and argument here was the traditional idea of salvation as deification *(theosis)*, although his mode of reasoning did not necessarily depend entirely upon it. For him as for Irenaeus and Origen and other early Christian theologians, the human problem was death because of sin, and the solution was deification by means of humanity and divinity being joined in the incarnation. It was Athanasius who provided the most famous expression of this "wonderful exchange" theory of salvation: "For He was made man that we might be made God; and He manifested Himself by a body that we might receive the idea of the unseen Father; and He endured the insolence of men that we might inherit immortality."[14]

Irenaeus had developed and exploited the concept of salvation as deification (partial participation in God's own immortal energy and life) in order to prove the necessity of Christ's humanity against the Gnostics. Athanasius exploited the idea in order to prove the necessity of Christ's deity against the Arians and semi-Arians.

Both Irenaeus and Athanasius, and many Christian theologians since them, have shared a common idea: that unless Jesus Christ was both "truly God" and "truly human," salvation simply could not occur. Of course Athanasius also plumbed the depths of Scripture to counter the interpretations of the Arians and other subordinationists and to substantiate from proof texts of the apostles' own writings that they considered Jesus Christ to be both divine and human. But Athanasius knew full well that Scripture could be twisted to mean many things. The ultimate argument had to come back to the reality of the gospel itself. The gospel is about salvation through Jesus Christ, and if Jesus Christ was not God *and* human, then he could not bring the two together. Salvation would then ultimately be reduced to living a good moral life (Christian moralism) or else gaining some secret knowledge (gnosticism) or merely having one's sins forgiven but being left in the same fallen and corrupt condition as before.

Here it will be beneficial to quote at some length from Athanasius's great classic text *On the Incarnation of the Word* in order to illustrate his vision of the connection between salvation and incarnation:

> He [the Logos] took pity on our race, and had mercy on our infirmity, and condescended to our corruption, and, unable to bear that death should have the mastery—lest the creature should perish, and His Father's handiwork in men be spent for nought—He takes unto Himself a body, and that of no different sort from ours. . . . And thus taking from our bodies one of like nature, because all were under penalty of the corruption of death He gave it over to death in the stead of all, and offered it to the Father—doing this, moreover, of His loving-kindness, to the end that, firstly, all being held to have died in Him, the law involving the ruin of men might be undone (inasmuch as its power was fully spent in the Lord's body, and had no longer holding-ground against men, his peers), and that, secondly, whereas men had turned toward corruption, He might turn them again toward incorruption, and quicken them from death by the appropriation of His body and by the grace of the Resurrection, banishing death from them like straw from the fire.[15]

On the one hand, this beautiful theological description of Christ's work on our behalf well illustrates why Athanasius considered it so essential that he be divine as well as human. If he were something less than truly God, his life could hardly banish death from mortal bodies. On the other hand, the statement also illustrates a problem in Athanasius's Christology. It leaves unanswered a question, and therein lies the "troubling legacy" Athanasius left behind for later theologians to wrestle with. The question is how Jesus Christ could accomplish the work of salvation if only his body or flesh was truly human and the divine Logos—the Son of God—remained immutable and impassible and even outside of the body throughout Jesus' life and death? Is this then a real incarnation? Did the Son of God actually experience birth, suffering and death? Athanasius's answer is that he only experienced such creaturely things through the human body that he took on. The Son of God was himself in no way limited or diminished or hindered or caused to change or suffer through the incarnation.

What kind of "incarnation" is that? one may fairly ask. Even during Athanasius's own lifetime another theologian named Apollinarius taught a view of the person of Jesus Christ nearly identical to Athanasius, and it was declared heretical at the Council of Constantinople in 381. It appears that Athanasius, as great as he was, was an "Apollinarian before Apollinarius."[16]

The third line of argument Athanasius pursued in order to defend the full and true deity of the Son of God was revelational. In order for Jesus Christ to be the true revelation of God and not merely another image or prophet as so many already were, he had to be God. Athanasius's reasoning here was that only God can truly reveal God: "If the Son is not one with God even as God the Father is, he cannot truly and genuinely reveal the Father."[17] Many events and persons had already come to reveal messages about and from God, but Jesus Christ is the self-revelation of God and not merely another messenger of God. Even the Arians and semi-Arians agreed on that point. Athanasius based his argument on this minimal common ground. If Jesus Christ is not God in human flesh, then God is not truly revealed in him: "For no longer, as in the former times, God has willed to be known by an image and shadow of wisdom, that namely which is the creatures, but He has made the true wisdom Itself to take flesh, and to become man, and to undergo the death of the cross; that by the faith in Him, henceforth all that believe may obtain salvation."[18]

So, Athanasius argued, if the Son of God who became Jesus Christ is not truly God as the Father is God, we humans are not being saved by him and our connection with him, *and* he does not truly reveal the Father to us. Furthermore, the Father has undergone change in begetting a Son, which is improper to the divine nature. All this adds up to the charge that Arianism and semi-Arianism constitute "another gospel" and not authentic Christianity at all. Christianity revolves around Jesus Christ as the real incarnation of God in human nature.

In his own trinitarian reflections Athanasius held on to a relic of subordinationism by affirming the "monarchy of the Father." In this he showed his true Origenist colors. The Son of God is begotten from the Father even if he is not created in time, Athanasius affirmed. Only the Father is completely unbegotten and without any source or origin in another. But the Son's begottenness is an eternal generation from the Father just like the radiance of the sun. Thus for Athanasius the Father was the principle of unity of the entire Trinity. He is source and fountain of all divinity, and both the Son and the Holy Spirit flow forth from him and owe their divine being and status to him. He owes his to none else. But Athanasius did not consider this monarchy of the Father in any way a concession to Arianism, nor would he even admit to call it a subordinationism. Everything that the Father has by way of attributes belongs to the Son by essence also. The only difference is that the Father's divine essence is uncaused, while the Son's and Spirit's are eternally taken from the Father's and thus in a sense caused by the Father through a process of "eternal begetting."

It should be clear, then, why Athanasius stubbornly refused to compromise on the terminology for the relationship of the Son to the Father. "What is at stake is not just a theological theory but people's salvation."[19] *Homoiousios* would mean that Jesus Christ was not truly God, and in that case, by confessing it as the correct way of expressing the relationship of the Son with the Father, we would be rejecting our own salvation and teaching a false gospel. But the full formulation of the doctrine of the Trinity, including the role of the Holy Spirit and the nature of the three persons and their unity in the Godhead, was not accomplished by Athanasius. He laid the foundation and others—namely, the Cappadocian fathers—built on it.

# CHAPTER 12

# The Cappadocian Fathers Settle the Issue

For *all practical purposes the great trinitarian controversy that swirled around* the Arian and Sabellian heresies throughout much of the fourth century ended at the Council of Constantinople in 381. It turned out to be the second ecumenical council of the Christian church and is noted for putting the finishing touches on the Nicene Creed, anathematizing (condemning and excluding) a variety of heresies and establishing the formal doctrine of the Trinity as worked out by Athanasius and his friends the Cappadocian fathers as the orthodox and catholic dogma binding on all clergy of the Great Church. From the council onward, denial of the orthodox doctrine of the Trinity as spelled out in the Nicene Creed has been considered by all major branches of Christianity (including most Protestants) as heresy and possibly even apostasy (loss of status as a Christian, if not loss of a state of grace).

A common modern misunderstanding about the process by which the doctrine of the Trinity was settled and about the formula of the doctrine itself is that all of it represents a kind of ivory-tower speculation by professional theologians who had nothing better to do and simply wanted to ignore mystery and rationalize Christian belief. Nothing could be further from the truth. In fact, the common folk of Christianity cared deeply about the issues and were constantly involved in the debates and struggles over theological correctness. One of the Cappadocian fathers, Gregory of Nyssa, wrote that in Constantinople about the time of the second ecumenical council "if you ask for change, someone philosophizes to you on the Begotten and the Unbegotten. If you ask the price of bread, you are told, 'The Father is Greater, and the Son inferior.' If you ask 'Is the bath ready?' someone answers 'The Son was created from nothing.' "[1]

The bishops and theologians of the early church were greatly concerned about the consensus and consent of the faithful people of God. Much theology was carved out in sermons and took into account the responses of ordinary people. At the same time, of course, theologians trained in philosophy and biblical interpretation held conferences and exchanged letters on a more sophisticated level of discussion. But they were not unconcerned about the beliefs, worship and Christian lives of the laity, and the laity were not unconcerned about the debates among the theologians. The situation has largely changed in modern Christianity, much to its impoverishment and detriment.

The impression that the theologians of the fourth century such as Athanasius and the Cappadocian fathers were attempting to rationalize away the mysteries of God is also completely mistaken. In fact, they were trying to protect the mystery of the gospel and the God of the gospel from false rationalization. The uses of extrabiblical and somewhat philosophical language such as *homoousios* in no way detracts from this. For them, *homoousios* and terms like it are expressions of mystery, not rationalizations that take away from the mystery of the Godhead. It was the Arians and Sabellians and other heretics who were attempting to make Christian belief too simple and too intelligible to human intellect by rejecting the mystery of God as one substance (being) and three distinct subsistences (persons). Exactly how that could be is not fully intelligible to human minds, and heresies reduced the mystery to something mundane and comprehensible and in the process robbed it of its majesty and glory. The orthodox defenders of the doctrine of the Trinity knew that they were standing before mystery when they examined the three-in-one God and the equality of Jesus Christ with the Father. If they sometimes used seemingly complicated and difficult-to-understand formulas and terminology, it was only to defend the mystery.

## The Cappadocians' Contribution

The Council of Constantinople with its resounding endorsement of the Nicene doctrine of the Trinity and its condemnation of the twin but opposite heresies of Arianism and Sabellianism could not have come about without the work of the three great Cappadocian fathers: Basil of Caesarea, Gregory of Nazianzus and Gregory of Nyssa. They are known as the Cappadocian fathers because all of them came from and held church offices in the region of Cappadocia in central Asia Minor (Turkey)—a stronghold of Christianity from the early days of Gentile

Christianity. They were all close friends of Athanasius and built on his theological thinking. In fact, as one historical theologian notes, "Without him, the work of the Cappadocians would have been impossible. Without the Cappadocians his work would not have come to its final fruition."[2]

When Athanasius died in 373 an Arian emperor ruled and various forms of Arianism—some moderate and some extreme—were influential among bishops. At least twelve different creeds expressing various kinds of Arianism had been written and promulgated since the Council of Nicaea and Constantine's defection from its accomplishment. None of the rival creeds stuck, but without the arguments and explanations of the Cappadocian fathers, it is possible that eventually an Arian or semi-Arian creed would have been accepted by the majority of bishops and by a powerful emperor and Christianity would be a different religion than it is.

The work of the three great Cappadocian fathers, then, "consisted in clarifying, defining, and defending trinitarian doctrine"[3] and in "systematizing the faith of the church and expounding it with as much logical clarity as is possible"[4] so that heresies could be exposed for what they were and the entire church could understand, accept and unite around the orthodox faith.

A particularly virulent and aggressive form of Arianism known as Eunomianism (after its main proponent, Eunomius) was gaining ground in the middle and late decades of the fourth century. In spite of Athanasius's heroic efforts and profound theological explanations, Eunomianism claimed with some persuasive success that full Trinitarianism denied the unity and immutability of God and was a disguised form of paganism—all arguments made in modern times by Jehovah's Witnesses. Sabellianism was still alive and well in the time of the Cappadocians (370s), and many bishops and other Christians still could not distinguish between modalism and Nicene orthodox Trinitarianism. The task and accomplishment of the Cappadocians was to explain the Trinity in a way that clearly distinguished it from these heresies and protected the mystery at its heart without leaving it as a sheer contradiction.

Another way to state their common task is that "Cappadocian theology is an attempt to interpret the central term *homoousios* in such a way as to insist on the full deity of the Son and of his eternal distinction from the Father."[5] Their efforts to this end diverged in details but converged on one essential and central point: God is one *ousia* and three *hypostases.* The meaning of this formula and its Greek words will be unfolded in this chapter. It is this concept and these words that became the core of the trinitarian belief of the Great Church from the Council of Constantinople onward.

**Basil of Caesarea**

Who were these Cappadocian fathers? Basil was born in about 330—just five years after the Council of Nicaea—to a wealthy Christian family in Cappadocia. He was raised mainly by his godly grandmother Macrina, after whom his influential sister was named. Basil's sister Macrina adopted the monastic life of a nun early and urged Basil and their young brother Gregory to take monastic vows as well. Basil and Gregory both gave their sister great credit for influencing them spiritually.

Before joining a monastery, however, Basil attended the best school of Greek culture and philosophy in the world at Athens. There he met and became a lifelong friend of Gregory of Nazianzus, who was the same age as him and was also from a wealthy Christian family of Cappadocia. Attending the Platonic academy with them was a future emperor—Julian—who turned his back on Christianity and during his brief reign (361-363) attempted to return the empire to paganism.

Basil was baptized and ordained in 357 and shortly afterward began visiting the hermit monks and nuns of the caves and small monasteries of the Cappadocian wilderness. Under his sister's influence, he renounced his family wealth and his legacy as eldest son of the family and founded his own monastery. His life of extreme asceticism contributed to both his poor health and his reputation for spiritual greatness.

In 370 the great Bishop Eusebius of Caesarea (in Cappadocia) died and Basil was appointed to succeed him. Caesarea was a major center of church life in the Eastern empire and so Basil became an archbishop over bishops of smaller sees. One of his major concerns as bishop was to counteract the influences of Arianism—especially its Eunomian form—and Sabellianism. Even before becoming archbishop, Basil had written a major critique of Arianism in five books entitled *Against Eunomius.* Besides his theological efforts on behalf of Nicene orthodoxy, Basil gained a great reputation as an able church administrator, monastic leader and spiritual counselor. He traveled widely in the Eastern empire and wrote numerous epistles to bishops, emperors and presbyters of churches attempting to persuade and even coerce them if possible to reject heresy and accept orthodoxy as he saw it. He worked tirelessly to bring about a new ecumenical council that would ratify the acts of Nicaea and put an end to the Arian heresy and strife it had caused. To this end he appointed bishops he could trust to help. Two he pressed into service were his friend Gregory of Nazianzus and his younger brother Gregory of Nyssa. Neither one distinguished himself as a great bishop in the same way Basil did, but both helped influence Christendom toward final and formal adoption of trinitarian orthodoxy.

One of Basil's most important theological works is *On the Holy Spirit,* which he wrote around 375. It was the first whole treatise on the person of the Holy Spirit by a Christian leader or theologian and greatly influenced the eventual revision of the Nicene Creed to include more about the third person of the Trinity.

Basil was concerned that in all the controversy over the relationship of the Son of God to the Father, the Holy Spirit had been ignored if not forgotten by the theologians and bishops involved in the debates over the Trinity. Also certain bishops had adopted a teaching about the Holy Spirit known as pneumatomachianism that denied the equality of the Spirit with Father and Son. This was a subordinationism of the Spirit and resulted in a "binity"[6] rather than a Trinity for those who adopted it. They worshiped the Father and the Son while rejecting worship of the Spirit as God. For them the Holy Spirit was simply a created force or power of God the Father sent into the world through the Son. By way of response, Basil plumbed the depths of both Scripture and worship in order to establish the third distinct person, or *hypostasis,* of the Godhead as "truly God" and equal with the Father and the Son.

Because of his work on behalf of the Holy Spirit, Basil came to be known in the church as the "theologian of the Holy Spirit," and because of his entire life's work he has come to be known in church history as Basil the Great. He died in 377 or 379. Like Athanasius, however, he was not alive to see the fruition of his endeavors at the great Council of Constantinople in 381. In all probability he did, however, anticipate it when Emperor Theodosius succeeded Valens. Even though Theodosius was no paragon of Christian virtue, he openly favored Nicene orthodoxy and opposed Arianism.

**Gregory of Nazianzus**

Gregory of Nazianzus—sometimes called Nazianzen—was unrelated to Basil but was the same age and his best friend. He was born in 329 or 330 and died well after Basil in about 391. Like his friends Basil and Gregory of Nyssa, Nazianzen was raised in a wealthy Christian family in Cappadocia. His father was the bishop of Nazianzus, and his mother, Nonna, was influential in his conversion to Christianity. After his studies in Athens with Basil, Gregory was ordained to the priesthood in 364. In spite of Basil's constant pestering and even occasional attempts at manipulation, Gregory resisted the appeal of monasticism—possibly because of a romantic attraction, although whether he ever married is unknown. At that time and place in church history, priests and bishops could be married; monks could not. That is still the rule in Eastern Orthodox Christianity.

Eventually Basil persuaded Gregory to accept a position as bishop of the small see of Sasima in Cappadocia under Basil. The relationship nearly ruined their friendship because Gregory did not relish the administrative work required of a bishop and longed for the simpler life of being a local parish priest and studying and writing. He was an ascetic at heart even if he never took monastic vows, and his neglect of his body's needs for nourishment, exercise and rest nearly killed him. Nevertheless, Gregory of Nazianzus gained a reputation as a great defender and explainer of trinitarian orthodoxy against all kinds of heresies because of his writings such as *Theological Orations.* These were first preached as sermons in the Church of the Resurrection in Constantinople after the new emperor Theodosius moved Gregory there in 380. According to one historian, these sermons constituted "a brilliant summary for the city congregation of what was becoming the accepted trinitarian orthodoxy. These statements were the height of Gregory's achievement."[7] The sermons and five books based on them argued against the Arians and paved the way for the coming Council of Constantinople.

When Emperor Theodosius formally convened the second ecumenical council in Constantinople in 381, he appointed Gregory of Nazianzus patriarch of the city—one of the highest positions in the entire church and virtually equal in honor with the bishop of Rome—and asked him to preside over the council itself. These honors immediately propelled the relatively shy and humble Gregory into a spotlight he did not want and could not handle. After a brief attempt to serve as best he could, Gregory resigned both positions and retired to his home city of Nazianzus, where he remained in obscurity until his death. The cause of his early and unexpected retirement is unknown but probably had to do with the great political wrangling over his appointment to the patriarchate of Constantinople and presidency of the ecumenical council. It is possible that his life was threatened. It is certain that Arian bishops and other opponents of orthodoxy falsely accused him of illegal acts and improprieties. A churchman with thicker skin might have stuck it out. Gregory withered under the barrage of criticism and faded away.

Because of his *Theological Orations* and contribution to the Council of Constantinople, Gregory of Nazianzus has come to be known in church history simply as "The Theologian." One commentator has said of the sermons he preached under that title, "In a few pages and in a few hours Gregory has summed up and closed the controversy of a whole century."[8] And yet Gregory Nazianzen is not considered the greatest or most brilliant of all the Cappadocians. Nor is Basil. That reputation falls to the youngest and least educated of the three friends—Basil's brother Gregory of Nyssa.

### Gregory of Nyssa

Gregory of Nyssa was born the third son and youngest child in the same family as

Basil. The exact year of his birth is unknown, as is the exact year of death. He was probably born about 340 and died around 393. It appears that he did not have the benefit of a great education such as Basil and their friend Gregory Nazianzen experienced at Athens. Julian, the latter two students' colleague in school, banned Christians from receiving the best pagan educations possible during his brief reign as emperor, which probably coincided with Gregory's youth. So he was taught at home by Basil and their sister Macrina. Yet "wherever he received his education he is scarcely inferior to the other two [Basil and Gregory Nazianzen] in the rhetorical skills admired in that period, and his philosophical ability is superior to that of his brother and his friend."[9] Somehow Gregory managed to garner a stellar knowledge and understanding of Greek philosophy and became extremely articulate and sharp in his thinking and communicating skills. Some scholars would argue that his genius is rivaled only by Origen's in all of early church history.

Gregory had a strong mystical bent and experienced remarkable dreams and visions and spiritual experiences that transcended intellectual explanation. One such dream or vision led to his conversion and baptism at a young age, after which he chose to retire from active life in the world and live the ascetic, monastic life with Macrina and Basil. Gregory spent much of his time reading and studying both Scripture and the writings of the Platonists and Neo-Platonists, those mystical pagan philosophers whose beliefs seemed so compatible with Christianity to many fourth- and fifth-century church fathers. Gregory soaked in their message about the absolute unity, spirituality and transcendence of God and sought to combine the best of it with his Christian reflections on the Trinity and attributes of God.

In 372 Basil prevailed upon his younger brother to become bishop of the very troublesome see at Nyssa in Cappadocia. That is the origin of his identification as "Gregory *of* Nyssa" in church history. His life as bishop was miserable, and he was constantly embroiled in conflicts and controversies and suffered a series of persecutions for his steadfast defense of trinitarian orthodoxy. When Basil died in 379, Gregory picked up his theological mantle as living leader of the anti-Arian cause and caught the attention of Emperor Theodosius, who highly regarded Gregory's mystical bent as well as his theological mind. He participated in the Council of Constantinople, delivered its inaugural address and helped guide it toward its final conclusion in favor of Nicene trinitarian orthodoxy. When the emperor's wife Placidia died, Gregory of Nyssa was asked to give her funeral oration. The details of his later life are unknown.

Gregory of Nyssa's theological writings make greater and more profound use of Greek philosophy than do those of the other two Cappadocian fathers. They breathe something of the speculative spirit of Origen but without the latter's flights of fancy into extraneous subjects such as preexistence of souls and *apokatastasis* (universal reconciliation). Like Origen, Gregory treated God as completely incomprehensible and ineffable in essence—beyond all human knowing except in mystical experience. At the same time, however, like Origen, Gregory did not hold back from borrowing from Greek metaphysics ("despoiling the Egyptians") to help explain the unity of God's being in harmony with the threeness of persons. For him, a "nature" *(ousia)* is like a Platonic "form"—a real universal that binds many individual things together. God's nature or essence, then, is like the form of human nature, and the form of human nature is like God's own substance. Many individual humans have distinctive qualities while sharing the most important thing about themselves in common—a universal nature, or essence. So Father, Son and Holy Spirit share a common *ousia* while remaining distinct but not separate persons. The background of Nyssa's way of explaining this against the heretics lies in Platonic philosophy with its stress on the reality of universals.

Gregory of Nyssa wrote many books and letters and delivered many sermons and orations, but three of his writings stand out as especially important in making an impact on the outcome of the great trinitarian controversy: *On the Holy Trinity, On Not Three Gods* and *Against Eunomius.* In all of his writings his concern was the same as Basil's and Nazianzen's: to provide a solid foundation and intelligible explanation of the mystery of the Trinity that would completely shatter the objections of its enemies and retain the mystery at its heart. This he did with unparalleled success.

**Basil the Great's Theology**

Whatever one finds that is notable in a Cappadocian father's theology is likely to have echoes in the others as well. It is clear that they collaborated a great deal and drew from the same wells of inspiration: Scripture, Plato, Origen and Athanasius. Their overall thrust and purpose unified—to establish once and for all the great mystery of the threeness and oneness of God as Christian orthodoxy. More specifically, their common mission and goal was to destroy Arianism and Sabellianism and establish as orthodox the belief that God is one infinite and incomprehensible essence *(ousia)* shared equally by three distinct but never separate identities, or persons *(hypostases)*. In the process of reaching this common goal the three Cappadocians carved out somewhat distinctive emphases and sometimes went off on tangents of their own that turned out to be important. Our method here will be to discuss each father in turn—in the order in which they were introduced—and describe his main theological ideas, mentioning along the way how they are similar to or different from the others'. At the conclusion we will discuss their common achievement and the great Council of Constantinople by which it was crowned.

Basil of Caesarea's main opponents were the Eunomians and pneumatomachians—both radical subordinationists. The Eunomians subordinated the Son of God to the Father, arguing that the Father's very essence is "unbegottenness." Since the Son is begotten, he cannot be equal with the Father and cannot be considered God. The Eunomians were radical Arians. The pneumatomachians (also known as Macedonians) subordinated the Holy Spirit to the Father and the Son, arguing that the Spirit is a created being—a force from God sent from the Father through the Son, Jesus Christ. In contrast to both types of subordinationism, Basil attempted to demonstrate from Scripture and reason that God can be and is one united being—not three Gods—eternally related within himself as three distinct persons.

The Eunomians' main assertion against the Trinity was that the essence of God is unbegottenness and thus the Son cannot be *homoousios* with the Father because the Son is begotten. In *Against Eunomius* Basil responded with four main arguments. First, he scoffed at Eunomius's claim to have grasped God's very essence. God's essence, Basil declared, is incomprehensible because God is holy and his ways are not our ways and his thoughts are not our thoughts. Here Basil relied on both Scripture and Greek philosophy, for the latter emphasized the human mind's incapacity to know the divine as it knows itself. Basil accused Eunomians (and by extension all the Arians) of hubris, that is, of pride in their own abilities. To claim to know God's essence as unbegottenness is the epitome of sinful pride, Basil argued. We can know God's revealed being and properties, but his infinite and eternal essence is beyond our finite comprehension. This idea of God's incomprehensible essence is found also in the two Gregories and became a major theological axiom for Eastern Christian thought.

The second argument Basil presented against Eunomius was his denial of the subordinationist analogy between divine begetting (generation) and human begetting. That is, just because human begetting is always in time and always implies a kind of inferiority of being of the begotten to the one who begets (infant to parent), that is no reason to draw the conclusion that God's begetting a Son necessarily implies inferiority of the latter to the former.

This leads directly into Basil's third line of argument, which was to counter Eunomius's claim that "unbegottenness" always goes together with "eternity" in such a way that to be begotten is to be temporal and not eternal. Basil went to great lengths to demonstrate logically that a generation (process of being begotten) can be eternal by appeal to analogies such as the sun's rays—a favorite of trinitarian church fathers. The rays of the sun are as old as the sun itself. There never was a time when the sun existed without its rays (radiance). Yet the sun generates (begets) its radiance. So the Father eternally generates the Son of God, and the Son of God is eternally begotten of the Father.

Basil expressly appealed to this analogy in a letter to his brother Gregory where he explained the unity-in-distinction of Father and Son using an image of sun and brightness:

> For just as the brightness is emitted by the flame, and the brightness is not after the flame, but at one and the same moment the flame shines and the light beams brightly, so does the Apostle mean the Son to be thought of as deriving existence from the Father, and yet the Only-begotten not to be divided from the existence of the Father by any intervening extension in space, but the caused to be always conceived of together with the cause.[10]

Finally, Basil argued that if the Son of God is merely a creature, as Eunomius claimed, then humanity is still without a true revelation of the divine. In the case of a personal being such as God, only the personal being himself can reveal himself. If Jesus Christ is not God, then God is not yet self-revealed. If Jesus Christ is merely a creature—however exalted—then humanity still does not have a true revelation of the face of God. And yet Eunomius and all the Christian subordinationists claimed that Jesus Christ is the Savior of the world and the true revelation of God. Basil showed the absurdity of such a claim. If he was nothing more than a great creature—like an archangel—then Jesus Christ was more like a prophet than like God self-revealed for us.

Basil's main work against the pneumatomachians, or Macedonians, who denied the deity and personhood of the Holy Spirit, is *On the Holy Spirit.* Basil explained their heresy: "It is not permissible, they assert, for the Holy Spirit to be ranked with the Father and the Son, on account of the difference of His nature and the inferiority of His dignity."[11] Against this argument Basil appealed to Scripture—especially Jesus' commandment of baptism at the end of Matthew's Gospel: "If . . . the Spirit is there conjoined with the Father and the Son, and no one is so shameless as to say anything else, then let them not lay blame on us for following the words of Scripture."[12] He also appealed to examples in the book of Acts where the Holy Spirit is said to be the only one who knows the things of God (Acts 5:9). He pointed out that even the pneumatomachians worshiped the Holy Spirit in their divine liturgies together with the Father and the Son, which would be blasphemy if he were not God.

Finally, Basil turned to Christian experience of salvation and argued against the subordinationists of the Spirit that since the Holy Spirit effects our salvation, he cannot be anything but God. Only God can save:

> Through the Holy Spirit comes our restoration to paradise, our ascension into the kingdom of heaven, our return to our adoption as sons, our liberty to call God our Father, our being made partakers of the grace of Christ, our being called children of light, our sharing in eternal glory, and, in a word, our being brought into a state of all "fullness of blessing," both in this world and in the world to come.[13]

In all things, then, the Holy Spirit is incapable of being parted from the Father and the Son. It is the Spirit who applies God's salvation to our lives. How can he be conceived as a creature and not as God himself? Of course, Basil was more than willing to allow a certain kind of subordination of the Spirit to the Father as the Father is the eternal fount of all divinity from whom the Son is generated and the Spirit proceeds. The analogy is to the sun and its light and warmth. The latter originate in and from the former without being inferior or "after" it. So the Son of God and the Spirit of God are God's eternal counterparts sharing in his very being and glory while being subordinate in position but not in being to God the Father.

Basil considered the pneumatomachians apostates because of their rejection of the deity of the Spirit, just as he considered the Eunomians and other Arians apostates due to their rejection of the deity of the Son of God. In *On the Holy Spirit* he declared theological war on those who would in any way deny the Spirit: "But we will not slacken in our defence of the truth. We will not cowardly abandon the cause. The Lord has delivered to us as a necessary and saving doctrine that the Holy Spirit is to be ranked with the Father."[14] Why was the deity of the Holy Spirit so important to Basil? Many modern Christians have trouble conceiving of the Holy Spirit as either a distinct person or as equal with God the Father and the Son. To them as to his ancient enemies, Basil would cry that to deny the Spirit's deity is to place a question mark beside the deity of the Father and the Son. In Scripture as in worship as in personal Christian experience, the Holy Spirit is always associated with them as sharing equal honor and dignity, and equal honor and dignity imply equal nature. One cannot be ontologically subordinated to the others without that impinging on the honor and dignity and glory of all the persons of the Godhead.

One of the accusations made by his opponents was that Basil's trinitarian view of God necessarily implies tritheism—belief in three Gods. The subordinationists and Sabellians argued that the whole idea of three equal persons *(hypostases)* necessarily implies three different natures, or substances *(ousia)*. Against all of them Basil declared, "Against those who cast it in our teeth that we are Tritheists, let it be answered that we confess one God not in number but in nature."[15]

Basil's explanation of this is echoed in the writings of the two Gregories, and no one can be certain which Cappadocian father influenced the others the most. Some scholars argue that Basil is the one who first expressed the all-important distinction between *ousia* (substance) and *hypostasis* (subsistence, person) in a letter to his brother Gregory of Nyssa. Other scholars argue that the letter itself was actually written by Gregory and somehow came to be attributed to Basil. The truth seems to be that around 375 both Basil and Gregory were simultaneously working out this distinction in order to correct the impression that Nicene trinitarian orthodoxy implied three Gods.

In any case, Basil argued against his accusers that there are two kinds of nouns that predicate: general and limited. General nouns indicate "the common nature" of more than one thing. In terms of later theological and philosophical discussions, Basil has in mind universals such as "human nature" and "circleness" and "redness" and "goodness." Limited nouns denote peculiarities of specific things such as "tall" and "oblong" and "dark" and "lesser of two evils."

Building on this distinction between general and limited nouns, Basil then attempted to refute the accusation of tritheism in trinitarian doctrine. He did this by using two words that in Greek were often used synonymously but could be distinguished: *ousia* and *hypostasis.*

> My statement, then, is this. That which is spoken of in a special and peculiar manner is indicated by the name of the hypostasis. . . . This then is the hypostasis, or "under-standing;" not the indefinite conception of the essence or substance *[ousia]*, which, because what is signified is general, finds no "standing," but the conception which by means of the expressed peculiarities gives *standing* and circumscription to the general and uncircumscribed.[16]

This is admittedly a dense statement. Basil used two analogies to help unpack its meaning. First, he illustrated the distinction between *ousia* and *hypostasis*—substance and subsistence—by referring to the common humanity of three hypothetical individual men: Peter, James and John. All three are human and they equally share in common the universal nature, or essence *(ousia)*, of humanity. At the same time all three have characteristics peculiar to them. Peter is taller than James or John. That has nothing to do with an essential inequality in their humanity. So it is with the *hypostases* of Father, Son and Holy Spirit: the Father is unbegotten, the Son is begotten, and the Spirit proceeds from the Father. The difference in no way detracts from their equal sharing in divine substance, Basil argued.

The other analogy he offered his brother (and by extension others who read the letter) is a rainbow: "The peculiar properties of the hypostases [of the Trinity], like colours seen in the Iris, flash their brightness on each of the Persons Whom we believe to exist in the Holy Trinity; but that of the proper nature no difference can be conceived as existing between one and the other, the peculiar characteristics shining, in community of essence, upon each."[17] Only a fool, in other words, would claim that a rainbow is several different things or substances. At the same time, only a fool would argue that there is no distinction within the rainbow between colors. The colors are not even parts that can be separated out leaving the rainbow intact. In the same way, God is one divine substance or being made up of three distinct but inseparable subsistences. The other Cappadocian fathers offered their own analogies, but they all made the same basic point.

Two things must be said about Basil's distinction between *ousia* and *hypostasis* as it applies to the Christian doctrine of the Trinity. First, even Basil and the other Cappadocian fathers knew that it had inherent problems. For one thing, the two terms could be understood as synonyms. *Hypostasis* was sometimes used instead of *ousia* in Greek culture for "substance." That is why Basil and the Gregories went to great pains to explain what they meant by *hypostasis.* For another thing, the only way in which the distinction could help make the case they wanted to make was if everyone thought like they did—as Platonists. For them, substance was a kind of Platonic form—a real universal in some sense "above" individual things. The Platonic form or universal "red," for example, was conceived to be real and in some sense higher and greater than individual red things. Basil and the two Gregories all thought along those lines about *ousia,* or substance. Human nature is a real thing—a real universal in which individual human people participate, and it is what makes them human. Father, Son and Holy Spirit are only not three Gods (tritheism) if their common substance—divinity—is conceived as somehow more real and "higher" than the individual persons that they are. Not everyone agrees with Plato's theory of the forms. In their own day, however, the Cappadocians could assume that it made sense to most people.

The second thing that must be said about Basil's distinction between substance and subsistence, or "person" *(hypostasis)*, is that modern-day people must understand that neither Basil nor the two Gregories thought of the latter concept individualistically. This point cannot be stressed enough. If a modern reader approaches this distinction with the modern, Western mindset that to be a "person" is to be an individual "self" in the sense of being self-actualized over against other persons, the tritheistic implications cannot be avoided. While the English word *person* is normally used to translate *hypostasis* in this context, it is not really a perfect translation because of the cultural baggage it carries. To the ancients—as to many people in non-Western cultures today—*person* did not mean "individual, self-actualized center of free will and conscious activity." *Person* was in some sense individual, but always in community as well. When Basil referred to the Father, Son and Holy Spirit as "three persons" (three *hypostases),* he meant that they are relations within the one Godhead that is an infinite, transcendent and perfectly simple (unified) being. Their community is thought of as in some sense more real than their individuality. That way of thinking is often foreign to modern Western people who tend to elevate individuality over community.

So for Basil, Father, Son and Holy Spirit are not three Gods, because they share equally in divine substance, and that substance is more real than their individualities without in any way detracting from their distinctiveness. For Basil (as for the Gregories) the *hypostases,* or persons of God, are inseparable and indivisible and yet not identical in every way. The main difference is source. The Father has no source. The Son and Spirit find their sources in the Father in different ways.

## The Theologies of the Two Gregories

Basil's great work was taken up by Gregory of Nazianzus and Gregory of Nyssa, each of whom added his own spin to it.[18] Gregory of Nazianzus's explanation of the triunity of God falls very much into line with Basil's. Like the latter Cappadocian father, Nazianzen strongly opposed all the various heresies that denied or distorted the essential oneness or personal threeness of Father, Son and Holy Spirit: subordinationism (Arian, semi-Arian, Eunomian, pneumatomachian), tritheism and Sabellianism. Like Basil he argued that salvation itself depends on there being one divine essence or substance *(ousia)* and three distinct but equal sharers in it *(hypostases).* More than Basil, he drove home with zeal the point that a being is always either God or a creature; there can be no in-between stages if God created all things out of nothing. Also, if a being is eternal, he must be divine (God). Any being that has a beginning in time must be a creature, and if a creature, different only in degree from other creatures. Thus if either the Son or the Spirit began to be in time, he is creaturely and therefore in the same "rank" with humans (even if existing before them) and therefore unable to save, for "if He is in the same rank with myself," Gregory asked, "how can He make me God, or join me with Godhead?"[19]

*Gregory of Nazianzus.* Together with Basil, Gregory of Nazianzus explained the three-in-oneness of God by using the concepts *ousia* (substance) and *hypostasis* (subsistence or person). While all three *hypostases* are consubstantial *(homoousios),* they are not identical. Gregory used a social analogy to explain this: just as Adam, Eve and

Seth (the first three humans) were one human family and shared the exact same nature and yet were three distinct identities, so Father, Son and Holy Spirit constitute one divine family sharing the same glory and essence and yet are distinct persons. Gregory concluded this sermon illustration with "Well, then, here it is an acknowledged fact that different persons may have the same substance."[20] Of course, this social analogy—used also by Basil and Gregory of Nyssa in their own ways—has come under severe criticism from heretics and orthodox theologians alike. Especially Western (Catholic and Protestant) theologians have tended to wince at it. The Cappadocians would respond that it is, after all, only an analogy and point out as well that it depends for its conceptual viability on a Platonic understanding of the reality of universals such as "humanity" and "deity."

But the real contribution of Gregory of Nazianzus to trinitarian thought lies not in his social analogy or use of *ousia* and *hypostases* but in his explanation of the latter—usually translated into English as "persons"—as relations. Within the Trinity itself, Gregory explained, there are not "three beings" but "three relations," and relations are neither substances (beings) nor merely actions (modes of activity).

The Eunomians and other heretics had posed this dilemma to the trinitarians: a reality is either a substance (being) or an action (event, mode of activity), and if the three in God are the former, then tritheism follows; and if the three in God are the latter, then Sabellianism is true. The Cappadocians rejected this dilemma, and especially Gregory of Nazianzus sought to provide a way out of it by explaining that a *hypostasis* (subsistence, person) is not necessarily either a substance or merely an activity. In God it designates a relation. Thus Gregory gave ontological status to relations. The Father's unique identity within the one divine being is his relatedness to Son and Holy Spirit as their begetter and source of procession. The Son's unique identity is as the one who is eternally generated from the Father as his express image and agent. The Holy Spirit's unique identity is as the one who eternally proceeds from the Father as his wisdom and power.

To those opponents who objected that these relations are not fully comprehensible, Gregory responded with exasperation: "What then is Procession? Do you tell me what is the Unbegottenness of the Father, and I will explain to you the physiology of the Generation of the Son and the Procession of the Spirit, and we shall both of us be frenzy-stricken for prying into the mystery of God!"[21] In other words, Gregory was saying, "There is a mystery here, you fool!" And he was implying that even the heretics could not explain all the mysteries of God, and so they should not have been blaming him or the other trinitarians for not being able perfectly to explain what the relations within the Godhead are.

Gregory's concept of *hypostasis* as relation became part of the common stock of ideas within the Eastern church's theology of the Trinity and appeared occasionally in the Latin West as well. While it may not be possible fully to conceive of a relation as a reality on the same level as a being (substance) or even an action (event), Gregory's great contribution was to introduce into the stream of Christian thought that very idea—the ontological reality of relationships. The three persons of God, then, are not to be understood as individual *selves,* as independent centers of consciousness and will (which would amount to a "committee analogy"), but rather as real interdependent relationships within one community of being and substance. Thus for Gregory, "the characteristic of the Father is that of not being begotten; . . . that of the Son is being begotten; . . . and that of the Spirit is procession. . . . With these terms, Gregory gave further meaning to the characteristic formula of the three Cappadocians: one *ousia* and three *hypostases.*"[22]

Gregory of Nazianzus's other main distinctive contribution to theology lay in his opposition to the new teaching about Jesus Christ presented by a fellow trinitarian theologian named Apollinarius. Apollinarius, who was bishop of Laodicea, was greatly influenced by Athanasius and like him vehemently rejected all forms of subordinationism, especially of the Son. He tended to trace all of the various forms of Arianism back to the Antiochene heresy of adoptionism, and in contrast to it he wanted very much to emphasize the real deity of Jesus Christ and of the Son of God who became incarnate in him. Apollinarius set out to explain to his contemporaries, shortly before the Council of Constantinople, how it is that Jesus Christ could be both *truly human* and *truly divine*—consubstantial *(homoousios)* with both God and humans. His explanation was heavily dependent on and reminiscent of Athanasius's in *On the Incarnation of the Word.* Apollinarius's opponents such as Gregory of Nazianzus, however, did not seem to notice this connection.

Apollinarius's view of the incarnation of the Son of God in Jesus Christ has been labeled Apollinarianism. It could just as well be labeled Athanasianism and probably had its true beginning in Origen's Christology. The basic idea is that human persons are composed of three distinct and even separable aspects: body, soul and rational soul, or spirit. This tripartite composition of humanity is borrowed more from Platonic philosophy than from Scripture, even though the New Testament does refer to all three aspects.

The especially Platonic nature of Apollinarius's anthropology appears in his identification of the body or physical nature as the lower nature and his identification of the rational soul or spirit as the higher nature. The soul is the animating life force that exists in nonhuman creatures as well as in humans. It is part of the lower nature. According to Apollinarius, Jesus Christ was divine in that the eternal

Logos—Son of God—took the place of a rational soul in him. His body and animating soul (life force) were human, but his spirit (mind, consciousness) was not. It was divine. The impression given by this Christology, of course, is of "God in a bod"—an omniscient being inhabiting a creaturely body and using it as a vehicle without actually becoming human and experiencing human limitations and sufferings. Of course, that was one of Apollinarius's motives—to show how Jesus Christ could be God (immutable, impassible, omniscient) and human (limited, finite, suffering, mortal) at the same time. He did not, however, think he was inventing any new idea. He thought he was just packaging Origen's and Athanasius's Christologies in a better way. He might have been right.

In any case, Apollinarius's Christology was catching on among both trinitarians and heretics of all kinds. It could "work" whether one believed the Son of God who dwelled in Jesus Christ as his rational soul was eternal God or created demigod. Gregory of Nazianzus began a campaign of letters and sermons against Apollinarius and the Apollinarian teaching. He wanted it condemned as heresy at the Council of Constantinople, and he got his way. The reason he so vigorously and uncompromisingly opposed it was that he saw it as undermining salvation. Gregory frequently used the term *theosis* (divinization or deification) for the process of salvation and, like Athanasius, considered salvation a process of grace transforming humans into partial participants in the divine nature through the "wonderful exchange" of the incarnation. In other words, for Gregory the Son of God came "in order that I too might be made God so far as He is made Man."[23]

Of course, as explained earlier the idea of salvation as *theosis,* or divinization, in Eastern Christian thought never means that humans can actually cross the divine-creature divide. Even Gregory did not think that humans can actually "become God" in exactly the same way that the Logos (or Son of God) is God. However, he did seem to believe that the ultimate goal of our salvation and reason for the incarnation is to bring humans to the same status as the *humanity* of Jesus Christ. His humanity—as Irenaeus had explained long before Gregory wrote—is the very same humanity that Adam had and that bore the image of God and was destined to share in God's glory in a creaturely way. Christ restored that lost potential, and that is what Scripture means when it describes him as the "first born among many brothers" and our example and when Paul explains in 1 Corinthians 15 that we will be like him in the resurrection.

So for Gregory, if Jesus Christ's humanity was not complete humanity, then our human nature cannot be wholly saved through it. The way Gregory expressed this was by the formula "What has not been assumed has not been healed."[24] In other words, if Jesus' humanity was not a whole human nature—body, soul and spirit—then the "wonderful exchange" could not work. The divine Son of God had to have joined his divine nature with a whole human nature—everything essential to being human—in order to heal or restore it. That part that was not human in him would not be healed in us. For Gregory, then, Apollinarianism undermined salvation itself and had to be rejected. What he did not seem to notice was that in rejecting it he was implicitly rejecting Athanasius's Christology.

Gregory's Christology won against the Apollinarian view at the Council of Constantinople. The orthodox view is well expressed by Nazianzen in his *Fourth Theological Oration:*

> So He [Jesus Christ] is called Man, not only that through His Body He may be apprehended by embodied creatures, whereas otherwise this would be impossible because of His incomprehensible nature; but also that by Himself He may sanctify humanity, and be as it were a leaven to the whole lump; and by uniting to Himself that which was condemned may release it from all condemnation, becoming for all men all things that we are, except sin, —body, soul, mind and all through which death reaches—and thus He became Man, who is the combination of all these.[25]

In order to save humanity, then, Jesus Christ has to be truly human, possessing all essential aspects of a human being, including a human mind and soul, and truly divine, possessing divine nature equal with God the Father's own being. Even Christians who do not accept the divinization idea of salvation or the "wonderful exchange" concept of the incarnation (including most Protestants) sympathize with Gregory's strong affirmation of Jesus' complete humanity and true divinity. How else could he provide sacrifice for sins and at the same time be our example in identification with us?

*Gregory of Nyssa.* Gregory of Nyssa's theology begins and ends and is entirely surrounded by a mystical sense of the utter incomprehensibility of God. More than any of the other Cappadocian fathers, Gregory was captivated by the majesty and otherness of the divine essence. Some scholars see in this emphasis an influence of Neo-Platonism, the popular and highly abstract philosophy stemming out of Alexandria that stressed the absolute oneness and infinite beyondness of the eternal divine source and origin of all things.

This influence of Neo-Platonism appears in several of Gregory's distinctive teachings. For example, Gregory argued that God's essence is so transcendent and incomprehensible that the only way in which humans can even begin to describe it is negatively—by declaring what it is *not* God's nature or essence is utterly mysterious—but we can at least describe it by stripping away improper creaturely characteristics. Thus God's essence is infinite (not limited), impassible (incapable of suffering), incomprehensible (not able to be defined).

This is known in the history of theology as "negative theology" and came to have a great deal of influence on later theologians both East and West. Mystics especially tended to revel in it. Others were often dissatisfied with it because it seems to imply a distant God with whom it would be difficult to have any kind of reasonable relationship. One could truly know such a God only by losing oneself in mystical experience. Gregory, however, did not reject rational discussion of God based on revelation so long as it did not destroy mystery.

Another aspect of Gregory's theology that may reflect influence by Neo-Platonism is his explanation of evil as the privation of goodness. According to Gregory and Neo-Platonic philosophy, the source of all evil in the world is not God (or in Neo-Platonism "the One") but humans' misuse of free will in turning away from spiritual toward material things. But evil is not a substance or even matter. It is the absence or lack of goodness, which is an aspect of being itself. God is the fullness of being and therefore perfectly good. God is perfectly good and therefore the fullness of being. Being and goodness are inseparable. For Gregory, evil was literally "nothingness"—the emptiness of being and goodness where they were intended to be. Evil is to good as darkness is to light. The influence of Neo-Platonism in this view of evil is clear especially when Gregory went further to equate the absence of the good with the pull of materiality away from spirituality and the drag of matter, multiplicity, change and time on the ascent of the spirit toward God, who is opposite of those things.

Yet Gregory held back from going all the way with Neo-Platonism. The pagan Neo-Platonists such as Plotinus and his followers saw the entire physical world, including bodies, as unconscious emanations of the One (their concept of God) that have gotten so far from their source that they have become a prison for spirits. Gregory did not have such a negative view of physical reality or human bodies.

Gregory's contribution to trinitarian thought lies in his attempt to overcome the charge of tritheism leveled against it by its enemies—both Arians (such as Eunomius) and Sabellians. Like Basil and Gregory Nazianzen, Gregory of Nyssa used the imagery of physical things that share a common nature to illustrate the mystery of the Trinity. One of his analogies does not seem to help his cause very much. That is the famous (or infamous) image of the gold coins.

In his book *On "Not Three Gods": To Ablabius*, Gregory asked the reader to imagine a pile of gold coins. All share the same substance while differing only in one aspect: that they are different instantiations (subsisting things) of that substance: "As, then, the golden staters [a type of coin] are many, but the gold is one, so too those who are exhibited to us severally in the nature of man, as Peter, James, and John, are many, yet the man [humanity] in them is one."[26] Then Gregory delivered the truth about God illustrated by the coins: "The Father is God; the Son is God; and yet by the same proclamation God is One, because no difference either of nature or of operation is contemplated in the Godhead."[27]

But Gregory was perceptive enough to know that his inquirer—someone named Ablabius who suspected the orthodox trinitarian doctrine of tritheism—would object to the illustration and its interpretation. Gregory stated the objection clearly, and it is worth quoting it at length here so that readers may know exactly what it was that Gregory was attempting to answer:

> The argument which you [Ablabius] state is something like this:—Peter, James and John, being in one human nature, are called three men: and there is no absurdity in describing those who are united in nature, if they are more than one, by the plural number of the name derived from their nature. If, then, in the above case, custom admits this . . . how is it that in the case of our statements of the mysteries of the Faith, though confessing the Three Persons, and acknowledging no difference of nature between them, we are in some sense at variance with our confession, when we say that the Godhead of the Father and of the Son and of the Holy Ghost is one and yet forbid men to say "there are three Gods?" The question is, as I said, very difficult to deal with.[28]

Gregory's answer also relies at least somewhat on Neo-Platonic conceptuality about the nature of being as oneness. Not only is being good and goodness being; being is also unity of operation and activity. If God is one being—one substance—and not three Gods, then the three persons *(hypostases)* must always act together in all things, and therein lies the key to the doctrine of the Trinity for Gregory.

According to Gregory, three humans share in the same nature, or essence, and yet at the same time are generally considered three beings because of their separate operations or actions. Peter, James and John are three separate beings not because one is more human than another (the humanity in them is the same Platonic form) but because they act separately and independently. In God, however, all activity is one. Gregory laid down the rule or dictum that orthodox trinitarian theology is to follow in order to avoid falling into tritheism: All operation is common to all three persons of the Godhead.

> In the case of the Divine nature we do not similarly learn that the Father does anything by Himself in which the Son does not work conjointly, or

> again that the Son has any special operation apart from the Holy Spirit; but every operation which extends from God to the Creation, and is named according to our variable conceptions of it, has its origin from the Father, and proceeds through the Son, and is perfected in the Holy Spirit.[29]

Thus, since every activity or operation of God is common to all three persons, we cannot call this "divine and superintending power" three Gods.

Gregory's rule has been adopted by most orthodox theologians of the ancient and medieval church and given the Latin translation *opera trinitatis ad extra indivisa sunt* (operations of the Trinity toward what is outside itself are indivisible). Gregory allowed that the exact modes of the operation may differ. Thus only the Son of God—the second person of the Trinity—actually took a human body and nature in the incarnation, but in this operation he was in no way independent of or separate from the Father and Holy Spirit. The three always act together and never independently. That is what makes them not three Gods in spite of the fact that they are three distinct persons.

Like Gregory of Nazianzus, Nyssa emphasized the persons as *relations* within the community of being that we honor and worship as God. This is where the distinction (not difference or separation) of the three comes into play. Though they are not three Gods, they are three distinct relations to one another. The Father is the eternal cause, ground and source of the Son and Holy Spirit. The Son is the one eternally begotten of the Father, and the Spirit proceeds from the Father eternally.

**The Cappadocians' Legacy**

Although the basic ideas of the Cappadocian fathers helped overcome the various antitrinitarian heresies and were adopted as at least semiofficial orthodoxy by most of the church and had great influence at the Council of Constantinople in 381, they also raised many questions and stirred up some controversy even among orthodox believers. For example, in the Latin West no clear distinction between *ousia* and *hypostasis* was recognized—both were translated into Latin as "substance." It appeared to many in the West, then, as if the Eastern theologians and bishops were reveling in contradiction when they affirmed one *ousia* and three *hypostases.* Careful correspondence and explanation of terms and flexible translation had to occur before many in the Latin-speaking half of the empire could accept the Cappadocians' contribution. Once it became clear to bishops and theologians in Rome and Carthage, for instance, that the Easterners were saying much the same thing as Tertullian long before, they were more ready and willing to accept it.

Another problem with the Cappadocians' trinitarian theology is more general. Throughout centuries of theology many critics have found it simply too ambiguous to accept without further clarification. When examined closely, it seems either that the Cappadocians were affirming God's oneness to the exclusion of real threeness or else affirming God's threeness to the exclusion of real oneness. Their analogies tend to emphasize threeness. Thus they are often treated as the source of the modern "social analogy" of the Trinity that sometimes seems to border on tritheism. But their abstract explanations tend to emphasize oneness. This is especially true of Gregory of Nyssa's principle of the indivisibility of divine operation. How are Father, Son and Holy Spirit truly distinct persons if their operations and activities are indistinguishable? Later theologians who follow the Cappadocians' line of thinking attempt to tidy this problem up just a bit by introducing the idea of "attributions" so that we humans may properly attribute certain operations to one person more than to another. That hardly solves the problem, however.

The main criticism leveled against the Cappadocians, especially by modern Christian theologians, is that they reveled too much in speculation about the immanent Trinity (the inner-trinitarian relations in eternity), while the New Testament restricts itself to the economic Trinity (the three persons active in salvation history). There is some truth to this accusation, but exclusive focus on the economic Trinity can also be a problem. It leaves unanswered the important question about the divine background of this saving activity of three divine persons in eternity. The move from the economic Trinity to the immanent Trinity and some limited speculation about it is justified so long as one reconnects the two and in the end returns to God's threefold activity in time and history as meaning something for God as well as for humans.

What does it all mean? Can the seemingly abstruse and speculative doctrine of the Trinity as it developed throughout the fourth century and as it was declared at the Council of Constantinople be made somewhat intelligible for ordinary people who are not scholars? Yes. The basic idea is to distinguish between "whatness" and "whoness"—substance and person—while carefully avoiding commonsense and culturally distorting ideas of what they mean. In his study of the Cappadocian fathers Anthony Meredith states it like this: "A crude paraphrase of this elegant expression [the Cappadocian doctrine of the Trinity] might read 'In Christ there are two "whats" and one "who"; in God there are three "whos" and one "what." ' "[30] In other words, the key to unlocking—but not destroying—the mystery of both the Trinity and the person of Jesus Christ is the distinction between whatness and whoness. Three "whos" can be one "what" so long as they are inseparable and function together. Two "whats" can exist in one "who" (Jesus Christ) so long as they are intimately united wholely and inseparably in him. But that is the topic of part four.

### The Council of Constantinople

The Council of Constantinople crowned the efforts of Athanasius and the Cappadocians by once and for all condemning all types of subordinationism and Sabellianism (modalism) and rewriting the Nicene Creed so that it included a "third article" about the Holy Spirit and the church. The complete Niceno-Constantinopolitan Creed—usually known simply as the Nicene Creed—says:

> *We believe* in one God
> the Father, *the Almighty,*
> maker of heaven and earth,
> of *all that is,* seen and unseen.
> *We believe* in one Lord, Jesus Christ,
> the *only* Son of God,
> *eternally* begotten of the Father,
> God from God, Light from Light,
> true God from true God,
> begotten, not made,
> *of one Being* with the Father.
> Through him all things were made.
> For us men and for our salvation
> he came down from heaven;
> *by the power of the Holy Spirit*
> *he became incarnate from the Virgin Mary,*
> and was made man.
> For our sake he was crucified under Pontius Pilate;
> he suffered *death* and was buried.
> On the third day he rose again
> *in accordance with* the Scriptures;
> He ascended into heaven
> and *is seated* at the right hand of the Father.
> He will come again in glory to judge the living and the dead,
> and his kingdom will have no end.
> *We believe* in the Holy Spirit,
> the Lord, the giver of life,

who proceeds from the Father *(and the Son).*
With the Father and the Son he is worshipped and glorified.
He has spoken through the Prophets.
*We believe* in one holy, catholic and apostolic Church.
*We acknowledge* one baptism for the forgiveness of sins.
*We look* for the resurrection of the dead,
and the life of the world to come. Amen.[31]

The Nicene Creed became the basic universal statement of faith binding on all Christian clergy by decree of the emperor Theodosius and was reaffirmed by the fourth ecumenical council at Chalcedon in 451. Other creeds and confessions of faith were written later, but all of them in the Orthodox, Catholic and magisterial, or mainline, Protestant traditions are meant to be elaborations and interpretations of this one. It is the universal creed of Christendom.

# PART IV

# Another Crisis Shakes the Church

## *The Conflict over the Person of Christ*

*The Council of Constantinople declared in 381 that true Christian orthodoxy* necessarily includes belief that Jesus Christ was and is both truly God and truly human—consubstantial with both God the Father and humans. For all practical purposes the debate over the Trinity ended there. From that second ecumenical council on, all Christians were expected to believe and confess God as a single divine being eternally existing as three distinct subsistences or persons. Although various kinds of Arians and Sabellians remained on the fringes of Christendom for a long time, the Great Church catholic and orthodox considered the matter settled. No one who dared question the equal divine dignity and glory of the three persons as one being had any serious chance of being a church leader or even priest or deacon within its ranks. Several Arian missionaries traveled to the so-called barbarian tribes of central Europe and evangelized them for Arian Christianity, and when some of those tribes contributed to the fall of the Roman Empire, Arianism reappeared in the centers of power—especially Rome and other places in the West. Eventually the victorious barbarians converted to orthodox, catholic Christianity, however, and Arianism died out until modern times.

The settlement of the great trinitarian debate and the establishment of the equality of the three persons did not, however, resolve certain other doctrinal questions and problems. As we saw in the last chapter, even at the Council of Constantinople there were rumblings of a new controversy arising among leading bishops and theologians of the Eastern churches. Apollinarius's teaching about the incarnation was condemned even though he clearly believed in the Trinity, and many Christians within the Alexandrian sphere of influence felt his condemnation was unjust. The bishop of Laodicea's father had been born and raised in Alexandria and he considered his own roots there even though Apollinarius himself lived near Antioch and lectured on theology in that city. Many in Antioch were so horrified by his way of explaining the incarnation—how Jesus Christ was both God and human—that they began investigating other Alexandrian theologians to see if others believed and taught similarly. Alexandrians, in turn, began to watch and listen to Antiochene theologians to see if the old heresy of adoptionism that was taught by Paul of Samosata in the middle of the third century was again rearing its ugly head.

Soon the bishops and theologians of Alexandria and Antioch and their followers throughout the empire were at one another's theological throats over the nature of the God-man, Jesus Christ. All agreed that Jesus Christ was God incarnate. The confession itself was not in debate. The question now—after the Council of Constantinople—became, How should Christians explain and express Jesus Christ's humanity and divinity? Are there ways of explaining it that are heretical because they actually undermine its truth? In other words, the problem surrounding this mystery was somewhat like the problem of the mystery of the Trinity in that Sabellians, for example, claimed to believe in the Trinity but expressed it through the language and imagery of modalism. The church decided that merely *saying* you believed in the Trinity was not good enough if the way in which you explained it to your congregation or catechetical students actually amounted to its denial.

It is easy to wish that the leaders of Christianity in the late fourth and early fifth centuries had all taken deep breaths and stepped back from the brink of all-out theological warfare and simply allowed one another to explain the mystery of Jesus' humanity and divinity in different ways. But the problem with this wish and the criticism implied in it is that some of the ways even leading bishops and patriarchs explained the incarnation of God in Christ amounted to denials of the mystery. Again, as with the leading defenders and promoters of the orthodox doctrine of the Trinity, the main orthodox bishops and theologians involved in the christological controversy were concerned to protect and preserve the mystery of the person of Jesus Christ against explanations that overrationalized it and explained it away. The champions of the doctrine known as the hypostatic union, which became the orthodox doctrine of the person of Christ at the Council of Chalcedon in 451, were defenders of mystery, not rationalists peering into mysteries better left alone in order to figure them out and make them rationally intelligible to human thinking. That is a popular caricature and is simply wrong.

At times the great controversy over the person of Jesus Christ did become highly technical and hairsplitting. That was probably inevitable given the complexity of the problem. It helps to have some patience with the terminology and concepts of the argument if one remembers that all involved were actually concerned with salvation. As in the case of the great trinitarian controversy, what they all saw as at stake was human salvation itself. If Jesus Christ was not both truly God (equal with the Father) and truly human (equal with us), then how could he save us? How could someone less than divine and other than human bridge the gap and bring the two together in reconciliation and saving union? That was the common core concern of all the fathers embroiled in this controversy. Sometimes their formulations and arguments seem very abstruse and speculative—even hairsplitting wrangles over semantics—but their concern was laudable and sound. It was to explain as far as possible for human minds what Christians mean when they confess the man Jesus to be both God and human at the same time in order to protect the gospel of salvation.

The unfortunate aspect of this great conflict and controversy is that it at times fell into dishonest intrigue with bishops spying on one another and monks threatening one another and churchmen actually lying to and about each other. The truly troubling aspect of this episode of the story of theology is not subtlety. One can learn to live with ambiguity and abstract language. Harder to accept is Christian bishops and theologians using theology to jockey for power and influence and using unethical means to do it. Not all involved in the christological controversy were guilty of that, but perhaps for the first time, some of it appears on all sides. Politics and theology became tangled with one another in a way never seen or anticipated before. God works in mysterious ways, however, and most Christians of all stripes believe that the eventual outcome of the controversy was a victory for truth, even if that truth remained something of a mystery.

As with the trinitarian controversy, the christological controversy had two great ecumenical councils as its "bookends." But unlike the other controversy, this one has an ecumenical council at its center as well. Three great ecumenical councils stand as transitions within this part of our story: the Council of Constantinople in 381, where the episode began; the Council of Ephesus in 431—the third ecumenical council—where the episode took a turn; and the Council of Chalcedon in 451, where it arrived at its denouement.

Chalcedon is considered the fourth ecumenical council of Christendom, and it produced a doctrinal "definition"—sometimes thought of as another creed—that declared the official dogma of the person of Jesus Christ. That dogma is known as the "hypostatic union." This chapter is the story of how the church came to carve out and declare that dogma and of the Chalcedonian Definition that expresses it as binding on all Christians. At the end of this section we will see that even though the Great Church considered the matter settled at Chalcedon in 451, various groups of Christians refused to accept it and continued to protest and appeal it. The catholic and orthodox church's response to that led it deeper and deeper into theological speculation about the person of Christ, and whereas many Protestants can and do follow the thinking of the church up to and through Chalcedon and its hypostatic-union doctrine, they stop there and do not consider the pronouncements that followed binding. That is to say, when even conservative Protestants look back on the processes of defining true doctrine in the early centuries of Christianity, most of them are not impressed with what goes under the label *orthodox* after Chalcedon. We will see why that is the case toward the end of this section and in the next one.

As with all great conflicts and controversies, finding the exact roots and causes of the christological controversy of the late fourth and early fifth centuries is exceedingly difficult. One can keep tracing causes and influences backward into almost an infinite regress. In order to explain it we will simply have to jump in midstream and begin with one major factor—the long-lasting and very deep-seated theological differences between two great cities of Eastern Christianity and the theologians that looked to them as their fountains of wisdom. They are Alexandria and Antioch. The first portion of the present episode of the story of Christian theology will begin with the rivalry between these two cities and show how it laid the foundation for the christological debate.

# CHAPTER 13

# The Schools of Antioch & Alexandria Clash over Christ

B*oth Antioch and Alexandria were ancient and venerable centers of Greek* and Roman culture as well as of Christian theology and church life. Alexandria was named after Alexander the Great and in the time of Christ was a thriving cosmopolitan center of education, culture, trade and commerce. At times it rivaled Rome as the cultural headquarters of the empire. Its stockpile of gold and grain was greater than Rome's and its great library and museum served as the centers of an early university where philosophers and religious scholars from far-flung parts of the world rubbed shoulders. Alexandria was the envy of many other cities and itself was envious of Constantinople, the new upstart capital of the empire under Constantine and his heirs. It wanted to dominate Constantinople because that was where the emperor and his court were headquartered. Whoever was the bishop of Constantinople (sometimes also known by its ancient name Byzantium) would automatically have a special influence over the rest of Christendom by virtue of proximity to the imperial court. Alexandrian leaders knew that their rivals in the other major Eastern city—Antioch—wanted to dominate the church of Constantinople. Long before the christological controversy brought matters to a head between the Christian leaders of the two cities, they were eyeing one another suspiciously for political reasons.

Antioch was not nearly as large or influential as Alexandria in the great scheme of things. However, it also had an ancient and venerable heritage both culturally and theologically. It was founded by one of Alexander's generals, Antiochus Epiphanes, and in the time of Christ and the apostles was a great center of trade and commerce. The Roman governor of Antioch ruled over Syria, the Roman territory that included Palestine. Christians were first called that in Antioch, and from that city's early Christian community, Paul's Gentile mission began and continued. For first-century Christians, Antioch was much more important than Alexandria. The focus of theological brilliance and creativity shifted to the latter city in the second and third centuries. Antioch also looked to the new imperial city of Constantinople—the "new Rome"—as a place to regain influence and power. Constantinople had no great ancient heritage and its Christian church was fairly new and relatively weak until Constantine began inviting Christian leaders there in the fourth century. In a sense, it represented a "mission field" for other churches—not so much in terms of evangelism as in terms of a power vacuum to be filled.

It sounds crude when put this way, but there can be no getting around the fact that both Antioch and Alexandria looked hungrily to Constantinople and sought to have their "favorite sons" rise to high positions as chaplains, presbyters, deacons and even as bishop—patriarch of Constantinople—in order to enhance their own city's reputation and influence and in order that their own distinctive brand of theology might be promoted. And their own brands of theology differed significantly.

**Differing Biblical Hermeneutics**

One major difference between Alexandrian and Antiochene theologies revolved around hermeneutics (biblical interpretation). The Alexandrian pattern had been established in the time of Christ by the Jewish theologian and biblical scholar Philo, who believed that the literal and historical references of the Hebrew Scriptures were of the least importance. He sought to discover and explicate the biblical narratives' allegorical or spiritual meaning. In other words, many passages of the Hebrew Bible seemed to be about one thing, while—according to Philo—they really referred to something else. As a person seeking to integrate Hebrew religion with Greek (especially Platonic) philosophy, Philo could not take literally much of what he read in the Prophets. He believed that through allegorical interpretation he could demonstrate the underlying unity of Greek ethical and philosophical thinking with Hebrew religion. Many early Christian thinkers borrowed their hermeneutical strategies from Philo, and that was nowhere truer than in Alexandria itself. Clement and Origen both sought to dig down through the various layers of meaning in the Bible to discover its hidden gems of spiritual truth separated from the crude literal and historical narratives and images.

When Alexandrian Christian scholars—whether living in Alexandria or elsewhere—read the Prophets and Apostles, they tended to find hidden references to the Logos and heavenly, spiritual existence everywhere. They could justify this method of interpretation by appealing to the apostle Paul himself. Paul used allegorical interpretation in Galatians when discussing the law and the gospel (Gal 4:21-31). Abraham's servant Hagar is equated with the giving of the law at Mount Sinai and Judaism under domination of law. The gospel to the Gentiles is equated with Abraham's wife Sarah—a free woman—who bore him a son (Isaac) according to promise. The way Paul described all of this is clearly allegory. An Old Testament character corresponds to a spiritual and theological reality in a very direct way so that one gets the impression that such correspondence—and the truth it reveals—is the main purpose of the story in the Old Testament. Alexandrian biblical scholars—both Jewish and Christian—were steeped in such methods of interpretation.

Antioch was noted for its more literal and historical hermeneutical method. Of course the theologians and biblical scholars of Antioch also recognized allegory as one legitimate way of communicating truth, but they tended to resist finding spiritual meanings by claiming that a biblical story is allegorical unless there was some good reason to believe the story was intended as allegory. One notable example of this Antiochene hermeneutical method is the great Christian scholar Theodore of Mopsuestia (died 428), who was Antioch's leading biblical commentator and theologian. Theodore wrote many commentaries on Scripture and always shied away from the allegorical interpretation unless clear evidence in the text itself directed him to it. Even the Hebrew book the Song of Songs (popularly known as the Song of Solomon), which is often treated as an allegory of Christ's love for the church even by modern conservative Protestants, was regarded as a literal love poem by Theodore. He saw no reason to interpret it allegorically. Theodore allowed that many Old Testament characters and events could be interpreted by Christians as types of Christ and the church, but he refused to impose New Testament or Greek philosophical meanings as the main references on narratives that clearly were describing historical events.

Thus Alexandrian and Antiochene theologies diverged at their very roots—biblical interpretation. The Antiochene historical-literal-grammatical method is the more influential one in modern, Western Christianity, whereas the Alexandrian allegorical-spiritual method tended to dominate much early Christian thinking and remained a powerful influence throughout the Middle Ages in both the East and the West. The differing mindsets regarding Scripture and its meaning set the stage for christological conflict as we will see. Alexandria tended to emphasize the divinity of Jesus as a spiritual gem hidden within the shell of his humanity. Docetism—denial of Christ's true humanity—lurked in the background of Alexandrian theology and was a constant danger in both its biblical scholarship and its Christology. The physical, historical, creaturely dimensions of both Scripture and the incarnation were scandals to many Alexandrians and they sought ways to minimize them without demonizing them as the Gnostics had.

The Antiochenes faced their own dangers. So captivated were they by the historical, literal realities of both the revelation in Scripture and in Jesus Christ that they had trouble doing full justice to the divinity of each. Of course, they *confessed* the divine inspiration of Scripture and the divinity of Christ. But they tended to minimize the spiritual and divine aspects of these mysteries without denying them, as Paul of Samosata had. How these two cities' approaches to biblical interpretation influenced their Christologies will become clearer as we explore that subject more directly.

### Diverging Soteriologies

A second difference between Alexandrian and Antiochene theologies had to do with soteriology—their views of salvation. Alexandrian soteriology was especially enamored with the traditional Eastern deification view of the process and ultimate goal of salvation. That is not to say Antiochenes rejected it, but the Alexandrian theologians placed it at the forefront and center of all their theological musings. Their basic approach to the person of Jesus Christ was colored by this prior commitment, as we have already seen with Origen and Athanasius. According to one leading modern scholar of Alexandrian thought, "Their fundamental thought, as their soteriological ideas are carried over into Christology, is that if our nature is to be filled with the divine life, the divine Logos must so unite it to himself, and make it his own, that in him is effected a real unification . . . of Godhead and manhood."[1] Thus Alexandrian thought about salvation emphasized the necessity of intimate unity of divine and human in Christ such that human nature can be transformed by the divine. At the same time, the Alexandrian emphasis on God's transcendence (otherness) and especially his immutability and impassibility required that this union of divinity and humanity not infect the divine nature with corruptions of creatureliness. Therein lay the problem. The typical Alexandrian approach was to say that in Jesus Christ a "wonderful exchange" took place so that our fallen human nature was healed by the perfect divine nature of the Logos in such a way that the Logos's divine nature was untouched by creaturely limitations or imperfections.

The Antiochene approach to soteriology was not entirely different from the Alexandrian approach. Both agreed that one major aspect of salvation involves deification or divinization—healing human nature so that it shares in some of the divine aspects or characteristics such as immortality. They also agreed on the essential difference between human and divine natures. Both Alexandrians and Antiochenes firmly rejected any idea of a "metamorphosis" of the human into divinity or of the divine into humanity. However, the Antiochenes were much more concerned than were the Alexandrians with the human role in salvation. While Alexandrians would affirm that the human person needs to receive God's healing power through the sacraments by free choice, the Antiochenes drew that all-important role of human free choice in salvation right back into the incarnation itself. The humanity of Jesus had to have free moral agency in order to achieve salvation for us.

One way of describing this difference is to say that the Alexandrian soteriology was more metaphysical and the Antiochene soteriology was more moral-ethical. Both drew in aspects of the other emphasis, but each one fell into a kind of obsessiveness with its own distinctive and blamed the other school of theology for neglecting it. Alexandrians saw salvation as a wonderful metaphysical mystery wrought by the Logos through union with humanity in Jesus Christ. Antiochenes saw salvation as a wonderful moral-ethical accomplishment wrought by a human being on our behalf through uniting his will with that of the divine Logos. Of course, at least after Paul of Samosata's adoptionism was declared a heresy, all the Antiochenes would affirm very strongly that the actual accomplishment of our salvation was a work of the Son of God in and through the man Jesus. But they especially wanted to make clear that this could not have happened without the will and mind of the man being wholly human and playing a role in the process. The humanity of Jesus Christ could not be conceived as a passive instrument, the Antiochenes never tired of arguing. If it was, then our human minds and wills are left without an exemplar to show us the way to please God and enter into that saving union with him by which we are healed.

## Two Approaches to Christology

These two modes of thinking about Scripture and salvation resulted in sometimes widely and wildly divergent ways of conceiving of the person of Jesus Christ. We have already seen how Athanasius understood the divinity and humanity of Christ. For him as for many other Alexandrians, the human nature *(ousia, physis)* of Christ was passive and impersonal. It was a vehicle—almost nothing more than an animal shell, as it were—for the use of the Son of God. It had to be real, but it did not have to have its own center of consciousness and will distinct from the Son of God's. Athanasius's and other Alexandrians' typical way of speaking about the incarnation and the unity of God and humanity in Christ is sometimes referred to as the Word-flesh Christology. That is, the Logos (Word) of God took on human flesh without actually entering into human existence in its fullness. The humanity of Jesus Christ was "flesh"—body and soul. Apollinarius put the finishing touches on that Christology by denying any active human intellect and will in Jesus Christ.

The Antiochenes were horrified by this Word-flesh Christology of Alexandria and regarded it as just as serious a heresy as the adoptionism of Paul of Samosata that had been so soundly condemned. The leading Antiochene theologians contemporary with Athanasius and Apollinarius were Eustathius of Antioch, Diodore of Tarsus and Theodore of Mopsuestia. All three of them emphasized the humanity of Jesus Christ and accused the Alexandrians of truncating it. Over against the Alexandrian Word-flesh Christology, they developed what has come to be called a Word-man Christology in which the humanity of Jesus Christ was not passive but active and was a whole and complete human person. Instead of emphasizing the unity of the divine and human in Jesus Christ, the Antiochenes emphasized the distinction of the two natures *(physes)* in him. This was both to protect the holy otherness of the Logos's divine nature over against everything creaturely and to emphasize the integrity of the human nature as able to obey God actively and not passively as a mere instrument. Diodore of Tarsus went so far as to talk about Jesus Christ as "two sons"—the Son of God and the Son of David.[2]

The Alexandrians were appalled at Diodore's Christology because to them it sounded so much like the old adoptionist heresy that had thrived in Antioch years earlier. It seemed to them a frank denial of the real, ontological union of God and humanity in Jesus Christ. How are we saved if divine and human natures have not become one nature in him? they asked. The Antiochenes argued back that if Jesus Christ was one nature and not two, then how was he "truly divine" and "truly human"—consubstantial with both God and humanity? God's being is one thing—completely different from any created being. It is eternal and not temporal. It is immutable and not changing. Human being is a form of created being. Even when redeemed it is not divine. It shares in divinity by becoming immortal. The deadly wound of sin and death is healed, but even completely redeemed saints in heaven are still creatures and not God. So, the Antiochenes argued, how can humanity and divinity become "one nature"? That would be not only a mystery but also a denial of fundamental Christian beliefs about God and salvation.

At the heart of this disagreement over Word-flesh versus Word-man Christologies lay differing views of salvation. According to the Alexandrian view, full salvation depends on a real incarnation but not on a full and true human nature exactly like ours. Above all, it did not have to have its own independent center of intellect, action and will. The humanity of Jesus Christ could be and was an impersonal human nature. According to the Antiochene view, full salvation depends on a real incarnation but not on an intimate union of humanity and divinity that would threaten their real distinction, and the real incarnation must include a fully personal human nature. Jesus Christ had to be a man just like any other man—just like Adam!—although without sin.

> Apollinarius and Cyril, whom we shall take as representing the Alexandrian school of thought, holding that man's salvation amounts to his deification, see that only the very God can save sinners, and, consequently, lay stress on the Christian confession that in Jesus Christ the divine Logos has united man's nature to himself, and made it his own: Jesus Christ is, then, one Person, the Logos himself in his incarnate state. The Antiochenes see the message of the Gospel from another point of view. These understood that if man is to be renewed in that state of obedience to the will of God which spells his salvation, the divine Logos must unite to himself the Man [of Christ], who though tried to the uttermost will succeed where the first Adam failed.[3]

**Apollinarius's "God-in-a-Bod" Heresy**

An excellent example of the early Alexandrian Word-flesh Christology is that of Apollinarius of Laodicea, the unfortunate Christian bishop and theologian so thoroughly criticized and condemned by Gregory of Nazianzus and the Council of Constantinople. His only error, according to orthodox Alexandrians and even Gregory himself, was that he denied the human rational soul *(nous)* of Jesus Christ and replaced it in him with the Logos. Against the Antiochene view, such as that held by Diodore of Tarsus, Apollinarius "was seeking to secure a true Incarnation, as opposed to the idea of a mere connection between the Logos and the man Jesus." The problem was that "he secured this organic unity between the human and the Divine only by a mutilation of the human."[4] The reason that Apollinarius "mutilated" the human in Jesus Christ was soteriological, of course. For him as for most Alexandrians, salvation as deification was only possible if the whole of Christ is thoroughly controlled by the divine will and power. If he had a human rational soul, or mind/spirit, he *might* have sinned and resisted the call of the Logos on his life, and that would imply no true incarnation. Furthermore, if he had a human rational soul, or mind/spirit, there would be two centers of consciousness, action and will in Jesus Christ—one divine and one human—and that is a false or incomplete union of divinity and humanity. Only a true natural union—two natures coming together in one person as one nature—can amount to an incarnation where the divine permeates and heals the human.

Apollinarius's Christology was condemned at the Council of Constantinople not because it included the idea of "one nature of the God-man after the union"—a common Alexandrian idea—but because it denied the whole and complete humanity of the Savior. Gregory of Nazianzus sympathized with the Alexandrian approach but could not allow it to be taken to the extreme to which Apollinarius took it. Thus in his most famous passage against Apollinarius, Gregory wrote:

> If anyone has put trust in Him [Jesus] as a Man without a human mind, he is really bereft of mind, and quite unworthy of salvation. For that which He has not assumed He has not healed; but that which is united to His Godhead is also saved. If only half Adam fell, then that which Christ assumes and saves may be half also; but if the whole of his nature fell, it must be united to the whole nature of Him that was begotten, and so be saved as a whole.[5]

The Council of Constantinople condemned as heretical Apollinarius's Christology without solving the problem to which it pointed. After that council it was necessary for orthodox Christians to agree with the Antiochene view that Jesus Christ had a whole human nature—body, soul and spirit—including a human mind. The Antiochenes such as Theodore of Mopsuestia considered this a great victory. Alexandrians considered it a defeat. They lurked around Constantinople watching and waiting to catch Antiochene theologians repeating the heresy of Paul of Samosata.

### Theodore of Mopsuestia's Dualistic Christology

The greatest early defender of the Antiochene God-man Christology was Theodore of Mopsuestia. He too was condemned as a heretic, but not until the sixth century and only because he was perceived to have been a precursor of another heresy. His fate was similar to Origen's. During his lifetime he was hailed as a great orthodox biblical scholar and theologian, especially in and around Antioch. But because his thinking seems to have led to a heresy, he was condemned as a heretic by a council more than one hundred years after his death.

Theodore's Christology was dominated by three main concerns: the immutability of the Logos, the freedom of the will in Jesus Christ and the reality of Jesus' human life of struggle and achievement. If the Logos is truly God—as orthodoxy teaches and as both the Nicene and Constantinopolitan councils affirmed—then whatever union he entered into with a human being must be a union in which the human changed and the Son of God did not. This cannot be a "natural union" (one nature) because in that case the Son of God would have changed through union with the human nature to form a "third something." Also if the humanity of Jesus Christ did not include a human mind and will *(nous)*, then he did not have free will and his achievement of union with God would not be anything like ours—it would be something static, automatic, and therefore no achievement at all. Finally, if he was not a full human person, then he could not identify with our struggles or be tempted—as he so clearly was. For Theodore, all this adds up to a strong case for God-man or Word-man Christology:

> He [Christ] is not God alone nor man alone, but He is truly both by nature, that is to say God and man: God the Word who assumed, and man who was assumed. The one who assumed is not the same as the one who was assumed nor is the one who was assumed the same as the one who assumed, but the one who assumed is God while the one who was assumed is a man. The one who assumed is by nature that which God the Father is by nature . . . while the one who was assumed is by nature that which David and Abraham, whose son and from whose seed he is, are by nature. This is the reason why He is both Lord and Son of David: Son of David because of his nature, and Lord because of the honour that came to him. And he is high above David his father because of the nature that assumed him.[6]

For Theodore, then, one must distinguish between the "man whom God put on" in the incarnation and the Logos who put on the man. The incarnation is this relationship of assumption of a human person by the Logos and the reciprocal obedience of the human person to the Logos. It is a union of "good pleasure" and of "disposition of will," not of nature or a matter of course. Theodore went to great lengths to emphasize the intimacy of this union, arguing that a more intimate union than the incarnation could not be conceived. He even used the phrase *one person (prosopon)* to describe the union. So closely together do the Son of God and the human person cooperate that their activity together as Jesus Christ cannot really be separated.

Naturally enough, Alexandrians felt that Theodore's explanation of the incarnation amounted to something like adoptionism. He spoke of the divinity of Christ as an "indwelling" of the Logos in the man and of the human person's freedom as a whole person in relation to the Logos. Unlike his predecessor Diodore, Theodore did not speak of "two sons," but he did seem to think of Jesus Christ as a kind of compound person. Alexandrians argued that the only difference between this Christology and Paul of Samosata's was that the latter saw the human person Jesus being assumed into a special relationship with God the Father as his special Son at his baptism. Theodore simply saw the union of a human person and a divine person as beginning at Jesus' conception and growing throughout his lifetime. In both cases, Alexandrians argued, the incarnation amounts to an adoption of a human by God rather than a true "becoming flesh" of a divine person.

As the Council of Constantinople adjourned and the bishops departed for their home sees, the differences and resentments between Alexandria and Antioch were just beginning to boil. An Alexandrian hero—Apollinarius—had been condemned but the basic Word-flesh Christology had not. How it could be developed further without falling into Apollinarius's "God-in-a-bod" heresy was unclear, but soon certain Alexandrians would attempt it. Theodore was firmly ensconced as a great theologian near Antioch, but his Word-man Christology was being quietly undermined and attacked as closet adoptionism by Alexandrians.

The Council of Constantinople had made official the use of terms and concepts like *nature* and *person* for explaining the Trinity. Both Alexandrians and Antiochenes were ready to employ these concepts and terms for their own Christologies. The former would argue more and more vehemently that just as the Trinity is one substance, or nature, and three persons so Jesus Christ is one nature and one person. In him the natures of God and humanity join so intimately that they form a compound or hybrid. The Antiochenes argued that Jesus Christ is two natures and two persons (even though Theodore himself never went that far) who can also be conceived as one person, just as many communities or societies of more than one person are corporate persons in the eyes of the law. When it comes to personhood, Antiochenes averred, two can become one while remaining two.

The stage was set for a theological blowout. Alexandrians were resentful that Apollinarius had been condemned. It seemed that such a decision could eventually lead to their greatest hero, Athanasius, being criticized if not condemned. Antiochenes were self-confident and ready to sweep into ecclesiastical power in Constantinople. They were also overly confident of the security of their greatest theologian, Theodore of Mopsuestia, and his God-man Christology. But they were keeping a wary eye on Alexandria.

The theological blowout came in 428. The orthodox patriarch of Constantinople, a man from Antioch named Nestorius, climbed the steps of the great pulpit in the cathedral and preached a sermon against calling Mary *Theotokos*. That started one of the greatest theological controversies and conflicts in Christian history.

# CHAPTER 14

# Nestorius & Cyril Bring the Controversy to a Head

W*hen visitors attend divine liturgy (worship) at an Eastern Orthodox* church that uses English, they are sometimes surprised and perplexed to read and hear certain words left in Greek. One Greek word heard often throughout the liturgy in all Eastern Orthodox churches is *Theotokos,* and it is clearly a title of the Virgin Mary. What does it mean and why is it left untranslated in Orthodox churches that are attempting to adapt to non-Greek cultures?

*Theotokos* is a highly symbolic relic of an ancient Christian debate and the doctrinal formula arising out of it. Its continued use fifteen hundred years after the debate consumed the attention and energies of Christians all over the Roman Empire reminds Orthodox believers that Christ is God. The title itself means "bearer of God" or "God-bearer." Sometimes *Theotokos* is translated as "mother of God," but that is not the preferred translation. Although both Eastern Orthodox and Roman Catholic traditions highly revere Mary, the *Theotokos* title is really a pointer to belief in Jesus' true divinity. When Mary gave birth to her little boy, she gave birth to God.

This kind of language about both Mary and Jesus was commonplace in Constantinople in the early fifth century. The faithful people of the city frequently spoke of Mary as *Theotokos* in songs and prayers. So it came as a great surprise to many of them when the newly appointed Patriarch Nestorius stood up in the cathedral and ordered them to stop it. Not only were the Christian folk of the city surprised and concerned, the Alexandrian spies were shocked and delighted at the same time. Here was their chance to get back at Antioch for helping arrange the condemnation of Apollinarius. They were going to make Nestorius suffer for the sins of all Antioch!

Little is known about the details of Nestorius's life except that he was born in or around Antioch sometime in the late fourth century and died in exile in the desert of North Africa around 450. He was probably a student of the great Antiochene theologian Theodore of Mopsuestia. At least he was influenced by him. In 428 Emperor Theodosius II, who favored the Antiochene theology over the Alexandrian, elevated Nestorius to the coveted position of bishop of Constantinople, which automatically made him patriarch of the region and honorary pope of the East (just as the bishop of Rome was widely honored as pope of the West). The appointment of Nestorius was a severe blow to Alexandrian dreams of domination. Furthermore, both the emperor and the patriarch tended to persecute any and all Christians in Constantinople who favored the Alexandrian theology. They treated Alexandrian clergy and theologians as if they were closet Apollinarians just waiting to revive that heresy.

There may have been some justification for that. The Alexandrians all insisted on preserving and promoting the Apollinarian formula of Jesus Christ as "one nature *[mia physis]* after the union." That is, Alexandrians readily acknowledged that the Son of God is one kind of being—divine—while the man Jesus Christ was human. But they insisted that due to the incarnation and right from its inception in the womb of Mary, this union of the Son of God with humanity resulted in the creation of a one-natured God-man. They reluctantly acknowledged that he had a human mind and soul, but these they downplayed, preferring to emphasize that he was the Logos in human flesh.

The Antiochene Christology was on the ascendancy in 428 when Antioch's favorite son, Nestorius, occupied the most powerful ecclesiastical position in the Eastern half of the Roman Empire. Back in Alexandria the bishop—also a patriarch due to the importance of the city—was a man named Cyril. Little is known about his birth or early years, but he became bishop of the Egyptian city in 412 and presided over the Christian churches there and in all of Egypt until his death in 444. Cyril is not regarded as one of the great saints of Christian history, although he has never been condemned either. His reputation is somewhat sullied by two factors. First, he almost certainly sent spies to Constantinople to lurk in the shadows of the great cathedral and attempt to catch Nestorius (and anyone else from Antioch) in heresy. He had his eyes on the seat of power occupied by the

Antiochene theologian. Second, Cyril is suspected of being a bridge between two heresies even though his own Christology was basically sound and received affirmation from two great ecumenical councils. The two heresies he seems to have bridged are Apollinarianism before his time and monophysitism afterward. The latter heresy arose after Cyril's death and represented an intense and uncompromising form of his own theology, especially his formula of Christ as "one nature."

On Christmas morning in 428, shortly after he arrived in Constantinople, Nestorius preached his infamous sermon condemning the Marian title *Theotokos.* He told the congregation—many of them visiting clergy and members of the imperial court—that Christians must not refer to Mary as "God-bearer" because it is wrong to give the name "God" to one who was two or three months old. The problem was not veneration of Mary. The problem was, according to Nestorius, confusion of the two different natures of Jesus Christ. Faithfully following Theodore of Mopsuestia's dualistic Christology to its logical conclusion, Nestorius argued that divine nature cannot be born any more than it can die. Divine nature is immutable, impassible, perfect and incorruptible. So, while the human nature of Jesus was born of Mary, the divine nature was not. Nestorius gave the congregation permission to call Mary *Christotokos,* which means "Christ-bearer." While it is theologically correct to say that "Christ was born of a woman," it is not, he averred, orthodox to say that "God was born of a woman."

It is important to carefully understand what Nestorius was saying and what he was not saying. Nestorius was not denying the deity of the Son of God. He was not Arian or subordinationist in any sense. He agreed wholeheartedly with the Nicene trinitarian theology of equal divinity and glory of Father, Son and Holy Spirit. The problem was that he believed so strongly in the divinity of the Logos, or Son of God, that he resisted any attribution to him of creaturely characteristics or experiences. (Arius would have jumped for joy and shouted, "See! This is what I knew would come of denial of the creaturely status of the Logos!") Nestorius also was not denying the virgin birth of Jesus Christ. For him, the Virgin Mary gave birth to the man Jesus Christ, who was from the moment of his conception intimately united with the eternal Logos of God. At first, anyway, he was simply interpreting and applying the classical Antiochene Christology of his mentor, Theodore of Mopsuestia.

It seems likely that Nestorius, also not one of the most beloved Christians of history, was using the *Theotokos* title to punish Alexandrians in Constantinople. They especially loved it. But he considered it crypto-Apollinarian. That is, as Nestorius viewed it, if one affirms Mary as God-bearer, then the one born of her was not fully human. In Nestorius's mind one being cannot be both fully human and fully divine. Like many Antiochenes he thought of these as mutually exclusive realities. And Jesus Christ clearly was and had to be completely human. So to say that Mary gave birth to God is to deny that Jesus Christ was human as the rest of us are human. Nestorius's motives in condemning the phrase were probably as mixed as Cyril's were in sending spies to Constantinople to catch him in heresy. Both were probably convinced that the distinctive approaches of their cities to the doctrine of Christ were correct and intimately linked to the gospel itself. To them and their cohorts, this was a battle for the gospel and for the true doctrine of Jesus Christ. But both were probably equally guilty of mixing that purely theological motive with impure political motives. Nestorius wanted to root out of Constantinople every vestige and remnant of Alexandrian influence. Cyril wanted to vindicate Alexandrian theology by delivering a body blow to Antiochene prestige equal to the blow to his own city's reputation delivered by Apollinarius's condemnation.

Nestorius wrote his arguments against *Theotokos* in his circular Easter letter in 429. That made it official. The patriarch of Constantinople now considered reference to Mary as *Theotokos* a heresy. The shadow of the emperor behind Nestorius made this especially fearful to Alexandrians and others, and Cyril saw his chance to pounce. At his direction two things began to happen.

First, Alexandrian agents in Constantinople began to set up anonymous placards around the city near churches juxtaposing phrases from Nestorius with sayings of the Antiochene heretic Paul of Samosata, whose adoptionist heresy had been condemned almost two hundred years earlier. Cyril considered Nestorius's Christology a sophisticated form of adoptionism, just as Nestorius considered Alexandrian Christology a sophisticated form of Apollinarianism. The placards drew attention, and people in Constantinople began to gossip about Nestorius's flawed orthodoxy.

The second thing that happened was a vigorous correspondence between Cyril and Nestorius and other bishops around the Roman Empire. Cyril wrote several letters to Nestorius, and Nestorius responded, explaining rather pointedly his Antiochene approach to the person of Jesus Christ. Cyril's letters to Nestorius were more cautious and strictly avoided extreme terms of Apollinarian Christology. Cyril acknowledged a human rational soul in Jesus Christ while at the same time continuing to affirm and argue for the union of God and humanity in Christ as "one nature." Nestorius insisted on the union as one of "two natures."

Neither Cyril nor Nestorius produced great classics of Christian theology. Most of what they wrote were lengthy epistles, and their writings and arguments seem quite muddled. Ambiguity plagues their formulations, and scholars of this dispute have argued endlessly over what each meant by key terms and whether perhaps they were actually saying the same things but with different words and phrases. Was it all just a big misunderstanding? a semantic wrangle? Without any doubt there was some of that. While their followers were probably more extreme, Nestorius and Cyril might have converged in their thinking given sufficient time. The official orthodox doctrine of the person of Christ is a kind of compromise between their two views that was carved out after their deaths. But there is no denying that they thought differently about certain absolutely crucial aspects of the incarnation. The difference between them cannot be reduced entirely to a verbal muddle.

Complicating interpretation of Cyril and Nestorius is the fact that their thinking developed and changed over time. Nestorius's only known book—*The Book of Heraclides*—was an apology for his theology written after he was deposed and exiled. It seems that he changed some of his views to cast them in a more favorable light. Some scholars argue that the book proves he did not even really hold or teach the heresy named after him—Nestorianism. More likely is that he changed his position in order to restore his reputation. Cyril's main works in Christology are letters to Nestorius, and some change and development can be seen in them. So it is difficult to pin down exactly what either patriarch believed and taught. Nevertheless, in spite of all uncertainty and ambiguity, there are certain generally acknowledged themes that can be labeled typical of Cyril and Nestorius. It is on them that we will concentrate without a great deal of discussion of details.

Nestorius's Christology may best be viewed as an attempt to carry Theodore of Mopsuestia's Christology to its logical conclusion. Ever since Paul of Samosata and the more orthodox Lucian of Antioch, Antiochene theologians had emphasized the humanity of Jesus Christ while attempting to do justice to his divinity as well. Nestorius was faced with the challenge of Cyril and his followers: "How can you say that Jesus Christ is consubstantial *(homoousios)* with God and with humans if you say that he was completely human?" His own challenge to Cyril and the Alexandrians was to ask, "How can you say that Jesus Christ is both truly God and truly human if you deny that he was the union of two different natures?" Nestorius tried to carve out a way of explaining Jesus' real humanity and real divinity that would preserve the natural integrity of both realities in him. He could not conceive of a human nature *(physis)* without a person *(prosopon)* attached to it. A basic axiom of Nestorius's thought was that real humanity cannot exist at all without a specific human individual person who is the center of the human nature. *Prosopon* (person) and *physis* (nature) go together in both humanity and divinity.

This meant, of course, that Nestorius had to affirm that Jesus Christ was two persons. Theodore had not gone so far, even though his conceptuality implied it.

Building on Theodore's idea of the incarnation as the Logos "assuming a man" and as a man being "assumed by the Logos," Nestorius argued that the incarnation is a mutual indwelling of two persons—the eternal Son of God and the mortal human Jesus. To that union we assign the name Jesus Christ, or just Christ, and consider the union itself as a "person" in the compound or corporate sense. Thus, for Nestorius, "in Jesus Christ, God has united the divine *prosopon* to a human nature—but this in no way destroys the two natural *prosopa* [persons], which correspond to each of the two 'complete natures' or *hypostases* which are united in Christ."[1]

How can two persons be one person? That was the dilemma facing Nestorius. In order to avoid adoptionism (in which the man Jesus Christ is merely a "divine pick-up"), Nestorius had to account for the true unity of divine and human in Jesus Christ. There had to be a way to say of Jesus Christ that although he is human, he is also truly divine. Nestorius's solution lay in positing a special kind of union that he called *synapheia*. In Latin it has been translated *conjunctio,* and thus in English Nestorius's idea has traditionally been called a "conjunction." Jesus Christ was a conjunction of divine nature-person and human nature-person: eternal divine Logos and human person Jesus in intimate union. According to Nestorius, such a conjunction can be so intimate and strong that it forms a new kind of entity like a whole that is greater than the sum of the parts. In his view "the unity of *prosopon* is based on the fact that the *prosopon* of the Logos makes use of the *prosopon* of Christ's manhood as an instrument, an *organon*. The whole is the union of the two natures, of an invisible and a visible element."[2]

Nestorius began to get himself into trouble when, in answering some of Cyril's questions, he attempted to go further to explain the conjunction idea of the incarnation. Cyril knew that if he could get Nestorius to keep attempting to explain it, he would eventually reveal it for what it was—a sophisticated form of adoptionism. The only real differences were in the person who adopted the man and the timing of the adoption. The key similarity lay in the fact that in both adoptionism and Nestorianism the Son of God never actually enters into human existence. The human person in the Nestorian conjunction remains not only distinct in nature but also a different person from the Son of God. Nestorius proved it when he (according to Cyril) used the analogy of marriage. Nestorius apparently argued that just as two independent persons come together to form a union transcending their differences in marriage, so in the incarnation the Son of God and the Son of David formed a union (initiated by the Son of God) that transcended their different natures. That union is a bond of fellowship and cooperation of wills that is stronger than any human friendship or marriage. Those can only provide a dim analogy for it.

Nestorius was also trapped by Cyril into denying one of Cyril's most beloved christological principles—the *communicatio idiomatum,* or "communication of attributes." According to Cyril, if Jesus Christ was truly the Word incarnate—God in flesh—then it must be theologically correct to attribute to him all the glory and majesty and power of deity, as well as to the Son of God who became human all the weakness and mortality and suffering of humanity.

Nestorius adamantly rejected this. For him, this was one of the main advantages of his conjunction idea of the incarnation. It made it possible to say that Jesus Christ is both truly God and truly human without mixing them. He wanted to be able to say that the God person of the union worked the miracles and the human person suffered. Divinity cannot suffer and humanity is incapable of altering the course of nature. Obviously two different persons were in him doing these things. But they always did them together.

He was horrified by Cyril's *communicatio idiomatum* idea and automatically rejected it as Apollinarian. Cyril wanted to say that the Son of God suffered and died (because of his union with human nature) and that the man Jesus walked on water and read people's minds (because of his divinity). To Nestorius this proved that Cyril was not properly distinguishing between the human and the divine—a heresy that for Nestorius corrupted everything about the Christian worldview.

One should be able to sympathize with Nestorius—up to a point. After all, the Great Church had just decided a half century earlier that the Trinity means one substance and three persons and accepted Gregory of Nyssa's view that the three persons, though distinct, are never separated and do everything in common. Why cannot the same conceptuality be applied to the incarnation? Nestorius's view seems at least superficially sound in light of the orthodox doctrine of the Trinity. The difference, though, is that the *hypostases* (persons) of the Trinity share a common *ousia* (nature), whereas the two *physeis* (natures) of the Nestorian Christ have different *prosopa* (persons) attached to them. That throws a stronger difference into the equation. In the case of the union that makes up Christ, the divine one is eternal and omnipotent, while the human one is mortal and weak. Their "union" cannot be as strong as that between the persons of the Godhead.

There is no doubt that Nestorius's intentions were sound. He wished to preserve the integrity of God's nature and human nature even in the incarnation by positing a "union of natures." He wanted also to do full justice to the humanity of Jesus Christ and not allow it to be swallowed up in the divinity or truncated or in anyway made less than like ours. After all, Nestorius would argue, does not Scripture itself say that Jesus Christ "increased in wisdom and in years, and in divine and human favor" (Lk 2:52 NRSV)? Yet in spite of his laudable intentions—

many of which were shared by more orthodox Christians—Nestorius could not account for the unity of Christ. In the end, in spite of his valiant attempt to explain how a conjunction of two persons could count as one person *(prosopon),* his Christ turns out to be two individuals and not one. The Son of God did not truly experience human existence "in the flesh" but only "through association with the man." Cyril was right to criticize Nestorius's Christology as little more than warmed-over and dressed-up adoptionism.

### Cyril of Alexandria's Christology

What about Cyril's Christology? Is Nestorius's accusation that it represents little more than warmed-over and dressed-up Apollinarianism accurate? It is hard to tell. Every scholar who studies and writes about Cyril's Christology admits the same thing: it is ambiguous. All one can do is explain its substance as the church has traditionally interpreted it while noting that many scholars point out tensions and conflicts within Cyril's writings.

Overall, so it seems, Cyril's unique contribution to Christology is the doctrine of the *hypostatic union*—at least in its basic outlines. This becomes the Great Church's foundation for explaining and expressing the mystery of the incarnation of God in Christ. In a nutshell it means that the subject of the life of Jesus Christ was the Son of God who took on himself a human nature and existence while remaining truly divine. In other words, according to Cyril, there was no human personal subject in the incarnation. The *hypostasis* (personal subsistence) of Jesus Christ was the eternal Son of God who condescended to take human flesh through Mary. Mary, Cyril argued, gave birth to God in flesh. That is the essence of the incarnation.

How does this differ from Apollinarianism? This is where the ambiguity enters Cyril's thought. On the one hand, Cyril and his Alexandrian colleagues admitted the human soul of Jesus. Unlike Apollinarianism, their Christology recognizes Jesus' human psychology so that he really did grow in wisdom and favor with God and humans and not only in "stature" (body): "The Cyril of the Nestorian controversy recognizes a real human psychology in Jesus Christ. Suffering is transferred to the soul, as well as the body, and above all, the significance of the human obedience and sacrificial action of Christ is seen. For the Alexandrians, too, the soul of Christ has become a theological factor."[3] However, in order to avoid "dividing the person" in Nestorian fashion, Cyril also emphasized the unity of the subject or person in Christ so that only the divine Logos is truly personal and active in him. The result is that for Cyril either Christ did not have a human personal center of consciousness and will or else it was inactive.

What is a rational soul without a free personality? That is the dilemma Cyril's Christology faced. For him, the Son of God formed the personality of Jesus Christ. He was it. The humanity appears *anhypostasia*—impersonal. But it is still more than a mere body and animal life force. The human nature of Jesus Christ included every aspect of true humanity—body, soul, spirit, mind, will. It just did not have any independent or autonomous personal being over against the Logos.

Cyril's favorite formula for expressing the incarnation was "God the Logos did not come into a man, but he 'truly' became man, while remaining God."[4] He completely rejected the conjunction idea of union and replaced it with hypostatic union—union of two realities in one *hypostasis* or personal subject—the Logos. For him, the Nestorian conjunction idea amounted to little or nothing more than a cooperation between two persons—one human and one divine. That's a type of adoptionism. That could be true of any prophet. So strong was the union of humanity and divinity in the one *hypostasis* of the Logos, Cyril argued, that one must speak of "one nature after the union." In other words, even though it is possible conceptually to think of Christ's humanity and divinity as two distinct *physeis*, or natures, in reality their union in the incarnation made them to become "one nature."

Because Jesus Christ was the one-natured God-man, Cyril could justify his *communicatio idiomatum* principle for speech about the incarnation. Through the incarnation the one personal subject of the Son of God was both divine and human (even though the human nature was not personal), and so it is correct to say that the Son of God was born, grew, suffered and died, and it is correct to say that the human Jesus worked miracles, forgave sins and defeated death. They are one and the same person with two modes of being. Of course, the Nestorians and some other Antiochenes could see in this nothing other than a mixing of divinity and humanity, and even Cyril himself denied that it meant that God actually suffered. He only suffered through the humanity that he took to himself as his instrument in the incarnation. Ambiguous.

Cyril wrote several letters to Nestorius urging him to see the error of his thoughts and change his Christology. Nestorius refused. His responses only widened the differences. Eventually Cyril appealed to the bishop of Rome—much to that person's delight!—and asked for a full ecumenical council to settle the controversy. The bishop of Rome investigated the matter and wrote a letter back to Cyril denouncing Nestorius and his heresy and urging that he be deposed from his position as patriarch of Constantinople. Cyril immediately used the pope's letter to pressure the emperor for a council to investigate and condemn Nestorius. The emperor was reluctant but agreed on the assumption that such a council would vindicate Nestorius and the entire Antiochene tradition. The council was to meet in Ephesus in 431 as soon as all the bishops could arrive.

## The Council of Ephesus

Cyril and his loyal bishops arrived first and waited for a few days. When no one else showed up, Cyril—the only patriarch present—called the council to order and began the proceedings in the absence of Nestorius or any other bishops loyal to Antioch. First, the gathered bishops read aloud and reaffirmed the Nicene Creed of Constantinople I and declared that it was sufficient as a creed and contained the essential truth of the orthodox Christology. Then Cyril's second letter to Nestorius was read. It contained his statements concerning the Son of God as the subject of the human life of Jesus Christ and harshly criticized Nestorius's christological dualism. The bishops voted to endorse it as the true and authoritative interpretation of the Nicene Creed as it pertains to the person of Jesus Christ. Finally, the council condemned Nestorius and his Christology as heresy. The official declaration against the patriarch of Constantinople said:

> The holy synod which, by the grace of God, in conformity with the ordinance . . . of our pious and Christ-loving kings, is assembled at Ephesus, to Nestorius, the new Judas! Know that because of your godless teachings . . . and disobedience towards the canons, in accordance with the decree of the statutes of the church on the 22nd of the current month of June you are condemned by the Holy Synod and dispossessed of any dignity in the church.[5]

The Council of Ephesus, generally regarded as the third ecumenical council of Christendom, did not promulgate any new creed, but it did endorse a belief and bind it on all Christians. It is a dogmatic formula taken almost word for word from Cyril's letters to Nestorius: "One and the same is the eternal Son of the Father and the Son of the Virgin Mary, born in time after the flesh; therefore she may rightly be called Mother of God."[6]

Shortly after the Council of Ephesus led by Cyril completed its work, the bishop of Antioch and his colleagues arrived. They immediately withdrew from the bishops already assembled and held a rival Council of Ephesus. They proceeded to condemn Cyril and his formulas and reconfirm Nestorius as patriarch of Constantinople. Before they finished, the bishops of the West and papal delegates arrived from Rome and joined Cyril and his council, which quickly ratified the earlier acts condemning and deposing Nestorius. It was all very confusing and ultimately up to the emperor to sort out.

True to form, the emperor did not like schism and strongly pressured all parties to compromise. However, he did support the council's deposition of Nestorius, who was sent into exile after John, the bishop of Antioch, agreed to that course of action if Cyril would agree to affirm the two-natures formula for orthodox Christology. Cyril reluctantly agreed so long as the two natures in Christ are not divided. For him, "A *distinction* of the natures is necessary, a *division* is reprehensible. To speak of *duo physeis* [two natures] makes a distinction, but does not of itself divide; it only has the latter effect if a reprehensible intention to divide is associated with it."[7]

Cyril clearly preferred the "one nature after the union" formula, and many of his Alexandrian colleagues and followers were dismayed by his compromise. They felt he had given away the farm, so to speak, by allowing any talk of two natures in Christ. After all, they argued, does not two natures imply two persons? Cyril defended his compromise with Antioch in a document known in church history as the Formula of Reunion (433) by insisting that the two natures are only distinct in thought and not in reality. It is highly unlikely that the Antiochenes agreed. For them the distinction of Christ's two natures was ontological and not merely mental.

The Formula of Reunion of 433 was signed by both Cyril of Alexandria and John of Antioch and ratified by the emperor. It avoided total schism between the two great cities. Each side got some of what it wanted. Alexandria saw Nestorius condemned and deposed and sent into exile, from which he never returned in spite of many efforts on his behalf. Antioch saw Alexandria affirm the incarnation as a union of two natures. Alexandria had its collective fingers crossed behind its back. Cyril clearly did not mean by this anything like what many Antiochenes meant. Nevertheless, many of his own people resented him for compromising and waited for the opportunity to take it back and reassert the one-nature formula they so dearly loved. While Cyril was alive, that seemed impossible.

After the Council of Ephesus and the Formula of Reunion, it became clear that not much that was positive had been decided. Two great christological heresies had been anathematized (condemned): Apollinarianism and Nestorianism. If you wanted to be part of the Great Church catholic and orthodox, you had to avoid denying the humanity of the rational soul of Christ and you had to avoid dividing his two natures into two persons. That meant that in 440 in order to be a catholic, orthodox Christian you had to believe that the Savior had a human mind and a divine mind but was not two persons! No wonder many people were still confused. No wonder the controversy was about to erupt all over again in a new form and require another ecumenical council to settle it once and for all.

# CHAPTER 15

# Chalcedon Protects the Mystery

C*hristians alive in 450 who could remember events surrounding the Arian* controversy that led up to the Council of Constantinople in 381 must have had a sense of déjà vu. Of course, there probably were not many of them around. But no doubt a few elderly monks and priests and lay Christians in Constantinople could remember the bitterness and feuding that went on seventy years earlier as the last remnants of the most damaging heresy were eradicated from the official church's doctrinal lists. Now, in the middle of the fifth century, it all seemed to be happening over again, only this time all sides to the dispute agreed on one thing—the doctrine of the Trinity.

This disagreement—just as bitter and divisive as the earlier one—was about the nature of the God-man, Jesus Christ. As always, that was the surface issue. Beneath the surface, wrangling over proper terminology for describing his person and being lay vastly different ideas of salvation. Jesus Christ's importance was as Savior of the world. Everyone agreed that in order to accomplish salvation he had to be truly God and truly human. Representatives of Antioch and of Alexandria both felt that the other side was continuing to express the doctrine of the incarnation in ways that undermined or even subtly destroyed Jesus Christ's ability to save. The conviction was that if the wrong doctrine set in and became universal, the gospel itself would be changed.

For example, even though blatant Nestorianism had been condemned at Ephesus I in 431, Antiochene theologians in Constantinople and other places continued to emphasize the two natures of Christ in a way that tended to make his humanity a distinct individuality over against his divine nature. In its extreme form this crypto-Nestorian Antiochene Christology could easily lead to the impression that Jesus Christ accomplished salvation by being a godly human person and cooperating perfectly with the divine Logos who assumed him.

A heretic from the West by the name of Pelagius—who will reappear in more detail later in our story—received refuge from Antiochenes in Syria and Palestine just before the Council of Ephesus. Pelagius believed that salvation is at least in part a matter of human achievement and not all of grace, or so at least his enemies claimed. Antioch's Alexandrian enemies pointed this situation out to their Western allies in Rome and argued that the sympathy shown Pelagius by Antiochenes proved that their Christology was intimately connected to a false gospel of salvation by good works. In other words, the suspicion was that by emphasizing the autonomous humanity of the Savior, Antiochenes were subtly portraying him as our human example rather than as our divine healer. Allegedly Pelagius recognized this compatibility between his own teaching and the Antiochene Christology and that is why he sought refuge and received it among the theologians of that party. The Alexandrians wondered why the Antiochene Christians would give refuge to such a heretic as Pelagius if they did not at least sympathize with his views on salvation? The refuge Pelagius found among Antiochenes in the East damaged both him and them. It helped Alexandria convince Rome and the Western bishops that Antiochene Christology was on the wrong path.

At the Council of Ephesus in 431 one of the conditions Rome and the bishops of the West laid down for being Alexandria's allies (when they finally arrived) was that the council had to condemn Pelagius. In return Rome promised to vote for Nestorius's condemnation and deposition as bishop of Constantinople. Cyril readily agreed, and in the final phase of the council both men were condemned as heretics and sent away into desert exile. By Alexandrian lights, they belonged together because their heresies were connected. Both emphasized the human role in salvation too much so that grace became a contingent reward for achievement. Nestorianism and Pelagianism (works righteousness) became forever linked in the minds of orthodox and catholic Christian theologians.

Alexandrian Christology manifested a different underlying view of salvation. Jesus Christ is the divine Savior as the Logos of God, not as a human person. Yes he had to have both divinity and humanity in order to accomplish salvation as the mediator between the two. But the saving operation in and through him was an activity of the Logos healing the wounds of sin and death in the humanity that becomes the new humanity for all who participate in him by faith and through sacraments. The Alexandrian soteriological emphasis was on grace rather than on human achievement. This should not, however, be misunderstood through the lens of later theological debates.

All parties in the great christological controversy believed in the role of free will in sinners benefiting from Christ's saving work. The question whether Jesus Christ himself had a *human* free will, however, was still unsettled. It seemed that for most Alexandrians—even Cyril—he did not. Even though Cyril reluctantly compromised with the Antiochenes after Ephesus I in the Formula of Reunion and allowed talk of two natures of Christ, he continued to favor the formula "one nature after the union" and it was clear to all that this one nature of Jesus Christ was more divine than human. This was the only way Cyril and his Alexandrian cohorts could see that the sheer graciousness of salvation as a work of God in Christ could be preserved. It is a "done deal" in the incarnation. All we humans have to do is accept it by being faithful and loyal followers of Christ through repentance and sacraments.

**The Controversy Continues After Ephesus**

The Council of Ephesus and the Formula of Reunion were temporary settlements. Each side got some of what it wanted. Rome got Pelagius condemned by an ecumenical council and won some prestige in the East when Cyril appealed to the bishop of Rome over the emperor's head. Cyril and Alexandria got Nestorius and his extreme Antiochene Christology condemned and Cyril's explanation of the incarnation canonized as true doctrine over against Nestorianism. Antioch got its dearly beloved two-natures formula accepted as orthodox by Cyril and its stamp of approval by the emperor. But the issues were far from settled. In many ways the situation was like that between Nicaea I in 325 and Constantinople I in 381. The council that was supposed to resolve the dispute and establish universal orthodoxy about the triunity of God opened up a greater conflict and forced another council to bring it to closure.

After the Council of Ephesus and the Formula of Reunion, Antiochene theologians began to assume that the two-natures idea of Jesus Christ was the one and only orthodox formula. They apparently thought that Cyril had made a quantum leap in Alexandrian Christology and would henceforth and forevermore speak and write about Jesus Christ as two natures—divine and human—after the union. Furthermore, Antioch learned at the Council of Ephesus and through correspondence afterward that Rome and much of the West considered Jesus Christ to be made up of two substances. Although there was no exact one-on-one translation of Greek and Latin terms, a comparison could indicate that the Latin formula for Christ going back to Tertullian was in many ways closer to Antioch's than to Alexandria's. Antiochene leaders simply began to act as if the old Alexandrian "one nature after the union" formula was sent off into the desert along with Nestorius. The two were viewed as equal and opposite extremes that deserved each other.

It is clear, however, that Alexandrian leaders did not view things in that way. Cyril thought that he had merely allowed Christians to speak of Christ as having two natures so long as they did not divide them. He merrily proceeded to continue preaching and teaching "the one incarnate nature of the Word" in Alexandria and never did address or resolve the ambiguity implicit in his Christology, where Christ appears to be both truly human and truly divine and yet one nature.

Cyril died in 444 in full fellowship with the bishops of Antioch, Rome and Constantinople. The Great Church seemed at peace in spite of tensions simmering just beneath the surface. It seems that Cyril was willing to live with mystery and ambiguity for the sake of peace. So was John, the bishop of Antioch. Rome had other things to think about, such as barbarian invaders sweeping out of central Europe down into Italy. But one other person was not willing to let things be.

Cyril's successor as bishop and patriarch of Alexandria was a rascal named Dioscorus. Few men in church history have been as universally disdained and scorned as this character. Soon after becoming Alexandria's leading churchman, he set about undoing the peace Cyril had helped establish with Antioch. A leading church historian reports that

> it was the policy of Cyril's successor, Dioscorus, who was ready to fling moderation to the winds, to destroy root and branch the doctrine of "two natures," and to proclaim to Christendom that the way of sound belief lay in the general acceptance of the Alexandrian doctrine of "one nature," as this had been propounded by the Fathers, and by Cyril himself, before he took the unfortunate step of entering into communion with the Orientals [Antiochenes] on the basis of their "Nestorianizing" formulary in the year 433.[1]

Dioscorus is not known for any other contribution to the story of Christian theology than that of renewing the doctrinal war between Alexandria and Antioch. In all probability his motives had as much to do with ousting Antiochene influence from Constantinople once and for all as with discovering and defending truth. In matters theological he was a radical Cyrillian. That is, while rejecting Apollinarian Christology by affirming a human soul and mind of Christ, Dioscorus also completely rejected talk of two natures of Christ as unavoidably Nestorian and insisted on the formulas “one incarnate nature of the divine Logos” and “after the union, one nature.”[2]

Dioscorus’s counterpart in Antioch was a theologian named Theodoret of Cyrus, who was Antioch’s favorite son and a likely candidate to become the next patriarch of Constantinople. Theodoret was one churchman who seemed to assume that the Formula of Reunion of 433 meant a one-sided victory for Antioch, and he treated the two-natures doctrine of Christ as orthodox to the exclusion of all talk of one nature after the union. Clearly, Dioscorus and Theodoret were on a collision course. All that was needed was a single spark to ignite a great theological conflagration. That spark appeared in the person of a certain humble monk of Constantinople named Eutyches.

### Eutyches and the Eutychian Controversy

Eutyches was a somewhat feeble-minded but influential elderly monk of Constantinople. As in the cases of so many people of ancient church history, Eutyches appeared on the scene, played a role in the drama and stepped off stage never to be heard from again. Almost nothing is known of his life apart from this episode during which he was briefly at center stage. Eutyches was a strong supporter of the Alexandrian cause, and after Cyril’s death, he sided with Dioscorus regarding the one nature of Christ. While it is difficult to ascertain exactly what Eutyches’ teaching about Christ was, it is clear that he went a step beyond the language of Cyril and affirmed of the process of incarnation that it involved “two natures *before* the union (of God and humanity) but only one nature *after* or as a result of the union.” Of itself this formula would not arouse much attention since Cyril could have said the same and most Alexandrians favored it. It clearly fit the Christology of Alexandria. What brought wrath down on Eutyches’ head and made him the center of a firestorm of controversy was that he refused to affirm that Christ was consubstantial with us humans, which appeared to the Antiochenes as a clear rejection of the faith of Nicaea, which had declared Jesus Christ both truly human and truly divine. Their response was, “There! See we told you what Alexandrian Christology would lead to—rejection of Christ’s very humanity.”

Eutyches did seem to reject the full and true humanity of Jesus Christ. While he did not repeat the exact heresy of Apollinarius, he did reduce Christ’s humanity to a “drop of wine in the ocean of his deity.” According to some historical theologians, “probably what Eutyches taught was that, because of the incarnation, the body of Christ was deified in such a way that it was no longer ‘consubstantial with us.’ ”[3] It seems that Eutyches took Cyril’s christological principle *communicatio idiomatum* to an extreme in a one-sided way. While he would allow recognition that divine characteristics and attributes permeated and transformed the humanity of Christ, he would not allow recognition of a reverse process. According to Eutyches' Christology, the human reality of Jesus Christ made no difference to the Logos and was even swallowed up in the incarnational union with him. It is difficult indeed to see how the Jesus of Eutyches' theology is truly or fully human at all. The specter of outright docetism loomed in Constantinople when he taught Christology.

Just as Nestorius and his teaching about Christ had confirmed the worst fears of Alexandrians concerning Antiochene theology, so Eutyches and his teaching confirmed the Antiochenes' worst fears about Alexandrian theology. Nestorius was implicitly guilty of a kind of adoptionism, even if he did not intend that. His language, concepts and imagery about Jesus Christ inexorably moved in that direction—right back to Paul of Samosata's heresy. That is why Nestorius and his doctrine of the person of Jesus Christ were condemned. But Eutyches was implicitly guilty of something very close to Apollinarianism if not outright docetism, even if he did not intend that. He went far beyond Cyril's hypostatic-union idea of the incarnation of God in Christ right into denial of the true humanity of Christ when he rejected his consubstantiality with us. Not only did Christ not have a human personality or individual human existence, for Eutyches he did not have a human nature like ours at all.

Perhaps Eutyches' Christology would not have been so terribly objectionable to many theological fence-sitters between Alexandria and Antioch if Eutyches and his followers had only claimed that Christ's humanity became divinized like ours will be if we receive grace through him. But that is not what Eutyches apparently taught. Instead he seems to have taught that right from the moment of conception in Mary, Jesus Christ was a hybrid of humanity and divinity—a single divine-human nature—that mixed together and mingled the two natures so that the human nature was overwhelmed and swallowed up by the divine. "If this were true, then how was he really our mediator?" critics asked. How could he go through that process of undoing the fall of Adam and recapitulating the human race about which Irenaeus spoke so eloquently? How could his death on the cross represent humanity? These soteriological questions leaped to the fore from many different quarters as soon as Eutyches' teaching became widely known.

## The Robber Synod

Enter the scheming Dioscorus from stage left. In 448 Dioscorus manipulated a synod of bishops in Constantinople to condemn Eutyches. Dioscorus's methods give meaning to the well-worn adjective *Byzantine,* which is frequently used to describe secretive, scheming, double-dealing political manipulation. When someone in power seems to be on one side but is really on the opposite and is temporarily trying to gain an advantage over political opponents by subtle and complicated scheming—that is called Byzantine behavior. Byzantium, of course, was the ancient name of the city that became Constantinople under Constantine, and it remained a common term for the city and the entire Eastern empire well into the Middle Ages. Dioscorus personified Byzantine behavior. His reason for bringing about Eutyches' condemnation was to offer the Constantinopolitan monk refuge and fellowship in Alexandria and then use his condemnation and subsequent communion with Alexandria to force a confrontation with Antioch's leaders and even with the patriarch of Constantinople himself.

During the months between his condemnation at the synod in Constantinople and an ecumenical council to be held in Ephesus in 449, Eutyches appealed to Leo the bishop of Rome for support and help. Meanwhile, Dioscorus was busy using Alexandrian wealth to sway the emperor to their side. The patriarch of Constantinople, a man named Flavian, was caught in the middle. He had to support the synod that had condemned Eutyches and his teaching because it was held in his see and under his supervision. Messengers scurried back and forth between Rome, Alexandria, Constantinople, Antioch and Ephesus before the planned fourth ecumenical council met in 449. By the time the council opened, Dioscorus thought he had it all sewed up. But just to be sure, he brought a gang of thugs, who happened to be Egyptian monks, with him to the meeting. If political maneuvering could not control the council, perhaps threats of violence would!

What happened at the would-be council led to its condemnation and cancellation later. Instead of being the fourth ecumenical council of Christendom, it has come to be known generally as the Robber Synod. Dioscorus arrived with his gang of heavily armed monks and quickly took control of the entire council. Eutyches' formula "two natures before the union; one nature after the union" was approved as orthodox, and the leading Antiochene representative Theodoret of Cyrus and other so-called Nestorianizers were condemned as "contenders with God" and deposed from their positions as church leaders. Some of the Alexandrian bishops and many of the monks present called for them to be burned. Worst of all, perhaps, Patriarch Flavian of Constantinople arrived at the council with a document from Bishop Leo of Rome against Eutyches. The epistle has come to be known in church history as *Leo's Tome* and later played a very important role in the solution and settlement of this most unfortunate doctrinal conflict. Pope Leo I—perhaps the first bishop of Rome to actually function as a pope in that he virtually ruled much of Italy as well as all of the Western church—had sent a lengthy doctrinal epistle to Flavian condemning Eutyches and charting out orthodox Christology. Flavian tried to read the letter from the pope, but Dioscorus's monks attacked and beat him up so badly that he died shortly afterward.

At the end of the Robber Synod in Ephesus, "the Bishop of Alexandria had every reason to be satisfied with the results of his attack against the doctrine of the school of Antioch."[4] Emperor Theodosius II had switched allegiance from Antioch to Alexandria and fully supported the acts of the synod. For a time it stood as the fourth ecumenical council—Ephesus II. The Alexandrian victory seemed complete. Eutychianism triumphed. The official orthodox and catholic doctrine of the person of Jesus Christ was that he is the "one-natured God-man" whose humanity was swallowed up in divinity. No one could be blamed for counting this a victory for docetism in that when a person would try to picture this, it was natural to think of Jesus Christ as the eternal Son of God pretending to be human. The Formula of Reunion of 433, which even Cyril had signed and supported, was undone. But worse, the faith of Nicaea itself was at stake. Eutyches had denied Jesus Christ's consubstantiality with us and gotten away with it.

Shortly after the Robber Synod adjourned, its victims began appealing to both the emperor and the bishop of Rome. Pope Leo was horrified at what he heard and immediately sent a letter to the emperor in Constantinople demanding that the council be reversed, Eutyches condemned, and Theodoret of Cyrus reconfirmed as leader of the church in Antioch. Leo also protested the death of Flavian and asked the emperor to vindicate him by arresting his murderers. Theodosius finally responded to Leo's appeal in 450. He refused all of Leo's demands and especially refused to call a new council to replace the Robber Synod as fourth ecumenical council.

Pope Leo's response was to begin the process of calling an ecumenical council to meet in the West without the emperor's support. By this time the two halves of the Roman Empire had fallen so far apart that the bishop of Rome in the West did not even have to worry very much about the Roman emperor, who stayed in the East and allowed the various barbarian tribes to take over the Western empire. The bishops of Rome, beginning with Leo I, gradually stepped into that political and cultural vacuum in the Latin West and took up the fallen imperial mantle to try to maintain a semblance of the old Roman order.

In July of 450 it appeared that the church was about to break in two just as the empire itself was falling apart. The bishop of Rome—the pope—was threatening to hold an ecumenical council without the emperor's approval, and the emperor was defending the acts of a violent synod that had ratified heresy as orthodoxy. Just as the church of the mid-fourth century almost made Arianism orthodox, so the church of the mid-fifth century almost made docetism orthodox. Then God intervened. Emperor Theodosius II was killed on July 28, 450, in a freak accident. He was thrown from his horse. The main power protecting heresy and holding back unity was quickly removed and succeeded by his sister Pulcheria and her consort, Marcian, who favored complete independence of Constantinople from domination by either Alexandria or Antioch.

Pulcheria and Marcian began the process of reversing the terrible acts of the Robber Synod of 449. They had Flavian's body brought to Constantinople from Ephesus and buried with full honors in the great cathedral of Hagia Sophia—"Holy Wisdom"—that stood at the center of the capital city. A new council to replace Ephesus II as fourth ecumenical council was called to meet at Chalcedon near Constantinople in May 451. All bishops of the Great Church of Christendom were ordered to attend and *Leo's Tome* was circulated to them in advance of the meeting. Leo himself found an excuse not to attend the Council of Chalcedon because he was upset that the fourth ecumenical council was not being held in the West. But he sent delegates to represent him. Dioscorus was ordered to attend, and while traveling to the new council, issued a letter excommunicating Leo of Rome: "Though he knew well what lay in store for him, it was to be a fight to a finish, so far as the Bishop of Alexandria was concerned."[5]

**The Council of Chalcedon and the Chalcedonian Definition**

The great ecumenical Council of Chalcedon opened with pomp and circumstance on October 8, 451, with five hundred bishops and eighteen high-state officials, including the imperial couple, in attendance. The followers of Leo and the Antiochenes sat on one side of the great hall and Dioscorus and his cohorts sat on the other side. Only the imperial power could get them inside the same building and keep them there. One of the first events of the first session of the council was the entrance of Theodoret of Cyprus, who had been condemned, deposed and nearly burned by the Robber Synod. A near riot ensued, but the empress and her guards quieted down the bishops and Theodoret was seated in honor. Then the acts of the Ephesian Robber Synod were read aloud and discussed. Gradually Dioscorus's supporters abandoned him and the Robber Synod and expressed remorse for their participation in the persecution of Theodoret and death of Flavian. Only Dioscorus stood defiantly for the validity of what had happened at Ephesus in 449 and defended its actions. At nightfall the bishops voted to depose Dioscorus as patriarch of Alexandria and exile him together with the ringleaders of the infamous Ephesian synod. The empress and emperor ratified their decision. Dioscorus was immediately sent into exile in the desert.

It was clear to all at the Council of Chalcedon that the Great Church needed a new statement of orthodox belief about the person of Jesus Christ and that it had somehow to bridge the gap between the sincere and faithful Christians of Alexandria and Antioch. The truth on both sides had to be preserved and expressed, while the extremes of both had to be avoided and even excluded. The empress and emperor and their commissioners ordered the bishops who were still in good standing to spend two days reflecting alone on their beliefs about Christ and then gather again on October 10 to decide once and for all on the "right faith":

> The bishops were directed to draw up in writing each his own statement of belief without fear and with God only before his eyes. To aid them in their task, it was pointed out that the Emperor upheld the decrees of Nicaea and Constantinople, together with the writings of the holy Fathers, Gregory, Basil, Hilary, Ambrose, and the two letters of Cyril which had been approved at the former Synod of Ephesus. It was pointed out, too, that the bishops now possessed the letter which Leo had written to Flavian of holy memory against the error of Eutyches. "We have read it," they replied.[6]

When the bishops reassembled on October 10, *Leo's Tome* was read to them aloud and discussed over several sessions. After much debate, a new formulary of faith was agreed upon based heavily on language and concepts in *Leo's Tome* and Cyril's letters to Nestorius and John of Antioch. Tertullian's writings on the person of Christ lay in the background of the discussion and the new statement of faith. The bishops wanted to make absolutely clear that the new Formulary of Chalcedon (more often known as the Definition of Chalcedon) was not a new creed but an interpretation and elaboration of the Nicene Creed of 381. It was finally approved and signed by the emperor and bishops on October 25, 451. The heart of the statement says:

> In agreement, therefore, with the holy fathers we all unanimously teach that we should confess that our Lord Jesus Christ is one and the same Son; the same perfect in Godhead and the same perfect in manhood, truly God and truly man, the same of a rational soul and body; consubstantial with the Father in Godhead and the same consubstantial with us in manhood; like us in all things except sin; begotten of the Father before all ages as regards his Godhead and in the last days the same, for us and for our salvation, begotten of the Virgin Mary the *Theotokos* as regards his manhood; one and the same Christ, Son, Lord, only-begotten, made known in two natures without confusion, without change, without division, without separation; the difference of the natures being by no means removed because of the union but

> the property of each nature being preserved and coalescing in one person *(prosopon)* and one *hypostasis,* not parted or divided into two persons but one and the same Son, only-begotten, divine Word, the Lord Jesus Christ; as the prophets of old and Jesus Christ himself have taught us about him, and the creed of our fathers has handed down.[7]

The bishops then proceeded to condemn both Nestorius (who was already dead) and Eutyches. The overall tenor of the Council of Chalcedon was decidedly anti-Alexandrian, and by its end that see's pretensions and dreams of domination had been dealt a severe blow. The council also elevated the office of patriarch of Constantinople to equality with Rome so that the two great patriarchates would stand side by side in honor above the rest. It threw the bishop of Rome a bone, however, by bestowing on his seat the empty honor of "first among equals." When Leo I heard of this, he rejected the entire declaration and continued to argue for Roman preeminence over all Christian bishops.

At the conclusion of the council on February 7, 452, the empress and her consort decreed that no further controversy about the "matters of faith" would be allowed and that all Christians would be required from then on to affirm the teachings of Nicaea, Constantinople and Chalcedon. Leo of Rome accepted the christological heart of the council—the Chalcedonian Definition—because it essentially expressed what he had written in his *Tome*. The ancient faith of Tertullian was accepted in the East: Jesus Christ as one person of two natures or substances. Just as Nicaea and Constantinople had declared God three whos and one what, so Chalcedon declared Jesus Christ one who and two whats. Many Antiochene theologians, however, regarded the Chalcedonian Definition as a victory for Alexandrian Christology because it so strongly affirmed *one Son* and rejected any separation or division of the two natures. Many Alexandrians regarded it as a victory for the Antiochene Christology because it so strongly affirmed *two natures* and forbade confusion or change in their union.

As we will see, the result of the Council of Chalcedon and its christological definition was permanent schism within the Eastern church. Significant portions of the churches of Syria and regions east of Syria (Persia and Arabia) refused to accept the new statement and split off from the Great Church to form their own separate Nestorian churches. They developed their own traditions and beliefs and isolated themselves from orthodox and catholic Christendom. Most of the Christian churches of Egypt also refused to accept the new faith and split off from the Great Church to form their own independent monophysite churches. (*Monophysite* means "believing in one nature.") The Coptic Church of Egypt is the modern remnant of that schism.

The Chalcedonian Formulary, or Chalcedonian Definition, became one of the landmarks of catholic and orthodox Christian belief in spite of the schisms resulting from it. The Eastern Orthodox family of churches accepts it as does the Roman Catholic Church. Most major Protestant denominations accept its essence even if they do not consider its language binding. The doctrine that it embodies and expresses is the hypostatic union slightly altered from Cyril's description. Nowhere is Cyril's *communicatio idiomatum* mentioned, even though Leo favored it and wrote it into his *Tome*. Nowhere, however, does Chalcedon reject or criticize it either. Perhaps the main reason for not including affirmation of the *communicatio idiomatum* in the statement of faith was to keep as many of the Antiochenes on board as possible. They could not accept that principle.

The definition of Chalcedon may sound esoteric or highly abstract and philosophical, but in fact it is simply an attempt to express and protect the mystery of the incarnation against distortions:

> It may be conceded at once that the Definition is not an explanation of the mystery of the Incarnation. The very failure of the Definition to solve the insolvable is its best recommendation to our careful consideration. The framers of the Definition were not concerned so much to formulate a theory as to safeguard the truth from two attempted solutions of an erroneous character, and to preserve for us the truth hidden in both those errors.[8]

A careful study of the wording of the Chalcedonian Formula reveals the ways in which it was both a compromise between two extremes and an attempt to protect the mystery of the incarnation. It clearly affirms with moderate Antiochene theology the real humanity of Jesus Christ and his two natures. But it states that the two natures are not to be divided or separated and that each nature—in its full integrity—is held together in one person. Antiochene Christology is right in what it affirms—two natures of the God-man—but wrong in what Nestorius denied—the unity and integrity of the person of Jesus Christ. Chalcedon also clearly affirms, against extreme Alexandrian Christology, that the two natures of Christ must not be confused (mingled or mixed) or thought to change through their intimate hypostatic union in the Logos. Alexandrian Christology is right in what it affirms—one person of Christ who is the Son of God—but wrong in what Eutyches denied—the completeness and integrity of the distinct natures of humanity and divinity even in their union in Jesus Christ.

The real heart of the Chalcedonian Definition is what is known as the four fences of Chalcedon—"without confusion, without change, without division, without separation." These four phrases serve as "fences" around the mystery of the hypostatic union—Christ's two full and complete natures in one person. "Without confusion, without change" protect the mystery from the heresy of Eutychianism and from monophysitism, which try to preserve the unity of person by creating a hybrid—*tertium quid* (third something)—out of divinity and humanity. "Without division, without separation" protect the mystery from the heresy of Nestorianism, which tries to emphasize the distinction between the humanity and divinity by tearing them apart into two different persons. The definition is saying, So long as you do not violate one of these fences, you may express the mystery of the incarnation in many different ways. All the definition really does is express and protect a mystery. It does not explain anything.

The two main thinkers behind the Chalcedonian Definition were Leo of Rome (who was heavily influenced by Tertullian) and Cyril (who was heavily influenced by Athanasius). When we read their letters carefully, we find that both of them conceived of the person of Jesus Christ as the eternal Logos of God who condescends to take upon himself a human nature that has no particular existence of its own (so *not* a human person). It is an *impersonal* human nature. The personal center of consciousness, will and action is the Logos, the eternal Son of God.

Thus orthodox-catholic Christian belief is that Jesus Christ was and is God with a human nature and not a man elevated into a special relationship with God or a hybrid of God's being and human being. The mystery lies in the fact that this is the only case in reality of a single individual personal being who is both human and divine bearing in his own being all the attributes essential to both natures. Many Christian theologians have attempted to explain how that can be conceived and explained intelligibly. Chalcedon allows speculation so long as it does not fall over a fence into either Nestorianism or Eutychianism.

Leo and Cyril also seem to have considered the divine person and nature of the Logos unaffected by his assumption of a human nature in his existence as Jesus Christ. This is where many Protestants and especially modern ones (and not a few Catholics as well) have difficulty with the Chalcedonian Christology insofar as it reflects that old principle of the immutability and impassibility of the divine. In his masterful *A Study in Christology* British historical theologian Maurice Relton found this to be the Achilles' heel of at least the classical interpretation of Chalcedon: "For both Leo and for Cyril it is the unlimited Logos Who is the centre of the God-man. It follows that, in the Incarnate Christ, His Divine Nature, having undergone no change, is incapable of suffering, and remains unchangeable and unalterable through all the experiences He undergoes in His Incarnate life."[9] According to Relton and many other modern Protestant theologians who accept the basic formula of Chalcedon, this aspect of classical Christology is more than a mystery—it is sheer nonsense. In other words, what is the point of an incarnation in which the Son of God is the one and only person and takes to himself a full and complete human nature but remains entirely and completely untouched and unaffected by the humanness? Is that, then, really an incarnation? Was not the victory of the doctrine of the hypostatic union a hollow one if it is interpreted as in this classical sense?

In other words, there seems to be a lingering ambiguity and unresolved tension in Chalcedon itself—or at least in the way in which its main proponents and interpreters have understood and explained it. If the subject of the union—the divine Logos, Son of God—is understood as unaffected by the union with humanity, then either the union of the two natures is being undermined or the human nature is being made passive and abstract. Clearly Jesus Christ was beset by temptations and fears and suffered many things that were mental and spiritual and not merely physical. According to the hypostatic-union doctrine of Chalcedon, who was tempted? Who experienced fear and mental and spiritual anguish? The only personal subject present is the divine Logos, but according to Leo and Cyril and most of their orthodox followers, divinity cannot suffer or change in any way. Can an "impersonal human nature" be tempted, fear and suffer anguish?

Classical Chalcedonian Christology follows Leo's *Tome* and Cyril's *Letters* in denying change or suffering to the personal subject of the incarnation—the Son of God. But does Chalcedon itself do that? That is less clear. During the Protestant Reformation in the sixteenth century, Martin Luther embraced both Nicaea and Chalcedon as respected landmarks of Christian doctrine and at the same time rejected belief in divine impassibility and attributed creaturely experiences to the Son of God in his incarnate state. For Luther it is no scandal to say "God was born" and "God suffered and died" and "God was crucified" and really *mean* it as more than mere figures of speech. Luther carried the *communicatio idiomatum* to its logical conclusion—something apparently neither Leo nor Cyril nor their orthodox and catholic interpreters did. They were still prisoners of the old Greek notion of the divine impassibility. This kept them from fully fleshing out the great mystery of the incarnation and caused the Chalcedonian doctrine of Christ to be interpreted more and more in a Nestorian sense after the council adjourned.

Even though the empress and her consort decreed that the Council of Chalcedon and its christological definition would end all debate and controversy over important matters of faith, debate erupted again soon afterward over what might seem like fairly minute details of christological interpretation. Bishops soon began asking, Did Christ have two wills or one? Well enough just couldn't be left alone, so it seems.

# CHAPTER 16

# Fallout from the Conflict Continues

Even though the Council of Chalcedon canceled the great controversy between Antioch and Alexandria over the person of Jesus Christ, it did not bring final closure to all argument and discussion of the doctrine. As we will see in this chapter, the aftermath of the council and its formula of orthodox belief in Christ was a long and gradual fallout of debate over its exact meaning. Once again, as so often before, emperors became involved and new councils were held to attempt once and for all to settle on a uniform belief about the incarnation of God in Christ. Most of the post-Chalcedonian controversy took place in the East, and the Western church ignored it unless it was forced to become involved by an emperor, as happened from time to time. As Maurice Relton notes:

> If the West, with its love for ecclesiastical orthodoxy, was content to leave the problem at the point to which the Chalcedonian Definition had carried it, the speculative spirit of the Eastern theologians urged them to further effort in their endeavors to unravel the mystery.[1]

Some of the debate in the East was indeed speculative, and it is sometimes difficult to follow its ins and outs. The bishops and theologians who frequently gathered in Constantinople from all over the Eastern empire wrangled endlessly over whether the Chalcedonian Definition favored Antioch or Alexandria and whether it required belief in two wills or only one will of Christ and how best to explain and express the mystery that lay at its heart. The ambiguity of the hypostatic-union doctrine was unsettling to many Eastern church leaders who sought complete intelligibility in theology or who had vested interests in promoting an Alexandrian or Antiochene interpretation.

**Theology in the West During the Christological Controversy in the East**

Before delving into the post-Chalcedonian christological controversy in the East, it will be helpful to stop and briefly survey what was happening in theology in the West during this time. The Latin West was consumed with its own theological problems all during the great christological controversy that lasted roughly from the First Council of Constantinople in 381 to the Third Council of Constantinople in 680/681. The most intense period of the Western theological debates, however, took place in the decades between Constantinople I and Chalcedon in 451. While the Eastern bishops and theologians debated the fine points of Christology, the Western church leaders were embroiled in a great controversy about the nature of salvation and especially whether the human person who is being saved plays any role in the process or whether its accomplishment is completely a work of God. As we will see in the next chapter, this Western debate was sparked by the contrary teachings of the great North African bishop and theologian Augustine (354-430) and his rival the British monk Pelagius (about 350-418). It led to intense debates between Augustine's defenders and Pelagius's moderate sympathizers in the so-called Semi-Pelagian Controversy that lasted well into the sixth century. Of course, bishop of Rome Leo I (Leo the Great) became involved in the Eastern controversy over Christology, but to most Western theologians, that all-consuming conflict and controversy in the East was of little concern. They believed that Tertullian had settled the issue long before and were pleased to see the Eastern church recognize this at the Council of Chalcedon.

Similarly, the Eastern bishops and theologians were less concerned about the great debate over grace and free will in the West than about their own christological issues. As we have seen, the two did connect at some points. The heretic Pelagius fled from Rome to the East hoping to find refuge there and was temporarily welcomed and given refuge in Syria and Palestine. Many Eastern church leaders thought that his teaching about sin and salvation was not as bad as Augustine and other Western theologians claimed. Nevertheless, they were willing to sacrifice him at the Council of Ephesus in 431 to please the bishop of Rome and get his support for the condemnation of Nestorius. In the outcome of the history of theology, East and West agreed that both Nestorius and Pelagius were heretics and that their teachings were not only unorthodox but damnable errors that undermined gospel itself. Yet it seems clear that the West never did consider Nestorius and

Nestorianism as evil as the East did and that the East never did consider Pelagius and Pelagianism as evil as the West did.

The Western church was also embroiled in battles over the schism known as Donatism, whose churches were numerous and powerful in North Africa in the late fourth and early fifth centuries. The Donatists insisted that the catholic and orthodox Great Church represented by the pope in Rome and the patriarchs of the East and linked with imperial power was apostate because many of its leading bishops had lapsed under persecution before Constantine and then been restored under him. The Donatists wanted a pure church untainted by traitors and immoral leaders, even ones who had repented and been restored through penance. They were moral and ecclesiastical rigorists who harked back to Tertullian and Cyprian. They had their own bishops and cathedrals and schools in the early fifth century, and try as they might, the Western bishops could not seem to stamp them out or bring them into the fold of the Great Church without the help of emperors. Eventually that is what happened. The Western church forced the Donatists underground and many of them became "guerrillas for God" in the North African deserts. They made travel between cities extremely hazardous for leaders of the Great Church.

While the Eastern church was caught up in christological controversy, the Western church was consumed by debates and conflicts over salvation and the true nature of the church. These different contexts of conflict contributed to the eventual parting of the ways between East and West. But another pattern was emerging that also contributed to the division. In the East the Roman emperors from Constantine onward tended to dominate the bishops and patriarchs. This method of church government has come to be known as caesaropapism, that is, "Caesar is pope." The Eastern church rejected this label and the claim that it had *de facto* allowed emperors to become rulers of both church and state. Nevertheless, certain emperors did dominate the church and even its theology. The pattern was established by Constantine, who declared himself "bishop of all the bishops" and "the thirteenth apostle" at the Council of Nicaea in 325. It came to its culmination in Emperor Justinian, who ruled in Constantinople from 527 until 565 and brought much of the Western empire that had been lost to barbarian kings back within the borders of the Roman Empire (which might better be known as the Byzantine Empire after Rome fell in the fifth century).

The West was left without any functioning emperor between about 410 until Justinian and then was divided up by barbarian kings again after his brief invasion and conquest of the West. During the long period of cultural and political decline and division in the Latin West, the bishops of Rome stepped forward to fill the vacuum of power and provide some semblance of unity. This process, begun by Leo I in about 410 and continued even more successfully by later popes such as Gregory I (590-604), set an entirely different precedent for church-state relations in the West. These two bishops have gone down in the annals of church history with the title "the Great" in part, at least, because they exercised power over both church and state. In many ways they functioned as emperors when no single office or person stood above the fray of barbarian battles and cultural dissolution in the West. Eventually, the popes became so powerful they crowned new Western emperors such as Charlemagne in 800. Struggles between secular rulers and popes always plagued the Western church and empire, but never did popes or the bishops of great Western sees acknowledge secular rulers as having power to determine true doctrine. They attempted to assert the church's independence over against the state and its superiority in doctrinal and ecclesiastical matters even when it meant imprisonment.

The continuing christological debates in the East after Chalcedon were virtually ignored by the West, which had its own all-consuming issues to deal with. The Eastern debates over the nature of Christ also came heavily to involve Byzantine emperors and especially the greatest one of all: Justinian. Unfortunately, many Western Christians—both Roman Catholic and Protestant—know little or nothing about the post-Chalcedonian christological controversies in the East, while Eastern Orthodox Christians are steeped in the concepts and terminology of those debates. Without any doubt, greater understanding between Western and Eastern Christians could be achieved if both sides came to know the other's theology better. A major mark of Eastern Christian thought is its struggle against the threats of monophysitism and iconoclasm. Iconoclasm will be discussed in a later chapter. Here we will look at the monophysite controversy and various debates and resolutions surrounding it in the East.

## The Controversy over Christ Continues in the East

One church historian has written that "Chalcedon has proved less a solution than the classic definition of a problem which constantly demands further elucidation."[2] While Chalcedon did propound theologically correct doctrine about Jesus Christ—in that its formula stood the test of time—"from the political point of view, the Council of Chalcedon was a failure" because "no sooner had the bishops departed from Chalcedon than dissentients began to give voice to their indignation."[3] As already noted, some Alexandrians (even outside of Egypt) broke away by refusing even to pay lip service to the Chalcedonian Definition, and they may be called the "radical monophysites" because they refused to compromise in any way with a church that would not declare Christ "one nature after the union." They rejected Eutyches and his error of denying Christ's very humanity as consubstantial with ours, but they would have no fellowship with anyone who claimed that Christ had two natures. Certain radical Antiochenes—really Nestorians—also broke away from the Great Church because the Chalcedonian Formula anathematized any division of the two natures and smacked of Eutychianism and monophysitism in emphasizing Christ's one person (*prosopon* and *hypostasis*).

But many of the bishops who had signed the Chalcedonian Definition became restless and dissatisfied afterward. They wanted to remain in the Great Church, connected with the emperor and patriarchs, but they felt that the Chalcedonian Christology was being interpreted wrongly. Of course, the Antiochenes believed its interpretation favored the Alexandrians and vice versa. The situation was very much like that after the Council of Nicaea in 325. Then bishops who had signed the Nicene Creed reconsidered the *homoousios* formula for describing the equality of Father and Son because it could be interpreted in a Sabellian or modalistic way. After Chalcedon many bishops regretted signing the Definition because it could be interpreted either in a Nestorian or Eutychian way. They feared that it was a victory for one heresy or the other. So "a work corresponding to that which the Cappadocian Fathers did for the Nicene theology was needed to commend the Chalcedonian Definition and to win for it full acceptance."[4]

A question left unresolved in many church leaders' minds was this: "What constitutes a complete manhood [humanity]? What is the minimum which it must retain if it is to be called complete? If the Logos had become the Ego of the manhood, in what sense could the manhood be said to have retained all its parts?"[5] This question was, of course, the main concern of the bishops who leaned toward the Antiochene side with its strong emphasis on the duality of the natures and genuine humanity of the Savior. The Alexandrian bishops had a different concern. They were pleased that the main interpretation of the Chalcedonian Definition was that the one person of the hypostatic union was the divine Son of God, and they wished to push the idea that the human nature was *anhypostasia*—impersonal. But their question was how the integrity and unity of the person of Christ as the divine Logos could be preserved in the long run if the two natures were kept so complete and distinct even after the union. "They believed that there was a contradiction and an open door to Nestorianism in a formula such as that of Chalcedon which distinguished between two natures while claiming that they subsisted in a single hypostasis."[6]

Actually the bishops and theologians of the East tended to fall into three main groups after Chalcedon. First, there were the strict *dyophysites*. (A dyophysite is one who believes in the two natures as radically distinct from one another while rejecting Nestorius's talk of two persons after the union.) These tended to be moderate Antiochenes who saw Chalcedon as a victory for the old Christology of Theodore of Mopsuestia, the theological hero of Antioch. They hoped Chalcedon would turn out to be a partial disavowal of Cyril and his Christology, even if it did endorse his "one person and hypostasis" principle. These dyophysites did not leave the Great Church as did the radical Nestorians. They stayed to fight for the Antiochene interpretation of the hypostatic union. Above all they wished to prevent Cyril's *communicatio idiomatum* principle from becoming the official interpretation of Chalcedon. Their hero after Chalcedon was Theodoret of Cyprus, who had been vindicated at Chalcedon.

A second party within the Great Church after Chalcedon were the moderate monophysites, who regarded Cyril as their great dead hero (even though he had slipped by allowing talk of two natures in his compromise with Antioch in 433) and Severus of Antioch as their living hero and main theologian. Not all monophysites lived in or around Alexandria. Monophysitism had invaded the very heart of Nestorian country—Antioch itself! Severus and his monophysite allies (most of whom were centered around Alexandria or lived in Constantinople) wished to promote Cyril's *communicatio idiomatum* idea of the incarnation and even tried to reinterpret Chalcedon so that the incarnation could be regarded as "one nature after the union." At first they quietly worked behind the scenes to get the Chalcedonian Definition revised—just as the semi-Arians had worked after Nicaea to get the Nicene Creed revised from *homoousios* to *homoiousios*. "The starting point of their Christology was the contemplation of the identity between the pre-existent Word and the incarnate Word; this identity was a soteriological necessity asserted by the Creed of Nicaea and by Cyril against Nestorius. For the Monophysites, it was expressed as an identity of nature or hypostasis, since these two terms were synonymous."[7] A leading monophysite by the name of Timothy Aelurus declared that "if there are two natures [in Christ], there are also necessarily two persons; but if there are two persons, there are also two Christs."[8] But the moderate monophysites rejected Eutychian mingling of divinity and humanity in Christ and argued for "one composite nature" of divinity and humanity through the hypostatic union. The distinction between the natures was to be kept while the union was to be emphasized. Their theology was probably not very different—if at all—from Cyril's.

The third post-Chalcedonian party was the neo-Chalcedonians, and their hero and victor became someone named Leontius. There is great confusion in church history about his identity. Some consider Leontius of Byzantium the person who worked out the officially approved interpretation of Chalcedon known as the *enhypostasia* principle. Others say the person who did that was a different Leontius—of Jerusalem. Here we will follow the tradition of considering the person who led the Great Church toward a solution at the Second Council of Constantinople in 553 Leontius of Byzantium. The neo-Chalcedonians wished to find a compromise between the moderate Antiochenes (dyophysites) and moderate Alexandrians (monophysites) while rejecting the radical wings of both parties. The path toward such a resolution of the seemingly interminable controversy lay for them in reaffirming the language of Chalcedon as "carved in stone" while interpreting it in such a way that the human nature of Christ is seen as real and genuine without giving it any independent status over against the Logos. In other words, somehow all the known categories of being *(physis, ousia)* and personhood *(prosopon, hypostasis)* had to be transcended in some great conceptual leap to a new category.

All parties in the great christological debates seemed locked into the belief that nature and person necessarily go together so that in order for a nature to be real and complete it has to have a person to give it real existence as opposed to abstract existence. At least this was nearly universally believed about human beings. An individual human nature without a human person simply could not be conceived as real and complete by anyone in the debate. That is why the Antiochenes tended to sacrifice the oneness of personhood to the duality of natures and why the Alexandrians tended to sacrifice the duality of natures to the oneness of personhood. Neither side could see how a human nature could be completely real and really complete without a distinct and individual human person. That presented the task for thought for the neo-Chalcedonians, and Leontius of Byzantium presented the solution, just as the Cappadocian fathers had presented the solution to the trinitarian dilemma a century and a half earlier.

### The Monophysite Controversy

In the overall scheme of things the monophysite party caused much greater trouble within both the church and empire than did the dyophysite or moderate Antiochene party. The latter group of theologians and bishops believed that Chalcedon generally represented a victory for their side and that their cause could best be served by fighting against monophysitism, which was very strong politically and ecclesiastically. The two leading monophysites in the post-Chalcedonian period were Severus of Antioch and the bishop of Alexandria, Timothy Aelurus. They and their cohorts were able to sway Emperor Zeno (476-491) to favor monophysitism for a time. Severus wrote the most important theological book of monophysitism, *The Lover of Truth,* and in it he strongly affirmed the real humanity and divinity of Christ while arguing that these coalesce into a single composite nature because of their union in the person of the Word or Son of God:

> He who was eternally consubstantial to him who begat him is the one who voluntarily descended and became consubstantial to this mother [Mary]. Thus, he became man, being God; he made himself that which he was not, while at the same time remaining that which he was, without any change. For he did not lose his divinity in his incarnation, and the body did not lose the tangible character of its nature.[9]

Yet even though Severus affirmed the dual realities of divinity and humanity in Jesus Christ, it is clear which one dominates: divinity in the person of the Logos dominates Jesus' humanity. He only mentioned the "tangible character" of the human body as an example of how he was human. Apollinarius could have said as much.

The leading monophysites argued against the classical interpretation of Chalcedon, which was increasingly dyophysite. They began to criticize not only the interpretation but the Definition itself, and that on three counts: First, the Definition had excluded the one and only formula that could successfully prevail against Nestorianism: "one incarnate nature of the divine Logos." Second, the Definition had neglected to mention the hypostatic union or *communicatio idiomatum*. Third, it had excluded the confession "out of two—one." Finally, when their moderate attempts to sway opinion toward their interpretation of Chalcedon failed, the leading monophysites openly repudiated it and Timothy Aelurus pronounced anathema against it: "As for us, we conform to the doctrine of the divine Scriptures and of the holy Doctors of the Church. We anathematize those who speak of two natures or of two *ousiai* [substances] in respect of Christ."[10]

While it was one thing for the emperor and leading patriarchs of Christendom to allow a few Nestorian and radical monophysite (Eutychian) churches in Syria and Egypt to depart from the Great Church in schism, it was another thing entirely to allow the powerful patriarch of Alexandria and a whole limb of the body of Christ to fall away over a few words when they openly repudiated all heresies and were only calling for reconsideration of some wording and interpretation of the Chalcedonian Definition. After all, the Definition itself was not a creed like the Nicene statement of faith. It was regarded even by its formulators as only an interpretation of the Nicene faith. During the early part of the sixth century, the monophysite forces grew within the Eastern church until they threatened to become more numerous and powerful than the other parties. In order to make clear that they were not heretics, they insistently proclaimed their disagreement with Eutyches and his radical monophysite followers and harked back to the great father Cyril so highly regarded by all.

In 527 a powerful new emperor was crowned in Constantinople—Justinian I, or Justinian the Great. Justinian is known for many reforms and innovations in law and government, as well as for building the great cathedral of Hagia Sophia that now stands as a converted mosque in the center of Istanbul, but in theology his claim to fame is resolving the monophysite controversy. Like the first Byzantine emperor, Constantine, he considered it his duty to keep the church united in doctrine as well as in polity. So one of his first acts was to require all Christian bishops throughout the empire to adhere strictly to Chalcedon. This seemed a blow to even moderate monophysitism. However, in order to bring at least the most moderate of the moderates back within the orthodox and catholic camp of the Great Church, Justinian agreed to call another council and make clear once and for all how Chalcedon was properly to be interpreted. He promised that the monophysites would be accommodated if they stayed within the church.

## Leontius of Byzantium and Orthodox Christology

Just as Empress Pulcheria and her consort and regent, Marcian, had circulated *Leo's Tome* to all bishops before the Council of Chalcedon to ensure a certain outcome there, so Justinian adopted a particular theologian's writings to promote among bishops in preparation for the new council that was to be held in Constantinople in 553 as the fifth ecumenical council of Christendom. The favored theologian was Leontius of Byzantium, who had been working away quietly in both Jerusalem and Constantinople between 529 and 536. Justinian had appointed him to call and preside over conferences of leading orthodox theologians to carve out a new concept of the hypostatic union that would remain fully consistent with the Chalcedonian Definition while at the same time bridging the gap between the moderate monophysites and dyophysites.

The details of Leontius's life are unknown. In fact, as noted earlier some scholars debate whether the person who accomplished this even was Leontius of Byzantium! Nevertheless, tradition has it that he was born around 485 in Byzantium of noble parentage—which is why Justinian knew him—and died in 543, probably in Jerusalem. Justinian and Leontius may have been related in some way. Early in life Leontius left his wealth and comfortable life in Constantinople and traveled to Syria, where he lived in a monastery and came under Nestorian influence. Eventually he freed himself of that heresy and became an ardent supporter of Chalcedon but with a decidedly Alexandrian spin to it.

Leontius of Byzantium's main surviving works have never been translated into

English. They are generally known in the West by their Latin titles: *Contra Nestorianos et Eutychianos (Against the Nestorians and the Eutychians), Capita Triginta Contra Severum (Thirty Chapters Against Severus)* and *Epilysis (Solutions* [to the arguments of Severus]). Besides presenting profound arguments against the various christological heresies and in favor of Chalcedonian Christology, Leontius achieved a conceptual leap that Justinian found eminently helpful in defending Chalcedon against its detractors: the principle of the *enhypostasia* of the human nature of Christ in the divine Word. This idea, soon to be explained here, represented a "distinct advance on what had gone before in Alexandrian christological thought"[11] and seemed to satisfy the demands of both moderate parties—Antiochenes as well as Alexandrians. The problem to which *enhypostasia* is the solution is expressed in this question: "If, as was everywhere agreed, a nature must have its [own] *hypostasis* [personal existence], how can one confess 'two natures in one *hypostasis*'?"[12] This seems to be the kernel of the entire debate—the unresolved and seemingly unresolvable dilemma that drove and kept Antioch and Alexandria apart.

Leontius agreed with the Alexandrians first and foremost that the eternal divine Logos/Word, the Son of God, is the subject of the incarnation. The one and only personality of Jesus is God the Son. But against the Alexandrian Christology, he rejected the idea of the impersonality of the humanity of Christ—Cyril's *anhypostasia* of the human nature—for "a nature without hypostasis would be an abstraction."[13] Must not two natures then involve two persons? No! Leontius argued that while a nature—even a human nature—cannot exist without a hypostasis, it need not have its own hypostasis. It can be "hypostatized" in another. In other words, for Leontius, "the human nature of Christ was not without hypostasis, but became hypostatic [personalized] in the Person of the Logos."[14] The human nature of Christ—a full and complete human nature—was not *anhypostatic* (impersonal), nor personal in itself, but *enhypostatic,* which means "personalized in the person of another."

According to Leontius, there are three ways in which any two beings or realities may be united. First, they may be merely juxtaposed side by side and closely related to one another as in a friendship or a marriage. This is how the Nestorians conceived the incarnation—humanity and divinity as two natures and two persons cooperating together. Second, they may be blended into a "third something"—a hybrid—so that out of their union a new nature appears that is a mixture of the two. That is how the Eutychians and radical monophysites conceived the incarnation—humanity and divinity as one personal entity that is a mixture of two natures, but neither one fully. Finally, "two things may be so united that their distinct natures subsist in a single hypostasis."[15] This was Leontius's vision of the incarnation, and he provided illustrations to support it. For example, a torch is both wood and flame—two natures—completely united by fire. Similarly, in a human being, body and soul are two distinct natures united as long as one lives by the person of the human being. Each nature in this third kind of union *can* have its own independent existence but does not. They interpenetrate without forming a third something because they are held together by the hypostasis or subsistence of one.

According to Leontius, the incarnation is the third kind of union. In the hypostatic union the human nature of Christ subsists—is personalized and given its concrete existence—in the hypostasis of his divine nature. "Thus, the hypostasis in Christ is that of the eternal Word, and in it the divine as well as the human subsist. It is for this reason that one may say that there is in Christ an 'enhypostatic union.' "[16] In other words, for Leontius the human nature of Christ had everything any other human has in its unfallen condition (pristine sinlessness) except independent personal existence apart from the person of the divine Word. Jesus Christ was and is the eternal second person of the Trinity—the Word, the Son of God—with a human nature as well as his own divine nature, and he is the "person" of both. Why didn't they think of that before?

Leontius's proposed solution was not an addition to the Nicene faith as interpreted by Chalcedon. All *enhypostasia* involves is an interpretation of Chalcedonian Christology that helps overcome the strenuous objections of Alexandrians and Antiochenes, even if the more obstinate advocates of both parties refused to give in and accept it. The important point is that neither Leontius nor Justinian nor the Second Council of Constantinople in 553 considered it in any way going beyond Chalcedon. Rather, with the *enhypostasia* principle

> Leontius . . . is but carrying forward the work of the Chalcedonian Fathers in seeking so to formulate the true faith that no room would be left for either the Nestorian or the Eutychian error. "Two natures must be confessed, since in Jesus Christ Godhead and manhood have been united in a personal union. But the manhood does not exist independently, as if it were that of 'another besides the Logos'." Rather, it has its existence, only it exists in the *hypostasis* of the Logos, who has united it to himself. And because each nature remains in its essential properties and qualities, the "difference of existence" being preserved, the conception that in Jesus Christ there is but one nature *(una substantia)* is rendered impossible.[17]

Leontius's Christology can accommodate the *communicatio idiomatum* so that both divine and human characteristics can be attributed to the divine Logos who formed the personal center of Jesus Christ. As Jesus Christ, he—the Word—both suffered and conquered death. Nevertheless, in this scheme it is still possible to say that divinity is incapable of suffering (impassible) by claiming that Jesus Christ only suffered "in his humanity." Also it is possible to say that humanity is whole and complete and being healed by the saving incarnation because the human nature of Jesus Christ had everything essential to a human nature.

At the Second Council of Constantinople in 553, Leontius of Byzantium's interpretation of Chalcedon was explained to all, and all bishops were required to reaffirm the Chalcedonian Definition. In other words, they were told by the emperor, "If you don't see that this new interpretation completely clears up your objections—be they Alexandrian or Antiochene—then you are just obstinate and unworthy to be a bishop of the Great Church." In order to get the monophysites to agree to reaffirm Chalcedon with this new interpretation, Justinian and the council condemned Antioch's hero Theodore of Mopsuestia posthumously. Also as a sideshow to the main purpose of the council, it condemned Origen—an Alexandrian. Clearly the main thrust of the fifth ecumenical council, dominated by Justinian, was to placate and accommodate the moderate Alexandrian monophysites while retaining and reaffirming the orthodoxy of Chalcedon. The Antiochenes lost this one. "In short, Antiochene Christology was condemned in all its forms, while Alexandrine Christology was rejected only in its most extreme form."[18]

Is there a bottom line to this story? What, after all is said and done, is a Christian supposed to believe about Jesus Christ? Cutting through all the dense undergrowth to find the hidden treasure, it is this: According to the doctrine of the hypostatic union as interpreted and affirmed by the fifth ecumenical council, "while one may embark on the mental process of seeing in their reality the two natures of Christ, one must always return to the fundamental truth that he is one Person, the Logos made man, to whom belong both divine and human properties, and whose are all the actions and sayings reported of him in Scripture, whether divine or human."[19]

With great patience one may follow the church's train of thought up to and through the christological decisions of the fifth council at Constantinople in 553. Few modern Protestant Christians, at least, can happily or without great frustration move on with the Eastern church from there to the christological decisions of the sixth ecumenical council, the council that is known in church history as the Third Council of Constantinople or Constantinople III. It was held in the Byzantine capital in 681 to settle a controversy of great importance to Eastern Orthodox Christians but virtually ignored by Western Christians. The Roman Catholic Church does recognize Constantinople III as one of the truly ecumenical councils of the undivided church, but few Catholics pay any attention to its acts or decisions. Between Constantinople II and 681 a teaching about Christ arose within orthodox ranks that was meant to bring schismatic monophysites in Syria and Egypt back into the fold of the Great Church. It has come to be known as monothelitism—belief in one will in Christ. The question that was subsequently debated was whether Christ had two wills—a divine one and a human one—or only one will, which would be divine.

One of the great heroes of Eastern Orthodox theology is the man who almost single-handedly defeated monothelitism: Maximus the Confessor (580-662). His story will be told in a later chapter. Because of his theological defense of dyothelitism (belief in two wills of Christ), and because of his heroic martyrdom because of it, the sixth ecumenical council condemned monothelitism and required belief in two wills as orthodox doctrine. This was a terrible defeat for monophysitism, which remained separated from the Great Church ever after.

If, at the end of this section on the great christological controversies and the councils that dealt with them, some readers feel that something went terribly wrong on the way to the fifth and especially the sixth ecumenical councils, they would not be alone. Many Protestants and not a few modern Catholics wonder if all this was really necessary. Was the gospel of Jesus Christ as Savior and Lord really at stake in these seemingly abstract and sometimes hairsplitting debates? Perhaps the best answer is both yes and no. Church historian Justo González sums it up best:

> Thus ended a long process of dogmatic development and clarification which had begun at least three centuries earlier. The result was the rejection of all extreme positions, the categorical assertion that Jesus Christ was totally and truly human as well as divine, and yet the claim that these two natures were closely bound together in a single hypostasis. In this process, the historical, loving Jesus of the New Testament was left aside, and the Savior had become an object of speculation and controversy; he was now described in terms totally alien to the vocabulary of the New Testament—"hypostasis," "nature," "energy," etc.; he had become a static object of discussion rather than the Lord of believers and of history. But one might ask whether any other road was open to the church once believers began applying their best intellectual faculties to the greatest mystery of the Christian faith. The way that was followed through six councils . . . did somehow manage to reject every simplistic attempt to rationalize the faith, and did point to the inscrutable mystery of the incarnation.[20]

The curtain closes on this great act of the drama of Christian theology. For all practical purposes, Christian orthodoxy was complete by the fifth or sixth ecumenical council. Eastern Orthodox Christians will want to include the seventh before bringing down the curtain on the development of orthodox doctrine. Roman Catholic Christians will perhaps point to later councils and decisions of popes, and some Protestants will no doubt argue that most of it was unnecessary because Christian orthodoxy was all established much, much earlier—perhaps as early as 325 at the Council of Nicaea if not earlier in the writings of the apostles and some of the church fathers. Nevertheless, the great heresies of gnosticism, adoptionism, Arianism, Sabellianism (modalism), Apollinarianism, Nestorianism and Eutychianism (monophysitism) had to be overcome, and that was a long and convoluted theological process. Would that it could have been simpler. Some systematic theologians argue that virtually every heresy of two thousand years of Christianity can be boiled down to one of those mentioned above. If that is true, then their defeat was essential even if it involved great confusion, some scandal, and highly technical debates and doctrinal formulas. If any one of the heresies mentioned had won the day and become the consensus of Christians worldwide, the result would have been a serious loss for the gospel. God works in mysterious ways—even through emperors such as Cyrus in the Old Testament era and Constantine and Justinian in the early church—to preserve truth.

Now it is time to turn to the story of theological developments in the West at the same time as the great christological controversy in the East. One name stands head and shoulders above all the rest of Western Christian thinkers. Perhaps it is not an exaggeration to suggest that Augustine was the most influential Western Christian theologian since the days of the apostles themselves. It is to his story and then to others that we will now turn.

# PART V

# A Tale of Two Churches

## *The Great Tradition Divides Between East & West*

*Up to this point the story of Christian theology has been the story of a relatively unified* Great Church, both catholic and orthodox. We have seen how heresies and temporary schisms threatened the unity of the early church and how the church sometimes used coercive power to enforce unity if not uniformity. In spite of these tensions, however, the church of the bishops in apostolic succession managed to remain one church. In the middle of the fifth century at the time of the Council of Chalcedon (451), the bishops of the great sees of Christendom were still in fellowship with one another, even if that fellowship was strained and threatening to break. After the council, the Great Church was identified with the bishops in fellowship with the emperor and patriarch of Constantinople in the East and the bishop of Rome (also considered a patriarch) in the West, and these three usually maintained communion and fellowship with each other.

We have also seen that the Great Church suffered several major defections in the fourth and fifth centuries. In the West the Donatist schism in North Africa developed its own fellowship of bishops and congregations and was only overcome by the power of the state forcing its adherents back within the fold of the Great Church or into exile and underground. In the East the Nestorian and monophysite schisms became more permanent on the fringes of the empire. At least as an ideal on paper, however, the Great Church and its Great Tradition of faith and fellowship remained relatively intact. But this was not to last indefinitely. Tensions between the churches of the West, which looked increasingly to the bishop of Rome as supreme patriarch of all Christendom, and the East, which looked to Constantinople (emperor and patriarch) as the center of Christendom, deepened over the centuries after the Council of Chalcedon for many reasons.

The great schism between East and West came officially and finally in 1054 when the patriarchs of Rome and Constantinople excommunicated one another. But in fact that had happened before. After 1054, however, the breach was never healed. From that time on, at least for nearly a millennium, there would be two major branches of Christianity, each claiming to be the one true apostolic church both catholic and orthodox. Most readers will recognize these two great traditions by the names Eastern Orthodoxy and Roman Catholicism. However, each tradition considers itself the continuation of the church of the apostles that was born on the day of Pentecost (Acts 2). Each one considers the other a schism away from the one true holy catholic and orthodox church.

A visible sign of this attitude is refusal of eucharistic fellowship. Members of the churches of Rome who look to the bishop of Rome as pope and "vicar of Christ" are not to partake of the Eucharist, or Lord's Supper, with members of the Eastern Orthodox family of churches. Members of the Eastern Orthodox family of churches (Greek, Russian, Romanian, etc.) are not to partake of the sacrament with members of the church of Rome. While each side acknowledges the other as Christian, they do not consider each other true churches of Jesus Christ. They are schisms in their rival's eyes. Each claims that the other broke the peace and unity of the body of Christ at least in 1054 if not earlier.

What led to this split? How did the undivided Great Church of the apostles and Roman Empire divide in this way? Why are there two great and ancient families of churches each claiming to represent the early church in the world today? This chapter will tell that story in several stages. It begins with the most important theologian of the Western tradition—Augustine of Hippo—who in many ways is the true father of the Western approach to theology. Even though he is counted a saint of the church and great teacher of Christians by the Eastern churches, he is also considered one who led the church astray in several crucial ways. His legacy included several deeply ingrained habits of thought in the West that Eastern Christians could not accept. Our story of the great schism between East and West will continue with consideration of several important, distinctive theologians of the East as well as of the West who contributed to the split in lesser ways than Augustine. We will conclude this portion of our story of Christian theology with consideration of the immediate factors causing the divide, such as the Western alteration of the Nicene Creed that the East interpreted as a heresy. By the end of this section, readers will know why the Great Church and its Great Tradition divided into the two branches known today as Eastern Orthodoxy and Roman Catholicism.

In order to tell this part of the story properly, we must back up in time before the ending of the part four. While the roots of the divide between East and West lie deep in issues of language and culture, the divorce between Rome and Constantinople seems to have become inevitable once one particular theologian became the standard and norm for theological thought in the West. His name was Augustinus Aurelius and he did not speak or read Greek. He read both the Bible and the earlier church fathers in rather poor Latin translations. He was steeped in the Latin traditions of thought and lived his whole life within the sphere of influence of Rome. For some reason his influence became pervasive in Western Christianity in his own lifetime and semiofficial within a few decades after his death.

Augustine may be compared with Origen in terms of genius, literary productivity and influence. What Origen was to the East (up until his undeserved condemnation in 553), Augustine is to the West. Even the great Protestant Reformers of the sixteenth century considered themselves followers and interpreters of Augustine. It would be almost impossible to exaggerate the influence of this one man's thinking on Western Christianity, both Roman Catholic and Protestant. His acceptance in the East has, however, been less enthusiastic. Eastern Orthodox theologians generally believe that interpretations of Augustine's theology, if not the thinking of the North African church father himself, led the Western churches down the path of schism and perhaps even heresy.

It is appropriate, then, to begin our story of the great schism between East and West with careful consideration of Augustine and his legacy. While he wrote books and letters about almost every conceivable theological, philosophical and ethical issue, our focus will be on Augustine's soteriology. His views on sin and salvation stand at the center of his controversial contribution to the story of theology. His views on the Trinity and the person of Jesus Christ have distinctive aspects, but overall he accepted the consensus of the church at Nicaea and Constantinople, and his writing on those subjects is not in any particular conflict with the orthodoxy declared at Ephesus and Chalcedon. Much has been made of Augustine's psychological model of the Trinity, and many have contrasted it with the dominant mode of thinking about the Trinity in the East. However, by no means was Augustine's overall theology of the Trinity or the incarnation unorthodox or out of line with the general Eastern forms of thinking. Here, then, we will focus on those aspects of Augustine's theology that more directly contributed to the East-West split and that came to shape the distinctive theology of salvation in the West that Eastern Christians find troubling.

# CHAPTER 17

# Augustine Confesses God's Glory & Human Depravity

*Church father, theologian and bishop Augustine stood at a major crossroad* of theology and pointed the entire West in a certain direction:

> Augustine is the end of one era as well as the beginning of another. He is the last of the ancient Christian writers, and the forerunner of medieval theology. The main currents of ancient theology converged in him, and from him flow the rivers, not only of medieval scholasticism, but also of sixteenth-century Protestant theology.[1]

Some have labeled the distinctive "river of theology" flowing from Augustine down the centuries of Western theology Augustinianism and rightly identified its main feature as "its emphasis on the absolute supremacy of God and the accompanying absolute helplessness and dependency of the human soul on the grace of God."[2]

This core of Augustine's theology was not entirely new with him, of course. Church fathers before him also believed in and taught God's supremacy and the human soul's dependency on grace. But Augustine contributed a new spin to these ideas and linked them together in a new way. As we will see, Augustinianism introduced into the stream of Christian thought something called monergism—the idea and belief that human agency is entirely passive and God's agency is all-determining in both universal history and individual salvation. Many people already know a part of this as "predestination" and automatically link it with the sixteenth-century Protestant Reformer John Calvin. However, the broader perspective is Augustine's monergistic ideas of providence and salvation in which God is the sole active agent and energy, and humans—both collectively and individually—are tools and instruments of God's grace or wrath.

Christian theology before Augustine tended to assume a view of the God-world relationship called synergism—the idea and belief that God's agency and human agency cooperate in some way to produce both history and salvation. Of course, orthodox Christians have always believed that God's power and grace are supreme, but pre-Augustinian theologians almost all assumed that God allows humans some degree of freedom to make certain crucial decisions. While Augustine never completely rejected human freedom, the overall tenor of his thought militates against any genuine freedom of humans to thwart God's perfect will. God always gets his way, even when humans sin and perform evil acts. Augustine's God is an "all-determining reality" whose power is his main characteristic:

> While Augustine makes a titanic effort to preserve both human freedom and the goodness of God, it is clear that his God is, above all, the imperial ruler of the universe, and what cannot be sacrificed at any price is the absolute *power* of that God. This is the guiding thread of Augustine's thought, that which gives shape to those doctrines most associated with his name.[3]

**Augustine's Life and Ministry**

Augustine's life is the best known of all early church fathers. In fact, we know more about Augustine's life than almost any other ancient person's. That is because he wrote one of the first fairly reliable and detailed autobiographies, known as his *Confessions.* Although it is written in the form of a prayer to recount his spiritual journey and give thanks to God, Augustine's *Confessions* reveals a great deal about his childhood, family, youth, early struggles, mental and physical health, conversion, theological development and life as a leading churchman in North Africa. Augustine hid little or nothing from his readers. He laid out in intimate detail his sins from almost infancy into adult life and emphasized at every point his own total depravity and the power of God's grace to heal and transform. The *Confessions* reveals that Augustine was a pessimist about humanity, including his own, and an optimist about grace.

In 354 Augustine was born Aurelius Augustinus in Thagaste, a small city of North Africa not far from Carthage. His mother, Monica, was a Christian, and in the *Confessions* Augustine gave her great credit for bringing him to repentance and faith through her unfailing prayers on his behalf. Augustine's father was a middle-class Roman civil servant with some standing in the community. He was also a pagan and not very interested in Monica's Christianity. Although he was raised as a Christian, Augustine wandered away from practicing the faith as an adolescent and especially as a young student at the academy in Carthage, where he alternated between trying to "scratch the itching sore of lust" and attempting to discover the meaning of life through studying philosophy and religion.

In Carthage he came under the influence of a relatively new religion—a cult of the day—known as Manichaeism. The Manichaeans were followers of a Persian prophet named Manes who had been martyred by the Romans much like Jesus Christ. Augustine was attracted to them for some time because they seemed intellectual and offered answers to life's ultimate questions that seemed to the young student superior to Christianity's or traditional paganism's answers. For instance, the Manichaeans believed in two eternal and equally powerful forces of good and evil locked in endless combat. Like gnostics they attributed evil to matter—the creation of the evil principle—and good to spirit created by the good God of heaven. This seemed to solve the riddle of evil. Eventually Augustine became disillusioned with this dualistic theology and spirituality and left North Africa for Rome and Milan.

Living as a pagan in Milan, the seat of the imperial court in the West, Augustine came under two life-transforming influences. While teaching rhetoric (communication) at the academy in Milan, Augustine began reading books of Neo-Platonism. These convinced him that there could be an infinite spiritual reality that is not material, and this was one quandary that had stopped him from accepting Christianity. Neo-Platonism also provided him with an insight about evil similar to that discovered and taught by Cappadocian father Gregory of Nyssa: evil is not a substance but the absence of the good. Augustine had come to believe that Christianity and biblical religion in general could not answer the problem of evil. If God is all-powerful and perfectly good, why is there so much evil in the world God created out of nothing? Did not God have to create evil, then? Does that not make God the author of evil? Neo-Platonism—a pagan philosophy—gave him one of the most important keys to unlock the door that opened onto his mother's religious faith.

Also while living and teaching in Milan, Augustine began studying the rhetorical style of northern Italy's greatest Christian preacher and bishop, the saintly Ambrose. Ambrose was noted for his great courage in confronting the emperor after he had ordered thousands of Greeks slain in a senseless and vindictive massacre.

He was also noted for his impressive homiletical skills, and Augustine began lurking in the back of the Christian cathedral in Milan to hear him preach. Eventually the message preached by Ambrose began to sink in and convince Augustine that he had been wrong about Christianity. He had too easily dismissed it as a religion for weak and silly people with no sophistication. Ambrose proved that one could be intellectual, articulate and courageous and be a Christian.

By early 386 Augustine was convinced of the truth of the Christian worldview but not yet ready to convert to his mother's faith. He knew that authentic Christianity transcends the merely intellectual, and his *Confessions* reveals a deep inner struggle with taking the step of repentance and faith in Jesus Christ. One of Augustine's ironic prayers had earlier been "Oh, God, give me the gift of chastity . . . but not yet." Now in Milan he was truly at the point of decision and yet not quite ready to give up his sinful and self-centered lifestyle.

Augustine's conversion is one of the most famous in the annals of church history. The story of it is the focal point of his *Confessions,* and it reveals that the event involved a radical break with his past life and a transformation that left him hardly the same person as before. One day in August of 386 Augustine sat in the garden of a rented villa he shared with some friends in Milan. His own account of what happened describes his conversion best. He and a friend named Alypius were reading a scroll of Paul's Epistle to the Romans and discussing the gospel preached and taught by the apostle to the Gentiles. Augustine was overcome with conviction:

> When a profound reflection had, from the secret depths of my soul, drawn together and heaped up all my misery before the sight of my heart, there arose a mighty storm, accompanied by as mighty a shower of tears. Which, that I might pour forth fully, with its natural expressions, I stole away from Alypius; for it suggested itself to me that solitude was fitter for the business of weeping. So I retired to such a distance that even his presence could not be oppressive to me. Thus it was with me at that time, and he perceived it; for something, I believe, I had spoken, wherein the sound of my voice appeared choked with weeping, and in that state had I risen up. He then remained where we had been sitting, most completely astonished. I flung myself down, how, I know not, under a certain fig-tree, giving free course to my tears, and the streams of mine eyes gushed out, an acceptable sacrifice unto Thee. And, not indeed in these words, yet to this effect, spake I much unto Thee—"But Thou, O lord, how long?" "How long, Lord? Wilt Thou be angry for ever? Oh, remember not against us former iniquities;" for I felt that I was enthralled by them. I sent up these sorrowful cries—"How long,

how long? To-morrow, and to-morrow? Why not now? Why is there not this hour an end to my uncleanness?"

I was saying these things and weeping in the most bitter contrition of my heart, when, lo, I heard the voice as of a boy or girl, I know not which, coming from a neighboring house, chanting, and oft repeating, "Take up and read; take up and read." Immediately my countenance was changed, and I began most earnestly to consider whether it was unusual for children in any kind of game to sing such words; nor could I remember ever to have heard the like. So, restraining the torrent of my tears, I rose up, interpreting it no other way than as a command to me from Heaven to open the book, and to read the first chapter I should light upon. . . . So quickly I returned to the place where Alypius was sitting; for there had I put down the volume of the apostles, when I rose thence. I grasped, opened, and in silence read that paragraph on which my eyes first fell—"Not in rioting and drunkenness, not in chambering and wantonness, not in strife and envying; but put ye on the Lord Jesus Christ and make not provision for the flesh, to fulfill the lusts thereof [Rom. 13:13-14]." No further would I read, nor did I need; for instantly, as the sentence ended—by a light, as it were, of security infused into my heart—all the gloom of doubt vanished away.[4]

Shortly after his conversion Augustine was baptized by Bishop Ambrose into the catholic and orthodox church in Milan. At first he tried to live the life of a monk by converting the small villa into a monastery for prayer, study and reflection. Eventually he decided to return to his home in North Africa and establish a monastery there. His mother, who had joined him in Milan, died on the trip home. After his arrival in North Africa, Augustine became famous among Christians in the area now known as Tunisia for his great intellectual and rhetorical skills. The Great Church there was still plagued by the schismatic Donatist Christians who continued to draw converts away from catholic and orthodox Christianity to their own churches. The Manichaeans were still growing and challenging Christianity. Paganism remained relatively strong. The Great Church itself was beset with many internal problems. In spite of himself Augustine was unable to live the life he desired—that of a reclusive, reflective Christian scholar steeped in meditation, study and prayer.

In 391 Augustine was virtually forced to receive ordination by the Christian congregation in Hippo. One Sunday while he was worshiping with them, they literally laid hands upon him and dragged him forward to be ordained by the bishop despite his tears and protests. Then when the elderly bishop of Hippo desired a cobishop, Augustine was once again pressed into service. Against his will he was consecrated bishop of Hippo in 395 and succeeded the bishop when he died the next year. Augustine was bishop of a leading see of North Africa at age forty-two, and he remained in that office for more than thirty years until he died in 430. During his tenure he became deeply embroiled in the affairs of church life and politics and gained a reputation as one of Christendom's wisest leaders. He also entered into debate with the Manichaeans, and through his writings, showed them to be a religion based on myths and filled with contradictions. He fought against the growing influence of Donatism and provided a theology of church life and the sacraments that eventually overwhelmed their objections to the validity of catholic hierarchy and sacraments. But most importantly for our story, the bishop of Hippo engaged in a protracted controversy and debate with a British monk in Rome named Pelagius and his followers. Out of these conflicts and controversies grew a whole library of Augustine's writings. Only Origen exceeded him in volume of written words. A Spanish theologian named Isidore of Seville is alleged to have placed the following inscription above the cabinet in which he kept all of Augustine's works: "He who claims to have read all this is a liar."[5]

So massive was Augustine's literary output that one can almost literally find anything there that one wants to find. He wrote on many topics and often anticipated philosophical, psychological and theological developments of later ages. Some commentators consider him the first psychologist in that he explored the subconscious realm of the human mind. His reflections on creation anticipate evolution in broad outline in that he rejected a literal seven-day creation and interpreted the "days" of creation as epochs or eras of indefinite length during which God worked through nature to bring forth living things. But more pertinent to our story is that, unfortunately, Augustine's writings contain many apparent contradictions. His thinking on many theological subjects developed and changed over time, so that it is important to notice transitions within his thought. For example, in his early theology he defended a libertarian idea of human freedom against the deterministic Manichaeans. That is, Augustine began by arguing that sin and evil are not in any way determined by God but are products of human free will misused. Later, in debate with Pelagius and the Pelagians (and so-called Semi-Pelagians) he changed his mind and began to interpret human freedom as the ability only to sin and commit evil apart from God's transforming grace. He elevated God's freedom and sovereignty over against all human freedom and debased human agency as always evil left to its own devices. Also early in his theological career, Augustine considered faith the human person's contribution to salvation—a synergistic idea. Later, in reaction to Pelagius he came to regard faith as a gift of God—an idea more compatible with monergism.

Augustine's theology is not so much inconsistent as it is developmental. One should not get the wrong idea. Although there remained unresolved tensions in his theology to the very end, Augustine always strove for the ideal of complete systematic consistency. Like the Cappadocian fathers, he acknowledged mystery. He is alleged to have commented that the doctrine of the Trinity is mysterious and dangerous because "if you deny it you will lose your salvation, but if you try to understand it you will lose your mind!" Of course that did not stop him from writing hundreds of pages exploring the mystery and attempting to make it as intelligible as possible. But during his career as a bishop and theologian, Augustine constantly allowed his thinking to be shaped by the needs of the moment under the authority of the Word of God. So, when confronted with a new heresy, he was willing to rethink his earlier theology in order to combat it. He freely admitted that he had written things early in his career that were inconsistent with his own mature thinking, and that was because of the appearance of Pelagius and Pelagianism in his context. When he looked deeply into that heresy, he felt that some of his own earlier views could be interpreted as supporting it, so he revised them. In fact, he swung to what many Christians even of his own time saw as an opposite extreme.

Here we will discuss only a few slices of Augustine's overall theology and focus primarily on his mature thought, which developed gradually through three major stages of controversy. First, his thinking was shaped by the need to combat Manichaeism. Against that cult he launched an all-out apologetic assault in which he used Neo-Platonism as an ally and weapon. Neo-Platonism in turn shaped his own subsequent thinking about God and God's relationship with the world. Second, Augustine was preoccupied with combating the Donatist schism in his own backyard. Against that he developed ideas about the church, priesthood and sacraments that became distinctive hallmarks of Catholic theology. Third and finally, Augustine debated Pelagius and his sympathizers and through that debate developed his own distinctive views about human depravity and God's sovereignty. The Catholic Church never completely came to terms with Augustine's own views but firmly rejected Pelagius's and those of his followers in large measure due to Augustine's influence. Augustine's own anti-Pelagian views became a constantly recurring source of creativity as well as controversy in both Catholic and Protestant thought. The Eastern churches have never accepted them.

**Augustine on Good and Evil**

When Augustine returned to North Africa a Christian, he discovered his former religion, Manichaeism, alive and well. As a young bishop he found it growing among the youth of Carthage and other urban areas because of its intellectual appeal. There are many interesting parallels between that situation and the rise of cults and new religions in America and other parts of the world in the present day. Many fast-growing religious cults attract university students because they claim to provide better answers to life's ultimate questions than are offered by "traditional organized religion."

Even though Manichaeism claimed to be intellectually sophisticated, it "must be reckoned among the strangest and most bizarre of the many strange and bizarre fantasies which the human mind has conceived."[6] Its worldview was similar in some ways to gnosticism, and many of its early converts were probably Christian gnostics. Manichaeism promoted a plethora of fantastic myths about the origins of the physical world out of a primeval fall and of cosmic combat between good and evil forces. The human soul or spirit was said to be a spark of the good power that had been stolen by the evil force and trapped in matter. Evil was explained as the product of an eternal evil force that had created matter. It is perpetuated by the existence of physical reality and the soul's attachment to that.

Augustine himself had abandoned the Manichaean religion after several attempts to discover its answers to some unresolved questions raised by its myths and worldview. For example, Manichaeism taught that matter is evil or the source of evil and at the same time held forth no conception whatever of a nonmaterial, spiritual reality. Augustine thought this was inconsistent since the religion believed in an all-good God of heaven. When he finally had the chance to interview its leading philosopher—a man named Faustus—Augustine left the movement in disgust, convinced that it did not have the answers it promised. He found them rather in "the books of the Platonists" (Neo-Platonism) and then in Christianity. As a bishop years later, he turned his formidable critical faculties to the task of debunking Manichaean claims.

Augustine's main book against the Manichaeans is *Concerning the Nature of Good,* which he wrote around 405. In it he drew on the Neo-Platonic ideas of the ontological unity of being and goodness and of evil as the privation of both in order to explain the Christian concept of God as Creator and how that is consistent with the existence of evil. In other words, he showed how one does not have to posit the existence of two equal forces or principles in the universe (dualism)—one good and one evil—in order to explain evil. According to Augustine, evil is not a nature or a substance but the corruption of God-created good nature:

> When accordingly it is inquired, whence is evil, it must first be inquired what is evil, which is nothing else than corruption, either of the measure, or the

> form, or the order, that belong to nature. Nature therefore which has been corrupted, is called evil, for assuredly when incorrupt it is good; but even when corrupt, so far as it is nature it is good, so far as it is corrupted it is evil.[7]

But how can a good nature created by God go wrong and become evil? This Augustine answered with both a metaphysical and a moral argument. He explained that any nature created *ex nihilo*—out of nothing—is automatically less than God and is therefore less than absolutely metaphysically perfect and is open to possible corruption. Only God's nature is absolutely incorruptible. Also, human nature possesses the gift of freedom, which can be misused in favor of a lesser good than the one God assigned it to seek and follow. This is the true source and origin of the corruption and absence of good we call evil—the misuse of free will: "Sin is not the striving after an evil nature, but the desertion of a better, and so the deed itself is evil, not the nature which the sinner uses amiss. For it is evil to use amiss that which is good."[8]

The upshot of Augustine's answer to and argument against the Manichaeans is that the only truly evil thing is an evil will, and it is not really a "thing" at all. Evil is actually a nothingness. Free will is not evil. The occasion for it to sin is not evil. Only the actual misuse of the will that makes it an evil will is evil. For this there is no explanation or cause. If there were, then it wouldn't be truly evil. For Augustine there is a "mystery of iniquity" that cannot be fully explained. But it is no excuse to fly into irrationality or "sacrilegious vaporings," as he labeled the Manichaean myths.

Augustine's use of Neo-Platonism against the Manichaeans is a classic example of a Christian church father "despoiling the Egyptians." Just as the Hebrews took their masters' valuables with them in the Exodus, so Christian theologians are free to make use of pagan ideas insofar as they are compatible with the gospel and useful for its promotion because all truth is God's truth. Again there is an analogy between Augustine and Origen. Although the latter was a more speculative thinker, like him Augustine saw much that is of value in pagan philosophy. He wielded Neo-Platonism like a sword against Manichaeism while using it very carefully:

> Thus, Augustine has taken from the Neo-Platonists a certain conception of Evil, which he has modified and developed in the light of Christian dogma in order to provide an effective weapon for demolishing the arguments of the Manichaeans. Created things are good; there can be a hierarchy of created things, some more and some less good, without necessarily involving any existence of Evil. Evil arises from the corruption of a nature which is

> essentially good. What is called evil is good corrupted; if it were not corrupted it would be wholly good; but even when it is corrupted, it is good in so far as it remains a natural thing, and bad only in so far as it is corrupted.[9]

Of course, Augustine strongly disagreed with Neo-Platonism about the personal nature of God and about the creation of the world. According to the philosophy, ultimate reality is an impersonal unity—the One—beyond all being and essence, from which all things flow by emanation unconsciously and automatically. There is no concept in Neo-Platonism of a personal God or purposeful creation out of nothing. Nevertheless Augustine found it to be less dangerous and more useful for the gospel than Manichaeism.

Interesting to note is Augustine's strong endorsement of human free will in his polemic against the Manichaeans. However, one must remember that in that polemic he was only attempting to refute their theology of evil's nature and origin. They attributed it to an eternal evil principle and its creation of matter. This had the effect, of course, of absolving humans of responsibility for sin and evil and of limiting God and removing his monopoly on creation. So Augustine focused his arguments on the larger and wider picture of human nature before the fall into sin. Then, Augustine believed, humans did have free will. They were able to do otherwise than they did. But since the Fall in the Garden of Eden our human wills are so corrupted that freedom not to sin is no longer possible. This doctrine of human depravity and bondage of the will was not fleshed out by Augustine, however, until his later debates with Pelagius.

Augustine demonstrated the rational superiority of Christianity to Manichaeism with the help of a Greek philosophy. In the process he was able to provide certain models for Christian thinking about God, creation, sin and evil that have become deeply ingrained in at least Western Christian thought ever since. God is infinite, absolutely omnipotent, perfectly spiritual and free from every defect metaphysical or moral. But evil as the privation of the good is inevitably a possibility in any creation and especially in one that includes morally free and responsible created agents such as angels and human beings. According to Augustine, sin and evil were not inevitable and they certainly were not in any way necessary, but they were possible, and that possibility was actualized by the first human pair and by heavenly beings before them.

Thus Augustine began to build up an intelligible picture of all reality from biblical and philosophical materials. So far, most of that picture is not particularly new or novel. One can find it or its basic materials in Origen, Gregory of Nyssa and other Eastern church fathers before and during Augustine's time, but the

North African bishop painted the picture in new and attractive ways that helped defeat the allure of Manichaeism and draw many people to Christianity.

**Augustine on the Church and Its Sacraments**

After debating and defeating the Manichaeans, Augustine turned his attention to the greater problem of Donatism. It was greater because in his time Donatism may have been larger in sheer numbers of adherents than the Great Church in parts of North Africa. As the emperors put more pressure on Donatism, it also became violent, and roving bands of radical Donatists made travel in North Africa nearly impossible at times. As with Manichaeism, many people considered Donatism better than catholic and orthodox Christianity. The people who were attracted to Donatism and its churches tended to be moral purists rather than intellectuals. They were Christians deeply rooted in the tradition of *Shepherd of Hermas* and Tertullian, and they believed that bishops who had sinned or cooperated with persecuting Roman authorities were not true Christian bishops and the men they ordained to priesthood were not true Christian priests. The schism had its roots all the way back in the persecutions of Christians under emperors Decius and Diocletion in the late third century. But it was perpetuated by the Donatists' view that the catholic bishops were immoral, corrupt men with no authority. They rejected their sacraments as invalid because of their lives and lineage.

When Augustine launched his drive to overcome Donatism in North Africa, three main issues immediately came to the fore as the crucial ones in the controversy: the nature of the church, the sacraments and their validity, and the relationship between church and state. The essence of the Donatist view of the church that forced them into schism had to do with its purity: "What is the nature of the Church of Christ? According to the Donatists, it is a congregation of the saints, on earth as in heaven, and for that reason it will always be a tiny remnant."[10] Augustine rejected this ecclesiology with vehemence. He argued in numerous letters that the Donatists were the "impure" ones for destroying the unity of the church and falling into the sin of schism. "To this Donatist dream of the church of the saints, Augustine opposes another: the Universal Church, spread throughout the world and containing within itself both good and evil until the final separation of the Last Day."[11]

A major sticking point between Donatists and Catholics had to do with the sacraments. Donatists rejected all sacraments performed by unworthy ministers or even by worthy ministers under the authority of unworthy bishops. A leader of the Donatists wrote,

> What we look for is the conscience of the giver, giving in holiness, to cleanse that of the recipient. For he who knowingly receives faith from the faithless receives not faith but guilt. For everything consists of an origin and a root, and if it have not something for a head, it is nothing, nor does anything well receive second birth, unless it is born again of a good seed.[12]

On the foundation of this theology of ministry and sacraments, the Donatists rejected the baptisms performed by ministers or bishops they considered impure or heretical in some way. This raised an unresolved question for Augustine both as a bishop and as a Christian theologian: What is the validity, if any, of a baptism performed by a priest living in sin or espousing heresy? Cyprian, whose authority was considered great by both sides, had rejected such baptisms and Eucharists as invalid. The catholic church had gradually come to accept them as valid without clear theological justification.

Augustine reflected on the nature of the sacraments and developed the view that was eventually adopted by the Great Church both catholic and orthodox. According to Augustine's sacramental theology, sacraments such as baptism and the Eucharist, or Lord's Supper, convey grace *ex opere operato,* which is loosely translated "by virtue of the act itself." In other words, the power and validity of the sacrament rest in Christ's holiness, and the priest who administers it is only an instrument of Christ's grace:

> Augustine's view of the sacraments is based upon the conception of Christ, the high priest without sin, who is the sole giver of sacramental grace because to Him alone belongs the power of conferring it, but who administers it by human agents. What these administer is the baptism of Christ, whose sanctity cannot be corrupted by unworthy ministers, any more than the light of the sun is corrupted by shining through a sewer.[13]

In this view, then, the priest and the bishop are able to administer sacraments that are efficacious in imparting grace and transforming lives so long as they are properly ordained in apostolic succession. A baptism performed by a self-appointed priest with no valid ordination would not be a sacrament. But a baptism performed by an immoral or heretical priest with valid ordination and in communion with the Great Church would be a true sacrament. That is the meaning of *ex opere operato.*

Augustine held a very high view of sacraments. He identified only baptism and the Eucharist explicitly as sacramental, but he treated other rites and ceremonies of the church as if they could be channels and instruments of God's regenerating and sanctifying grace. According to Augustine, children are born guilty of Adam and Eve's sin and are corrupt from birth. Baptism is necessary to wash away that guilt, heal that corruption and introduce a person into the life of salvation within the church. This belief about baptism is known in theology as "baptismal regeneration." In his doctrinal handbook *The Enchiridion* Augustine wrote that "even infants who are baptized into Christ die to sin."[14] Elsewhere he wrote that an infant who dies unbaptized is damned even where no baptism is possible: "Rightly, therefore, by virtue of that condemnation which runs throughout the mass [of humanity], is he not admitted into the kingdom of heaven, although he was not only not a Christian, but was unable to become one."[15] Later Augustine suggested that unbaptized infants who die may go to a place called "Limbo," which is neither Paradise nor Hades (hell)—neither bliss nor suffering—but merely a holding place on the outskirts of hell for unregenerated persons without personal guilt. Although Augustine's idea of Limbo became a popular explanation, it has never become the official doctrine of any church.

**Augustine on Grace and Free Will**

From his own conversion on, Augustine tended to place great emphasis on the grace and power of God in salvation. It seemed to him that God's action in his own experience of conversion was so overwhelming that he could not really resist it. He did not choose God; God chose him. He believed that this impression was confirmed by the apostle Paul's teaching in passages such as Romans 9—11. In the *Confessions* he praised and thanked God for sovereignly changing him and gave all the glory to God while acknowledging his own helplessness to do anything good. He wrote, "My whole hope is in Thy exceeding great mercy and that alone. Give what Thou commandest and command what Thou wilt. Thou commandest continence from us, and when I knew, as it is said, that no one could be continent unless God gave it to him, even this was a point of wisdom, to know whose gift it was."[16]

When the British monk Pelagius arrived in Rome sometime around 405, he noticed that many Christians were living morally indecent lives and many others seemed unconcerned about growing indifference to moral purity and obedience in the church. He began inquiring about the possible causes of this, and when he heard or read Augustine's prayer quoted above, he was horrified and immediately convinced that this was the root cause of the problem. If Christians became convinced that they could not be continent (abstaining from immorality) unless God gave them that gift, then it should not surprise anyone if they practice incontinence. That was Pelagius's argument. Pelagius then composed *On Nature*, a book which condemned Augustine's view and argued that humans can live sinless lives through their "natural endowments" and are responsible to do so. This was the catalyst that set off the great controversy over original sin, free will, and grace that consumed the Western church off and on for over a hundred years and echoes down through the subsequent centuries.

**Pelagius and the Pelagian Heresy**

Pelagius was born somewhere in Britain in about 350. Like so many heretics of early Christianity, his life is shrouded in mystery and many of his writings are known only through quotations and allusions in the books that oppose and condemn him. He arrived in Rome sometime around 405 and traveled to North Africa, where he could have met with Augustine but did not. He then went to Palestine and wrote two books on sin, free will, and grace: *On Nature* and *On Free Will.* His views were viciously attacked by Augustine and his friend the Bible translator and commentator Jerome, who lived in Bethlehem. Pelagius was acquitted of heresy by a synod of bishops at Diospolis in Palestine in 415 but condemned as a heretic by the bishop of Rome in 417 and 418 and by the Council of Ephesus in 431. His exact year of death is unknown but was probably sometime not long after 423. His condemnation by the Council of Ephesus was probably posthumous.

"The reluctant heretic" is what one modern writer labels Pelagius.[17] He did not intend to preach a false gospel or any other gospel than the one he learned growing up in Britain. He did not ever actually deny any doctrine or dogma of the Christian faith—at least not any that had already been declared orthodox. He was fundamentally a Christian moralist—a person concerned with promoting strong moral attitudes and behavior in the churches—and he opposed certain common beliefs and practices of his day. He accepted infant baptism but denied its efficacy in washing away an inherited guilt. He completely rejected that notion of original sin. He was certainly not alone. Most of the Eastern Christians also rejected the idea of original or inherited guilt. He believed fervently in free will and the necessity of grace for salvation, but he viewed part of grace as a human person's natural equipment and part as the divine revelation of God's will through the law.

Although he was not always consistent with himself, Pelagius seems to have taught that human beings can indeed simply choose to obey God all of the time and never sin willfully and guiltily. If sin in the sense of guilt that condemns is inevitable, he argued, then how can we be held responsible for it? And why not simply relax and sin more if it is inevitable? And if any good that we can do is always a gift of God, why blame people if they sin while waiting for the gift of goodness to arrive?

Pelagius's opponents—led by Augustine—accused him of three heresies. First, they claimed that he denied original sin. Second, they charged him with denying that God's grace is essential for salvation. Third, they said that he preached sinless perfection through free will apart from grace. There is certainly truth in all three accusations so far as we can tell.

On the other hand, the matter is not as simple as it seems. When Pelagius denied original sin, he was denying Augustine's view of original sin, but not as clearly was he denying the view of original sin common in the Eastern churches. That is one reason he found some acceptance and refuge in the East. So what exactly did Pelagius teach? It is important to establish that as far as possible in order to understand Augustine's mature theology of sin and salvation, which was largely carved out in dispute with Pelagius.

Without doubt Pelagius did deny original sin as inherited guilt. He did not believe that infants are born responsible before God for their ancestor Adam's sin. In his book *On Free Will* he wrote that "evil is not born with us, and we are procreated without fault."[18] He did believe that we are all born into a world corrupted by sin and we all tend to sin due to the bad examples shown us by our parents and peers. This might be called an incubator model of original sin as opposed to Augustine's biological and legal models. If we sin, it is because we choose willfully and knowingly to sin, and it is always a matter of free will if we are held accountable for it. Pelagius would go so far as to deny sin's inevitability. If everyone does sin, it is simply because they freely and willfully choose to repeat what Adam did. There is no inborn bent or predisposition to sin. There are only sinful examples that lure people to sin. Metaphorically speaking, for Pelagius sin was a social disease, not a genetic one.

When it came to the necessity of God's grace, Pelagius remained ambivalent and ambiguous. He affirmed the human person's need of God's assistance in order to do anything good but seemed to regard the giving of the law and conscience sufficient assistance. He wrote that "God helps us by his teaching and revelation, opening the eyes of our heart, pointing us to the future so that we may not be absorbed in the present, discovering to us the snares of the devil, enlightening us with the manifold and ineffable gift of heavenly grace."[19] In other words, the grace of God's Word and our own conscience is all that we need. Any baptized Christian can simply choose to follow God's will all of the time and never need any further special enabling from God to live sinlessly. Pelagius did not claim as much for non-Christians. He held to the necessity of baptism for the establishment of a right relationship with God. There does seem to be some inconsistency in his theology at this point.

Clearly Pelagius did affirm that a Christian person can be without sin if he or she wishes. A baptized infant can and really should live so that he or she never needs to beg God for forgiveness. Forgiveness is there if one stumbles and falls into sin or even if one sins willfully, but Pelagius considered that unnecessary if a person would live rightly by free will according to the light given in God's Word and in conscience. However, when pressed by bishops at the Synod of Diospolis in 415, Pelagius seemed to affirm this potential to live sinlessly as a theoretical and not an actual possibility. That is, he stated that while such perfect obedience is a possible achievement for any person, it may not ever have actually been achieved by anyone other than Christ:

> I did indeed say that a man can be without sin and keep the commandments of God, if he wishes; for this ability has been given to him by God. However, I did not say that any man can be found who has never sinned from his infancy to his old age but that, having been converted from his sins, he can be without sin by his own efforts and God's grace, yet not even by this means is he incapable of change in future.[20]

In all three cases of the accusations of heresy brought against him, it is difficult to ascertain exactly what Pelagius did believe and teach. Not so difficult to ascertain is what he denied. He denied inherited guilt and the inevitability of sin. He denied the absolute necessity of supernatural assisting grace for obedience to God's law and affirmed the power of free will. He denied that perfect obedience to God's law is absolutely impossible for fallen humans. Yet even then it was possible for Pelagius to claim that these denials were only theoretical and that no one except Jesus Christ himself had ever actually lived a life to maturity in perfect conformity with God's will and law. In other words, he could claim that he was only arguing that sinless perfection apart from special assisting grace must be a possibility or else it would be unjust for God to demand it and hold humans accountable for not achieving it. The famous modern German philosopher Immanuel Kant paraphrased Pelagius's basic attitude in his aphorism "ought implies can."

### Augustine's Response to Pelagius

In response to Pelagius's perceived teachings about sin, free will, and grace, Augustine developed his own strong theology of human depravity and God's sovereignty and grace. His major anti-Pelagian works include *On the Spirit and the Letter* (412), *On Nature and Grace* (415), *On the Grace of Christ and on Original Sin* (418), *On Grace and Free Will* (427) and *On the Predestination of the Saints* (429). He also worked his own views on the relevant issues into many other writings, including *The Enchiridion: On Faith, Hope and Love* (421) and his magnum opus, *The City of God*, which he completed shortly before his death in 430. Some of these books were written after Pelagius's condemnation by the pope (418) and his death shortly thereafter, and were directed not so much at Pelagius himself as at certain monks and theologians who defended aspects of Pelagius's teaching against Augustine's own developing monergism. In other words, Augustine ended up attempting to refute not only Pelagius's alleged heresy of sinless perfection apart from assisting grace but also all forms of synergism. By the end of his life and career, Augustine would allow only his own monergism as the basis of an orthodox doctrine of salvation. The debate over this extended well past his own lifetime and into the next century and continues to echo down through the centuries of Christian theology.

Augustine's entire soteriology flows from two major beliefs: the absolute and total depravity of human beings after the Fall, and the absolute and total power and sovereignty of God. The ways in which Augustine interpreted these doctrines both developed out of and conditioned his debate with Pelagius and his moderate defenders, the so-called Semi-Pelagians. Augustine's view of original sin and human depravity is as strong as any can possibly be. According to him, all humans alive at any given time (with the sole exception of the God-man, Jesus Christ) are included in a "mass of perdition" and are altogether guilty and damned by God on account of Adam's primal sin. As the Puritans phrased it in the seventeenth century: "In Adam's fall we sinned all." Augustine himself expressed it more wordily:

> Thence, after his sin, he [Adam] was driven into exile, and by his sin the whole race of which he was the root was corrupted in him, and thereby subjected to the penalty of death. And so it happens that all descended from him, and from the woman who had led him into sin, and was condemned at the same time with him—being the offspring of carnal lust on which the same punishment of disobedience was visited—were tainted with the original sin, and were drawn through divers errors and sufferings into that last and endless punishment which they suffer in common with the fallen angels, their corrupters and masters, and the partakers of their doom.[21]

Furthermore, "the fault of our nature remains in our offspring so deeply impressed as to make it guilty, even when the guilt of the self-same fault has been washed away in the parents by the remission of sins."[22] Thus for Augustine even infants born of Christian parents are born guilty and entirely corrupt by Adam's sin and the fallen nature inherited from him.

Contrary to Pelagius and most theologians of the Eastern churches, then, Augustine believed that all humans except Christ himself are born not only corrupt, so that sin is inevitable, but also guilty of Adam's sin and deserving of eternal damnation unless they are baptized for the remission of sins and continue in that grace through faith and love. Augustine based his doctrine of original sin as universal inherited guilt on a proof text in Paul's Epistle to the Romans. The Greek of Romans 5:12 says that death passed to all human beings "inasmuch as all sinned." But Augustine did not read Greek and used a very poor Latin translation of Romans that mistranslated the verse to read *in quo omnes peccaverunt,* or "in whom [that is, Adam] all sinned." In other words, when Augustine read Romans 5:12, he saw the message that death spread to all humans beings inasmuch as all sinned in Adam. But this is not what the verse says in the original language. Of course, Augustine would argue that the entirety of Romans 5 and of the epistle to the Romans and the very gospel itself teach that we humans are all born of Adam's race and therefore inherit his guilt and corruption. Why else would Jesus Christ have to be born of a virgin? Augustine believed it could only be because the guilt and corruption of sin are passed down the generations through sexual procreation, and only if Christ was conceived without the natural process could his human nature be sinless.

Augustine's doctrine of original sin may appropriately be labeled one of "seminal identity" between the human being and ancestor Adam. The newborn infant as well as the middle-aged person as well as the elderly man or woman is corrupt and guilty because of the connection with Adam. That connection may be temporarily broken by baptism, but it returns immediately when a person sins again after baptism and must be broken again by repentance and sacramental grace. Augustine believed that this process of transforming grace could include genuine progress so that a person might actually come eventually to enjoy a life of unbroken fellowship with God virtually free of the condemnation and corruption of original sin, but such a life would be entirely a work of God's grace and in no way a product of human effort or free will apart from assisting grace. Furthermore, even such a saint would produce children both guilty and corrupt and in need of baptismal grace to enjoy their own fellowship with God.

Because of the inherited depravity and corruption of sin, Augustine argued, fallen humans are not free not to sin: "A man's free will," he wrote against Pelagius, "avails for nothing except to sin."[23] Before Adam's disobedience, he had the power not to sin. His condition then was *posse non peccare:* it was possible not to sin. After the disobedience and because of it, Adam's condition and that of all his posterity except Jesus Christ became *non posse non peccare:* not possible not to sin.

Augustine argued that two conclusions may *not* be drawn from this. First, he denied that his view implies any absolute necessity of sin. Sin and evil are products of the misuse of freedom and are not metaphysically necessary. Once the first human pair disobeyed, however, sin became inevitable in their own lives and in the lives of their posterity. Augustine insisted on a distinction between necessity and inevitability. Even now—long after Adam's transgression—sin is inevitable but not necessary.

The other wrong conclusion Augustine denied is that his view implies complete loss of free will. Augustine argued that human beings retain free will even after the Fall. But that free will is conditioned by sin so that it is always turned toward disobedience unless God's grace intervenes and turns the will in another direction. Even in choosing to sin—which is inevitable—the human being born of Adam's race is choosing freely.

How can this be? Augustine defined free will simply as doing what one wants to do. For him, "In brief, then, I am free with respect to any action (or that action is in my power) to the extent that my wanting and choosing to perform that action are sufficient for my performing it."[24] Just so long as a person does what she wants to do, her action is "free." This is quite different, of course, from defining free will as "ability to do otherwise," which is probably the view Pelagius and his followers held. For Augustine, people are free to sin but not free not to sin. That is because they want to sin. The Fall has so corrupted their motives and desires that sinning is all they want to do apart from God's intervening grace. Thus they are sinning "freely." Pelagius and his followers would almost certainly reject this idea of free will and argue that a person is only truly free if he could either sin or not sin.

Thus we come to a fundamental parting of the ways in theology. Almost all Christian theologians believe in free will, but some follow Augustine in seeing it as compatible with determinism because it is there whenever we do what we want to do even if our wants and wishes are predetermined by something other than ourselves. Other Christian theologians believe that free will is incompatible with determinism and is there only when we face genuine alternatives of decision and action. It is the ability to do otherwise.

Why did Augustine define free will in such a counterintuitive way? He gave us a strong clue in On Grace and Free Will when he discussed the sovereignty of God in relation to human decisions and actions: "For the Almighty [God] sets in motion even in the innermost hearts of men the movement of their will, so that He does through their agency whatsoever He wishes to perform through them."[25] In other words, for Augustine God alone is the all-determining reality and whatever happens, including human sins, must be rooted in his sovereign will and power. In order for humans to be responsible, they must have free will in their sinning. But in order for God to be sovereign, every event must be under his control, for "if we maintain that the will of a human being is not in God's power but is controlled wholly by the person, then it is possible for God to be frustrated. And that is just absurd."[26] The only solution is to define free will as doing what one wants to do. But for Augustine God is the source of those wants. In whatever happens God's will is being done.

Grace then is absolutely necessary for any truly good decisions or actions of any fallen human person. Augustine argued this against Pelagius and his followers on several counts. First, humans are so utterly depraved that unless God gives them the gift of faith by grace, they would never even think to do anything good. In his own words, "the Spirit of grace, therefore, causes us to have faith, in order that through faith we may, on praying for it, obtain the ability to do what we are commanded. On this account the apostle himself constantly puts faith before the law; since we are not able to do what the law commands unless we obtain strength to do it by the prayer of faith."[27] Any other view, he argued, would weaken belief in our depravity and in the sole sufficiency of God's grace, including Christ's death on the cross. That is his second reason for insisting that grace is the sole cause of anything truly good that we do. If anyone could obtain any measure of righteousness by nature and free will alone, apart from supernatural assisting grace, then Christ died in vain: "If, however, Christ did not die in vain, then human nature cannot by any means be justified and redeemed from God's most righteous wrath—in a word, from punishment—except by faith and the sacrament of the blood of Christ."[28]

If any good thing humans can do is a gift of God, and if every desire of the human will is a work of God, and if God is the all-determining reality, then the only natural conclusion that one can draw is that God sovereignly predestines everything that happens, including both sin and evil on the one hand, and salvation and righteousness on the other hand. Augustine was reluctant to attribute sin and evil to God, but the inner logic of his overall theology moves in that direction. In his final work, *On the Predestination of the Saints,* Augustine affirmed what later generations of theologians would come to call "unconditional election" and "irresistible grace." That is, God chooses some out of the human mass of perdition to receive the gift of faith by grace and leaves others to their deserved damnation. Those whom he chooses to receive the gifts of grace cannot resist. Why does God not save all? Augustine said that "the reason why one person is assisted by grace and another is not helped, must be referred to the secret judgments of God."[29] This is true even of the reason why some infants are baptized and others are not. It lies only in "the hidden determinations of God."[30]

**Augustine's Monergistic Doctrine of God and Salvation**

Of course all this raises the question of God's goodness to an intense pitch. Did God predestine the fall of Adam and Eve and even the fall of Satan and the angels who rebelled with him? Augustine could hardly draw back at that point. The die was cast; he had to follow the logic. And yet he never did blatantly attribute the source of evil to God. He left it in the realm of mystery. "Thus, apparently, the answer to the question why the first created wills [Satan's, Adam's] chose to turn to sin is that that is just what they did and that there was no cause of their turning."[31] But throughout his later writings Augustine constantly insisted that God—and God alone—is the ultimate cause of all things. He left no room for creaturely autonomy to thwart the will of God. In the final analysis, then, it is difficult to see how he could "get God off the hook," so to speak. Even the inclinations of the will that caused Satan and Adam and Eve to rebel against and disobey God *must* have been imparted to them.

Would this make God evil or even the author of evil? Augustine would have none of it. He only stated that God permits evil and never attributed evil itself to God's causation. Why does God permit evil? He explained: "Although, therefore, evil, in so far as it is evil, is not a good, yet the fact that evil as well as good exists, is a good."[32] But if the fact that evil exists is good, and if God is the source of all goodness (which Augustine could not deny), then does it not inexorably follow that God is the source of the existence of evil? Yes. But only in the sense that he permits it.

Augustine scholar T. Kermit Scott is quite correct that in the final analysis the key to understanding Augustine is his obsession with the absolute and unconditional power of God. Whether he is correct that Augustine wrongly fell victim to an "imperial myth" of creating God in the image of a perfect Roman emperor is more debatable. However, one can only agree when he concludes that "the omnipotence doctrine is the heart of Augustine's imperial myth, and when 'push comes to shove,' it is the doctrine that cannot be compromised. God is the absolute ruler of the universe whose will directs every event in creation. That fundamental certainty cannot be qualified in any way, regardless of any consequences it may have."[33]

One consequence would seem to be that Augustine could only affirm God's absolute and unqualified goodness by refusing to answer the question whether God is the source and cause of the evil inclinations of will that led Satan to fall and Adam and Eve to disobey. If God is not their source and cause, then there is something in the universe that is outside of God's control. Merely "permitting" evil inclinations is not the same as directing and controlling them. But if God is their source and cause, then either they are not so evil after all (because they serve a higher good) or else God himself is not so good after all. Augustine came right up against the ultimate questions raised by his monergism and flew into mystery. Apparently he could not conceive of a self-limitation of God's power such that God could allow free creatures to do what is against his own perfect will.

As we will see in the next chapter, Augustine's radically monergistic view of salvation was never completely accepted by the church in the West. It was rejected by the Eastern church. The magisterial Protestant Reformers of the sixteenth century tended to accept it. Some Protestants, especially those in the free-church tradition, however, rejected it. The great English revivalist John Wesley rejected it in favor of an evangelical synergism that Augustinians would consider at best Semi-Pelagian. We will come to those episodes of the story of theology in due time. For now, suffice it to say that Augustine's theology made a profound impact on Western Christian theology by introducing the idea of monergism into it. Since he was hailed by virtually all popes and the major Protestant Reformers as the greatest of all the church fathers, anyone who wished to promote monergism could appeal to his authority.

Augustine also wrote a great treatise on the Trinity titled *De Trinitatis*, or *On the Trinity*. Its main contribution to the story of theology was to introduce the so-called psychological model in which God's unity is compared with the unity of a human person and God's threeness is compared with three aspects of human personality such as memory, understanding and will. Because of Augustine, Western theology tended to emphasize the unity of God's essence over his threeness, whereas Eastern theology, under the influence of the Cappadocian fathers, tended to emphasize the threeness over the oneness.

Augustine's greatest work—his magnum opus—was *The City of God*, a massive book on divine providence and human history in which Augustine explained that from a Christian perspective, no human civilization is God's kingdom. Human civilizations rise and fall but God's kingdom lasts forever. God's kingdom is the church, and by God's grace and power, it will eventually replace the earthly kingdoms in the heavenly city after Christ returns. Until then it is a hidden kingdom of a fundamentally spiritual nature and exists whenever and wherever God's will is being done among people. This interpretation of history and civilizations was a great inspiration and comfort to many Christians who observed the once great Roman Empire crumbling and falling into ruins around them. Even many Christians had come to identify the Christianized Roman Empire with the kingdom of God, and its fall to barbarian tribes was a great disillusionment. To them Augustine said, "Don't worry. God's kingdom is not affected by the demise of the Roman

Empire, for it is not of this world."

Shortly after Augustine's death the invading barbarian tribes of central Europe did destroy the last vestiges of the Roman Empire in the West. The bishop of Rome increasingly filled the vacuum of central authority and unified the culture left in its wake. Monks and monasteries converted the barbarian tribes to catholic and orthodox Christianity and preserved the writings of Greek and Roman philosophers and church fathers during the so-called Dark Ages that followed Rome's fall in the West. Augustine became the touchstone of catholic orthodoxy—*the* catholic theologian, whose sayings and teachings always carried great authority. Yet even during his own later years, some leading monks and theologians in the region around Marseilles in southern Gaul (France) were challenging that authority. This so-called Semi-Pelagian controversy deeply affected the church of Rome, helping it to become the Roman Catholic Church. As we examine the rise and development of that tradition of Christianity, we will find the answer to the question How did the Latin Western half of Christendom become *Roman* Catholic?

# CHAPTER 18

# The Western Church Becomes Roman Catholic

H*ow did the Great Church in the West become the Roman Catholic* Church? From a Roman Catholic perspective, that is an improper question. According to the Roman Catholic account of the history of Christian theology, the Great Church catholic and orthodox lived on from the apostles to today in the West and all bishops that remained in fellowship with the bishop of Rome have constituted its hierarchy. There was no break, as it were, of the Roman Catholic Church from something else. In this way of seeing and telling the story, the Eastern bishops broke away from the Great Church gradually throughout the centuries after Augustine and officially in 1054. Similarly, in this view all Protestant denominations are not true churches of Jesus Christ at all but religious sects that need to return to the mother church of Rome. However, as we will see later, the Eastern Orthodox family of churches tells the story of the Great Church differently, with itself as the continuous existence of the one true Great Church of Jesus Christ from the apostles to today, and the Roman Catholic Church and the various Protestant denominations as schismatic sects that need to return to fellowship with the patriarch of Constantinople and the other Eastern bishops and patriarchs.

Protestants generally interpret the story of Christian theology as a gradual demise of true, apostolic Christianity during the time of Cyprian and then Constantine and afterward. This decline was continuous with the rise of the penitential system, the authority of the great Christian patriarchs of the Roman Empire, and the loss of the gospel of free grace by faith alone and the priesthood of all believers. Only from a Protestant perspective, in other words, does the story of theology include an episode of "the rise of Roman Catholicism." One might wish for a neutral account of the story, but there really can be no such thing. Everyone tells the story from some perspective. But that does not mean it has to be told in a highly biased way. By the "rise of the Roman Catholic Church," I do not mean, as some Protestants do, the complete apostasy of the Western church. I merely mean that a new development took place sometime after Augustine's death and before the end of the first millennium that can properly be described as the appearance in Europe of what today is generally known as the Roman Catholic tradition and fellowship of churches. Long before the official split between Rome and Constantinople in 1054, the Western church took on certain characteristic features that mark it as distinct both from the East and from the early church. That is as much as to say that here it is regarded as one denomination of Christianity with a beginning after the apostles and even after Constantine and Augustine, although with earlier roots.

Between Augustine and the rise of scholasticism in the eleventh century, Latin Christian theology fell into a kind of lethargy. For over six hundred years, during the so-called Dark Ages, the church in the West produced little in the way of great theological innovation, and no theological giants stalked the land. Much of the theological debate in the West revolved around interpretations of Augustine's theology, and the Latin theologians could find justification for almost any view there, if willing to ignore the development of his thinking. In other words, synergists—defenders of free will—could appeal to Augustine's early writings against the Manichaeans. Defenders of monergism—meticulous providence and predestination—could appeal to Augustine's later writings against Pelagius's sympathizers. During the six hundred years after the great bishop of Hippo's death, popes "baptized" his theology as semiofficial, Eastern theologians questioned its orthodoxy, and many in both halves of Christendom misinterpreted it. Even during the Middle Ages, the Renaissance and the Reformation, Christian theologians of many stripes called themselves Augustinian or appealed to his memory to defend their own theological proposals.

**Semi-Pelagianism**

The greatest debate of all over Augustine's theology and its ramifications took place within the century after his death. Its outcome—like so many in the history of theology—was ambiguous. The Roman Catholic Church decided in favor of some aspects of Augustinianism and against other aspects of it, and remained neutral about some issues of the debate. In the end, at the Synod of

Orange in 529 (in what is now France), some of Augustine's most ardent supporters as well as some of his most fervent opponents lost their causes. The church took a mediating and somewhat inconsistent position with relation to the great questions of sin, free will and grace. The form of Christianity known especially to outsiders as Roman Catholicism was deeply influenced by this debate and its outcome. The irony is that what it said on paper in its official pronouncements was not carried out in practice by some of its most influential leaders. It has always remained somewhat torn between moderate Augustinianism and moderate Semi-Pelagianism. This portion of the story of Christian theology will deal with that so-called Semi-Pelagian controversy and its outcome as well as other important factors contributing to the rise of the branch of Christianity known as Roman Catholicism around the same time.

One of the most vexed questions in the history of theology has been what role, if any, humans play in their own salvation. All Christians have always attributed salvation to God's grace and placed Christ and his cross at the center of the gospel as the very basis of forgiveness and transformation. But the debate between Augustine and Pelagius raised the question to new levels of vexation. For the sake of preserving the all-sufficiency of grace, Augustine ended up making salvation such an exclusive work of God that humans play virtually no role at all. If they are saved, it is solely because God chose them and gave them the gift of grace—including faith itself—apart from any decision they might make or action they might undertake. Of course, even Augustine insisted on baptism as an instrument of salvation, but he taught that anyone who is baptized and thereby receives saving grace was foreordained by God to receive it. It is never accidental. Everything is completely controlled by God's eternal wisdom, decree and power. Pelagius, on the other hand, reacted against Augustine's budding monergism in the *Confessions* and developed a doctrine of salvation that opened the door to a genuine human contribution to salvation such that any supernatural assisting grace might be unnecessary.

The church condemned Pelagius's denial of the necessity and all-sufficiency of supernatural, assisting grace first in 418 and then again at the Council of Ephesus in 431. But the church did not decide the issue in favor of Augustine, although some of Augustine's followers interpreted it that way. While sheer Pelagianism was no longer an option for catholic, orthodox Christians after 431, many theologians sought mediating positions between Augustine's monergism and Pelagius's works righteousness. Surely, they thought, there is much room in the middle for carving out a doctrine of salvation that would do justice to both the sovereignty of grace and the free decision and action of the human person.

The leader of the Semi-Pelagian party of theologians was a monk of Marseilles

(France) named John Cassian. He was born about 360 and entered a monastery in Bethlehem in Palestine as a young man. He traveled to monasteries in the Egyptian desert and other places around the Roman Empire for at least seven years and eventually founded his own monastery in Marseilles in 410. His claim to fame in church history is more as the founder of Western monasticism than as the main theologian of the Semi-Pelagian controversy. According to Cassian's English translator, "although his fame has been overshadowed by that of the greatest of Western monks, St. Benedict of Nursia, yet his is really the credit for being, not indeed the actual founder, but the first organizer and systematizer of Western monachism [monasticism]."[1] Benedict of Nursia, who formulated the official rule for Western monks in The Rule of St. Benedict around 600, was greatly influenced by and indebted to Cassian. John Cassian died in 432—just a couple of years after Augustine and at the height of the great Semi-Pelagian controversy. He has never been canonized as a saint by the Western church (Roman Catholic) but is considered a saint in the East (Eastern Orthodoxy).

John Cassian's monastery in Marseilles became home to a number of moderately brilliant and productive theological scholars, and through them it became a hotbed of opposition to Augustine's strong monergistic view of salvation. Two theological monks who worked with Cassian to refute that doctrine were Vincent of Lérins and Faustus of Riez. These three together made up the core of the loyal catholic opposition especially to Augustine's and his followers' belief in divine predestination. They have been labeled Semi-Pelagians by later generations. At the time of the controversy (fifth and early sixth centuries), they considered themselves completely orthodox theologians of the Great Church who wished only to fight off this Augustinian innovation of monergism. They knew, for instance, that the entire Eastern church held an essentially synergistic view of the God-human relationship in salvation where grace held the preeminent role but human decision and effort had to cooperate with grace for salvation to result. This, they believed, was the ancient faith of the church, and they were almost certainly right.

The problem is that traditional synergism had never been clearly worked out in distinction from Pelagianism. And the fact that Pelagius had found refuge in the East and had been exonerated by a synod of bishops in Palestine before his ultimate condemnation at the third ecumenical council contributed to the Augustinians' argument that synergism was essentially flawed and led to Pelagianism. It was up to Cassian and his colleagues to work out the subtle differences between orthodox synergism and Pelagianism in order to present to the catholic church a viable alternative to Augustinian monergism.

John Cassian's main theological works were all written at Marseilles and include

*On the Institution of Monasticism, Spiritual Discourses,* and *On the Incarnation of the Lord Against Nestorius.* He also wrote a series of *Conferences* in which he created dialogues between various abbots of monasteries he had visited and attempted thereby to show the shortcomings and novelty of Augustine's views on salvation. But Cassian went beyond pointing out the errors in Augustine's views. He attempted to carve out the alternative to both monergism and Pelagianism by developing an orthodox catholic synergism. According to the Western church, he failed. However, his failure became the widely accepted folk theology of much of medieval Roman Catholicism.

What was this Semi-Pelagian synergism of John Cassian?

> They [Semi-Pelagians] believed in the doctrine of the Fall; they acknowledged the necessity of real grace in order to man's restoration; they even admitted that this grace must somehow be "prevenient" to such acts of will as resulted in Christian good works: but some of them thought—and herein consisted the error called Semi-Pelagianism—that [human] nature, unaided, could take the first step towards its recovery, by desiring to be healed through faith in Christ. If it could not,—if the very beginnings of all good were strictly a Divine act,—exhortations seemed to them to be idle, and censure [for sins] unjust, in regard to those on whom no such act had been wrought, and who, therefore, until it should be wrought, were helpless, and so far guiltless, in the matter. Of the party which took up this position Cassian was the recognized head.[2]

In other words, Cassian and the other Massilians taught that a human being can only be saved by God through grace, but that such salvation could begin with the initiative of a good will toward God in the human heart. Their view of the beginning of salvation can be summed up by the expression "God helps those who help themselves" or at least by the saying "If you will take one step toward God, he will come the rest of the way to you." This was the Achilles' heel of their theology and the cause of its condemnation at the Synod of Orange in 529. The church judged this emphasis on human initiative to be too close to outright Pelagianism even though the Massilians all affirmed the absolute necessity of assisting grace for full salvation and righteousness.

Some question remains, however, whether John Cassian himself actually held the view so widely vilified as Semi-Pelagianism. That Faustus of Riez did is not debated. He clearly argued in *On the Grace of God and Free Will* that the *initium fidei* (beginning of faith) belongs to the human side and is not enabled by grace. Cassian himself, however, presented a more ambiguous face in his *Conferences.* He could be interpreted as supporting either his colleague Faustus's view or a more nuanced position. The key passages appear in his *Third Conference of Abbot Chaeremon*. One problem with any dialogue, of course, is determining which party is supposed to represent the view of the author. Were Cassian's own beliefs being expressed by Abbot Chaeremon or by Abbot Cermanus—Chaeremon's dialogue partner? Or did Cassian simply intend the dialogue to stimulate further theological discussion by clarifying the issues? In any case, Abbot Chaeremon poses the central issue of the entire Semi-Pelagian dispute: "does God have compassion upon us because we have shown the beginning of a good will, or does the beginning of a good will follow because God has had compassion on us?"[3] Chaeremon goes on to answer the question himself, which is why many readers suspect his is the proxy for Cassian's own voice.

Abbot Chaeremon's—perhaps Cassian's—answer is complex and difficult to interpret. It is certainly not as simple as Faustus's blatant attribution of the initiative in salvation to the human will. He begins by stating that we must understand that the grace of God and the free will of the human person are not opposed to one another. And by free will here is clearly meant "ability to do otherwise" rather than Augustine's mere "doing what one wants to do." Cassian said that grace and free will are both necessary for salvation to occur and they are in harmony with each other, "for when God sees us inclined to will what is good, He meets, guides, and strengthens us: . . . And again, if He finds that we are unwilling or have grown cold, He stirs our hearts with salutory exhortations, by which a good will is either renewed or formed in us."[4] It seems that Cassian wished to leave the door open both ways: to the possibility of either the divine initiative of grace or the initiative of human free will with grace responding. This dual desire is clearly expressed in the most famous of Cassian's sayings upon which his Augustinian opponents pounced: "And when He [God] sees in us some beginnings of a good will, He at once enlightens it and strengthens it and urges it on towards salvation, increasing that which He Himself implanted or which He sees to have arisen from our own efforts."[5] If Cassian had stopped writing after "which He Himself implanted [i.e., grace]" all would be well. His affirmation of free will and denial of predestination were not problems for most catholic Christians. But when he went on to write "or which He sees to have arisen from our own efforts," he handed his Augustinian opponents such as Prosper of Aquitaine a mile of rope with which to hang him. This was clearly an opening to Pelagianism. This is what is labeled Semi-Pelagianism in the history of Christian theology: the idea that human nature and effort alone—apart from supernatural assisting grace—can cause God to respond with saving grace. It may be far from outright Pelagianism, but it is the beginning of a slippery slope down into it.

John Cassian seems to have recognized that his words could be interpreted in a Pelagian way and so he went on to affirm the preeminence of grace in everything. However, nothing could undo the damage done. Because of the slightest openness to human initiative in salvation, Cassian would forever be remembered as the founder of Semi-Pelagianism. One should, however, read and take into account what else he wrote:

> But let no one imagine that we have brought forward these instances to try to make out that the chief share in our salvation rests with our faith, according to the profane notion of some who attribute everything to free will and lay down that the grace of God is dispensed in accordance with the desert of each man: but we plainly assert our unconditional opinion that the grace of God is superabounding and sometimes overflows the narrow limits of man's lack of faith.[6]

In the end, Cassian affirmed mystery at the heart of the God-human interaction in salvation. Without giving any ground to predestination, he said that God's ways in salvation are many and inscrutable and "how God works all things in us and yet everything can be ascribed to free will, cannot be fully grasped by the mind and reason of man."[7]

Augustine's defenders responded to Cassian and the other Massilians by attacking their belief in the possibility of a human initiative in salvation and arguing that this denies the absolute necessity of grace and turns grace into something less than a sheer gift. Augustinians such as Prosper of Aquitaine compiled selections of Augustine's teachings to refute Semi-Pelagianism, and these selections tended to neglect or ignore predestination. Most later catholic bishops and theologians were only familiar with Augustine's soteriology through Prosper's selections and did not bother to read all of Augustine and so never knew that it included a version of monergism that completely excluded free will as ability to do otherwise.

The Semi-Pelagian controversy finally ended in 529 with a gathering of Western bishops known as the Synod of Orange. Sometimes it is called the Council of Orange, but it is not listed among the ecumenical councils of the church by either East or West. At Orange the catholic bishops condemned key aspects of Semi-Pelagianism, endorsed Augustine's vision of the necessity and all-sufficiency of grace, and condemned belief in divine predestination to evil or damnation. Since Augustine had never actually affirmed that God foreordains anyone to sin or to hell, his own teaching came through the Synod of Orange unscathed but also not fully affirmed. The synod did not endorse predestination at all. It did, however, require belief that any goodness or righteousness humans can have is a result of

God's grace working in them. Orthodox Catholic theology would henceforth include the ideas that God's grace is the sole basis and cause of any human righteousness and that humans cannot produce works that merit salvation apart from assisting grace. Since the Synod of Orange left the door open to human free cooperation with grace, though, the Catholic Church went on to include and emphasize a system of meritorious works that are necessary as proofs of grace, and it tended to favor a kind of synergism in which free will must cooperate with grace in order for salvation to attain its full completion.[8]

Although Semi-Pelagianism was a heresy after 529, it had already deeply imbedded itself in certain common popular beliefs and customs of Western spirituality. Throughout the Middle Ages—from the sixth to the sixteenth century—many monks and priests of the Roman Catholic Church practiced a kind of Semi-Pelagianism even if on paper the church opposed it. That is, a great burden of religious effort and spiritual performance was laid upon the laity as necessary for grace to work fully in their lives. The penitential system going back to Cyprian in the third century leans in that direction. In a sense it is inherently Semi-Pelagian. The church's official teaching, however, was that even as a person is being converted through baptism and growing as a Christian through sanctification (penance, sacraments, etc.), God's grace is actually the sole efficient cause of the entire process. At best the human decisions and efforts are merely instrumental causes that would be impossible without God's prevenient grace going before and enabling them. How many medieval Christians were aware of this is unknown. It seems likely that few understood it. How many Protestants understand the doctrines of grace of the great Reformers? The cavil that Roman Catholics believe in and teach "works righteousness" is just that—a cavil. It is not to be taken seriously except as a commentary on many Catholics' lack of theological understanding and many Protestants' lack of awareness of Catholic theology.

**Pope Gregory the Great**

When attempting to answer the question "How did the Western church become Roman Catholic?" one name comes to the fore as an essential part of any historical answer: Gregory I, also known as Gregory the Great. Gregory was one of the most important popes and theologians in the history of the Roman Catholic tradition and a major contributor—unwittingly—to the divisions between that tradition and both Eastern Orthodoxy and Protestantism. He was a very influential pope at a crucial turning point in the Western church's history as well as a major interpreter of Augustine's theology and promoter of monastic piety and lifestyle. Gregory is considered one of the four great doctors of the church by the Roman Catholic tradition. The others are Ambrose of Milan, Jerome and Augustine. He is often considered by church historians the last church father as well as the first medieval pope and theologian in the West.

Gregory was born into an aristocratic family in Rome about 540 and spent his early life in a monastery, where he received his education and spiritual training. He traveled widely around the Mediterranean world and stayed for a time in Constantinople. He firmly rejected the Byzantine claim of equality between the patriarchs of that city and Rome, however, and as bishop of Rome promoted the absolute superiority and primacy of that see over all others. Gregory wished to live the life of a scholarly and ascetic monk in Rome but was drafted by the people as pope on September 3, 590. His gifts as a scholar, mediator, administrator and gifted spiritual adviser won him the position against his will.

He became pope at a time when Rome and the Western empire in general were in decay. The barbarian kings had failed to unite and were constantly at war with one another. Byzantine emperor Justinian had failed in his attempt to reunify the old Roman Empire. The Roman senate that had tried to rule again had disbanded, and there was a desperate need for someone to step into the vacuum of cultural and political power. Like Leo I before him, Gregory provided the needed authority, at least in Italy if not throughout all of Europe:

> In the vacuum left by the senatorial flight, the church became a directing force in and around Rome, securing supplies and distributions of food to the poor as best it could. As bishops of Rome had been doing this since the fifth century at least, it followed an established pattern and was expected by the local population. But the failure of other authorities to assist was more marked. It was to their own bishop that Romans looked for the city's protection and their own well-being.[9]

During his tenure as bishop of Rome, Pope Gregory I provided a rule (set of guidelines) for all Western bishops that is summarized in his major existing work, *The Book of Pastoral Rule*. He also launched a great missionary effort to convert the pagan peoples of Britain and the Arian barbarian tribes of Europe to Catholic Christianity. He built up monastic communities and gave them charters to control vast territories of Europe for the purpose of establishing firm Christian footholds throughout it. He also baptized Benedict of Nursia's monastic movement and the Rule of St. Benedict as official and binding for the Western church. From Gregory on, all Catholic monastic orders were some form of Benedictine monasticism. Gregory also sought to reach accommodation with pagan cultures and religions in Europe for the sake of evangelism. He also approved and promoted many traditional spiritual beliefs and practices of lay Christians in the West having to do with veneration of saints and self-sacrificial penance and observances of feast days. These and many other of Gregory's approved Catholic beliefs and practices came to play a major role in the Protestant Reformation of the sixteenth century. Protestants generally rejected them as examples of syncretism between paganism and Christianity. Finally, Gregory created a hybrid of Augustine's monergistic view of salvation and John Cassian's synergism that deeply influenced Roman Catholic theology ever after.

Gregory was a prolific writer and preferred to communicate his ideas through letters. About 850 of his letters are known today. Many of them contain fascinating insights into his own views on Christian spirituality, leadership, evangelism and church order. His letters reveal a deeply ascetic man—almost mystical in some ways—who was also highly political. He insisted that his ecclesiastical inferiors refer to him as "servant of the servants" rather than with honorific titles befitting a virtual ruler of vestiges of the old Roman Empire. On the other hand, Gregory also tirelessly promoted the spiritual and temporal primacy of the holy see of Rome over all other orders of church and society. His letters also show his strong interest in practical matters of Christianity and a distinct distaste for philosophical speculation in theology, even though his own theology was clearly influenced by Greek (Platonic) ideas.

Gregory reigned as pope over the Western church and ruler over much of Italy for only fourteen years. He died in 604. His legacy to medieval Christendom, however, is incalculable. He left an indelible stamp of his own spiritual and theological preferences on Roman Catholicism for at least a thousand years.

## Gregory's View of Salvation

Most pertinent for our telling of the story of Christian theology is Gregory's soteriology. In him come together and then flow out into medieval Catholic theology two seemingly disparate streams of thought about salvation. On the one hand, he strongly favored Augustine as the greatest church father of all. On the other hand, he read and interpreted Augustine through—of all people—John Cassian. Gregory's interpretation and application of Augustine's theology is thoroughly synergistic:

> Gregory's significance for the history of Christian thought is not his originality—which was rather meager—but rather in his influence on medieval theology, and the manner in which he served as a filter through which that theology read the works of Augustine. His thought is Augustinian, at least in its formulas. And yet, when one reads his works after having read those of Augustine, one cannot help but feel that there is a chasm between the two.[10]

Catholic scholars tend to consider Gregory a Semi-Augustinian, whereas Protestants came to regard him and the soteriology that he formulated as more Semi-Pelagian. The truth is that he was not a slave to consistency—foolish or otherwise. When Gregory wished to emphasize the sovereignty of God and his grace and denigrate the self-assertion of sinful human beings, he could sound very much like Augustine. When he wanted to warn Christians against taking grace for granted and urge them to greater efforts of self-sacrificing piety (what modern Christians call discipleship), Gregory could sound very much like Pelagius. His own advice to bishops in *The Book of Pastoral Rule* was that preaching involved two tasks: comforting the afflicted and afflicting the comfortable. Gregory's soteriology is filled with tensions in part, at least, because he sometimes wrote to comfort those who felt they could never please God no matter how many works they performed, and to them he emphasized the all-sufficiency of grace as a gift of God, while at other times he wrote to afflict those who he believed were reveling in "cheap grace," and to them he emphasized the absolute necessity of cooperation with grace through human effort.

One statement of Gregory's stands out as particularly revealing of the duality and tension within his soteriology. After emphasizing grace to the point where he *almost* affirmed monergism with Augustine, Gregory wrote, "Even the predestination itself to the eternal kingdom is so arranged by the omnipotent God that the elect attain it from their own effort."[11] For Gregory, "prayers, penance, masses, intercession, works—all are forms of human effort mediating with the divine."[12] On the other hand, no one would be capable of performing these efforts in any redemptive way apart from assisting grace. But when a person's will and effort cooperate with that grace so that the person perseveres to the end and goes to the eternal kingdom, the result is that such a person may be said to have been "predestined to salvation." Electing grace must be activated. In Gregory's mind there was nothing automatic about it.

What is it, then, that a person must do to activate grace so that he or she becomes one of God's elect? According to Gregory, one must be crucified with Christ in order to benefit from Christ's cross and its grace: "Indeed . . . Christ did not fulfill everything for us. To be sure, he redeemed everyone through the Cross, but it is left that he who strives to be redeemed and reign with him should be crucified with him."[13] According to Gregory, being crucified with Christ means extreme repentance, including penitential acts of self-sacrifice, a general rational self-denial of bodily pleasures that hinder spirituality, active participation in the sacramental life of the church, and works of love, such as giving to the poor. The person who truly wishes to please God, become assured of divine election and escape from the pangs of purgatory ought to live the life of a monk, which is the life of the "perfect penitent." For Gregory physical pleasure itself is an enticement to sin if not actual sin. Sexual intercourse even within marriage is a sin except for the purpose of procreation, and even then, if the act involves any lust or bodily pleasure, it may involve guilt.[14] If a person wishes to be a "perfect penitent" and be "secure of pardon" and assured of heaven, he or she will surely join a monastic order and deny the body all kinds of pleasures that may be technically allowed by God but contain within themselves the seeds of temptation.

Because of Gregory's strong emphasis on extreme asceticism (self-denial), acts of penance, works of love, and free cooperation with assisting grace, and because of his denial of assurance and security of salvation (apart from exceptional cases), Protestants have come to consider Gregory a Semi-Pelagian even though he affirmed the necessity of assisting supernatural grace for any righteousness a person may attain. He clearly was a synergist if not a legalist in his approach to salvation and Christian living. His theology had the effect—perhaps unintended—of destroying any sense of assurance or security about salvation for most medieval Christians.

When Luther joined the Augustinian monastery seeking a gracious God, it was Gregory's version of Augustinianism that he was taught. He was plagued by an idea of God as wrathful and impossible to please. He tried flagellating himself to punish himself for his own sins, thus completing the work of Christ on his behalf through self-sacrifice. Eventually he came to hate God rather than love him. Then he had his great tower experience of realizing the sole sufficiency of grace and efficacy of faith alone for achieving forgiveness. He stopped trying to be Gregory's perfect penitent and relaxed in grace, finding assurance in the biblical statement that the "righteous shall live by faith." In large measure Luther's Protestant theology was a reaction against Gregory's doctrine of salvation.

The Eastern church did not so much react against Gregory's synergism as against his rather inflexible assertions of the superiority of the Roman bishop over their bishops and even over the patriarch of Constantinople. It also objected to many of his innovations in Christian teaching and practice. While Gregory by no means created the gulf between the East and the West, he did little to bridge it and may have contributed to its widening. At least from Gregory's papacy onward the Western church went on its way undisturbed by the fact of Eastern Christianity and the Byzantine Empire. The two halves of Christendom rarely read one another's works, and their relationship grew colder and more distant with each passing decade and century.

# CHAPTER 19

# The Eastern Church Becomes Eastern Orthodox

The Western church that became Roman Catholic has always also considered itself the Roman Orthodox Church. The Eastern church that became what we today call Eastern Orthodox has always considered itself also the Eastern Catholic Church. It is merely by convention that people have come to call one "Catholic" and the other "Orthodox." By no means do members of the church of Rome concede that the Eastern church is more orthodox than it is. Nor do members of the Eastern Orthodox Church consider the church of Rome more catholic than it is. Since 1054, both consider themselves the one, true Great Church that is catholic and orthodox. Each considers the other a schismatic sect that is neither fully catholic nor fully orthodox.

We have seen some of the factors that contributed to the drift of the Western church away from the Eastern church so that by the early Middle Ages it often acted on its own as if the Eastern church did not exist. That split was not formal or official, however. If asked, the bishops of the Western church would have acknowledged the Eastern bishops as genuine Christians, even if a bit odd in their beliefs and practices. The same would have been true of the Eastern bishops if asked about the Western ones. However, the two halves of the Great Church faced their own unique problems and dealt with them in different ways.

Just as there were certain pivotal figures and controversies that helped create what we now call Roman Catholicism, so the Eastern church experienced its own controversies and had its own uniquely Byzantine thinkers who shaped it into the Eastern Orthodox tradition and family of churches. The towering figure in the West behind everyone and everything—in some ways the main human character in its theological story—was Augustine of Hippo. Even when his ideas were being misinterpreted and misapplied to problems, he remained the theologian every Western Christian thinker had to reckon with. The Eastern Church also had a towering figure like Augustine. We have already met him. His name was Origen.

**The Enduring Influence of Origen**

The church of the Byzantine Empire (from Emperor Justinian until the late Middle Ages) had a love-hate relationship with Origen and his theology, which is labeled Origenism. Even though Origen and Origenism were condemned by the fifth ecumenical council at Constantinople in 553, they remained powerfully influential in Eastern Christian thought. According to a leading modern Eastern Orthodox thinker, "Origenism . . . remained at the center of the theological thought of post-Chalcedonian Eastern Christianity, and its influence on spirituality and theological terminology did not end with the condemnation of the Origenistic *system* in 553, but continued at least until the iconoclastic crisis of the eighth century."[1] Among other things, Origenism stamped the Eastern church and its theology with a strongly synergistic view of salvation that emphasizes human free will cooperating with grace and a rational-mystical doctrine of God that emphasizes divine ineffability and immutability. Origenist soteriology centers on the idea of saving incarnation, in which the Logos, by becoming human in Christ, transforms creation itself, overcoming sin and death. Origen's permanent and pervasive influence in Eastern thought cannot be denied or overlooked.

Two great controversies and three great theologians played particularly crucial roles in the development of Eastern Orthodoxy as a branch of Christian theology distinct from the Roman Catholic. The two controversies were the monothelite controversy and the iconoclastic controversy. These disputes and their outcomes through two ecumenical councils deeply affected Eastern Christian belief and worship. The three theologians were John Chrysostom, who came to be called Golden Mouth because of his great homiletical skills; Maximus the Confessor, who was martyred by a Byzantine emperor for his uncompromising opposition to monothelitism; and John of Damascus, who provided a great summary of Orthodox faith and defended the church's use of icons (holy images) in worship against those who tried to outlaw them.

**Liturgy and Tradition**

It is very difficult for Western Christians—both Roman Catholic and Protestant—to tell or understand the story of Eastern Orthodox theology. Radically differing mindsets gradually developed as the Roman Empire split apart. Theology in the West after Augustine tended to look to objective, written authorities such as Scripture, creeds, canonical law (the code by which the Roman Catholic Church governs itself) to settle disputes and guide its development. Western Christians came more and more to see theology as a kind of philosophy, even if one that recognizes an element of mystery in God's relationship with the world. Salvation was regarded increasingly in judicial terms as God's legal favor or judgment upon souls. Although Protestants sought to reform what they saw as abuses in Roman Catholic theology and practice as it had developed during the Middle Ages, by and large they inherited the basic mindset of the Western church. For example, overall the Western branches of Christianity tend to see worship as an outgrowth of reflection on Scripture and theology. The Eastern approach is quite different.

Eastern Orthodox theology is never divorced from divine liturgy—that is, worship by the faithful people of God. In fact, leading spokespersons for the Eastern tradition argue that its theology is an outgrowth of its tradition of worship:

> While a Western Christian generally checked his faith against external authority (the magisterium or the Bible), the Byzantine Christian considered the liturgy both a source and an expression of his theology; hence, the very great conservatism which often prevailed both in Byzantium itself and in post-Byzantine times in matters of liturgical tradition and practice. The liturgy maintained the Church's identity and continuity in the midst of a changing world.[2]

The worship of the church is considered by Eastern Orthodox Christians to be a—perhaps *the*—major aspect of tradition, which is the ultimate source and norm of all theology. Scripture is also part of tradition. Especially Protestants often have great difficulty understanding and accepting this different mindset regarding the source of truth for faith and practice. For Eastern Christians, tradition governs the entire church as well as individuals' Christian lives. It is the overall story into which God inserts converts' lives (even infants converted by baptism) so that their individual stories become part of the great story of divine revelation from the Old Testament through the early church and its martyrs, heroes, councils, creeds, and identification of the canon of Scripture and true worship.

The key question for any Eastern Orthodox theologian when confronting a controversial issue is, What does tradition say about it? And Christian tradition virtually came to a close for Eastern Orthodox Christians around 787 at the seventh and final ecumenical council, Nicaea II.[3] That is why the Eastern church is sometimes known as The Church of the Seven Councils. At the heart of tradition stands worship, and the rule of Eastern Orthodox theology is *Lex Orandi, Lex Credendi*—"The law of worship is the law of belief." Worship did evolve throughout the early centuries. No Eastern Orthodox believer would argue that divine liturgy today is exactly as it was in the first-century Christian churches in Rome or Antioch. Eastern Orthodoxy does believe, however, that the development of its worship primarily in Constantinople throughout the centuries from Constantine to the Second Council of Nicaea and especially during the reign of Emperor Justinian was divinely inspired. The "Great Church" of the Eastern capital—the Hagia Sophia—played a central role in this process. "The adoption of a liturgical practice or tradition by the 'Great Church' meant a final sanction and, ultimately, a quasi-guarantee of universal acceptance."[4]

Eastern Orthodox theology is reflection on tradition, and that means interpretation of worship as well as Scripture. It does not take the form of great systematic summaries of doctrinal propositions such as developed in the West, especially in the medieval period and later. At least according to Eastern Orthodox spokespersons, its theology resists both speculation beyond divine revelation in tradition and rationalistic systematization. It recognizes, if not revels in, mystery and allows beliefs to be stated as antinomies or paradoxes. Many of the necessary distinctions it insists upon are beyond human comprehension and may even appear to the rational Western mind as incomprehensible. For example, Western Christians often find it difficult to see the distinction between salvation as deification and a kind of pantheistic oneness of God with all creation. Especially Maximus the Confessor promoted such a distinction while strongly emphasizing the ultimate deification of the entire universe—not just humans—through the incarnation. A related distinction that is also difficult for Westerners to grasp is that between God's "essence" and "energies." It is absolutely crucial to Eastern Orthodox theology but can hardly be expressed rationally.

To the Western mind, Eastern theology often appears mystical and even paradoxical without objective, written authority by which to judge it. One is hard-pressed to find any Eastern Orthodox systematic theologies such as crowd the shelves of Roman Catholic and Protestant seminary libraries. Leading modern Eastern Orthodox theologian John Meyendorff traces this difference back at least to the Byzantine era and argues that Eastern Christianity's lack of systematic theology

> does not mean . . . that behind the issues debated by theologians there was not a basic unity of inspiration, and the sense of a single, consistent tradition

> of faith. Of course, the East was less prone than the West to conceptualize or to dogmatize this unity of tradition. It preferred to maintain its faithfulness to the "mind of Christ" through the liturgy of the Church, through the tradition of holiness, through a living *gnosis* of the Truth.[5]

**John Chrysostom: The Golden Mouth**

Because of this uniquely Eastern approach to theology, it is well to begin our story of its development during the Byzantine era with a pre-Byzantine saint and bishop highly revered by the Eastern Orthodox tradition. John Chrysostom typifies the preference for theology solidly rooted in worship, including practical preaching of the "mind of Christ" as expressed in tradition (including Scripture). Chrysostom was a contemporary of Augustine's. He was born in Antioch in about 349 to a moderately wealthy family of some social standing. At an early age he showed great promise as a spiritual leader and joined a monastic community in Antioch. He became a noted preacher and teacher of Scripture and wrote as well as delivered orally numerous sermons and commentaries on books of the Bible. The approach that he took was typically Antiochene in that he would begin with the historical-literal meaning of Scripture and move from it to the typological meaning, keeping the latter firmly grounded in the former. A leading modern Western scholar of the early church says that "John's sermon-commentaries . . . form the most impressive, and also most readable, collection of patristic expositions of scripture."[6] Although the masses loved his preaching and teaching, Chrysostom's reputation with the ruling cultural elite of Antioch was not always favorable because many of his sermons attacked their conspicuous consumption and selfishly affluent lifestyles. Nevertheless, he was so popular and widely regarded that in October 397 he was appointed bishop of Constantinople by Emperor Theodosius I.

Once installed in Constantinople as its patriarch, John Chrysostom launched an all-out effort to clean up and reform the clergy and monks of the city. He believed that the favoritism the emperor and imperial court showed to Christianity had led to a moral and spiritual lethargy and that he was called by God to shape up the church and set it back on the right track. He began almost immediately to preach powerful sermons in the great cathedral against the dominance of the emperor over the church—what in the West has come to be called caesaropapism. He asserted the independence of the bishops from the imperial court and from the civil servant bureaucracy that had grown up around it, and condemned the wealth and opulence that existed side by side with abject poverty in Constantinople. He also ordered the monks and clergy to work and tend their flocks and quit living luxuriantly off the incomes of the wealthy who patronized them. An excellent example of his preaching is offered by his modern biographer:

> What senselessness, what madness is this! The church has so many poor standing around it, and has also so many children who are rich; yet she is unable to give relief to one poor person. "One man is hungry, another gets drunk" (1 Corinthians 11:21); one man defecates in a silver pot, another has not so much as a crust of bread.[7]

Needless to say, Chrysostom quickly became a hero with the poor and downtrodden masses, both Christian and pagan, who flocked to hear him. They gave him the title "Golden Tongue" or "Golden Mouth" because his preaching was so sweet to their ears. On several occasions he had to harshly forbid applause of his sermons from the enthusiastic congregation who demanded that he preach more often and longer. His preaching skill was even noted by a contemporary pagan writer named Zosimas, who wrote of Chrysostom, "The fellow was quite clever at bringing the ignorant masses under his spell."[8] Eventually, of course, the emperor and empress and their court began to criticize the great preacher-bishop. The straw that broke the proverbial camel's back may have come when Chrysostom publicly compared Empress Eudoxia to Jezebel in a sermon preached in 401. He seemed bent on provoking rulers like an Old Testament prophet.

Chrysostom's downfall began with attacks against him by fellow bishop Epiphanios of Cyprus (367 to 403), who launched a campaign to smear him as an "Origenist heretic." The campaign against him was primarily politically motivated as his theology was completely orthodox. In fact, his theology consisted primarily of biblical expositions and condemnations of cultural accommodations by Christians to paganism. In September 403 Chrysostom was condemned by an ecclesiastical court and his deposition as a bishop was confirmed by the Synod of the Oak in the same year. His forced exile from Constantinople was accompanied by open rioting in the streets and inside the cathedral. The emperor had to send in soldiers to put down the rebellion. After a series of temporary restorations and returns—during which he always picked up where he left off preaching against corruption—Chrysostom died during a forced march into distant exile from Constantinople on September 14, 406. He died from malnutrition and exposure. It was clearly an execution by Emperor Arkadios, who wanted the Golden Mouth out of his way forever.

John Chrysostom is remembered as one of the great heroes of Eastern Orthodoxy even though his contribution to theology as such was minimal. Because of his courageous preaching and reforms of both church and state, and because of his martyrdom, he is regarded as a saint and teacher of the church. Many Eastern Orthodox churches are named after him. Why tell his story in a book on the history of Christian theology? Simply because it illustrates something about Eastern Orthodox theology. A great and courageous preacher, reformer of worship and church life, spiritual guide and prophet to the powerful is considered the paradigm of a good theologian even though he never wrote a book of systematic theology or speculated about how many angels can dance on the head of a pin. According to Eastern Orthodoxy, he who prays and preaches well is the best theologian.

Two other heroes of Eastern Orthodox theology from the Byzantine era are Maximus the Confessor and John of Damascus. Their stories are wrapped up with the stories of two great controversies that were all-consuming in the Eastern church during that time. Maximus's story is entangled with the great monothelite controversy over the wills of Christ. John of Damascus's story is part of the great iconoclastic controversy over the use of holy images in worship. These stories are at the heart of the larger story of Eastern Orthodox theology. To a large extent, that branch of Christianity is what it is because of these controversies and the theologians who helped settle them.

**Maximus the Confessor and Monothelitism**

Earlier we surveyed the monosphysite controversy of the post-Chalcedonian era. The monophysites were those Christians under the influence of Alexandria who believed that the Chalcedonian Definition actually violated the spirit of the hypostatic-union doctrine of Cyril of Alexandria. They saw it as favoring the Antiochene idea of two natures and two persons in Christ. In other words, they believed it did not go far enough to exclude Nestorianism. Various emperors in Constantinople tried to mollify the monophysites—to little avail. They remained a powerful force to reckon with in the Byzantine Empire. During the fifth and sixth centuries, many emperors and leading bishops of the East strove for union between orthodox and monophysite Christians. One seemingly attractive proposal to bridge the gap was *monothelitism*—the idea that even though Jesus Christ was one integral person with two complete but inseparable natures, he had only one will—a divine one. Monothelites and their sympathizers hoped that this compromise would reunite the church, and after all, it seemed like such a small measure of compromise for both sides.

Maximus—like John Chrysostom before him—was born of a family of high reputation. The exact year of his birth in Constantinople is unknown, but it was probably around 580. He grew up to become a highly regarded and successful civil servant and was invited by Emperor Heraclius to become his personal secretary of state. After a short while in that position, though, Maximus left the imperial service to become a monk, and after living in several monasteries, he arrived in Carthage in 632. It was there that he first heard of monothelitism and began his lifelong fight against it that eventually led to his execution. His struggle against monothelitism and for *dyothelitism*—belief in two natural wills of Christ—took him to Rome, where he lobbied popes to stand firmly against the compromises advocated by Byzantine emperors. Like Athanasius before him, Maximus believed that this one little compromise would destroy the entire edifice of orthodox Christology. It would amount to a return to monophysitism and thus a denial of Christ's two natures and thus of his true and full humanity and divinity. In the end it would, he believed and argued, make Apollinarianism or Eutychianism orthodox because if Christ had only one will, it certainly had to be divine, and then the humanity would be mutilated. And as Gregory of Nazianzus had declared, "What the Son of God has not assumed has not been healed."

While in Rome, Maximus was captured along with Pope Martin by Byzantine soldiers invading the West to attempt to reunify the once great Roman Empire. Taken to Constantinople for trial in May of 655, he was condemned for crimes against the state because he had openly denounced the emperor's authority over church and theology. Maximus had written, "I think not of the unity or division of Romans and Greeks, but I must not retreat from the correct faith. . . . It is the business of priests, not emperors, to investigate and define the salutary dogmas of the Catholic Church."[9] After refusing to recant his dyothelite views and compromise with the monothelites, Maximus was tortured to death by the emperor's orders on August 13, 661. Later he was recognized as a great defender of the Chalcedonian faith by emperors, bishops and laypeople alike and given the honorific title "the Confessor." His writings on theology were also rehabilitated and became standard works for teaching and interpreting the orthodox faith. One leading modern Eastern Orthodox theologian says that

> Maximus can be called the real father of Byzantine theology. Only through his system, in which the valid traditions of the past found their legitimate place, were the ideas of Origen, Evagrius, the Cappadocians, Cyril, and Pseudo-Dionysius preserved within Eastern Christianity. . . . It remains impossible . . . to understand the whole of Byzantine theology without becoming aware of Maximus' synthesis.[10]

In spite of his great importance for Eastern Orthodox theology, interpreting Maximus is no easy task—even for Easterners. He did not provide a systematic exposition of his theology but expressed his ideas in letters, oral arguments and in fragments of intended books and written debates with opponents. Pulling it all together and summarizing it is a daunting task also because so many of his phrases and concepts are enigmatic and quasi-mystical. What he was aiming at was much more than merely a defense of Chalcedonian Christology against the threat of monothelitism. That was just the tip of the iceberg. Maximus's larger goal—never set forth in completeness—was an orthodox Christian worldview centered entirely around the incarnation. For him the incarnation of God in Jesus Christ was and is the ultimate purpose for everything—not just a way of getting Jesus to the cross so he could die for the sins of the world and not even just a way of recapitulating Adam in order to reverse the effects of the Fall. For Maximus the incarnation was the very crown of creation and would have taken place even if humans had never fallen into sin. Eastern Orthodoxy accepted that view from him.

**Maximus's Theandric Vision of Reality**

Maximus's Christian vision of reality—his ontology—begins with the idea that everything in creation is in some sense a revelation of God because "the whole world is the attire of the Logos."[11] Because of creation by and through the Logos, and especially because of the incarnation of the Logos in humanity, "everything in the world is spiritual in its depths. One can recognize the fabric of the Logos everywhere."[12] The world was created by God as an expression of himself and vehicle of his presence, and it was to be united with God through the Logos—the second person of the Trinity. This would have been a natural progression reaching its culmination in the incarnation had the first humans not sinned. In Maximus's own words,

> He who founded the existence—origin, "genesis"—of all creation, visible and invisible, by a single act of his will, ineffably had, before all ages, and any beginning of the created world, good counsel, a decision, that he himself should inalterably unite with human nature through a true unity of hypostases. And he inalterably united human nature with himself—so that he himself should become a man, as he himself knows, and so that he should make man a god through union with himself.[13]

By sinning, humans introduced into the world confusion and death, which interrupted the unification of all things with God through the Logos. Humanity was to stand at the center of that God-cosmic unity filled with the Logos in a special way. But because of sin and its resultant corruption, humanity lost its connection with God, and the entire cosmos was affected by that. A curse, as it were, fell upon the creation. The incarnation of the Logos, which was to be the natural goal and fulfillment of creation, became its rescue operation instead.

Nevertheless, the incarnation of the Logos was more than a rescue operation. According to Maximus, it was also the resumption of the original plan and project of God to unite all creation with himself. In a sense, through the particular incarnation of the Logos in Christ, God was aiming at a universal incarnation of the Logos in all creation. And because of the incarnation the Logos has a foothold, as it were, in everything and especially in humanity. Nothing has true being apart from the Logos. Apart from the Logos, everything is emptiness and on its way to nothingness.

At the center of this vision of reality in the process of being divinized by God stands the human being. For Maximus humans have a special place in creation between nature and God. God's assignment to humanity was and is to play a pivotal role in uniting and harmonizing all the diverse aspects of reality—physical and spiritual—so that creation as a whole may be a fit vehicle of God's dwelling. It is not automatic. Universal incarnation depends on human cooperation. For the goal of God in creation to be crowned with completion, the human creature must respond to God properly through free submission to God's will and being open to God's indwelling.

In order for human beings to accomplish their designated purpose in the divine plan, the incarnation is necessary. Maximus saw the incarnation as the charge that reenergizes the human creature to become active with God in cosmic deification. This recharging and reenergizing of humanity by the Logos is what Maximus called the theandric dimension of the incarnation. That is, God and humanity belong together, and the incarnation both reveals it and makes it possible. For Maximus,

> "theandric" designates the entirely unique and new relationship that is established in Jesus Christ as being both fully human and fully divine: God and man as cooperating for the benefit of the whole creation; not separated and yet not mixed, not confused and yet in full harmony. . . . Maximus is among the first Christian writers to use the term frequently and freely. Thereby he introduces a whole tradition of Eastern Christian thinking, for which the reality behind the term is of the utmost importance: life itself is marked by Christ's incarnation to such an extent that there is always a theandric dimension to it.[14]

In order for this theandric dimension to work, however, humans must freely cooperate with the "spark" of divine grace in the energizing incarnation. God's own divine energies (not God's essence) are available to fill and transform every created thing if humans will play their role freely by bringing every thought captive to Christ and, through sacrament and worship, be filled with his Spirit.

This theandric vision of reality is the background for Maximus's uncompromising opposition to monothelitism: "The whole polemic of St. Maximus the Confessor with the Monothelites, strictly speaking, comes down to this interpretation that the will is a necessary feature of human nature, and that without will and freedom, human nature would be incomplete and not authentic."[15] Thus, Maximus argued, the theandric dimension so necessary for the ultimate completion of God's plan of creation and redemption would not be possible if Christ did not have a human will. His humanity *had* to cooperate freely with the divine call of the Logos in order for humanity to transcend its mere creatureliness and enter into deified existence. But Maximus argued that Christ's human will was a "natural will" and not a fallen "Adamic will" turned against God. At every point in Jesus' life his human will chose freely to cooperate with the Logos. The two wills were fully coordinated in such a way that the Logos led the way and the human will freely obeyed and followed.

One possible tension in Maximus's dyothelite Christology lies in his definition of *will.* On the one hand, like Origen and the entire Eastern Christian tradition, he assumed that human beings have free will in the sense of ability to obey or disobey God. He held a clearly synergistic view of salvation as well in which human beings may either cooperate with God's grace or reject it. For Maximus, as for the entire Eastern tradition, free will meant "ability to do otherwise" and not Augustine's "freedom to do what one wants to do." There was no inevitability of the Fall. And humans now must freely choose to participate in redemption. On the other hand, when dealing with the problem of how one person (Christ) could have two wills, Maximus redefined *will* so that it does not necessarily involve free choice. He clearly did not believe that Christ could have sinned. Christ had a human will—something essential to a human nature—but not human free choice. Furthermore, his human nature, including his human will, was deified by the union with the Logos so that it always chose to adhere to the good.[16]

But if free choice (ability to do otherwise) is an essential part of human nature—and how else was it that Adam and Eve sinned?—did not Christ have to have free choice in order to be fully human and achieve the theandric dimension? It would seem so. Yet Maximus was not willing to affirm that. How meaningful, then, is affirmation of two wills in Christ if it does not imply two sets of choices? In practice, does not Maximus's Christology come down to one active and operative will? It seems so.

One way out of the dilemma taken by some non-Eastern Orthodox theologians is to suggest that a will is a function of person and not of nature. Thus building on Leontius of Byzantium's *enhypostasia* idea of the incarnation, Jesus Christ had only one will and it was the will of the Son of God who formed his unifying personhood. It was a divine will under the conditions of humanity because of the incarnation. It was a will that was opened to temptation (if not sin) by the lowering process (kenosis) involved in the Son of God's descent into the conditions of creatureliness.

But this is also something Maximus and the entire Eastern tradition could not accept. For Maximus and the tradition so deeply influenced by him, the Logos underwent no change whatever in becoming incarnate. He suffered "through the humanity" without undergoing any alteration or change. He remained immutable and impassible.

This is what many Western Christian theologians—especially modern Protestants—find unacceptable and unnecessary. They believe that many of the dilemmas of ancient and Byzantine theology could have been cleared up if the theologians had been willing to soften their position on divine immutability and impassibility.

Long after Maximus's martyrdom, his Christology was vindicated by the sixth ecumenical council called by Emperor Constantine IV. Known as the Third Council of Constantinople or Constantinople III, it met from 680 to 681 and condemned monothelitism and affirmed two natural wills in Christ. From then on, Maximus's reputation as a great hero of Orthodoxy has been firmly upheld. His vision of cosmic redemption is generally accepted as valid by Eastern Orthodox Christians.

**John of Damascus and the Iconoclasm**

The story of Byzantine Eastern Orthodox theology reaches its climax of tension, conflict and resolution with the great iconoclastic controversy of the eighth century. The Orthodox hero of this episode of the story is John of Damascus, also known as "the Damascene." The resolution is found in a final ecumenical council that capped off the process of authoritative tradition for Eastern Orthodoxy in 787 with the declaration that holy images—icons—must not be rejected and indeed ought to be used in Christian worship.

Icons are simply pictures of Christ and saints used as focal points of meditation and prayer in worship. In Eastern Orthodox worship and devotion they play a crucial role as "windows into heaven" that the faithful use as a point of contact in praying to the Trinity or to saints. Saints are regarded simply as accessible intercessors—a portion of the great "cloud of witnesses" in heaven—who take living Christians' petitions to God. Icons have never been regarded by Eastern

Orthodox or Roman Catholic theologians as idols. They are never worshiped. In fact, worship of them has always been strictly forbidden by those traditions. However, from ancient times such pictures have been used as aids to prayer, worship and devotion. As early as the sixth century in the East, icons were being used as "books for the illiterate." Their teaching and reminding functions were considered essential for those who could not read Scripture or Christian books for themselves.

By the early eighth century Constantinople and other Christian cities of the Byzantine Empire were overflowing with icons. Iconography was a major industry, especially among monks. Every household and every church possessed several and perhaps many elaborate icons before which the faithful of Orthodoxy meditated and worshiped. Some leaders of both church and state feared that the practice was getting out of hand, and one emperor in particular, Leo III (717), ordered the destruction of icons throughout the empire.

The conflict that ensued lasted for decades and led to rioting among monks, martyrdoms of leading defenders of icons as well as of leading iconoclasts (opponents of icons), and a general state of turmoil and confusion in the entire Byzantine Empire and church. The iconoclasts argued that images of Christ violated the spirit of the biblical prohibition of idolatry and implied a defective Christology:

> According to them, the divine nature [of Christ] cannot be circumscribed. Therefore, if one represents the humanity of the Savior in an image it will be necessary to represent it apart from his divinity, and this would immediately lead to that division of the two natures for which Nestorianism was condemned. If, on the other hand, one claims that in representing the humanity of Christ one also represents his divinity, this would imply circumscribing his divinity, and it would lead to the confusion of the two natures for which monophysism *[sic]* was condemned.[17]

For some time during the eighth century the iconoclasts were in power and churches throughout the Eastern empire were stripped of images, and many of their defenders—known as iconophiles—were persecuted.

John of Damascus is noted in the history of theology for several contributions but most of all for providing the theological rationale and justification for the use of icons in worship. Through his writings in favor of icons, the Eastern church found a way to reinstitute them without implying idolatry.

John was born in Damascus, Syria, sometime between 645 and 675 and died around 750. He spent at least some of his adult life in a monastery called St. Sabas near Jerusalem. His "remarkable addresses in defense of holy ikons *[sic]* drew universal attention to him" throughout the Byzantine Empire.[18] These addresses came to be known as *Discourses Against the Iconoclasts* and were written by John between 726 and 730. In them the monk emphasized the radical change that took place in the relationship between God and the visible, physical world through the incarnation. God gave to material existence a new function and dignity such that physical objects could reflect his incarnate being. According to John, "in former times, God, without body or form, could in no way be represented. But today, since God has appeared in the flesh and lived among men, I can represent what is visible in God. . . . I do not venerate matter, but I venerate the creator of matter, who became matter for my sake, who assumed life in the flesh, and who, through matter, accomplished my salvation."[19]

John went on to justify the use of icons in worship by making a subtle but important distinction between actual worship of a person or object and mere veneration—a kind of respect for something because it is dedicated to God and permeated by his spiritual energies. Absolute worship, which John designated by the Greek word *latria,* is due only to God, whereas *proskynesis,* or reverence, may be offered to holy images because they are sacramental channels of the divine energies. John's view of icons had a profound impact on the Second Council of Nicaea in 787, which was the seventh and last ecumenical council, according to Eastern Orthodoxy. The bishops gathered there concluded by condemning the iconoclasts: "Anathema to those who do not salute [venerate] the holy and venerable images. Anathema to those who call the sacred images idols."[20]

John of Damascus is also known as the last of the great church fathers of the Eastern Orthodox tradition. He not only defended icons and provided their theological justification—something crucial for Eastern Orthodox worship—but he also wrote the first great summary of Orthodox theology, known as *Exposition of the Orthodox Faith.* In it he attempted to bring together all essential Christian truth and express it in as timeless a way as possible. While there is nothing original in it, the *Exposition* remains a standard of Eastern Orthodox theology that emphasizes the saving incarnation, deification of humanity through Christ and ineffable essence of God beyond all human comprehension.

Even though the Western church that looked to Rome as its center recognized and accepted the sixth and seventh ecumenical councils and considered both Maximus and the Damascene to be great expositors of the faith, by the end of the eighth century the two branches of the Great Church were irreparably broken apart over differences of governance, worship styles and views of the trinitarian creed. The final episode in our story of these two great churches' parting of the ways will focus on the final and ultimate causes of the separation, especially the great controversy over the *filioque* clause that crept into the Nicene Creed in the West.

# CHAPTER 20

# The Great Schism Creates Two Traditions Out of One

B*y the end of the eighth century and beginning of the ninth, the two halves of* Christendom had developed their own ecclesiastical and theological cultures to such an extent that true communication and understanding between them was almost impossible. Of course bishops and theologians traveled back and forth between Constantinople and Rome, but such exchanges often led to greater misunderstandings and even animosities. As usual, politics played a major role in this rift. The Byzantine emperors of Constantinople still considered their realm—increasingly shrinking due to Muslim invasions—the one true Christian empire. As far as they and their bishops were concerned, the Christian Roman Empire of Constantine, Theodosius and Justinian still existed and ought to include the West. The popes of Rome, however, increasingly looked to Christianized barbarian tribes such as the Franks of central Europe to reestablish the old Roman Empire in the West. On Christmas day 800 a pope crowned the Frankish king Charles the Great—Charlemagne—emperor of the new, revived Holy Roman Empire. The Byzantine emperor was dismayed, to say the least.

Here, however, we will focus on the theological aspects of the story of the Great Schism between Eastern and Western Christianity.[1] Many differences exist between the two traditions that are not particularly theological. For example, the Eastern church always allowed priests to be married. Clerical celibacy is required only of monks. Eastern Orthodox bishops are traditionally chosen from the ranks of the monks, so they are always celibate. The ordinary parish priest, however, is allowed to marry before ordination. If he is single at the time of his ordination, he must remain so. The Roman Catholic tradition gradually developed the practice of universal clerical celibacy so that all priests of the church must be single and chaste. There are, however, exceptions to this rule. The canon law of Roman Catholicism allows for "special dispensations"—exceptions to rules—and that is why some priests are married. The norm, however, is clerical celibacy. This is not a major theological difference between the two branches. It played little or no significant role in the schism that tore them apart. Likewise, there are numerous other fairly minor differences of worship styles, interpretations and practice of sacraments, and beliefs about the canon of Scripture, life after death, and saints that East and West probably could have learned to live with. The real reasons for the schism lay elsewhere than these observable and fairly superficial differences.

Perhaps the most fundamental cause of the schism was what church historian Jaroslav Pelikan calls "intellectual alienation." In other words, the two sides simply drifted so far apart in their basic attitudes and mindsets that they could no longer understand one another. Each tended to read and quote only its own church fathers. Augustine dominated in the West, even if read and interpreted through Gregory the Great's rather distorted version of Augustinianism. The East looked to Irenaeus, Origen, Athanasius, the Cappadocian fathers, Cyril, Maximus the Confessor and other fathers and theologians steeped in a kind of mystical, speculative theology. The West insisted on the sole sovereignty of grace and allowed modified monergism. The East insisted on free will and a synergistic view of salvation. But even more, as Pelikan notes, "Not simply this or that theological idea of Greeks, but their very method of theologizing, was foreign to the Latins."[2] The same could be said the other way around, simply substituting "Latins" for "Greeks" and vice versa. The Greek Eastern pattern of theologizing was more mystical and speculative and emphasized the authorities of worship, popular piety, and the informal and unwritten accumulation of Eastern Christian tradition. The Latin Western pattern of theologizing was more legalistic and practical and emphasized the authorities of written codes and objective norms.

Perhaps the immediate theological causes of the schism could have been overcome were it not for the deeper differences of culture, politics and mindsets between East and West. Both sides, however, attribute the ultimate schism in which each one excommunicated the other to two major controversies: papal authority and *filioque*. To this day the bishops of the Eastern Orthodox Church and the bishops of the Roman Catholic Church cannot arrive at agreement on these major issues, even though they have come to regard one another as the "two halves of Christendom." As of the time this is being written, however, they still do not have eucharistic fellowship.

**The Controversy over the Papacy**

Western Christians of the ninth and tenth centuries looked to the East and saw an emperor ruling the church. They labeled this caesaropapism—"Caesar is pope." They firmly believed that the bishop of Rome stood as Peter's successor in apostolic succession because Peter had been the first bishop of Rome according to church tradition. Since Jesus had given the keys of the kingdom of heaven to Peter (Mt 16:18-19) and promised to build his church upon "this rock" (which the church of Rome interpreted as Peter), they believed that all bishops of Rome have primacy over the entire church of Jesus Christ until he returns. The Western bishops, then, resisted imperial power over church and theology and insisted that even emperors such as Charlemagne ought to bow to the authority of the pope in spiritual if not also in temporal matters.

Eastern Christians of the ninth and tenth centuries looked to the West and saw a bishop of one great see of Christendom attempting to dominate all the rest illegitimately. They accused the Latins of attempting to force a "monarchy of the pope" on all Christendom and resisted the bishop of Rome's attempts to dominate the East. From Origen on, the Eastern bishops and theologians had interpreted "the rock" Jesus spoke of as Peter's faith and not Peter as a man and certainly not the bishops of Rome, even if Peter was the first. According to Eastern Orthodox theologian John Meyendorff, "The whole ecclesiastical debate between East and West is thus reducible to the issue of whether the faith depends on Peter, or Peter on the faith."[3] The Eastern church considered every orthodox bishop a true successor of Peter, not just the bishop of Rome, and it considered the great sees of Christianity—Rome, Constantinople, Antioch, Alexandria and Jerusalem—equal in dignity, power and authority. The East was willing to acknowledge the patriarch of Rome as "first among equals," but considered that a purely honorary title. The Roman patriarch rejected it.

Thus Meyendorff says the basic cause of the disruption and reason it could never be healed came down to different attitudes toward church government: "The medieval development of the Roman primacy as the ultimate reference in doctrinal matters stood in obvious contrast with the concept of the church prevailing in the East. Thus, there could not be agreement on the issues themselves, or on the manner of solving them, as long as there was divergence on the notion of authority in the church."[4]

An example of a seemingly minor issue that could not be healed due to this basic difference over ecclesiastical authority is the ninth-century dispute between Eastern and Western churches over use of unleavened bread *(azymes)* in the Eucharist. This seems rather minor to modern-day Christians—especially Protestants—but was symbolic of a deeper issue at that time. The Western churches used *azymes*, or unleavened bread, in the Communion, while the Eastern churches used leavened bread. Each side considered the other's practice an innovation within Christian tradition, and the West accused the East of departing from scriptural practices, while the East accused the West of insisting on unleavened bread because it was stuck in Jewish practices and had not discovered the freedom of the new covenant. Both sides felt that this difference was significant enough that it had to be reconciled, but the Roman bishop insisted that the decision should be his and the Eastern bishops insisted that he had no right to dictate eucharistic practices to them.

**The *Filioque* Controversy**

Without any doubt the greatest theological argument between East and West contributing to their ultimate mutual excommunication was that over the *filioque* clause in the Latin version of the Nicene Creed. Virtually everyone agrees that the original Greek version of the Niceno-Constantinopolitan Creed of 381 did not contain the phrase "and the Son" *(filioque)* after the portion in which the Holy Spirit is said to proceed "from the Father":

> We believe in the Holy Spirit,
> the Lord, the giver of life,
> who proceeds from the Father *(and the Son)*.
> With the Father and the Son he is worshiped and glorified.
> He has spoken through the Prophets.

The phrase in parentheses—*and the Son*—is an English translation of the Latin *filioque* and appears in almost all Western versions of the Nicene Creed. How did it come to be there? That is what no one knows for sure. And the Eastern bishops, when they heard about it in Constantinople around 850, insisted that it be taken out for two reasons. First, they loudly protested that the West had no right to alter the basic creed of Christendom without consulting the Eastern church. Second, they argued that it revealed a deep theological difference between Eastern ideas of the Trinity, which they considered the only truly orthodox ones, and Western ideas of the Trinity rooted in Augustinian thinking, which they considered heterodox (unorthodox verging on heretical). Meyendorff expresses the Eastern view even of today:

> The Byzantines considered the *Filioque* issue as the central point of the disagreement [between East and West]. In their eyes, the Latin Church, by accepting an interpolated creed, was both opposing a text adopted by the ecumenical councils as the expression of the universal Christian faith, and giving dogmatic authority to an incorrect concept of the Trinity.[5]

Exactly what happened when and where and who did what in this entire *filioque* controversy is shrouded in mystery. The historical sources are not clear. The Eastern church historians offer a different story than do the Western church historians. All that can be said with certainty is that the phrase was officially added to the creed in its Latin translation in the West by a Spanish synod of bishops meeting in Toledo in 589. Before that it had already become common among monks in the West, and some argue that Augustine himself promoted it, which is unlikely, although in *On the Trinity* he did assert the procession of the Spirit from the Son. In any case, the Byzantines first heard of it in Jerusalem when a group of Latin monks from Europe came there on pilgrimage and recited the creed with the interpolated phrase. By sometime in the middle of the ninth century, word of the change in the Western version of the creed had reached Constantinople and the emperor and patriarch there were both livid about it. While they agreed that the Spirit may be said in theology to proceed "from the Father *through* the Son," they condemned the West's unilateral addition of *filioque* to the creed and argued that it is heretical to say that the Spirit proceeds "from the Father *and* the Son."

In 809 a European synod of bishops at Aachen in Germany declared the Greek version of the Nicene Creed that omitted the phrase "and the Son" heretical and required that all Christians everywhere affirm it and add it to the creed. Even the pope at that time rejected this extreme measure and tried to avoid open schism with the East by promoting use of the Apostles' Creed or Old Roman Symbol, rather than the Nicene Creed. It was too late for that, however. The Nicene Creed with the *filioque* clause had caught on in the West and was widely considered orthodox. In response to the Western church's condemnation of omitting the phrase from the creed, the Eastern bishops and emperors began hurling accusations of heresy against the pope and bishops of the West. In the end, the two churches declared one another excommunicated from the Great Church. The patriarch of Constantinople in 1054 was Michael Cerularius, who declared of the bishop of Rome, "The pope is a heretic!"[6] Pope Leo IX's representatives in Constantinople entered the Hagia Sophia cathedral and placed a declaration of excommunication against the patriarch and the bishops in fellowship with him on the high altar and stalked out. The rift has never been healed.

What was truly at stake in the *filioque* controversy? Certainly there was a great deal of resentment over the West's unilateral alteration of the creed on the part of the East. And there was the bitterness over the East's unwillingness to acknowledge the West's right to have its own traditions on the part of Latin bishops. But the deeper causes of the conflict go to the heart of trinitarian theology. Gradually, almost unnoticed, the two halves of Christendom had developed different ways of thinking and talking about the triune God.

The Western approach was rooted in Augustine's theology. The Eastern approach was rooted in Origen's and the Cappadocian fathers' theologies. The Western theology of the Trinity tended to begin with the divine unity of substance and move on from there to explication of the threeness. The emphasis was placed on the one being of God behind and within the persons of Father, Son and Holy Spirit. The three persons were often regarded as manifestations of the one divine being that all three share equally and in common. The Holy Spirit was treated as the bond of love between Father and Son. Augustine could say in *On the Trinity* that the Spirit proceeds from the Father and the Son because of this unifying function of the Spirit's being. Within the eternal Godhead the Spirit is the unifying principle and thus in a sense "comes forth from" Father toward Son and Son toward Father. It would be natural, then, to say that the Spirit is sent into the world by both Father and Son.

To the East, which is rooted in Origen's and the Cappadocian fathers' theologies, this Western view of the Trinity implied a subordinationism of the Spirit. In fact, it seemed to Easterners to depersonalize the Holy Spirit. Their own tradition of trinitarian thinking was to emphasize the monarchy of the Father so that both Son and Spirit find their source, principle and cause eternally in the Father. The Western idea of the Spirit proceeding from the Son seemed to them to imply that the Spirit finds his source, principle and cause in him as much as in the Father. This detracts from the monarchy of the Father and implies that the Spirit is a "son" of the Son of God even as the Son of God is the Son of the Father. A complete distortion of the traditional order of the triune community would follow from that. To Easterners it is insulting to both the Father and the Spirit and confuses the Son with the Father.

Eastern bishops and theologians, then, looked at the addition of the *filioque* clause to the Nicene Creed in the West as evidence of an unorthodox doctrine of the Trinity. To them it manifested an almost modalistic model of the Trinity (Sabellianism) because it did not do justice to the distinctness of the three persons in their relationships and tended to identify the divinity of the three persons with some common abstract substance rather than with the Father himself. To them it also manifested a subordinationism of the Holy Spirit such that the Spirit could hardly be recognized as a distinct person alongside the Son in his own right.

Western bishops and theologians, in return, looked at the East's rejection of the *filioque* clause from the Nicene Creed as evidence of its own unorthodox doctrine of the Trinity. They pointed to passages in the New Testament that clearly speak of the Spirit as sent by Jesus to the church and they accused the East of subordinating both Son and Spirit to the Father.

Some modern theologians—especially Protestants—have suggested that the entire controversy rests on some basic misunderstandings as well as on attempts to peer too closely into the inner, eternal life of the Trinity (immanent Trinity). They suggest that *filioque* ought to be affirmed when Christians are referring to the economic Trinity—the relations of the triune persons toward the world in history and for salvation. In that set of statements about the Trinity the Spirit is confessed as being sent by the Son, and even the Eastern Orthodox Church itself affirms that the Spirit proceeds "from the Father *through* the Son." But, say the modern Protestant thinkers, when referring to the immanent Trinity—the inner life of the Godhead in eternity apart from the world—it is probably best to stick with the original wording of the Nicene Creed and simply say that the Spirit proceeds out of the Father even as the Son is eternally generated (begotten) by the Father. So whether or not the phrase *and the Son* should be used depends on the context of meaning.

With the schism between East and West the story of the church fathers ends. Some would say it ended much earlier, but for our purposes we see it as drawing to a close at least then. That is not, however, the end of the story of Christian theology. The story continues after 1054 in the West with a renaissance of creative theology known as scholasticism that lasted throughout the medieval period. This is a transitional phase in the story of theology, however, because very little that was truly innovative happened in Christian doctrine during that time. The scholastic theologians were not at all interested in promoting development of Catholic theology but rather only in systematizing and summarizing it and showing how it is consistent with the best of philosophy. But the "best of philosophy" was now becoming synonymous with the Greek thinker Aristotle—Plato's pupil in ancient Athens. We move on to that transitional phase in the story of Christian theology as we wend our way toward the story of the great Reformers of the church.

# PART VI

# The Saga of the Queen of Sciences

## *Scholastics Revive & Enthrone Theology*

*After a long drought of creative Christian theology, a new flowering of intellectual* reflection on God and salvation began in the West in the eleventh century. Scholastic theology, as this renaissance of thought is generally known, grew out of the great reforming monastic orders founded in Europe and flourished in the new universities such as those at Paris and Oxford. The universities were at first simply collections of independent scholars who gathered around schools of great cathedrals and monasteries. Some of them were monks, but increasingly many of the scholars of the medieval era were laypersons who had gained a classical education in the cathedrals' chapter schools or in monasteries but never took vows and never were ordained. They were expected to live like priests and monks nevertheless. Celibacy was the norm even for them, as were chastity, poverty and obedience to the church. Gradually, though, men of great education, wisdom and teaching ability formed guilds to support one another and settled down together in close proximity to share students and enrich each other. These groupings of scholars and students developed into the universities of medieval Europe.

Out of the cathedral and monastic schools and universities arose a new kind of theology known as scholasticism. Its intellectuals and teachers are known as the scholastics. The term itself derives from the Latin word for school—*schola*. It is, of course, the same word from which we get *scholar* and *scholarly.* But scholasticism itself designates a particular approach to Christian theology that gradually came to dominate in the West from about 1100 until its decline during the fourteenth and fifteenth centuries. Church historians and historical theologians are not in unanimous agreement about the exact definition or even universal characteristics of scholasticism. Its general contours are more definite, however. Most would agree that "scholasticism was essentially a movement which attempted a methodological and philosophical demonstration of Christian theology as inherently rational and consistent"[1] within the cultural context of medieval Europe. As we have already seen, rationality had been an ideal of many of the church fathers. Certainly Augustine believed in and strove for a consistent and coherent account of Christian belief in his writings. Medieval scholastic theology, however, pushed this concern for rationality in theology to new heights.

For many of the medieval scholastic theologians and philosophers, human reason could, with the help of God's grace, discover the answers to virtually all conceivable questions of any real importance. Its epistemology (theory of human knowledge) was optimistic. Some critics would say it was overly idealistic and subtly placed the human intellect at the center of all theological reflection so that eventually faith and mystery and even divine revelation were pushed aside or subjugated to logic and speculation. That criticism is not entirely fair to all of the scholastics. Some of them sought to use reason to critique itself and show that revelation and faith are necessary in order to understand God, the world and salvation in their depths. Nevertheless, as a generalization it is true that "at the height of scholasticism, virtually everything was deemed accessible to human cognition and classification."[2] All of the great Christian scholastic thinkers agreed that human reason must operate at its best within the realm of faith and upon the foundation of divine revelation through Scripture and the church's tradition. In varying degrees, however, they attempted to build great "cathedrals of ideas"—architectonic edifices of propositions about God, the world and salvation—to stand at the center of the curricula of medieval universities. Theology was to be enthroned as the Queen of the Sciences so that all the disciplines *(scientia)* of the universities would be guided if not ruled by it.

Three common characteristics of medieval scholasticism stand out as important in attempting to understand its nature and contribution to the story of Christian theology. First, as already noted, it passionately embraced human reason as the route to knowledge even within theology. The motto of most scholastics would be "faith seeking understanding" or "I believe in order that I may understand." Augustine had said the same thing, but the medieval scholastics (all of whom highly regarded Augustine) underlined and emphasized the "understand" part and interpreted it as the rational, intellectual activity of the human mind guided by strict rules of logic.

A second common characteristic of medieval scholasticism was its overwhelming concern with discovering the correct relationship between non-Christian philosophies and divine revelation. At the high point of scholasticism in the thirteenth century, the works of the ancient Greek philosopher Aristotle were being rediscovered and translated into Latin. Most of Christian theology had looked to Plato and various forms of Platonism as its main philosophical conversation partner. Scholasticism came to wrestle more with Aristotle, who had been Plato's pupil in ancient Athens and who broke with his mentor over several major philosophical issues. As Aristotle's philosophy was being rediscovered in the Muslim and Christian universities of Europe, scholastic theologians attempted to demonstrate the inner compatibility between the philosopher's main insights and the truths of Christianity.

The third and final common characteristic of medieval scholastic theology was the use of a certain style of teaching and writing that focused on great commentaries on past theologians and philosophers and discussed them by means of dialectic—the method of posing a problem or question and then discussing its various aspects, including objections to standard answers, and then setting forth the solution. The first great scholastic theologian, Anselm of Canterbury, wrote in the form of prayers and dialogues. In both he included many questions—sometimes addressed to God and sometimes addressed to an imaginary conversation partner—and then proceeded through discussion of all the possible answers to discover the true solutions by reducing others to logical absurdity. The greatest scholastic thinker of all, Thomas Aquinas, wrote by setting forth a proposition or question, posing objections and traditional answers from accepted authorities, and then arguing for the one and only possible logical truth.

All of the medieval scholastics valued logic very highly. No illogical assertions or propositions could be considered true. Logic was viewed as a primary tool of theology in arriving at correct answers to all conceivable questions as well as in eliminating false answers. All scholastics assumed that logic was a gift of God to the human mind that connected it to the world and to God himself. All assumed that it would be possible for the human mind to construct a comprehensive and completely coherent system of propositions about all reality—including God—that would be Christian in the sense of being faithful to divine revelation and tradition *and* intellectually superior to all competing and alternative worldviews. Scholasticism, then, aimed at a great synthesis of truth as a foundation for the structure of the unified culture of Catholic Europe. Put another way, "medieval scholasticism intended to demonstrate the complete harmony of Christian theology with the rest of human thought and opinion by a minute re-examination of every aspect of Christian theology in light of philosophy."[3]

One should not assume that scholasticism was a monolithic approach to truth. The scholastic theologians disagreed among themselves about many issues. Some, such as Anselm, wished to use logic alone as the servant and tool of divine revelation in constructing proofs and propositional systems of Christian ideas. Under the influence of Platonic and Augustinian notions of knowledge and reality, Anselm and others like him viewed the physical world as inimical to spiritual reality and to the search for ultimate truth and was suspicious of the five senses because they are unreliable and locked into examining the physical world. Thomas Aquinas, on the other hand, under the influence of the newly discovered philosophy of Aristotle, viewed the five senses operating upon the physical world as the basic "stuff" of philosophy and theology. Logic was useful only in interpreting the data given to the five senses or to the mind through divine revelation. Without data, logic has nothing to work with. For Anselm, on the contrary, without logic the mind is mired hopelessly in the confusion of data.

It is important to realize that both Anselm and Aquinas were concerned largely with what has come to be called natural theology. That is, a dominating feature of their scholastic theologies was investigation of the grounds for Christian belief in a kind of philosophical theology. Both readily accepted that God reveals truths that can be known only through special, supernatural revelation. The doctrine of the Trinity would be one example. Both would agree that the Trinity must be accepted as true by faith and through the authority of Scripture and church tradition. They would also agree that it is not ultimately mysterious and certainly not illogical. But neither is it something the human mind can discover on its own apart from special revelation. When the scholastics disagreed about the roles of logic versus empirical evidence, they were primarily disagreeing about the foundations of theology in prerevelational knowledge. What can the human mind know about God apart from special revelation? What can the human mind know about the human soul and life after death and other universal questions that all philosophies and religions wrestle with? The scholastics agreed that the human mind can know much. They disagreed about *how* it knows it.

Another area of diversity within medieval scholasticism was in the issue of universals. Universals are concepts such as "redness" and "humanness" that transcend individual things. The universal redness is what all red things have in common. The universal humanness is what all humans have in common. The ancient Greek philosopher Plato discussed the nature of universals and developed the theory of forms, which suggests that universals have real existence above and apart from individual things. For Plato redness is a reality in which red things participate. How else do we know that something is more or less red? But Plato was mainly concerned with forms or ideals such as truth, beauty and goodness.

So were the medieval scholastics. One of their main concerns in philosophical theology came to be how to conceive universals in a Christian way. What are truth, beauty and goodness? How should Christians regard such universals? Is beauty really only in the eye of the beholder? Or is beauty a real norm of some kind outside the human mind? Or is it just a name (term) we humans assign to things that we perceive to be pleasing? What about truth? Is there a real norm of truth, or is truth also relative? The same questions can be asked about goodness. All these questions are crucial for philosophy and therefore also for theology, according to the scholastics, who refused to divide and separate the two disciplines. But they could not agree among themselves on the thorny and controversial issue of the nature of universals, and that disagreement eventually contributed to scholasticism's downfall as a dominating method of theological reflection.

Not all Christian thinkers of the medieval period can automatically be labeled scholastics. Some monks and bishops, especially those inclined toward mysticism, harshly criticized the scholastic methods and concerns as overly intellectual, dry and irrelevant to the spiritual life. During the end of the medieval era, as it shaded into the Renaissance of the fifteenth century (just before the Protestant Reformation), many Catholic Christian thinkers called themselves humanists, which often meant "antischolastics." Christian humanists like Erasmus of Rotterdam believed that scholasticism was a sterile and arid approach to Christian truth that focused  too much and too long on speculation about totally impractical issues and questions. Against it he posed his own "philosophy of Christ" that placed ethics and spirituality at the center of theology and philosophy with Christ's teachings as the model for fruitful Christian reflection. Nevertheless, "from the thirteenth century onwards all significant church debates were carried out in university scholastic style. . . . Even those who could afford to ridicule scholasticism had to acknowledge its intellectual presence—and engage with it directly."[4] That is why we place it at the center of this transitional chapter in the story of Christian theology. Even Martin Luther, who loved to refer to medieval scholasticism as "that great whore" that seduces Christian theology into absurd speculation, was influenced by it and had to reckon with it. His and the other Reformers' contributions cannot be understood without some knowledge and understanding of medieval scholastic theology.

# CHAPTER 21

# Anselm & Abelard Speculate About God's Ways

S*ome historians of Christian theology would count Anselm and Abelard as* mere forerunners of true scholasticism. Others consider them to be the first scholastics. All agree that they are two of the earliest great Christian thinkers of the second millennium of the story of Christian theology. Justo González writes, "Anselm was without any doubt the greatest theologian of his time. [He] paved the way for the great scholastics of the thirteenth century. . . . With Anselm a new era began in the history of Christian thought."[1] Anselm's claim to fame in the history of Western philosophy is his formulation of the so-called ontological argument for the existence of God, about which many books have been written. It constitutes a marvelous example of scholastic rationalism as well as of Anselm's genius. To Christian theology he contributed a new model of the atonement (Christ's sacrifice on the cross) and how it reconciles God and humanity. Although this theory finds adumbrations earlier in patristic theology, Anselm's version of it, known as the satisfaction theory of the atonement, represents a quantum leap beyond any doctrine of Christ's reconciling work on behalf of God and humanity before it. Anselm is also known for his staunch opposition to secular or lay control of the church by kings. As archbishop of Canterbury, head of the Catholic church in England under the pope, Anselm suffered exile twice for refusing to grant the Norman king of England authority over church affairs.

**Anselm of Canterbury's Life and Career**

Anselm was born in 1033 in the Alpine town of Aosta in Italy. His early preoccupation with God and religion may have been the result of his godly mother Ermenberga's influence. In childhood and youth he studied with the Benedictine monks and left home for good in 1056 to study at the famous Benedictine monastery at Bec in Normandy (France). He became a monk at age twenty-seven and was named prior of the monastery in 1063 at age thirty. Because of his great reputation as a thinker, writer and administrator, Anselm was forced against his will to become abbot of the monastery at Bec in 1078. While serving in that capacity he began his stellar writing career with his two greatest books of philosophical theology—the *Monologion* (*Monologue* or *Soliloquy*) and the *Proslogion (Discourse)*. These contain versions of his famous ontological proof of God's existence and are still regularly published as well as read and discussed even in secular philosophy courses. He also wrote his *Epistle on the Incarnation of the Word* while abbot of Bec.

In 1093 Anselm was elevated against his will to the high position of archbishop of Canterbury—primate (head clergyman) of all England. At that time, of course, the English church was Roman Catholic. Anselm wanted to refuse the position but was forced to take it under his vow of obedience as a monk. The pope wanted him to serve in that role and he was unable to decline. The reason Anselm did not want to be archbishop of Canterbury was because the kings of England from William the Conqueror on attempted to control the church by appointing bishops themselves. Anselm refused to allow this "lay investiture" and fell into continuous conflict with the secular rulers of the kingdom. Twice English kings forced him into exile, and he retired to the monastery at Bec and to retreats in the Italian Alps of his childhood. During these exiles he wrote several books, including his famous work on the atonement *Cur Deus Homo? (Why God Became Man)*, as well as *On the Virginal Conception and Original Sin* and *On the Procession of the Holy Spirit*. In his final years back in Canterbury, Anselm produced a great scholastic work, *On the Agreement of Foreknowledge, Predestination, and Grace with Free Will*, in which he took a position very much like Augustine's. In fact, Anselm always considered the great North African bishop his theological mentor and hero, and his overall theology was strongly influenced by Augustine's.

Anselm returned to Canterbury from his final exile in 1107. During his last two years Anselm worked to enforce clerical celibacy and debated with the archbishop of York over the primacy of Canterbury. Anselm died in 1109. Anselm's main passion in life was solving intellectual problems. Even though he was a gifted church leader and administrator, those activities were clearly secondary to him.

A modern translator of Anselm's books illustrates this with a story:

> In 1109, when he was told he was dying, Anselm expressed his submission to God's will, but he added that he would welcome the prolongation of his life for a little while, until he could solve the problem of the origin of the soul. It was characteristic of the man that his last thoughts were not about politics nor even about the organization of the Church of England, but about the truths regarding God and His manifestations and His dealings with His creatures.[2]

**Anselm's Ontological Argument for God's Existence**

Anselm is best known in intellectual history generally for his formulations of the proof of God's existence known as the ontological argument. One story about the origin of this argument recounts how Anselm received it in an experience of illumination while chanting the evening service with the other monks at Bec in 1076. He had been asked by someone to provide an explanation and defense of the basic teachings of Christian faith, and he was contemplating God's existence and why the psalmist says in Psalm 14, "Fools say in their hearts, 'There is no God.' " There were no overt atheists in Anselm's day. Blatant denial of God's existence would bring quick and severe punishment down on anyone's neck. The church and state cooperated to enforce blasphemy laws, and atheism was considered blasphemy. Yet Anselm was intrinsically interested in the question of why atheism is so foolish. And he was curious about whether an airtight logical proof of God's reality could be developed that would in no way depend on faith in divine revelation.

The illumination that occurred to him was written down in two books entitled *Monologion* and *Proslogion,* written in 1076 and 1078 respectively. These two books together constitute "the first systematic treatise of 'natural theology' or the philosophical study of God" in the history of Christian theology.[3] Anselm's entire purpose in these books was to provide a wholly rational account and defense of the foundations of Christian belief without any appeal to faith or divine revelation. This was a new project for Christian thought. "What was new and significant in the method of this book *[Monologion]* was the effort to convince readers of the truth of his conclusions about God's essence and attributes *by rational arguments,* and not by adducing the authority of Holy Scripture."[4] If anyone other than the great abbot of Bec had attempted such a rationalistic endeavor, he would have suffered far more criticism. As it was, Anselm reaped a backlash from those who disagreed both with his methodology and with the logic of his argument for God's existence.

Anselm prevented greater criticism by writing his natural theology in the form of prayer. Both *Monologion* and *Proslogion* are addressed to God in the form of questions, reflections on possible answers, and praise to God for his great wisdom and for sharing it with humans through reason. Throughout them Anselm made clear both to God and his readers that he was not beginning with doubt and seeking to understand in order that he might believe in God. Not at all. He wrote in *Proslogion,* "I do not endeavor, O Lord, to penetrate thy sublimity, for in no wise do I compare my understanding with that; but I long to understand in some degree thy truth, which my heart believes and loves. For I do not seek to understand that I may believe, but I believe in order to understand. For this also I believe,—that unless I believed, I should not understand."[5] Anselm's basic theological method, then, was not extreme rationalism, as some have supposed, but an attempt to use logic in the service of divine revelation to strengthen faith.

Of course, Anselm no doubt had a hidden agenda as well. His natural theology aimed at refuting the subtle skepticisms slowly arising in some intellectual circles in Europe as well as the alternative theologies and philosophies of the Jews and Muslims. In Anselm's time Spain contained flourishing Muslim and Jewish communities with their own schools and intellectual communities. Their challenges to Christian beliefs were beginning to be felt in the rest of Europe. Anselm believed that the time had come to provide a comprehensive, systematic explanation and defense of Christian belief that did not rely on Christian sources alone. So in *Monologion* and *Proslogion* he never appealed to Scripture or Christian tradition but only to the light of reason. Later on he followed much the same method in *Cur Deus Homo? (Why God Became Man),* where he attempted to prove the doctrine of the incarnation from the need for salvation and its provision by Jesus Christ. Throughout his great theological works, then, Anselm "endeavors believingly to understand and understandingly to believe."[6]

In *Monologion* and *Proslogion* Anselm offered at least two distinct versions of his argument for the existence of God. The first is in *Monologion* and argues that God's existence is necessary because of degrees of goodness in creation. In very Platonic fashion Anselm attempted to demonstrate that there must be a perfectly good highest being in order for humans to be able to discern and truly believe in degrees of goodness in the world around them. Without a perfectly objective standard of goodness, there would be no way of telling "better" from "worse" in things: "There is, then, some one being which alone exists in the greatest and highest degree of all. But that which is greatest of all, and through which exists whatever is good or great, and, in short, whatever has any existence—that must be supremely good, and supremely great, and the highest of all existing beings."[7]

In other words, Anselm was beginning with the assumption that people *do* distinguish between greater and lesser goods in life: "This is better; that is not as good." Such judgments are universal and in many cases are meant to be propositions of objective fact and not merely expressions of personal taste. According to Anselm, such assertions cannot be objective facts if there is no God. Only a being such as God is believed to be could provide the ultimate standard or norm for measuring individual things as to their degrees of goodness. A thing is good insofar as it reflects God's being and character and fulfills its intended reason for existence from God. A thing is not so good to the extent that it falls short of reflecting God's character and what it was intended to be in God's created order.

Anselm was not entirely satisfied with his first version of the ontological argument for God's existence. So he moved on in *Proslogion* to a second version that has come to be identified with the whole argument itself. When most people mention the ontological argument for the existence of God, they are referring to this version or some later expression of it. It is somewhat subtle and usually takes some time to sink in after a first reading. Anselm began in typical scholastic fashion by stating a proposition: "Truly there is a God, although the fool hath said in his heart, There is no God." In the form of prayer he proceeded to explain why the proposition is true. He praised God for giving understanding to faith and then confessed that "we believe that thou art a being than which nothing greater can be conceived."[8] This confession and the definition of God contained in it is absolutely crucial for Anselm's entire argument. If anyone does not agree that the God Anselm is attempting to prove may be understood to be "a being than which nothing greater can be conceived," then the argument cannot work. But Anselm simply believed that this was a self-evident definition of God. It is not an exhaustive description of God, of course, but at the very least the word *God* must include "being greater than any other conceivable being."

Anselm then proceeded to distinguish between existence in the understanding alone and existence in reality. His point is that to exist in reality outside the understanding (mind, intellect) is greater than merely to exist in the mind as a thought. He illustrated his point with the example of a painter who first imagines a painting and then performs it. His point is that the actual painting is greater than the image of it in the painter's mind. Then Anselm delivered the argument:

> Hence, even the fool [atheist] is convinced that something exists in the understanding, at least, than which nothing greater can be conceived. For, when he hears this, he understands it. And whatever is understood, exists in the understanding. And assuredly that, than which nothing greater can be

> conceived, cannot exist in the understanding alone. For, suppose it exists in the understanding alone: then it can be conceived to exist in reality; which is greater.
>
> Therefore, if that, than which nothing greater can be conceived, exists in the understanding alone, the very being, than which nothing greater can be conceived, is one, than which a greater can be conceived. But obviously this is impossible. Hence, there is no doubt that there exists a being, than which nothing greater can be conceived, and it exists both in the understanding and in reality.[9]

Anselm went on in the next chapter of *Proslogion* to explain the point of the argument: that God—as the being greater than which none can be conceived—cannot be conceived not to exist. Thus anyone who denies God's existence is a fool because such a person is attempting to deny the very being whose existence is contained in its definition. If one can conceive of a being greater than which none can be conceived (and anyone can), then that person must admit that such a being actually exists or else he could conceive of a greater one—one that actually exists.

Many critics have suggested that Anselm was lost in word games. That is simply not true. He was very much concerned to demonstrate that the God who created all reality, including our human minds, has made it impossible to deny his existence and remain in the realm of logic. For Anselm logic is a "signal of transcendence"—a link between our own thoughts and God's. If it were possible logically to deny the existence of God, then, Anselm believed, there would be a flaw in God's good creation. Logic at its best points to God. That is why the Bible declares that only a fool can deny God's existence. A fool is one who is irrational. Denying God's existence is irrational.

During Anselm's own lifetime, some critics attempted to undermine his argument. A monk named Gaunilo, or Gaunilon, wrote a treatise against Anselm's argument entitled *On Behalf of the Fool.* However, Anselm responded by showing the flaws in Gaunilo's objections, and most logicians agree with Anselm over against the critic, even if they do not accept the absolute validity of his ontological argument. Later theologians and philosophers have wrestled with the ontological argument for God's existence with no clear consensus emerging about its logical force. In any case, Anselm was apparently the first Christian theologian who attempted to develop an account of basic Christian beliefs entirely on the foundation of logic with no appeal to divine revelation or faith. That is one of his main contributions to the story of Christian theology.

### God's Nature According to Anselm

After providing his logical proof of God's existence, Anselm went on to explain who this God is whose existence is necessary. Without appealing to Scripture or any other special revelation, he attempted to show the attributes such a being must have. Such a being must be "the Supreme Good," he argued, and the Supreme Good must be both compassionate and passionless (impassible). If God were not compassionate, he would not be supremely good, but if he has passions (emotions), then he would be affected by creatures and therefore dependent on them, which is improper to the being greater than which none can be conceived. Thus in a famous passage on God's nature and character Anselm offered his solution:

> But how art thou compassionate, and, at the same time, passionless? For, if thou art passionless, thou doest not feel sympathy; and if thou dost not feel sympathy, thy heart is not wretched from sympathy for the wretched; but this it is to be compassionate. But if thou art not compassionate, whence cometh so great consolation to the wretched? How, then, art thou compassionate and not compassionate, O Lord, unless because thou art compassionate in terms of our experience, and not compassionate in terms of thy being.
>
> Truly, thou art so in terms of our experience, but thou art not so in terms of thine own. For, when thou beholdest us in our wretchedness, we experience the effect of compassion, but thou dost not experience the feeling. Therefore, thou art both compassionate, because thou dost save the wretched, and spare those who sin against thee; and not compassionate, because thou art affected by no sympathy for wretchedness.[10]

According to Anselm, God does not feel any emotions. Neither does God have discursive thoughts—ideas that "occur" to him by a process of deduction or are received through a process of investigation or information. All of that would imply that God is finite and dependent. For Anselm and most other scholastics God was a simple, timeless, unchanging and unfeeling essence or substance without limits, body, parts or passions. God acts, but is never acted upon.

### Anselm's Satisfaction Theory of the Atonement

Anselm's second great contribution to the story of Christian theology lies in his new model of the atonement. *Atonement* simply means "reconciliation," and in theology it usually refers to the act of God in Jesus Christ or the act of Jesus Christ as a human being on the cross by which humans are reconciled to God and vice versa. In Anselm's age most Christians in the West thought of Christ's great sacrifice on the cross along the lines of what is known as the ransom theory. It was laid out in its clearest form by Pope Gregory the Great around 600, although many before him and after him put their own individual touches on it. Gregory used many images to explain the effect of Christ's death on the cross upon humanity, but his favorite one was the cross as the "fishhook" upon which God placed the "bait" of Jesus Christ in order to snare the devil and free humanity held captive by him. According to Gregory,

> matching deceit with deceit, Christ frees man by tricking the devil into overstepping his authority. Christ becomes a "fishhook": his humanity is the bait, his divinity the hook, and Leviathan [Satan] is snared. Because the devil is proud, he cannot understand Christ's humility and so believes he tempts and kills a mere man. But in inflicting a sinless man with death, the devil loses his rights over man from his "excess of presumption," Christ conquers the devil's kingdom of sin, liberating captives from the devil's tyranny. Order is reinstated when man returns to serve God, his true master.[11]

Anselm considered this theory of the atonement—which had become almost universal in the preaching of the Roman Catholic Church throughout the so-called Dark Ages—an insult to God. As the being greater than which none can be conceived, God does not have to trick the devil, because he is in no way beholden to him. If the only problem is that humanity has become captive to Satan and his kingdom, God could simply invade and conquer them and release humanity from captivity. He would not have to bargain with or trick Satan. Another version of the ransom theory of the atonement said that God offered Christ to Satan as a ransom for humanity but that Satan did not know that he could not keep Christ in hell. In whatever version it appeared, Anselm rejected the ransom theory as improper to God's great deity. It tended to place God and Satan too much on the same plane.

Anselm sought an explanation of the atonement that would explain why Jesus Christ had to be both truly human and truly divine and that would be both rational and fully consistent with Scripture and the church's tradition. An exile from Canterbury in 1098 afforded Anselm the leisure time and opportunity to write *Cur Deus Homo?* or *Why God Became Man*. The book is written in the form of a dialogue between Anselm and a friend named Dom Boso. The key question they are discussing in the book is "Why, and with what necessity, did God become man, and redeem human beings by his death, although he could have accomplished this by other means?"[12] In typical scholastic fashion the answer unfolds almost painfully gradually with many tangents and possible objections discussed along the way.

Anselm's alternative to the ransom theory has come to be called the satisfaction theory of the atonement because it centers upon the medieval concept of a vassal paying "satisfaction" to a lord when he has broken the feudal contract. Anselm found in this custom the perfect analogy for explaining why God sent his Son in the form of a human being to die a sinner's death when he was not at all a sinner. In essence, the theory says that Christ paid a debt that all humanity owes to God because of disobedience. God's justice demands payment of a satisfaction or else the order of the universe would be disrupted. The needed satisfaction is like a debt to God's honor that humanity must repay, but humanity is incapable of repaying it without suffering complete loss in hell. God in his mercy provides a perfect substitutionary sacrifice that satisfies his own honor and preserves the moral order of the universe.

Toward the end of *Cur Deus Homo?* Anselm placed in Boso's mouth a summary of the satisfaction theory of the atonement:

> The nub of the question was why God became man, to save man by His death, when it would seem He could do this in some other way. In answering this question, you showed, by many conclusive arguments, that the restoration of human nature ought not to be neglected, and that it could not be accomplished unless man paid to God what he owed for sin. But this debt was so great that, although man alone owed the debt, still God alone was able to pay it, so that the same person would have to be both man and God. Hence it was necessary that God assume human nature into the unity of His person, so that the one who in his nature owed the debt and could not pay it, should be, in His Person, able to pay it. Then you showed that that man who was God had to be taken from a virgin, and by the person of the Son of God, and you showed how He could be taken from the sinful mass without sin. Besides, you very clearly established that the life of this man was so sublime, so precious, that it can suffice to pay what is owed for the sins of the whole world, and infinitely more.[13]

Anselm's model of the atonement pictures Christ's death on the cross as an objective transaction between God the Father and the Son of God, Jesus Christ, in his humanity. The voluntary death of a sinless human being who is at the same time the very God of the universe reconciles God's love and his wrath because justice is fulfilled mercifully. Sinful disobedience is not swept under the rug, so to speak, but neither do all sinners have to die eternal deaths to pay for it. God's honor is fully satisfied, cosmic justice is restored, and humans who embrace Christ's sacrifice through repentance, faith and the sacraments reap its full benefits and are forgiven by God.

Justo González notes that "this treatise by Anselm was epoch-making. Although they did not follow it at every turn, most later medieval theologians interpreted the work of Christ in the light of this treatise."[14] The satisfaction theory virtually replaced the ransom theory in Roman Catholic theology because of Anselm. Furthermore, during the Protestant Reformation in the sixteenth century, John Calvin presented a completely biblical version of Anselm's model that has come to be called the penal substitution theory of the atonement. In many ways it is simply an updated version of Anselm's theory stripped of feudal imagery.

Many critics have dissented from Anselm's and Calvin's thinking about the atoning death of Christ. To some it seems too objective to include any human activity in the process so that humans appear to be pawns in a great cosmic transaction between God the Father and Jesus Christ. Others find it too judicial or legalistic to bring out the love of God. For them it focuses too much on God's honor—portraying God the Father as a feudal king and Jesus Christ as our compassionate friend who pays the debt for the rest of us humans. In that way it would also seem to the same critics to divide the Trinity between Father and Son and leave the Spirit totally out of the equation. Anselm's satisfaction theory of the atonement has been much debated, but its overall impact on theology in the West (Catholic and Protestant) has been profound because it seems both biblical and rational in spite of its flaws.

**Peter Abelard's Life and Misfortunes**

One dissenter near to Anselm's own time in the story of theology was the great medieval scholastic genius Peter Abelard. We probably know more about Abelard's personal life than about any other ancient or medieval Christian thinker's except Augustine's. That is because Abelard wrote an autobiography—a rare event before modern times—that is still published under the title *The Story of My Misfortunes*. Abelard's tormented and tortured life was even made into a Hollywood feature movie, which unfortunately tended to focus all too much on the lurid aspects of his love affair with the lovely Héloïse. By all accounts Abelard was one of the great geniuses of Christian theology and a prominent philosopher as well. Apparently he was also a man of great personal charm and attraction—what would today be called a charismatic personality. Such traits often combine to create a life of tragedy, and such was the case for Abelard. People either loved him passionately and devoted intense loyalty to him and his teachings or else hated him and sought to destroy him. Few who knew him were indifferent.

Peter Abelard was born in 1079 in Brittany (France) and died in 1142 at the famous Cluny monastery in France while on his way to Rome to defend himself against charges of heresy. His lifetime coincided with the era of great Gothic cathedral building throughout Europe. It was also the beginning of the flowering of scholastic philosophy and theology. After studying philosophy and theology under some of the most reputable teachers in France, Abelard established his own teaching practice in Paris. To some extent, at least, his fame as a teacher and great reputation as a scholar helped establish the University of Paris as students arrived from all over Europe to study with him and other independent scholars there. In Paris, Abelard was regarded as a young Turk among the schoolmen of the monastic orders, whose theological lectures were considered dusty and boring as they commented endlessly on the traditions of the church fathers and earlier medieval thinkers. Abelard's lectures challenged revered traditions, and his students were often quite rowdy and disrespectful to the accepted traditions of the church.

In order to support himself Abelard tutored the teenaged daughter of a leading citizen of Paris. Abelard and Héloïse fell in love and began a passionate love affair that resulted in the birth of a son. Even though they married secretly so that the boy would be legitimate, the scandal broke out and Héloïse's uncle and guardian, Fulbert, hired thugs to break into Abelard's quarters and castrate him. Soon everyone in Paris knew all about it and, according to Abelard, crowds began gathering in the street outside his apartment loudly expressing sympathy and calling for revenge against Fulbert. Abelard eventually left Paris in humiliation and became a monk and then abbot of a monastery in Brittany, where he was born. He moved back and forth between Paris and various monasteries and retreats throughout his lifetime and carried on a correspondence with Héloïse, who had taken vows as a nun and joined a convent. Her letters to him are still published and considered classics of medieval love poetry.

### Abelard's Philosophical Style

Needless to say, Abelard was controversial during his lifetime. But surprisingly to many today, that was not so much because of his love affair and punishment by the girl's uncle, but because of his style of teaching and writing and his great popularity among the students who were restless and tired of the traditional ways of thinking. Abelard did not hesitate to challenge what he considered to be illogical or unbiblical beliefs no matter how traditional they might be. His writings included the highly controversial *Sic et Non (Yes and No)* wherein he set forth contrary propositions contained in accepted authoritative writings of Christian theology and philosophy in order to show that there were still many unresolved problems for him and other Christian thinkers to work on. He opposed the mentality that the only tasks of theology and philosophy were to repeat and interpret accepted authoritative writings of the past. Of course, opponents like the great abbot and mystic Bernard of Clairvaux (1090-1153) used this against him and accused Abelard of subtly attempting to undermine authoritative Christian tradition.

Abelard also wrote a volume entitled *Christian Theology* immediately after *Sic et Non* (1123-1124) in which he attempted to solve some of the unresolved problems of tradition. Abelard's project was to demonstrate the consistency between Christian truth and the truth of philosophy. He believed that even though reason may not be able to solve every possible theological problem and certainly could not even hope to do so without faith, the basic truths of Christianity are implicit in the human mind and can be reached and understood with the help of rational thought. Ultimately, for Abelard there could be no conflict between philosophical truth and theological truth, even though reaching their perfect reconciliation may never be achieved within history. For example in *Christian Theology* Abelard argued that although the Trinity cannot be discovered or understood completely by human reason alone, nothing about it conflicts with reason. In fact, he argued that the basic contours of trinitarian belief can be found implicit in the Jewish prophets and Greek philosophers before Christ.

Throughout Abelard's teaching and writing one finds a new way of thinking about universals that breaks radically with the realism of Anselm and Augustine and foreshadows the rise of what came to be known as nominalism later in medieval theology and philosophy. As already seen, Anselm treated universals as having ontological reality apart from the human mind. He certainly regarded them as more than names or terms or even mental concepts. That is the idea of universals in realism. Abelard was trained in this kind of philosophy and broke decisively with it. He came to regard universals as concepts with real being that exist neither above nor apart from individual things nor merely in the mind as conventional terms. If Plato's philosophy of forms stands behind realism, Aristotle's philosophy of form and matter stands behind Abelard's conceptualism, which is often regarded as a step toward later medieval nominalism which treated universals as mere names or terms. According to Abelard,

> the solution [to the problem of universals] is to be found by realizing that universals are not "things"—that is, they cannot subsist in themselves except by an abstraction. They are real in a manner similar to that in which form exists in matter—one can abstract form from matter, but form is never actually given without matter. Similarly, universals can be abstracted from individuals—and one must do so in order to think—but they are never given apart from concrete particular things.[15]

Abelard's theory of universals, then, may be considered a medium between extreme realism and the extreme nominalism that would appear later in medieval thought. But overall his view was perceived as closer to nominalism, which was another cause for criticism during his lifetime. Many theologians and church leaders considered realism essential to catholic and orthodox theology.

**Abelard's Moral Influence Theory of the Atonement**

Abelard's most striking innovation in theology was his doctrine of the atonement. In *Christian Theology,* and even more so in a book entitled *Exposition of the Epistle to the Romans,* he openly disagreed with the traditional ransom theory as well as the newer satisfaction theory of Anselm and developed his own view, which has been called the moral influence or moral example theory of how Christ's death on the cross reconciles humanity with God. For many of his critics this was the straw that broke the proverbial camel's back. Bernard of Clairvaux—without doubt the most influential church leader of the day—preached against Abelard in Paris and called for his condemnation by the pope. A synod of bishops in Paris condemned many of Abelard's views, and Pope Innocent III issued an edict that agreed with the synod. Abelard hoped to get the condemnation lifted by appearing directly before the pope to personally plead his cause, but he fell ill and died while en route to Rome. In a letter to Héloïse shortly before his death Abelard wrote, "I do not wish to be a philosopher by dissociating myself from Paul; I do not wish to be an Aristotle by separating myself from Christ, since there is no other name under heaven by which I can be saved."[16] Just before death overtook him, Abelard officially submitted himself to the pope and reconciled with Bernard of Clairvaux by letter. He died at peace with the church that condemned and persecuted him. Abbot Peter the Venerable of Cluny observed Abelard's last days and wrote an account of them in which he praised Abelard's humility and called him "the Socrates of the Gauls, the great Plato of the West, *our* Aristotle."[17]

Abelard's model of the atonement emphasized God's love rather than God's honor or wrath. According to Abelard, what humanity needs is a new motive for action, not a compensation paid to God on its behalf. He considered that the satisfaction theory as well as the ransom theory left humanity out of the process of reconciliation altogether and portrayed the God of the cross as concerned only with his own honor and cosmic justice. Abelard's mind was captivated by Jesus' parable of the prodigal son whose father was always waiting for him to return. Thus for the maverick theologian the cross is God's demonstration to sinful humans of his loving heart *and* it is the Son of God's communication to them of his own merits won before God by this radical obedience. The effect of the cross is toward humanity, not toward God. God, according to Abelard, does not need to be reconciled to humanity. God already loves us. Our problem is that we do not realize this and because of our sin and ignorance live in alienating fear of God. The cross of Jesus is an act of God's love that inspires new motives into our actions so that we see how much God loves us and we begin to love in return:

> It seems to us that we are justified in the blood of Christ and reconciled to God in this, that through the singular grace manifested to us in that his Son took our nature and that teaching us by both word and example he persevered even unto death, Jesus bound us closer to himself by love, so that, fired by so great a benefit of divine grace, true charity would no longer be afraid to endure anything for his sake.
>
> Every man is made more just, that is more loving towards God, after the Passion of Christ than he had been before, because men are incited to love by a benefit actually received more than by one hoped for. And so our redemption is that great love for us shewn in the Passion of Christ which not only frees us from the bondage of sin, but acquires for us the true liberty of the sons of God, so that we should fulfil all things not so much through fear as through our love for him who shewed towards us a favour than which, as he himself says, none greater can be found: "Greater love hath no man than this, that a man lay down his life for his friends."[18]

Notice that Abelard's account of the atonement strips it of all connotations of legal transaction. That is why some critics have dubbed it the "subjective theory." According to them, in Abelard's theory no objective change occurred in the alienation situation between God and humanity because of sin and guilt when Christ died on the cross. The only real change occurs when and if sinful humans happen to be impacted by the example of God's love in the death of Christ. And exactly how people "dead in trespasses and sins" are turned around by a mere moral example is lost on many critics of Abelard's theory. To them it seems that Abelard's view necessarily also implies a Pelagian denial of original sin and encourages the idea that all humans really need to do is turn over a new leaf of life by seeing how much God loves them so they will begin to love as well.

There is some truth to this criticism. On the other hand, Abelard did affirm original sin and included in his overall view of the atonement that Christ's death gained merit before God because of his obedience as a man and that his merit can be communicated to all sinners who come to him by repentance and faith and through sacraments.[19] That brings something of an objective view of the cross back into Abelard's picture of the atonement. Nevertheless, Abelard's main line of thinking was that the cross was the event by which God demonstrated his great love to humanity and thereby transformed our hearts so that we act out of love rather than fear. In that case, then, the real atonement takes place within us, not on the cross.

It takes place when sinful humans repent and begin to act out of love rather than when Christ died. That is because God, according to Abelard, never did need reconciling to us by a bloody sacrifice. It is rather we who need reconciling to God, and that happens when we are affected by the cross through a moral change within ourselves. A modern commentator on Abelard sums up his view succinctly: "The purpose of the Crucifixion, then, was to pour charity [love] into our hearts, and charity is given us by Christ, who makes us thereby sons of God, not his slaves in fear. In this manner a new motive is infused into our actions, which accordingly becomes meritorious."[20]

Anselm's satisfaction theory of the atonement has remained a standard for much conservative Christian theology in the West. Some conservative Catholic and Protestant thinkers consider it the biblical and orthodox view of the atonement. Abelard's theory was rejected in his own lifetime but has been rediscovered and hailed as the "enlightened" Christian view of the cross by many liberal Protestant thinkers of the nineteenth and twentieth centuries. Some mediating theologians believe that no single theory of the atonement can capture all the truth, that both Anselm and Abelard were correct and that, in fact, their two models complement one another. Abelard's subjective approach emphasizes the moral effect of Christ's cross within history and in each person who repents and begins to live in love. Anselm's objective approach emphasizes the legal effect of Christ's cross within the cosmos and upon God himself, who can only truly forgive sinners because a great debt has been paid. Taken alone it is difficult to see how Abelard's theory can do justice to human responsibility for sin or to God's holiness. Taken alone it is difficult to see how Anselm's theory can do justice to human involvement in the reconciliation process or explain how the cross affects human lives. It is unfortunate that the two theories were ever seen as necessarily incompatible or in competition with one another. It would seem rather that they are complementary accounts of the cross.

Anselm and Abelard represent the earliest stage of scholastic theology in medieval Western Christianity. Most of scholasticism's concerns and methods are at least foreshadowed in them. The great realist-nominalist controversy that would help bring down scholasticism as a method in the late Middle Ages began to appear already with them. Their focus on the rationality of Christian belief and desire to demonstrate its compatibility with the best of philosophy illustrates their scholastic mindsets. But the greatest scholastic theologian and philosopher was yet to come. The crown jewel of scholasticism and the greatest thinker of medieval theology appeared in Paris in the thirteenth century. The Angelic Doctor of Catholic thought started out as the "dumb ox" of the University of Paris and became the standard and norm of Roman Catholic thought for centuries to come.

# CHAPTER 22

# Thomas Aquinas Summarizes Christian Truth

O*ne name stands out above all others as the scholastic thinker par excellence:* Thomas Aquinas. It is impossible to overestimate his importance for the story of Christian theology and especially for the story of Roman Catholic theology. There he remains the standard, the norm, well into the twentieth century. That is not to say, of course, that every Catholic theologian agrees wholeheartedly with every single proposition or viewpoint found in Aquinas's massive corpus of writings. Rather, his basic approach to theology and its foundational ideas and methods remain those with which every Catholic theologian is expected to know and interact with. To disagree openly with them may result in some measure of censure from the Vatican's theological watchdogs. In 1879 Pope Leo XIII made Aquinas's theology the norm for Catholic theology in his encyclical letter *Aeterni Patris.* But that act only made official what had been unofficially the general view of Catholic leaders for centuries. He had already been canonized to sainthood in 1323 and given the title Angelic Doctor by the Roman Catholic hierarchy. Pope Pius V gave Thomas Aquinas the title Universal Doctor of the Church in 1567 during the Council of Trent. With all these official accolades and affirmations, Thomas Aquinas cannot be considered anything other than the single greatest theologian of the Western Catholic tradition between Augustine in the fifth century and Karl Rahner of Austria in the late twentieth century.

## The Theological Context of Aquinas's Work

Before delving into Aquinas's life story and his particular theological contribution it will be helpful to reflect a bit further on the theological milieu in which he worked. Aquinas was a scholastic theologian, and that meant that he was a philosopher as well. Especially for the scholastic theologians of the thirteenth and fourteenth centuries at universities such as Oxford and Paris, theology and philosophy were inseparable. Their aim was to synthesize the two disciplines without losing theology in philosophy. Theology was to become the "Queen of the Sciences" and philosophy was to be her necessary servant, or handmaid. Understanding the scholastics' view of the relationship between theology and philosophy is absolutely crucial to grasping what they were all about and aiming at:

> The scholastics of the thirteenth and fourteenth centuries were theologians essentially, philosophers only incidentally. Their reasoning was a concentrated effort to penetrate the mysteries of the Christian faith; their philosophy was the handmaid of theology. None the less, it is a striking historical fact that these great theologians were equally great as philosophers. Being theologians, they did not care to start by developing a complete philosophy. Rather they developed their theology and philosophy in organic integration, so that theology was constantly fertilised by philosophic speculation and philosophy remained under the guidance of Christian dogma.[1]

This description of scholastic method certainly applies to Thomas Aquinas's approach. At first glance his theology may seem very speculative and philosophical and one may wonder where the theological reflection on divine revelation comes into play. Deeper and further into study of his writings, however, what becomes clear is his overriding concern with salvation as the very heart of his entire project. The great theological-philosophical synthesis he attempted to construct like a massive medieval cathedral of ideas had at its very heart the altar of Christ's broken body and the grace of redemption found upon it. Getting to that altar past the flying buttresses and elaborate vestibules of natural theology is a task, and many never make it there. But for those who persevere, there can be no doubt that Aquinas—if not all scholastics—cared deeply about the mysteries of salvation and that it was for their sake that he taught and wrote.

## Aquinas's Life and Career

Thomas Aquinas was born in either 1224 or 1225 in his family's castle near Roccasecca, Italy. His father, Landulf de Aquino, was a wealthy member of the landed gentry and expected his sons to follow in his prosperous and influential footsteps. Thomas received his primary education at the mother house of the entire Benedictine movement—the monastery at Monte Cassino founded by Benedict of Nursia himself. As a youth he matriculated at the relatively new University of Naples, where he came into contact with two forces that changed his life. The newly discovered philosophy of Aristotle was creating controversy there, and Aquinas quickly latched onto it and spent the rest of his life attempting to reconcile it with divine revelation because "Aristotle became for him a paradigm of sound reasoning."[2] That means he did not consider Plato and Platonism the paradigm of sound reasoning even though they had been so judged by most Catholic thinkers for centuries. Even the great Anselm had been Platonist in his basic philosophical orientation.

The second force that changed Aquinas's life at Naples was the relatively new order of friars known as the Dominicans. These followers of the mendicant preacher Dominic (1170-1221) were quickly becoming a proud and popular religious renewal movement with strong appeal among young intellectuals. They were considered fanatics by many of the wealthy and powerful elite of society, however, and Aquinas's father was appalled at his association with them. In 1242 the young university student joined the Dominican order as a novice friar and moved into their house. His father sent his brothers to kidnap him and carry out what modern people would call a deprogramming so that he would return to his senses and play his assigned role in the family and society. The Aquinas family held Thomas in confinement in their castle for two years without persuading him to give up his dream of becoming an Aristotelian scholar among the Dominican friars. They finally let him go and he immediately rejoined the order.

Aquinas left Italy as soon as possible—to avoid being recaptured by his family—and settled into student life at the University of Cologne in central Europe, where he studied under the great scholastic master of theology Albert Magnus (Albert the Great, 1193-1280), who is supposed to have declared about Aquinas in front of all the students, "We call this lad a dumb ox, but I tell you that the whole world is going to hear his bellowing."[3] Legend has it that Aquinas was very portly and shy and that is why his fellow students dubbed him "the dumb ox." Albert, however, recognized his potential, and Aquinas went on to supersede the master himself.

After Cologne, Aquinas studied theology and philosophy at the University of Paris, which had become a hotbed of the controversy over Aristotle's philosophy. The Franciscan friars, who had a large house in Paris and many of whom taught at the University's School of Theology, opposed Aristotle and condemned Christian use of his thought. They tended to view Platonism as the "mind's road to God." The Dominicans were more favorable toward Aristotle and some went so far as to talk about "two truths"—one of divine revelation in Scripture and tradition and one of Aristotle's philosophy. The Catholic church condemned the two-truths theory, and Aquinas's entire life project as a scholar was to overcome it by showing that Aristotle's basic philosophical insights were not in conflict with basic Christian truth.

In 1256 Aquinas began his teaching career as a master of theology at Paris. He produced many works of theology, but the two most notable are the multivolume sets known as *Summa contra Gentiles* and *Summa Theologica* (or *Summa Theologiae*). A "summa" is a system of propositions that is supposed to sum up the truth about a particular discipline. *Summa contra Gentiles* was Aquinas's apologetic defense of Christian truth against the criticisms of Muslim scholars in Spain and North Africa. *Summa Theologica* was his systematic theology. While teaching at Paris, Aquinas became famous and highly regarded by leaders of both church and nation. He was, however, something of an eccentric—the epitome of the absent-minded scholarly professor continually lost in thought:

> One of the most famous [stories] concerns an occasion in 1269 when he was dining with King Louis IX of France. According to his biographer Bernard Gui, Aquinas, who seemed often to be "rapt out of himself" when thinking, spent most of the meal pondering on the Manichees (a religious sect dating from the third century AD). Suddenly he struck the table and exclaimed, "That settles the Manichees!", whereupon he called for his secretary to come and take dictation. He explained to the alarmed dinner guests, "I thought I was at my desk."[4]

Another often-repeated story about Aquinas has to do with his dying days. He died on March 7, 1274, in Paris, but less than a year before that date he suddenly stopped writing altogether for no apparent reason. His colleagues and aides urged him to return to his work, and Aquinas is supposed to have replied, "I cannot, because all that I have written seems like straw to me." Some versions of the story include an ending to the reply: "compared to the things being revealed to me." The implication is that he was having mystical experiences that were foretastes of the great "beatific vision" that he had written so much about as the goal of human redemption—to see God face-to-face.

Like Augustine, Aquinas wrote on almost every conceivable topic related to the university curriculum. He was a true encyclopedist and therefore it is difficult, if not impossible, to touch on even many of his ideas and contributions. Here our task will be only to describe his major distinctive theological methods and concepts, especially those that have come to have great influence in Roman Catholic theology generally and that are somehow different from the ideas and methods of Augustine and Anselm—the two earlier major Western Christian thinkers. Our description of Aquinas's theological contribution will focus on his thoughts about theological method and especially natural theology, his ideas about nature and grace including the relationship between reason and revelation, his concept of God's nature and attributes, his view of language about God as analogical speech, and his doctrine of divine providence, including predestination. In each area—as in many others—Aquinas paved the road ahead for Catholic theology and set the stage for Protestant reaction during the Reformation of the sixteenth century. While most of the Reformers respected Aquinas as a great genius, they regarded his theology as a serious diversion away from the biblical faith into philosophical speculation under the spell of Aristotelian philosophy.

### Aquinas's Theological Method

Aquinas's style of writing in both *Summas* is typically scholastic. He begins with a disputed or debatable question such as "Whether, Besides the Philosophical Sciences, Any Further Doctrine is Required" and then proceeds to discuss objections such as "Objection 1: It seems that, besides the philosophical sciences, we have no need of any further knowledge."[5] After stating all the important negative answers to the question, he sets forth his own view, which usually begins with phrases such as "On the contrary" or "I answer that" or "Reply to objection 1." Often, as part of his own view, Aquinas cites traditional authorities such as scriptural passages, statements by church fathers and quotations from councils and creeds. Interestingly he often simply quotes Augustine as the authority in place of citing any scriptural passages. He also sometimes quotes or refers to "the Philosopher," by which he always means Aristotle.

One does not read very far into Aquinas's *Summas* without realizing that he regarded Aristotle both as authority and as problem. For him Aristotle's basic logic and metaphysic were correct and were helpful guides to Christian natural theology. At the same time, however, Aristotle held views that clearly conflict with Christian doctrines. One notable example with which Aquinas wrestled valiantly is the origin of the universe. Aristotle believed that the universe is both eternal and caused by an Uncaused Cause at the same time. In other words, he believed that a metaphysically all-powerful and eternal Uncaused Cause and Unmoved Mover has eternally brought about the existence of the universe. Aristotle had no place in this thought for any notion of *creatio ex nihilo* or even a creation in time. Some philosophers of the medieval universities were suggesting that a Christian philosopher had to agree with both the church fathers and Aristotle, and that was one example of the two-truths theory against which the church fought and Aquinas argued. On that score he simply had to disagree with Aristotle. On others, though, he found Aristotle a great ally of Christian theology, much as many of the early church fathers looked to Plato and the Platonists in their apologetic writings.

Aquinas's theological method begins with the relationship between natural knowledge (philosophy and the other nontheological sciences) and divine revelation in discovering knowledge of God. Like earlier scholastics, such as Anselm and Abelard, Aquinas refused to set them over against one another in any essential conflict. However, unlike Anselm at least, Aquinas did not make faith essential to understanding, at least not in the sphere of knowing that God exists and knowing some of God's nature and attributes. Anselm's motto was "faith seeking understanding" or "I believe in order that I may understand." Aquinas would not necessarily reject that attitude, but he was seeking to discover and firmly establish a realm of natural knowledge of God that in no way presupposes Christian faith. Of course, Anselm also believed that pure reason apart from revelation or faith can prove God's existence and essence. But Anselm considered logic itself a kind of revelation or at least a gift of God. He did not really acknowledge a natural realm devoid of grace. No clear distinction between "natural" and "supernatural" appears in Anselm's or Abelard's Christian philosophical theologies such as Aquinas introduced and insisted upon.

### Aquinas's View of Faith and Reason and Natural Theology

One of Aquinas's most controversial contributions to Christian theology was his claim of a natural realm of knowledge about God and the human soul that is distinct from any realm of special gracious, supernatural activity of God. Every Christian thinker before him, including Anselm and Abelard, had thought of natural theology as an elevation of the human mind by grace. Even Anselm's ontological argument for the existence of God was supposed by Anselm to be a work of God through logic and the intellect. There was no recognizable line between special divine revelatory activity and reason generally. Reason was one of the mind's roads to God, but the road itself was paved by grace. Aquinas wanted to show that there is a natural world and a natural knowledge that is not wholly dependent on grace so that even a non-Christian entirely devoid of faith—such as Aristotle—could follow a purely natural path to knowledge of God. Of course, for him this operation of reason, natural as it is, is the image of God in humans: "Now the intellect or mind is that whereby the rational creature excels other creatures. Hence, this image of God is not found even in the rational creature except in the mind."[6] Thus it is not entirely independent of God—nothing could possibly be that if God is the creator of all. However, reason has its own sphere of activity and competency apart from supernatural gracious activity of God. This was new and controversial in the story of Christian theology.

One way to picture Aquinas's scheme lying at the very foundation of his entire theology is like this:

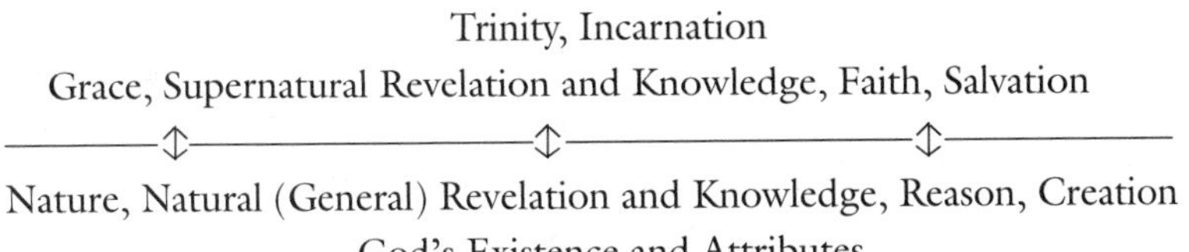


For Aquinas, the lower realm is basically Aristotle's philosophy, and the upper realm is supernatural, divine revelation. One cannot be saved and achieve the "beatific vision of God" in heaven (similar to divinization) without arising to the second story, but one can know and understand God truly as to his existence and attributes on the basis of reason examining the natural order of creation. Through reason alone one can never know that God is triune, but belief in the Trinity is not irrational. It simply transcends what reason alone can know and is revealed by God's grace through Scripture and church tradition. Both Anselm and Abelard had believed and argued that God's triunity—like every other important Christian belief—is both revealed and rationally discoverable. The only reason people do not discover it rationally, they would say, is due to the effect of sin on the human mind. Aquinas was saying something different. For him, reason has a sphere distinct from grace and revelation—nature. Likewise, faith has a sphere distinct from and above nature—supernature. The arrows also represent an important part of Aquinas's scheme. Nature points upward toward grace; reason is fulfilled in revelation. Grace and the supernatural activity of God for salvation elevate nature; revelation fulfills and completes reason. The two spheres do not contradict one another. They are separate but complementary.

God's existence is not the only theological and spiritual truth that reason alone, unaided by grace, can discover. According to Aquinas, reason operating completely in the natural sphere can also discover the immortality of the soul and basic ethical and moral laws. These truths he found well developed in Aristotle, even if the philosopher did not know all that can be known about them with the help of supernatural revelation and faith. An excellent example of Aquinas's Aristotelian natural theology is the natural knowledge of God. He believed and argued that while God's existence is not self-evident, as Anselm had said, it can be demonstrated by natural reason.[7] Aquinas rejected Anselm's ontological argument because it does not begin with the senses and, basing his argument on Aristotle's disagreement with his mentor Plato, Aquinas averred that all natural knowledge begins with sensory experience.

Aquinas presented five ways of rationally demonstrating the existence of God, and all five of them may be found in some form in Aristotle's philosophy. All five ways appeal to experiences human minds have in relation to the natural world and state that if God did not exist, these experiences would be meaningless or impossible. In fact, what is being experienced would not exist. Because they do, God also must exist. Stated another way, God is known naturally through his natural effects as their necessary cause: "From effects not proportioned to the cause no perfect knowledge of that cause can be obtained. Yet, from every effect the existence of the cause can be clearly demonstrated, and so we can demonstrate the existence of God from His effects; though from them we cannot know God perfectly as He is in His essence."[8]

The first way Aquinas attempted to demonstrate God's existence was from the phenomenon of natural motion. Everything moved must have a mover, and there cannot be an infinite chain of regress in motion. "Therefore it is necessary to arrive at a first mover, moved by no other; and this everyone understands to be God."[9] Within this argument, or "proof," Aquinas introduced a very important Aristotelian distinction between two modes of being: actuality and potentiality. In every movement something potential is becoming actual. But actuality can never arrive out of potentiality without a cause, and such a cause has to be already fully actual itself. Thus, the ultimate first mover of everything in the natural world must be pure actuality—*actus purus.* This, though, becomes clear later in Aquinas's discussion of God's nature and attributes. In the first way he was simply interested in noting that the first mover of all must be "moved by no other." He is Aristotle's Unmoved Mover.

The second way Aquinas attempted to prove God's existence was by appealing to causation. In a manner very similar to the first way, he argued that everything in the universe is caused and therefore there must be a "first efficient cause, which everyone gives the name God."[10]

The third way is generally considered to be the most forceful of Aquinas's five ways of demonstrating God's existence, so we will save it for last consideration.

The fourth way focuses on gradations found in things and concludes that "there must . . . be something which is to all beings the cause of their being, goodness, and every other perfection; and this we call God."[11] This is very similar to Anselm's first argument for God's existence in *Monologion.*

Aquinas's fifth and final way is by appeal to purposes in things within the natural order: "Some intelligent being exists by whom all natural things are directed to their end; and this being we call God."[12] This is a version of what some call the argument from design and has been known in philosophical theology as the teleological argument. It is not well developed in Aquinas's thinking.

Aquinas's third way is generally considered the heart of his natural theology. Since it is a clear example both of scholastic thinking and Thomist natural theological reasoning, it will be quoted here in its entirety:

> We find in nature things that are possible to be and not to be, since they are found to be generated, and to be corrupted, and consequently, it is possible for them to be and not to be. But it is impossible for these always to exist, for that which can not-be at some time is not. Therefore, if everything can not-be, then at one time there was nothing in existence. Now if this were true, even now there would be nothing in existence, because that which does not exist begins to exist only through something already existing. Therefore, if at one time nothing was in existence, it would have been impossible for anything to have begun to exist; and thus even now nothing would be in existence—which is absurd. Therefore, not all beings are merely possible, but there must exist something the existence of which is necessary. But every necessary thing either has its necessity caused by another, or not. Now it is impossible to go on to infinity in necessary things which have their necessity caused by another, as has been already proved in regard to efficient causes. Therefore we cannot but admit the existence of some being having of itself its own necessity, and not receiving it from another, but rather causing in others their necessity. This all men speak of as God.[13]

In other words, even if the world were eternal, as Aristotle claimed, it would nevertheless need explanation because it is made up of finite, dependent things that beg explanation for their existence. They are dependent and caused, and if the entirety of reality were made up of such dependent and caused things, then it would not exist. The world needs an uncaused cause for its continuing existence if not for its beginning.

Aquinas thought that the beginning of the natural world in time (or at a beginning of time) and especially *ex nihilo* (out of nothing) could not be demonstrated philosophically. As a Christian he believed in those truths on the basis of faith in divine revelation, but he argued that even someone like Aristotle who did not believe them had to conclude that the world requires an uncaused cause for its explanation. In this way Aristotle knew of God's existence even though he was a pagan and believed in the eternity of the world. All of Aquinas's proofs of God's existence "work" even if Aristotle was right and the world is eternal. For him, "that God exists is a judgment well grounded in sound philosophical thinking. But the existence of God does not follow from what we must suppose to have happened in the past. Philosophically speaking, God is required to account for what we can now observe, and he accounts for it in its presentness as we observe it."[14]

**Thomas Aquinas's Doctrine of God**

Aquinas proceeded from the five ways of demonstrating God's existence to an explanation of what God's essence must be if he is the first cause of everything. He believed that much of God's nature and attributes could be known by reason from nature alone. For example, if God is the unmoved mover and first cause of everything, he must be pure actuality without potentiality, for otherwise he would require a mover and a cause himself. For Aquinas there can be no potentiality in God.[15] "Absolute perfection must be pure act, for potency implies non-realized being. That is why God is pure act."[16] Another way of saying this is that God's essence and existence are identical, and that is unique to God as the first cause of all things. *What* God is, is also *that* God is and vice versa. There is nothing that God ought to be or may become that he is not already. To imply otherwise, Aquinas argued, would be to suggest that there is some lack in God, and anything lacking something cannot be the first cause of everything else because it would itself have to have a cause to fill up its lack. Not only is God pure actuality without potentiality—pure being without any becoming—God is also absolutely simple. God's essence is not composed of more than one thing. Perfect being, such as God must be to function as the first cause, must be noncomposite, unmoved, complete and lacking nothing: "God is absolutely simple, for there is in God no body, or hylomorphic composition. God is pure act in whom essence and existence are identical; the perfection of all being; and the highest good."[17]

In the final analysis, Aquinas's God turns out to be very nearly like Anselm's—immutable, impassible, simple substance, being and never becoming, altogether unlike anything finite, creaturely and mortal. Together their portraits of God constitute the pinnacle of what is sometimes called classical Christian theism. The God of classical Christian theism is pure actuality but cannot be acted upon. All his acts are timeless and self-determining and no creaturely act or plea can move him unless he has already decided to move, and that motion would never be away from what he already was. Some modern critics have wondered how such a God can even be considered personal. He does not seem capable of responding or interacting with anything outside himself. The same could be said of Anselm's and

Aquinas's God. Both portraits of God as static and nonrelational result from their natural theologies. In order for God to be "that than which nothing greater can be conceived" or "the first efficient cause of everything," he must be being without becoming, pure actuality without potentiality and thus impervious to being acted upon from outside himself. Is that the God of the Bible? It was against just such a portrait of God that the great seventeenth-century Christian philosopher and mystic Blaise Pascal wrote, "The God of the philosophers is not the God of Abraham, Isaac, and Jacob."

On the other hand, Aquinas's doctrine of God has been hailed by many scholars—both Christian and non-Christian—as a work of genius and the only one that truly does justice to God's majesty and glory. Its defenders bristle at the accusation that the Thomist God is "static." How can "pure actuality" and "pure act of existence" be static, they ask? This God is very active, and that is hardly characteristic of a static being. They also point to the later portions of Aquinas's *Summa Theologica* where he discusses God's attributes of love and goodness and object to any implication that such a God is uncaring or cold or distant, as some critics charge against classical Christian theism. Whichever side of the argument is right, one thing is clear beyond debate: Aquinas's "uncaused cause," God, is impermeable to any change whatsoever. His "God is being itself, of itself subsistent. Consequently, He must contain within Himself the whole perfection of being."[18] This necessarily implies within Aquinas's system of thought that God cannot change, and any being affected is a kind of change. Aquinas steadfastly affirmed and defended God's absolute immutability:

> Here is the proof that God is altogether immutable. First, because it was shown above that there is some first being, whom we call God, and that this first being must be pure act, without admixture of any potentiality, for the reason that, absolutely, potentiality is posterior to act. Now everything which is in any way changed, is in some way in potentiality. Hence it is evident that it is impossible for God to change in any way.[19]

Immutability is one thing. It simply means "unchangeable," and many theologians—perhaps most—before Aquinas also attributed it to God. The problem many modern theologians have with Aquinas's God is the deeper, more intense sense of God's unrelatedness that comes out in his discussion of God's being. Because of God's utter simplicity of essence and complete actuality of being, God is not really related to creatures at all. Relatedness itself would imply a kind of lack or need or imperfection in God. In Aquinas's own words, "Since God is altogether outside the order of creatures, since they are ordered to him but not he to them, it is clear that being related to God is a reality in creatures, but being related to creatures is not a reality in God."[20] Modern Aquinas interpreter Brian Davies concludes that for Aquinas, "the fact that there are creatures makes no difference to God. . . . In Aquinas's view, God is unchangeably himself and he remains this way even though it is true that there are creatures created and sustained by him."[21] Aquinas's view is very reminiscent of Anselm's and seems to combine Aristotle's idea of the Unmoved Mover as "Thought thinking itself" and Augustine's idea of God as the timeless, all-determining reality. According to Davies, Aquinas even denied that mercy in God is any sort of feeling. "'To feel sad about another's misery,' he writes, 'is no attribute of God' . . . For Aquinas, God's mercy lies in what he brings about, not in what something brings about in him."[22]

It would seem that Aquinas allowed his natural theology to determine his doctrine of God. Yet the portrait of God that evolves out of it is not dissimilar to earlier Christian ones. What Aquinas did was nail down classical Christian theism, which had already evolved from the apologists on through Augustine and Anselm. But this portrait of God seems quite foreign to the God of the scriptural narrative, who genuinely grieves and sorrows and even repents (relents) when people pray. All these characteristics and emotions of God have been dismissed as mere anthropomorphisms by defenders of the classical theist view, but one has to wonder what kind of God it is who loves (not an anthropomorphism) but does not genuinely feel compassion, mercy, sorrow and grief when his creatures suffer or rebel.

**Aquinas's View of Religious Language as Analogical Speech**

Another area where Aquinas provided some innovative suggestions in theology is the nature of religious language, that is, "God talk." The problem he attempted to solve was how human speech about God could be meaningful and actually describe God if God's being is so radically different from all creaturely being. Like many theologians of both East and West before him, Aquinas never tired of saying that God's essence is incomprehensible. We can know some of God's attributes, but we cannot penetrate the mystery of the divine life to describe it directly or literally. Yet Aquinas was not satisfied with the apophatic theology of some mystics and theologians in which God can only be described negatively, by saying what he is *not*. Aquinas believed that the clue to right thinking about human language about God lay in the cause-and-effect relationships by which God is known in natural theology: "Effects are like their causes, he holds, because they are that in which the operation and nature of their causes is played out or is manifest. Because they come from what their causes are, they reveal what brought them about."[23] Thus there is an "analogy of being" between causes and effects that makes it possible to describe an unseen and unknown cause by examining its effects.

Aquinas's solution to the problem of language about God, then, revolves around the concept of analogy. An analogy is a figure of speech that lies between "univocal" predication, in which a word literally describes a thing, and "equivocal" predication, in which a word does not describe at all but merely evokes certain feelings. An example of univocal speech would be the assertion that a rock is hard. The term *hard* is not being used in any metaphorical or poetic sense. It is meant literally. What *hard* means is what a rock is. There is a one-to-one correspondence between the normal meaning of *rock* and the normal meaning of *hard*. An example of equivocal speech would be the assertion that "the moon is a ghostly galleon." There is really nothing about a ghostly sea ship that resembles the moon or vice versa. It is a poetic figure of speech meant to evoke a certain spooky sensation. Aquinas argued that when we speak in theology of the attributes of God, we are speaking neither univocally, for God is always greater than any creaturely thing, nor equivocally, or else we would not know anything at all about God. Rather, all our theological speech about God is analogical.

An analogy is a description of something where the describing term is both like and unlike the thing it describes, just as an effect is both like and unlike its cause.

> Whatever is said of God and creatures is said according as there is some relation of the creature to God as to its principle and cause, wherein all the perfections of things pre-exist excellently. Now this mode of communication is a mean between pure equivocation and simple univocation. For in analogies the idea is not, as it is in univocals, one and the same; yet it is not totally diverse as in equivocation; but the name which is thus used in a multiple sense signifies various proportions to some one thing: e.g., healthy, applied to urine, signifies the sign of animal health; but applied to medicine, it signifies the cause of the same health.[24]

In other words, *healthy* is an analogy when used of urine and of medicine but in different ways. When applying the theory of analogous speech to God, Aquinas chose the adjective *wise* and said that when it is used of both God and a human being, it is used analogically. There is an analogy, in other words, between human wisdom and divine wisdom. They are neither wholly different nor wholly alike.

> In short, in speaking of God we use words which are normally employed with respect to things in the world. But, insofar as we speak truly, we will be latching on to something (God) whose way of being what we say it is differs from that of anything else we describe in the same manner. In this sense, we both do and do not understand what we are saying when we talk about God.[25]

Aquinas's theory of language about God has been widely influential in Western theological traditions. Many Protestants as well as Roman Catholics embrace it. Like so many other suggestions of Aquinas, it echoes Aristotle as much as the Bible. Aristotle promoted the idea of the right and the good as the "golden mean" between extremes. Courage is the golden mean between cowardice and foolhardiness. So Aquinas was once again borrowing from a pagan—"despoiling the Egyptians"—as many Christian thinkers before him had done. But there is certainly nothing unbiblical about his theory of religious language and it can be used far beyond the confines of Thomism[26] or any other particular philosophy or theology.

## Aquinas's Teaching About Salvation

What about Aquinas's view of salvation? At the opening of this chapter, we noted that even though his philosophical theology may seem highly technical and even speculative at times, his ultimate aim was to protect and promote salvation. In this area Aquinas moved entirely above the line between nature and grace. Salvation cannot be found or experienced without God's supernatural grace, which is "God's action in leading us to union with him."[27] This transformation by grace is similar to the Eastern Orthodox view of salvation as divinization *(theosis)*. For Aquinas, grace "is a work of God in human beings raising them above their human nature to the point where they become sharers in the divine nature."[28] Two things are absolutely essential to keep in mind about Aquinas's view of this gracious transformation in salvation. First, for him, it does not destroy nature but elevates and fulfills it. Human nature, according to Aquinas, was not ruined by the Fall of humanity in the primeval garden. Human nature may be damaged goods, so to speak, but the basic image of God, which is reason, is intact in spite of original sin. What the Fall destroyed was "original righteousness," not the image of God. Thus the grace of salvation, which becomes active through baptism, faith, the sacraments and works of love, raises human nature up but does not change or restore it. It simply restores what was lost, which was a right relationship with God. It does this by imparting the theological virtues of faith, hope and love and eventually bringing the human person to a vision of God in heaven.

The second important thing to remember about Aquinas's view of the grace of salvation is that it can never be forced. It is a sheer gift imparted by God and cannot be earned. God can never be made a human person's debtor. For Aquinas, as for Augustine, even faith is a gift of God's grace. Also like Augustine, Aquinas understood faith as faithfulness—not just a decision to trust in God alone but a lifelong dedication to God in obedience. This "habit" is a gift of God infused into a person through the sacraments. No good work can cause it. Only God can cause it. This process of salvation through grace is both *justification* and *sanctification.* The first word emphasizes the judicial side of salvation in which the person being saved is made right with God. The second term is the other side of the coin and designates the inward side of the process in which a person is actually made more and more godly. The two are inseparable for Aquinas. They are simply two ways of describing the same process of grace transforming a person's life toward the ultimate goal of beholding God in heaven.

One of the most common Protestant misunderstandings of Aquinas's theology is that he taught salvation by works, or works righteousness. There is a sense in which this is correct and another sense in which it is not correct. Aquinas did believe that participation in the sacraments such as baptism, Eucharist and penance are essential aspects of the process of being increasingly justified and sanctified. And he believed that a human person must exercise free will and some effort to make use of these means of grace. From the outside, then, it appears that he believed good works can cause salvation.

From the inside of his thought, however, at a profounder level, Aquinas clearly denied that any human effort or performance can cause grace to come into one's life or keep it there. In the final analysis it is all God's work, even the human decision and effort. For Aquinas,

> justification is in no way a consequence of "works." He certainly does not think that we can get to God by confronting him with a righteousness that obliges him to reward us. He thinks that we are justified by God on the basis of sheer liberality. For him, our repentance, and what follows that in the way we behave (our "works"), are the projection into history of God's eternal love making and sustaining goodness where there is no prior claim obliging him to do so.[29]

The theological background necessary for understanding Aquinas's view of salvation is his overall view of God's providence, including predestination. Aquinas followed Augustine very closely in these doctrines, while adding his own theological spin to them. With regard to providence he averred that God ordains everything that happens and is the ultimate cause of absolutely everything except evil, which is merely a lack of goodness. But Aquinas added to Augustine's thought the idea that God works in nature and history through secondary causes. That is, although God is the primary cause of everything's existence, he uses created things to bring about many individual events. Not everything that happens is directly caused by God, and yet everything in reality is within God's overall plan, purpose, knowledge and control. Free will choices provide a good example of Aquinas's notion of secondary causation. Human beings act, and in acting think they are really causing something to happen that would not happen otherwise. There is some truth to this, even for Aquinas, but the greater truth is that they would never have chosen or acted as they did if God had not ordained it and put in motion a chain of causation that ended up rendering it certain that they would pray, repent, do a good deed or praise him:

> God, therefore, is the first cause, who moves causes both natural and voluntary. And just as by moving natural causes He does not prevent their actions from being natural, so by moving voluntary causes He does not deprive their actions of being voluntary; but rather is He the cause of this very thing in them, for He operates in each thing according to its own nature.[30]

In nature and history God generally works through *natural* secondary causes; in redemption God works through *supernatural* secondary causes. The grace of salvation must invade and elevate nature without destroying it. Reason is part of human natural equipment and can lead a person to know that God exists and to seek him. Even that would be a work of God's providence. For the human person to achieve salvation, however, requires a special gracious act of God that transcends reason alone without contradicting it. If this happens in a person's life, it can only be because God has decreed it from all eternity. All of God's decisions and acts are timeless, so it is absurd to suggest that God somehow arbitrarily selects anyone to be saved in time. Rather, God has eternally, sovereignly chosen certain humans to be saved and imparts to them the grace necessary for that transformation. That they pray for it is in no way contingent or free in the sense that it could happen otherwise (noncompatibilist free will). Rather for Aquinas as for Augustine, free will is merely doing what one wants and decides to do, and that is compatible with not being able to do otherwise. For him, then, predestination is compatible with free will.

Not all Roman Catholic theologians followed Aquinas in his doctrine of predestination. After him, controversy broke out among them over this very issue, and the Jesuits—an order of priests founded during the sixteenth-century Reformation—generally rejected monergism in favor of synergism. Many Roman Catholic theologians, like many Protestants, prefer to leave the answers to these questions of free will and divine sovereignty in the realm of mystery. But it is clear where Aquinas stood—squarely with Augustine in favor of monergism. Nothing God wills can ever be because of influence that begins with human or any other creaturely agency. Creaturely agency, such as deciding to pray and then asking God for something, is itself indirectly a result of God's eternal decree and agency:

> According to Aquinas, then, providence governs all, but everything does not happen in accordance with natural necessity, and we need to allow for human freedom. Yet even human freedom falls within the scope of providence since God works in everything. He does not do so as an item in the world, as something acting to bring about change in a context which it inhabits itself. He does so as calling into being all the changing things we know or can comprehend.[31]

With this background in mind, it seems highly ironic that some Protestants accuse Aquinas of Semi-Pelagianism! That is only a surface appearance due to his strong emphasis on habitual grace transforming a person's life in a process that involves works of love. Beneath the surface, though, Aquinas's scheme includes the all-determining agency of God that foreordains and causes those works of love.

Protestant complaints about Aquinas's soteriology ought to focus on the proper issue, which is the distinction between justification and sanctification. Aquinas refused to separate them. A person is only justified—right with God—insofar as he or she is internally sanctified to godliness. During the Reformation of the sixteenth century, all the Protestant Reformers insisted on a clear separation between justification (as God's declaration of a person as righteous) and sanctification (as God's transforming work creating inward righteousness). Within a monergistic framework, however, it makes little real difference whether they are separated or not. In the end, both are absolutely assured apart from any contingent effort or decision a human person makes. Logically, within such a framework, justification as God's making a person right with himself happens in eternity in the foreordination of God. Only within a synergistic soteriology does it really matter whether or not one clearly distinguishes between justification and sanctification, and in Luther's day, most Roman Catholics had embraced synergism while paying lip service to Augustine and Aquinas as their great theological heroes. It was really against the synergistic Catholic thought of his own time that Luther rebelled.

It is to that story of post-Aquinian Roman Catholic theology that we must now turn our attention. While Aquinas dominated the thinking of the Western church for hundreds of years after his death, some later medieval Catholic theologians diverged from his basic theological and philosophical framework and helped lay the foundation for the Reformation. Three in particular stand out as especially important in the transitional epoch between Aquinas and Luther: William of Ockham, John Wycliffe and Desiderius Erasmus. Each in his own way challenged the assumptions of medieval scholasticism, while standing on its shoulders, and helped pave the way for the Protestant and Catholic reformations of the sixteenth century.

# CHAPTER 23

# Nominalists, Reformers & Humanists Challenge the Scholastic Synthesis

E*uropean culture was in a state of turmoil throughout the fourteenth and* fifteenth centuries. Nationalism was on the rise, the bubonic plague was decimating the population, and the church was falling into ruin. The once great dream of a totally unified Europe led by the pope and emperor working together under God was fading quickly as the church fell under the control of the French kings and the papacy moved to Avignon in France (1309-1377) and as kings of nations that were supposed to be part of the Holy Roman Empire went to war against one another. The nadir of the medieval church and its respect and authority was reached in the Great Schism of the West when two and then three men managed successfully to lay claim to the office of pope (1378-1417). In such a milieu of cultural and religious confusion and chaos, it is no wonder that some Christian theologians began to align themselves more with a king under whose protection they could flourish as they called for reforms in both church structure and theology.

**The Renaissance and Three Pre-Reformation Reformers**

Besides the turmoil of nationalism and ecclesiastical corruption, another phenomenon helped pave the way toward radical change in the church and culture generally—the Renaissance. The Renaissance was not a single movement. It certainly had no headquarters, although some have treated Florence, Italy, as if it were that. Rather, the Renaissance was a mood among the cultural elite in Europe that began in the fourteenth century, gathered strength in the fifteenth and came to a head in the sixteenth century. It was a mood of reaction against the stifling control of culture by corrupt and self-serving rulers and clergymen; a mood of individualism in which artists signed their works and literary geniuses wrote autobiographies and revered human creativity; a mood of freedom, education, emphasis on the arts and humanities, and restless searching for something new to move European civilization out of the Dark Ages (as Renaissance leaders regarded the entire medieval era) and into a new era of prosperity, beauty and enlightenment.

The mood of the Renaissance can be summed up in one word: humanism. The humanism of the Renaissance, however, was not "secular." Rather, it was simply a belief in the cultural creativity of the human person that rejected the Augustinian pessimism about humanity that had reigned supreme for a thousand years. It included an intense interest in the arts and sciences that came to be known as the humanities. That is the true origin of the word *humanism*—interest in the humanities. In Italy humanism took on a distinctly pagan flavor as intellectuals and artists reached back to pre-Christian Hellenistic sources of inspiration. Along the Rhine River in northern Europe, humanism remained more solidly Christian while moving away from scholasticism and even openly disagreeing with Augustine about original sin as total depravity. The northern Renaissance led to sweeping changes in theology and eventually contributed heavily to the Protestant Reformation.

Three theologians stand out above all the rest of this two-hundred-year transitional era between the high Middle Ages and the Reformation: William of Ockham, John Wycliffe and Desiderius Erasmus. The first two reacted against the stifling authority of pope and church hierarchy as well as against scholasticism in philosophy and theology. Yet they were scholastics themselves compared to Erasmus, who came after them and became the most influential thinker of the northern Renaissance and of Christian humanism. Ockham's stature in the story of Christian theology lies in his renewing of nominalism, which in turn helped give birth to a reform movement within the Catholic church known as conciliarism. It also indirectly influenced the birth of Protestant theology through Martin Luther, whose philosophical and theological training was heavily nominalistic.

Wycliffe's claim to fame lies not so much in his Bible translation work as in his ideas about the church and salvation that influenced the great Bohemian reformer John Hus, who was burned at the stake in 1417 but left a legacy that resulted in Luther's being known as "the Saxon Hus." Thus Wycliffe's theology also indirectly influenced Luther as well as the Church of England. His followers in England, known as Lollards, helped bring about the Reformation there two hundred years after his death. Erasmus's claim to fame lies in his "philosophy of Christ," which was his alternative to medieval scholastic philosophy and theology. A popular saying of the sixteenth century was that "Erasmus laid the egg that Luther hatched." All three men—Ockham, Wycliffe and Erasmus—served as bridges between medieval scholasticism and Protestantism. Along the way, however, the bridge burned down so that once Protestant theology was constructed, it bore little or no real similarity to medieval scholasticism.

**William of Ockham and Nominalism**

William of Ockham (sometimes spelled Occam) was born about 1280 or 1290 near the village of Guildford in Surrey County, England. Little is known about his early life, but his public life began with his studies at Oxford University, where he became a Franciscan friar and also taught philosophy and theology until 1324. He wrote the usual scholarly commentary on medieval theologian Peter Lombard's *Sentences*, which was a collection of authoritative statements of the Bible, church fathers and especially Augustine. *Sentences* was composed around 1150 and became a standard work of theology throughout the Middle Ages in Europe. Almost every ambitious young theological scholar had to write a commentary on it. Ockham's was not well received by some of his colleagues or by the church authorities. In 1324 his commentary was condemned as unorthodox by a synod of bishops and theologians in England, and he was ordered to go to Avignon, France, where the pope resided, to defend himself before the Curia, or papal court.

Arriving in Avignon, Ockham was confined to the Franciscans' house (like a monastery in the city) and held for two years before he was finally condemned as a heretic in 1326. One of the reasons for Ockham's condemnation was his support for a group of radical Franciscans who wished to return to Francis of Assisi's ideals of poverty. These "poor Franciscans" were in the habit of harshly criticizing the pope's and the church's power and wealth and comparing them unfavorably with Jesus Christ's lifestyle. Pope John XXII launched a campaign against the radical Franciscans and all Franciscans who sympathized with them.

Ockham escaped his confinement in Avignon and managed to make his way to the court of King Louis of Bavaria in Munich, Germany. Louis was also emperor of the Holy Roman Empire at the time and therefore a powerful protector. He happened to be in a heated dispute with the pope and more than willing to provide refuge to dissidents such as Ockham. In return for protection and patronage, the Franciscan friar and theologian wrote treatises arguing for the supreme authority of the emperor over both church and state. The result was that "Ockham was solemnly excommunicated upon joining himself with the monarch against whom the pope had already exhausted his spiritual maledictions."[1]

Also while residing and teaching in Munich, Ockham wrote most of his great works of logic, theology and ethics. He is probably best known outside theological circles for his development and use of a principle that has come to be known as "Ockham's Razor." There are many versions of the principle, but it is basically a rule of economy of explanation that is widely considered one of the most important breakthroughs in the early stages of modern science. Ockham argued throughout his writings that "to employ a number of principles [to explain phenomena] when it is possible to use a few is a waste of time."[2] In other words, if a particular event in nature can be explained by reference to a single causal antecedent, it is superfluous to posit more than that one. Ockham's Razor worked against the tendency for church leaders to posit dual causation for things—one natural and one spiritual. Thus, according to Ockham, if a law of nature explains why a rock fell down a mountainside, there is no point in also claiming an angel or a demon pushed it.

Ockham is also known in general intellectual history for his development and defense of a version of nominalism. Whether he actually was a nominalist or not is hotly debated. Many prefer rightly to call his theory of universals "conceptualism." In many ways it echoes Abelard's theory developed against extreme realism two centuries earlier. It is more correct to call Ockham's followers nominalists, for many of them took his theories further than he did. Nevertheless, for better or for worse Ockham is generally considered the philosopher and theologian of moderate nominalism in the later Middle Ages. In any case, what is clear is that "Ockham . . . categorically rejected all forms of realism, and grounded knowledge on direct apprehension of individual objects."[3] In his time that was a revolutionary step, and many historians trace the beginning of modern science back to him. They refer to a *via moderna*—a "modern path" of knowledge—that began with Ockham and continued after him up through Copernicus, Galileo, Kepler and Newton.[4]

Toward the end of his life, Ockham found his status at Munich weakening as Emperor Louis the Bavarian tried to reconcile with the Avignon popes. Ockham died of the plague in 1349, before having to flee Munich. He never reconciled with the church and died a condemned and excommunicated heretic. His influence was felt everywhere in northern Europe anyway. It led to a widespread disillusionment with the traditional realism favored by the church's hierarchy and thus helped undermine the church's status. It helped inspire and fuel conciliarism, which sought rule of the church by councils rather than popes. It also subtly drove a wedge between faith and reason, thereby undermining the dominance of the scholastic method of coordinating them in theology. Overall, there can be no denial that Ockham was a revolutionary figure in spite of the fact that he did not develop or promote any new doctrines. Rather, "his logical criticisms shook the foundations of scholasticism, and the dialectics of the following centuries revolved around the problems which he had raised."[5]

At the foundation of every other innovation Ockham brought about in any area of intellectual life lies his theory of universals. This entire area of philosophy seems so abstract and abstruse to many modern people that it would be well to review what the controversy was about and why it was considered so important throughout much of the Middle Ages. A "universal" is a quality or characteristic attributed to several individual things. The controversy among realists and nominalists and the various *via media,* or moderating views, had to do with the ontological status of universals—their existence and being. Are universals such as "redness" and "beauty" and "goodness" real in some sense apart from the individual things in which they inhere? Realists of all stripes said universals were real and insisted that no other view could possibly support a rational and ordered view of the universe. If universals are not real above and apart from individual things, realists argued, the order in reality is merely a construction of the human mind imposed on things, not an order discovered by the human mind already inherent in things. Take away ontologically real universals and all you have left is a "blooming, buzzing confusion" of individual things in nature.

Realists argued that their view of universals was inextricably linked with the Christian worldview and theology. For example, did not Christ take on real human nature in the incarnation? What was that if not a universal? It had no *hypostasis* of its own. It was hypostatized in the Logos (Leontius's doctrine of *enhypostasia*). Any nonrealist or antirealist view, such as nominalism, would seem to make the incarnation impossible. And what of the one divine substance of the Trinity? Would not denial of ontologically real universals result in tritheism? But the main flash point of controversy between realists and nominalists in the high and late Middle Ages in Europe had to do with the church. The Roman Catholic Church had come to think of the church—the body of Christ—as something real apart from the aggregate of individuals that compose it. It is "mystical." In other words, it is spiritual, transcendent, supernatural. This ecclesiology would seem to assume realism as its basis. Realists looked upon any radical rejection of realism as virtual heresy because of the effects it would eventually have on the entire system of Christian belief and on society. Realists were convinced that their view of universals was the only bulwark against relativism—the idea that there are no absolute values or ethical and moral principles.

William of Ockham may not have been a nominalist in the sense many scholars mean by that term. *Nominalism* is often understood to be a radical denial of the reality of universals such that they are reduced to mere sounds invented by humans to describe similarities of individual things. Whether Ockham went so far in his view of universals is doubtful. Other nominalists did. But Ockham did follow Abelard in arguing that "the generality in our thinking is subjective."[6] In other words, as one leading medievalist contends, "The pervading note of Ockham's philosophical discussions is the rejection of all facets of realism. Universals have no existence in reality. They are convenient mental fictions, signs standing for many particulars at once."[7] One reason Ockham rejected ontologically real universals is because belief in them violates his "razor." Reality can be adequately described without reference to them and therefore they are superfluous. He also considered belief in universals as realists understood them self-contradictory. Realists describe them as individual entities existing in multiple things, but Ockham argued, an individual thing cannot exist in many individual things simultaneously and still be an individual thing. Thus, realism is illogical.

So what was Ockham's view of universals? That is less clear than one would hope. His thought about universals seems to have developed throughout his career. At one time he considered them mere fictions, which implies something invented by the mind. Later, however, he refined this view so that universals are mental concepts that have real existence, but only in the mind as ideas. Modern people tend to assume that ideas are unreal because they are not measurable or tangible. People before modern times did not assume such. For Ockham and nearly everyone else in late medieval Europe, a concept can have ontological reality even if it cannot be weighed. That is where he eventually settled with regard to universals. He believed and argued that they are real concepts shared by many minds at once and neither real things outside the mind (as in realism) nor mere arbitrary and conventional noises (as in extreme nominalism). Some kind of reality attaches to general ideas even though that reality is not objective in the sense of having being independent of minds. All that exist objectively are individuals. Thus for Ockham, "There is no whiteness, only different white things. Mental signs cannot then resemble general entities, for there are none such."[8] Historians of ideas call this revolutionary and epoch-making—a Copernican revolution in philosophy.

Our main interest is in Ockham as a theologian. His nominalism, or conceptualism, had far-reaching effects on theology. First, it tended to drive a wedge between faith and reason and led in the direction of fideism, or "faith alone," as the basis for Christian belief. The scholastic faith in reason was seriously undermined by Ockham's philosophy. Second, Ockham's philosophy and theology emphasized God's will over God's nature and reason. That emphasis in theology is known as voluntarism. God does not command certain things because they are good; certain things are good simply because God commands them. God could just as well command other things. Everything exists as it does merely because God voluntarily chooses for it to exist, not because God follows some eternal pattern outside or inside his own being. Third, Ockham's thinking helped establish conciliarism in ecclesiology.

Ockham's rejection of objectively real universals led him away from natural theology, which tended to draw conclusions about God and spiritual realities from a logical order inherent in the universe and perceived by the mind. In other words, realism underlies most scholastic natural theology. Ockham believed that only one truth about God can be conclusively established by reason alone, and that is that God exists. Even belief in only one God cannot be conclusively proved from reason alone. Faith in the truth of divine revelation is the basis for that and almost all other Christian beliefs.[9]

Ockham set the standard of proof higher than many others would, but nevertheless he rejected rational proofs of most Christian beliefs because they depend on a kind of knowledge that is simply unavailable to the human mind without special revelation—knowledge of invisible, spiritual realities. Also such proofs as Anselm's relied on lead to concepts, but concepts do not necessarily imply existence. "In a word, conclusive philosophical knowledge of God cannot be attained. Our concepts of Him suffer the defect of all concepts; they cannot establish existence. In order to know God as an existent being we should have to apprehend Him in intuition [sense experience]; and this is impossible."[10] Natural theology, then, was out of the question for Ockham. He took everything below the line in Aquinas's double-decked scheme of theological knowledge and moved it above the line—except God's existence. That hardly constitutes a natural theology, however, especially when natural reason cannot establish that only one God exists.

Ockham's philosophical theology led him to distinguish between two powers of God: *potentia absoluta* and *potentia ordinata*—God's absolute and unlimited power and God's actual ordered power as it works in the world. This is the theological basis of voluntarism. God's power is not limited by anything other than the strictest laws of logic such as the law of noncontradiction: *A* cannot equal not-*A*. But Ockham did not really consider this any limitation, for a being that could act against the law of noncontradiction is a completely arbitrary and meaningless being. One could not possibly even know anything about or discuss such a being. On that one point Ockham agreed with the entire realist tradition of theology. Beyond that, Ockham would not limit God in any way. In other words, for Ockham there was no rhyme or reason to the way God creates and acts within creation other than that he so wills.

God's *potentia absoluta* is his power to will otherwise than he does, and it is virtually unrestricted. God's *potentia ordinata* is his power to will what he does and that also is virtually unrestricted. So for Ockham God could have become incarnate in a rock, a tree or a donkey. He chose to become incarnate in a human person. But more importantly, Ockham believed that when God commands something—such as repentance and belief—it is not because there is some eternal and immutable structure to reality that makes such things good. Rather, they are simply good because God wills and commands them.

Thus for Ockham "a human act is good or moral, not because it is in conformity with an eternal law which exists of itself and even governs the will of God, but simply because it is ordained and commanded by the will of God. Hence what God wills is good, what he forbids is bad."[11] That means God *could* will something other than he does. God *could* will evil. Ethics and morality and the way of salvation itself are all grounded in God's will and not in God's nature or eternal structures in reality that reflect God's nature.

Ockham's opponents recognized that this would seem to make a rational ethic or any kind of philosophical justification for Christian morality impossible. One must obey God's commands simply because God commands it. No reason beyond that can generally be given. In his *potentia absoluta* God could change his mind and command hatred and murder tomorrow. In his *potentia ordinata* he does not. He chooses to command love and peace instead. "The distinction itself was understood by all to mean that, given the divine omnipotence, God could act otherwise than reason expects or requires, and that therefore it is futile to attempt to prove by arguments of logical necessity what is in fact true only because God has chosen to make it so."[12]

Ockham's voluntarism flowed right out of his nominalism (or conceptualism) because "it points to the productive will of God as the ground of the universe [including laws], rather than to His unchangeable essence."[13] God, according to Ockham, has no unchangeable essence that would in any way limit his will and power. If he did, it would be a universal with objective, ontological reality. Such do not exist. So Ockham concluded that even God is an individual—one with absolute, unconditioned power to do whatever he wills to do.

Like his rejection of natural theology, Ockham's voluntarism influenced Luther two hundred years later. Luther hailed Ockham as a hero for knocking down scholasticism and affirming God's absolute power, which cannot be limited or comprehended by human reason. Luther wrote about the "hidden God" with

Ockham's *potentia absoluta* in mind as the untamed God of the Bible who can never be tied down by the human mind. To realists—whether Catholic or Protestant—this God appears arbitrary, irrational and dangerous. But in reaction to medieval scholasticism, Luther wanted a more unpredictable and uncontrollable God and found in Ockham an ally.

No area of Ockham's theology was more radical for its time and more controversial than his ecclesiology. Ockham reacted against the entire medieval hierarchical structure of the church and its tendency to identify the body of Christ with the clergy almost to the exclusion of the laity. He especially criticized the role of the bishop of Rome—the pope, or supreme pontiff—in his own time and sought a return to a more biblical model of church leadership. "According to Ockham, in organized religion only believers, Scripture and sacraments, the most essential aspects, exist. Thus, he argued, the traditional hierarchical system of the Church had given a priority totally unfounded in scripture to a single pontiff."[14] On the basis of his nominalist or conceptualist view of universals, Ockham denied the invisible essence of the church that was supposed to reside in the pope and his appointed bishops, archbishops and cardinals and instead identified the church with the individual believers who compose it. For him, "the Church comprises the whole of all believers—the community of Christians. . . . Every believer is a member of the Christian community."[15]

"Conciliarists" were those churchmen like Marsilius of Padua (1275-1342) who combined Ockham's nominalism with his theories of church and state with his focus on individuals and their personal judgments in ethics and declared that the church should be governed by councils and not by a single individual. Conciliarism became very popular during the Renaissance, and its ideas helped prepare European church and society for the Protestant Reformation. Beyond that, of course, it also foreshadowed and laid some of the groundwork for modern democratic movements. The Roman Catholic Church itself rejected conciliarism, just as it rejected Ockham, but both profoundly affected all of European society nevertheless.

### John Wycliffe and the Lollards

John Wycliffe was born in William of Ockham's homeland, England, about the time the excommunicated exile died in Munich of plague. Although they came to many of the same conclusions regarding the church, Wycliffe and Ockham differed greatly in their basic philosophical and theological approaches. Wycliffe was a realist with regard to universals, but like Ockham, he believed the pope was corrupt and the church should be governed by the people of God through their representatives rather than by the hierarchical structure of clergy.

Wycliffe was born in about 1330 at Lutterworth in Yorkshire, England. He died there in 1384 as the parish minister, after being driven away from Oxford University by his colleagues and the church leaders due to his radical teachings. At a fairly young age Wycliffe became a master of Balliol College at Oxford University and quickly rose to a prominent position and acquired a wide reputation as a scholar and outspoken advocate of church reform. While teaching at Oxford, Wycliffe, like many other scholars, was an employee of the king of England and received protection from him as long as his views comported with the royal view. He served as a mediator between the church and the royal court in disputes over church property, taxes and other matters of conflict between church and state and wrote two great volumes on government, *On Divine Lordship* and *On Civil Lordship*. He also wrote *On the King's Office, On the Truth of the Holy Scriptures, On the Church, On the Power of the Pope, On the Eucharist* and *On the Pastoral Office*. He advocated translation of the entire Bible into the language of the people so that all Christians could read and study it for themselves. For that he has been memorialized in the name of the modern world's largest Bible translation society.

Wycliffe was anything but diplomatic and compromising on those issues he felt strongly about. He railed against the corruptions and abuses within the church and harshly condemned the popes of his day for their secularity and apparent obsession with power and money. An example of his invective against the pope gives a taste of Wycliffe's polemical bent: "So the wicked pope is anti-Christian and a devil, for he is both falsehood itself and the father of lies."[16] He called the ubiquitous friars of his land "adulterers of the Word of God in prostitutes's robes and coloured veils."[17] Wycliffe anticipated Luther's attacks on the corruptions of the church and nowhere better than in his critique of indulgences. Indulgences were scripts of remittance for the temporal punishment of sins (such as purgatory) sold by Roman Catholic agents of the popes. Wycliffe harshly condemned this practice, as Luther did in his day. Of the Oxford theologian's virulent criticisms of the church of his time, a modern Wycliffe biographer writes, "Such an attack was a necessary prelude to Reform and was no small part of Wycliffe's contribution. Indeed it can be claimed that Wycliffe's onslaught was so well-directed and so devastating that he saved the Reformers of the sixteenth century the trouble of doing the job themselves."[18]

In 1377 eighteen "errors" of Wycliffe's were condemned by the pope at the behest of some of his Oxford colleagues. He was ordered to appear before England's bishops to respond. He was able to avoid a showdown in that instance only because the queen mother strongly supported him. In 1378 Wycliffe began denouncing the Western Great Schism in which two and then three men claimed to be pope. He did not stop with criticizing the papacy, however. He extended his criticism to key Catholic doctrines such as transubstantiation, which had become the semiofficial dogma of the church regarding the Eucharist at the Fourth Lateran Council in 1215. The royal family supported and protected Wycliffe until he openly sympathized with the peasants during an uprising in 1381. Under great pressure from the faculty at Oxford and the bishops of England, Wycliffe retired to his home parish in Lutterworth, where he spent the rest of his days writing and organizing a society of poor lay preachers known as Lollards. He died of a stroke while leading in worship on the last day of 1384 and was condemned as a heretic and officially excommunicated by the Council of Constance in 1415, where his devoted Bohemian follower John Hus was burned at the stake. Wycliffe's remains were exhumed, burned and scattered in the River Swift by the bishop of Lincoln in 1428.

Unlike Ockham, Wycliffe was an ardent realist with regard to universals. In this as in many other matters, he looked back to the Platonic Christian tradition of the early church and Augustine and stood with Anselm. He used scholastic logic but had little use for the Aristotelianism of Aquinas or the nominalism of Ockham. Wycliffe's realism manifested itself in several areas of his theology, but nowhere more forcefully than in his critique of the doctrine of transubstantiation. According to that doctrine, when the priest pronounces the words of consecration in the service of the mass, the bread changes substance and becomes the literal, physical flesh of Jesus Christ and the wine changes and becomes his literal blood. The "accidents," or outward qualities, of the bread and wine remain the same, but the inner substance changes so that the person partaking of the Eucharist is believed actually to be eating and drinking Christ's physical body and blood. Although this doctrine of the Eucharist would not be made finally and formally a dogma—beyond debate—until the Council of Trent in the sixteenth century, it had become the accepted belief and teaching of the Roman Catholic Church already in Wycliffe's day. He fought ferociously against it and used realism as his ally.

In *On the Eucharist* Wycliffe raised many objections against the doctrine of transubstantiation and even labeled it "faithless and baseless imaginings" and argued that it leads to idolatrous worship of food. But his most profound argument against it was based on realist metaphysics. The doctrine implies that a substance—such as bread or wine—can be destroyed and that "accidents" can exist without attachment to a substance. Such a belief would dishonor God, who is the author of all substances, Wycliffe argued. In addition, it violates basic metaphysical and logical rules. In any realist metaphysic, where a substance or universal is destroyed, so are its accidents. Or so Wycliffe believed and argued.

In any case, Wycliffe presented his own view of the Eucharist as an alternative to what he called "the modern heresy" of transubstantiation. In his view the substances of bread and wine remain while the Spirit of the living God enters them so that they bear a "real presence" of Jesus Christ while remaining bread and wine. In his own words, "As Christ is two substances, namely earthly and divine, so this sacrament is the body of sensible bread and the body of Christ."[19] Wycliffe rejected the idea that any sacrament is efficacious *ex opere operato*. On this score he broke with his beloved church father Augustine and insisted that for a sacrament to be truly sacramental in conveying grace, faith must be present. Wycliffe's view of the sacraments—especially the eucharistic meal—foreshadowed that of the great magisterial Protestant Reformers Luther and Calvin. His doctrine of Christ's real presence through the Spirit especially anticipates Calvin's.

Wycliffe's rejection of medieval Roman Catholic doctrine and practice went far beyond his criticism of transubstantiation. Even more fundamental to his reforming efforts were his views of ministry and authority. The Oxford theologian argued that the primary responsibility of the Christian minister—the priest—is to proclaim the gospel, and that this duty exceeds all others: "Preaching the gospel exceeds prayer and administration of the sacraments, to an infinite degree. . . . Spreading the gospel has far wider and more evident benefit; it is thus the most precious activity of the Church. . . . Thus those preaching the gospel truly are to be set apart by the authority of the Lord."[20]

How are they to be set apart? Wycliffe went so far as to advocate that the people of a parish choose their own priest—a truly radical idea in his time. He had become deeply disillusioned with the power, wealth, corruption and abuses of authority of the church's leaders and looked away from them to the people of God as the voice of God's will in church government. Although he was a realist, his ecclesiology converges with Ockham's at some points. Like the nominalist of Munich, Wycliffe advocated radical reform of the clergy and even abolition of the papacy in any recognizable form.

Perhaps Wycliffe's main achievement in theology was his advocacy of the supreme authority of Scripture for all of faith and life. The medieval Roman Catholic Church had come to treat the Great Tradition as equal in authority with Scripture. The word of the pope was regarded by many priests and bishops as God's own word, even though Catholic theology did not necessarily require this. The dogma of papal infallibility was not officially promulgated until the nineteenth century, but in practice the words and deeds of medieval popes were treated as having absolute authority. Wycliffe entirely rejected this and after 1380 began to refer to the popes as antichrists. Even the pope must be held to an "evangelical standard" of teaching and practice derived entirely from Scripture, and insofar as a pope fails to be truly evangelical, he is not even part of the true church of Jesus Christ and his lordship both temporal and spiritual is disregarded.

Wycliffe wrote a treatise titled *De veritate sacrae Scripturae (On the Truth of the Holy Scriptures)* in 1378—the year that the Western Great Schism began. In it he set forth the thesis that "Holy Scripture is the highest authority for every Christian and the standard of faith and of all human perfection."[21] He also affirmed the infallibility of Scripture, its self-interpretation and the role of the Holy Spirit in illuminating readers' minds as they read and study it. In other words, like the major Protestant Reformers later, Wycliffe rejected the necessity of an authoritative *magisterium,* or teaching and interpreting office of the church. The Bible as God's inspired Word takes the place of such an office and stands over all ecclesiastical agencies.

Wycliffe also rejected the medieval penitential system of salvation. Throughout the centuries after Pope Gregory the Great, the Western church and especially the monks had developed an elaborate and burdensome system of penances, or acts of contrition that Christians had to follow in order to gain merit before God. While Wycliffe did not achieve a full recognition of the Protestant gospel of justification by grace through faith alone, he anticipated Luther and Calvin and other Reformers of the sixteenth century by condemning all human efforts at gaining merit before God. Without ever criticizing or abandoning genuine works of love as part of the Christian life, Wycliffe placed the entire burden of merit upon Christ alone and emphasized grace and faith in a way not heard in the church for centuries. He also firmly endorsed belief in predestination and leaned toward monergism in his view of God's action in relation to human agency. He based this on Scripture and not on a scholastic metaphysic or natural theology.

Many reasons justify Wycliffe's reputation as a precursor of the Protestant Reformation. None is more important, however, than his emphasis on the Bible as infinitely superior in truth and authority to any human tradition or office. "One hundred and fifty years before the time [of the Protestant Reformation], Wycliffe seized on the one authority adequate for Reform, gave it the central place in his work and did his best to bring knowledge of it to the people, both by translation and insistence on the preaching of the Word."[22]

In his last years at Lutterworth he organized the group of lay evangelists and preachers later known as Lollards who helped set the stage for the Reformation in England. He also advocated the translation of the Bible into English, and his efforts produced among his followers the first English Bible known as the Oxford Bible. His books and teachings spread to Prague in Bohemia, where the great reforming preacher

John Hus used them to establish a permanent pre-Protestant movement there. Eventually Luther stood on the shoulders of both Hus and Wycliffe in his successful bid to reform theology and church life in Europe.

**Erasmus and Christian Humanism**

Desiderius Erasmus did not consider himself a theologian. The title was an insult because it was virtually synonymous with "scholastic speculative thinker." To Erasmus, "insipid theology" was a tautology. For him, "all subtle contentions of theological speculation arise from a dangerous curiosity and lead to impious audacity."[23] Yet Erasmus of Rotterdam is often considered one of the greatest theologians of the transitional age known as the Renaissance. He lived well into the era of the Protestant Reformation and debated with Luther. He also had one foot firmly planted in the medieval Catholic tradition of thought. He is a classical example of a transitional figure. His "philosophy of Christ" was in actuality a kind of theology, even if he refused to call it that. It was his alternative to the theology of the medieval schoolmen who still dominated the university theology faculties in the late fifteenth and early sixteenth centuries. It was also his alternative to what he considered the fanatical evangelicalism of the Protestant Reformers of the mid-sixteenth century.

Erasmus was truly a theologian without a home—a free thinker who refused to be tied down. Like an independent prophet, he stalked Europe throughout the first half of the sixteenth century, tirelessly urging reform of both church and state while refusing to join any party of reform. Without any doubt, however, Erasmus's writings and influence as a cultural hero helped bring about reforms both Catholic and Protestant.

Erasmus was born in about 1466 in Rotterdam, Holland. His parents died when he was a child, and when he was nine, his guardian sent him to a church school operated by a reforming mystical order of lay Christians who called themselves the Brethren of the Common Life. There he imbibed their *devotio moderna,* or "modern way of being spiritual," which centered on the practical aspects of Christian spirituality such as prayer, meditation, following Christ's example and the study of Scripture. Undoubtedly Erasmus's entire life of seeking reform in Christendom was given impetus by this peaceful, spiritual order of Christians who ran schools all over Europe. Eventually the young scholar joined an Augustinian monastery, somewhat against his will. His guardian chose the monastic life for him, and Erasmus always resented that. He was a free and independent spirit who highly valued personal self-determination. He managed to receive special permission from the church hierarchy to stay away from the monastery much of his life.

The young Dutch monk received ordination to the priesthood in 1492, the year Columbus "sailed the ocean blue," and Erasmus went on to study Greek, church history, theology and various other disciplines at a variety of European universities. He was much more of a scholar than a churchman and devoted his life to traveling, writing and lecturing and to his lifelong love of learning. Erasmus soaked in the new spirit of humanism, which was transforming the intellectual and cultural life of Europe, and integrated with it his love for the way of Jesus Christ. Humanism involved a rediscovery of the ancient sources of philosophy, including Socrates. "So far as Erasmus was concerned, there existed neither a moral nor an unbridgeable antagonism between Jesus and Socrates, between Christian teaching and the wisdom of classical antiquity, between piety and ethics."[24] He came to refer to the ancient Greek teacher of Plato as "Saint Socrates" and held him up as a model of natural wisdom along with Jesus as the model of supernatural wisdom and goodness. Erasmus's lifelong dream was to reform the Roman Catholic Church without breaking it apart. He believed that the way to accomplish that was through spreading the gospel of his philosophy of Christ, which meant a practical and peaceful Christian spirituality centered on the example of Jesus.

Erasmus became famous throughout early sixteenth-century Europe when he published his first book, known as *Adagia,* a collection of witty and stimulating thoughts that clearly reflect the mind of a Christian humanist. Embedded within it is a subtle critique of medieval society and church, and people all over Europe were soon quoting Erasmus. Soon after it he published *Colloquia,* a series of dialogues and vignettes that poked fun at popular superstitions promoted by the church. Some of the colloquies describe conversations between people who have been on pilgrimages to holy sites of Christendom, and it is clear that Erasmus considered the entire custom of pilgrimages to view relics ignorant if not immoral. In one colloquy Erasmus described a future encounter between Saint Peter and the pope, Julius II, at the gate of heaven. Julius, who was more interested in war than theology, appears in the dialogue dressed in full battle armor and is rejected from heaven by the poor and humble Peter, who does not recognize him as his successor. Erasmus had to apologize to the pope for the satirical farce, but it had its effect. Many educated people of Europe agreed with Erasmus that the popular piety promoted by the church had become mere religious superstition and that the hierarchy of the church of Rome had become little more than a secular power with no moral or spiritual authority.

Two of Erasmus's most influential works were *Enchiridion (Handbook of the Militant Christian)* (1503) and *The Praise of Folly* (1509). The first book is written to a Christian military man whose wife asked for a simple and straightforward exposition of the Christian life. It has become a classic of Renaissance Catholic devotional instruction and contains the best examples of Erasmus's philosophy of Christ. In it he advocated two "weapons of spiritual warfare," prayer and knowledge, and urges the Christian to follow Jesus Christ as his moral example and shun the seductive ways of the secular world as well as the superstitions of ignorant priests and monks: "You gaze in dumb amazement at the tunic or sweat cloth reputedly Christ's, yet half asleep you read the utterances of Christ? You believe it to be much more important that you possess a small piece of the cross in your house. Yet this latter is nothing in comparison with bearing the mystery of the cross in your breast."[25]

Erasmus's view of the Christian life in the *Enchiridion* clearly reflects the influence of the Alexandrian school of early Christian thought—the theologies of Clement and Origen. While neglecting the tendency toward gnostic speculation in that way of thinking, he drew deeply at its well of allegorical interpretation of Scripture and spiritualizing of the Christian life and relationship with God. For Erasmus, as for Clement and Origen, the way of Christ is an intellectual-mystical path that shuns the allures of the world and passions of the flesh and seeks to dwell constantly in the realm of the mind and spirit.

In *Praise of Folly* Erasmus took on the entire medieval Roman Catholic pattern of outward spirituality, including pilgrimages, relics, asceticism, monasticism, penitential acts and the hierarchical structure of the church. "Folly" is the sum of all that, and in order to make his point humorously and avoid retaliation by the powers of the church, Erasmus pretended to praise it. In fact, however, even a simple-minded reader knows immediately that the book is pure satire ridiculing popular piety and ecclesiastical pomposity as superstition and corruption.

Like the *Enchiridion,* it became wildly popular almost overnight, and together the two books provided reform-minded Christians throughout Europe a pattern for change. *Praise of Folly* clearly spelled out the problems. *Enchiridion* clearly spelled out Erasmus's solution. Instead of either ignorance or fanaticism, the scholar advocated inward and intellectual piety demonstrated in moral living patterned after Christ's example.

Perhaps the most important of all Erasmus's contributions was his production of a critical Greek New Testament in 1514. "The influence of this work on the Reformation was incalculable."[26] It became the basis for Luther's German translation and provided all scholars throughout Christendom with a touchstone for interpretation as well as translation work. Before Erasmus's Greek New Testament appeared, the only Bible most scholars had was the Latin Vulgate, which was the authoritative text of the Roman Catholic Church. Erasmus's text showed it to be a relatively poor translation, and that stimulated and equipped the growing movement toward translating the Bible into the vernacular languages of the peoples of Europe. Erasmus wanted everyone in Christendom to read the Bible for themselves. It was not just for the clergy and a few educated scholars, he insisted. Rather, the Bible should be read by every milkmaid and peasant. This came true in part, of course, because of his labors.

When Martin Luther launched the Protestant Reformation that split the church in Europe in half in 1517, Erasmus was without doubt the most influential scholar on the continent. He was in demand to advise kings and the emperor. Leading universities sought him out, and bishops and archbishops were wary of him. He was a cultural icon in his forties—a force to be reckoned with. According to his modern biographer, "never did a man . . . enjoy so great a prestige in Europe, a prestige due entirely to his intellectual acquirements."[27] And yet Erasmus was a man without a home. He considered himself a "citizen of the world" rather than a nationalist. He harshly criticized war and called for peace and unity among the peoples of Europe. At the same time, he wanted reform of the church that would not divide it into two churches. He abhorred both ignorance and fanaticism and hoped that his philosophy of Christ—another word for a lofty, humane and rational morality—would win the day and unify Christendom. It was not to be. Luther's prince, Frederick of Saxony, sought Erasmus's advice. Luther wrote to him. The pope and other sovereigns and churchmen virtually demanded a decisive statement from Erasmus about the events taking place in the church and empire.

Erasmus quietly supported Luther behind the scenes while refusing openly to side with him or his Protestant Reformation. He agreed with the German Reformer on many issues, but considered him a bit of a fanatic and a revolutionary for splitting the church and refusing to obey the emperor's and pope's orders to recant his heresies. To Frederick of Saxony, Erasmus quietly communicated the message that Luther should be protected. But in response to demands that he publicly declare which side he was on, "his resolution was unshakable, and so he kept pope, emperor, kings, and reformers like Luther, Melancthon, and Dürer, waiting year after year, and none of them was able ever to force from his lips the decisive word they expected. He smiled politely down upon his interlocutors, but his mouth remained sealed forever."[28] Or so it seemed. In private correspondence and in verbal communication to friends, Erasmus harshly condemned Luther and other Protestant Reformers for splitting the church and for holding fanatical views that did not correspond with the enlightened spirit of the age. Publicly he said little because he did not want to give the impression of supporting the corruptions of Rome. Erasmus's vacillation during such a crisis worked against him, and tremendous pressure was brought on him by everyone to write something about Luther.

Finally, reluctantly, Erasmus penned a critique of Luther's theology entitled *De libero arbitrio (On the Freedom of the Will)* in 1524. Many were surprised that he chose this issue for debate with the Protestant Reformer. Luther was delighted and congratulated the Dutch scholar's perspicacity for going right to the heart of their differences—the old issue of monergism versus synergism. Even though an Augustinian monk, Erasmus considered strict monergism incompatible with reasonable Christianity and argued for the human person's freedom to choose or reject God's grace. He knew where Luther stood on this. Luther had also been an Augustinian monk before his excommunication by the pope, and he considered the North African church father correct on this matter because he agreed with Paul in Romans 9—11. Luther was a monergist and believed God to be the all-determining reality and declared human beings nothing more than horses ridden by either God or the devil—at God's whim.

Erasmus considered Luther's teaching on free will and grace ludicrous and fanatical. He also considered it contrary to Scripture and the testimony of the church fathers before Augustine. He even accused Luther of Manichaeism. His basic position on this crucial issue is that

> although free choice is damaged by sin, it is nevertheless not extinguished by it. And although it has become so lame in the process that before we receive grace we are more readily inclined toward evil than good, yet it is not altogether cut out, except that the enormity of crimes which have become a kind of second nature so clouds the judgment and overwhelms the freedom of the will that the one seems to be destroyed and the other utterly lost.[29]

In order to avoid the charge of Pelagianism, Erasmus readily conceded that a kind of assisting grace—"cooperating grace"—is absolutely essential for the fallen human person's free will to do any truly good or righteous deeds. But he insisted that with the help of grace, damaged free will *can* choose to play a part in salvation. Thus he affirmed a synergism with grace as the dominant partner in the cooperative effort.

Luther responded with a harsh book entitled *On the Bondage of the Will* in which he reaffirmed his monergism and accused Erasmus of falling into Semi-Pelagianism if not outright Pelagian heresy. Later in life Luther wrote to a friend that if he had to sweep away all his other works, he would insist on keeping his *Smaller Catechism* and *On the Bondage of the Will*, as these two sum up his entire life's teaching. He firmly repudiated synergism of all kinds and argued that *only* evangelical monergism could possibly preserve the New Testament doctrine of salvation as sheer gift and do justice to God's majesty. He affirmed free will *only* of God and not of human beings and argued that because of the Fall the human will is bound to sin and Satan unless God chooses to overtake it:

> Thus the human will is placed between the two like a beast of burden. If God rides it, it wills and goes where God wills, as the psalm says: "I am become as a beast (before thee) and I am always with thee" (Ps. 73:22 f.). If Satan rides it, it wills and goes where Satan wills; nor can it choose to run to either of the two riders or to seek him out, but the riders themselves contend for the possession and control of it.[30]

Toward the end of his life Erasmus became despondent about his failure to bring about true reform—as he saw reform—without splitting the church. In 1533, in exile from his chosen hometown of Basel, Switzerland, and living in Freiburg, Germany, Erasmus penned what may be his most mature thoughts on the church, true reform and theology generally. Its English title is *On Mending the Peace of the Church,* and while Erasmus's hope expressed in the title never was fulfilled, the little book nevertheless contributed much to the Catholic Reformation and perhaps even more to modern Catholic theology and spirituality.

As he looked at the divided church of his day, Erasmus's diagnosis was quite different from Luther's. The latter regarded the chief problems as theological ones. And so long as the Roman Catholic Church would not radically alter its theology, he believed true Christians had to dust off their shoes and depart from it. Erasmus saw things differently. According to him, "the chief source of the disturbance is a breakdown of morals."[31] True morality, he averred, is in the heart and not merely in outward behavior, and the way toward Christian renewal and revitalization of a unified church is a new heart given by God's Spirit through grace.

Whereas Luther believed that it was necessary to use strong language to force reconsideration of once-settled issues, and whereas the defenders of Catholic tradition returned the favor against Luther and his followers, Erasmus called for civil and rational dialogue. The church's hierarchy called Luther "a wild boar in the vineyard of the Lord," and Luther called them antichrists and "fleas in God's overcoat." Erasmus wrote to both sides: "Tone down the filthy brawling of your insane quarrels."[32] He tried to reach a middle ground with regard to salvation by affirming both free will and human cooperation on the one hand and the absolute necessity of grace and faith as sheer gifts on the other hand. To fellow Catholics he wrote, "They who look at their own wisdom, their own strength, their own merits, who look only to ceremonies, privileges, and papal documents, never arrive at that blessedness [of heavenly things]"[33] because "true confidence can be placed only in the grace of God and his promises."[34] To Lutherans and other Protestants, Erasmus wrote, "The expressions reward or merit ought not to be rejected because God accepts and weighs that grace that is in us or operates through us"[35] and "Let us agree that we are justified by faith, i.e., the hearts of the faithful are thereby purified, provided we admit that the works of charity are necessary for salvation. Nor is true faith inoperative since it is the font and garden of all good works."[36]

Erasmus died three years after writing *On Mending the Peace of the Church.* He died without seeing the goal he had set before himself—a unified and reformed Catholic church of all Europe. Nevertheless, he left a legacy of liberal Christian humanism that, while controversial, has deeply influenced Protestants and Catholics alike. Luther's own right-hand man Philipp Melanchthon (1497-1560) was greatly influenced by Erasmus even though he could not show it until after Luther's death in 1546. He and some other Lutherans leaned toward a kind of evangelical synergism with regard to salvation and sought peace if not reconciliation with the church of Rome. On the Catholic side, Erasmus strongly influenced many moderate reformers, and his writings without doubt impacted the great reforming Council of Trent (1545-1563), even though he would not have been happy with its ultimate outcome.

Erasmus's legacy was nowhere more influential and permanent than in England, where he had lived for several years among the humanist scholars of the English Renaissance. The Church of England (now Anglican) tried to combine the best of the Roman Catholic tradition with the best of Protestantism in a fashion Erasmus would have loved. Within its bosom, his philosophy of Christ—including his synergism of salvation—took root and grew. Almost without doubt, if he had lived long enough, Erasmus would have smiled upon the Elizabethan Church of England of Shakespeare's day with approval.

"Erasmus laid the egg that Luther hatched" goes the popular saying. Of course, as we have seen, it was not only Erasmus who "laid the egg" of reformation in theology and church life. Ockham played his role in the process, as did Wycliffe. Lesser lights certainly contributed much. But whereas Erasmus was a reformer, Martin Luther was more than a reformer. He was a revolutionary. He turned his world upside down. While Dr. Erasmus tried to perform delicate surgery on the church and barely touched the vital nerves of theology, Dr. Luther performed radical surgery that involved amputation and reconstruction so that the patient emerged radically different. It is to that story that we must now turn.

# PART VII

# A New Twist in the Narrative

## *The Western Church Reforms & Divides*

*At the dawn of the sixteenth century, Christian theology in Europe was in trouble.* It might not even be an exaggeration to say that the story had lost most people's interest. The great Christian humanist Erasmus used *theology* as a synonym for pointless speculation and *theologian* for an ivory-tower thinker who had lost touch with reality. Of course, Erasmus was a theologian in his own way, but for many people like him, theology was to be equated with scholasticism in its various late medieval forms. It was also looked upon as a science—if it deserved that title—under the complete domination of the papal Curia, the Vatican bureaucracy that dictated what everyone had to think. And most enlightened people like Erasmus considered the Curia almost hopelessly irrelevant and corrupt.

Erasmus offered his "philosophy of Christ" as the solution for the lethargy of Christian thought and life. It would, he hoped, breathe new life into the dead science of theology by focusing it on practical matters of morality, ethical living by the example of Jesus, and real-world concerns of peace and harmony among all people. In the early decades of the 1500s few rivals for Erasmus's program appeared. And yet his voluminous and popular writings did not seem to be making a dent in the traditionalism and corruption of the official theology of Rome. The time was ripe for more radical solutions than Erasmus had to offer. The great

Bohemian reformer of Prague, John Hus, had prophesied just such a solution almost one hundred years earlier, shortly before his martyrdom at the Council of Constance (1415). So similar was Martin Luther's theology to Hus's that many labeled him "the Saxon Hus" because he was from the principality of Saxony in eastern Germany. Martin Luther did not just breathe new life into Western Christian theology, however; he revolutionized it. Compared to calm, patient Erasmus, the German Reformer was like a bull in a china shop. To bold, decisive Luther, Erasmus was like a little voice crying in the wilderness of worldliness, heresy, corruption and an almost total eclipse of the true gospel of Jesus Christ.

**Backgrounds of the Reformations**

Most historians date the dawn of the great sixteenth-century Reformation of church and theology to a single day in 1517. On October 31 of that year an Augustinian monk and professor of theology at the University of Wittenberg named Martin Luther nailed ninety-five theses (points for debate) to the cathedral church door in the city where he taught. His theses implied that the only official church of Western Christendom—the church of Rome—was in serious error. Within months all of Europe was reading Luther's theses due to the new invention of Gutenberg—the movable-type printing press. Pope Leo X read them and declared that the Saxon monk must be drunk. Later he called Luther "a wild boar in the vineyard of the Lord" and excommunicated him. But Luther's Reformation train had already left the station and there was no stopping it.

Soon other leading voices were raised against the standard theology of Western Christendom, and city after city joined Wittenberg in banning masses and reforming worship and theology. Zurich, Geneva and Strasbourg jumped onto the Protestant bandwagon, as did many leading German cities and principalities. Eventually all of Scandinavia joined the new movement, and within a few years Scotland and England were Protestant as well.

A third Great Schism was taking place in Christendom. The first was the split between East and West in 1054. The second was the medieval struggle between two and then three popes from 1378 to 1417. Now the third was the division between Roman Catholic and Protestant churches in Europe beginning around 1520 with Luther's excommunication from the church of Rome.

All the Protestant Reformers had certain common beliefs and aims. Three major Protestant principles are usually identified as setting them apart from the church of Rome and its official theology: *sola gratia et fides* (salvation by grace through faith alone), *sola scriptura* (Scripture above all other authorities for Christian faith and practice) and the priesthood of all believers. Each Protestant leader interpreted these in his own way, but all shared them in common and sought to give Christianity a new foundation in them. Their uniform aim was to return the church of Jesus Christ to its true New Testament foundation and rid it of all false teachings and corrupt practices. Unfortunately, they could not agree on how to do that, and a unified Protestant theology and church were never achieved. Nevertheless, in spite of differences, all the major Protestant Reformers and the churches they led held to and proclaimed the same basic message: the Word of God over all human traditions, salvation by grace through faith alone and every true Christian a priest unto God without need of a special mediator other than Jesus Christ.

The Protestant movement provoked a reaction from the church of Rome, which decided it needed to do two things: rid itself of the worst abuses and corruptions that had led some princes of the Holy Roman Empire to support the Protestants, and firm up its own theology by deciding and declaring once and for all what Christian truth would be regarding Scripture and tradition, salvation and the church. To that end the pope called a new council to respond to Protestantism. The Council of Trent is considered the nineteenth ecumenical council of the church by Rome, and it met off and on from 1545 to 1563. It is often considered the heart of the Catholic Counter-Reformation, and although it abolished many of the abuses that had helped spark the Protestant movement, it also baptized as dogma many of the unofficial and informal beliefs of the Roman Catholic tradition against which Luther and other Protestants had reacted. Ultimately, it deepened the divide within Western Christendom. Only in the second half of the twentieth century did that chasm narrow so that Catholic and Protestant theologians could conduct dialogue with one another and begin to regard one another as authentic Christians.

To one degree or another, all the major Protestant theologians of the 1520s through the 1540s thought that the church of Rome and scholastic theology had simply buried the gospel under layers of human tradition. They were generally not willing to say that there were no Christians within its fold, but they were more or less agreed that the leaders and teachers of the church had gone so far astray from anything recognizable as apostolic Christianity that it was beyond reform. A new start had to be made, especially once the pope began excommunicating Protestant leaders right and left.

It is extremely important to recognize that the Protestants were mainly concerned with theology and not just with the structure and practices of the medieval Catholic church. While the Reformation may have begun with Luther's protest against the selling of indulgences by papal hawkers, that and other concrete disputes over particular practices of Rome were symptoms of a deeper disagreement over the very nature of the God-human relationship. Luther and the leading Reformers of Switzerland, Zwingli and Calvin, believed that the church of Rome could justify the sale of indulgences (exemption from time in purgatory) because it misunderstood the nature of God's righteousness and human sinfulness. At the deepest level, then, the dispute was about soteriology and not specific corrupt practices.

The Protestant Reformation revolutionized Western Christianity. From 1520 on, no single church has existed to unify Western society, and in that sense Christendom died. The medieval synthesis of the one church headquartered in Rome ceased to exist. The era of denominationalism was ushered in against Luther's own wishes. He had no intention of dividing Christendom. His own theology did not advocate splitting the church up into warring or mutually ignoring factions. It happened nevertheless. Gradually, over the decades and centuries, Western Christianity splintered as Protestantism took on ever new forms.

In its first generation, Protestant Christian theology existed in four distinct branches. All four still exist, but even they have divided within themselves. The four were and are Lutheran (or *Evangelische* in German), Reformed ("the Swiss" to Luther), Anabaptist (considered the major part of the Radical Reformation), and Anglican (the Church of England). Each had its own distinct emphases that differed from the others, while all shared the three main Protestant principles. In part seven we will explore the story of how these forms of Protestant theology came about and what their distinctives were in the sixteenth century. We will also examine the Roman Catholic Church's reformation—the so-called Counter-Reformation—in response to Protestantism.

Before plunging into that rather complicated plot, it will be helpful first to delineate the situation in church and theology at the beginning of the Protestant revolution. That is because to a large extent Protestantism was just what its name implies—a *protest* against something. Luther and the other Protestants were protesting the condition of the church of Rome. Although on paper the official theology of the Roman Catholic Church was solidly anti-Pelagian and even anti-Semi-Pelagian, and although some of its leading thinkers strongly advocated Augustinian monergism, the popular theology of the church had fallen into a nonevangelical synergism that would have had both Augustine and Aquinas spinning in their graves. At the very least, church leaders and even some leading theologians of Roman Catholicism were implying that grace was a commodity to be earned or even bought. *Merit* had become a key term in Catholic soteriology. One could be truly saved only to the extent that he or she had gained sufficient merit before God through faith and works of love. *Faith* had come to be interpreted as faithfulness to the teachings and practices of the official church, and *works of love* had come to be interpreted as buying indulgences, paying for masses for souls in purgatory and taking expensive pilgrimages to view relics as well as giving alms to the poor, doing penance, participating in the sacraments and carrying out devotional practices such as prayer and meditation.

The implication behind this system of salvation as well as the explicit theoretical support it received from some late medieval Roman Catholic theologians was that humans can and must add their own efforts to the grace of God in order to achieve salvation. Salvation was increasingly being viewed as a reward that one received for cooperating with grace. Even though all Catholic theologians affirmed that the initiative in salvation lay with the grace of God in baptism, many went on to emphasize "habitual grace" that increased gradually within a baptized person's life through works of love. Only as this grace did its work of transforming the person from sinner into saint—actually holy and righteous within—could God "justify," or "declare righteous." "Generally, the medieval church defined the righteousness of God as the demanding justice of God."[1] God could and would declare one completely forgiven and fit for heaven when that person was no longer a sinner but was transformed into a holy person by cooperating with grace by all means possible. For most late medieval Catholic Christians, that meant enduring eons in purgatory after bodily death. The result for many—including Luther in the monastery before his recovery of the gospel of grace by faith alone—was fear of God's judgment that destroyed all assurance of salvation. For some it resulted in self-righteousness as they congratulated themselves for their spiritual achievements. All the Protestant Reformers (and some Catholics) considered this soteriology implicitly Pelagian—a moralistic and legalistic works righteousness completely contrary to the New Testament proclamation of God's righteousness given as a gift by grace through faith alone.

Of course there were many other important issues that came to divide the Protestants from the Roman Catholic Church, and many of them were also theological in nature. But no single issue so captured the imagination and created as much furor as soteriology and especially the question of God's righteousness and how humans gain a share in it or benefit from it for salvation. When challenged to produce the biblical support for their soteriology, the Catholic leaders appealed to the unwritten tradition of the church alongside Scripture. The medieval church had come to consider informal and unwritten tradition as equally authoritative as the Bible. Luther and the other Protestants rejected two sources of authority for the church and declared Scripture above all human traditions. When Luther stepped onto the stage of Christian theology from about 1513 to 1518, that was the condition in which he found himself and all Western Christendom: captive to an informal, unwritten tradition controlled by a corrupt pope and Curia in Rome and caught up in a near-Pelagian, synergistic soteriology of merits and works of love. His major sources of inspiration in correcting that condition became Scripture (especially Paul's epistles), Augustine's theology and some aspects of nominalism.

Luther's story is the opening act of the story of the sixteenth-century Reformation. Few individual Christian thinkers have affected the development of Christian belief so profoundly. And yet many modern Christians who think they know Luther do not know his theology very well at all. That he rebelled against the pope and rediscovered the authority of Scripture and the gospel of salvation by grace through faith alone is well known to almost every Protestant confirmation student. But how he did what he did and why are neither widely known nor understood. It is well, then, to devote an entire chapter of this story to the one actor Martin Luther, who saw himself as only a humble monk and theology professor but who turned the world upside down.

# CHAPTER 24

# Luther Rediscovers the Gospel & Divides the Church

*Martin Luther was born on November 10, 1483, in Eisleben, Germany.* He died in the same town while traveling through it on February 18, 1546. His father was an upper-middle-class mine owner and a strict disciplinarian. His mother was a deeply religious but also superstitious woman about whom Luther said and wrote little later in life. He received as good an education as his parents could afford. By about age fourteen he was living away from his parents in order to get the best possible education. At least a portion of it was under the instruction of the Brethren of the Common Life, the same lay religious order that educated Erasmus.

Luther's father wanted him to become a lawyer, and so he entered the University of Erfurt. He often walked the miles between his home in Eisleben and Erfurt on weekends. According to Luther's own memoirs much later in life, he was almost killed by a bolt of lightning one summer afternoon in 1505 while walking the road alone. The lightning knocked him to the ground, and in fear he cried out to his patron saint, "Saint Anne, help me! I shall become a monk!" Soon after that the young university student sold all his law books and knocked on the door of the Augustinian monastery in Erfurt. While a novice and young monk, Luther experienced attacks of what he called *Anfechtungen*—severe spiritual anxiety about his soul. He was not certain about the sincerity of his own sorrow and repentance, and so he punished himself in order to make up for that and to gain merit before God. He said later that his whole life in the monastery was a "search for a gracious God." But instead of loving God and finding him to be a gracious heavenly Father, he feared God and came to hate him because he sensed only his wrath and not his love.

Luther's confessor in the monastery was a man named Johannes Staupitz, who was also the vicar-general of the Augustinian order of monks in Germany. Luther later traced many of his own theological insights back to his lengthy sessions with "Lord Staupitz" in the monastery. So often did the young monk go to confession that the confessor admonished him to stop it until he had something really sinful to confess. But Luther was always worried that he had forgotten to confess some possibly sinful thought, motive or deed. The spiritual environment of Luther's time contributed to his anxieties. The general belief was that

> although God is merciful and Christ has died for the sins of the world . . . the responsibility of the sinner [is] to act on behalf of his own soul by rigorous self-examination, by good works and self-denial, by prayer and pious exercises. God is willing to forgive the sinner, but there are conditions which must be met and which lie within the power of the sinner to perform. Above all, the sinner must be truly contrite and must make a sincere and complete confession.[1]

Staupitz did not entirely agree with this and took a more lenient approach, emphasizing God's grace and mercy. Luther took the most severe approach possible, perhaps just to be on the safe side and relieve his doubts about God's mercy. Eventually Staupitz sent Luther out of the monastery to study philosophy, theology and the Bible at the University of Erfurt, and he also sent him to Rome on business for the Augustinian order.

At the university Luther was given a thoroughly nominalist education. According to leading Luther scholar Heiko Oberman, "There is no question that Luther was trained as a nominalist in Erfurt; but the implications of his academic training are still contested and under debate."[2] Later Luther's nominalistic education shows up at least in his emphasis on God's absolute freedom to do whatever he will do—expressed as the "hidden God" *(Deus absconditus)* behind the God who actually reveals himself in grace, love and mercy. Nominalism also probably helped turn Luther away from the scholastic tradition of Thomas Aquinas and away from natural theology toward a greater emphasis on faith as the mind's road toward God. Luther came to refer to scholasticism and natural theology, especially reliance on Aristotle, as a "great whore" that seduces the mind away from Christ.

In 1511 Luther went to Rome for the Augustinian order of monks. This was for any good Catholic the trip of a lifetime—an opportunity to visit the holy shrines of the apostles and the great church of the pope and soak in the spiritual aura of the most holy city of all Christendom. It turned out to be the greatest disappointment of Luther's life. In Rome he found only filth, immorality, blasphemy, squalor and spiritual apathy. His description of the city in 1511 fits with other contemporary accounts. Even some of the popes of the sixteenth century called for renovation of Rome—both spiritually and physically. Luther returned to Germany disillusioned and dismayed and probably inwardly determined to find some solution to the spiritual and theological lethargy that had led to such an abysmal situation in the holy city.

Luther earned his doctorate of theology degree from the relatively new University of Wittenberg in 1512 and began teaching biblical studies there at the same time. While preparing lectures on Paul's Epistle to the Romans in his tower room at the university, he experienced a series of intellectual-spiritual breakthroughs that have come to be compressed together by his biographers as his "tower experience." These happened between 1513 and 1518. The newly appointed young professor was still struggling with the issues of God's graciousness and righteousness. How could one God be both? What did Paul mean when he wrote about God's righteousness and about faith as the way of life of the just? Later in life Luther testified that he felt "born again" when the true meaning of Paul's words finally sunk into his mind and heart:

> At last, by the mercy of God, meditating day and night, I gave heed to the context of the words, namely, "In it the righteousness of God is revealed, as it is written, 'He who through faith is righteous shall live'." There I began to understand that the righteousness of God is that by which the righteous lives by a gift of God, namely by faith. And this is the meaning: the righteousness of God is revealed by the gospel, namely, the passive righteousness with which merciful God justifies us by faith, as it is written, "He who through faith is righteous shall live." Here I felt that I was altogether born again and had entered paradise itself through open gates. There a totally other face of the entire Scripture showed itself to me.[3]

Luther's view of God and salvation was revolutionized by his new interpretation of the righteousness of God and the gospel of justification by grace through faith alone. Soon he was lecturing about it and writing tracts and treatises explaining it in contrast to the standard ways of interpreting the gospel of salvation in his own time. The crisis came in 1517 when a seller of indulgences arrived in a town near Wittenberg with the message "As soon as the coin in the coffer rings another soul from purgatory springs!" Luther was not the only opponent of such crass methods of raising funds for the pope's new cathedral in Rome, but he was the only one who wrote up ninety-five theses for debate and nailed them to the castle church door. The theses condemned more than merely indulgences. They contained implicit condemnations of many of the popular beliefs and practices promoted by the church. Thesis 82 especially must have drawn the pope's attention to the Saxon monk: "Why does not the pope liberate everyone from purgatory for the sake of love (a most holy thing) and because of the supreme necessity of their souls? This would be morally the best of all reasons. Meanwhile he redeems innumerable souls for money."[4]

Within months Luther was a German folk hero for challenging the foreign power of Rome that was draining money away from Germany. He also became a man marked by the Vatican for careful examination and possible excommunication. From 1518 until 1520 Luther engaged in debates with leading Roman Catholic scholars who defended the authority of the pope to sell indulgences and remit the temporal consequences of sins (e.g., purgatory). He also wrote several reforming treatises on the church and its theology and appealed to the German princes to side with him against Rome. Luther was excommunicated by the pope in 1520 and called to appear before the emperor Charles V at his imperial court (Diet) in the city of Worms in 1521. When ordered by the pope's representative to recant his "heretical" views, Luther declared, "My conscience is captive to the Word of God. Thus I cannot and will not recant, for going against my conscience is neither safe nor salutary. I can do no other, here I stand, God help me. Amen."[5]

Luther was banned as an outlaw by the emperor but protected by his prince, Frederick "The Wise" of Saxony. Back in Wittenberg after a year in hiding, Luther carried on his reforming work through a flood of books and letters. All the eyes of Europe were upon him. Almost everyone either loved or hated him. Few individuals in history have succeeded in dividing a continent as thoroughly as Martin Luther.

Luther was a controversialist. He insisted that people either side entirely with him—because of what he saw as the great danger of the church of Rome and the papacy—or else get away from him and become his enemies. His attitude was expressed in this: "If they are not one hundred percent with us and for us, they are against us." After his excommunication by the pope, Luther unleashed his fury on the Vatican, the Curia and the papacy, calling them "Babylon"—holding the true church captive—and "the antichrist"—seeking to destroy God's true work. But some of his strongest invectives were reserved for other Protestants who broke ranks with him over issues such as the sacraments and obedience to the state. One of his favorite names for a theologian who disagreed with him was "pig-theologian," and he referred to more radical Reformers as "those fanatics" *(die Schwärmer)*. Occasionally when responding to a fellow Reformer such as Ulrich Zwingli of Switzerland, Luther would break out in a furious volley of insults. To Zwingli, who disagreed with him about the "real presence" of Christ in the Lord's Supper, Luther wrote, "Get out of here, you stupid fanatic, with your worthless ideas! If you cannot think in higher and other terms than this, then sit behind the stove and stew pears and apples, and leave such subjects alone."[6]

The only defense of Luther's offensive to opposition is that he saw the very gospel as at stake in the theological battles surrounding him. He felt that if the gospel of salvation by grace through faith alone was to be recovered once and for all, *all* Protestants needed to unite around him and stop breaking rank over minor matters. Such disunity only served to strengthen the enemy, which he saw as the Vatican and the papacy. Of course, Zwingli and other Reformers did not think they were breaking rank with Luther! Zwingli claimed that he had come to the same breakthrough and rediscovery of the gospel as Luther had at the same time and completely independently of him. Nevertheless, one must take into account Luther's siege mentality when reading his polemics against fellow Protestants and even against Jews. As Oberman reminds us, "Luther never styled himself a 'reformer.' He did not, however, shrink from being seen as a prophet; he wanted to spread the Gospel as an evangelist."[7] To him it was desperately important that others follow and unite behind his leadership. But he also thought he was right about the doctrines under dispute and considered all others who were in serious doctrinal error as little better than the pope and the Curia.

### Luther's Theology of the Cross

Luther was not a systematic theologian and never produced a systematic theology. He was a dialectical thinker, meaning he revelled in the paradoxical nature of truth. He believed that God's Word reveals a message beyond human reason or comprehension and that its truth is often couched in apparent contradictions. It would be up to later Protestant Reformers such as Luther's right-hand man Philipp Melanchthon and the French-born Swiss Reformed theologian John Calvin to systematize Protestant doctrine. Luther would have none of that. Most of his writings were *ad hoc* treatises aimed at a particular issue or controversy or else biblical commentaries or sermons. He did pen two catechisms for the instruction of Christians by Protestant ministers and worked on two fairly detailed statements of Evangelical belief—the Augsburg Confession and the Schmalkald Articles.

Due to the nature of his writings, one has to discern Luther's main doctrinal principles rather than merely "look them up." Among his major emphases are the theology of the cross (versus the theology of glory), knowledge of God through God's Word and Spirit, the hidden and revealed God, justification by grace through faith alone, the priesthood of every believer, and baptism and the Lord's Supper as efficacious signs and instruments of God's grace and faith. These then will form the outline for this chapter and through them we will attempt to elucidate Luther's contribution to the story of theology.

Before delving into Luther's theological contribution in detail, it will be helpful momentarily to step back and ask whether it can be summed up in a nutshell. Many Luther scholars believe that it can. One way of summarizing Luther is offered by David C. Steinmetz, who says that for Luther, "the gospel is not 'give me your virtue and I will crown it with grace' but 'despise your sin and I will shower you with mercy.' "[8] Paul Althaus expands on that by saying that for Luther "man is not only unable to gain merit before God in fact, but he is also unable to do so in principle. In every case, he is dependent on God's unspeakable mercy for his salvation."[9] Was this insight and contribution really new? Oberman argues that

> Luther's discovery was not only new, it was unheard of; it rent the very fabric of Christian ethics. Reward and merit, so long undisputed as the basic motivation for all human action, were robbed of their efficacy. Good works, which church doctrine maintained as indispensable, were deprived of their basis in Scripture. This turnaround touched on more than individual faith and righteousness; the totality of life was affected and thus had to be reconsidered. Throughout the coming years of confrontation and conflict, there was only one objective: to unfold the implications of this discovery and to see to it that they gained a wide hearing.[10]

The heart and essence of Luther's theological contribution, then, was salvation as a free gift of divine mercy for which the human person can do nothing. Many modern Protestants and even some Catholics take this idea for granted as if it has always been believed. But that is to ignore the revolutionary role played by Luther in recovering what had been largely lost and ignored for over one thousand years.

If anyone were to ask Luther himself what was his most basic theological idea, he might not have named the doctrine of salvation by grace through faith alone. That came to be his most significant idea in terms of overall impact. However, Luther himself might have responded to such a question by noting that beneath everything else lay his idea of the "theology of the cross," which can only be understood by contrasting it with its opposite, the "theology of glory." The distinction between these two opposite approaches to theology was delineated in his Heidelberg Disputation of 1518.

Less than a year after posting the ninety-five theses in Wittenberg, Luther was invited to the Augustinian monastery in Heidelberg to explain his program for theological reform and renewal. He decided to penetrate right to the heart of his differences with scholasticism—the greatest enemy of his own theology of gospel restoration. He labeled any approach that tried to discover God through human reason unaided by supernatural grace and the gift of faith a "theology of glory":

> It is certain that man must utterly despair of his own ability before he is prepared to receive the grace of Christ. . . . That person does not deserve to be called a theologian who looks upon the invisible things of God as if they were clearly perceptible in those things which have actually happened (Romans 1:20). . . . He deserves to be called a theologian, however, who comprehends the visible and manifest things of God seen through suffering and the cross. . . . A theologian of glory calls evil good and good evil. A theologian of the cross calls the thing what it actually is.[11]

Paul Althaus expresses this distinction succinctly: "The theology of glory knows God from his works; the theology of the cross knows him from his sufferings."[12] Luther was thinking of Paul's astounding statements in 1 Corinthians about the gospel of the cross being a "scandal" and a "stumbling block," and was comparing that with what he perceived to be scholastic natural theology's attempt to circumvent the scandal through reason apart from faith and grace. God, according to Luther, is revealed supremely in Jesus Christ and his cross. That is precisely the scandal of the gospel of the New Testament. The great creator God of the universe humbled himself to suffer on a Roman cross and therein be revealed as love and mercy. Of course Luther did not deny that all people everywhere have an innate sense of the existence of a supreme being, but he was inquiring about Christian theology and its beginning point. For Luther, following Paul, it is Jesus Christ and his cross and not nature and reason. That is because God has chosen this scandalous (to reason) self-disclosure and because human reason is too corrupted by sin to arrive at a true knowledge of God by itself. Luther believed that if Christian theology begins with scholasticism's lower level of Thomas Aquinas's two-tiered scheme of theology, it never really arrives at the second story, where gospel truth is to be found. Since God has revealed himself in the cross of Jesus Christ, why start our Christian thinking about God anywhere else?

Luther believed that the theology of glory, with its focus on human reason and what it can know about God from nature alone, inevitably leads to a moralistic spirituality of works righteousness because that is more rational to the fallen, sinful human intellect than the gospel of righteousness by Christ's death gained by grace through faith alone:

> The theology of glory seeks to know God directly in his obviously divine power, wisdom, and glory; whereas the theology of the cross paradoxically recognizes him precisely where he has hidden himself, in his sufferings and in all that which the theology of glory considers to be weakness and foolishness. The theology of glory leads man to stand before God and strike a bargain on the basis of his ethical achievement in fulfilling the law, whereas the theology of the cross views man as one who has been called to suffer.[13]

The theology of glory, then, is a human-centered theology that leads to an overestimation of natural human power and ability. The theology of the cross shows the true condition of humans as helpless sinners alienated from God in mind and heart and desperately in need of God's rescue mission, the cross of Christ. The theology of glory implies that humans can pull themselves up to God by their own bootstraps, so to speak, and leads to projects of self-salvation and theological speculation. The theology of the cross proclaims that humans are totally dependent and unable to figure out anything about God apart from God's own self-disclosure and leads to discipleship marked by suffering for God and others.

Even though he did not explicitly refer to it everywhere, "the theology of the cross permeates all of Luther's theological thinking."[14] It lies behind and beneath his frequently scornful rejections of theological rationalism and his warm embrace of paradox and mystery in theology. It is the foundation of his focus on human sinfulness and divine transcendence as well as of his emphasis on God's completely unpredictable, uncontrollable grace and mercy and human dependence. When he looked at the church of Rome, Luther saw a concrete manifestation of the theology of glory. He wanted to reject everything of that without destroying Christendom itself. He could accept a pope that stood at the head of the church as a suffering servant, but he could not accept one who ruled over all as wealthy, powerful and majestic. He could accept a theology that saw its sole purpose as proclaiming the gospel of grace, but he could not accept one controlled by Aristotle that aimed at speculation and rational explication of the divine mysteries apart from faith.

Luther also considered belief in human free will with regard to salvation an example of theology of glory. With some rare exceptions, most of the late medieval scholastic theologians and humanists accepted the freedom of the will as part of their synergistic view of salvation. Luther regarded this as just one more manifestation of human pride standing against the cross that proclaims human helplessness.

Luther believed strongly in the bondage of the will due to the Fall and original sin, but he believed this because of the cross and not as a result of metaphysical speculation. His theology of the cross also led him to a passionate defense of the doctrine of predestination—monergism of salvation—which he considered "very strong wine, and solid food for the strong."[15] Although Luther found many reasons to believe in predestination, at rock bottom his belief in it was based on the cross and he thought it could only be approached through the cross and not through rational theological or philosophical argumentation:

> Luther's doctrine of predestination was not motivated by speculative or metaphysical concerns. It was a window into the gracious will of God who freely bound Himself to humanity in Jesus Christ. Predestination, like the nature of God Himself, could only be approached through the cross, through the "wounds of Jesus" to which Staupitz had directed young Luther in his early struggles.[16]

For Luther, belief in freedom of the will—whether in its scholastic or humanist version—evidenced a refusal to accept God's action on our behalf as the sole hope for salvation. The cross is the great event and symbol of human helplessness and divine intervention. The only proper response to it is acknowledgment of complete unworthiness and dependence on God's grace.

In his own time Luther saw only two options for Christian theology: either some version of a theology of glory or a theology of the cross. In his estimation all of his opponents—including the church of Rome and the humanists as well as the "fanatics" among the Protestants—were guilty of a theology of glory. Only he could see the centrality of the cross and the paradox of God's power and suffering that lies at the heart of the gospel as he understood it. Everything else of Luther's theological contribution flows from there and returns to it continually.

Of course, extraneous theological and philosophical elements influenced him in ways he was not entirely aware of. One notable example of that is the influence of nominalism on his doctrine of God, and at least some Luther scholars and critics have argued that it was as much a factor in his monergism of salvation as was his theology of the cross. Like Ockham earlier, Luther tended to identify God's being with his sheer freedom of will. Human wills are bound and determined by God. As Luther declared to Erasmus in his response to the humanist's question in *On the Freedom of the Will* regarding the reason for God's foreordination of sin and evil:

> He is God, and for his will there is no cause or reason that can be laid down as a rule or measure for it, since there is nothing equal or superior to it, but

> it is itself the rule of all things. For if there were any rule or standard for it, either as cause or reason, it could no longer be the will of God. For it is not because he is or was obliged so to will that what he wills is right, but on the contrary, because he himself so wills, therefore what happens must be right. Cause and reason can be assigned for a creature's will, but not for the will of the Creator, unless you set up over him another creator.[17]

There could hardly be a clearer statement of a nominalist doctrine of God.

**Knowledge of God According to Luther**

According to Luther, if God is to be known at all, he must reveal himself. Thus the basis of all true knowledge of God can only be God's self-disclosure by his Word and through his Spirit. While natural theology would be a possibility before and apart from sin, according to Luther, the Fall destroyed not only freedom of the will but also the intellect's ability to know God through natural reason apart from special revelation. Because of sin, Luther averred, "Anyone who has a god, but does not have his Word, has no god at all," and whoever seeks God outside of Jesus Christ as God's Word in person finds the devil and not God.[18] That is because, according to Luther, reason itself needs miraculous healing and renewal by the grace of God and the Holy Spirit in order to believe in God rightly. Sin has so corrupted the human person that the very image of God itself is little more than a shattered mirror or a relic of what it was intended to be. Reason is a prime damaged faculty of the sinner. Although evidence of God's existence, power and goodness lies all around in nature, because of sin the human mind sees only idols and rejects the true worship of God in favor of idolatry. Luther looked to Paul in Romans 1 for support of his rejection of any true natural knowledge of God.

Needless to say, the German Reformer had no use whatsoever for scholasticism's natural knowledge of God, and especially none for the emphasis on Aristotle's philosophy among the Thomists (followers of Thomas Aquinas). For one thing, Luther argued, that approach to knowledge of God does not take sin seriously enough. For another thing, it takes philosophy too seriously. When Luther railed against reason as a "great whore," he generally meant Aristotle and any philosophy or theology attempting to gain knowledge of God and the gospel through means alien to God's Word. In his estimation "the whole of Aristotle is to theology as shadow is to light"[19] and "philosophy can express nothing but the limited content of human reason."[20]

Again, two reasons seem to lie behind Luther's view, and scholars debate endlessly which was the primary influence on his thinking about knowledge of God. On the one hand, Luther appealed to the gospel and Scripture for support. Here, the doctrines of original sin and God's transcendence over and above human reasoning come into play. On the other hand, Luther was clearly under the sway of Ockham and nominalism here as well as elsewhere. Ockham found little positive help for theology in natural reason (other than logic itself). The great medieval nominalist emphasized faith alone as the instrument of grasping God's nature and the mysteries of divine revelation.

So if reason and philosophy apart from grace and revelation are of little or no use, where did Luther look to find a body of knowledge about God from which to draw and establish true doctrine? Against the theology of the church of Rome, he appealed to Scripture alone—*sola scriptura*—as the ultimate guide, norm and authority for Christian faith and practice. The Catholic church of Luther's day taught that unwritten tradition could be just as authoritative as Scripture. Furthermore, it taught that the Bible is the church's creation and therefore only the church hierarchy can properly interpret it. Luther, on the other hand, viewed the gospel and the Scripture through which it shines as being on an entirely higher level of authority than either philosophy or tradition, both of which can and often do err.

That is not to say, however, that he discarded tradition entirely. Luther held Christian tradition, unlike philosophy, in high esteem and sought to rescue and preserve as much of it as possible. One of his complaints against the more radical Reformers was that they threw the baby out with the bath water when they reacted against the church's heritage of tradition in theology and worship. Comparing the church's accumulated tradition of creeds and liturgy with a temple, Luther wrote against the radicals, "One needs a more cautious, discreet spirit, which attacks the accretion which threatens the temple without destroying the temple of God itself."[21]

For Luther the ultimate standard and touchstone of all truth is the gospel of Jesus Christ, and that is first and foremost a spoken message—God's Word—and not a "dead letter." Luther did not simply equate God's Word with the Bible. On the other hand, he did not relegate the Bible to some lesser or unimportant status either. We only know and hear the gospel through the Bible, which is God's chosen instrument used by the Holy Spirit to bring Jesus Christ to us and teach us the gospel. For Luther, the Bible was the cradle that holds Christ. But the Bible is not God and it is not Jesus Christ and it is not even the gospel. All are above the book, and the book's value lies only in the fact that God uses it to instruct his people. But he does use it as no other book, and therefore its authority stands over all human authorities. According to Luther, "The gospel . . . is nothing but the preaching about Christ, Son of God and of David, true God and true man, who by his death and resurrection has overcome for us the sin, death, and hell of all men who believe in him."[22] It is, in other words, a message—the Word of God. Before there was a New Testament, it was preached by the apostles. And it forms the core and inner standard of truth even within Scripture itself.

Luther's approach to the Bible was rather ambiguous and even paradoxical. Some critics would say it is an excellent example of his tendency toward inconsistency if not downright contradiction. On the one hand, against the Catholic elevation of tradition alongside Scripture as an equal authority, he put the Bible on a higher plane and insisted that no person or church has the right to judge Scripture. At times in his writings he virtually equated it with God's Word and condemned all criticism of it or subordination of it to the church's authority. He referred to the Bible as "the queen" and declared that "this queen must rule, and everyone must obey, and be subject to her. The Pope, Luther, Augustine, Paul, or even an angel from heaven—these should not be masters, judges, or arbiters but only witnesses, disciples, and confessors of Scripture."[23] On the other hand, Luther could also state quite unequivocally that not everything in Scripture is equally valuable and he felt free to debase certain books of the Bible as having little or no value for the soul.

The classic example of this is the epistle of James, of which Luther wrote, "Away with James. . . . His authority is not great enough to cause me to abandon the doctrine of faith and to deviate from the authority of the other apostles and the entire Scripture."[24] Luther worked with the gospel message—God's Word—as a "canon within the canon" so that James and certain other books and portions of Scripture are not equal in authority:

> In a word, St. John's Gospel and his first epistle, St. Paul's epistles, especially Romans, Galatians, and Ephesians, and St. Peter's first epistle are the books that show you Christ and teach you all that is necessary and salvatory for you to know, even if you were never to see or hear any other book or doctrine. Therefore St. James' epistle is really an epistle of straw, compared to these others, for it has nothing of the nature of the gospel about it.[25]

For Luther, then, even Scripture has levels of authority within it and the test for determining them and the touchstone for interpreting all of Scripture is *was Christum treibt*—what promotes (or pushes) Christ—in other words, the gospel message about Christ, his cross and our salvation by grace through faith alone. Contrary to some misconceptions, Luther did not put James out of the New

Testament. But he did discourage its use in worship and teaching, and he forbade Lutheran ministers in training from preaching from it or the book of Revelation, which he considered obscure. He also expelled the intertestamental books known as the Apocrypha from Protestant Bibles and produced a German translation of Scripture from Erasmus's critical Greek New Testament. There is no doubt about Luther's passionate devotion to Scripture as the authoritative Word of God. But there is also no doubt that his doctrine of Scripture is highly ambiguous and raises almost as many questions as it answers.

The ultimate religious and spiritual authority, according to Luther, was the "external Word" of the gospel that shines through Scripture as the Holy Spirit uses it to call, convict, convert and instruct sinners as they become believers. Against the church of Rome, he placed the Bible on a pedestal above church tradition as judge of all belief and practice. Only those aspects of tradition that accord with Scripture are to be retained. Against the mystics and spiritualists of his time, Luther firmly tied the Spirit to the external Word and to the Bible and argued that the Holy Spirit teaches nothing other than what the Bible teaches. For him "Word and Spirit . . . not only belong together but constitute an indissoluble unity."[26] The only validation for Scripture's truth and authority is the testimony of the Holy Spirit through it. For Luther that was sufficient. No rational arguments can add anything to it.

**Luther's God Hidden and Revealed**

Another basic principle of Luther's theology has to do with the being of God. Luther is famous for hinting often and enigmatically at his belief in the "hidden God." For him, the true God is both hidden and revealed, and this is a paradox. Luther's concept of God's hiddenness implies much more than the kind of commonsense or popular notion that not everything about God is comprehensible to the human mind even when it grasps divine revelation. That is virtually a truism without any special interest. Luther's idea of God's hiddenness says much more, but exactly what it says and implies is disputed. Some critics find it incoherent. Some Luther admirers find it to be one of his greatest achievements.

For Luther there were two senses in which God is hidden as well as revealed in the gospel and through Scripture. On the one hand, God sovereignly chooses to disclose himself under his opposite in the humanity of Jesus Christ and the suffering of his cross. This sense of God's hiddenness was Luther's way of expressing God's condescension in his self-revelation. He chooses what is ungodlike and even ungodly (the Godforsakenness of Jesus Christ on the cross due to his bearing the sins of the world) to encounter humanity. His greatness and power are revealed through weakness and suffering and sin bearing. How God can be God and go through all of this is incomprehensible to the human mind. It is part of the scandal of the theology of the cross that is an offense and stumbling block to the natural mind.

The more puzzling sense of God's hiddenness has to do with Luther's affirmation that somehow above and behind God's revelation of himself in the gospel lies a mysterious power that is almost totally unknown to humans. On the one hand, God reveals himself in Jesus Christ as loving brother and friend and in the gospel as grace and mercy. In the gospel God is all compassion and perfect goodness without any hint of arbitrariness or capriciousness. This is God "for us." This is the only side or aspect of God we are supposed to concern ourselves with. God revealed through the gospel opposes sin and evil and seeks to overcome them by defeating sin, death and Satan through the cross. God for us in the gospel is our only business in proclamation. According to Luther, we should focus on this God, who is very much like the waiting father in Jesus' parable of the prodigal son.

On the other hand, paradoxically, Luther wished to warn us that this is not all there is to God. Behind the waiting Father of loving face and outstretched arms lies the hidden, dark, mysterious God of all-determining power who is the very cause of every evil thing as well as every good thing in nature and history. Even though this dark divine force has little to do with the gospel message, Luther pointed to it as the necessary background to all of history. Nothing whatever can exist or happen apart from God's direct plan and causation. Here Luther's monergism goes beyond even Augustine's. For Luther the devil was both God's enemy and God's instrument, "The devil is 'God's devil.' "[27] God works all in all and even in and through Satan and the godless. "We should know then that in everything bad that happens to us it is God himself who is at work through instruments."[28]

Luther related his doctrine of double predestination—that God foreordains some angels and humans to heaven and some to hell—to God's hiddenness. Such a terrible idea seems contrary to the gospel, yet it cannot be escaped, so Luther believed. As both hidden and revealed, God has two wills that seem completely in conflict to finite human minds. On the one hand, God wills the salvation of all. On the other hand, God wills to work evil (although it is not evil for him to do it!) and create Satan, cause his fall and use him as an instrument. Without any attempt to smooth out the apparent contradictions in this doctrine, Luther simply spoke of God's hiddenness and urged Christians to acknowledge it while keeping their focus on God's self-revelation in Christ.

Many critics and scholars see Luther's "hidden God" as further evidence of his nominalism. On the one hand, his rediscovery of the gospel pointed ineluctably to God's great compassion, mercy and goodness. On the other hand, Luther could not bring himself to limit the doctrine of God to that since to do so would be to imply that God is somehow a prisoner of his relationship with humanity and that there are powers—Satan, sin and evil—outside of God's control. Luther experienced Satan very vividly as his and God's enemy and opponent of the gospel. On the other hand, he experienced God as all-powerful Lord of the universe who calls all of the shots all of the time. The solution lay in positing a hidden God behind the loving, personal God of the gospel who opposes Satan and is humanity's friend. This hidden God is nearly identical with nominalism's completely free divine will and power *(potentia absoluta)* and with Augustine's emperor of the universe. The result for Luther's theology is a Janus-like God with two faces.

Even sympathetic Luther scholars such as Paul Althaus are dismayed that Luther held so tenaciously to the hidden God when his commitment to the gospel should have revolutionized even the doctrine of the divine being.[29] Instead of God's power being subordinated to God's love—as the gospel would indicate—Luther's hidden God concept seems to imply either a sheer conflict between divine love and power or else subordination of love to power.

**Justification: The Doctrine on Which the Church Stands or Falls**

Luther's best-known contribution to theology is his doctrine of righteousness, or "justification by grace through faith alone." Justification is the act by which God declares a person to be in a right relationship with himself, that is, righteous. Luther considered this the heart of soteriology and considered soteriology the heart of all theology. For him, "The doctrine of justification is not simply one doctrine among others but the basic and chief article of faith with which the church stands or falls, and on which its entire doctrine depends."[30] In order to understand Luther's concept of justification, it is essential to understand the medieval Catholic teaching against which it reacted. According to Catholic doctrine—stretching back at least a thousand years to Augustine—justification is the gradual process by which a sinner is made actually righteous internally by having God's own righteousness infused through the grace of baptism, faith, works of love and the entire penitential life. Only when the sinner is so transformed that he or she is no longer really a sinner at all does God justify in the full and complete sense. Baptismal grace that washes away the guilt of original sin must become habitual grace that grows within through sacraments and penance and must eventually become sinless perfection. Justification comes gradually all through the salvation process, but ultimately and perfectly only at its end. For medieval Catholics it extended into purgatory.

Luther despaired of ever finding justification this way. He had been baptized and had become the "perfect penitent" by entering a monastery and going to confession in true contrition several times daily. He had even tried whipping himself and half starving himself as well as sleeping on the cold, stone floor of his monastery cell. Yet his conscience was still troubled, and God's countenance still seemed angry so long as he considered it in light of his own imperfect goodness. He felt that he could never fully please God no matter how hard he tried. His own study of Scripture led him to a much deeper sense of human sinfulness than the medieval Catholic system of salvation presupposed. Luther came to believe that "Man . . . sins even when he does the best he can, even in his best works."[31] Where then could there be any hope for justification? His alternative doctrine began with his insights that "I am not good and righteous, but Christ is" and that there is a "sweet and joyful exchange" between Christ's goodness and righteousness and the human person's own sinfulness and unrighteousness on the cross that is of full benefit the moment one has faith and believes in it. "As bride and bridegroom exchange possessions in a marriage, so the sinner receives justification from Christ, and Christ takes over the Christian's sins."[32]

This joyful exchange takes place both on the cross through Christ's death and in the Christian's life as soon as he or she believes the Word of God and trusts in Christ alone for salvation. Nothing is necessary for it other than the cross in history, the gospel proclaimed and faith in the heart of the sinner. No penitential acts can add anything. The merits of Christ imputed to the sinner by God cannot be increased. The righteousness gained is Christ's, therefore it is "alien" and "imputed": "through faith in Christ . . . Christ's righteousness becomes our righteousness and all that he has becomes ours, he himself becomes ours."[33] Luther made clear in the context that this justifying righteousness never becomes a person's own possession. It remains forever completely Christ's. Furthermore, it does not change the person receiving it into an actually righteous person, although it provides a new motive for pleasing God—gratitude. Rather, the person receiving Christ's righteousness through imputation (a bookkeeping or legal metaphor) remains a sinner through and through. Such a person is in a constant state in this life of being *simul justus et peccator*—"simultaneously righteous and a sinner." Because of Christ received by faith, God sees the sinner as righteous while the sinner is still just that—a sinner: "thus a Christian man is both righteous and a sinner, holy and profane, an enemy of God and yet a child of God."[34]

For Luther, then, justification involved two movements. First, on account of faith and by his grace alone, God forgives the sinner. Second, and beyond mere forgiveness, God imputes Christ's righteousness to the sinner as if it were the sinner's own. This is a two-step event that happens at once—usually at baptism—and daily throughout life as the sinner-believer daily renews repentance and faith. But there is no insecurity in the daily aspect of justification, for it is a sheer gift and not in any way contingent on progress in actual righteousness. The only condition for maintaining it is continuing faith, and faith, according to Luther, is the opposite of a "work." "For Luther . . . faith means accepting God's promise from the heart and taking a chance on it."[35] Faith's essence is simple belief and trust in God's promise made in Christ on the cross. The moment one has that—and it is a gift of God to the elect—the sweet and joyful exchange is complete and the sinner is no longer a sinner under condemnation in God's sight.

Luther's opponents accused him of opening the door to the old heresy of antinomianism—rejection of all law and obedience. They charged that his teaching on justification would cut the heart out of Christian living. People would "sin more that grace may abound" and go to hell for neglecting growth toward perfection through the penitential system. Luther met this criticism with fear and trembling because he knew there was a kernel of truth in it in that some people would no doubt misunderstand the gospel and turn liberty into license as they had in Paul's time.

Luther accounted for Christian good works in his own way. Good works, such as acts of love for God and neighbor, would flow naturally from the new heart that a person receives from being forgiven and justified freely by grace. The same faith that grasps grace and the same grace that justifies will inevitably begin to change the person within and produce fruits of righteousness. Of this Luther was sure. But he did not dwell too long on good works lest it lead back into works righteousness. For him, the amount of good works and the degree to which a person actually is conformed to Christ in behavior have nothing to do with his or her justification. In the final analysis, they are all "filthy rags" compared with Christ's perfect righteousness and therefore in no way a support or cause for justification.

### Luther on Priesthood and Sacraments

Because they are justified by grace through faith alone, according to Luther, all Christians are priests unto God. That is another of his basic theological principles. Whereas the medieval church had elevated a certain class of men called priests to a special spiritual status as mediators between sinners and God with supernatural powers to absolve guilt and perform sacraments, Luther elevated every true believer to the same special spiritual status. He referred to the entire church as the "communion of saints" and the "evangelical priesthood." Because of grace and faith, Luther asserted,

> Not only are we the freest of kings, we are also priests forever, which is far more excellent than being kings, for as priests we are worthy to appear before God to pray for others and to teach one another divine things. . . . Christ has made it possible for us, provided we believe in him, to be not only his brethren, co-heirs, and fellow-kings, but also his fellow-priests. Therefore we may boldly come into the presence of God in the spirit of faith . . . and cry "Abba, Father!" pray for one another, and do all things which we see done and foreshadowed in the outer and visible works of priests.[36]

Luther did not denigrate the office of the minister as shepherd of the congregation by elevating all believers to priesthood. He affirmed the teaching office of ministers as servants trained to interpret and teach God's Word. However, he believed that ministers ought always to be called and chosen by God's people and not imposed upon them by a hierarchical officer of the church, and he taught that any ordinary Christian may in an emergency perform either of the two sacraments—baptism and the Lord's Supper—and preach and teach God's Word to the congregation. The priesthood of all believers means two things. First, all true believers in Jesus Christ may go directly to God in supplication for others as well as for themselves. Second, no special spiritual status places ministers above the rest of God's people to lord it over them.

A great deal of the controversy surrounding Luther and his reforming theology had to do with the sacraments. The medieval Catholic church of Rome had emphasized the value and importance of seven acts of Christ through the church for individuals' salvation. The debate during the Reformation revolved around two of them: baptism and the Lord's Supper. The latter is called Eucharist by the Eastern Orthodox and Roman Catholic churches as well as by some Protestant denominations. Luther preferred to call it simply the Lord's Supper or Holy Communion.

Much to the dismay of the church of Rome, Luther reduced the number of sacraments to those two. For a time early in his reforming work he considered penance (confession and absolution) a third sacrament, but eventually he removed it from that category. For Luther, in order for a ceremony to be a true sacrament and strengthen faith, "the symbolic act must be instituted by God and combined with a promise. Sacramental character ultimately depends on the presence of a divine Word of promise."[37] Only baptism and the Lord's Supper fit the criteria.

Furthermore, against the prevailing Catholic view Luther insisted that in order for a sacrament to be efficacious in strengthening faith, faith must be present. Sacraments do not work *ex opere operato*. It is not enough merely not to put an impediment in the way of a sacrament's efficacy, as Augustine claimed and the church taught. Rather, the person receiving the sacrament must have faith to benefit from the sacrament.

In contrast to the Roman Catholic teaching regarding baptism, Luther rejected the idea that it merely restores the original righteousness lost by Adam and Eve and all their descendants through the Fall and begins the process of habitual growth in grace. Instead, he averred that baptism, when performed and received by faith, fully justifies the sinner through the Word of God that is mysteriously bound to the water. In contrast to the Roman Catholic teaching regarding the Lord's Supper, Luther rejected the idea that it represents a resacrificing of Christ as well as the belief in transubstantiation, which claimed that bread and wine actually become the body and blood of Christ in substance.

On the other hand, Luther fought most of his battles over baptism and the Lord's Supper with other Protestants. Ulrich Zwingli in Switzerland opposed Luther's own view of the Lord's Supper, and the Anabaptists and other radical Reformers rejected his view of baptism. The theological battles among Protestants over these sacraments, or "ordinances," kept them divided as nothing else did. Luther was harsh and uncompromising in his debates with both Catholics and non-Lutheran Protestants.

The Anabaptists accused Luther of inconsistency. If the efficacy of a sacrament depends on faith, then how can an infant receive true Christian baptism? The Anabaptists wanted a thorough reform of the church, and they thought Luther and other magisterial Protestant leaders were stopping halfway. For them infant baptism was both a relic of the church's fall away from apostolic Christianity and inconsistent with the gospel of salvation by grace through faith alone. Because Luther defended infant baptism, they accused him of inconsistency and remaining stuck in Catholic tradition. They believed that only persons who had reached the awakening of conscience, or age of accountability, could repent and express faith, and only when this is done is baptism effective as a sign and symbol of conversion.

*Anabaptist* means "rebaptizers" and it was meant as an insult. Of course, the Anabaptists, who called themselves Brethren, did not believe in "rebaptizing" anyone. They did not consider infant baptism true baptism at all.

Luther was unsympathetic with the Anabaptists and responded to their questions and implied accusations with vitriolic fervor. His own view was close to what may be called "baptismal regeneration"—the belief that "in baptism we are immediately given complete forgiveness of sin."[38] For Luther, baptism was "the visible sign of unmerited justification through God's grace. Baptism performs the justification through God's grace. Baptism performs the 'joyful exchange' through which a sinner receives the righteousness of Christ and Christ takes over his sins."[39] He insisted, however, that an infant must have faith in order to receive salvation by baptism.

How can a child have faith? Luther considered that an almost blasphemous question because for him faith is simply trust, and it is a gift of God. Who better to have it than a child? Even though he did believe and argue that an infant can have faith, Luther did not hang the validity of infant baptism on that. Rather, he held that infant baptism is legitimate because it is traditional:

> Since our baptizing has been thus from the beginning of Christianity and the custom has been to baptize children, and since no one can prove with good reasons that they do not have faith, we should not make changes and build on such weak arguments. For if we are going to change or do away with customs that are traditional, it is necessary to prove convincingly that these are contrary to the Word of God.[40]

The Anabaptists were dissatisfied with Luther's final appeal to tradition. They believed infant baptism to be contrary to the Word of God, and they argued that it had not always been practiced by Christians but had been introduced in the late second or early third centuries and was still controversial at the time of Tertullian. Luther's doctrine of infant baptism and his defense of it seem at best tenuous in light of his strong emphasis on personal faith as belief and trust in the work of Christ as necessary for justification and his tendency to reject traditions that in any way conflict with the gospel and do not find clear support in Scripture.

**The Divided Protestant House: Luther Versus Zwingli on the Lord's Supper**

Perhaps the most unfortunate incident in Luther's interactions with fellow Protestants happened in October 1529 in the German city of Marburg. It was a conference known as the Marburg Colloquy, and the ardently Protestant prince Philip of Hesse had brought Luther, Zwingli and Martin Bucer of Strasbourg there to try to achieve consensus about the sacrament of the Lord's Supper. Zwingli, the Reformer of Zurich, had been teaching the Swiss Protestants that the Lord's Supper is simply a commemoration of Christ's death and that there is no "real presence" of the body of Christ in it. Luther had been teaching that although the Roman Catholic doctrine of transubstantiation was unbiblical, Christ's words "this is my body" at his last meal with the disciples proves that there is a "real presence" of Christ's body "in, with and under" the elements of bread and wine. Although Luther did not give his doctrine of the Lord's Supper label, later church historians called it consubstantiation. That is, for Luther the two natures of physical food and of Christ's glorified human body come together and feed the faithful soul in the sacramental meal. "Just as the incomprehensible and omnipresent God draws near to a man in the humanity of Jesus Christ, so the incomprehensible and omnipresent humanity of Christ again draws near to and can be grasped by men in the Lord's Supper."[41]

At the Marburg Colloquy, Zwingli argued that Scripture teaches that "flesh and blood avail for nothing" (John 6:63) and that Luther's insistence on Christ's bodily presence in the sacrament takes Jesus' words "this is my body" too literally and is too close for comfort to the Catholic doctrine of transubstantiation. Zwingli also argued that the very idea of eating flesh and blood is a disgusting, pagan notion. To this Luther replied, "I would eat dung if God demanded it,"[42] and accused Zwingli of not taking Scripture seriously and of attempting to rationalize a mystery. Needless to say, the meeting was unsuccessful. The participants went home more divided than ever, and Luther's attitude toward Zwingli hardened. To colleagues he commented of Zwingli and his supporters, "I suppose God has blinded them,"[43] and made clear through his writings that he could hardly consider them saved at all.

Much of the difference between Luther's and Zwingli's doctrines of the sacrament of the Lord's Supper centered on their differing Christologies. Zwingli believed that because of the incarnation, Jesus Christ is localized in heaven and not omnipresent. The resurrected and glorified human body of Jesus Christ cannot be everywhere at once except "by the Spirit." Otherwise it would not be truly human. Luther, on the other hand, believed strongly in the *communicatio idiomatum* of Cyril and Leo I and argued that because of the incarnation, the humanity of Jesus Christ is glorified and "Christ is around us and in us and in all places" at once.[44] The two great Reformers charged each other with christological error as well as with seriously misunderstanding the Lord's Supper. One of the major differences between Protestants ever since has been over this issue. Another Swiss Reformer—John Calvin—tried to discover a middle ground, as we will see in the next chapter.

Luther believed that like baptism, the Lord's Supper is a real sacrament that mediates the forgiveness of sins when faith is present. Why he did not advocate Communion for infants after baptism is a mystery, but he did not. In any case, Luther held a very high view of the two sacraments and in general tied justification to them. On the other hand, he readily admitted when pressed that one could be justified fully apart from participation in the sacraments. He did not believe that unbaptized infants automatically miss heaven, let alone go to hell. And while he encouraged frequent participation in the Lord's Supper, he did not make it a requirement for maintaining justification. On the other hand, Luther warned that rejecting baptism and willfully neglecting the Lord's Supper could lead to loss of fellowship with God. That would only be true, of course, if God had foreordained it. Such rejection and neglect of the sacraments would simply be a sure sign that such a person is not one of God's elect.

At the same time Luther was beginning his reform of church and theology in Germany another Reformer was inaugurating a Protestant revolution in Switzerland. Ulrich Zwingli is considered by the Swiss a national hero, and Swiss Protestants generally believe that his breakthrough to Protestantism was completely independent of Luther. The same cannot be said of his younger French-born Swiss colleague John Calvin of Geneva. He was influenced by Lutheran teachings while a university student in Paris. Together Zwingli and Calvin helped reform Switzerland and establish what is known as the Reformed branch of Protestantism—the major European counterpart to Lutheranism—that spawned the Presbyterian and Puritan movements in Great Britain. Their stories come next.

# CHAPTER 25

# Zwingli & Calvin Organize Protestant Thought

L*uther never published a systematic theology, and his thoughts remained* largely inchoate if not incoherent. Paradox was his normal mode of expression because he believed that God and God's Word are ultimately mysterious and beyond human comprehension. The Swiss Reformers were more intent on organizing and systematizing the new Protestant theology. In the process of doing that they added their own unique spin, so that the theology stemming from their works is usually identified as Reformed, while that stemming from Luther is called Lutheran or Evangelical. (In some places in Europe *Evangelical* simply means "Protestant" as opposed to Roman Catholic.) Reformed theology is that form of Protestant thought that finds its roots in the teachings of Ulrich (or Huldreich) Zwingli and John Calvin. Lesser lights of Reformed theology revolved around these two great stars, and some spun off and led major reforming movements in Holland, Scotland, England and other places around Europe. All were dependent, however, on Zwingli and Calvin.

**Reformed Theology**

What is Reformed theology? It is a form of Protestant theology and therefore shares with Luther and other Protestant Reformers the three great Protestant principles of salvation by grace through faith alone, the special, ultimate authority of Scripture and the priesthood of every believer. However, Reformed Protestant theology has its own theological flavor. While entirely in agreement with Luther on most issues, it puts a distinctive spin on several doctrinal issues, interpreting and emphasizing them in its own unique way.

One often hears the generalization that Reformed theology is that branch of Protestant thought that especially emphasizes God's sovereignty. As we have already noted in the story of Christian theology, however, many theologians long before the Swiss Reformation highlighted God's sovereignty over nature and history. Monergism and meticulous providence characterized Augustine's mature theology, and medieval scholastics Anselm and Thomas Aquinas taught them as well. Luther denied free will and argued that God is only truly God if he rules over everything in such a way that nothing happens in either nature or history that is not planned and brought about by God. It seems incorrect, then, to make divine sovereignty in providence and predestination a special contribution of Reformed Protestant theology.

Perhaps the popular (and sometimes scholarly) identification of Reformed theology with emphasis on the sovereignty of God, including monergistic providence and predestination, results from the fact that later Lutheran theology tended to soften Luther's similarly strong emphasis. Lutheran theology after Luther was influenced by Luther's lieutenant Philipp Melanchthon (1497-1560), who leaned toward synergism and was somewhat Erasmian in temperament and theology. Anabaptists and Anglicans (Church of England) were either divided over the issue or leaned strongly toward synergism—especially in the seventeenth and eighteenth centuries. Thus Reformed theology flowing out of Switzerland eventually came to be especially linked with the doctrine of God's absolute sovereignty. Certainly, however, it holds no monopoly on that doctrine in the story of Christian theology.

Swiss and later all Reformed theologians diverged from Luther in three main areas of theology: soteriology, ecclesiology (doctrine of the church) and sacramental theology. The distinctive flavor of Reformed thought in these three loci of theology permeated its entire ethos so that over time Reformed theology appeared to be quite different from Lutheran theology. Many leaders of both church and state during the Reformation of the sixteenth century could not see why the Swiss Reformed and German Lutheran's could not unite. Martin Bucer (1491-1551), Reformer of Strasbourg, worked tirelessly to bring them together. Philip of Hesse, prince and elector of Marburg, also strove to unite the two main wings of Protestantism. All attempts failed until the eighteenth century when a Prussian king forced the Lutheran and Reformed churches in his area of Germany into a union. Within it, however, the two types of Protestantism were simply like two boards glued together. No theological synthesis was achieved. In the late twentieth century in North America, major Lutheran and Reformed denominations finally agreed to accept each other's ministries and sacraments without formally uniting into one denomination. While recognizing the incommensurability of their theological cultures, each side arrived at acceptance of the other through much dialogue and cooperation.

**Ulrich Zwingli's Life and Reforming Career**

The true father of Reformed Protestant theology is Ulrich Zwingli. Unfortunately for him, he has been overshadowed in history by his younger French-Swiss counterpart John Calvin. Calvin's great claim to fame, however, is simply that he organized, systematized and articulated Reformed theology as never before. In doing so he stood firmly on the shoulders of Luther and Zwingli. It would be difficult to find any doctrinal insights or contributions in Calvin's work that were not already discovered and articulated by Luther and Zwingli. The two first-generation Reformers simply did not have Calvin's great gifts of organization, and they did not influence the English-speaking world as did Calvin through the Presbyterians and Puritans of Great Britain and the American colonies, whose founders studied under Calvin in Geneva and considered that city under Calvin "the most perfect school of Christ since the days of the apostles."

Ulrich Zwingli was born in Glarus, Switzerland, on New Year's Day 1484. His family was upper-middle class and well connected, and he received a fine humanist education, including university studies at Vienna and Basel. He received his master of arts degree in theology from Basel in 1506 and almost immediately purchased a pastorate[1] in his home city. There and in the pilgrimage town of Einsiedeln the young Swiss nationalist and humanist scholar distinguished himself as a renowned preacher, writer and patriot. A turning point came in Zwingli's life when he met Erasmus in the spring of 1516. He became a devoted follower of the great humanist Reformer and promoter of his philosophy of Christ and "could be considered an unreserved Erasmian and outstanding adherent of biblical humanism when he arrived in Zurich on January 1, 1519."[2] In the Swiss Confederacy's most important city Zwingli became the "people's priest" at the Great Minster (cathedral) church on his thirty-fifth birthday.

During his tenure in Zurich, Zwingli worked with the other religious leaders and the city council to bring about major reforms in both the church and state. At his urging the city council abolished masses and substituted Protestant worship services in all the churches in and around Zurich. Throughout the decade of the

1520s, the pace of Protestant Reformation in Zurich and other northern Swiss cities such as Berne and Basel increased so that by 1530 virtually all vestiges of Roman Catholicism had been abolished. The churches were stripped of statues, and the ministers changed vestments so that they wore robes like those found in university lecture halls rather than at Catholic altars. Veneration of saints and of Mary was banned as were indulgences, prayers for the dead (Zwingli denied purgatory) and many other traditional Catholic practices.

The process of purging the Swiss Reformed churches of traditional Roman Catholic practices went much further than Luther allowed in German Protestant churches. Someone has referred to Swiss Reformed churches as "four bare walls and a sermon." Lutheran churches, at least in Germany, retained many of the external trappings of the medieval Catholic heritage, including bishops, although these were seen by Luther as administrators rather than holders of special spiritual status.

To Luther, Zwingli and his followers were "fanatics" because they stripped the churches of all tradition and because they denied the efficacy of the two sacraments in strengthening faith. They also rejected the real presence of Christ's body in the Lord's Supper and reduced the ceremony to a meal of remembrance. To the Catholic hierarchy, Zwingli and the other Swiss Protestants under his tutelage were dangerous rebels. However, the independent cities where they pastored and taught protected them from Catholic forces. But Zwingli was not radical enough for some of his own followers, as we will see in the next chapter. Certain of Zwingli's followers in Zurich wanted to abolish infant baptism and accused the Reformer of not carrying out his reforming principles consistently. These Anabaptists, as they were called by their enemies, began refusing water baptism for their newborn infants and baptizing each other by immersion or pouring in Zurich in 1525. They also rejected Zwingli's acknowledgment of the city council's authority over church affairs as just another form of Constantinianism or caesaropapism and advocated total separation of church and state. Zwingli and the Zurich city council persecuted these radical Reformers by having them arrested and sometimes drowned in Swiss rivers.

Zwingli was a prolific writer as well as articulate preacher and debater. He held public disputations with Catholic opponents in Zurich and engaged in wars of pamphlets with Catholic, Anabaptist and Lutheran critics. He also wrote declarations of Reformed doctrine for the king of France and Emperor Charles V. His best-known theological works include *On the Providence of God* (1531), *On True and False Religion* (1525), *An Account of the Faith of Zwingli* (1530) and *A Short and Clear Exposition of the Christian Faith* (1531). There is no doubt that these and other essays and books by Zwingli profoundly influenced other Reformed theologians. *On True and False Religion* is generally considered the first Reformed dogmatics (systematic theology).[3] John Calvin borrowed heavily from Zwingli's works, and through Calvin as well as other Swiss Reformers, Zwingli left an indelible mark on the entire Reformed branch of Protestantism.

In 1531 tensions between the Protestant and Catholic cantons (counties) of Switzerland had mounted to the point of open conflict. The city of Zurich decided to go to war with five Catholic cantons to the south, and several of Zurich's ministers went into battle with the men of the city. The Second Kappel War lasted one day—October 11, 1531—and Zwingli was killed in the fighting along with several hundred Zuricher men and about two dozen Protestant preachers. Zurich survived as an independent state nevertheless, but southern Switzerland remained primarily Catholic and Protestantism was confined for the most part to northern and far western Switzerland. From there it spread into France (where it was later all but eradicated), southwestern Germany, cities along the Rhine River such as Strasbourg, Holland, Scotland and England. The Puritans of England and the New England colonies were followers of Zwingli's and Calvin's Reformed theology.

**Zwingli's Theology**

Like Luther, Zwingli strongly emphasized the Scripture principle—that the Bible is the ultimate authority for Christian faith and practice and stands entirely above all human traditions, which must be judged by it.[4] One slight difference between the German and the Swiss Reformers lies in their implicit doctrines of Scripture. Luther felt free to recognize a "canon within the canon" and to relegate portions of the Bible to secondary status when they did not "promote Christ" in the right way. Zwingli, on the other hand, virtually identified the entire Bible with God's Word. The Bible took on a special status in Zwingli and Reformed theology that Luther did not accord it. Luther very carefully distinguished between the book and the Word of God itself, which he equated with the gospel and with Jesus Christ. Zwingli tied them all together. At least for us the distinction is relatively unimportant. Christ and the gospel come to us only through the Bible, and therefore the Bible *is* God's Word to us. Zwingli recognized no canon within the canon and refused to elevate any portion of Scripture over any other. Like Luther, though, Zwingli emphasized that the power and clarity of Scripture come from the Holy Spirit. For both Reformers, as for Calvin later, the Word and the Spirit are bound inseparably together so that only by the Spirit of God is the Bible God's Word, and the Spirit speaks nothing outside of or against the Bible.

In spite of his strong appeal to the authority of Scripture, Zwingli also placed a positive value on philosophy in a way totally foreign to Luther's antiphilosophical method in theology. Zwingli was steeped in humanism and Greek thought. He was trained in Plato, Aristotle and Stoicism, and one of his favorite ancient writers and thinkers was the Roman poet and orator Seneca. Like the Alexandrian school of early Christianity, Zwingli believed that all truth is God's truth and that insofar as the Greek philosophers thought and spoke truth that is helpful to Christian theology, they are to be highly regarded and valued. No doubt this was a vestige of his Erasmian period of thinking. In his book *On Providence* Zwingli began with natural theology to establish the existence and nature of God as the all-determining reality ruling sovereignly over both nature and history. His first principle was heavily influenced by Greek thought, as was his method of reasoning deductively from it. Beginning with the concept of the supreme good (similar to Plato's form of the Good), Zwingli deduced that "Providence must exist, because the supreme good necessarily cares for and regulates all things,"[5] and through a carefully argued series of deductions, concluded that "Providence exists and must exist [and] it is clear that He not only knows all things, but regulates, orders and disposes all things."[6] Throughout the essay Zwingli wove together Greek philosophy, Christian natural theology (heavily influenced by Thomas Aquinas), Aristotelian logic, biblical theology and appeal to Christian tradition. The theology of Augustine was especially influential on Zwingli's doctrine of divine providence.

While Luther believed and taught that God is the all-determining reality, Zwingli placed the sovereignty of God in a special position within Christian theology. Luther treated God's sovereignty as a part of the gospel of grace, even though it was also influenced by his nominalism. Zwingli, and later Calvin, treated God's sovereignty as a first principle of Christian thought. That is not to say it appears first in his system of theology. Rather, it has a certain pride of place among all the doctrines as Reformed theology's central organizing theme—the hub that holds everything together. For Luther, that would be the doctrine of salvation (justification) by grace through faith alone. For Zwingli and Calvin and their Reformed colleagues, it became the doctrine of God's all-determining sovereignty and power.

On the basis of reason and Scripture, Zwingli arrived at the strongest conceivable doctrine of God's meticulous providential and sovereign rule over everything. If God is God, he argued, then absolutely nothing else can have any independent power or determination. Zwingli wrote in *On Providence,* "I defined Providence as the rule over and direction of all things in the universe. For if anything were guided by its own power or insight, just so far would the wisdom and power of our Deity be deficient."[7] God's providential rule is eternal and unchangeable, the cause of everything that happens, including both good and evil, and rules out anything as contingent, fortuitous or accidental. God and God alone is the "sole cause" over everything, and all other so-called causes are merely "instruments of the divine working."[8]

Zwingli carried his monergistic belief in God's relationship with the created order almost to a heretical conclusion. That is, he freely admitted that if no created being has any independent self-determination, then there is a sense in which everything is a manifestation of God. Some critics have accused Zwingli of falling into a kind of Stoic rationalism and pantheism.[9] At the very least he affirmed what may be called a theopanism—belief in God as the one actor and energy in everything. In *On Providence* he wrote of created powers, "This power is said to have been created, I say, because it is a manifestation of the general, all-embracing power in a new individual form. Moses, Paul, Plato, Seneca are witnesses."[10] Even the fall of Adam and Eve was foreordained and brought about by God's providential power "so that we might learn by the Fall and by erring what could not have been done by earnest striving and endeavor."[11]

For Zwingli, predestination was both a biblical doctrine and the only view of God's role in salvation consistent with the rationally deduced doctrine of providence. He thought that Thomas Aquinas and the entire medieval Catholic tradition based God's foreordination of people to heaven or hell on God's foreknowledge of their free decisions, and he rejected that most emphatically in favor of God's election and predestination as the basis of his foreknowledge. God *knows* because he *predetermines.* And Zwingli did not hesitate to affirm that those individuals who end up damned forever in hell are also eternally determined by God for that fate: "Thus election is attributed to those who are to be blessed, but those who are to be damned are not said to be elected, though the Divine Will makes a disposition with regard to them also, but he rejects, expels, and repudiates them, that they may become examples of His righteousness."[12] *Election* refers only to those foreordained to be saved and to their destiny in heaven. All others are not merely left to their freely chosen damnation, as later Reformed Christians would often say, but they also are predestined (but not elected) to their destiny in hell.

Zwingli averred that God is in no way "stained" by the sin and evil that the reprobate commit. Even though God directs a person to kill or commit adultery, for instance, God is in no way liable, for "the same deed which is done at the instigation and direction of God, brings honor to Him, while it is a crime and sin to man" and "although He impels men to some deed which is a wickedness unto the instrument that performs it, yet it is not such unto Himself."[13] Ultimately

Zwingli reasoned that God is not responsible or guilty for the sin and evil he himself plans and causes because "He is not under the law."[14] But he also argued that God brings something good out of every evil, and even the eternal suffering of the wicked manifests his righteousness and justice and is therefore a necessary part of God's overall good plan.

Zwingli agreed completely and wholeheartedly with Luther about salvation by grace through faith alone. He also defined faith in much the same way as Luther and rejected any idea that a person's right standing with God (justification) could be merited by works of any kind. Faith is a gift of God given to the elect and is the sole basis for the efficacy of grace. But Zwingli deviated from Luther (or Luther deviated from Zwingli) in two significant ways with regard to salvation. First, whereas Luther defined the law of God (for example, the Ten Commandments) negatively and contrasted it with the gospel, Zwingli taught that the law and the gospel are inseparable and complementary. For him, the law of God was the expression of God's will for righteous and holy living and therefore a guide for the Christian in knowing how best to please God. While Luther saw this as a subtle accommodation to works righteousness, Zwingli saw it as the only way to avoid antinomianism and know how best to serve God in gratitude. Reformed theology from Zwingli on tended to emphasize sanctification and the life of discipleship as one of obedience to God's revealed law in a way Luther did not. By no means, however, did Zwingli or Calvin mitigate the gospel of salvation by grace through faith alone by stressing the positive role of the law of God in the Christian's life. For them obedience to the law of God was simply a "sign of grace and gratitude" and not at all a condition or cause of the sinner's justification.

**Zwingli Versus Luther on the Sacraments**

The second soteriological difference between Zwingli and Luther revolved around the sacraments. Zwingli disliked the term *sacrament* because it connotes a material means of grace, and he believed that saving grace comes only to faith by the Holy Spirit. One of his favorite Scripture passages was John 6:63: "The flesh is of no avail." He interpreted this as meaning that material substances cannot convey spiritual blessing and especially that the bread and wine of the Lord's Supper cannot capture and communicate Christ's body and that even if they could it would serve no purpose. Only the Spirit feeds and strengthens the soul, and the only channel of the Holy Spirit to the soul is faith. Therefore, for Zwingli, the so-called sacraments of baptism and the Lord's Supper were symbolic ceremonies (later called "ordinances") rather than actual means of grace: "Sacraments are . . . signs or ceremonies . . . by which men offer themselves before the church as soldiers or disciples of Christ. The sacraments assure the church of a man's faith far more than they do the man himself. If faith is not real without a ceremonial act to certify it, it is not true faith. True faith rests unshakably, solidly, and wholly upon the mercy of God, as Paul repeatedly points out."[15]

A sacrament, or ordinance, is a sign or symbol of a divine reality. They exist for the church and proclaim and commemorate Christ's saving act and its effect upon the individual. They strengthen faith only in the sense that they bring to mind the gospel in a visible way as object lessons. But that does not mean they are dispensable. For Zwingli, we humans need such visible words and ceremonies to help us remember and proclaim Christ's work and our faith. In response to Catholic and Lutheran critics who claimed that he demeaned the sacraments, Zwingli replied, "But we venerate and cherish the sacraments as signs and symbols of sacred things, not as if they were themselves the things of which they are signs. For who can be so ignorant as to say that a sign is the thing it signifies?"[16] Zwingli believed that the Holy Spirit is actually present in a special way in and through the ceremonies of baptism and the Lord's Supper, but the Spirit's presence is on account of the faith of the person receiving the ordinance and because of the church's faith. No faith and certainly no saving grace or forgiveness are tied to the ceremonies themselves. "With an anti-Lutheran and anti-Catholic thrust, he [Zwingli] denied their grace-imparting power."[17]

Zwingli equated baptism with circumcision in the old covenant of God's relationship with Israel. It is the new covenant ceremony of initiation into the people of God. In Zwingli's Reformed theology, infants of Christian parents are simply assumed to be "in the covenant" with God as part of God's elect people the church. Election by God precedes faith; faith is a gift imparted by God to the elect. Baptism is simply the sign and seal—like circumcision—of election and inclusion. It does not save or strengthen faith or impart grace. Zwingli radically rejected any hint of baptismal regeneration. On the other hand, he also radically rejected what he called "rebaptism" practiced by the Anabaptists. Zwingli explained his view in *An Account of the Faith of Zwingli*, which he submitted to the emperor Charles V in preparation for the Diet (Parliament) of Augsburg in 1530:

> The sacraments are given as a public testimony of that grace which is previously present to every individual. Thus baptism is administered in the presence of the Church to one who before receiving it either confessed the religion of Christ or has the word of promise, whereby he is known to belong to the Church. Hence it is that when we baptize an adult we ask him whether he believes. And only when he answers "yes," then he receives baptism. Faith,

> therefore, has been present before he receives baptism, and is not given by baptism. But when an infant is offered, the question is asked whether its parents offer it for baptism. When they have answered through witnesses that they wish it baptized, then the infant is baptized. Here the promise of God precedes, that He regards our infants, no less than those of the Hebrews, as belonging to the Church. For when members of the Church offer it, the infant is baptized under the law that, since it has been born of Christians, it is regarded by the divine promise among the members of the Church. By baptism, therefore, the Church publicly receives one who has previously been received through grace. Hence baptism does not convey grace but the Church certifies that grace has been given to him to whom it is administered.[18]

It hardly needs to be stated that Zwingli did not believe that infants are born guilty of Adam's sin. For him, original sin is an inherited disease of corruption, depravity and death. It does not carry guilt with it because Christ's death on the cross wiped out the guilt of Adam's sin for all his posterity. Inherited sin is slavery but not guilt. It includes such a strong tendency toward actual sin that guilt is inevitable for those who grow and mature to an age of accountability, but infants who die outside the covenant (unbaptized) before the age of moral accountability should not be assumed to be under condemnation.[19] They are simply in God's hands and we should not presume to know their fate or destiny. If they are elect, they will be saved. Baptized children may all be assumed to be saved even though they will need to confirm their election for themselves at the age of conscience by public confession of faith.

Zwingli also disagreed strongly with both Luther and the Roman Catholic tradition about the Lord's Supper. Together with Luther he rejected transubstantiation and the theory that the Eucharist conveys grace *ex opere operato*. He also denied that it is a resacrificing of Christ. Against Luther, however, he argued that Christ's resurrected and glorified human body is localized in heaven and is *not* omnipresent. Therefore, Zwingli concluded, there is no real presence of Christ's body in, with or under the elements of bread and wine in the meal. Luther's first error, Zwingli claimed, was believing that any external thing—whether water in baptism or bread in Eucharist—can actually convey grace or faith. "The flesh is of no avail." Furthermore, Zwingli averred, Luther erred by teaching that Christ's body is in the sacrament. For the Swiss Reformer the two Lutheran claims amount to idolatry and christological heresy. The humanity of Christ means that his body—although raised and glorified—is *not* omnipresent. An omnipresent body would be divine and not human. Zwingli saw in Luther's teaching about Christ's bodily omnipresence more than a hint of the old heresy of Eutychianism. Of course, Luther saw in Zwingli's teaching about Christ's "localized body" in heaven more than a hint of the old heresy of Nestorianism, for Zwingli was willing to acknowledge Christ's divine nature as omnipresent. Only his human nature—tied to a body—is localized in heaven.[20]

For Zwingli the Lord's Supper is a memorial meal in which the body of Christ on earth—the church—remembers and proclaims his death. As baptism is for the church as much or more than it is for the recipient, so the Lord's Supper is for the church. In it Christians do "eat Christ," but only spiritually, not physically:

> To eat the body of Christ spiritually is nothing else than to trust in spirit and heart upon the mercy and goodness of God through Christ, that is, to be sure with unshaken faith that God is going to give us pardon for our sins and the joy of everlasting blessedness on account of His Son, who was made wholly ours, was offered for us, and reconciled the divine righteousness to us.[21]

Why is this sacramental meal necessary, according to Zwingli? "Because each Christian must make it clear to other Christians that he is a member of the body of Christ and each Christian must know that the others are members of the body, too."[22] Zwingli's view of the Lord's Supper as a memorial meal and of the elements of bread and wine as symbols was later modified by most of the Reformed churches. They adopted Calvin's mediating view of the sacrament, which was meant to take the best and omit the worst from both Zwingli and Luther. The Zwinglian view of the Lord's Supper became the standard view among Anabaptists and later among Baptists and other free-church Protestants in England and North America.

This brief sketch of Zwingli's role in the story of Christian theology hardly does him justice. It only points out some of the distinctive notes of his theology and indicates his historical role as the founder of the Reformed tradition of Protestantism. In the main he agreed with Luther. Their deep and corrosive disagreement over the Lord's Supper remains one of the most unfortunate and divisive episodes of the entire Protestant Reformation. Zwingli has largely been overshadowed by the other two great magisterial Reformers of European Protestantism, Luther and Calvin. *Calvinism* is a widely used label for Reformed theology. It could just as well be called *Zwinglianism,* except that by odd exigencies of history that label has come to be used almost exclusively for agreement with the Zurich Reformer's view of the Lord's Supper. Ironically, even Free Will Baptists, who reject Zwingli's Reformed theology of providence, predestination and infant baptism, are called Zwinglian simply because they agree with his doctrine of the Lord's Supper! It is time that Zwingli's important role in the history of Christian theology is rediscovered and highlighted more than has been the case for hundreds of years. Although he was not inclined to acknowledge his debt to Zwingli, John Calvin was his disciple in many ways (through the influence of Zwingli's successor Heinrich Bullinger on Calvin) and hardly contributed anything to theology that cannot be found earlier in Zwingli's own works.

**John Calvin's Life and Reforming Career**

John Calvin was born near Noyon, France, on July 10, 1509. He died in Geneva, Switzerland, on May 27, 1564. In Geneva, an independent republic that later became part of Switzerland, Calvin virtually ruled as "chief pastor"; the French Protestant Reformer established the Genevan Academy to which Protestants flocked from all over Europe. Throughout the times of Protestant persecutions in Scotland and England, the seminary in Geneva attracted future Reformers such as John Knox (1514-1572), who succeeded in turning Scotland into a nation modeled after the Swiss city. It was Knox who proclaimed Geneva and its academy under Calvin and his successor, Theodore Beza, "the most perfect school of Christ since the days of the apostles." Through men like Knox, Calvinism became a synonym for Reformed theology in English-speaking lands. The Puritans of England and New England considered themselves Calvinists, as did the Reformed "divines" (preachers) of Holland, even though their theologies and spiritualities took on their own distinctive flavors. For better or worse, Calvinism became the common label for Reformed theology in the English-speaking world. That is not in any way to belittle John Calvin's role in the Protestant Reformation and its theology, but only to say that it is perhaps not as great in fact as in popular conception. Certainly *Reformed* and *Calvinist* are not identical terms. But Calvin did become the great hero of most Reformed theologians after him.

Almost certainly Calvin's great reputation is due to his personal passion and leadership and his magnificent systematic mind as it is expressed in his magnum opus, *Institutes of the Christian Religion,* published in several editions over his lifetime. It became *the* textbook for Reformed theology for centuries and is still published, analyzed, interpreted and debated. Calvin also wrote numerous commentaries on biblical books as well as sermons for all occasions and letters to other Reformers on almost every conceivable subject. Beyond theology his influence on politics, economics and social ethics has been profound in Protestant cultures and especially those like Holland and Scotland where his theology dominated a national church.

As a young student in Orléans and Paris, Calvin studied law, philosophy and theology. He came into contact with humanists and Lutherans and converted to Protestant thought sometime around 1530. When persecution broke out against Protestants in Paris, Calvin fled to Basel, Switzerland, which was in the process of becoming a Reformed city like Zurich. There Calvin wrote the first edition of his *Institutes,* which was published in 1536. He was only twenty-five years old and yet had "not only given genuine dogmatic form to the cardinal doctrines of the Reformation: he had molded those doctrines into one of the classic presentations of the Christian faith."[23] The book was almost immediately recognized by friends and foes of the Protestant Reformation as the work of a young genius destined to become one of the movement's leading lights.

In 1537 Calvin attempted to travel to Strasbourg, one of the leading Protestant cities of Europe, to study with Martin Bucer. Because of war, the most direct route had been blocked, and so the young Frenchman went by way of Geneva, a city that had become Protestant and a republic less than a year earlier. Calvin planned to stay there only one night, but a leading Protestant named Guillaume Farel came to him and begged him to stay and help complete the Reformation of the city. Later Calvin remembered,

> After learning that my heart was set upon devoting myself to private studies, for which I wished to keep myself free from other pursuits, and finding that he gained nothing by entreaties, he [Farel] proceeded to utter the imprecation that God would curse my retirement and the tranquillity of the studies which I sought, if I should withdraw and refuse to help, when the necessity was so urgent. By this imprecation I was so terror-struck, that I gave up the journey I had undertaken.[24]

To shorten a very long and complex story, Calvin remained in Geneva the rest of his life, apart from one brief hiatus during which he lived and studied in Strasbourg. During his time in Geneva, he served officially only as its chief pastor. In fact, he reigned as virtual dictator of the city. He was its prophet, and the city council and leading citizens for the most part feared and respected the self-styled "servant of Geneva" so much that they usually obeyed his commands.

Calvin's Geneva was to be a "godly city"—a theocratic republic that modeled on earth God's kingdom in heaven. At least that was Calvin's ideal and goal for Geneva. Many individuals and factions within the city resisted his authoritarian discipline, but Calvin repeatedly won in confrontations with them and managed to get his way by threatening to leave if the city council did not support him. A strict lifestyle based on biblical law was imposed on the city, and offenders were severely punished and sometimes banished for loud partying or for openly criticizing Calvin. At least one heretic was burned at the stake in Geneva in 1553. Michael Servetus had been warned to stay away from the city by Calvin himself, but he had dared to come and sit in the church, listening to Calvin preach. Calvin wanted him beheaded as a more merciful punishment for his blatant denial of the Trinity, but the city council chose to burn him instead. Calvin did not always get his way in the small matters, but his grip on the principles and beliefs by which the church and the city were run was firm.

### Calvin's Theology

Calvin's theology built on and borrowed heavily from both Luther and Zwingli as well as the Strasbourg Reformer Bucer. Calvin rejected natural theology in favor of God's Word as the surest path to knowledge of God and elevated Scripture, inspired and illuminated by the Holy Spirit, as the sole supreme authority for Christian faith and practice. Although God is adequately revealed in nature and in his Word, sin has so blinded humans that they cannot gain a true knowledge of God apart from a special illumination of the Holy Spirit that Calvin called the inner testimony of the Spirit, which is given only to the elect when they are regenerated (born again). Calvin based his doctrinal arguments and beliefs entirely on Scripture and seldom appealed to philosophy or Christian tradition as absolute authorities, because both err frequently in matters pertaining to God and salvation.

Calvin's doctrine of God is thoroughly Augustinian, which he considered thoroughly biblical. Like Augustine, Luther and Zwingli, he viewed God as the all-determining reality and taught God's meticulous providence over nature and history. Sometimes Calvin referred certain events in history to God's "permission," but overall he saw God as the ultimate cause of everything and taught that absolutely nothing happens or can happen apart from God's determination "by his decree." Like Zwingli, Calvin denied the reality of contingency; nothing happens by accident. Nor does God merely foresee or foreknow what is going to happen in the future. Rather, "God by the bridle of his providence turns every event whatever way he wills,"[25] and "what for us seems a contingency, faith recognizes to have been a secret impulse from God."[26] Does this mean that even the fall of Adam and Eve was foreordained by God? Calvin denied any real distinction between God's will and his permission, such as some scholastic theologians posited. Rather he affirmed, "The first man fell because the Lord had judged it to be expedient; why he so judged is hidden from us. Yet it is certain that he so judged because he saw that thereby the glory of his name is duly revealed."[27] For Calvin, everything that happens redounds to God's glory, even if we humans cannot see how, and God's glory is the purpose why everything happens, even if we are unable to reconcile it with love, mercy or justice.

Even though belief in double predestination is often simply called Calvinism and many people have thought it to be the central organizing principle of Calvin's theology and his greatest contribution, "on closer examination, one is impressed with the unoriginality of Calvin's doctrine of election. His teaching on this subject is in all essentials identical to what we have already observed in Luther and Zwingli."[28] Calvin affirmed that in both Scripture and Christian tradition "God is said to have ordained from eternity those whom he wills to embrace in love, and those upon whom he wills to vent his wrath."[29] He acknowledged an apparent conflict between this doctrine and 1 Timothy 2:3-4 and 2 Peter 3:9, both of which suggest a universal will of God for salvation. Calvin's solution was to posit a dual will of God—one revealed and one secret. God's revealed will offers mercy and pardon to all who repent and believe. God's secret will foreordains some to eternal damnation and render it certain that they will sin and never repent. Calvin had no patience with those who objected to this doctrine of two wills and double predestination as unjust and declared, "For as Augustine truly contends, they who measure divine justice by the standard of human justice are acting perversely."[30]

Many critics of monergism raise the objection that if God has foreordained and brought about humanity's Fall and an individual's reprobation (sin and eternal damnation), how can the reprobate be held responsible and God not held responsible for sin? Where is the justice in that? One anti-Calvinist wag produced a bit of doggerel about a famous sixteenth-century Dutch Calvinist named Franciscus Gomarus, who taught that supralapsarianism—a particularly extreme form of Calvinism—is the true form of Christian monergism:

> Franciscus Gomarus was a supralapsarius;
> He actually gave Adam an excuse.
> God had decreed, foreordained Adam's deed.
> God had precooked Adam's goose!

Calvin attempted to answer such objections against double predestination—objections that he called "wicked excuses." "But I admit," he wrote, "this cannot be so done that impiety will not always growl and mutter." His definitive answer in the *Institutes of the Christian Religion* is that "even though by God's eternal providence man has been created to undergo that calamity to which he is subject [the Fall, sin, death], it still takes its occasion from man himself, not from God, since the only reason for his ruin is that he has degenerated from God's pure creation into vicious and impure perversity."[31] Calvin's opponents and critics can hardly be blamed if they are not persuaded by this answer. It appears to contain a sheer logical contradiction in light of Calvin's clear rejection of any distinction between divine will and divine permission.

One area of doctrine where Calvin diverged from both Luther and Zwingli was the Lord's Supper. While agreeing with Zwingli about baptism, he disagreed with the Zurich theologian about the Lord's Supper as a memorial meal lacking any real bodily presence of Christ. Yet Calvin vehemently rejected the Catholic doctrine of transubstantiation and Luther's consubstantiation version of real presence. As with his doctrine of predestination and human responsibility for sin, Calvin's teaching about the Lord's Supper appears contradictory. With Zwingli and against Luther he affirmed a spatial limitation of Christ's body in heaven and denied the omnipresence or ubiquity of Christ's humanity: "For as we do not doubt that Christ's body is limited by the general characteristics common to all human bodies, and is contained in heaven (where it was once for all received) until Christ return in judgment, . . . so we deem it utterly unlawful to draw it back under these corruptible elements or to imagine it to be present everywhere."[32] However, against Zwingli and with Luther, Calvin affirmed a real presence of Christ *bodily* in the sacrament of the Lord's Supper: "For why should the Lord put in your hand the symbol of his body, except to assure you of a true participation in it? But if it is true that a visible sign is given us to seal the gift of a thing invisible, when we have received the symbol of the body, let us no less surely trust that the body itself is also given to us."[33]

Calvin wanted to have Christ's body in heaven and eat it in the sacramental meal too! His solution to this apparent contradiction was that the Holy Spirit mystically and spiritually draws together the body of Jesus Christ and the faithful believer through the symbols of bread and wine in the Lord's Supper: "For us the manner [of real presence] is spiritual because the secret power of the Spirit is the bond of our union with Christ."[34] What Calvin denied is much clearer than what he affirmed. He rejected both Luther's view and Zwingli's view. His own view was that the Lord's Supper is a sacrament of real presence that strengthens believers' faith when they participate in it with faith and that it effects a stronger union of the believer with Christ through the Holy Spirit.

Largely due to the influence of John Calvin, Reformed theology has profoundly affected Protestantism in Western Europe and North America and, through missionary movements, around the world. Presbyterianism is simply Scottish Calvinism which takes its name from the form of church government favored by Calvin and brought to Scotland by John Knox. Swiss, French and Dutch Reformed churches have greatly influenced all areas of life in Europe, as well as South Africa and North America. The Puritans of England sought to establish a godly commonwealth modeled after Calvin's Geneva in the New World, and both American Presbyterianism and Congregationalism adopted forms of Calvinist theology. When the earliest Baptist congregations emerged out of Puritan Congregationalism in England and North America, many of them declared themselves "Particular Baptists," meaning that they believed in and taught "particular election"—a form of double predestination. All of these Protestant traditions looked back to Calvin more than to Zwingli or any other Protestant Reformer, even though to a large extent all Calvin did was mediate Zwingli's Reformed theology to the rest of the world.

# CHAPTER 26

# Anabaptists Go Back to the Roots of Christianity

---

T*he entire collection of Protestant Reformers and their followers in the* sixteenth century may be divided into two major categories: the Magisterial Reformation and the Radical Reformation. *Radical* simply means "going back to the roots," and of course, all of the Protestants intended to recover the true New Testament gospel from the layers of medieval tradition that they saw surrounding and burying it. Yet one diverse group of Protestant Reformers were more radical than the rest and they have come to be lumped together as "the Radical Reformation" or simply "radical Protestants" because of their common characteristics.[1]

The main magisterial Reformers included Luther, Zwingli, Calvin and Thomas Cranmer, the leading Protestant Reformer of England and architect of the post-Catholic Church of England. Their associates and followers in various European cities and countries constituted the magisterial Reformation because they all intended to establish one true Christian church and commonwealth in their countries with the support of *magistrates*—a general term for secular authorities such as princes, judges and city council members. The magisterial Reformers envisioned some form of cooperation between church and state and sought to drive out of their territories all Romanists (Roman Catholics) and heretics. For the most part these magisterial Protestants, whether Lutheran, Reformed or

Anglican, recognized a relative authority of the earliest creeds of Christendom, insisted on infant baptism, allowed only one legal form of Christianity in their territories and advocated the power of the secular authorities to wage war and persecute religious nonconformists.

**The Radical Reformation and Anabaptists**

The Radical Reformation includes all those Protestants of sixteenth-century Europe who believed in the principle of separation of church and state, renounced coercion in matters of religious belief, rejected infant baptism in favor of believers' baptism or Spirit baptism, and emphasized the experience of regeneration (being "born again") by the Spirit of God over forensic justification. They eschewed Christian magistrates and often sought to live apart from the rest of society as much as possible. Some founded Christian communes. Most embraced Christian pacifism and simple lifestyles. Some rejected formal theological training and professional clergy. All emphasized practical Christian living more than creeds and confessions of doctrinal belief.

Needless to say, the radical Protestants were the "Protestants of Protestantism." They protested what they saw as the halfway measures taken by Luther and the other magisterial Reformers in purifying the church of Roman Catholic elements. Their ideal was to restore the New Testament church as a persecuted remnant as it was in the Roman Empire before Constantine. To them, the magisterial Reformers were all stuck in Constantinianism and Augustinianism. These were the two main diseases of medieval Christianity that the radical Reformers wished to eradicate from their own independent and autonomous congregations, if not from Christianity itself.

The Radical Reformation includes three distinct subgroups: Anabaptists, spirituals (or spiritualists) and anti-trinitarian rationalists. The latter group, which included Michael Servetus, who was burned at the stake in Calvin's Geneva, was composed mainly of individuals and small groups who for the most part had to worship and teach in secret. They later emerged in organized form in late eighteenth-century England and New England as the Unitarians. The spirituals included people like Caspar Schwenkfeld (1489-1561), who taught a mystical form of Protestant Christianity that emphasized the "inner light" of God's Spirit within everyone. The English Quaker movement emerged as an organized form of this spiritual radical Protestantism in the eighteenth century.

The largest and most influential group of radical Reformers were the Anabaptists, and they left the most significant mark on Christian theology through leaders like Balthasar Hubmaier and Menno Simons. Beginning under Zwingli in Zurich in 1525, they called themselves "Swiss Brethren" and later spread throughout Europe. One group of Anabaptists became known as Mennonites after their founder, Menno Simons, and another group formed communistic colonies known as Hutterites after their leader, Jacob Hutter. The main groups of Anabaptists in the modern world are the various Mennonites, Amish and Hutterite colonies and the Churches of the Brethren. In varying degrees they all seek to continue the unique theological and practical distinctives of their sixteenth-century founders.

Because the Anabaptists were the most influential of all the radical Reformers on Christian theology, we will focus exclusively on their story. Two Anabaptist thinkers of the Reformation period stand out as particularly creative and influential: Balthasar Hubmaier and Menno Simons. Each left his unique mark on Anabaptist life and thought as well as indirectly on the entire free-church tradition that rejected official state churches in favor of separation of church and state.

Before examining the theology of Anabaptism, it will be helpful to explain the beginning of the movement.[2] According to Anabaptist historian William R. Estep, "the most revolutionary act of the Reformation" took place in Zurich on January 21, 1525.[3] A former Catholic priest turned Protestant named George Blaurock met secretly with other radical followers of Zwingli. They were dissatisfied with the slow, cautious pace of reform in Zurich. Two of Zwingli's bright young followers named Felix Manz and Conrad Grebel were among them. After careful thought and prayer, they decided to baptize one another. While that may not seem a particularly courageous thing to do now, at the time it was. Refusing infants baptism and rebaptizing persons was illegal because it was considered both heretical and seditious. These Brethren, as they called themselves, had all experienced life-changing conversions and after careful study of the New Testament had come to believe that infant baptism is not true baptism because it precedes repentance and faith. Zwingli had refused their efforts to abolish it and the Zurich city council had threatened them with punishment if they acted on their beliefs. The first to be baptized by pouring was Blaurock. He was the first true Anabaptist. Afterward he baptized Grebel and Manz.

"With the birth of Anabaptism a new and dynamic religious movement found expression in Europe."[4] The young radicals went around the countryside and towns of northern Switzerland and southern Germany preaching the necessity of repentance and personal faith *before* baptism and "rebaptizing" hundreds of Catholics and Protestants. "The Brethren emphasized the absolute necessity of a personal commitment to Christ as essential to salvation and a prerequisite to baptism."[5] In the town of Waldshut, Balthasar Hubmaier's entire Protestant congregation underwent believers' baptism after confessing their faith publicly.

Back in Zurich, Zwingli and the city council passed laws against the Anabaptists and urged the civil authorities throughout Europe to hunt them down and arrest them. Felix Manz, Zwingli's onetime star pupil and protégé, was the first Anabaptist martyr. He was arrested and taken to Zurich for trial. Zwingli consented to the sentence: drowning. This so-called third baptism became the punishment of choice for Anabaptists among both Catholics and Protestants. On January 5, 1527, Manz, the leader of the budding Swiss Brethren movement, was bound and thrown into the Limmat River in the center of Zurich. During the next few years, thousands of Anabaptists were hunted down by the special police known as *Täuferjäger* (Anabaptist-hunters), and many, including women, were executed. Children of Anabaptists were taken away and given to families of officially recognized church bodies.

The Anabaptists were viewed by authorities of church and state as dangerous rebels as well as heretics.[6] A few fanatics among them did take over the German city of Münster in 1534. Although most Anabaptists were pacifists and had nothing to do with the Münster Rebellion, all were blamed for it. Furthermore, refusing to baptize infants or even encouraging others not to baptize their newborn children was considered a form of child abuse at a time when a child's spiritual well-being was considered just as important as his or her physical well-being. The Anabaptists' separation from the state churches and their frequent sermons against them were viewed with suspicion by magisterial Protestants and Roman Catholics, who believed that church and state must work hand in hand. The whole idea of freedom of conscience and dissent was viewed as a dangerous novelty that could only lead to anarchy. At least that is how the guardians of the national churches viewed the matter. Besides, many of the Anabaptists were fairly confrontational in their methods of winning converts and defiant of what they considered apostate religious and civil authorities. George Blaurock was not untypical. Before being arrested and burned at the stake in 1529, he made a habit of interrupting Reformed church services in Switzerland in order to proclaim the gospel of personal repentance, conversion and subsequent baptism.

Because of the widespread persecution against them, and because most of their leaders did not live very long, the Anabaptist Brethren produced little in the way of formal theology. Besides, they were for the most part uninterested in dogmatic theology and philosophical speculation. The earliest Anabaptists simply took the great doctrines of Christianity for granted and saw little need to explore or defend them further. They believed in the Trinity and humanity and divinity of Jesus Christ. With Luther and Zwingli and other Protestants, they accepted salvation by grace through faith alone, the final authority of Scripture and the priesthood of all believers. They just did not think the magisterial Protestants went far enough with these Protestant principles in practice and they saw them as mired in Constantinianism and Augustinianism. In their minds the mainline Protestant Reformers were not reformed enough. Most of the Anabaptists' writings focused on defending believers' baptism and freedom of conscience from coercion. They often wrote sermons and hymns that emphasized personal decision and discipleship, and their essays and letters were mostly directed toward reconstituting the church along New Testament lines apart from official sanction from governments. No Anabaptist leader of the first generation produced a comprehensive system of theology or doctrine. Only much later did they have the leisure or freedom to do that.

**Balthasar Hubmaier's Life and Reforming Career**

Perhaps the greatest intellect of the early Anabaptist movement was the pastor of Waldshut who led his entire congregation in believers' baptism after conversion. His name was Balthasar Hubmaier and he was born in 1481. He was burned at the stake in Vienna in 1528. Three days later his wife was drowned in the Danube River. Hubmaier was considered especially radical and dangerous by religious and civil authorities throughout Europe because he had been a noted Catholic scholar before becoming a Protestant and then joining the Brethren. In 1515 he had been appointed vice-rector of the University of Ingolstadt in Germany. In 1516 he became priest of the cathedral of Regensburg, an important city of Bavaria in southern Germany. Through his teaching, preaching and scholarly writing, Hubmaier became one of Europe's best-known Catholic leaders at a time when Luther was beginning his reforming work in northern Germany. In 1522 Hubmaier converted to Protestantism and was forced out of his position at Regensburg. He took the pastorate of a small Reformed congregation at Waldshut near Zurich in Switzerland and participated in the reforms taking place under Zwingli. Protestants throughout Europe regarded his conversion to their cause as a great coup.

In early 1525 Hubmaier began to preach and publish his opposition to infant baptism. Exactly what or who influenced him in this regard is unclear, but probably he had been communicating with Zwingli's radical young followers who formed the core of the Swiss Brethren movement of Anabaptists. Hubmaier's Waldshut church became the first Anabaptist congregation when on Easter Sunday in April, 1525, he baptized three hundred adults out of a milk pail. (Most Anabaptists baptized by effusion—pouring—rather than immersion.) In May Zwingli published an attack against the Anabaptists, and Hubmaier responded with the first Anabaptist treatise, titled *The Christian Baptism of Believers.* After that, Zwingli and Hubmaier engaged in a pamphlet war. When the emperor's police came to Waldshut looking for Hubmaier, he fled to Zurich and engaged in a public debate with Zwingli, who then had him arrested and tortured. "While stretched on the rack, he [Hubmaier] uttered the required recantation and afterwards committed it to writing as demanded by Zwingli."[7] He was then allowed to leave Zurich and he settled in the Moravian city of Nikolsburg, where Anabaptists and other dissenters enjoyed limited freedom. There Hubmaier engaged in extensive ministry and baptized at least six thousand persons, including members of the ruling family. Eventually, however, the emperor's *Täuferjäger* captured him and took him to Vienna for trial and execution.

Hubmaier agreed heartily with the leading magisterial Reformers over against the prevailing theology and practices of the Roman Catholic Church, but he very strongly believed that Luther and Zwingli had not broken free of the debilitating diseases of Constantinianism and Augustinianism. While he did not actually use those labels in his writings, it is clear that these were the syndromes he opposed. Under their continuing influence, even the magisterial Protestant churches of Europe were not true New Testament "believers' churches" but state churches dominated by secular authorities in which it was impossible to distinguish between genuine and false believers because everyone has been baptized at birth. Church and society are coextensive in that model of Christendom, and this is what Hubmaier and all Anabaptists opposed. The church is to be the *ekklesia* of God—the "called out ones" who stand apart and are set aside from the rest of society by faith and discipleship.

Without rejecting the authority of secular government, Hubmaier harshly criticized its coercion of conscience and enforcement of beliefs and condemned the burning of heretics. He also criticized those Protestant leaders like Zwingli who turned dissenters over to magistrates for torture and execution. Referring to both Catholic and Protestant heretic-hunters *(Ketzermeister)*, Hubmaier wrote that "the inquisitors are the greatest heretics of all, because counter to the teaching and example of Jesus they condemn heretics to fire. . . . For Christ did not come to slaughter, kill, burn, but so that those who live should live yet more abundantly."[8] He urged especially religious authorities to use only the weapon of God's Word against those they perceive as heretics and to hope and pray for their repentance rather than kill them.

These sentiments seem commonplace to many modern Western people, but in the early sixteenth century, they were considered radical and even dangerous. Hubmaier was constantly accused by his enemies of wanting to abolish all government—something he denied. Indeed, his writings show that he urged respect for and obedience to princes and magistrates so long as they did not require Christians to go against God's Word. On the other hand, it is also clear that he did not believe official ties between churches and governments were legitimate because they were nowhere sanctioned by Jesus or the apostles.

**Hubmaier's Theology**

Hubmaier's anti-Augustinian attitudes manifest in his views on salvation and the sacraments. He explicitly blamed Augustine for a thousand years of Christian failure to regard biblical truth about these matters.[9] Against Luther's and Zwingli's monergistic views of salvation, Hubmaier sided with Erasmus in affirming free will and synergism. Against their views of baptism, he sided with the Zurich radicals Grebel and Manz. With regard to the Lord's Supper, he sided entirely with Zwingli over against Luther. At the heart of Hubmaier's theology lies one overriding concern that governs everything else: individual conversion. Again, he did not use that phrase, but it is a fitting label for his conviction about the necessary beginning of the Christian life. Throughout his writings—especially about baptism—Hubmaier presupposed that faith is a free decision to believe the gospel and trust in Jesus Christ and his grace alone for salvation.[10] It involves hearing God's Word, becoming convicted of sin, believing the gospel of Christ, confessing sinfulness and repenting, trusting in Christ alone for salvation, committing to live according to Christ's commands, being baptized in water ("external baptism"), and participating in the life of the church, including the Lord's Supper. In and through this experience, Hubmaier said, God gives the gifts of forgiveness and the Holy Spirit ("internal baptism"), and that is what makes a person a Christian. Only truly converted persons—"believers"—should be members of Christian congregations.

According to Hubmaier, the New Testament order of salvation requires that "where these things proceed correctly, faith must precede baptism" or else people assume that they are true believers merely because they have been baptized as infants. According to the New Testament pattern, he argued, "no one should be baptized with water unless beforehand he confesses faith and knows how he stands with God."[11] Speaking for all Anabaptists, he wrote, "Thus we confess openly that we were not baptized in childhood"[12] and "infant baptism is a trick which is invented and introduced by human beings."[13] According to Hubmaier, baptism is simply a public testimony of previous conversion and regeneration by God's Spirit and must follow them or else it is not genuine baptism at all. That is why he and other Anabaptists rejected the term *rebaptism* for their practice of baptizing mature believers who had been "washed" as infants. For them that practice was not rebaptism but the first genuine baptism. Although in his debates with Zwingli and his various treatises on the subject of baptism, Hubmaier presented detailed interpretations of all pertinent biblical passages, his opposition to infant baptism rested ultimately upon his vision of true Christian initiation. One simply does not become a Christian on the basis of birth in a Christian family or because of the faith of parents or the church. Nor can an infant have faith in the full and true sense of personal repentance and confession of trust in Christ alone.

In the year of his death Hubmaier composed *A Christian Catechism* for Anabaptists, and in it he laid out the persecuted movement's basic beliefs, including three kinds of baptism: Spirit baptism, water baptism, and baptism of blood.[14] Spirit baptism comes first and is "an inner illumination of our hearts that takes place by the Holy Spirit, through the living Word of God." The overall context of Hubmaier's theology makes clear that in this he included conversion and regeneration on the basis of repentance and faith. It is the "internal baptism" and absolutely must come first. Water baptism "is an outward and public testimony of the inner baptism in the Spirit, which a person gives by receiving water, with which one confesses one's sins before all people." This is the ceremony by which a new believer enters into the fellowship of the church and pledges to live life for Christ. Finally, the baptism of blood "is a daily mortification of the flesh until death" (sanctification). The second baptism—water baptism—is the bridge between the first and the third baptisms. It is not a sacrament, nor does it convey a gift of faith or grace. Yet it is necessary because Christ commanded it as outward testimony and pledge and the church needs it to know who properly belongs within its fellowship and who does not.

If anything is clear in Hubmaier's theology it is his passionate belief—more presupposed that explicitly stated—that authentic Christian life begins with a free decision made by the individual in response to God's gracious act in Jesus Christ. Such a free and personal response of the will cannot happen within an infant. It involves belief, sorrow, trust and commitment. Although infants are born innocent of sin because of Christ's restoration of fallen human nature by his life, death and resurrection, no one can know whether they will grow up to become true believers or not. Hubmaier likened infant baptism to an inn hanging out a sign announcing its fine wine before the growing season. It is presumptuous. Of course, Luther and Zwingli both defended infant baptism on the ground that faith is a gift of God and not a contingent, free decision. Their monergistic views of salvation form at least part of their foundations for the practice. Hubmaier eventually came to reject Augustinian monergism, including predestination, in favor of Erasmian synergism, including free will. In his first essay, *Freedom of the Will,* he wrote, "Now the human being can also help himself through the power of the Word or he can willfully neglect [it]; that is up to him. Therefore, one says: God has created you without your help, but without your help he will not save you."[15]

Hubmaier's defense of free will follows Erasmus's in *On the Freedom of the Will* very closely except that the Anabaptist Reformer attributed human free will to Christ's and the Holy Spirit's action rather than to a natural capacity that survives the Fall into sin. According to Hubmaier, by sinning Adam and Eve and all their posterity lost free will and fell into bondage to sin: "If now God the heavenly Father had not come to our help with a new and special grace through Jesus Christ, his most beloved Son, our Lord, we would all have to remain in this blindness, die and be eternally lost."[16] God's revealed will for universal salvation is clear in Scripture, however, and "he . . . sends to all people his Word and after that gives them the power, freedom, and choice so that they can accept or reject the same."[17] What Hubmaier was proclaiming as the basis of free will is what other theologians call prevenient grace—the resistible grace of God that calls, convicts and enables. Hubmaier also claimed that God's election and predestination are based entirely on his foreknowledge of which individuals will respond to grace and how. He was adamantly opposed to unconditional predestination—the monergism of Augustine, Luther, Zwingli and Calvin: "That would be a perfidious God who would invite all people to a supper, offer his mercy to everyone with exalted earnestness, and would yet not want them to come, Luke 14:16ff; Matt. 22:2ff. That would be a false God who would say with the mouth, 'Come here,' but would think secretly in the heart, 'Stay there.' "[18]

Not only was Hubmaier the first Anabaptist theologian; he was also the first evangelical synergist. That is, he was the first Protestant thinker openly to espouse belief in free will on the basis of a work of God in Christ and through the Holy Spirit. Free will, destroyed by the Fall, is restored by Christ and by the Spirit of God working through the Word of God. Only because they have free will are people rightly held responsible by God and by the church for their decisions and actions. But whatever they do, they cannot boast because any right decision they make or good action they take is enabled only by grace and is not a product of some innate goodness of nature or character. This is basically the same theology of salvation that the Dutch Remonstrants—followers of Jacob Arminius—later developed in the early seventeenth century. Hubmaier, then, was an "Arminian before Arminius," just as Augustine was a "Calvinist before Calvin."

Although Balthasar Hubmaier was not the founder of any particular church or group of Anabaptists, his legacy was profoundly influential among all Anabaptists. During his two to three years as a leader of the radical Protestant movement, he gave it a theological foundation upon which to build. For the most part, later influential

Anabaptists like Menno Simons built on that foundation so that they remained committed to basic Protestant principles in a radical perspective and with a strongly synergistic flavor. Their emphasis was on individual conversion and communal discipleship as well as separation from the world and freedom of conscience.

**Menno Simons's Life and Reforming Career**

Menno Simons was born in 1496 in the Lowlands and died of natural causes in 1561. He was one of Anabaptism's greatest organizers, and a significant number of congregations took their name from him and are thus known as Mennonites. They are probably the most numerous of all the existing Anabaptist groups in the modern world, although they are broken up into several denominations scattered throughout Europe and the Americas. Menno's claim to fame lies in his courageous leadership among persecuted Anabaptists in northern Europe during the last twenty-five years of his life. Because of his role in organizing and teaching them, "Menno Simons was the most outstanding leader of the Anabaptist branch of the Radical Reformation."[19] Menno was ordained to the priesthood in the Roman Catholic Church in 1524 and served as parish priest in his hometown, where, by his own later confession, he lived an immoral life and was popular with the local partying crowd. Sometime between 1530 and 1535 he began to read Luther's and Zwingli's books and encountered a number of radical Protestants. In 1535 Menno's brother Peter became an Anabaptist and was killed by the authorities. This event brought the young priest to a crisis of faith, and after much agony of spirit, he experienced a conversion:

> My heart trembled within me. I prayed to God with sighs and tears that He would give to me, a sorrowing sinner, the gift of His grace, create within me a clean heart, and graciously through the merits of the crimson blood of Christ forgive my unclean walk and frivolous easy life and bestow upon me wisdom, Spirit, courage, and a manly spirit so that I might preach His exalted and adorable name and holy Word in purity, and make known His truth to His glory.[20]

Menno's heartfelt conversion involving conscious repentance and trust in Jesus Christ followed by a filling of the Holy Spirit became the paradigm for the early Anabaptist theology of salvation.

After his conversion experience, Menno began meeting secretly with underground Anabaptist groups and helped shape them into permanent congregations. So successful was he that Emperor Charles V issued a warrant and reward for his capture. Somehow Menno managed to evade arrest and traveled around northern Europe for twenty-five years, preaching, establishing Anabaptist congregations, and writing about twenty-five books and major tracts as well as numerous sermons, hymns and letters. Unlike Hubmaier, Menno was not a scholar, but he became steeped in the Bible and taught his followers to study and memorize the Scriptures so that when they were arrested and interrogated they often astonished the magistrates and leaders of the state churches by their superior grasp of the New Testament. Clearly, Menno was a theologian even though he was not formally trained in theology and did not write a systematic theology: "Menno never had the leisure to produce learned tomes or to develop a systematic theology. Yet he wrote with vigor and insight, drawing on the earlier Anabaptist heritage and the wider Christian tradition but primarily on his own intensive engagement with the Scripture."[21] Among his better-known writings is an influential treatise titled *The Foundation of Christian Doctrine,* which Menno wrote first in 1540 and then revised in 1558. While not a systematic theology by any definition, it does provide a summary of major Anabaptist beliefs both for Anabaptists themselves and for the non-Anabaptist society that misunderstood and persecuted them.

### Menno's Theology

Like Balthasar Hubmaier and other early Anabaptist leaders, Menno Simons's theology centered around the experience of salvation. He took for granted the absolute authority of Scripture and tended to elevate the New Testament above the Old Testament as having a higher doctrinal authority for Christian teaching. He also took for granted the magisterial Reformers' accomplishments in overthrowing the authority of tradition and purifying the church of medieval accretions of that tradition such as purgatory, indulgences and prayers to saints. Menno's main concern was that the magisterial Protestants did not go far enough in discarding the unbiblical traditions of the church, and he insisted that infant baptism was one of those that should be discarded. However, his main reason for wishing to abolish infant baptism was not that it was an addition to early Christian practice but that it was inconsistent with a true gospel understanding and experience of salvation. For Simons, genuine salvation always involves conscious repentance and faith and always results in radical conversion of life, which includes regeneration (being born again of God's Spirit) and results in sanctification (a life of following Christ in discipleship). Since baptism is a testimony of regeneration and pledge of discipleship, it cannot precede conversion.

According to Menno, children are born without guilt and need neither conversion nor baptism until they reach the age of moral discretion, which is what later Baptists came to refer to as the age of accountability. Menno wrote, "To innocent and minor children sin is for Jesus' sake not imputed."[22] He believed that Adam's sin corrupted human nature so that all are included in Adam's fall and would be held responsible for it were it not for Jesus Christ and his life, death and resurrection. But because of Christ's atonement, all of humanity is pardoned by God spiritually. Menno did not deny original sin, but he interpreted Paul as teaching in Romans 5 that Christ's death sets aside the guilt of original sin for everyone until they commit actual sins consciously and willfully. He believed that everyone who reaches the age of maturity does sin responsibly and then incurs both objective guilt and a guilty conscience and needs conversion through repentance and faith. He felt that the magisterial Reformers emphasized faith to the neglect of repentance, and so he never tired of writing that "such repentance we teach and no other, namely that no one can or may piously glory in the grace of God, the forgiveness of sins, the merits of Christ, unless he has truly repented."[23]

For Menno, baptism of infants (pedobaptism) is an "abomination and idolatry" because infants cannot hear the gospel, understand and repent and because nowhere in the New Testament does Christ command infant baptism.[24] Clear from his words is Menno's belief that baptizing infants inevitably implies that they do not need to repent and be converted later in life and that this will lead them down to destruction. It also makes it impossible to tell who truly belongs in the church and who does not, and since Menno and all the Anabaptists insisted that the true church consists only of genuine believers who have experienced conversion and regeneration, baptism is the act of testimony and commitment that marks entrance into the body of Christ. Since infants cannot be believers, they are not fully members of the body of Christ even though if they die they will, according to Menno, be saved and go to heaven.

In his doctrine of salvation Menno Simons tended to neglect Luther's strong emphasis on justification as imputed righteousness, and he never affirmed the typical Lutheran doctrine of *simul justus et peccator*—simultaneously righteous and a sinner. Like Hubmaier, Menno also rejected predestination, and for the same reasons. Neither of these Anabaptist theologians ever denied that salvation is by grace through faith alone, but they "did not accept Luther's forensic doctrine of justification by faith alone because they saw it as an impediment to the true doctrine of a 'lively' faith which issues in holy living."[25] The key word is *forensic*. That is, the Anabaptists did not like the doctrine that righteousness is only *imputed* to sinners who repent. They wished to emphasis regeneration, which includes the impartation of the Holy Spirit and union with Christ so that the born-again sinner actually begins to become righteous within. Genuine, heartfelt faith, Menno argued, always results in righteous living, even though there is no perfection before death.

Menno may have been unfair in his attacks on Luther's doctrine of salvation because he accused it of involving only a "head faith" or "historical faith" that neglects the heart and inward righteousness. Luther spoke of "two kinds of righteousness." The second one involves inward transformation through Christ, but it is true that Luther emphasized the first kind of righteousness, which is passive and imputed, not imparted. It is an "alien righteousness." It is questionable whether Menno or other Anabaptists accepted alien righteousness at all, although they did affirm complete and full forgiveness of sins at conversion when there is true repentance of the heart.

Catholic critics condemned the Anabaptists because they rejected the penitential system and the sacraments. Like Menno, all the leading Anabaptists focused their attention on an inward conversion and outward testimony. Magisterial Protestant critics condemned the Anabaptists because they rejected monergism (predestination), infant baptism and forensic justification. Like Menno, all the leading Anabaptists focused their attention more on personal decision and holy living than on passive reception of salvation. To the magisterial Protestant followers of Luther and Zwingli, Menno and other Anabaptists seemed to be more Catholic than truly Protestant in their soteriology. The Anabaptists like Menno were clearly frustrated in their attempts to free theology of what they saw as the chains of traditional categories and recover the simple New Testament Christianity they sought. Overall, however, it must be said that Anabaptists like Hubmaier and Menno Simons were more Protestant than Catholic in spite of the harsh attacks of men like Luther, Zwingli and Calvin. There can be no doubt about their firm and unshakable faith in God's mercy and grace through Christ as all-sufficient and in forgiveness of sins without need of priest, penance or good works whenever anyone truly repents.

Two very controversial concepts of Menno Simons must also be mentioned in any account of his theological contribution. Largely due to his influence the Anabaptist movement accepted pacifism as the norm for their Christian lives. Hubmaier had earlier argued against militant Anabaptists that Christians should never use "the sword" (coercion of any kind) to spread the gospel or attempt to establish God's kingdom as a few had done. But Hubmaier and other early Anabaptist leaders had not required complete nonresistance by Christians. Menno did. In *Foundation of Christian Doctrine* he wrote that "all who are moved by the Spirit of Christ know of no sword but the Word of the Lord"[26] and "we teach and acknowledge no other sword, nor tumult in the kingdom or church of Christ than the sharp sword of the Spirit, God's Word."[27] From Menno on, Anabaptists rejected violence and coercion of any kind while acknowledging the right and necessity of the secular state to use them to protect the innocent and punish evildoers. But Christians, they argued, are not permitted by Christ to participate in that and so must never bear arms or do battle, even to protect themselves or anyone else. For that reason Mennonite and other Anabaptist churches are known as peace churches. Many have been imprisoned for refusing to serve in the military, and entire congregations have migrated from place to place seeking a nation where they will be free to worship and live their nonconformist, pacifist form of Christianity.

Another controversial aspect of Menno Simons's teaching had to do with Christology. It is hardly worth mentioning because it did not become an accepted part of Menno's theological legacy among Anabaptists or any other group. However, both Catholic and magisterial Protestants frequently used it to argue that Menno and Mennonites were heretics. In 1554 Menno wrote a treatise entitled *The Incarnation of Our Lord* in which he attempted to explain his own interpretation of the person of Jesus Christ. Without explicitly rejecting Chalcedonian two-natures Christology (hypostatic union), Menno did criticize Reformed theologians of his own day who seemed to interpret it as implying a Nestorian-like division of Jesus Christ into two persons. To summarize Menno's alternative view: the entire man Jesus Christ had his origin in heaven and took nothing essential from Mary other than his entrance into earthly life from heavenly existence.[28] Some critics have described his alleged heresy as Eutychian or monophysite because he seems to have believed in the heavenly or celestial flesh (human nature) of Christ and thereby may have unwittingly denied Jesus' authentic humanity. What Menno was trying to do, however, was guard and protect Jesus' humanity from sinfulness and at the same time avoid dividing him into two persons in Nestorianlike fashion.

Menno's view of the person of Christ and incarnation is not entirely clear and has been hotly debated. What is clear is that Menno denied that Jesus' humanity was taken from Mary. Whether he denied any true humanity of Jesus Christ is less clear as he did affirm Jesus' true sufferings and death. Apparently he believed that if Jesus received his human nature from Mary, it would be "fallen, Adamic flesh," and therefore Jesus could not be the sinless Savior of the world. Jesus' human nature was a creation of God the Father in heaven, and it was placed in Mary by the Holy Spirit through whom it entered into the world without taking anything substantial from Mary. While this would be unorthodox compared to traditional Christology, "Menno had no intention of denying the true humanity of Christ,"[29] and unlike most representatives of classical Christology he at least taught that Jesus

Christ truly suffered as the Word, the Son of God, and not merely "according to his human nature." However strange his doctrine of the incarnation may have been, it was not identical with any known heresy and was not adopted by any Anabaptist group as its official Christology.

Anabaptist theology may be summarized by saying that it was an attempt by radical Protestant Reformers to complete the Protestant Reformation by recovering the Christianity of the apostolic era. It was radically anti-Constantinian in its view of the church and its relations with secular rulers. It was radically anti-Augustinian in its view of salvation and the Christian life. The Anabaptists emphasized personal, conscious decision of repentance and faith and holy living as disciples of Christ to the exclusion of any idea of salvation as a gift imparted sacramentally. They extended Zwingli's symbolic interpretation of the Lord's Supper to baptism and insisted that since infants cannot repent or believe the gospel, baptism should be given only to those who repent after reaching the age of accountability. Clearly both the Anabaptist vision of salvation and the church and the magisterial Protestant vision—especially in its Reformed version—have strongly influenced modern evangelicalism. The tensions between the two visions remain within it as well.

The sixteenth-century reformations include more than Lutherans, Reformed and Anabaptists. The Reformation in England had an entirely different beginning and development and came to incorporate aspects of Catholic, Lutheran and Reformed theologies. The Church of England that emerged out of the English Reformation is in many ways a hybrid of all three. The Roman Catholic Church experienced its own Reformation in the sixteenth century. It is sometimes known as the Counter-Reformation because it was perceived by Protestants, at least, as reactionary in response to their own reforming work. Its centerpiece was the great Council of Trent that met in the Italian city of that name from 1545 to 1563. It is to the stories of the English and Catholic reformations that we next turn in our continuing narrative of historical theology.

# CHAPTER 27

# Rome & Canterbury Go Separate but Parallel Ways

T*he reformations of the Church of England and the Church of Rome were* complex processes covering decades of the sixteenth century and involving numerous persons, movements and events. Neither reformation was led by a single outstanding theologian or ecclesiastical reformer. Both reformations were looked upon as somewhat less than satisfactory by the magisterial and radical Reformers of Germany and Switzerland. The Reformation in England was primarily theological in nature, with the structure of the church's government and liturgy left largely as they were before that Reformation began. The reformation of the Roman Catholic Church was primarily ecclesiastical in nature, involving changes in practice, with the church's traditional theology and liturgy affirmed and even hardened. All Protestants were dismayed and even appalled by the so-called Counter-Reformation within the church of Rome, and its result was a deepening of the division within Christendom caused by corruption within that church as well as by the Protestant Reformation. Especially the Reformed theologians of Geneva and Strasbourg as well as other parts of Europe were dismayed by the eventual outcome of the English Reformation because it seemed stuck in a compromise with Catholicism.

Because both the English Reformation and the Catholic Reformation contributed little truly new to the story of Christian theology, here we will treat them in a single chapter and highlight those areas where each one achieved some new or distinct emphasis. We will also focus on those aspects of each that particularly agreed or disagreed with other branches of the sixteenth-century Reformation. Before continuing to the theologies of these reformations, however, it will be useful to survey their main historical backgrounds and contours. Neither the English nor the Catholic Reformation can be understood without some acquaintance with the political and ecclesiastical forces and events that shaped them.

### Historical Background of the English Reformation

The English Reformation began very differently than the other Protestant Reformations in Europe. King Henry VIII (1491-1547) wanted to divorce his wife and marry another. This was strictly forbidden by Roman Catholic canon law, and yet Henry, a devout Catholic and ardent opponent of Protestantism, wanted a son to succeed him. His wife bore him only daughters and had several miscarriages. Eventually Henry broke off the official relationship between the Church of England and Rome and appointed a sympathetic English theologian as primate of all England. Thomas Cranmer (1489-1556) of Cambridge University became archbishop of Canterbury in 1533. Cranmer legitimized Henry's divorce and remarriage and proceeded cautiously to reform England, as much as Henry would allow, along Lutheran lines. Henry was distinctly not sympathetic to the Protestant cause in spite of his gratitude to Cranmer. In 1534 the King declared himself "Supreme Head" of the English Catholic Church with the archbishop of Canterbury as his subordinate and burned at the stake both Roman Catholics and Protestants who would not recognize his supremacy. Under Henry the theology of the Church of England remained solidly Catholic but independent of Rome and the pope.

Henry died in 1547 and was succeeded by his nine-year-old son Edward VI, who lived only until 1553. During that time, Protestantism of various kinds flourished in England. Archbishop Cranmer was in the thick of the fast-paced Protestant movement, and at his side were a number of leading Lutheran and Reformed theologians from Europe. Martin Bucer, for example, came from Strasbourg to encourage and advise the flowering Protestant Reformation in England. Cranmer himself had lived for a time in Nuremburg, Germany, and had even secretly married the niece of that city's Lutheran Reformer, Andreas Osiander. In 1549 Cranmer produced a Protestant-inspired English Prayer Book to be used as the uniform worship manual throughout the Church of England. He revised it as the Book of Common Prayer in 1552, and even though it has gone through many revisions since then, it has remained the distinctive published centerpiece of English

Protestantism ever since. England was flooded with Protestants from Europe during the brief reign of Edward VI. The Church of England under Cranmer was headed toward becoming a Protestant church with a monarch and an archbishop working hand in hand.

The boy king died suddenly in 1553 and was succeeded by his fanatically Roman Catholic half-sister Mary, dubbed "Bloody Mary" by later generations. Under her five-year reign, England reverted to Roman Catholicism. Cranmer and over three hundred other leading Protestant churchmen and theologians were burned at the stake or beheaded. Under torture and threat of death, the archbishop of Canterbury and architect of English Protestantism recanted his "heresies" and embraced the faith of Rome once again. He was sentenced to die anyway and held the hand that had signed the recantation in the flames as a sign of his retraction of the recantation when he was burned publicly on March 21, 1556. Many Protestant leaders fled England to live in Geneva and Strasbourg and other Protestant cities during Mary's reign of terror. There they drank deeply at Reformed theological wells and decided that if they ever regained power and influence in their homeland, it would be thoroughly Calvinistic and Reformed in politics and theology.

Bloody Mary died in 1558 and was succeeded by her half-sister Elizabeth, who reigned as Elizabeth I until her death in 1603. She was a Protestant but had little sympathy with Reformed theology and none with Reformed polity, which was known in Scotland as Presbyterianism. Elizabeth wanted a *via media* for her English Church, and she wanted it to be the sole church of her realm. The compromise—known as the Elizabethan Settlement—was to allow a moderately Protestant theology within a moderately Catholic polity and liturgy. The form of church government under Elizabeth and her appointed archbishops of Canterbury would be episcopal with bishops under a monarch as supreme governor of the entire Church of England. A revised Book of Common Prayer would be imposed on every church in the realm and all priests would affirm a doctrinal statement known as the Thirty-Nine Articles of Religion. This Anglican church would appear very Catholic to European Protestants, especially Reformed theologians and divines (ministers) who looked to Calvin's Geneva as their model for what the church should be. On the other hand, Rome condemned it as too Protestant because it had no role whatsoever for the papacy or typical Catholic doctrines and practices such as transubstantiation, purgatory, penance and meritorious works of love. Elizabeth's Anglican church affirmed justification by grace through faith alone unequivocally while at the same time rejecting the more radical aspects of European Reformed Protestantism.

Throughout the sixteenth century, England was a separate kingdom from

Scotland. The two joined under one monarch only early in the seventeenth century when Elizabeth died. The importance of this lies in the fact that the kingdom of Scotland became the first whole nation to adopt the Calvinist, Reformed version of Protestantism as its national religion under the Reformer John Knox (1514-1572) around 1560. Knox, who referred to Geneva under Calvin and his successor, Theodore Beza, as "the most perfect school of Christ since the days of the apostles," wanted all of Scotland to follow the Genevan model both theologically and politically. Many within the Church of England under Elizabeth wanted that nation to follow Knox's and Scotland's example. Others wanted it to be as Catholic as possible, while yet others looked more to Lutheran models in Germany. Elizabeth abhorred and feared John Knox, who returned the favor. Referring to her and to her cousin Mary, Queen of Scots, Knox published a tract entitled "The First Blast of the Trumpet Against the Monstrous Regiment of Women" and called for abolition of all monarchy and establishment of a Presbyterian national church with a strongly Calvinistic theology throughout both Scotland and England.

In England only Elizabeth I's power held the Anglican church together as high-church and low-church parties struggled against one another. The former consisted of the so-called prayer-book men who fought to keep the English church as Catholic in polity and liturgy as possible.[1] They defended apostolic succession as the true order of ministry and argued for a special spiritual authority for priests within the church. While affirming typical Protestant doctrines of Scripture and salvation, they wanted a hierarchical church with bishops tied closely to the crown and formal liturgy using a uniform worship book. The low-church party were the heirs of the "hot gospelers" of Cranmer's day, most of whom were either burned at the stake or exiled to the European continent under Bloody Mary. They wanted England to emulate Knox's reformation of Scotland. Increasingly they called for abolition of the Book of Common Prayer, bishops, priesthood and apostolic succession, and highly liturgical worship. As they wanted to purify the Anglican Church of remaining Catholic elements, they came eventually to be known as Puritans. Those with a high-church theology were called Anglicans.

The leading Anglican theologian under Elizabeth I was Richard Hooker (1554-1600), who was raised Reformed but converted to Anglicanism with strong Catholic sympathies while studying at Oxford University. In 1584 Hooker was appointed Master of the Temple in London by the Queen. This was one of the most prestigious preaching positions in the kingdom. Hooker found himself working with an associate minister named Walter Travers (1548-1635), who was an ardent and outspoken Puritan critic of Anglicanism and the Elizabethan Settlement. Hooker expounded his moderate catholic episcopalianism in the morning and Travers contradicted him in the afternoon. As one twentieth-century historian puts it: "The forenoon spoke Canterbury and the afternoon Geneva."[2]

Leading members of London society listened to both. Hooker presented meticulously reasoned defenses of high-church polity and liturgy and argued that Catholic thought, though heretical in some ways, was not entirely wrong. For example, he emphasized the scholastic idea that grace fulfills nature rather than contradicts it. And he defended belief in free will and a moderately synergistic view of salvation. He even dared to suggest that Roman Catholics, though errant in their beliefs, might enjoy heaven nevertheless. Travers preached predestination as well as hellfire and brimstone against all Catholics—open or closeted—in his afternoon sermons and declared from the Temple pulpit that the Book of Common Prayer, priestly vestments, statues of saints and every other relic and remnant of the Catholic heritage of the church ought to be abolished.

Travers and Hooker represented two sides of the Church of England that eventually began persecuting one another to such an extent that civil war erupted nearly a century later. Even to this day the Church of England and the Anglican communion of churches worldwide (all of which look to the archbishop of Canterbury as spiritual leader) hold within themselves moderate high- and low-church parties. Extremists of both sides have left Anglicanism over the years for either Rome or various Reformed denominations.

**Historical Background of the Catholic Reformation**

In the 1520s and 1530s various Roman Catholic leaders and theologians called for a new ecumenical council to respond to the sweeping Protestant revolution and to reform the church from within. Erasmus of Rotterdam was by far the most influential Catholic Reformer, but others calling for change within the church were leaders such as cardinals Gasparo Contarini (1483-1542) and Jacopo Sadoleto (1477-1547), both of whom hoped for reunion between Rome and the Lutherans. Most of the Roman Catholic leaders of the sixteenth century were thoroughly disgusted with the conditions into which the church had fallen. They wanted clergy to be educated, truly celibate, resident in their parishes and preachers of the gospel—Roman-style. They wanted the popes to focus their attention on spiritual matters and leave war and politics to secular rulers, and they hoped for the day when church positions would never again be bought and sold (simony) or given to relatives (nepotism). Finally, they wanted the church to state clearly and officially what it believed and what was required of good Catholic Christians in terms of doctrine and practice. Many of the typical Catholic beliefs challenged by Protestants had never been made official dogmas by Rome. So it was unclear exactly what divided them necessarily and what divided them unnecessarily.

On November 11, 1544, Pope Paul III issued a decree calling the nineteenth ecumenical council of the church to meet at the Italian city of Trent beginning in March of the next year. The location was a compromise between the pope and Emperor Charles V. Trent was an insignificant town lying exactly on the border between the papal estates of Italy and the Holy Roman Empire. The emperor hoped that the council would bring about reconciliation between Protestants and Roman Catholics and reunite Christendom. He insisted that Lutheran representatives be invited. The pope wanted the council to spell out the differences between Protestants and the church of Rome and make clear that the former were heretics and the latter represented the one true church. Both pope and emperor wanted the council to rid the church of abuses and corruption.

Several ecumenical councils had met already to settle problems within the church and establish true Catholic dogma. None of the previous reforming councils had been spectacular successes. The Council of Constance (1414-1418) is considered the sixteenth ecumenical council by the Roman Catholic Church. It settled the great papal schism by deposing all three rival popes and electing Martin V as the one true pope. His first act after the council was to ratify all its acts except the final one that deposed the others and declared him pope. That conciliar act he rejected because it implied that a council can depose a pope. The Council of Constance seemed a triumph for the conciliar movement, but because of Martin V's successful repudiation of its key actions, it turned out to be less than successful in reforming the church. It was also the council that burned the Bohemian Reformer John Hus. The Council of Florence met in that Italian city from 1438 to 1445. Considered the seventeenth ecumenical council by Rome, it achieved a brief reunion between Eastern Orthodoxy and the Western church. The eighteenth council met in Rome from 1512 to 1517 and is known in church history as the Fifth Lateran Council. ("Lateran" was the name of the pope's official church in Rome before St. Peter's Cathedral was built.) Without much success it attempted to cleanse the church of the kinds of abuses Luther observed and decried when he visited Rome. The best that can be said is the council brought attention to the need for reform of church structures and practices.

The Council of Trent was a spectacular success compared with the immediately preceding three ecumenical gatherings. Hundreds of bishops, abbots and generals of special orders within the church met in several sessions across almost twenty years. The council was interrupted by plagues, wars and controversies between the delegates. The pope who called it died during the council, which was concluded by Pius IV, a virulently anti-Protestant pontiff. Far from achieving reunion of Christendom, Trent further divided it. It did, however, strengthen Roman Catholicism and gave impetus to its revitalization and resurgence. Catholic leaders now knew what every good Catholic was to believe and fight for. Besides ridding the church of corruption, the council produced a set of decrees and a creed that made Catholic dogma uniform and condemned all those like Luther and other Protestants who rejected any part of it. The anathemas of Trent declared Luther and the other Protestant Reformers and their followers heretics, and those condemnations still stand.[3]

With this background in church history it will now be easier to understand the unfolding stories of the English Reformers' theologies and of the theology of the Roman Catholic Counter-Reformation. Here we will focus attention on only two leading English Reformers and their theological contributions—Cranmer and Hooker—and the Council of Trent on the Catholic side. Certainly many church leaders and thinkers influenced these reformations, but time and space permits consideration only of these, and they are, by all accounts, the most important representative examples. We will also concentrate on these Reformers' and Trent's views on the three major principles in discussion and dispute during the sixteenth-century Reformations: *sola scriptura* (Scripture as final authority for Christian faith and practice), *sola gratia et fides* (salvation by grace through faith alone) and the priesthood of all believers. Many other issues played pivotal roles in the Catholic and English reformations, but time and space constraints require that we restrict the story to its main line and leave all tangents and subplots aside.

**The Father of the English Reformation: Thomas Cranmer**

The English Reformers affirmed the all-sufficiency and sole supremacy of the Bible for Christian faith and practice without discarding tradition. In the final analysis, Richard Hooker's Anglican theology, as expressed in his magisterial work *Laws of Ecclesiastical Polity,* preserved more of the Catholic tradition than any other form of Protestant theology. Yet both Cranmer and Hooker required that any retained traditional beliefs and practices be compatible with the Bible. Similarly, the English Reformers promoted the Protestant doctrine of justification by grace through faith alone while also emphasizing the importance of sanctification and good works. Finally, they taught that every believer in Jesus Christ is able to go directly to God in prayer on his or her own behalf as well as on behalf of others without mediation of clergy or saints. At the same time they held to a very high view of ordination and priesthood, including apostolic succession and indelible spiritual characteristics conveyed upon the minister by proper ordination. The third Protestant principle—priesthood of all believers—was the one most weakly held by the English Reformers, according to their Puritan foes. The latter saw the Book of Common Prayer, apostolic succession and priestly vestments and benedictions as sure signs of latent "popery" in Hooker and his Anglican ecclesiology. Nevertheless, there can be no doubt that Cranmer and Hooker and the other early and later architects of Anglican theology were Protestants, even if their Protestantism came with a decidedly traditionalist flavor.[4]

Thomas Cranmer is generally regarded as the founder of English Protestantism. "If he was not a theologian of the first rank, he certainly exercised a decisive and lasting influence."[5] Cranmer produced few formal theological writings, but he was responsible for a great deal of "indirect theology" through his policy of opening the Bible to all the people as well as through his work on the Book of Common Prayer. He also influenced the theology of England through his production of the Church of England's Articles of Religion. In June of 1553, the year he was martyred, Cranmer wrote the Forty-Two Articles of Religion, which became the basis for the later Thirty-Nine Articles of Religion. As one modern Cranmer interpreter notes, "He gave to his church a Bible, biblical preaching, a catechism, a Prayer Book and a confession of faith. If he has nothing much to offer in the way of dogmatic treatises, the reforms for which he himself was in the main responsible are all at the theological level."[6] The main theological influences upon Cranmer's thinking and reforming work were Lutheran and Reformed. Especially crucial was his friendship with Martin Bucer, who had tried unsuccessfully to unite Continental Protestants and also attempted to chart a middle course between Zwingli and Luther on the presence of Christ in the Lord's Supper. No doubt Cranmer's Lutheran wife and her uncle Andreas Osiander of Nuremburg also influenced his thinking.

With regard to Scripture, Cranmer's actions speak louder than his written words. Soon after being installed as Henry VIII's archbishop of Canterbury, he introduced the first English Bible, known as The Great Bible, into the churches of the kingdom. Even though Cranmer was not the translator, it also became known as Cranmer's Bible because he wrote its preface and engineered its distribution in all the churches. In that preface the archbishop urged everyone to read the Bible and referred to it as "the Word of God, the most precious jewel, the most holy relic that remaineth upon earth."[7] For Cranmer, Scripture was the "very foundation of the Reformed [Protestant] faith" and "whatever is found in Holy Scripture . . . 'must be taken for a most sure ground and an infallible truth; and whatsoever cannot be grounded upon the same, touching our faith, is man's device, changeable and uncertain.' "[8] All "unwritten verities" (human religious traditions not found in

Scripture) must be subjected to testing by Scripture and are to be rejected insofar as they conflict with its plain statements or broad principles.

On the other hand, unlike many in the Reformed tradition, Cranmer held in high regard all tradition that is compatible with Scripture and often appealed to the church fathers as authorities in matters where Scripture is silent: "He could grant that patristic utterances are dispensable and may even be wrong if they are not grounded in the Word of God. But against that he could also maintain that "every exposition of the Scripture, whereinsoever the old, holy, and true church did agree, is necessary to be believed."[9] Cranmer and other English Reformers of the sixteenth century sought to find and maintain a delicate balance between the supreme authority of Scripture and respect for ancient Christian tradition. This is one of the hallmarks of the English Reformation: respect for the subsidiary authority of the church fathers and the creeds of the first few centuries of Christianity, especially in matters of ceremony and order within the church.

Cranmer's commitment to the Protestant principle of *sola gratia et fides* (salvation by grace through faith alone) shines clearly through his published sermon "A Homily on Salvation" (1547), which "belongs in a special way to the official teaching of the Church of England."[10] There the Reformer of England criticized and condemned the Roman Catholic doctrine of imparted or infused righteousness through faith, sacraments and meritorious works, and affirmed that "our justification doth come freely by the mere mercy of God" and not on account of any works that we do but only by a "true and living faith, which nevertheless is the gift of God."[11] Cranmer's doctrine of salvation is nearly identical with that of the Continental Reformers Luther, Zwingli and Calvin. However, he set the pace for the future Anglican theology of Hooker and other theologians of the Elizabethan Settlement by emphasizing sanctification as a life of holiness and good works that results naturally and necessarily from the "true and living faith" of justification. Unlike Luther, Cranmer highly valued the epistle of James and saw no conflict between its message and Paul's regarding salvation: "For that faith which bringeth forth (without repentance) either evil works or no good works is not a right, pure, and lively faith, but a dead, devilish, counterfeit, and feigned faith as St. Paul and St. James call it."[12]

Finally, Cranmer had little to say directly about the priesthood of all believers, but he indirectly affirmed it no less than *sola scriptura* and *sola gratia et fides*, even though in a distinctively English Protestant style. Cranmer and the other English Reformers stood shoulder to shoulder with their counterparts in Europe in rejecting the Roman Catholic concept of sacerdotal clericalism—the belief in a special spiritual power invested in priests by the sacrament of ordination.[13] They especially rejected the traditional Catholic belief that priests alone are capable of absolving sins and of offering Christ anew in the sacrifice of the mass. In a treatise entitled *Defence of the True and Catholic Doctrine of the Sacrament,* Cranmer condemned the sacerdotalism of the papal church and treated it as "the very tap-root of the tree of error which he and his fellow Reformers felt it essential to extirpate."[14] In contrast to that he sought to retain the terminology of minister as "priest"—only because it was an English translation of the New Testament term for "elder" *(presbyteros)*—and invest it with new meaning. For him the priest was the person ordained by the church to preach and teach God's Word, serve in pastoral labor the spiritual needs of the congregation and administer the sacraments of baptism and Holy Communion. The office of priest in the Church of England was envisioned as not distinctively priestly in nature but rather as prophetic and pastoral. According to Cranmer, only Christ is our true priest who mediates between God and the believer in intercession, forgiveness and imparting grace.

Some of Cranmer's critics felt that what he gave with one hand he took away with the other. That is, although he rejected sacerdotalism and indirectly affirmed the priesthood of every believer, he also held on to the hierarchical structure of the medieval church and its Constantinianism. For Cranmer and the later Anglicans, the monarch of England was the supreme governor of the Church of England even though Christ is its sole head. The king or queen was recognized as a secular minister of God over the entire commonwealth—both civil and religious—and had the right and power to appoint the chief minister the archbishop of Canterbury. The church itself was led by a hierarchy of bishops, priests and deacons under the monarch and archbishop, and true ordination had to take place within the order of apostolic succession. For all practical purposes bishops alone were invested with the authority to sanction sacraments and ordain and appoint clergy to their parishes. This highly episcopal form of church polity was laid out and defended by Richard Hooker in his magisterial *Laws of Ecclesiastical Polity,* but it was initially kept in place (from the Roman Catholic heritage of the Church of England) by Cranmer. To low-church and especially Puritan English Protestants, this order and the ceremonies retained by the Church of England from Roman Catholicism smacked of sacerdotalism even if priests were not said to have special spiritual powers.

Cranmer shaped the Church of England's doctrine of the sacraments through his treatise *The Defence of the True and Catholic Doctrine of the Sacraments* and through the Book of Common Prayer and Articles of Religion. The course he set and the foundation he laid were consciously intended to avoid the internecine theological warfare over the sacraments that he so deplored among European Reformers. The exact wording of the ceremonies for baptism and the Lord's Supper that Cranmer wrote in the Book of Common Prayer, as well as the doctrinal statements he included in the Articles of Religion, leave room for various interpretations while excluding the typical Roman Catholic doctrines as well as the Zwinglian and Anabaptist interpretations and practices. Cranmer's ideas of both sacraments were most comparable with those of Calvin and Bucer. With regard to baptism, he affirmed infant baptism and baptismal regeneration when faith is present or later confirmed by the maturing baptized child. Like the Reformed theologians, Cranmer compared baptism with circumcision and assumed that baptized children of Christian parents are truly saved. Also with Reformed theology, he argued for the spiritual real presence of Christ in the sacrament of Holy Communion when faith is in the partakers' hearts and minds.

**The Architect of Anglicanism: Richard Hooker**

Although Thomas Cranmer was the true historical founder of English Protestantism, the theological architect of Anglicanism—as the mature English church of the Elizabethan Settlement may be called—was Richard Hooker. It was Hooker who picked up and magnified those elements of Cranmer's thought that were favorable to high-church tradition, including formal liturgy and hierarchical polity. He also combined these with a moderately scholastic vision of nature and grace, including natural theology, and an emphasis upon human free will and participation in the process of salvation (synergism). If Cranmer's vision of English Protestantism had been interpreted and imposed by the low-church party of Puritans within the Church of England, such as Walter Travers and Thomas Cartwright (1535-1603), that branch of Protestantism may never have become Anglican and would have looked very different. That was not to be, however. Elizabeth I clearly favored churchmen like Richard Hooker who leaned heavily toward Catholic traditionalism without falling into medieval Catholic doctrine and practice contrary to the basic impulses of the European Protestant Reformation. Through his sermons and writings, especially his multivolumed *Laws of Ecclesiastical Polity,* Hooker became "the best exponent of the theology behind the Elizabethan Settlement."[15] That settlement and Hooker's theology created the half-Protestant, half-Catholic Anglican Church and theology so despised and rejected by Puritans, Presbyterians and miscellaneous other nonconformist Protestants of Great Britain who looked to Geneva for their inspiration.

Without any doubt Hooker agreed wholeheartedly with Cranmer and the magisterial Reformers in general about the first two main Protestant principles: *sola scriptura* and *sola gratia et fides.* But he put his own distinctive spin on them.

In addition, he so neglected the third Protestant principle of the priesthood of all believers that his Puritan enemies considered him a closeted Catholic. With regard to the Scripture principle, Hooker held to the official teaching of the Church of England as expressed in the Thirty-Nine Articles of Religion. Article VI of that authoritative doctrinal confession of the English church affirms the supreme sufficiency and authority of Holy Scripture for Christian faith and practice. On the other hand, without denying Scripture's special status as source and norm for Christian theology and life, Hooker recognized multiple authorities, ranging in degrees from God on down through the Bible to national laws and individual conscience. He always thought in terms of degrees and gradations of everything—including authorities—and rejected what he saw as the tendency toward black-and-white, either-or thinking on the part of Puritans, who appealed to Scripture alone and often rejected all other authorities.[16] Hooker readily appealed to Plato, the early church fathers, creeds of the church, declarations of monarchs, philosophers and lawyers in those areas where Scripture is silent or ambiguous. He sought a broad, reasonable approach to authority that avoided what he saw as extremes of rationalism and narrow-minded dogmatism.

Perhaps most offensive to Puritans was Hooker's use of medieval scholastic natural theology. For the most part the European Reformers, including Luther, Zwingli and Calvin, had repudiated scholasticism as part and parcel of the Catholic theology they rejected. Hooker, however, believed in a Thomist-like scheme in which grace (the supernatural realm) fulfills rather than contradicts nature. Twentieth-century Hooker admirer and commentator Lionel Thornton sums up the Anglican divine's thought: "Man [to Hooker] is the crown of the natural order and that which gives him his unique position in that order is his possession of moral freedom. He possesses a natural light of reason whereby he can recognize the Good and a free-will whereby he can choose the Good and identify himself with it."[17] In other words, according to Hooker, human nature is not so damaged by the Fall and original sin that it cannot reach up to grace and cooperate with it by the help of grace. Reason and free will at their best are preparations for true knowledge of God and salvation, and when divine revelation and saving grace appear, human nature is elevated into participation in the life of God and not recreated. This means that the natural human mind observing the order of nature even apart from special revelation can see something of God and his grace, for "the whole order of nature is a mirror in which God can be seen and known."[18] This entire metaphysical and epistemological scheme was seen by Hooker's Reformed opponents as anti-Protestant and as a throwback to medieval Catholic foundations.

Hooker's agreement with the Protestant principle of justification by grace through faith alone was without qualification. In his treatise *A Learned Discourse of Justification* the architect of Anglican theology distinguished between two kinds of righteousness in a manner very reminiscent of Luther and completely contrary to official Roman Catholic teaching as that had already been declared by the Council of Trent. For Hooker, "justifying righteousness" is neither inherent in nor infused into the soul as is "sanctifying righteousness."[19] The former is always only imputed by God by his free mercy and grace on account of Christ's death and because of our faith. The latter is not a meritorious cause of a right relationship with God (as in Catholic thought), even though the two are inextricably linked. In all this Hooker agreed completely with Luther and Cranmer and the Thirty-Nine Articles of Religion, which in Article XI clearly affirms justification by grace through faith alone. As in the case of Hooker's doctrine of Scripture, however, his Calvinist opponents in the Church of England were dissatisfied with his doctrine of salvation because he believed that Roman Catholics who denied justification by grace through faith alone out of ignorance could be saved and that human persons participate in their own salvation by freely accepting God's grace. While he spoke of election and even predestination, he seemed in the end to base them on God's foreknowledge rather than on eternal divine foreordination.

Perhaps the most troubling aspect of Hooker's soteriology for low-church Protestants within the Church of England was his endorsement of the catholic and orthodox idea of salvation as deification.[20] Even though he taught the Protestant doctrine of initial salvation as a once-and-for-all declaration of forgiveness and imputed righteousness (forensic justification), Hooker also tended to describe salvation as a process by which human nature is gradually brought to participation in the divine nature through the sacraments. While rejecting the classical Catholic idea that the sacraments of baptism and Eucharist, or Holy Communion, infuse grace *ex opere operato,* Hooker accepted the classical orthodox and catholic belief that the sacraments unite the person with God and transform the person into one truly holy and immortal. He simply added that faith must be present for this to happen and that the completion of the process is heavenly and not earthly. Thus Hooker held to the Protestant view of justification and combined it with the classical catholic and orthodox view of sanctification with the result that many of his English Protestant critics accused him of accommodating to Roman Catholicism and watering down the Reformation principle of *simul justus et peccator* (always righteous and sinner at the same time).

Hooker paid lip service to the principle of the priesthood of all believers while shoring up the Catholic clericalism within the developing Anglican tradition as much as possible. Of course, he did not deny that every true, baptized believer can approach God directly for forgiveness and help, nor did he affirm any necessity of a special priesthood to absolve sins or perform sacrifices as in the Roman Catholic doctrine of the Mass. Nevertheless, at least in the eyes of his detractors within the Church of England, Hooker's doctrine of ministry came dangerously close to Catholic sacerdotalism in that Hooker accepted and defended "the Catholic doctrine of Church government by Bishops possessing apostolic authority through a visible succession."[21] The low-church party felt that this hierarchical and Catholic view of polity within the church would inevitably lead back to the smothering embrace of Rome. In reaction to the Anglican emphasis on the authority of bishops, the Puritans more and more called for that office's abolition within the church. Hooker defended and strengthened it and went even further. Building on Cranmer's earlier endorsement of the monarch as supreme governor of the national English Church, Hooker brought the civil and religious orders as close as possible in *Laws of Ecclesiastical Polity* so that "Church and state are one society under two aspects."[22] In this one society with two authorities Hooker gave preeminence to the sovereign (monarch) so that Elizabeth I played the same role in England as Constantine the Great or Charlemagne played in the patristic and medieval churches.

Hooker's views on ecclesiastical polity did not overtly deny the universal priesthood of believers, but they did undermine it. The inevitable tendency was for lay Christians to look up to spiritual authorities over them as mediators of grace in Hooker's Anglican sacramental system. Hooker's modern interpreter and defender Thornton admits that the Anglican theologian was as much Catholic as Protestant and that Hooker was moving in the Catholic direction throughout his career. This is especially true with regard to ecclesiology—the doctrine of the church.[23] And yet Hooker never even toyed with the idea of a reunion between the Church of England and Rome. His *Laws of Ecclesiastical Polity* was being worked out in response to what he saw as two destructive extremes: Puritanism and Roman Catholic traditionalism. He wanted to be the architect of a *via media*—a middle way that would be true to the basic Protestant recovery of New Testament doctrine and at the same time faithful to the best of orthodox and catholic tradition. This compromise satisfied neither set of Hooker's opponents, but it did forge a lasting and durable national church for the English realm.

It would be highly improper to leave behind a discussion of Anglicanism without at least touching on two of its main published hallmarks: the Book of Common Prayer and the Thirty-Nine Articles of Religion. Both have already received some attention in this story of the English Reformation, but their importance to that story has not been given its due. The Book of Common Prayer was inaugurated by

Cranmer in 1549 and has gone through many revisions since then. To a certain extent each autonomous, national body of the Anglican communion such as the Episcopal Church in America (which became separate from the Church of England during the American Revolutionary War) has its own Book of Common Prayer, but all share much in common. The BCP (as I will now refer to it) was intended to replace and simplify the enormously complex liturgies of the Roman Catholic Church in England as well as to give the English people a uniform liturgy and set of devotions and ceremonies in their own language. It prescribes sermon texts for Sundays of the year as well as readings, litanies, forms for special services and sacraments. It also contains prayers for collective and private use. The purpose of the BCP is to unify the church and avoid religious individualism. Anglicans around the world agree that God is glorified in beautiful, uniform, collective worship and not glorified in worship and devotion that are merely inventions of the moment disconnected from any Great Tradition of Christianity. Of course, Puritans of all kinds found the BCP stifling, too Catholic, and they resented its imposition by law. Eventually it became the flash point for open rebellion as more and more Puritan English congregations refused to use it.

The Thirty-Nine Articles of Religion represents the official doctrinal confession of Anglicanism worldwide. As with the BCP, various national bodies of that communion may modify it somewhat, but it remains for all a unifying doctrinal standard. Some of the articles have already been mentioned, especially those that affirm the supreme authority of Scripture and salvation by grace through faith alone. The first article deals with faith in the holy Trinity, and the second affirms the two natures of Christ. Article VIII gives special authority to the Apostles' Creed, the Nicene Creed and the Athanasian Creed. (The American revision omits the latter.) Article XVII, "Of Predestination and Election," avoids double predestination and leaves open the possibility of basing predestination on foreknowledge (as many Anglicans and Episcopalians do). Article XXII condemns belief in purgatory, and following articles deal with correct belief about the sacraments. The final article allows Christians to "swear when the Magistrate requires" even though in general Christ forbid using of "vain and rash swearing."[24] As in the case of some others, the final article is a reaction to Anabaptists, who refused to use oaths even in court.

The flavor of the Thirty-Nine Articles is overwhelmingly Protestant, even though Puritans considered parts of it too Catholic. On the other hand, aspects of the Church of England's polity and theology, including the BCP, are subtly or overtly Catholic, even if Anglicans like Hooker denied it. Church historian Justo González sums up the situation well:

> The Elizabethan settlement may then be seen as an attempt to develop a middle way between Roman Catholicism and the shape that the Protestant Reformation was taking on the Continent. As a result it had to struggle with the more radical elements within it—and this struggle did result in political upheavals. But in the long run, the Anglican via media would survive as the most characteristic form of Christianity in England, while other forms—from Roman Catholic to extreme Protestant—would continue existing alongside it.[25]

**The Jewel of the Catholic Reformation: The Council of Trent**

The centerpiece of the Catholic Reformation was the great Council of Trent. As one cardinal of the church described it, "no Council in the history of the Church has determined so many questions, established so many points of doctrine or made so many laws."[26] When the council finally reached its end on December 4, 1563, its numerous decrees were solemnly signed by four papal legates, three patriarchs, twenty-five archbishops, one hundred sixty-nine bishops, seven abbots, seven generals of Catholic orders, ten episcopal procurators and the ambassadors of all the Catholic powers of Europe. Pope Pius IV, confined to a sick bed, responded to news of the council's conclusion: "All was done by God's inspiration."[27] One modern Catholic traditionalist concludes that

> on all essential points of difference between Catholic tradition and heretical doctrine the Council speaks and resolutely determines what is to be believed. Its achievement is of capital importance, assuring to the Church stability of her foundations, removing revealed truth from the arena of debate, establishing rules which none henceforward can reject without thereby lapsing into error.[28]

To Roman Catholics, Trent was a magnificent achievement that defined dogma and unified the church against the heresies of the many Protestant sects. To Protestants of all stripes it was a reactionary power play by the papacy that hardened Catholic categories and condemned as heresy the very gospel the Reformers were attempting to recover.

The Council of Trent promulgated many doctrinal decrees and canons—affirmations of official belief (dogmas) and condemnations of their denials. Luther and his followers were specifically named as teachers of heresies and their beliefs were anathematized (condemned as heresy). What is the legal status of these decrees and canons for Roman Catholics after Trent? Authoritative Catholic scholar Daniel-Rops explains: "On the dogmatic plane the decisions of the Council are binding on all Catholics: to reject them is heresy. In the field of discipline, on the other hand, he who disputes or refuses to subscribe to them is rash and rebellious, even schismatic, but does not thereby put himself outside the Church."[29] In other words, Trent defined with final authority what Catholics must believe. To reject any one of its decrees or canons amounts to heresy. Although many modern Roman Catholics question and debate some of Trent's decrees and canons, they still must be very cautious and guarded so that they are not interpreted as rejecting them. Especially for Catholic theologians and priests such rejection can be grounds for discipline if not excommunication.

As the Council of Trent dealt with so many issues of belief and practice, I will limit the discussion to its major decisions relating to the three main Protestant principles. One of the first issues discussed and decided by the council was the authority of Scripture and tradition. Although the Roman Catholic Church had never officially stated the weight of tradition's authority in relation to Scripture, it had treated unwritten tradition as equal with the Bible. When challenged by Protestants to prove the truth of extrabiblical teachings and practices such as prayers for the dead and transubstantiation, Rome had appealed to an oral tradition handed down from the apostles to their successors, the bishops. Protestants rejected such unwritten tradition as having no binding authority and argued that only those beliefs and practices specifically taught in Scripture itself could be required of Christians. Trent responded to the Protestant challenge by declaring that Christian doctrine and practice have two sources of authority as special revelation itself comes in two forms:

> The council follows the example of the orthodox Fathers and with the same sense of devotion and reverence with which it accepts and venerates all the books of both the Old and the New Testament, since one God is the author of both, it also accepts and venerates traditions concerned with faith and morals as having been received orally from Christ or inspired by the Holy Spirit and continuously preserved in the Catholic Church.[30]

Not only did Trent affirm the authority of extrabiblical traditions, it also anathematized, or condemned, any person who knowingly and willfully rejects or insults them. Furthermore, the council identified the Latin Vulgate as the authentic edition of the Bible (including the so-called apocryphal books) and authorized the Mother Church (Rome) as the final judge of Scripture's meaning.

As in the case of the decree on Scripture and tradition, Trent responded to Protestantism by "baptizing" as dogma the standard Roman Catholic doctrine of justification. The council's sixth session, which lasted almost a year (1546-1547) produced after long debate the decree on justification, which defined it as "a passing from the state in which man is born of the first Adam, to the state of grace and adoption as sons of God . . . through the second Adam, Jesus Christ our Savior. After the promulgation of the gospel this passing cannot take place without the water of regeneration [baptism] or the desire for it."[31] Furthermore, the council decreed that "justification is not only the remission of sins, but sanctification and renovation of the interior man through the voluntary reception of grace and gifts, whereby a man becomes just instead of unjust and a friend instead of an enemy, that he may be an heir in the hope of life everlasting."[32] Thus Trent identified justification with sanctification, treating them as two sides of the same coin of salvation. The decree also treated justification as infusion of faith, hope and charity (love) by the indwelling of the Holy Spirit at baptism and rejected the idea that saved persons are only "considered just [righteous]." According to the decree on justification, persons who are saved receive justice (righteousness) within themselves as their own "according to the disposition and cooperation of each one."[33] In effect then the council repudiated forensic or alien righteousness as well as monergism. Protestants interpreted this as meaning that Christians are only as justified as they are sanctified, and since sanctification is a matter of cooperation with God's grace, justification itself must be a work of the human person. However, Trent nowhere stated it so blatantly.

After the decree on justification, the Council of Trent pronounced thirty-three canons on justification that amount to condemnations (anathemas) of contrary views. Canon nine states:

> If anyone says that a sinful man is justified by faith alone, meaning that no other cooperation is required to obtain the grace of justification, and that it is not at all necessary that he be prepared and disposed by the action of his will: let him be anathema.[34]

Canon eleven says:

> If anyone says that men are justified either through the imputation of Christ's justice [righteousness] alone, or through the remission of sins alone, excluding grace and charity [love] which is poured forth in their hearts by the Holy Spirit and inheres in them, or also that the grace which justifies us is only the good will of God: let him be anathema.[35]

To Protestants the clearest offense against the gospel (as they understood it) came in canon thirty-two:

> If anyone says that the good works of a justified man are gifts of God to such an extent that they are not also the good merits of the justified man himself;

> or that, by the good works he performs through the grace of God and the merits of Jesus Christ . . . the justified man does not truly merit an increase of grace, life everlasting, and, provided that he dies in the state of grace, the attainment of that life everlasting, and even an increase of glory: let him be anathema.[36]

This seemed to Protestants sure proof that the Roman Catholic Church was embracing works righteousness.

The upshot of Trent's decree and canons on justification was the rejection of Protestant soteriology and alienation of Protestants themselves. Although cautiously stated and carefully nuanced, Trent clearly denied salvation by grace through faith alone and made justification a process involving human cooperation of the will and meritorious good works. Of course Trent also affirmed the priority of grace over all. Without God's prevenient grace going before and enabling, no human person would ever be capable of producing truly good works. But the righteousness of justification is not a sheer gift. The ability to merit and possess it may be a gift, but it is itself partly earned. Protestants recoiled in horror from this just as Roman Catholics recoiled in horror from the Protestant's forensic righteousness that appeared to be a "legal fiction."

Trent's utter rejection of the priesthood of all believers is blatant. In a decree on "Holy Orders" (ordination) the council stated that

> in the sacrament of orders [ordination], just as in baptism and in confirmation, a character is imprinted which can neither be blotted out nor taken away. Therefore, this holy council rightly condemns the opinion of those who say that the priests of the New Testament have merely temporary power, and that once they have been duly ordained they can become laymen again, if they do not exercise the ministry of the word of God. But if anyone says that all Christians without exception are priests of the New Testament or are endowed with equal spiritual power it is apparent that he upsets the ecclesiastical hierarchy.[37]

The council reaffirmed the traditional hierarchy of the church, including pope, bishops, priests and deacons and condemned anyone who rejects it.

The Council of Trent produced decrees affirming the traditional teaching of Rome concerning purgatory, transubstantiation and indulgences. In its disciplinary decrees and canons it corrected abuses and corruption, including the sale of indulgences for money. As already noted, the result of Trent for Christendom was a vast strengthening of the Roman Church's position and a deeper division between it and all Protestants, who were for all practical purposes excommunicated as heretics by its canons. Only at the Second Vatican Council (1963-1965), known as the twenty-first ecumenical council, were Protestants accorded the more favorable status of "separated brethren" by Rome. Of course, one must remember that well before Trent anathematized Protestants, the leading Protestant Reformers and many of their followers were routinely referring to the pope as the antichrist and consigning his entire flock to hell.

Partly in response to the Council of Trent and its anticipated decrees and canons, the magisterial Protestant communions of Europe began promulgating their own formal doctrinal confessions. Luther wrote the Schmalkald Articles in 1537 to summarize clearly and succinctly his version of Christian doctrine for the new council that was in the offing. Soon after Trent's closure, Lutheran leaders produced the Formula of Concord (1577), which is a more detailed statement of official Lutheran teaching. Toward the end of the Council of Trent, the Dutch Reformed Christians wrote the Belgic Confession (1561) and the Swiss Reformed churches embraced the Heidelberg Catechism (1562), which became the basis for most later Reformed confessions of faith, including the Presbyterian Westminster Confession and Catechism (1647/1648).

The great Reformation chapter of the story of Christian theology ended in chaos, with a church and civilization deeply divided. Christendom no longer existed as before and never would again. The great medieval vision of a unified Christian society had its echo in England under Elizabeth I, but as a dream for Europe as a whole it had faded hopelessly away in the smoke of theological warfare. Soon theological warfare would turn into armed warfare as Protestant and Catholic territories engaged in death struggles throughout Europe in the late sixteenth and early seventeenth centuries. The Thirty Years War raged between Catholics and Protestants in central Europe from 1618 to 1648. Smaller national conflicts broke out around the same time in France and England.

Not only was Christendom divided at the end of the Reformation era, but Protestantism was splintering even further than anyone had dreamed possible. In Great Britain (England and Scotland) the Church of England gave rise to numerous splinter groups out of the original Puritan movement. Most of them were offshoots of Puritanism or Scottish Presbyterianism and therefore Reformed in theology. But they disagreed among themselves over church government and other secondary issues. The influence of Puritan theology was greatest in North America, where thousands of Puritans of various kinds emigrated to escape persecution in England and establish a Geneva-like Christian commonwealth after failing to establish it in their homeland. In Holland the Reformed Church divided over the doctrine of predestination, and a new form of Protestant theology known as Arminianism (after Jacob Arminius) arose. Some Protestants became so impressed with the advances of reason and science in the seventeenth century and so depressed and disillusioned by the wars of religion that they sought to discover a religion of pure reason, and thus Deism was born. Finally, out of the ashes of the wars of religion and the rebellion against the rationalism and dead orthodoxy into which much of Protestant theology had fallen, a Christianity of the heart was born in the sixteenth century. This new movement, known as Pietism, focused attention on experience over doctrine and gave rise to revivalism in the early eighteenth century.

Out of all this post-Reformation ferment, new denominations and new forms of Christianity were born. Methodism and all its offshoots arose out of Pietism and revivalism. The Baptist movement arose out of Puritan contact with European Anabaptists in Holland. The Unitarian Church, to which several United States presidents have belonged, was the result of Deism and the natural, rational religion of the Enlightenment. Dutch Arminian theology deeply influenced the early Methodists, many Baptists and the Church of England and its American offshoot, the Episcopal Church. The next chapters of our story of Christian theology will recount how Protestantism fell apart by going back to the roots of its numerous denominations in sixteenth-century theological debates and controversies.

# PART VIII

# The Center of the Story Falls Apart

## *Protestants Follow Diverse Paths*

*Two great divisions have so far occurred in the story of Christian theology. The first* parting among catholic and orthodox Christians took place gradually over several centuries and culminated in the as yet unhealed breach between East and West in 1054. The second break was in the West during the sixteenth century and officially began with the excommunication of Martin Luther by the pope in 1520. Protestants disagreed among themselves over many fairly minor matters, but they managed to present a relatively united front to the monolithic power of the church of Rome. For all their secondary differences, Lutheran, Reformed and Anglican theologians stood together theologically if not politically. While they enjoyed casting aspersions at each other over their differences regarding the sacraments and forms of church government and followed different political leaders, these Magisterial Reformation families were unified in faith and doctrine throughout much of the sixteenth century. The fourth Protestant family—the Anabaptists—were so persecuted and marginalized by everyone that they all but faded out of public view and played little or no role in the ongoing story of Christian theology for a very long time.

The seventeenth century saw large theological cracks opening not only between but also within these Protestant families. Early in that post-Reformation century the Reformed followers of Zwingli and Calvin fell into conflict and controversy among themselves over the details of the doctrine of predestination. A major, enduring split occurred around 1610 as the followers of Dutch Reformed theologian Jacob Arminius rejected the classical Zwinglian and Calvinist doctrine entirely in favor of a more Erasmian and Anabaptist belief in synergism and free will. A new theological stream branched off the Reformed tributary: Arminianism. It is basically synonymous with Protestant synergism and the rejection of classical Augustinian-Zwinglian-Calvinist belief in meticulous providence and absolute predestination. Lutheranism in Germany and Scandinavia experienced a great spiritual renewal movement in the middle of the seventeenth century known as Pietism that led to tremendous conflict and controversy among Luther's followers and then also among other Protestants.

The Church of England went through a wrenching theological and political battle between Anglicans and Puritans with many of the latter leaving the mother church and founding several different dissenting and nonconformist denominations based on Reformed theology. In the eighteenth century the Church of England and worldwide Anglican community experienced another major defection as John Wesley's followers broke away to found the Methodist movement. Finally, a new cultural mood known as the Enlightenment arose in Europe at the end of the religious wars in the middle of the seventeenth century. It gave rise to an entirely new form of religious thought that began out of no one Reformation theological family but eventually impacted all of them. It is known variously as Deism and natural religion. Most of its early adherents and promoters were Protestants, but many of its later generations wandered off into skepticism and agnosticism. The influence of Deism both within and from outside the established Protestant churches profoundly challenged Protestant orthodoxy and laid the foundation for the rise of liberal Protestant theology in the next century.

Luther never dreamed that his call for reform, his excommunication and the establishment of a rival form of Christianity would eventually lead to the complete splintering not only of Christendom but also of Christian theology. His vision was to restore the one true orthodox and catholic church of the apostles and church fathers. That was also Zwingli's, Calvin's, Bucer's and Cranmer's common goal. One hundred years after their deaths, however, the Protestant project unraveled. That is not to say it failed completely. The vision of visible unity failed, but then that should not be surprising. All of the first-generation Reformers broke that visible unity when they rejected Rome—and with what they considered good reasons. That set a precedent, however, and their theological children, stepchildren and grandchildren followed in their footsteps of reforming by dividing. In this section I will tell the story of that post-Reformation splintering of Protestant theology and begin with the continuing story of the Reformed branch of Protestantism in which John Calvin had emerged as the great guru over all. Wherever Reformed theology went, his influence followed. And yet some of his closest disciples interpreted Calvin in ways that seem foreign to the spirit of the great "servant of Geneva." It was in the Netherlands that this led to an attempt to reform Reformed theology that broke it wide open and led to a new form of Protestant theology.

# CHAPTER 28

# Arminians Attempt to Reform Reformed Theology

*Arminian theology derives from the Dutch Reformed theologian Jacob* (James) Arminius, who was born in 1560 and died at age forty-nine in 1609.[1] Arminius and his theology were controversial throughout the Netherlands as well as Great Britain and other countries where Reformed theology was dominant or influential. At one point during the controversy, rioting broke out in the major cities of Holland and the other provinces of the Netherlands. During his lifetime Arminius's teachings created such a deep split within the Reformed community that the Dutch government became involved. Although he was once exonerated of heresy by the highest governing body of the land, Arminius died in the middle of another crisis of church and state that swirled around his public criticism of Calvinist doctrines. His followers, known as the Remonstrants (protesters), picked up his fallen banner and continued the challenge. Eventually they were excommunicated from the Reformed church of the Netherlands by the Synod of Dort (1618-1619), and their leaders were sent into exile by the Dutch government. One of them who had served for many years as a leading statesman of the Netherlands was imprisoned and publicly beheaded in part, at least, due to his intransigent support for the "heresy" of Arminianism.

For centuries after the Remonstrant controversy died down, Arminianism was virtually synonymous with Pelagianism among Puritans and other conservative

Calvinists. And yet Jacob Arminius himself expressly denied being a Pelagian or having any sympathies with that heresy of salvation apart from assisting supernatural grace. More cautious opponents have equated Arminian theology with Semi-Pelagianism even though Arminius himself affirmed that the initiative in salvation is completely God's and that all of salvation is by grace alone through faith alone. Arminius saw himself as a faithful Protestant of the Reformed Church of Holland who just happened to disagree with certain viewpoints of Calvinism. He especially rejected the extreme version of Calvinism known as supralapsarianism, but he ended up rejecting all forms of belief in unconditional divine election or predestination of individual persons to heaven or hell. Because many Calvinists of his day (and since) equated the Protestant doctrine of justification by grace through faith alone with monergism and equated synergism with Roman Catholic doctrine, Arminius was accused of being a secret sympathizer with Rome. Arminius and his followers vehemently denied that monergism is the only view of God's relationship with fallen, sinful human beings that does justice to salvation as a sheer gift. While rejecting unconditional election and irresistible grace, they upheld the central Protestant principles and affirmed that Christ's righteousness is imputed to sinners for their salvation on account of faith alone.

Without doubt or debate, Arminius is one of the most unfairly neglected and grossly misunderstood theologians in the story of Christian theology. Both he and his theology are "frequently assessed according to superficial hearsay."[2] A modern Reformed commentator and critic has noted that "the theology of Jacob Arminius has been neglected both by his admirers and by his detractors"[3] and says of Arminius that he is "one of a dozen or so theologians in the history of the Christian church who has given lasting direction to the theological tradition and who, as a result, has stamped his name upon a particular doctrinal or confessional viewpoint,"[4] which makes it doubly ironic that he is also "one of the most neglected of the major Protestant theologians."[5] In order to understand Arminius and his theology and the deep division it has caused within Protestant theology, it is necessary to go back before Arminius himself and examine the development of Reformed theology after Calvin.

### Reformed Scholasticism and Supralapsarianism

Although the major first-generation Protestant Reformers such as Luther, Zwingli and Calvin reacted against scholasticism and scholastic theology, their immediate followers fell back into a kind of scholastic thinking that placed a great deal more emphasis on philosophy and logic and sought to use these to construct highly coherent systems of Protestant doctrine. This tendency of post-Reformation

Protestant thinkers has earned them the dubious label of "Protestant scholastics," and their theology is often vaguely characterized as Protestant scholasticism. What many of them tried to do was discover and carve into stone a rigid Protestant orthodoxy that could repel all heresy, including attacks by skeptics and Roman Catholic critics. Thus whereas Luther and Calvin had been comfortable with some degree of mystery in theology, these Protestant scholastics tended to expunge mystery, uncertainty and ambiguity from Protestant theology by imitating the style of Thomas Aquinas, who tried to use Scripture, tradition and reason to develop a comprehensive system of all truth. Of course, most of the sixteenth- and seventeenth-century Protestant scholastics were not aware of the similarities between their own theological projects and that of Thomas Aquinas and other medieval Catholic theologians. Nevertheless, later historical theologians examining them cannot help but notice the comparison.

Richard Muller, a leading modern scholar of Protestant scholasticism, defines it as "a school theology, identified by its careful division of topics and definition of component parts and by its interest in pressing the logical and metaphysical questions raised by theology toward rational answers."[6] Muller accurately describes this post-Reformation Protestant theology toward the end of the sixteenth century (just when Arminius was beginning his ministry in Amsterdam) as "a confessional orthodoxy more strictly defined in its doctrinal boundaries than the theology of the early Reformers but, at the same time, broader and more diverse in its use of the materials of the Christian tradition, particularly the materials provided by the medieval doctors [of theology]."[7] While few, if any, of these practitioners of Protestant scholasticism would have explicitly acknowledged their indebtedness to Roman Catholic sources, their developing Protestant orthodox systems of thought borrowed heavily from them and especially from their methods of logical deduction and metaphysical speculation.

One of the prime examples of this budding Protestant scholasticism is Calvin's successor in Geneva, Theodore Beza (1519-1605). Upon Calvin's death in 1564 "the full weight of Calvin's responsibility came upon Beza. Beza was the head of the [Genevan] academy, a teacher there, moderator of the Company of Pastors, a powerful influence with the magistrates of Geneva, and the spokesman and defender of the Reformed Protestant position."[8] Like numerous other Reformed pastors and theologians from all over Britain and Europe, Jacob Arminius studied under Beza for a time. Later, of course, he came to reject Beza's conclusions if not his scholastic methods of arriving at them. Beza is best known in the history of theology as one of the founders of the extreme type of Calvinist theology known as supralapsarianism. Many of the Reformed scholastics like Beza were fascinated with questions about the decrees of God. Zwingli and Calvin both had emphasized that everything that happens—including the fall of Adam and Eve and the election of some humans to salvation and others to damnation—is decreed by God. In other words, both Swiss Reformed theologians had asserted, nothing at all happens or can happen accidently or even contingently. Everything that happens outside of God himself happens by divine decree. God foreknows what will happen because he foreordains everything that happens, and he foreordains because he decrees it all from eternity.

Beza and other post-Calvin Reformed theologians began to wonder and speculate about the "order of the divine decrees." In other words, they were concerned with the ultimate purposes of God in everything. Why did God create the world? Is his decree to create the world logically prior to his decree to predestine some persons to salvation and other persons to eternal damnation, or is it the other way around? They agreed that all of God's decrees are simultaneous and eternal because they accepted Augustine's notion of eternity as an "eternal now" in which all times—past, present and future—are simultaneous. For God, they believed, there is no separation or even succession of moments. Everything is eternally present. Thus God does not decree something and then wait to see what happens and then decree something else in response. All of God's decrees in relation to what is outside of God (creation) are simultaneous and timeless. Thus when Beza and other Protestant scholastics speculated and debated about the "order of the divine decrees," they were referring to their logical order and not to some chronological order. So the question was, What is the proper logical order of the decrees of God concerning creation and redemption? It matters because how one views God's ultimate purposes for things depends on how one views the order of the divine decrees and vice versa.

Beza and certain other Calvinists were obsessed with the doctrine of predestination more than Calvin himself ever had been. Whereas Calvin located the doctrine within the category of redemption as part of the gracious activity of God and admitted mystery regarding God's purposes in divine election and reprobation, Beza located predestination within the doctrine of God as a direct deduction from God's power, knowledge and providential rule.[9] In this way he was closer to Zwingli than to Calvin. Beza and most other Calvinists also deduced the doctrine of limited atonement—that Christ died only for the elect and not for the reprobate—from the doctrine of God's providence and electing decrees. That deduction, though logical, cannot be found in Calvin himself. In order to protect the doctrine of predestination from any erosion by synergism, Beza and other rigid Calvinists of the sixteenth century developed supralapsarianism. *Supra* indicates logical priority to something else. *Lapsarianism* indicates reference to the fall of humanity (from the same root as *lapse*—to "fall"). Thus *supralapsarianism* literally means "something prior to the Fall." That hardly explains its theological significance, however.

Theologically, supralapsarianism is a certain way of ordering the divine decrees so that God's decision and decree concerning predestination of humans to either heaven or hell precedes his decrees to create humans and allow them to fall. Here is the typical order of the divine decrees according to supralapsarianism:

1. The decree of God to predestine some creatures to salvation and eternal life and some other creatures to damnation and everlasting punishment in hell.

2. The decree of God to create.

3. The decree of God to allow human creatures to fall into sin.

4. The decree of God to provide the means of salvation (Christ and the gospel) for the elect.

5. The decree of God to apply salvation (the righteousness of Christ) to the elect.

The supralapsarian order of the divine decrees makes clear that God's first and foremost purpose in his relation with the world is to glorify himself (always God's main motive in everything) by saving some creatures and damning others. Double predestination, then, logically precedes creation, the Fall and everything else, including Christ's incarnation and atonement in the mind and purpose of God.

Beza and the other supralapsarian Calvinists thought they were merely working out the logical details of Calvin's own doctrine of election. Whether that is true or not is debatable. Some scholars believe Calvin would have approved. Others think he would have rejected supralapsarianism in favor of its rival, infralapsarianism. *Infra* indicates subsequence to something else. In this case, infralapsarianism subordinates the divine decree of predestination to the decree to allow the fall of humanity into sin. According to infralapsarian Calvinists, God's ultimate purpose in his overall plan is not to elect some and damn others but to glorify himself by creating the world. Only because humans fell into sin did God subsequently (in logical order) decree double predestination. Thus the typical order of the divine decrees in infralapsarianism is as follows:

1. The decree of God to create the world and humanity in it.

2. The decree of God to allow the Fall of humanity.

3. The decree of God to elect some fallen humans to salvation and eternal life and predestine others to damnation and everlasting punishment.

4. The decree of God to provide the means of salvation (Christ) for the elect.

5. The decree of God to apply salvation to the elect and leave the reprobate

(those predestined to damnation) to their deserved fate.

Both supralapsarians and infralapsarians agreed on many things. They agreed that Calvin had the right basic vision of God's plan and purpose with regard to creation: to glorify himself through everything. They agreed that God controls everything that happens in both creation and redemption and that nothing happens without God's decreeing it and bringing it about. They agreed that the fall of humanity and individual humans' ultimate destinies in heaven or hell are predestined by God and not merely foreknown or foreseen. They agreed that God is not responsible for sin or evil in the sense of bearing any burden of guilt for them, because God is above human law and notions of fairness. Everything that God does is right because it glorifies God and, as Beza is supposed to have declared, "Those who suffer for eternity in hell can at least take comfort in the fact that they are there for the greater glory of God."

What supralapsarians and infralapsarians disagreed about was whether God's first (ultimate) purpose was to glorify himself through predestination or through creation. Another way of putting it is that supralapsarians regarded God's predestining decree as applying to humans as creatures completely apart from their also being sinners, while infralapsarians regarded God's predestining decree as applying only to humans as fallen sinners. In either case, however, both the saved and the damned are such as they are because God has so decided it from eternity.

### The Calvinist Doctrinal Consensus

Throughout the second half of the sixteenth century, the Reformed Protestant scholastics of both schools of thought—supralapsarian and infralapsarian—gradually developed a system of Calvinist doctrine that later came to be described according to the acronym TULIP. These five points of Calvinism were never laid out in this exact manner before the great Arminian controversy and its conclusion at the Synod of Dort in 1618-1619. It was at that Calvinist synod in Holland that they were pronounced and made official doctrine—at least for the Dutch Reformed churches. Once that happened, Reformed Protestants everywhere tended to accept them. The acronym caught on and its five points have been correctly seen as valid for most Reformed scholastics—both supralapsarians and infralapsarians—even before Dort canonized them. These five points are what Arminius questioned and his followers the Remonstrants rejected, and the latter were excommunicated and exiled from Holland for that. Arminius himself almost certainly would have suffered the same fate had he lived long enough. Here are the five points in a nutshell:

□ Total depravity—humans are dead in trespasses and sins before God sovereignly regenerates them and gives them the gift of salvation. (This usually implies a denial of free will.)

□ Unconditional election—God chooses some humans to save before and apart from anything they do on their own. (This leaves open the question of whether God actively predestines some to damnation or merely leaves them to their deserved damnation.)

□ Limited atonement—Christ died only to save the elect, and his atoning death is not universal for all of humanity.

□ Irresistible grace—God's grace cannot be resisted. The elect will receive it and be saved by it. The damned never receive it.

□ Perseverance—The elect will inevitably persevere unto final salvation (eternal security).

This is a partial picture of Calvinist Reformed theology around 1600, even though the acronym TULIP itself was coined later. Wherever one went in Britain or on the European continent, those who considered themselves Reformed and followers of John Calvin agreed at least on these five axioms of doctrine in addition to the Nicene Creed. Whether Calvin himself would have agreed with all five is debatable. Reformed theologians and divines (preachers) also generally agreed that part and parcel of the whole system was belief in God's meticulous providence over all—that everything that happens in nature and history is decreed by God. Any other view such as synergism was equated by most Calvinists with Roman Catholic doctrine. Supralapsarians tolerated infralapsarians but thought that their interpretation of the Calvinist theology was weak at best and an opening to synergism at worst. Beza tolerated infralapsarianism in Geneva and even among the faculty of the Genevan Academy.

### Jacob Arminius and the Remonstrant Controversy

The Holland in which Jacob Arminius was born and raised was struggling with its Roman Catholic heritage and the domination of Catholic Spain. A small group of rebels had united several provinces of the Netherlands against Spanish rule and established a shaky alliance known as the United Provinces (of the Netherlands). Holland was the largest and most influential of the provinces. At the same time that the Dutch were liberating themselves from Spain, they were establishing their own national Protestant church. The Reformed Church of Amsterdam was established in 1566, and its leading ministers and laymen held to the three main Protestant principles without allying themselves with any one particular branch of Protestantism. Earliest Dutch Protestantism was a *sui generis* type of Protestantism that was not rigidly locked into either Lutheranism or Calvinism.[10]

Arminius was raised a Protestant in the small town of Oudewater between Utrecht and Rotterdam, but his early Christian formation was not heavily Calvinistic. When he was fifteen years old, he was sent to Marburg in Germany for education. While he was there, his hometown suffered an invasion and massacre by Catholic soldiers loyal to Spain. His entire family was killed in one day. The young student was taken in by a leading Dutch minister in Amsterdam and eventually became one of the first students to enroll in the newly established Protestant university at Leiden. The Reformed Church of Amsterdam considered Arminius one of its most promising young candidates for ministry and so paid for his education at Leiden and then in Switzerland. There he studied for a time at the "Mecca" of Reformed theology—the Genevan Academy under Beza.

In 1588 Arminius began his ministry in the Reformed Church of Amsterdam at the age of twenty-nine. By all accounts his tenure there was an illustrious one. As one biographer notes, "Arminius was the first Dutch pastor of the Dutch Reformed Church of the greatest Dutch city, just when it was emerging out of its medieval past and bursting into its Golden Age."[11] He was clearly well liked and respected as both a pastor and a preacher and quickly became one of the most influential men in all of Holland. He married a daughter of one of Amsterdam's leading citizens and joined the ranks of the privileged and powerful. And yet there is no indication of any arrogance or ambition on his part. Even his critics never accused him of abusing his pastoral position or of any other personal or spiritual faults. They only accused him of heresy because as pastor of one of Holland's most influential churches, he began openly to criticize supralapsarianism, which was on the rise as more and more Dutch ministers returned from studying under Beza in Geneva. Arminius was of the "old school" of independent-minded Dutch Protestantism that refused to canonize any particular brand of Protestant theology as orthodox. Some though, were increasingly insisting that supralapsarianism was the only truly orthodox Protestant theology and that every other view was somehow an accommodation to Roman Catholic theology and therefore a potential ally of the Netherlands's political enemy Spain.

Throughout the 1590s Arminius and rigid Calvinists in Holland came into increasing conflict. Some scholars have suggested that Arminius changed his mind during this time. Their assumption is that he had once been a "high Calvinist" if not a supralapsarian himself. That assumption seems to be based merely on the fact that he had studied under Beza. The leading modern interpreter of Arminius contradicts this notion of Arminius's alleged change of mind: "All [the] evidence points to one conclusion: namely, that Arminius was not in agreement with Beza's doctrine of predestination when he undertook his ministry at Amsterdam; indeed, he probably never had agreed with it."[12] In the course of a series of sermons on Paul's *Epistle to the Romans,* the young preacher openly began to contradict not only supralapsarianism but unconditional election and irresistible grace as well. He interpreted Romans 9, for instance, as referring not to individuals but to classes—believers and unbelievers—as predestined by God. He affirmed individuals' free will to include themselves in those classes of "elect" and "reprobate" and based God's predestination of individuals on his foreknowledge of their free choices, appealing to Romans 8:29 for support. As Arminius's biographer and interpreter Carl Bangs notes, the Dutch theologian showed in his 1590's sermons a desire to strike a balance between sovereign grace and human free will: "The objective was a theology of grace which does not leave man 'a stock or a stone'."[13]

Arminius's rigid Calvinist opponents in Amsterdam and elsewhere quickly sniffed out the dreaded error of synergism in his preaching and teaching and publicly accused him of heresy to the officials of the church and the city, who looked into the matter and cleared Arminius of the charges. Arminius had appealed to the Dutch Protestant tradition of independence from specific theological systems and tolerance of diversity on details of doctrine. The officials agreed. Arminius's supralapsarian opponents seethed with resentment and determined to undermine him in whatever way possible. They suffered a major defeat when Arminius was appointed to the prestigious position of professor of theology at the University of Leiden in 1603. The other professor of theology at that time was Franciscus Gomarus, who was perhaps the most outspoken and rigid supralapsarian Calvinist in all of Europe. Not only did Gomarus consider every other view, including infralapsarianism, defective if not heretical, but also "in his temperament he was, by almost all accounts, fractious in the extreme."[14]

Almost immediately Gomarus began a campaign of accusation against Arminius. Some of the accusations were true. For instance, Arminius was quite open about his rejection not only of supralapsarianism but the classical Calvinist doctrine of predestination in general. Gomarus twisted this to imply both publicly and behind Arminius's back that he was a secret sympathizer with the Jesuits—a particularly feared order of Roman Catholic priests who have been called the "shock troops of the Counter-Reformation." This and other of Gomarus's allegations were blatantly false. For instance, he accused Arminius of Socinianism, which was a denial of the Trinity and virtually every other classical Christian doctrine. No matter what Arminius wrote or said in his own defense, he found himself constantly attacked by rumors and under a cloud of suspicion. "As the controversy passed beyond the bounds of academic halls to pulpits and streets, it made no difference what defense he made. It was enough to conclude that 'where there is smoke, there is fire.' "[15] The controversy escalated to the point that it threatened to lead to civil war between the provinces of the Netherlands. Some of them supported Arminius. Some of them supported Gomarus. The conflict raged from 1604 when Gomarus first openly accused Arminius of heresy until after Arminius's death in 1609 of tuberculosis. He died in the midst of a public inquisition of his theology by religious and political leaders. At his funeral one of his closest friends uttered the eulogy over Arminius's body: "There lived in Holland a man whom they who did not know could not sufficiently esteem, whom they who did not esteem had never sufficiently known."[16]

After Arminius's death, forty-six leading Dutch ministers and laymen composed a document known as the "Remonstrance" that summarized Arminius's and their own opposition to rigid Calvinism in five points. After the title of their document, the Arminians came to be known as the Remonstrants. Among them were Dutch statesmen and political leaders who had helped liberate the Netherlands from Spain. Their enemies accused them of secretly supporting the Jesuits and Roman Catholic theology and of sympathizing with Spain—all because they agreed with Arminius against Gomarus on the doctrines of predestination! There is no evidence whatever that any of them actually were even remotely guilty of the political charges leveled against them. Nevertheless, rioting broke out in several Dutch cities as sermons were preached against the Remonstrants and as pamphlets appeared defaming them as heretics and traitors. Eventually the leading political power of the Netherlands, Prince Maurice of Nassau, stepped into the fray on the side of the Calvinists against the Remonstrants. In 1618 he ordered the leading Arminians arrested and jailed pending the outcome of a national synod of divines and theologians. The Synod of Dort met from November 1618 until January 1619 and was attended by over one hundred delegates, including some from England and Scotland, France and Switzerland. "John Bogerman, a Calvinist preacher of extreme views who had written in favor of the punishment of heresy with death, was chosen as President."[17]

Predictably, in spite of eloquent defenses of Arminianism by leading Remonstrants, the synod concluded by condemning as heretics all of the Remonstrant leaders. At least two hundred were deposed from ministry in church and state and about eighty were sent into exile or imprisoned. One of them—the elder statesman and philosopher Hugo Grotius (1583-1645)—was thrown into a dungeon from which he later escaped. Another statesman was publicly beheaded. A modern historian of the controversy concludes that "[Prince] Maurice's treatment of the

Arminian statesmen can only be regarded as one of the great crimes of history."[18]

The Synod of Dort promulgated a set of standard doctrines for the Dutch Reformed church that has become the basis for the common acronym TULIP. Each canon, as the doctrines were called, was based on one of the five points of the "Remonstrance." What the Arminians denied Dort canonized as official doctrine required of all Reformed Protestant believers. It did not, however, decide between supralapsarianism and infralapsarianism, and both have continued to exist within the Calvinist consensus expressed at the Synod of Dort ever since. After the death of Prince Maurice in 1625, Arminianism was gradually accepted back into Dutch life. By 1634 many of the exiles had returned and organized the Remonstrant Brotherhood, which evolved into the Remonstrant Reformed Church, which still exists. It was not in the Netherlands, however, where Arminian theology would have its greatest impact. That happened instead in England and North America through the influences of leading Anglican ministers, General Baptists, Methodists and other sects and denominations that sprang up throughout the seventeenth and eighteenth centuries. John Wesley (1703-1791) became the most influential Arminian of all time. His Methodist movement adopted Arminianism as its official theology, and through it Arminianism moved into the mainstream of Protestant life in Great Britain and North America.

## Arminius's Critique of Reformed Theology

Arminius expressed his theology in a number of published treatises, which when bound together form three large volumes.[19] His main doctrinal works bearing on issues related to the Arminian controversy (God's decrees, providence, predestination) are *Examination of Dr. Perkins's Pamphlet on Predestination* (1602), *A Declaration of Sentiments* (1608), *A Letter Addressed to Hippolytus A Collibus* (1608) and *Certain Articles to Be Diligently Examined and Weighed* (date unknown). Of course, Arminius wrote numerous other important works, including commentaries on Romans 7 and Romans 9, but these four treatises adequately summarize and clearly express his basic ideas regarding God, humanity, sin and salvation.

One of the charges frequently made against Arminius and his followers was that they deviated from classical Protestant theology. They were accused of rejecting the fundamental tenets of the Protestant Reformation. One still sometimes hears or reads that claim, especially from traditionalist Calvinists. Arminius himself went to great lengths to prove his Protestant theological commitments and credentials. For example, with regard to *sola scriptura* Arminius affirmed the supreme authority of Holy Scripture above all other sources and norms. He explicitly rejected equality of either tradition or reason with Scripture and called for reexamination of every human theological formulation in the light of the Bible:

> The rule of Theological Verity is not two-fold, one *Primary* and the other *Secondary;* but it is one and simple, the Sacred Scriptures. . . . The Scriptures are the rule of all Divine Verity, from themselves, in themselves, and through themselves. . . . No writing composed by men,—by one man, by few men, or by many men,—(with the exception of the Holy Scriptures,) . . . is . . . exempted from an examination to be instituted by means of the Scriptures. . . . It is tyrannical and Popish to bind the consciences of men by human writings, and to hinder them from being submitted to a legitimate examination, under what pretext soever such tyrannical conduct is adopted.[20]

In addition to explicit statements such as these, evidence of Arminius's commitment to the Protestant Scripture principle lies in the fact that he never contradicted or disagreed with Scripture or appealed to some extrabiblical tradition or philosophical idea over against it. He openly disagreed with certain traditional interpretations of Scripture, but he never disagreed with what he understood the teaching of Scripture to be. In fact, he accused his Calvinist opponents of violating the Scripture principle by treating certain Reformed confessional statements as equal in dignity and authority to the Bible and refusing to reconsider or revise them.

As with the Scripture principle Arminius never tired of affirming his own allegiance to the basic Protestant principle of *sola gratia et fides*—salvation by grace through faith alone. Modern Reformed theologian Alan Sell states that "on the question of justification, Arminius finds himself at one with all the Reformed and Protestant churches."[21] Of course, if one simply assumes from the outset that any form of synergism is incompatible with the Protestant doctrine of justification by faith alone, then Arminius's doctrine of salvation is ruled out a priori. But Arminius himself contested that assumption and tirelessly argued that even though he denied the monergistic theology of Augustine, Zwingli and Calvin, he could nevertheless hold to the classical Protestant doctrine of salvation. In his *Declaration of Sentiments* he wrote, "I am not conscious to myself, of having taught or entertained any other sentiments concerning *the justification of man before God,* than those which are held unanimously by the Reformed and Protestant churches, and which are in complete agreement with their expressed opinions."[22] Because he had been publicly accused of implicitly denying justification by grace through faith alone, Arminius included a confessional statement regarding that doctrine in his *Sentiments,* which he delivered to the Dutch government during the controversy just before his death:

> For the present, I will only briefly say, "I believe that sinners are accounted righteous solely by the obedience of Christ; and that the righteousness of Christ is the only meritorious cause on account of which God pardons the sins of believers and reckons them as righteous as if they had perfectly fulfilled the law. But since God imputes the righteousness of Christ to none except believers, I conclude, that in this sense it may be well and properly said, *To a man who believes Faith is imputed for righteousness through grace,*—because God hath set forth his Son Jesus Christ to be a propitiation, a throne of grace, [or mercy-seat] through faith in his blood,"—Whatever interpretation may be put upon these expressions, none of our divines [ministers] blames Calvin, or considers him to be heterodox on this point; yet my opinion is not so widely different from his as to prevent me from employing the signature of my own hand in subscribing to those things which he has delivered on this subject, in the Third Book of his *Institutes;* this I am prepared to do at any time, and to give them my full approval.[23]

In many other places and ways Arminius affirmed his belief that salvation is by God's grace and through faith alone. The calumny that he denied it—so common in his own day and not infrequent ever since—is one of the greatest injustices in the history of Christian theology.

Why then did Arminius's opponents and enemies accuse him and his followers of denying the principle of salvation by grace through faith alone? It can only be because he openly opposed the doctrines of Calvinism that they so closely associated with it. They believed that salvation can only be a sheer gift—unearned—if the human person is totally passive in regeneration, conversion and justification. That is, by their way of thinking salvation can only be truly by grace if its acceptance by sinners is not freely and actively chosen but given unconditionally and irresistibly. And that can only be true if it is foreordained and eternally decreed. Thus, to see the sinner who is being saved as in any way active in salvation is to give place to boasting because it implies that the person who makes the free decision to accept grace unto salvation is somehow earning it. To the traditional Calvinist mindset, it also robs God of his sovereignty and makes his decision of whom to save dependent on creaturely decisions and actions. Arminius rejected this entire line of reasoning and interpreted the key Scripture passage Romans 9 differently than Calvinists did.

Arminius did not reject predestination as such. In fact, he affirmed belief in predestination. He did, however, reject supralapsarianism, which he considered a most pernicious doctrine. He summarized Gomarus's supralapsarian version of Calvinism this way:

> God by an eternal and immutable decree has predestined, from among men, (whom he did not consider as being then *created,* much less as being *fallen,*) certain individuals to everlasting life, and others to eternal destruction, without any regard whatever to righteousness or sin, to obedience or disobedience, but purely of his own good pleasure, to demonstrate the glory of his justice and mercy:—or, (as others assert,) to demonstrate his saving grace, wisdom and free uncontrollable power.[24]

In his *Declaration of Sentiments* Arminius presented twenty objections to this supralapsarianism. Some of them apply to any version of Calvinist belief in predestination, including infralapsarianism. He argued that it is contrary to the nature of the gospel itself since it treats people as being saved or not saved completely apart from their being sinners or believers. They are saved or damned first (in God's first decree) and only then made believers or sinners. He also argued that this doctrine is a novelty in the history of theology because it had never been heard before Gomarus and his immediate predecessors (e.g., Beza). Furthermore, it is repugnant to God's nature as love and to human nature as free. Perhaps Arminius's strongest objection was that supralapsarianism (and, by extension, any doctrine of unconditional election) is "injurious to the glory of God" because "from these premises we deduce, as a further conclusion, that God really sins . . . that God is the only sinner . . . that sin is not sin."[25] Arminius never tired of arguing that the strong Calvinist doctrine of predestination cannot help making God the author of sin, and if God is the author of sin, then sin is not truly sin because whatever God authors is good. Arminius was a metaphysical realist.

When he turned to examining infralapsarianism, Arminius was not much more generous than with supralapsarianism. Even though it does not place God's decree of election and reprobation prior to creation and the Fall, it still nevertheless makes the fall of humanity necessary and God its author.[26] In the final analysis, according to Arminius, any monergistic doctrine of salvation makes God the author of sin and thus a hypocrite "because it imputes hypocrisy to God, as if, in His exhortation to faith addressed to such, He requires them to believe in Christ, whom, however, He has not set forth as a Savior to them."[27] Arminius appealed to John 3:16 and argued throughout his writings that the universality of God's will of salvation must be taken seriously and that predestination must be so understood that it is compatible with God's love and goodness and with human free will.

### Arminius's Doctrine of Predestination

Arminius was not averse to discussing the decrees of God. He was just opposed to the particular ordering of the divine decrees found in both major branches of Calvinism. Both of them, he believed, were open to several of the same devastating criticisms. For example, neither one placed God's decree to send Jesus Christ as the Savior of the world first and foremost, while the gospel is first and foremost about Jesus Christ. In his *Declaration of Sentiments* Arminius proposed an alternative scheme of four divine decrees regarding salvation under the heading "My Own Sentiments on Predestination":

> I. The First absolute decree of God concerning the salvation of sinful man, is that by which he decreed to appoint his Son Jesus Christ for a Mediator, Redeemer, Saviour, Priest and King. . . .
>
> II. The Second precise and absolute decree of God, is that in which he decreed to receive into favour *those who repent and believe,* and, in Christ . . . to effect the salvation of such penitents and believers as persevered to the end; but to leave in sin and under wrath *all impenitent persons and unbelievers,* and to damn them as aliens from Christ.
>
> III. The Third Divine decree is that by which God decreed to administer *in a sufficient and efficacious manner* the means which were necessary for repentance and faith. . . .
>
> IV. To these succeeds the Fourth decree, by which God decreed to save and damn certain particular persons. This decree has its foundation in the foreknowledge of God, by which he knew from all eternity those individuals who *would,* through preventing [prevenient] grace, *believe,* and, through his subsequent grace *would persevere.*[28]

Thus for Arminius predestination was first of all of Jesus Christ and not primarily of individual persons outside of him.

Important to remember is that Arminius insisted that the whole matter of predestination must be related to the fallen condition of humans in need of redemption. God's decree to permit the Fall, in other words, was for Arminius not one of the divine decrees respecting salvation. The decrees of God respecting salvation come after (logically posterior to) God's permission of the fall of Adam and Eve. How did Arminius conceive of the Fall? He made that clear in his treatise on *Certain Articles to be Diligently Examined and Weighed:* "Adam did not fall through the decree of God, neither through being ordained to fall nor through desertion, but through the mere permission of God, which is placed in subordination to no predestination either to salvation or to death, but which belongs to providence so far as it is distinguished in opposition to predestination."[29] In other words, God's providence includes some decrees and God's predestination includes other decrees. The two must be kept separate. In his providence God decreed to permit the fall of Adam and Eve and all of humanity with them. In his *Examination of Dr. Perkins's Pamphlet* Arminius said clearly that God could not prevent the Fall once he created humans and gave them the gift of free will. Arminius believed in God's self-limitation and self-binding and in genuine human liberty within the overarching covenantal relationship.[30] Thus, the decrees of God regarding predestination relate only to humans as sinners after the Fall and not at all to the Fall itself. God foreknew that humans would fall, but he in no way decreed or foreordained it.

Once humans fell, Arminius argued, the first decree of God in relation to them was to provide Jesus Christ as their Savior. Then, subsequent to that, he decreed to save all who repent and believe by means of Christ and leave to their deserved damnation those who refuse salvation. This is where Arminius began to discuss predestination of fallen humans. First and foremost it is of classes or groups and not of individuals. That is, God decrees to save believers—all of them. The object of election to salvation is an indefinite group of persons—all believers. The object of reprobation to damnation is also an indefinite group of persons—all unbelievers. This is how Arminius interpreted Paul's language in Romans 9: as applying to classes or groups and not to individuals. "Arminius understands Romans 9 in terms of a 'predestination to classes'—'those who seek righteousness by works and those who seek it by faith': Esau is a type of those who seek righteousness by works while Jacob is a type of those who seek righteousness by faith."[31] But Arminius also had a place for a conditional predestination of individuals. In his absolute foreknowledge God knows who will believe and who will not believe.[32] As Paul said in Romans 8:29, "Those whom he foreknew he also predestined to be conformed to the image of his Son, in order that he might be the firstborn within a large family" (NRSV). Predestination of groups, then, is unconditional. Predestination of individuals is conditional and based on God's foreknowledge of what they will freely do with the liberty God gives them. This is the essence of Arminius's second and fourth decrees above.

### Arminius's Evangelical Synergism

What about grace? Whereas classical Calvinists argued that saving grace is always irresistible, Arminius believed that grace meant to save is resistible and that many even in Scripture resisted the grace of God. But how can salvation be "all of grace" if humans are free either to accept or reject it? If this seems like an unreasonable question to someone, then he or she is probably already an Arminian! Calvinists and other monergists believe that in order for salvation to be completely of grace, as Paul asserted in Ephesians 2, it must be a gift not received "freely" in the sense of contingently. In other words, if the person receiving the grace unto salvation could do otherwise, then in accepting it that person is doing a "good work," earning a part of salvation, and thus able to boast. That also implies a Pelagian-like ability to contribute to one's own salvation, so monergists claim. Arminius's solution to this thorny problem lay in the key concept of "prevenient grace." Arminius was always cautious to attribute all of salvation to grace and none of it to good works. Typical of this concern is the section on grace and free will in his *Letter Addressed to Hippolytus A Collibus:* "That teacher [of theology] obtains my highest approbation who ascribes as much as possible to Divine Grace; provided he so pleads the cause of Grace, as not to inflict an injury on the Justice of God, and not to take away the *free will to that which is evil.*"[33] How is this possible, though? Arminius explained:

> Concerning Grace and Free Will, this is what I teach according to the Scriptures and orthodox consent:—Free Will is unable to begin or to perfect any true spiritual good, without Grace. That I may not be said, like Pelagius, to practice delusion with regard to the word "Grace," I mean by it that which is the Grace of Christ and which belongs to regeneration: I affirm, therefore, that this grace is simply and absolutely necessary for the illumination of the mind, the due ordering of the affections, and the inclination of the will to that which is good. It is the grace which . . . bends the will to carry into execution good thoughts and good desires. This grace . . . goes before, accompanies, and follows; it excites, assists, operates that we will, co-operates lest we will in vain. It averts temptations, assists and grants succour in the midst of temptations, sustains man against the flesh, the world, and Satan, and in this great contest grants to man the enjoyment of the victory. . . . This grace commences salvation, promotes it, and perfects and consummates it. I confess that the mind of . . . a natural and carnal man is obscure and dark, that his affections are corrupt and inordinate, that his will is stubborn and disobedient, and that the man himself is dead in sins.[34]

The grace Arminius described in that rather lengthy statement is prevenient grace. It is the grace God offers and extends to everyone in some degree, and it is absolutely necessary for fallen sinners—dead in sins and in bondage of the will—to believe and be saved. It is the supernatural, assisting and enabling grace of Jesus Christ. But as prevenient (going before) grace, it is resistible. So long as one does not resist it but allows it to work in his or her life by faith, prevenient grace becomes justifying grace. That change is "conversion" and is not a good work but simple acceptance. This is where Arminius's synergism appears. The human will liberated by prevenient grace (an operation of the Holy Spirit within a person) must cooperate by merely accepting the need of salvation and allowing God to give the gift of faith. God will not impose it. Neither can the sinner earn it. It can only be freely accepted, but even the ability to desire and accept it is made possible by grace. The concept of prevenient grace allows Arminius's soteriology to be synergistic (involving both divine and human wills and agencies) without falling into Pelagianism or Semi-Pelagianism. Unlike the latter, Arminius's synergism places all the initiative and ability in salvation on God's side and acknowledges the human person's complete inability to do anything whatever for salvation apart from the supernatural assisting grace of Christ.

Clearly then Arminius rejected not only supralapsarianism but also any monergistic view of salvation. He denied at the very least unconditional election, limited atonement and irresistible grace. Whether he denied total depravity is more debatable. The quote from his *Letter to Hippolytus* above indicates that he did believe in it. Some of the Remonstrants clearly did not, and this became a flash point of controversy after Arminius's death. Arminius did not deny perseverance (eternal security of the saints), but argued that it is an unsettled issue and warned against false security and assurance. As with total depravity, many Arminians later rejected unconditional perseverance and taught that a person can lose salvation through neglect as well as conscious rejection of grace. Many other Arminians came to believe in the eternal security of those truly regenerated and justified by grace.

**The Legacy of Arminianism**

One question that is still debated among Arminius scholars is whether his theology was an *alternative* to Reformed theology or an *adjustment* within it. Richard Muller argues for the former viewpoint and points to Arminius's strong emphasis on God's self-limitation as proof. Reformed theologians from Calvin on acknowledged God's condescension in revelation, but uniformly denied any self-limitation of God in providence or predestination.[35] Carl Bangs argues for the view that Arminius's theology represents an adjustment and development within Reformed theology.[36] While Arminius himself almost certainly understood his theology that way, Muller is nearer to the truth of the matter. Arminius's theology is thoroughly Protestant but not Reformed. The Dutch theologian set out to reform Reformed theology and ended up creating a different Protestant paradigm altogether. Anabaptists would argue with good cause that it was a paradigm Balthasar Hubmaier and other Anabaptist thinkers had begun developing almost a century earlier. It may be labeled "evangelical synergism."

Though politically suppressed and later marginalized in the country of its birth, Arminianism took root and flourished on English soil in the late sixteenth century. Many leaders of the Church of England at first sympathized with it and then openly espoused it. Even though the Church of England's Thirty-Nine Articles of Religion includes affirmation of predestination, Arminianism became a permanent option within the Anglican tradition. During the eighteenth century—an era of both rationalism and revivalism in England and New England—Arminians divided between two types: Arminians of the head and Arminians of the heart. The former leaned in the direction of Deism and natural religion, and the latter leaned in the direction of Pietism and revivalism. The stories of these movements will be told in later chapters. Suffice it to say that in the modern age in English-speaking Christianity, at least, one may be either a liberal Arminian or an evangelical Arminian. The early Methodist movement founded by John and Charles Wesley and many early Baptists represented the latter type of Arminianism, while the Deists and liberal Protestant thinkers of the eighteenth and nineteenth centuries represented the former type. Through these movements Arminian theology gradually filtered into the mainstream of Protestant thought in England and the United States—much to the chagrin of more traditional Reformed Protestants.

As we have seen, after the original Reformers died, their orthodox, scholastic heirs tended to elevate to prime importance issues of doctrinal and liturgical correctness. Some critics would say that the magisterial Protestant national churches of Europe and Great Britain declined into "dead orthodoxy," belief in baptismal regeneration, clericalism, and Constantinianism. This situation led to a reaction among ministers within the state churches known as Pietism. Among other things it sought to link justification with personal conversion and regeneration with the beginning of a life of true sanctification. It also decried overemphasis on doctrinal correctness to the neglect of spiritual experience as the hallmark of authentic Christianity and created slogans such as "A live heresy is better than a dead orthodoxy!" It is to the story of Pietism and its attempt to reform Protestant theology in the sixteenth and seventeenth centuries that we now turn.

# CHAPTER 29

# Pietists Seek to Renew Lutheran Theology

According to its leading modern interpreter, "one of the least understood movements in the history of Christianity has undoubtedly been that of Pietism."[1] Another historian of Pietism notes that the label has generally been used by theologians in a negative sense: "Pietism connoted subjectivism, individualism, and otherworldliness."[2] In popular usage a pietist is often a self-righteous person with a "holier-than-thou" attitude toward others or a super-spiritual person too heavenly minded to be of any earthly good. But these are misconceptions and stereotypes almost completely without relation to the historical movement known as Pietism that arose in the seventeenth and eighteenth centuries primarily among Lutherans in Germany. Pietism was a renewal movement that aimed at a completion of the Protestant Reformation begun by Martin Luther. Its major thinkers and leaders were Lutheran clergy who gave wholehearted assent to the main Protestant principles of *sola scriptura, sola gratia et fides* and the priesthood of all believers. Seldom if ever did they break with the primary confessional statements of the Lutheran heritage. They held up Luther as a great hero and quoted him often, even if they neglected some of his distinctive ideas such as the hidden God. The basic thrust of Pietism was that the Lutheran Reformation had been an excellent beginning of a renewal movement left incomplete. "Pietism reiterated the motif that the reformation of doctrine which had been initiated by

Luther must be consummated by a new reformation of life."[3]

Even if one strips away the distortions and misconceptions of pietism, there remain the problems of defining the term and identifying the exact contours of the movement. When did it begin? Which thinkers and ideas does it encompass? What were its chief characteristics and distinctive ideas? Many people, including some scholars, use the term *pietism* for any form of experiential religion, especially experiential Christianity. Thus, insofar as a particular Christian thinker or leader emphasizes experience of God over intellectual understanding of God, or personal devotion over doctrinal belief, that person is considered by some a pietist. The great French Catholic mathematician and freelance philosopher Blaise Pascal (1623-1662) is sometimes considered a pietist in that broadest sense.

More careful and precise scholars of theological history, however, restrict Pietism (capital *P*) to a specific movement within German Protestantism in the sixteenth and seventeenth centuries that had lasting effects and left a significant legacy for later Protestant Christianity. Those modern Christians who follow in the footsteps of the leaders of that reform and renewal movement are truly pietists in this historical sense. Here we will focus on that specific historical movement and use the term *Pietism* exclusively for it. It never was and is not today a specific denomination or even a movement with a headquarters. Rather, Pietism was and is a "spirit" or "ethos" more than any socially perceptible form.[4] Today almost every Protestant denomination has its pietistic wing whether called that or not. There are also certain denominations alive and well that look back to the Pietist movement of the post-Reformation period as their wellspring and source. A paradigmatic example of the latter is the Evangelical Covenant Church in America, which began in Sweden among Pietist Lutherans who separated from the Swedish Lutheran Church over issues related to Pietism.

What was and is the distinctive note of Protestant Pietism? One modern interpreter identifies it by saying that "Pietism stressed personal religious experience, especially repentance (the experience of one's own unworthiness before God and of one's own need for grace) and sanctification (the experience of personal growth in holiness, involving progress towards complete or perfect fulfillment of God's intention)."[5] Luther had emphasized the objective work of God "for us" in Jesus Christ, and his distinctive note in theology had been salvation as a forensic declaration of forgiveness and imputation of Christ's righteousness to the sinner. In other words, Luther stressed justification by grace through faith alone—salvation as an objective change in a person's legal relationship with God. Of course, one can find in Luther other notes and emphases. Luther nowhere denied the rebirth and renewal of the justified person by the power of God's Holy Spirit. In some places he acknowledged it. He tended to equate that experience of personal regeneration with baptism. The original Pietists agreed completely with Luther about the doctrine of justification, although like most Lutherans after Luther, they muted his monergism and embraced either a paradoxical doctrine of divine sovereignty and human free will or turned more toward evangelical synergism. In any case, the Pietists agreed with Luther than salvation is solely God's work and a gift that a human person cannot earn in any way.

Pietists simply believed that Luther had been a bit one-sided in his emphasis on the objective aspects of salvation and that Lutherans tended to neglect even more the subjective, inward side of salvation. They saw it as their task to complete and bring to its final consummation the Protestant Reformation begun by Luther by highlighting the gracious work of God within the believer that transforms him or her into a new creation in Christ Jesus. Personal experience of God, then, was the Pietists' focus and emphasis. For all of them, the true beginning point of Christian existence may be baptism, but baptism alone is insufficient, even when accompanied by faith. A change of life called conversion must take place at some point at or after an age of awakening of conscience, and it must be accompanied by a transformed heart—a new set of affections for godly things—or else it is not genuine and authentic Christianity does not exist in that person. Whether Luther himself would have agreed with this is unclear. The Pietists thought he would have. Their critics insisted that Luther would have rejected this doctrine of personal conversion as a necessary aspect of Christian initiation.

**Background in Lutheran Orthodoxy**

Just as Arminianism was a reaction to and rejection of post-Calvin Reformed theology (Reformed scholasticism and supralapsarianism), so Pietism was a reaction to and rejection of post-Luther Lutheran orthodoxy. It is impossible to understand historical Protestant Pietism without some knowledge of Lutheran theology and the Lutheran state churches in the seventeenth century. "Lutheran orthodoxy" is a phrase coined by historians of theology to describe the general hardening of doctrinal categories within that branch of Protestantism after Luther. It closely parallels Reformed scholasticism. In fact, the latter may just as well be called "Reformed orthodoxy" and the former "Lutheran scholasticism." A generation or two after Luther's death, leading Lutheran theologians began to engage in a project of rational systematizing of doctrine that often included natural theology, Aristotelian logic and extreme fine-tuning and hairsplitting with regard to doctrinal formulations. The work of theology in major Lutheran universities "became increasingly stale and objectified, as if the significance of theology were to be found primarily in a series of truths that could be formally stated in propositions to be transmitted from one generation to another."[6]

Alongside the scholastic and rationalistic tendencies of Lutheran orthodoxy was the rise of a polemical approach to preaching and teaching. That is, because the leading theologians of that dominant type of theology in seventeenth-century Germany engaged in heated arguments against Reformed Christianity and against one another, the mark of a truly great theologian increasingly became his prowess at devastating his opponents by showing flaws in their theology. Little or nothing constructive was accomplished by this type of theology except new ways of arranging and rearranging classical doctrines. Most energy was spent on criticism of other doctrinal formulations and systems of theology. This was the type of theology in which most German Lutheran pastors were trained in the German universities of the seventeenth century. The result was that

> the scholastic spirit [of Lutheran orthodoxy] cast a pall of intellectualism over the Christian faith. Persons were left with the impression that Christianity consisted of the reception of God's saving Word through preaching and the sacraments along with loyal adherence to the Lutheran confessions. It was stated that with few exceptions, pastors avoided any stress upon inwardness.[7]

Increasingly throughout the post-Reformation century, Lutheran Christianity in Germany fell into a state of spiritual, moral and theological lethargy. There were notable exceptions, of course. Overall, however, authentic Christianity was identified with doctrinal and sacramental correctness so that

> the popular idea within the territorial churches was that a Christian is anyone who has been baptized and who maintains some formal connection with the church by making use at least occasionally of the means of grace and who believes in general the truths laid down in the doctrinal symbols [creeds and confessions] of his communion and adheres to its cultic [liturgical] forms.[8]

A notable example of this tendency was the increase in belief in baptismal regeneration, including an implicit acceptance of the old *ex opere operato* idea that baptism automatically effects salvation so long as there is not conscious resistance to divine grace. Luther had opposed that Catholic doctrine, but his own teaching about implicit or infantile faith seemed eccentric to many people. Thus they fell back into reliance on infant baptism as an automatic guarantee of salvation. In addition, Luther's strong emphasis on the forensic aspect of justification was interpreted by many ministers and laypeople as obviating the need for personal holiness of life or even moral improvement.

Pietism was a movement that arose within the context of Lutheran orthodoxy, which many Pietists came to refer to as "dead orthodoxy." To them, at least, there seemed to be no real spiritual life in it. The popular Pietist motto "Better a live heresy than a dead orthodoxy" may be an abbreviation of a lengthier declaration of one of Pietism's founders who asked fellow ministers of the German Lutheran state church, "What does it help if our hearers are free from all papal, Reformed, Socinian, etc. errors, and yet with it have a dead faith through which they are more severely condemned than all those grievously heterodox better lives?"[9] Fundamental to Pietism, then, was a strong distinction and visible difference between authentic and inauthentic Christianity or between a living and a dead Christian faith. Lutheran orthodoxy tended to neglect such a distinction unless it was made along doctrinal lines. Authentic Christianity was equated with proper baptism, worship and doctrine within the Lutheran tradition. The Pietists rejected this as shallow and superficial. They wished to identify authentic Christianity more in terms of genuine experience of inward transformation by God's Spirit. For them, then, the true criteria of authentic Christianity were orthopathy (right feelings) and orthopraxy (right living) along with orthodoxy (right believing). For Pietists, the three can never be separated. Furthermore, they believed and argued that the most reliable means of ensuring orthodoxy were by promoting orthopathy and orthopraxy. Right experience and right living would inevitably lead to right believing.

## Four Movers and Shapers of Pietism

*Johann Arndt.* The Pietist movement had no single leader. Instead, four figures stand out as its representative thinkers and promoters in seventeenth and eighteenth centuries in Germany. The precursor of Pietism was Johann Arndt (1555-1621), a shadowy figure who wrote a widely influential book that many historians consider the "Bible" of Pietism: *Four Books on True Christianity* (1610). Little is known about Arndt's life other than that he was a highly respected if somewhat controversial Lutheran minister who had mystical leanings and pastored churches in Eisleben (Luther's hometown) and Celle in Germany. Between 1606 and 1609, he wrote his devotional book, which came to be known throughout Germany simply as *True Christianity.* For many years it was the most widely read and influential religious volume in German after the Bible itself. Arndt emphasized every Christian's need for personal renewal through repentance and faith and the experience of a new birth. Instead of stressing justification by faith (which he never denied), the forerunner of Pietism wrote and preached about union with Christ and a transformation he called "new life." According to Arndt, there is in each Christian person both the "old man" and a "new inner man." The two are locked in a deadly struggle, and the victory of the latter—which is the image of Christ within—is dependent upon genuine repentance and true faith.

Arndt distinguished between external (false) repentance and internal (true) repentance: "This is true repentance when the heart internally through sorrow and regret is broken down, destroyed, laid low, and by faith and forgiveness of sins is made holy, consoled, purified, changed, and made better so that an external improvement in life follows."[10] He also distinguished between false and true faith. He wrote of true faith, "By this deep trust and heartfelt assent, man gives his heart completely and utterly to God, rests in God alone, gives himself over to God, clings to God alone, unites himself with God."[11] Both true repentance and true faith, then, involve the anthropological center identified by all Pietists as "the heart." They also involve feelings and emotions, even though Arndt did not write in any detail about these.

The point is that for him, as for later pietists, true Christianity cannot be purely objective, outward conformity to formulas of doctrine or sacraments or liturgy. It manifests itself in visible changes in the attitudes, affections and lifestyle of the Christian person. True knowledge of God lies first on the affective field of the heart and only secondarily on the intellectual plane. In *True Christianity* Arndt argued in typical Pietist fashion that purity of teaching and doctrine would be maintained better by true repentance and holy living than by theological disputations and books of systematic theology. Notably missing from Arndt's reflections is emphasis on baptism. Lutheran orthodoxy argued that true Christianity is daily renewal of one's baptism by confession of God's promises regarding it. Arndt's neglect of baptism as a major component in true Christianity is more than an oversight.

Arndt's influence on Pietism was profound. Some scholars consider him the true father of Pietism and date the beginning of the movement from the publication of his *True Christianity*. One such historian of theology writes that "Arndt's relation to Lutheran Pietism is to be found in the fact that he initiated it. As a result of his influence it quickly began to flourish and then eventuated in the contributions of Spener and Francke."[12] Other scholars consider Arndt a precursor and forerunner of Lutheran Pietism.[13] The latter view is probably better simply because Arndt proposed no program for pietistic reform of Protestantism or the Lutheran state church and led no movement. He simply wrote a book that helped lay the foundation for later reform and renewal. Others built on it.

*Philipp Jakob Spener.* The patriarch of Pietism is Philipp Jakob Spener, who was born in Alsace along the Rhine River between Germany and France in 1635.[14] As a child Spener was taken under wing by a wealthy, powerful and deeply spiritual woman named Countess Agatha von Rappoltstein, who lived in a castle near Spener's home. There the lad read and discussed Arndt's *True Christianity* and was nurtured in that type of heartfelt Christianity by his spiritual mentor. The countess helped arrange and pay for Spener's theological education at Strasbourg and Basel. He spent some time as well in Geneva and there came under the influence of a mystical Reformed preacher named Jean de Labadie (1610-1674), who urged his followers to rely on inner experience more than outward sacraments for assurance of salvation. By the time he received his first ministerial appointment in Frankfurt, Germany, Spener was a convinced "heart Christian" who felt strongly that the church life and theology of his country needed reform.

From the platform of his influential post as senior minister of the entire ministerium of Frankfurt, Spener began a program of renewal by founding *collegia pietatis* (gatherings for piety), which also became known as the "Frankfurt conventicles." These were small groups of Christians that met in homes and in the churches for prayer, Bible study and discussion of sermons and Christian living. In our day most people take such small groups for granted. Many even substitute them for formal church affiliation. In 1670, however, they were considered a radical innovation and quickly became controversial. Many pastors and rulers outside Frankfurt opposed this conventicle movement because it seemed to diminish the distance between clergy and laity and opened the door to lay interpretation and exposition of Scripture and doctrine. Spener, however, was a strong believer in the Protestant principle of the priesthood of all believers and thought that it was being neglected in the atmosphere of Lutheran orthodoxy within the state churches. While he insisted that conventicles be led by trained members of the Lutheran clergy, he also mandated participation by laypeople so that they prayed and read Scripture and discussed the meanings of sermons openly. The aim of these *collegia pietatis* was inculcation of "heart Christianity"—a deeper life of devotion to Christ and increase in personal holiness. Critics saw this as a subtle denial of the Lutheran doctrine of *simul justus et peccator* (always saved and sinner simultaneously).

Many historians date the beginning of Pietism proper from the publication of Spener's little volume *Pia Desideria* in 1675. The title means "pious desires" and the book contains a scathing critique of conditions in the Lutheran state church and a program for its reform. This is considered the classic text of Pietism and has been translated into many languages. It is still in publication three centuries after it was written. The whole title of the volume is *Pia Desideria, or Heartfelt Desire for a God-Pleasing Reform of the True Evangelical Church, Together with Several Simple Christian Proposals Looking Toward this End.* Typical of the entire book is this reminder to ministers:

> Let us remember that in the last judgment we shall not be asked [by God] how learned we were and whether we displayed our learning before the world; to what extent we enjoyed the favor of men and knew how to keep it; with what honors we were exalted and how great a reputation in the world we left behind us; or how many treasures of earthly goods we amassed for our children and thereby drew a curse upon ourselves. Instead, we shall be asked how faithfully and with how pure and godly a teaching and how worthy an example we tried to edify our hearers amid the scorn of the world, denial of self, taking up the cross, and imitation of our Savior; with what zeal we opposed not only error but also wickedness of life; or with what constancy and cheerfulness we endured the persecution or adversity thrust upon us by the manifestly godless world or by false brethren, and amid such suffering praised our God.[15]

Spener boldly condemned the defects of both civil and religious authority in Germany in his day. Among them he named rampant immorality, lack of signs of true Christian conversion among even the clergy, love of controversy and overreliance on "human ingenuity" in theology and church life and underreliance on divine illumination of the Holy Spirit. He condemned the "shameful illusion" of *opus operatum* (automatic efficacy) in baptism and decried formal, nominal Christianity that left the heart untouched and the life untransformed.

Far from rejecting Lutheranism per se, Spener wrote, "The teaching of our church is not to blame for any of this, for it vigorously opposes such illusions."[16] He praised infant baptism even while condemning the false assurance some people based on it. Spener called for greater church discipline and set forth a specific program for reformation and renewal of authentic Christianity within the state church. The program is laid out in a section titled "Proposals to Correct Conditions in the Church" and contains six concrete steps, including widespread use of the *collegia pietatis,* spiritual accountability, a more irenic spirit in religious controversies and greater emphasis on spiritual life in ministerial training. Above all Spener advocated restricting the office of ministry to persons who were truly converted Christians and who showed definite signs of that: "It would not be a bad thing if all students were required to bring from their universities testimonials concerning their piety as well as their diligence and skill."[17]

Toward the end of *Pia Desideria* the author revealed the true thrust of his

Pietism: the doctrine of the "inner man," or "new man." This comes directly from Arndt. Spener redefined authentic Christianity away from centering on baptism and orthodoxy toward revolving around experience of inner transformation: "Our whole Christian religion consists of the inner man or the new man, whose soul is faith and whose expressions are the fruits of life, and all sermons should be aimed at this" and

> it is not enough that we hear the Word with our outward ear, but we must let it penetrate to our heart, so that we may hear the Holy Spirit speak there, that is, with vibrant emotion and comfort feel the sealing of the Spirit and the power of the Word. Nor is it enough to be baptized, but the inner man, where we have put on Christ in Baptism, must also keep Christ on and bear witness to him in our outward life.[18]

Eventually Spener was driven from Frankfurt by controversy. In 1686 he became court chaplain to the Prince of Saxony, Elector Johann Georg III in Dresden. There he continued his fervent and prophetic advocacy of heart Christianity and eventually fell into disfavor with the worldly prince. In 1691 Spener moved to Berlin, where he became pastor of the influential Lutheran Nikolaikirche (St. Nicholas Church) and helped younger leaders of Pietism spread the movement around Germany and Scandinavia. Spener died in 1705 in Berlin and, by his request, was buried in a white robe and coffin as a symbol of his hope for his own future in heaven and for the future of Christendom. His biographer notes that "by the time of his death, Pietism was a flourishing movement in the Lutheran churches throughout Germany."[19]

*August Hermann Francke.* If Spener was Pietism's patriarch, August Hermann Francke was its organizing genius.[20] Francke was born in 1663 in the university city of Lübeck into a home deeply influenced by Spener's Pietism. His family was also one with strong intellectual traditions and ties to Lutheran orthodoxy. In 1684 Francke began theological study at the University of Leipzig, which was "the universally recognized bastion of Lutheran orthodoxy."[21] He quickly assumed a leading role in a pietistic movement there known as the *collegium philobiblicum*, or "group of Bible lovers." In 1687 he experienced a dramatic conversion that was accompanied by great struggle and emotion. He had been asked to preach at a church and the night before his sermon realized that he was not even a true believer in God and Jesus Christ. He had only a "head knowledge" and no "heart experience," as Pietists would say. In his autobiography he wrote, "With great care and doubt I had fallen to my knees but with an unspeakable joy and a great certainty I stood up again. When I knelt down I did not believe there was a God but when I stood up I believed it to the point of giving up my blood without fear or doubt."[22] Francke made his own conversion experience of *Sturm und Drang* (storm and distress) the norm for all genuine Christian initiation, even though he did not insist that everyone be able to give the exact date of it as he could. The centerpiece of his own theological writing became what he called the experience of *Busskampf*—"struggle of repentance." Anyone who did not experience it in some degree simply could not be assured of authentic Christian faith.

Francke was soon drawn into the Spener circle and devoted himself to Spener's program for reform of the Lutheran state church. After graduation he became a popular preacher and teacher and the center of no little controversy. His colleagues at Leipzig complained and charged him and Spener with over six hundred heresies! Without any doubt their accusations were based more on professional jealousy and misunderstanding than on any true awareness of his teaching. In 1690 Francke helped found the new Pietist University of Halle, where Spener was a strong influence. He also pastored a Lutheran church there and founded several charitable institutions, which became known as the Franckean Institutions. They included schools for both rich and poor, an orphanage, a publishing house and a missionary center. Francke gained the patronage of the king of Denmark for many of his charitable and missionary endeavors, and with his support sent the first Protestant foreign missionaries to India. Francke was a man of great personal charm, charisma, integrity and dedication and eventually became the most highly respected and sought-after educator in Germany. He moved easily among both the rich and powerful and poor and downtrodden and had a heart for the latter even though he curried the favor of the former in order to gain their financial and political support. When he died in 1727, he was known throughout Germany and much of Europe as Pietism's leader and one of the strongest forces in Protestant Christianity. As one historian notes, "he was the originator, founder, and life-long head of a charitable enterprise which has caught the imagination and elicited the admiration of people the world over. Nothing like it could be found in the long history of the Christian church."[23]

*Nikolaus Ludwig von Zinzendorf.* One of the most unique personalities in the entire story of Christian theology is Nikolaus Ludwig von Zinzendorf, or Count Zinzendorf. His official name, including noble title, was Nikolaus Ludwig, Count and Lord of Zinzendorf and Pottendorf, and he was born in 1700 in Dresden while Spener's influence was still strong there. If Spener was Pietism's patriarch and Francke was its organizing genius, Zinzendorf was its eccentric prophet. In some ways he took Pietism to its extreme while remaining within the parameters of Lutheran orthodox theology. Noted modern Lutheran theologian and church historian George Forell calls

Zinzendorf "the noble 'Jesus freak' " and makes the remarkable statement that he was "the most influential German theologian between Luther and Schleiermacher . . . and who, by the way, never studied theology."[24] Another historian calls Zinzendorf a "many-faceted genius" and "one of the most controversial figures of his age."[25]

Zinzendorf was a remarkable child who was raised by his Pietist grandmother Henrietta von Gerstorff, who was in the thick of the Spener-Francke Pietist movement in Saxony. Spener was Zinzendorf's godfather. From a very young age the count absorbed his grandmother's rich devotional life and had his own deep spiritual experiences. He wrote love poems to Christ at age six and conducted prayer meetings for family and friends as a preadolescent. By all accounts he was a spiritual prodigy destined for religious leadership of some kind. At age ten Zinzendorf began studying under Francke at Halle. His experience there was "hard and bitter" as his classmates considered him odd. Francke also treated him harshly because he detected a spiritual pride in the young nobleman. At sixteen Zinzendorf moved on to study law at the University of Wittenberg and there helped found a Pietist group known as the "Order of the Grain of Mustard Seed." After graduation he worked for the government and purchased his own estate at Bethelsdorf, which he renamed *Herrnhut*—"the Lord's Watch."

In 1727 Zinzendorf invited a band of religious exiles from Bohemia to settle on his estate. They were persecuted members of a church known as *Unitas Fratrum*, or Unity of the Brethren, that traced its roots back to the pre-Protestant reformer John Hus, who was burned at the stake at the Council of Constance in 1415. The Bohemian Brethren had settled for a while in Moravia and thus were called "Moravians" in Germany. For all practical purposes they constituted their own tiny branch of Protestantism. Several hundred Brethren settled on Zinzendorf's estate, and he became their feudal lord and protector. Eventually he also became their bishop and spiritual leader. The eccentric German count was definitely a frustrated preacher and theologian and managed to teach himself enough theology to become ordained within the Lutheran state church. Thus he was an ordained clergyman of Lutheranism *and* bishop of a separate religious organization—the Moravian Brethren Church, whose members (including Zinzendorf) became known popularly throughout the world as the Herrnhutters.

The Moravian Brethren were much closer to Pietism in their Christian form of life than was the state church in which Zinzendorf was ordained. The count was a rabid critic of Lutheran orthodoxy and formal, systematic theology. He declared, "As soon as truth becomes a system, one does not possess it."[26] Through his many sermons and letters Zinzendorf placed Christian experience and godly feelings at the center of authentic Christianity and pushed formal theology and doctrine out to its periphery. "Heart religion" became the ideal for which he and the Moravians strove in all their endeavors. To them, theoretical judgments and intellectual concepts about God were foreign to the true essence of Christianity, which was experiencing God with emotional fervor. Zinzendorf's and the Moravians' legacy lies in the entire line of Christianity afterward that revels in emotion and spiritual feelings.

> Not only did [Zinzendorf] help to thrust upon his age a new understanding of the nature of religion, but a new understanding of religious apprehension. The only valid road to personally meaningful religious reality is here considered to be "feeling." The meaning of religious affirmations is to be found basically in the way in which they meet the religious needs of the believer.[27]

Zinzendorf and the Moravians founded communities like Herrnhut throughout Europe and the American colonies. They developed their own unique practices, such as regular observance of "love feasts," song services especially for hymn singing, all-night New Year's Eve services called "watchnight services" and Easter "sunrise services." Some of these were considered fanatical at first but became widely accepted later among self-styled evangelical groups. They also engaged in foot-washing ceremonies like the Anabaptists and insisted on radical conversion experiences for recognition as full members of their churches. They gained the sympathy of the king of Denmark, who supported their missionary endeavors. The Moravians sent missionaries to many parts of the world untouched by any Christian witness. John Wesley, founder of the Methodist movement in England and North America, credited Moravian missionaries with stimulating him to a spiritual awakening.

Zinzendorf and the Moravians focused their worship and devotional life on the suffering of Jesus. Without in any way denying or neglecting Christ's divinity or his resurrection, they believed that the best way to true repentance, conversion and personal holiness was to become obsessed with love for the wounds of Jesus. Meditation and preaching on the image of the suffering Savior replaced formal liturgy and theology. Zinzendorf preached that "a soul most tenderly in love with the Savior may be ignorant of a hundred truths and only concentrate most simply on Jesus' wounds and death."[28] He was convinced that anyone who truly falls in love with the Savior will naturally seek to please him in all of life, and therefore he saw no need to preach moralistic sermons and he firmly eschewed legalism as much as doctrinaire orthodoxy.

Two misconceptions about Zinzendorf and the early Moravians must be avoided. First, they were not Pentecostal or charismatic in the modern senses of those words. They did not condone emotional outbursts or excesses. Their meetings were generally quiet and the most emotional display might be open but quiet weeping. To say that they reveled in emotion means that they experienced deep, inner feelings, not ecstatic outbursts. Second, Zinzendorf and the Moravians did not throw out correct doctrine. They simply demoted it from a position of all-importance to secondary status. Zinzendorf himself affirmed all the classical Christian creeds and Lutheran confessions of faith, but he did not believe that one had to affirm them in order to be a Christian. Much more important to him was repentance, personal faith and what modern evangelical Christians call a "personal relationship with Jesus Christ." The Moravians had previously embraced the Nicene Creed and under Zinzendorf came to affirm the Lutheran Augsburg Confession. What they did reject was outward doctrinal confession as having any value whatever apart from personal experience of God in Jesus Christ. Zinzendorf declared:

> A confession always comes out of my own heart, out of my own knowledge of the matter. It presupposes that I myself have done something, that I myself have been somewhere, that I myself have seen or heard something which other people would like to know from me. Therefore, whoever wants to be a confessor [of doctrine] . . . he must himself have had, seen, felt, experienced and enjoyed the matter.[29]

Without doubt Zinzendorf displayed tendencies toward emotionalism and anti-intellectualism, but he never encouraged or condoned fanaticism or obscurantism.

Zinzendorf died in Herrnhut in 1760. He left behind a highly organized and well-established, albeit relatively small, Moravian community spread throughout the world. The Moravian Church of North America still exists as a denomination and traces its roots directly back to Zinzendorf's visit to Pennsylvania in the 1740s. Throughout the world one can find pockets of Moravians where missionaries arrived from Herrnhut and other Moravian centers. But the influence of Zinzendorf and his Pietist movement is much greater than that. His emphasis on nondoctrinal, experiential "intimacy with Jesus" as the true heart of authentic Christianity has bled into and permeated much of Protestant Christianity in North America. Wherever people gather to sing gospel songs or to share their personal testimonies or to watch missionaries' slides or to hold an Easter sunrise service or a New Year's Eve watchnight service or to watch a passion play, Zinzendorf's legacy lives on.

### Major Themes of Pietism

The Pietist movement was not interested in introducing new doctrines or even in radically altering the beliefs of German Lutheranism. And yet it was more than merely a movement for spiritual renewal. Its unique emphases amounted to a shift in theology even though that shift was for the most part unconscious and unintended. The shift may be summed up by saying that before Pietism, Protestant theology focused by and large on the objective nature of salvation—what God has done *for* people—whereas Pietist theology focused more on the subjective nature of salvation—what God does *within* people. Especially Lutheran theology had emphasized the objective nature of God's work of redemption and had largely eschewed interest in spiritual experiences of a subjective nature. Believers were encouraged to accept and affirm God's word of promise given in Jesus Christ through Scripture and the water of baptism quite apart from any emotions they might experience. When a person came to a minister of the Lutheran state church and confessed feelings of guilt, condemnation and lack of assurance of salvation, the minister would likely ask, "Have you been baptized?" If the answer was affirmative, the church member would be encouraged to renew the faith of baptism and trust God's promise of forgiveness through its water and the accompanying Word. Baptism was the "landmark" of the believer's relationship with God. Pietists, on the other hand, would ask such a person, "Have you been converted?" and "How is your devotional life?" For them, the "landmark" of true Christianity became personal conversion rather than water baptism, and assurance rested in conversional piety rather than in daily renewal of baptismal faith.

The first hallmark of Pietism, then, is inward, experiential Christianity. Another way of expressing that is by the phrase "conversional piety." That is, for the Pietists, true Christian piety—devotion, discipleship, sanctification—begins with a distinct conversion experience not identical with baptism. All of the Lutheran Pietists of the seventeenth and eighteenth centuries believed that infants of Christian parents receive forgiveness and new birth at baptism but inevitably fall away from that grace as they arrive at the age of the awakening of conscience.[30] In true Lutheran fashion Spener even referred to baptism as "the bath of regeneration," but at the same time he emphasized the need for later personal conversion and regeneration through conscious repentance and faith. Francke followed the same general view of Christian initiation. Dale Brown notes, "The Pietists' need for subjective appropriation made it possible for some of the followers of Spener and Francke to minimize infant baptism in favor of later conversion experience and to circumvent the objective efficacy of the sacrament. Francke and Spener, however, attempted to avoid this tendency."[31] Indeed, many later pietists of the eighteenth and nineteenth centuries departed from the Lutheran churches of Germany and Scandinavia and formed "free churches" that either embraced believers' baptism or gave parents a choice between infant baptism and baptism after conversion.[32] Spener and Francke, however, sought to combine Lutheran sacramentalism and Pietist conversionism within their movement. F. Ernest Stoeffler notes, "It evidently did not occur to him [Spener] that he was holding to two more or less disparate views of salvation. The one is based on sacramentally infused grace, or at least a sacramentally induced change in God's attitude, the other upon a personal faith commitment."[33] The same could be said of Francke, Zinzendorf and the entire Pietist movement insofar as it remained within the magisterial Protestant churches and did not move out and toward Anabaptism and "sectarianism" (as magisterial Protestants call the free churches that separated from the state churches of northern Europe and Great Britain).

In any case, the real emphasis and heart of Pietism is conversional piety and not sacramental piety. Conversional piety emphasizes two distinct but related experiences in the order of salvation: regeneration and sanctification. Both terms played roles in previous theology, but they took on new meanings and new emphasis in Pietism. Whereas classical Protestant theology tended to see the new birth (regeneration) and holiness of life (sanctification) as outgrowths of justification (which normally happened at baptism), the Pietists treated justification (God's forensic declaration of forgiveness and imputation of Christ's righteousness) as secondary to regeneration, which is the beginning of sanctification. In other words, while the objective aspect of salvation—justification—was never denied by the Pietists, they did tend to emphasize the inward renewal of spiritual rebirth—regeneration—in a way that overshadowed justification. Their main concern became the experience of being "born again" by God's grace through conscious decisions of repentance and faith accompanied by clear feelings of sorrow, trust and joy resulting in a transformed lifestyle in imitation of Christ by the power of the Holy Spirit. Spener emphasized feeling states of individuals less than did Francke, and Zinzendorf emphasized them more than either of his Pietist predecessors.

The second hallmark of Pietism is tolerant, irenic Christianity. Fed up with the harsh polemics and theological heresy hunting of Lutheran orthodoxy, Spener, Francke and Zinzendorf called for a new, irenic spirit among Christians, especially in secondary matters:

> Their position was summarized in the popular Latin saying: *in necessarii veritas (unitas), in non necessarii libertas, in omnibus caritas* ("in necessary things, truth [or unity], in things not necessary, liberty, in all things, love"). . . . Spener, Francke, and their colleagues desired to walk the middle ground between dogmatic inflexibility and dogmatic indifference.[34]

The saying mentioned in the above excerpt has been widely translated into English as "in essentials unity, in non-essentials liberty, in all things charity." The trajectory of Pietism was toward complete freedom of conscience in religious matters. The later Pietists such as Zinzendorf especially rejected state coercion of religious belief and practice without advocating complete separation of church and state. Even Spener, though, criticized what he saw as caesaropapism—rule of civil authorities in church affairs—and an overemphasis on details of doctrine by theologians and church leaders. None of the original founders of Pietism, however, rejected doctrine. Their belief was that a true personal experience of Jesus Christ and the illumination of the Holy Spirit that accompanies it inevitably enlightens people concerning true doctrine, so it is better to fight heresy with renewal of heart religion rather than polemics and threats of excommunication.

Clearly, for Pietists, doctrinal propositions took on a new status as "second-order language" whose value lies in service to the first-order language of Christian experience. The enduring essence of Christianity is understood by all Pietists as what we have here labeled conversional piety. To them it matters less what denomination or theological tradition a person identifies with than what kind of experience of God that person has. Orthopathy and orthopraxy take precedence over orthodoxy without excluding it.

The classical Protestant Pietists such as Spener, Francke and Zinzendorf and their followers were conservative in theology. Long after them, however, a kind of liberal pietism developed beginning with Friedrich Schleiermacher (1768-1834), who was raised under the influence of Pietism but came to reject many orthodox doctrines. Orthodox detractors of Pietism blame it for his defection from conservative belief. Pietists like his own father and sister, however, attributed it to a cold heart toward God and lack of close, personal relationship with Jesus Christ. Perhaps no greater damage has been done to pietism than Schleiermacher's own statement as a liberal theologian that he remained a pietist "of a higher sort."

The third hallmark theme of Pietism is visible Christianity. This means a Christianity that is apparent in the converted person's lifestyle. The Pietists were convinced that authentic Christianity—as opposed to dead orthodoxy and the nominal Christianity of church membership alone—would always display itself in Christians' attitudes and conduct. Genuine Christian initiation would always begin with a vivid conversion including regeneration. Regeneration, so Pietists believed, would instill in the convert a "complete existential reorientation" of life such that a new pattern of living would result. Francke especially focused attention on this aspect of authentic Christianity. He developed and expounded five marks of this new pattern of living: trials, cross-bearing, obedience to God's law, trust in

God and joy.[35] These visible signs of new life would increase insofar as a believer engaged in five means of living the authentic Christian life: self-examination, daily repentance, prayer, hearing the Word and participation in the sacraments.[36] Thus sanctification became a special emphasis among Pietists as they sought to distance themselves from what they perceived to be the ethical and moral indifference of many professing Christians within the state churches.

The Pietists developed two main ways of promoting and encouraging visible Christianity. First, beginning with Spener they all established and led something like conventicles within the structure of the state church. These small groups of "heart Christians" held members accountable for spiritual growth toward the ideal of perfection. Second, they all emphasized individual, personal devotional life with something like a daily quiet time of prayer, Bible reading and meditation.

Zinzendorf had his own method of helping heart Christians achieve visible Christianity. For him, intimacy with the Savior was the surest way for Christians to make their life of piety and devotion strong and apparent. He eschewed all moralism and legalism in favor of continually strengthening "connection with Christ" through meditation on Jesus' blood and wounds. "What he insisted on was that the heart of Christian piety must not be considered a set of regulations but a joyful, affective, unutterably satisfying, personal relationship with 'the Savior.' "[37] Zinzendorf's followers—the Moravians—manifested their Christianity to the whole world by being completely unafraid of death. This was their way of making Christianity visible, and it so impressed John Wesley that he began to sense his own need of a deep, inner experience of Christ. Before his own spiritual awakening, he traveled to the American colonies to pastor an Anglican church and the ship almost sank during a violent storm in the middle of the Atlantic Ocean. Wesley observed that a group of Moravian emigrants were calm in the midst of the storm and in the face of death, and he felt his own fear of death as a sign that he was not as spiritual as they were even though he was an ordained minister of the Church of England.

The Pietists were accused of the heresy of perfectionism because they so stressed progress in sanctification that it seemed to undermine Luther's principle of simul justus et peccator. Yet all of the great Pietist thinkers rejected perfectionism even as they rejected satisfaction with mere forgiveness of sins. Francke and Zinzendorf actually went out of their way to criticize Christian perfectionism. Francke wrote a treatise titled *On Christian Perfection* in which he stated that "perfection is nothing other than faith in the Lord Jesus and is not in us or ours but in Christ or of Christ for whose sake we are considered perfect before God and thus his perfection is ours by ascription [imputation].[38] In the same essay, however, he also made clear that progress toward perfection of life is a possibility and a reality in sanctification. The truly converted Christian person will inevitably show the marks of "maturing faith." "From this it follows," Francke wrote, "that both the following statements are true in a certain sense: We are perfect, and we are not perfect."[39] In other words, our perfection of life rests in Christ alone and in our being led by him toward perfect Christlikeness. Our imperfection lies in our persistent failure in this life to achieve complete conformity to Christ. Zinzendorf engaged in a famous debate with John Wesley about Christian perfection after Wesley was spiritually awakened through contact with Moravians in London. The German count rejected Wesley's doctrine of "entire sanctification" and insisted that the Christian is always only holy "in Christ" by faith and never holy "in himself."[40]

The fourth and final hallmark theme of Pietism is active Christianity. Unfortunately, Pietism has often been confused with "quietism" and has been made a synonym for it. Quietism is the view that authentic, strong Christian spirituality leads one to be completely detached from the affairs of this world. A quietist does not seek to transform society and culture. The original Pietists were not quietists. Francke, for instance, established his Franckean Institutions in Halle and urged his followers everywhere to emulate his efforts by establishing similar charitable institutions for education, care of the poor and sick, and dissemination of the gospel. One modern historian writes of Francke: "Lives changed, a church renewed, a nation reformed, a world evangelized—these were the great objectives in the realization of which he meant to employ his energies."[41] Zinzendorf also displayed great interest in world transformation, primarily through missions and world evangelism. He also had a lifelong vision of a unified Christian church that he even gave a name: the Congregation of God in the Spirit. Such an ecumenical church transcending all denominational barriers never came about, but Zinzendorf saw its achievement as a means toward world transformation. Far from being quietists so "heavenly minded they were no earthly good," the leading Pietists were people of action who believed that authentic Christianity could not help but make a difference in society.

### Pietism's Legacy

The Pietist movement began with Spener as a "second Reformation" or completion of the original Protestant Reformation. Its opponents such as the very powerful Lutheran orthodox pastor Johann Friedrich Mayer of Hamburg campaigned against it as a fanatical and heretical movement. In spite of opposition, however, pietism gradually became a permanent ingredient in the Protestant tradition both through quiet penetration of the major Protestant denominations and through establishment of separatist sects and religious organizations. Its greatest impact has been in North America and through nineteenth-century American missions around the world. In Europe it remained relatively small and distinct—a fringe of the Protestant state churches. In North America it became *the* main form of Protestantism, completely dominating and overshadowing sacramentalism, confessionalism and liturgical traditionalism. Every Protestant denomination in North America was affected by the rising tide of pietism in the eighteenth and nineteenth centuries as it became the grassroots form of religion there. Even Episcopalian, Lutheran and Presbyterian denominations were affected by it so that in North America they tend to have a pietist flavor generally absent or barely discernible in Europe and Great Britain. Unfortunately, in North America pietism has often gone to seed in gross religious individualism, emotionalism and anti-intellectualism. Whether or not these distortions are necessary end points of the Pietist trajectory is hotly debated.

Pietism began as a distinct movement among Lutherans. As German and Scandinavian Lutherans emigrated to the American colonies and then the United States of America, they often formed distinct pietist Lutheran denominations. One notable example was the large and influential Augustana Lutheran Synod of North America, which eventually merged into another Lutheran denomination and finally was swallowed up in the ecumenical mergers leading to the denomination known as the Evangelical Lutheran Church of America. Its pietist emphasis serves, however, as a leaven within that otherwise mainline and often theologically liberal denomination. Many North American Lutheran congregations proudly proclaim themselves "evangelical" in a special sense and participate in evangelism and devotional life endeavors. Some have become charismatic in orientation. Beyond Lutheranism, Pietism influenced North American Methodism and the Baptist conventions and formed the foundation of various free churches such as the Evangelical Free Church of America. The entire revivalist movement, including the holiness and Pentecostal groups such as the Nazarenes and Assemblies of God, may be seen as radical extensions of Christian pietism.

Perhaps nowhere has Pietism's legacy been more concretely manifested than in the developments of devotional literature and gospel music. Bestselling Christian books such as *My Utmost for His Highest* by Oswald Chambers and *The Christian's Secret of a Happy Life* by Hannah Whitall Smith are pietist in nature and have served to promote its vision of authentic Christianity and the possibilities of the individual's relationship with God here and now. The gospel songs of Fannie Crosby such as "Blessed Assurance" and "I Am Thine, O Lord" exude pietism and have also helped make its theology widely accepted in the English-speaking world.

Pietism began as a movement for reform and renewal within the German Lutheran branch of Protestant Christianity, but it changed the very face of Protestantism itself, especially outside of European Protestantism. It gave rise to several distinct denominations—some rooted in Lutheranism and some not. The English branch of the Protestant Reformation experienced two reform and renewal movements of its own that led eventually to entirely new forms of Protestantism. The seventeenth and eighteenth centuries witnessed the rise in England of Puritanism and Methodism—two very different movements that began within the bosom of the Church of England but eventually split off from it while leaving traces of their influences behind.

# CHAPTER 30

# Puritans & Methodists Struggle to Revive English Theology

Perhaps a better, more descriptive title for this chapter would be "Puritans and Methodists Struggle to Revive the Theology of the Church of England but Fail and Split Away." But that would be too long. Also some Puritans and followers of Methodist founder John Wesley chose to stay within the Church of England. These two post-Reformation renewal and reform movements arose first within the Church of England as attempts to alter its character. That Anglican character was determined by the Elizabethan Settlement and best exemplified in the theology of Richard Hooker, author of the *Laws of Ecclesiastical Polity*. Puritanism began as the opposition party to Anglicanism within the Church of England under Queen Elizabeth I. Puritans like Walter Travers—associate minister of the Temple in London under Richard Hooker—were the heirs of the "hot gospelers" of the early days of the English Reformation. Their theology was deeply indebted to John Calvin and his successor in Geneva, Theodore Beza. They were also influenced by the Reformer of Scotland, John Knox, who functioned in that kingdom as Calvin did in Geneva and helped establish the Presbyterian Church (modeled after Calvin's theology and form of church government) as the national church of Scotland.

Puritanism took on its own character as it struggled for dominance in the Church of England. Although basically Calvinistic in theology, it did not match perfectly any other form of Calvinism but developed a flavor all its own. Even though the original Puritan movement failed in its quest to transform the English national church and state into an English Calvinist commonwealth, it succeeded in leaving a lasting impression on the North American landscape, where thousands of English Puritans sought a new beginning and fresh opportunity to build God's kingdom as they envisioned it. Everyone in the English-speaking world has some passing acquaintance with Puritanism, however distorted their images of it may be. Public-school curricula and the mass media in North America have managed to create a caricature of Puritanism so that most people in our day have very little accurate knowledge of these reforming Protestants of England and the British colonies.[1] The very terms *Puritan* and *puritanical* conjure images of strangely dressed men and women oppressing American Indians, burning and hanging women wrongly accused of witchcraft, and locking people in stocks for minor infractions of church rules. They are virtually synonyms for moral strictness and religious intolerance. Like all caricatures, these images contain an element of truth, but they do not tell the whole story of Puritanism. And it would be impossible to tell that whole story here.

In this chapter our only purpose will be to describe Puritan theology and that only insofar as it displayed unique features setting it apart from forms of Protestant theology already described and discussed. Puritanism as a distinct movement for theological reform began in England within the bosom of the Anglican Church and ended with the greatest Puritan preacher and thinker of all, Jonathan Edwards of New England. By the time the Puritan movement petered out in the mid-eighteenth century, almost all had given up on the Church of England and formed new dissenting denominations. Edwards bridged the two main Puritan groups in New England: Presbyterianism and Congregationalism. Much of our retelling of the story of Puritan theology will focus on Edwards, even though he appeared at the tail end of Puritanism's history. He might even be called both the last and greatest Puritan. Most often the great movers and shapers of a movement appear near its beginning. Edwards's case is the exception.

Another renewal and reform movement arose within the Church of England just as Puritanism was losing steam. The so-called Great Awakening in England and its North American colonies in the 1740s helped bring about Puritanism's demise and Methodism's birth. Methodism began as a pietist and revivalist movement to breathe new life back into the increasingly cold, formal and rationalistic Anglican tradition. Brothers John and Charles Wesley and their friend

George Whitefield were its founders. They had no intention of leading a schism or starting a new denomination, but eventually strained relations between their Methodist societies and the mother church forced John Wesley to allow his lieutenants to split away from the Church of England. The Methodist Episcopal Church was born in the United States of America in 1784, less than a decade before John Wesley's death in 1791. In England the movement became officially independent of the Church of England as a "dissenting church" in 1787. Wesley himself maintained the illusion that his movement would transform the Church of England until he was nearly on his deathbed. Only then did he reluctantly admit that he had founded a new Protestant denomination.

As in the case of Puritanism, the story of Methodism is extremely complex and cannot be recounted in any detail here. Here our focus will be on its theology and especially on those aspects of John Wesley's theology that set it apart as distinctive compared to other forms of Protestant theology. Just as Puritanism's theology was a form of Calvinism with a strong evangelical flavor (emphasis on conversional piety), so Wesley's and Methodism's early theology was a form of Arminianism with a strong evangelical flavor. There were Calvinist Methodists like George Whitefield at the beginning, and a few hung on along the fringes of Methodism, but Wesley himself was an Arminian and stamped the mainstream of Methodism in his own theological image. Here our attention will be on Wesley's unique and distinctive contribution to what we have previously called evangelical synergism. Wesley's Christian perfectionism may not be totally new in the history of Christian thought, but it certainly created a new flavor to add to the increasingly diverse set of choices facing Protestants in the eighteenth and nineteenth centuries.

## The Puritan Movement and Its Theology

Who were the Puritans and why were they called that? As usual, pat and simple answers are elusive. Scholars still discuss and debate the true essence and limits of Puritanism. Some, for example, hail Jonathan Edwards as the "Prince of Puritans," while others see him as appearing too late to be considered a true Puritan. Some scholars date Puritanism's beginnings with John Calvin and the Genevan Reformation. Others—more soberly—insist that no one before Walter Travers should be considered truly a Puritan in the historical-theological sense. Here we will follow the more sober course and treat Puritanism as a distinct, yet somewhat diverse, movement of British Protestants who reacted against the Elizabethan Settlement in the English church beginning in the second half of the sixteenth century, and we will treat Jonathan Edwards as the last and greatest Puritan theologian. As our story unfolds we will see that Edwards died shortly after his inauguration as president of what is now known as Princeton University in 1758. Thus Puritanism's history spanned about two centuries and was confined primarily to territories dominated by Great Britain. Of course, it had earlier roots and later effects.

The earliest Puritans were all English Calvinists who hoped to turn the entire Church of England into a Presbyterian national church—like Scotland's—and all of England into a Christian commonwealth modeled after Geneva. As the Elizabethan Settlement became clearer and more firmly entrenched, they raised their voices in protest against what they considered "popish" elements in the Anglican theology, worship and polity. That is, they considered the Church of England under Elizabeth and Hooker and the various archbishops of Canterbury too close to Roman Catholicism, and they sought to purge it and purify it of those "Romish" beliefs and practices. All of them wanted to abolish the office of bishop and allow congregations to have greater say in choosing their ministers. They despised the Book of Common Prayer and sought simpler worship centered upon sermons. Most of them saw priestly vestments, incense, high altars, kneeling and genuflecting, and statues in churches as pernicious symbols representing unbiblical, Catholic tendencies in the English churches. The label "Puritan" was attached to them because of their desire to purify the English church of such traditions and bring it into conformity with their own vision of true Reformed theology and practice.

In the early decades of the seventeenth century the Puritans began to quarrel among themselves over the exact nature of the ideal church. Some of them wanted to stay with the Church of England no matter what and keep trying to reform it. Others insisted that the state church was hopelessly corrupt and polluted and beyond reforming. These Puritans separated from the Anglican church and formed independent churches that followed a congregational form of church polity. Each church would be autonomous and self-governing, calling its own pastor and deciding on its own worship and practices. Among these radical, separatist Puritans were the so-called Pilgrims who settled first in Holland to escape persecution from the English government and then traveled on the Mayflower to Massachusetts Bay in New England and founded Plymouth Colony in 1620. During the decade of the 1630s, thousands of Puritans left England and settled in New England with the hope of establishing a Christian commonwealth. Most of them became congregationalists when they arrived in the New World, whereas the favored church polity of most Puritans in England was presbyterian.

The Puritans who remained in England after the great diaspora of the 1630s packed Parliament, deposed and beheaded King Charles I and established a Puritan republic under Oliver Cromwell. After Cromwell's death in 1658, Great Britain returned to a monarchy and reestablished the Church of England with freedom of religion for nonconformists and dissenters. At the beginning of the civil war against the crown, the Puritan parliament called a national assembly of divines (Puritan ministers and theologians) to meet at Westminster Abbey in London. The 1640s Westminster Assembly constituted a synod of 151 Puritan and Presbyterian leaders who intended to lay the foundation for a Reformed national church of England modeled after the national church of Scotland.

The Assembly's greatest achievements were the Westminster Confession of Faith and the Larger and Shorter Westminster Catechisms. These became the semiofficial doctrinal statements for all Presbyterians and many Puritans from that time forward. The first question and answer of the Westminster Shorter Catechism is famous for its timeless expression of "the chief end of man," which is to "glorify God and enjoy him forever." The Westminster Confession is thoroughly Calvinistic with a distinctly Puritan spin. It emphasizes the verbal inspiration and inerrancy of Scripture, the absolute sovereignty of God, God's eternal decrees of election and reprobation (damnation), and humans' total depravity and complete dependence on God's grace. The Puritan flavor appears in the Confession's use of federal, or covenant, theology to explain the relationship between God and humanity.

In England the Puritans ended up a divided camp scattered in several different denominations. The Church of England remained Anglican in theology, worship and polity with Richard Hooker as its main formative influence. Some die-hard Puritans remained in its fold, hoping to reform it gradually from within. Others who did not emigrate to America settled into nonconforming denominations, becoming Congregationalists, Presbyterians and even Baptists. The Baptists were those separatistic, congregational Puritans who chose to give up on infant baptism and embrace the Anabaptist practice of believers' baptism. In New England, Puritanism mutated and thrived for about a century. Even after its demise as the dominant cultural force, it left indelible marks on the American cultural landscape. Among the latter was the idea of "manifest destiny" for American colonists and the post-Revolutionary republic of the United States—a secularized version of the Puritan vision of a godly commonwealth on earth.

By the 1730s and 1740s Puritanism had weakened considerably in New England. Congregational or Presbyterian churches stood at the centers of every city and town, but their influence had dwindled. Most citizens were not faithful followers of the original Puritan ideals, and the grip of the Puritan preachers on the reins of civil power had loosened. Whereas the original New England Puritans had sought to avoid the curse of "mixed assemblies" (churches where true believers and unbelievers mingled), it had invaded their churches in the early and mid-eighteenth century. Jonathan Edwards sought to reverse the trend through evangelistic fervor, strong Christian intellectual endeavor and church discipline. But it was too late. Nevertheless, in his struggle to return New England Puritanism to its first love, Edwards became the greatest Puritan thinker and preacher of all.

Puritan theology was thoroughly and persistently Calvinistic. Some Puritan divines preached supralapsarianism; some preached infralapsarianism. All proclaimed the absolute sovereignty of God and total depravity of humanity. They would have agreed heartily with the five theological points of the Synod of Dort (TULIP), and they condemned Arminianism as a "gangrenous" disease on Christian theology. The only thing that a Puritan theologian loved as much as examining and extolling the mysterious ways of providence in history was exploring and proclaiming the stages and aspects of Christian experience in the believing individual. Beyond Calvinism, Puritan theology was characterized by three universal theological ideas that together compose the Puritan consensus: a pure church, a covenant relationship between God and the elect, and a Christianized society. Each idea was at least foreshadowed in earlier Protestant theologies, but the Puritans emphasized each one in a unique way and combined all three in a distinctly Puritan recipe found nowhere else in the story of Christian theology.

One of the distinctive hallmarks of Puritan theology was the ideal of a pure church. To Puritan reformers in the Church of England under the Elizabethan Settlement, this meant two things: ridding the church of remaining vestiges of Roman Catholicism and cleansing its ministerium and membership of unbelievers. To them, the true church of Jesus Christ was more than an arm of the state or a support group for sinners. It was to be the body of Christ on earth, the communal presence of God's kingdom in history, and a city set on a hill shining as light for all to see. Thus the church needed to be composed of and led by true saints of God whose beliefs were correct and lives pure. That does not mean that only perfect people could belong to the church, but it did mean that merely nominal Christians with no genuine experience of God by true repentance and faith should not be full members. Such should be allowed—even required—to attend church, but they should not be admitted to full membership. The Puritans came to regard the Church of England as a "mixed assembly" that made no effort to distinguish between believers and unbelievers. Merely being an orderly citizen of the kingdom baptized into the church at birth made one a full member with all the rights that implied. The Puritans looked around and thought they saw priests and bishops who made little or no pretense of being true Christians. So they set out to purify the church not only of what they regarded as lingering "popish" practices but also of persons without any evidence of true Christian belief and devotion.

This Puritan ideal of a believers' church created a dilemma. "Who was worthy to join the company and who must be left out or cast out into the world? This question, which at first seemed simple, proved increasingly difficult to answer."[2] A few answered it by adopting what seemed to most a radical and unacceptable solution—believers' baptism. These few Puritan separatist congregations eventually became known as Baptist and grew in strength in post-Revolutionary America. But they represented a tiny minority of British and American Puritans in the seventeenth and eighteenth centuries. A larger number of Puritans sought to solve the dilemma by identifying "signs of grace" that could be observed in true believers' lives and requiring candidates for full membership in the church to display them and make public professions of belief. The vast majority of Puritans—whether remaining within the Church of England or separatistic Congregationalists or Presbyterians—defended infant baptism but combined it with a requirement of later public entrance to the church as full adult members. Persons who could neither explain their beliefs nor give satisfactory account of their personal "acquisition of faith" would be rejected from full membership. As this was against policy within the Church of England (which required only a confirmation ceremony in which one confirmed his or her baptism publicly), more and more Puritans separated from the state church, suffering persecution for doing so.

Puritans who emigrated to New England during the 1630s and 1640s developed their own forms of Puritan ecclesiology. Nearly all of their churches were congregational in polity with strong fraternal ties of connection between them. The Puritans left England for the most part presbyterian but quickly adopted congregationalism once they settled in Massachusetts Bay Colony. This is the beginning in North America of the old American Congregational Church, which eventually merged with several other Protestant denominations to form what is now known as the United Church of Christ. The New England Puritans, unhindered by the church and state laws of England, began requiring candidates for membership to go beyond merely making a confession of orthodox Calvinist belief to giving detailed accounts of their conversions and displaying the signs of grace in their lives. Unlike the German Pietists, the New England Puritans did not emphasize feelings and distrusted psychological states. When they asked candidates for church membership about their conversions, they wanted to hear about their contrition, repentance, belief, trust and assurance of forgiveness. And when they asked about or looked for signs of grace, they did not seek perfection of life. Instead, they wanted to observe earnest dedication to the church, orderly participation in society, solid family life and genuine interest in hearing and studying Scripture.

In many Puritan churches only persons who met the qualifications for membership were admitted to the Lord's Supper and only their children were baptized.

Others—often the majority of citizens and church attenders—were relegated to secondary status as observers rather than full participants in the life of the church. If and when they acquired true saving faith, they would be considered for full membership. This strategy for ensuring a pure church created a dilemma for the New England Puritans. While it went far toward avoiding the much-hated "mixed assembly" of the state church of England, it raised the specter of the ancient heresy of Donatism. The Donatists of North Africa in the time of Augustine (fourth and fifth centuries) also wanted a pure church. Both the Roman Catholic and magisterial Protestant leaders for over one thousand years had condemned Donatism as too extreme and perfectionistic. While the Puritans did not want to be Donatists (they considered Augustine a great hero of church history), their ecclesiology leaned heavily in that direction, and their opponents and critics in the Church of England never let them forget it. They were accused of being schismatic, heretical and fanatical by the Anglican bishops. Even the Scottish Presbyterians and moderate Puritans who stayed within the Church of England looked askance at the New England Puritans and considered them sectarians for their separatistic and seemingly perfectionistic beliefs and practices.

Another problem created by the believers'-church model developed by New England Puritans was the issue of church members' children who were baptized and grew up in the church but never experienced conversion and signs of grace. Should the children of these unconverted church attenders be baptized? Should they be admitted to the Lord's Supper? By 1700 the majority of citizens of New England were not members of the established churches even though they were required to attend church regularly. The Puritan ideal of a pure church had inadvertently led to a decline in church membership as well as to the dilemma of whether to baptize infants born to nonmembers who grew up in the church. As one historian of Puritanism notes, "The Puritans had in fact moved the church so far from the world that it would no longer fit the biological facts of life."[3] Throughout the last quarter of the seventeenth century and first quarter of the eighteenth century, an interesting solution was found that changed Puritanism profoundly. One of the leading Puritan ministers of New England, Jonathan Edwards's grandfather Solomon Stoddard (1643-1729), helped introduce the Half-way Covenant, which allowed children of nonmembers raised in the church to be baptized. Many, including Edwards, who succeeded his grandfather as minister of the influential Northampton Church, saw this as a serious deviation from the Puritan ideal and attempted to reverse it. But it was too late. The Puritan ideal of a true believers' church lived on mainly among Baptists.

The second hallmark of Puritan theology was a covenant relationship between

God and the elect. Puritan divines faced one of the dilemmas of Calvinism head-on and sought to solve it through what is known as *federal,* or *covenant*, theology. While this type of thinking about God's relationship with humanity was developed among Calvinists before the heyday of Puritanism, it was the Puritans—especially in New England—who made it central to their whole theology. One dilemma faced especially by Puritan Calvinists of New England was this: If humans are to strive for conversion and sanctification (signs of grace), how is this compatible with divine sovereignty in predestination? In other words, how may strong belief in predestination be reconciled with equally strong insistence on Puritan piety? For "if predestination affirms the ultimacy and final efficiency of God's choice, piety urges at least some effective free participation on the part of the human subject."[4] A related dilemma was this: If God is so sovereign that his will is not bound by anything, including his own nature and character, how can believers ever be sure of their election? The underlying nominalism or at least divine voluntarism within high Calvinism raised this question intensely for Puritans who sought assurance of election through signs of grace. How can one trust God not to be capricious? Are the elect secure, or might God change his mind?

The solution to these and other problems was found in covenant theology, which affirms that God has initiated and bound himself to contracts with humans. The first covenant God offered to Adam and Eve was the *covenant of works.* God promised to bless them in paradise so long as they obeyed him and did not eat of the tree of the knowledge of good and evil. The covenant of works was broken by humans and the result was exactly what the contract required—condemnation and corruption for covenant breakers. The Puritans assumed that all of Adam and Eve's posterity were born covenant breakers. They accepted the strong Augustinian idea that, as they put it, "in Adam's fall we sinned all." Part of the covenant of works was the condition that if the original humans failed in their obligations, their posterity would suffer corruption and condemnation. God's covenants are not just with individuals. They are collective and apply to groups in history.

Covenant theology posited a second contract God mercifully established with fallen humanity—the *covenant of grace.* According to it, "God's promises of redemption and renewal are to those who will receive them in faith and respond to them in obedience. The good news is proclaimed but a requirement is exacted."[5] The covenant of grace requires only that humans be sorrowful for their sinfulness, believe God and trust in his promises (e.g., to provide a perfect sacrifice for sin), and strive to glorify him in their lives. As the nineteenth-century gospel song says, "Trust and obey."

According to Puritan theology, the covenant of grace, which extends from at least Abraham until Christ returns, is both conditional and absolute. It is conditional in that humans as individuals and as groups (i.e., Israel, the church) are required to participate in it freely and voluntarily. If they do accept its conditions, signs of grace will appear in their lives. For Puritans, this theology provided assurance because it settled the latent concern about God's possible capriciousness and solved the riddle of assurance of election. Who are the elect? Whoever is truly converted and demonstrating signs of grace in daily life. Why? Because God has bound himself through the covenant of grace to give them salvation. But how does this avoid Arminianism or even Pelagianism—two of the most hated "heresies" to Puritans? It would seem that covenant theology could easily be interpreted as leaning toward synergism and away from monergism.

The Puritans insisted that the covenant of grace is not only conditional but also absolute. Hidden behind the conditional aspect is the mystery of God's eternal decrees of predestination. If a person is indeed keeping the human side of the contract, it is because God has foreordained it and given to that person the will and the means to keep it: "So the covenant of grace is likewise an absolute covenant, dependent upon the final sovereignty of God's action, and the centrality of that conviction must likewise be recognized in the interpretation of covenant theology. The use of the idea of covenant did not lead Puritan theologians to abandon their Calvinism or to diminish their belief in the reality of God's free election."[6]

Ultimately, covenant theology rests on a paradox. The Puritans neither denied it nor sought to relieve it. For the most part they simply left it as an unrelieved paradox. God established a conditional covenant with humanity that requires free and voluntary assent and participation, but only those whom he has eternally chosen and irresistibly called can fulfill it. The rest are damned for eternity because they are covenant breakers. They broke the covenant of works (and could not do otherwise) and failed to keep the human side of the covenant of grace (and could not do otherwise). It is no wonder that Arminians—whose numbers were growing within the Church of England throughout the seventeenth and eighteenth centuries—objected to covenant theology as irrational and unfair. The Puritans responded that the Arminians were "rationalists" bent on destroying the mysteriousness of God's ways. Arminians objected that Puritan covenant theology was an imposition of a human construct on Scripture, which nowhere teaches it, and an absurdity because it tried to combine the conditional and the absolute. Either the covenant of grace is conditional or absolute, they argued. It cannot be both. Jonathan Edwards tried to stem the growing tide of Arminianism in New England by countering that an absolute covenant is the only kind of covenant a holy God can establish and that Arminian belief in free will is absurd. In his passion to counter Arminianism, Edwards ended up denying the conditional aspect of the covenant of grace altogether—either a deviation from or correction of classical Puritan theology, depending on one's point of view.

What was the point of the Puritan covenant theology? For Puritans, as convinced Calvinists and evangelicals, it provided the connecting link between monergism and synergism and established the ground of assurance for persons concerned about their election. The covenant of grace is established and supervised entirely by God and at the same time humans have a role to play. In order to be "in the covenant" they have to be visibly converted and growing in sanctification. If they are visibly converted and growing in sanctification (displaying signs of grace), it is because they are God's elect.

The third hallmark of Puritan theology was the ideal of a Christianized society. New England Puritans especially believed fervently in what has been called theonomy, or "kingdom now theology." That is, they believed that one of God's promises in the covenant is not only to bless individuals, families and the church for trusting and obeying but also to bless human society if it will strive for godliness in its order. The Puritans believed that God's promises of blessing to Israel applied to them as the extension of Israel under the second phase of the covenant of grace known as the new covenant. The church is the "new Israel" and the kingdom of God on earth is promised to it if it permeates all of human society and brings social structures into conformity with God's law. When the Puritans exiled themselves from England in the 1630s, they sought a New World where this Christian commonwealth (modeled after Calvin's Geneva) could be built unhindered by the godless crown and impure state church. They saw North America as the promised land and sought to occupy it for God and his kingdom.

Every high-school student now knows of the dark side of the Puritan effort to create God's kingdom on North American soil. What is seldom taught or understood, however, is how the Puritan ideal entered into the mainstream of American life in both religious and secular forms. Puritan optimism and activism fueled later non-Puritan efforts at mission and social transformation and deeply imbued the American psyche with a belief in that country's higher calling.

When the original Puritan ideal flickered and threatened to die out or become crass belief in prosperity and dominance, Jonathan Edwards arose as a Puritan prophet to call it back to its true impulses. In the process, he reinterpreted it. He insisted that New Englanders not only "multiply and subdue" the wild paradise of the New World but that they also treat the inhabitants they found there with justice and love. Specifically, he condemned mistreatment of American Indians and called for payments to their tribes for the lands taken from them. Shortly afterward, he was asked to leave his Northampton pulpit and went off into the wilderness to live among the Indians. The Puritan vision of a Christianized social order took many forms, but it always hoped for and believed in a kingdom of God on earth *before* the visible return of Jesus Christ (postmillennialism).

**Jonathan Edwards: Prince of Puritans**

Jonathan Edwards was born in 1703 in Connecticut. His maternal grandfather was Solomon Stoddard, one of New England's most influential Puritan divines. Even though the grandson was a precocious child and earnest student, few would have anticipated that he would grow up to overshadow his grandfather, whose associate minister Jonathan became on graduation from Yale College in 1724. Edwards's life was a remarkable one, worthy of a narrative longer than is possible here. Terribly unfair to him is his reputation promoted by public-school curricula in the United States as a fire-and-brimstone preacher whose single contribution was the frighteningly judgmental sermon "Sinners in the Hands of an Angry God." That sermon is often included in anthologies of American literature as an example of Puritan preaching, and many students graduate from high school knowing nothing else about the man Yale University philosophy professor John E. Smith calls "unquestionably the major theologian of American Puritanism [and] the most acute philosophical thinker on the American scene up to the time of Charles Peirce"[7] and eminent American Lutheran theologian Robert W. Jenson calls "America's theologian."[8]

Edwards wrote over six hundred sermons that still exist in manuscript form. Few of them are hellfire and brimstone in nature, and eyewitnesses say that when Edwards preached, he was articulate but not particularly emotional. He engaged actively in almost every controversy in New England and read and wrote widely on a variety of subjects, including philosophy, ethics and science. Many of his books are still in print and excerpts are included in collections and anthologies. Among his most influential and important works are *On the Nature of True Virtue, On Freedom of the Will, The Great Christian Doctrine of Original Sin Defended* and *A Treatise Concerning Religious Affections.*

He was a revivalist who stood at the center of the Great Awakening that swept through the colonies in the 1740s, and he helped found the science of psychology of religion through his careful and critical examinations of religious experiences. He was a philosopher who was among the first in the New World to read and study the Enlightenment philosophy of John Locke and the cosmology of Isaac Newton. Above all Edwards was a theologian who ardently defended the Puritan Calvinist doctrines against "creeping Arminianism" and rationalism in theology. Through his writings Edwards created a distinctively American form of Reformed theology that has stood as a landmark for intellectual Protestant Christians of evangelical faith for over two centuries. Many North American Christians who call themselves evangelicals look back to Edwards as their hero—a kind of Augustine of North America—the formulator of a Christian worldview for the New World and a standard for integrating deep Christian faith with rigorous and disciplined intellectual life.[9]

After leading his Northampton congregation, which he inherited from his grandfather, in revival during the Great Awakening, Edwards was unceremoniously discharged by its consistory in 1750 for his prophetic sermons about the fair treatment of the Indians and for closing Communion to unconverted church attenders. He then settled in the frontier community of Stockbridge, Massachusetts, as minister and missionary to the Indians. In 1757 he was called to be president of Princeton College in New Jersey. One month after his inauguration he died of smallpox contracted from a botched vaccination. Although he was an ardent opponent of Arminian theology and other views opposed to the Puritan heritage, Edwards never engaged in the stereotypical witch-hunts that obsess the minds of so many modern critics of Puritanism. He was a civil man concerned with truth, justice and virtue. He was a reflective man who gave deep thought to complex issues before declaring what he believed. He was a man of great devotion and profound piety, who agreed with the German Pietists (whether he read them or not) that true Christianity lies in the heart more than in the intellect.

Jonathan Edwards's theology was a hybrid of Calvinism and pietism in that it was not so different from classical Puritan thought, although the pietist emphasis on religious feeling is more pronounced in Edwards than in earlier Puritan divines. His preaching was revivalist and aimed at appealing to the hearts of hearers to bring them to religious awakening. It sometimes resulted in tumultuous emotional responses that frightened even him. His theological writings bear three main consistent marks: the glory and freedom of God, the depravity and bondage of humans, and the heart or affections as the anthropological center. As is so often the case, Edwards's theology evolved through conflict and controversy. He did not preach or write in a vacuum. The distinctive notes of his Calvinist elevation of God's glory and human depravity were impelled by his fear of Arminian theology. His emphasis on the heart over mind and will was partly a result of his fear of religious rationalism. Thus Edwards's theology was forged against the dangers he saw in a rising tide of "Arminianism of the head" in New England. It does not appear that he was really aware of or recognized any other kind of Arminian theology or evangelical synergism. To him, Arminianism was inherently rationalistic and humanistic and thus contrary to the true gospel of Jesus Christ and teaching of the great Protestant Reformers.

No theologian in the history of Christianity held a higher or stronger view of God's majesty, sovereignty, glory and power than Jonathan Edwards. Edwards focused his entire thought on those themes and demanded stringently that every idea be brought back to them and tested by them. For him, God is the all-determining reality in the most unconditional sense possible and always acts for his own glory and honor. Why did God create anything outside himself? According to Edwards, who wrote a treatise on that subject, God's only motive was self-glory. In his *Dissertation Concerning the End for Which God Created the World* the Puritan preacher declared that "it appears that all that is ever spoken of in Scripture as an ultimate end of God's works, is included in that one phrase, *the glory of God;* which is the name by which the last end of God's works is most commonly called in Scripture."[10] In and of itself, this strong sense of God's glory is not particularly new in the history of theology. But Edwards went on to posit that if God is truly God, then he must be the one power, cause and being of everything. Nothing can exist or act without God's immediate presence not only sustaining it but directly causing it. So strong was Edwards's doctrine of God's agency as all-determining that some interpreters have detected within it the danger of pantheism (God as identical with nature). Surely that was not Edwards's intention, but he did espouse a view of God's relationship with the world for which the term theopanism would not be too strong. God does everything and does it all for his own glory. God is the one cause; creatures and their actions are the effects. *Creatio ex nihilo* is true not only of the original creation but of the entire creation and every individual being in it at each and every moment.[11]

Contrary to what one might suppose, Edwards did not merely suggest his view of God's universal being and agency as one possible idea among others. He saw it as the one and only truly biblical doctrine of God. According to the Bible, God is sovereign. God's sovereignty is his deity. Contingency and libertarian freedom and even secondary causation detract from God's sovereignty. Thus any view but his own leads inevitably to atheism. John E. Smith states that for Edwards, "God's immediate conduct, whether in acting or forbearing, is the 'original' in the series of subsequent events. Despite the great length and the intricacies of Edward's argument, his position rests, like a huge tower, on one foundation: God alone is *the* cause of all, and to allow 'secondary causes' is tantamount to denying the reality of God altogether."[12] Of course, this view clashed especially with Arminianism with its doctrine of God's self-limitation and libertarian free will. It also conflicted with previous and contemporary monergisms that introduced layers of causation between God and human agency. It even was incompatible with classical Puritan covenant theology insofar as it represented God as binding himself conditionally to human responses. For Edwards, a Christian cannot emphasize too strongly the absoluteness of God and the dependency of every creature, including the human person.

The second major theme of Edwards's theology is the depravity and bondage of humans. Not only are human beings, like all creatures, totally dependent on God in the most direct and immediate way conceivable, they are also totally depraved and bound to sin until and unless God sovereignly saves them. Even then they are free only to do what God wills them to do. Against the rising tide of Arminian theology among Anglicans and some Congregationalists, Edwards staunchly defended the doctrines of total depravity, unconditional election and irresistible grace. If God chooses to include all humans in Adam and hold them responsible for Adam's fall, God is free to do that. According to Edwards, God constituted humanity so that there is strict identity between Adam and each of his descendants until God breaks that identity by imparting a new being to a person. Free will, Edwards argued, makes no sense whatever except that people—whether sinners or saved—do what they want to do. They follow their God-instilled inclinations. Every reality must have a cause, Edwards argued in *On the Freedom of the Will,* and the Arminian doctrine of libertarian freedom posits an uncaused event—the free decision of the human agent. Uncaused events are irrational and thus "this Arminian notion of Liberty of the Will, consisting of the Will's *self-determination,* is repugnant to itself, and shuts itself wholly out of the world."[13]

Of course, Edwards never did solve the dilemma this argument creates for his own doctrine of God. He believed fervently in God's freedom in relation to what is outside himself. That is, God's creation and redemption of the world are in no way determined. God did not have to create a world or redeem it. Otherwise, the world would be part of God and then God would not be infinite and sovereign. But Edwards's critique of Arminian theology raises a question for his own doctrine of God: Does *God* have libertarian freedom? If not, how is he sovereign and how is his decision to create the world not necessary? If so, why could God not share that libertarian freedom with humans as a gift and part of the divine image? And why is belief in libertarian freedom for humans irrational and absurd (as Edwards claimed) while belief in it for God is not? Edwards's critique of libertarian freedom would seem to land him on the horns of a dilemma, but he did not acknowledge that.

For Edwards it is not only sin that binds the will of sinners, but creatureliness itself makes free will impossible and inconceivable to the rational mind. All humans are sinners because God includes them all in Adam. The elect are redeemed because God includes them in Christ. God foreordains and causes it all. But how is God just in including all in Adam? In his treatise *The Doctrine of Original Sin Defended* Edwards argued that all identity, including each individual person's own self-identity, is completely constituted by God. Without God as the "glue" holding momentary experiences and ideas together, individual self-identity would fall apart. The only reason that a person is still the same person and responsible for evil acts committed years before is God's "divine establishment" of the continuance of that oneness called "self." Thus in answer to the question of God's fairness with regard to imputing Adam's sin to all of humanity, Edwards responded,

> I am persuaded, no solid reason can be given, why God, who constitutes all other created union or oneness, according to his pleasure, and for what purposes, communications, and effects, he pleases, may not establish a constitution whereby the natural posterity of Adam, proceeding from him, much as the buds and branches from the stock and root of a tree, should be treated as *one* with him, for the derivation, either of righteousness, and communion in rewards, or of the loss of righteousness, and consequent corruption and guilt.[14]

Edwards's radically monergistic vision of God and creation answers some questions and raises others. Why are things as they are? Because God glorifies himself by making it so. What provides order and continuity and coherence to the booming, buzzing confusion of the world? God. But unanswered and perhaps unanswerable from within Edwards's system are questions such as "Exactly wherein lies the difference between divine and human being if their agency is the same?" and "If God immediately and directly causes all that happens, why is anyone other than God responsible for sin and evil?" and "How is God glorified in creatures suffering eternally in hell?" Needless to say, Arminians were not satisfied with Edwards's answers or lack of answers to these questions. They chose to live with the mystery of libertarian free will rather than live with these questions unanswered and unanswerable.

The third theme of Edwards's theology is the affections as the "anthropological center." The anthropological center refers to the core of human personality out of which identity and actions flow. Three main candidates for that crucial central faculty had been posed before Edwards: mind, will and heart. In seventeenth-century New England a new rationalism that elevated the mind or reason to supremacy over human action was gaining in influence and popularity. Its advocates tended to be harshly critical of the great revivals sweeping through the colonies in the 1730s and 1740s as emotional, irrational and therefore against the best impulses of human nature. Some of the more fanatical proponents of revival insisted that the heart or emotions should guide people and rule over reason and will, especially in religious matters.

Jonathan Edwards developed a psychology of the human person that transcended the known alternatives. Instead of mind, will or heart, he suggested, a faculty he called "affections" rules personal actions. People do what their affections lead them to do. Affections are not the same as passions or emotions but guide them. Neither are they thoughts or decisions. Rather, affections are what determine a person's beliefs and choices. Affections are more like deep, inner motives. Essentially, they are what one loves, or better put, they *are* one's loves. Edwards himself explained affections as inclinations in his *Treatise Concerning Religious Affections:* "The affections are no other than the more vigorous and sensible exercises of the inclination and will of the soul . . . that by which the soul does not merely perceive and view things, but is some way inclined with respect to the things it views or considers; either is inclined *to* them, or is disinclined and averse *from* them."[15]

Edwards went to great lengths to distinguish true from false affections in religion. Ultimately, he argued, true affections are those that glorify God, and the one affection God seeks most to instill in the elect is benevolence toward being, because that is God's own basic affection. That is the "nature of true virtue" and the highest and best sign of grace. Genuine revival of religion results in it more than in emotional outbursts, even though according to Edwards, the latter are unavoidable whenever people are deeply moved. Needless to say, the rationalists of his day were shocked at Edwards's psychology of affections. They feared it would lead to irrationalism and religious emotionalism. But modern psychology has by and large vindicated Edwards's insights into human personality if not his theological interpretations, which included that God is the ultimate cause of all affections—both good and evil.

Jonathan Edwards is without doubt one of the most important theologians of American evangelicalism. Many of those Protestant Christians of modern America who call themselves evangelicals look back to him as the quintessence of solid biblical reflection and belief combined with deep personal piety. The other major theologian in evangelicalism's background is Jonathan Edwards's younger English counterpart John Wesley. While Calvinist evangelicals hold Edwards in higher esteem, Arminian evangelicals tend to tout Wesley as a paradigm.

**John Wesley: Founder of Methodism**

The Puritans tried to reform the Church of England along Calvinist lines and ended up separating into Congregational, Presbyterian and Baptist denominations. Without the strong Puritan influence, the Anglican churches drifted toward cold rationalism, including what modern Reformed theologian Alan P. F. Sell refers to as "Arminianism of the head."[16] John Wesley was determined to revive the evangelical spirit within the Church of England, but not by imposing Reformed theology on everyone. Instead, his theology was what Sell calls "Arminianism of the heart"—an Arminianism combined with pietism and burning with revival fire. Eventually Wesley's movement, called Methodism, separated from the Church of England. Like Puritanism and Edwards, Methodism and Wesley left an indelible impression on North American evangelical theology.

John Wesley was born into the home of an Anglican rector in Epworth, England, in 1703.[17] He grew up as one of sixteen children of Samuel and Susanna Wesley.[18] When John was a small child, the parsonage caught fire and he was saved by being thrown out a window into someone's arms. According to his journal, he often considered himself a "brand plucked from the burning"—a reference from two Old Testament prophets. John had a prophetic self-consciousness as one specially chosen and called by God to revive true Christianity in England.

Wesley's life story is fascinating and extremely complex and cannot be told here in any detail. Suffice it to say that he attended Oxford University, where he studied for the ministry in the Church of England and got into trouble for fraternizing with persons such as George Whitefield (1714-1770), who was from a different class of English society. With Whitefield and his own brother Charles, John founded what they called the "Holy Club," which was similar to a Pietist conventicle. Their critics labeled them "Methodists" because they were perceived as trying to discover and practice a method of spirituality. After his ordination John traveled to the North American colony of Georgia as a kind of missionary to English settlers there. On the sea voyage across the Atlantic a storm nearly sunk the ship, and Wesley was deeply troubled by his own fear of death as compared with the calmness and serenity of a band of Moravian Pietists.

Wesley's brief pastorate in Georgia was a disaster and he returned to England humbled. He increasingly sensed his own need for a spiritual awakening that would give him assurance of salvation and freedom from the tumult of temptations that besieged him daily. On May 24, 1738, the young Anglican minister attended a religious meeting in a rented hall on Aldersgate Street in London. Scholars believe it was a meeting of Moravians. There, according to Wesley, he listened as someone read from Luther's preface to his *Commentary on the Epistle to the Romans* and while listening experienced the much-needed religious awakening: "I felt my heart strangely warmed. I felt I did trust in Christ, Christ alone for my salvation; and an assurance was given me that He had taken *my* sins, even *mine* and saved *me* from the law of sin and death."[19]

Scholars have debated for 250 years whether that experience constituted Wesley's conversion to Christianity or whether it was a special, momentary event of sanctification. In any case, it was a turning point in his spiritual life and ministerial career. Afterward he began a long series of evangelistic campaigns together with his friend George Whitefield and brother Charles Wesley.

John Wesley traveled thousands of miles on horseback preaching to crowds in churches when possible and in the open air or rented halls when Anglican churches turned him away. In one famous incident he arrived to preach at his father's church in Epworth after his father's death. The rector barred Wesley from preaching in his own father's pulpit, so he stood on the older Wesley's headstone in the graveyard next to the church and preached his evangelistic message to the gathered crowd. During his itinerant evangelistic career, Wesley preached over twenty thousand sermons, many of which were published in books and magazines or as tracts. His brother Charles (1707-1788) wrote hundreds of hymns, many of which are still widely used in Protestant churches around the world. Together the three friends launched the Great Awakening in England that spread to the American colonies. Some historians have argued that the Wesleyan revivals in England helped prevent a bloody revolution like the one that boiled over in France at the end of the eighteenth century. Wesley preached conversion and holiness to the masses who felt excluded from the formal atmosphere of the state church. In order to accommodate and disciple the numerous new converts to Christianity, Wesley founded Methodist societies that were like the German Lutheran Pietists' *collegia pietatis,* or conventicles of heart Christians. He organized them, led them and eventually reluctantly appointed ministers and even bishops to lead them. By the time he died in 1791, Methodism was a full-blown dissenting denomination in England. In North America, where it was a tiny new sect at the time of the American Revolution, it grew to be the dominant Christian denomination by the time of the Civil War in mid-nineteenth century.

Wesley never wrote a systematic theology. In fact, he was actively uninterested in such an endeavor, believing that enough compendiums of doctrine and theological speculation had already been written by Protestants. However, he did have his own theology and it is clearly reflected in his sermons, journals, notes and commentaries, the Methodist Book of Discipline, and treatises such as *A Plain Account of Christian Perfection.* Wesley was strongly indebted to an eclectic band of precursors: Richard Hooker, Jacob Arminius, Nikolaus Ludwig von Zinzendorf and Puritans such as Richard Baxter and William Perkins. He considered himself orthodox and catholic as well as thoroughly Protestant. He always insisted that he accepted the classical Protestant principles of *sola scriptura, sola fides* and the priesthood of all believers, even though his opponents and critics still criticize him for interpreting these hallmarks of Protestant theology in his own way.

Wesley's theology was thoroughly Arminian at a time when many evangelicals, including his friend and fellow evangelist George Whitefield, considered Arminianism almost a heresy. This led to a split between the Wesley brothers and Whitefield and a divide within Methodism. Whitefield led a small band of Calvinist Methodists away from the main body who followed Wesley in his teaching about free will and resistible grace. Whitefield became a close friend of Jonathan Edwards during his evangelistic tour of the American colonies, and the Wesleys drew closer to the synergistic theology of Zinzendorf and the German and Scandinavian Pietists.

One way of getting at the difference between John Wesley's evangelical theology and the evangelical theology of Jonathan Edwards is to say that Wesley placed God's love at the center of his preaching and teaching whereas Edwards made everything revolve around God's glory. Every evangelical Protestant wants to hold these two together. As the famous children's prayer begins, "God is great and God is good." Wesley never denied or questioned God's majesty and greatness, but he tended to subordinate it to God's love. Edwards never denied or questioned God's love, but he tended to subordinate it to God's majesty and glory. As a result, Edwards considered Arminianism of any kind—even Wesley's warm-hearted, evangelical Arminian theology—an implicit denial of God's greatness and a step down the slippery slope toward atheism. On the other hand, Wesley considered Calvinism's doctrines of unconditional election, irresistible grace and double predestination offensive to God's character as love. He went so far as to state his opinion that these doctrines amount to blasphemy because they make it difficult to distinguish God from the devil.[20] Needless to say, Wesley and his Puritan counterparts in the evangelical revivals of the eighteenth century had great difficulty cooperating. The monergism-synergism split kept them apart, aloof and suspicious of one another. Both sides insisted that they could love the other while abhorring and repudiating its doctrines. That divide has remained within Anglo-American evangelical Protestant Christianity until today and promises to continue providing occasion for theological warfare into the indefinite future.[21]

Wesley's special contribution to the story of Protestant theology lies in his distinctive interpretations of two of its classical principles. While affirming *sola scriptura* he also developed a view of authority for Christian faith and practice known as the Wesleyan quadrilateral. While affirming *sola gratia et fides,* he also emphasized the real possibility of Christian perfection through entire sanctification. These two amendments to classical Protestant theology were controversial in Wesley's own lifetime, have deeply influenced Methodism and through it much of Protestant Christianity, and continue to be matters of debate within contemporary Christianity. Wesley's attitude toward the priesthood of all believers was thoroughly Protestant in theory even though some critics thought he qualified it by retaining the office of bishop and an episcopal polity in his Methodist movement.

Without debate, Wesley himself held to the supreme authority of Scripture over every other source and norm for Christian preaching and living. On the other hand, he included reason, tradition and experience as essential interpretive tools for doing theology. This is the Wesleyan quadrilateral: four essential sources and tools of theology—Scripture, reason, tradition and experience.[22] Wesley derived the strong emphasis on reason and tradition from Anglican theologian Richard Hooker, and from Pietism the stress on experience. He believed that all these inevitably play roles in Christian thought and that rather than rejecting them, Christians ought to acknowledge their proper place as tools of scriptural interpretation and value the contributions they can make to formulating biblical doctrines that are truly catholic (faithful to the spirit of the church fathers and Reformers), reasonable (coherent, intelligible) and practical (relevant to experience). But Wesley's quadrilateral of sources and tools for theological method was no equilateral. He never tired of emphasizing the supreme authority of Scripture and never allowed tradition, reason or experience to overshadow or control it. According to one of Wesley's most authoritative modern interpreters, Thomas C. Oden, "Wesley repeatedly held 'the written word of God to be the only and sufficient rule both of Christian faith and practice.' "[23] But Wesley insisted that no one reads the Bible alone. That is, everyone reads more than the Bible (whether they know it or not), and everyone interprets the Bible (whether they are aware of it or not).

By setting forth his quadrilateral Wesley was simply stating what the proper tools of good biblical interpretation are and how they should be used. By no means was he attempting to qualify Scripture's authority. Proper biblical interpretation and theological method combine absolute submission to the Bible as God's inspired Word with respect for the Great Tradition of Christian teaching, a reasonable mind that uses logic and a warm heart and mind illumined by the Holy Spirit.

The second distinctive contribution of Wesley is his belief in Christian perfection through entire sanctification. Some critics in his own century and since have accused Wesley of denying the classical Protestant doctrine of justification by grace through faith alone not only because he attempted to combine it with synergism but also because he stressed regeneration and sanctification more than justification. He did so because, along with the German Lutheran Pietists, he took justification for granted. It was a doctrine already firmly implanted in Protestant theology. What was neglected, Wesley believed, was the experiential side of Christian initiation into salvation, and in this he was at one with Francke and Zinzendorf and other "heart Christians" of Pietism. Like them, Wesley firmly defended infant baptism against Anabaptists and Baptists, but he tended to interpret the rite more as a means of prevenient (and resistible) grace than a regenerative sacrament. In some of his writings and sermons he came close to reducing infant baptism to a dedicatory ceremony, and that is how many later Methodists came to interpret it. Without any doubt Wesley's main emphasis in soteriology fell on conversion, including regeneration—being born again of the Spirit of God through conscious faith in Jesus Christ. This everyone must have to be a "real Christian." It is a work of God by grace through faith and includes justification.[24] But his most controversial soteriological teaching—even among pietists and other revivalists—was in the area of sanctification.

In a little book titled *A Plain Account of Christian Perfection* Wesley claimed that, contrary to classical Protestant theology, sanctification is not always a process without progress or completion in this life. Initially Wesley taught that the normal Christian life may reach a stage of sanctification in which the war with temptation is over. But he later abandoned the idea, noting that even Jesus was not free from temptation. In "Brief Thoughts on Christian Perfection," an appendix to his book dated 1767, the evangelist explained his view:

> Some thoughts occurred to my mind this morning concerning Christian perfection, and the manner and time of receiving it, which I believe may be useful to set down. 1. By perfection I mean the humble, gentle, patient love of God and our neighbour, ruling our tempers, words, and actions. I do not include an impossibility of falling from it, either in part or in whole. Therefore, I retract several expressions in our hymns, which partly express, partly imply such an impossibility. And I do not contend for the term *sinless,* though I do not object against it. 2. As to the manner. I believe this perfection is always wrought in the soul by a simple act of faith; consequently in an instant. But I believe in a gradual work both preceding and following that instant. 3. As to the time. I believe this instant generally is the instant of death, the moment before the soul leaves the body. But I believe it may be

> ten, twenty, or forty years before. I believe it is usually many years after justification; but that it may be within five years or five months after it, I know no conclusive argument to the contrary. If it must be many years after justification, I would be glad to know how many.[25]

In other words, Wesley came to the point of wishing simply to leave it as a real possibility that a Christian may and perhaps should arrive at "perfection in love" within this life before or at death.

To be sure, Wesley's doctrine of entire sanctification is open to several interpretations. But whichever way one interprets it, there is no escaping its inherent conflict with Luther's *simul justus et peccator* (always both righteous and sinner). Protestants who insist that justification by faith alone is intrinsically linked with that principle oppose Wesley's doctrine of sanctification as more Catholic than Protestant. Wesley did not see it that way. He taught that every good a person has is always a gift from God received freely by faith. That is as true of sanctification as of regeneration as of justification. In response to those who accused him of qualifying the Protestant principle of *sola fides,* Wesley wrote in exasperation:

> I believe justification by faith alone, as much as I believe there is a God. I declared this in a sermon, preached before the University of Oxford, eight-and-twenty years ago. I declared it to all the world eighteen years ago, in a sermon written expressly on the subject ["Salvation by Faith"]. I have never varied from it, no, not an hair's breadth, from 1738 to this day.[26]

Equally vehemently he attributed all of Christian experience to grace and claimed that faith alone and not works or human effort is the sole instrument by which grace works goodness in human life. But according to Wesley and contrary to monergists of every kind, grace is resistible and faith is simply the free decision—enabled by prevenient grace—not to resist it but to put all trust and hope in grace and allow the Holy Spirit to transform one's being into a child of God. Thus Wesley's soteriology is another form of evangelical synergism. It is thoroughly Protestant even if not monergistic because it rejects human meritorious works from any role whatever in salvation.

One other area where some critics have found Wesley's theology insufficiently Protestant is the priesthood of all believers. Some low-church evangelical Protestants, including some of Wesley's own nineteenth-century "holiness" heirs in offshoots of Methodism, reject his ecclesiology and especially his episcopal polity as inconsistent with believers' priesthood. Wesley, like Luther and the entire Anglican tradition, retained bishops in Methodism and rejected both congregational and presbyterian polity. Methodist churches are not autonomous and do not choose their pastors. Pastors are generally appointed by Methodist bishops and are frequently moved. Methodist congregations have neither complete freedom to determine their own forms of worship nor to control their own affairs. While Methodist bishops do not have any special spiritual authority (as in Roman Catholicism and some portions of Anglicanism) and do not stand in apostolic succession, they do maintain order in the churches and to that end may suspend pastors and boards of churches. Through contact with other free-church traditions in America, however, Methodism like Lutheranism has seriously watered down the role of bishops so that they are now little more than administrators. In essence, then, Wesley's theology and Methodism do not seriously diminish the priesthood of all believers unless one insists that no form of church polity except congregationalism (for example) is compatible with it.

## The Legacies of Puritanism and Methodism

In this chapter we have examined the roles of Puritanism, including Jonathan Edwards, and Methodism, especially founder John Wesley, in the story of Christian theology. Why? What legacies did they leave behind for later generations of Christians? These two renewal and reform movements have had the deepest and most lasting influence on North American theology and, subsequently through North American missions, on much of the world. British theology has also been influenced by them, although less profoundly. Both set out to revive and reform the theology and life of the Church of England and ended up creating new forms of Protestant theology. One way to describe their legacies is to point to contemporary evangelical Christianity in North America and movements stemming from it.

Evangelical Christianity is a multifaceted subculture notoriously difficult to pin down. But two things especially characterize it, and they are the living legacies of Edwards the Puritan and Wesley the Methodist. First, evangelical theology and life are doctrinally conservative in the sense of seeking to preserve and maintain classical Christian doctrines of the church fathers and Reformers. Both Edwards and Wesley resisted what they saw as impulses toward rationalism, heresy and accommodation to culture. They were committed to Christian orthodoxy.

The second legacy bequeathed by both Edwards and Wesley to contemporary evangelicalism is "orthodoxy on fire." That is, both of them averred that mere nominal Christian assent to doctrinal correctness does not automatically make one a real Christian. Transforming experience of God is what makes one a real Christian and is the best assurance of orthodoxy. They rejected sacramentalism, confessionalism and religious rationalism in favor of conversional piety, faith as trust and not merely assent, and belief in a supernatural God who works immediately in the world in often mysterious ways. At the same time, neither Edwards nor Wesley was a crass literalist in interpretation of Scripture and both eschewed mindless obscurantism and separation from culture. They were not what in the modern world people call "fundamentalists." Edwards and Wesley stand together in spite of their deep differences over grace and free will as the twin roots or pillars of contemporary Anglo-American evangelical thought and life.

At the same time that Edwards and Wesley were creating modern evangelical Christianity, other religious reformers were trying to move Protestantism in a totally new and different direction led by reason rather than the heart. Deism, or natural religion, was a movement of the seventeenth and early eighteenth centuries that tried to reform Protestant theology to make it reasonable and compatible with the budding modern world. It is to the very important story of this renewal movement in theology that we now turn.

# CHAPTER 31

# Deists Try to Transform Protestant Theology

A*ll of the movements whose stories are told in this section have one thing in* common. They regarded the Protestant Reformation as either incomplete or somehow off track and tried to complete it or get it back on the right track. In other words, they all attempted to reform the Reformation. Each movement and its leaders had a different vision of what was wrong with Protestant theology in the seventeenth and eighteenth centuries and a different program for correcting it or completing it. Arminius and the Remonstrants reacted to Protestant orthodoxy's "hardening of the categories," especially to post-Reformation Reformed theology's scholastic treatment of the doctrine of predestination. The Arminians wished to correct Reformed theology by moving it off the monergistic track and onto a track of evangelical synergism. Pietism responded to a perceived problem of "dead orthodoxy" in post-Reformation Lutheranism in Germany, especially to the tendency of many seventeenth-century Protestant theologians to equate authentic Christianity with assent to correct doctrinal formulas and systems. They wanted to complete the Reformation by emphasizing a neglected component of Protestant soteriology: Christian experience of regeneration and sanctification. Puritans and Methodists in very different ways tried to complete and correct the Protestant Reformation of English-speaking Christianity. The Puritans saw the correct path as lying in a distinctly British form of Reformed theology and ecclesiology. The Methodists charted a course for renewal that included an emphasis on Christian experience of conversion and the ideal of Christian perfection.

Another movement arose within the bosom of post-Reformation Protestant theology with an entirely different vision of how best to complete the Protestant Reformation. It emphasized the authority of reason in all matters, including religion, and dreamed of a reasonable, universal religion that would overcome sectarian strife, superstition and irrational, arbitrary authority, and usher Christianity into a modern age of peace, enlightenment and toleration. This movement, known variously as natural religion or Deism, had no single prophet or founder and no formal organization. Its adherents remained relatively few in number. Many spokespersons for organized Protestant Christianity condemned it as atheism and its leaders as infidels. And yet Deism managed to leave an indelible stamp on Christianity and religion in general in western Europe and North America. Many of the movers and shapers of modern nationalism in Britain, France and the United States sympathized with it. A small but influential denomination known as Unitarianism was founded in England and New England in the late eighteenth century largely on its ideas. In spite of great opposition from all branches of traditional Christianity, including the other reforming movements, and in spite of failure to establish its dream of a universal, natural and rational religion, Deism subtly filtered into the warp and woof of modern Western theology and became one precursor of what came to be known as liberal Protestant theology in the nineteenth and twentieth centuries.

## Toward a Definition of Deism

The old problems of misconceptions and misuses of terminology plague any discussion of Deism. The case is similar to those of Pietism and Puritanism. Over centuries a popular misconception of Deism has gradually emerged and become so deeply ingrained that it may now be quixotic even to attempt its correction. For many people Deism is the religion of an "absentee God" who is uninvolved in the world of nature and history. To them, the Deists were skeptics who denied miracles in the name of natural laws and rejected anything supernatural. As in the cases of Pietism and Puritanism, there is a kernel of truth in this popular stereotype of Deism. But only a kernel. For the most part the leading Deists of the seventeenth and eighteenth centuries considered themselves Christians, even if of a "higher order." They did not always or often outrightly reject everything supernatural even though they tended to take a skeptical attitude toward miracles and special revelations. Finally, contrary to even some uninformed scholarly opinion, the leading Deists did not exclude God from the world and relegate him to the roles of an "original architect" or "moral governor" who never intervenes in the world or interacts with humans. Certainly they did not consider God uninterested or uninvolved.

So what was Deism? It is simpler to correct misconceptions and misinformation than to nail down exactly what Deism was. The best way to describe it is not to deliver a pat definition but rather to delineate its history by telling its story. That will be my purpose here. However, so that readers may know whose story is being told and what the story is about, I will attempt a preliminary definition and description of the post-Reformation phenomenon known as Deism. Most simply put, the Deists were those religious thinkers of Europe and North America in the post-Reformation period who elevated human reason and natural religion over faith and special revelation, even in Christianity. Deism was not so much a doctrine of God, as many mistakenly suppose, as a view of religious knowledge that placed common principles of human reason and common religious ideas of humanity at the center and judged all claims to special revelation by them. The Deists thought this new, rational approach to religion most consistent with the basic impulses both of Protestantism and the new philosophy and science of the Enlightenment. The basic principle of Deism may be summed up this way: "Nothing should be accepted as true by an intelligent being, such as man, unless it is grounded in the nature of things and is in harmony with right reason."[1] This principle may express the universal impulse of the Enlightenment generally. Deism applied it to religion and even to Christianity.

Deism was an effort to demonstrate Christianity to be the highest and best expression of a purely natural religion of reason. In order to carry out this project, the Deists had to lop off much of traditional Christian theology or radically reinterpret it. In some cases, in order to avoid prosecution under blasphemy laws they merely neglected certain doctrines they considered inconsistent with natural religion and universal reason. The deity of Jesus Christ and the Trinity were two closely related dogmas of classical Christianity that many if not most Deists gladly neglected. Once blasphemy laws were no longer enforced in England and North America, most Deists openly denied such doctrines or relegated them to obscurity as unimportant at best.

At the most basic level, then, Deism's distinctive nature among Protestant movements of theology had to do with its view of religious authority. All the other Protestant theologies were theologies of Word and Spirit. Luther, Calvin, Zwingli, Cranmer, Hooker and the Anabaptists all emphasized the dialectic of Word and Spirit as the true Christian authority for faith and practice. The Word of God, especially as expressed in Holy Scripture, was seen as the objective, infallible special revelation of God delivered through the agency of the Holy Spirit by a supernatural operation known as inspiration. But the Word without the Spirit illuminating it to readers' minds and hearts would remain a "dead letter," and so the Holy Spirit is also crucial to Christian authority. All the major first-generation Protestant Reformers agreed that the Holy Spirit does not deliver new doctrinal truths after the completion of Scripture but does illumine it to readers of faith and impress its truth on them through the *testimonium internum Spiritus Sancti*—the "internal witness of the Holy Spirit." When classical Protestant Reformers and theologians spoke or wrote about the authority of Scripture, they based it on the Holy Spirit's inspiration of the authors and words and on the contemporary witness of the Spirit in and through its reading and proclamation. This is what they meant by the Bible's self-authenticating nature. To them it was really authenticated by the Holy Spirit.

After the Protestant Reformation, a tendency set in to break apart this delicate balance of Word and Spirit. Protestant orthodoxy tended to emphasize the Word only so that its authority resided in the inerrancy of its propositions (truth claims) and their inner coherence. The Holy Spirit came to play less and less of a role in its vision of Christian authority. Appeal to the inerrancy of Scripture's claims and to its inner consistency replaced appeal to the inner testimony of the Spirit. Protestant experientialism (including Pietism and Methodism as well as more radical movements such as Quakerism) emphasized the Spirit without neglecting the Word. Some of the more radical "religious enthusiasts" around its fringes advocated new revelations to supplement Scripture. All the Protestant movements saw reason as corrupted by sin and in need of healing by grace in order to grasp divine truths other than the few basic items of natural theology such as God's existence and the immortality of the soul. They did not place very much emphasis on natural reason's role in religious knowledge. At best reason provided a helpful tool in understanding Scripture and arguing against false religions and heresies. None of the main Protestant Reformers or theologians of the sixteenth through the eighteenth centuries considered natural reason apart from grace very useful in theology.

Deism arose out of dissatisfaction and disillusionment with that approach to religious and Christian authority. Two main catalysts sparked that dissatisfaction and disillusionment and set the natural religionists on their search for a new approach. The first was the sectarian strife of the seventeenth century. In central Europe, Catholics and Protestants engaged in the Thirty Years War that eventually led to Protestants fighting against fellow Protestants on German soil. In France, Catholics and Protestants engaged in a protracted civil war that led to massacres and mass exiles. In England, Puritans rose up against the monarch in a vicious civil war that involved the public beheadings of the archbishop of Canterbury and the king himself. Even after the restoration of the monarchy and reestablishment of the Church of England, the various Protestant sects engaged in verbal battles that one wag labeled *rabies theologicum*—a disease where theologians fight with one another like mad dogs. In the face of all of this strife, many of the educated people of Europe began to wonder if perhaps natural reason and not faith in special revelation should be the basis for religious unity and progress as it seemed to be so fruitful in uniting and energizing science, philosophy and politics.

The second catalyst for the Deists' search for a religion of natural reason was the Enlightenment—a general term for the new mood of culture that began in Europe around 1650. Some interpreters consider Deism simply the "religion of the Enlightenment" in the sense that most of the major thinkers of the Enlightenment came to sympathize with natural religion. Another way of viewing the matter, though, is that the Enlightenment provided a new cultural and philosophical context, and the Deists were those Christian thinkers who, like certain early church fathers and medieval theologians with Greek culture and philosophy, quickly adopted Enlightenment views and adapted Christian thought to them. To the minds of more traditional Protestant theologians and church leaders, of course, the Deists were guilty of shallow accommodation of Christianity to Enlightenment modes of thought. The Enlightenment may be summed up in a statement of three characteristic ideas:

1. an emphasis on the power of "reason" to discover the truth about humanity and the world
2. skepticism toward the venerable institutions and traditions of the past
3. emergence of a scientific way of thinking that offered intellectuals a viable alternative approach to knowledge from that which had dominated medieval thought[2]

The major intellectual catalysts of the Enlightenment were philosopher René Descartes (1596-1650) and scientist-mathematician Isaac Newton (1642-1717). Separately they laid the foundation for a new way of thinking and a new view of the natural world that emphasized doubt over faith and uniformity over divine interventions. Both considered themselves Christians, but their methods and ideas were antithetical in many ways to traditional Christian customs of thinking and viewing nature. As a result of the Enlightenment, no longer was it as easy or acceptable for educated, intellectual people to say with the majority of Christian thinkers through the ages, "I believe in order that I may understand."

No longer was the principle of "faith seeking understanding" taken for granted. Now these were being replaced for many people with "I will believe only what I can understand" and "faith follows understanding."

Disillusioned by sectarian strife, turned off by religious intolerance and controversy, and energized by a new vision of culture, science and philosophy sparked by the Enlightenment, the Deists attempted to reconstruct Christian thought. They were convinced that unless Christianity could be shown to be thoroughly reasonable in terms of the criteria used by Enlightenment thought, it would eventually become irrelevant and die out. They were also convinced that unless it could be shown to be in its essence a universal, rational, natural religion for all thinking people everywhere, it would continue to split apart into warring factions. What the Deists needed was a nonmysterious, rational and universal Christianity that transcended denominational and confessional boundaries and had no need of suprarational faith or internal testimonies of the Holy Spirit to persuade and convince people of its truth. What they ended up with was a generic religion that was a pale theism stripped of almost everything distinctively Christian. It looked very much like Thomas Aquinas's lower sphere of theology—a collection of concepts about God, the soul and morality knowable by reason apart from grace, faith and special revelation.

## Precursors and Proponents of Deism

Settling Deism's exact boundaries with any certainty is just as difficult as giving it a precise definition. Which religious thinkers of the seventeenth and eighteenth centuries truly count as Deists? There is no universal agreement on that. Authoritative interpreters provided different lists, but all of them include at least two eighteenth-century thinkers: John Toland and Matthew Tindal. Each Englishman wrote one major book that contributed heavily to the rise of Deism. These, then, are our two chief proponents of Deism, and soon we will turn to their personal stories and the roles they play in the overall story. As we have seen already in this story of Christian theology, every theological movement has its precursors. Luther had his Hus and his Erasmus. Spener had his Arndt. Wesley had his Hooker and his Arminius. Deism had its precursors as well, and some scholars include them in the movement itself. Here we will treat Lord Herbert of Cherbury and John Locke as Deism's precursors, whereas others may treat one or both as actual Deists.[3] In any case, chronologically the story of Deism must begin with Lord Herbert.

*Lord Herbert of Cherbury.* One reason Lord Herbert of Cherbury, whose Christian name was Edward, is sometimes identified as a precursor rather than as a proponent of Deism is his separation in time from that movement's heyday. Lord

Herbert was born in England to a wealthy and powerful family in 1583. He died in 1648 after living a rather rakish life as a free thinker, duelist, ladies' man and country squire. His brother George was a well-known poet whose verses often appear in anthologies of English literature. Lord Herbert wrote a little volume in Latin entitled *De veritate (On Truth)*, which was published in Paris in 1624 and is often considered the first essay outlining what would later come to be known as natural religion. In it the English nobleman attacked blind faith in special revelations, sectarian strife over points of doctrine, and all irrationalism in religion as in any other sphere of life. Positively he set forth five "Common Notions of Religion" that he supposed to be universal, rational and completely in accordance with what is known of nature:

1. There is a Supreme God;
2. This Sovereign Deity ought to be worshipped;
3. The connection of virtue with piety, defined . . . as the right conformation of the faculties, is and always has been held to be, the most important part of religious practice;
4. The minds of men have always been filled with horror for their wickedness. Their vices and crimes have been obvious to them. They must be expiated by repentance;
5. There is reward or punishment after this life.[4]

According to Lord Herbert, "The only Catholic and uniform church is the doctrine of Common Notions which comprehend all places and all men."[5]

The context of the entire book makes clear that Lord Herbert did not intend to reject as false everything believed by Christians except the five common notions. Rather, he proposed these as the foundation upon which all other "dictates of faith may rest . . . as a roof is supported on a house."[6] However, the tone of *De veritate* toward all particular doctrines of Christian denominations and even toward classical dogmas not clearly spelled out in Scripture or implied by the five common notions is skeptical. The Trinity is an example of a classical Christian dogma Lord Herbert treated skeptically. The main point of the essay is that whatever people believe as religious truth ought to be judged by the five common religious notions that are supposed to reside everywhere in human history and throughout all cultures.

Of course Lord Herbert's little book created a furor after its publication. Many accused the author of atheism, which was no more accurate than the Romans' accusation of the same against the early Christians. Clearly Lord Herbert believed in God. What was unclear was whether he believed in the Trinity or the deity of Jesus Christ. Clearly he believed in miracles and special revelations. He wrote in later autobiographical reflections that he published *De veritate* in spite of some anxiety because while he was considering it he heard a loud noise from a cloudless sky and took that as a heavenly sign to publish the book. Whether he believed in all the biblical miracles is less clear. *De veritate* was widely read during the middle and late seventeenth century and laid the groundwork for Deism: "The importance of *De Veritate* is that it made it possible for subsequent thinkers to profess belief in God, yet to abjure revealed religion and established Christianity; the liberating effects of such a possibility for thinkers immersed in the daring discoveries of the new scientific age should not be underestimated."[7]

*John Locke.* The second precursor of Deism was the much more important and influential philosopher John Locke.[8] Locke was born in England in 1632 and died in 1704. He made his living as a special assistant and tutor to leading English families and once had to flee England to Holland when his employer was implicated in a conspiracy to overthrow the king. Locke was without doubt the most influential intellectual of England and perhaps the Western world during his lifetime and for decades afterward. Few people in intellectual history have attained his stature and influence. Locke was the Erasmus of his own time. Everyone listened to him and sought his advice and counsel on matters philosophical, religious and political. His all-important *Essay Concerning Human Understanding* was revolutionary in Enlightenment philosophy. He started the empirical school of philosophy, which, combined with Isaac Newton's discoveries in physics, helped shape modern science. Locke's writings influenced people as diverse as Jonathan Edwards and Thomas Jefferson. What many teachers and students of Locke's philosophy ignore or fail to learn is that, like Newton and even like Descartes, Locke was mainly interested in religious questions. Only a modern bias against religion leads to such "learned ignorance." These men who are known as the movers and shapers of modern thought were obsessed with issues of religion and all considered themselves not only believers in God but also Christians, even if unconventional ones.

Locke's most important religious treatise is *The Reasonableness of Christianity,* which was published in 1695. Other relevant Lockean writings include *A Discourse of Miracles* and a portion of *A Third Letter Concerning Toleration.* Apparently Locke was well aware of a trend among certain religious thinkers toward Deism. He was well aware, of course, of Lord Herbert's protodeistic philosophy of religion and its influence. In *The Reasonableness of Christianity* Locke attempted to justify the basic beliefs of Christianity at the bar of reason. As one author has described Locke's contribution, "the lion of rationalism is made to lie down in peace with the lamb of traditionalism and not devour it."[9] That may be expressing it too generously. A more critical assessment of Locke's project and its outcome might be that the lion of rationalism made the lamb of Christian traditionalism lie down and be very quiet. While it is true that "Locke . . . was always of the mind that his writings did full justice to the Christian faith,"[10] a more objective evaluation will inevitably notice that key doctrines of the Christian tradition are neglected in Locke's defense. Locke had little or nothing to say about the Trinity or the deity of Christ. In any case, what Locke attempted to do in the book and other apologetic writings was demonstrate that the essence of divine revelation, and Christian belief that is based on it, is fully consistent with reason.

Why would such a project be controversial? Why do many critics allege that against Locke's own intentions *The Reasonableness of Christianity* made Deism inevitable? First, Locke treated religion, including Christianity, altogether as a matter of intellectual belief. His Christianity was what some modern pietists would call a religious "head trip." Rational assent to reasonable beliefs was what Locke meant by Christian faith. He payed lip service to repentance and emphasized the importance of living a good life, but overall, believing in God and in Jesus as the Messiah is what makes one a Christian. Locke argued that such belief is confirmed by Jesus' miracles and that his miracles and messiahship require that rational people do their best to follow his teachings. Thus far, only ordinary evidentialist apologetics is in view. But almost hidden between the lines of Locke's writings was a radical notion. Locke assumed and sometimes argued very subtly that anything in divine revelation that is not completely consistent with natural human reason is simply unbelievable. A very telling principle appears in *A Discourse of Miracles:*

> That no mission can be looked on to be divine, that delivers any thing derogating from the honour of the one, only, true, invisible God, or inconsistent with natural religion and the rules of morality: because God having discovered to men the unity and majesty of his eternal Godhead, and the truths of natural religion and morality by the light of reason, he cannot be supposed to back the contrary by revelation, for that would be to destroy the evidence and the use of reason, without which men cannot be able to distinguish divine revelation from diabolical imposture.[11]

The radical principle proposed by Locke was that "whatever God has revealed is true and must be the object of our faith; but what actually counts as having been revealed by God, *that* must be judged by reason."[12] Instead of natural reason serving as a tool in the hands of faith, for Locke it became the ultimate judge of revelation itself. There may be truths of revelation that transcend reason, but only reason can determine which truths those may be. Thomas Aquinas's lower sphere was in Locke beginning to rise up and dominate the upper sphere. But did Locke actually find anything in divine revelation that had to be rejected by reason? One answer to that is that for Locke nothing could be a divine revelation that is rejected by reason. So, rephrasing the question, did Locke actually reject any crucial doctrine of classical Christianity based on divine revelation? He did not. Locke was very cautious in this matter. We cannot read his mind, so we do not know why he hardly mentioned the Trinity, the deity of Christ or the atonement. He seemed to believe that authentic Christianity boils down to belief in Jesus as Messiah (unique prophet of God), repentance and trying to live a good life according to Jesus' teachings. Did he consider many of the dogmas of traditional Christianity contrary to reason and therefore not of Christianity's essence? One can only suspect it.

Locke's project of developing and defending reasonable Christianity cannot be labeled Deism outrightly. However, it opened the door and paved the road to it. One commentator notes that

> Locke's attempt to defend both the "reasonableness" of Christianity and hold to an empirical epistemology opened a gap between revealed religion and that which may be derived from reason without special revelation. Through that gap came the horses and carriage of deism, initially in the form of the Irishman John Toland (1670-1722).[13]

*John Toland.* John Toland was perhaps the first true Deist. He was an admirer of Locke and considered the famous English philosopher his mentor. One year after the appearance of *The Reasonableness of Christianity* Toland published his controversial book *Christianity Not Mysterious,* which argued that nothing contrary to a purely rational, natural religion accessible to all people may be considered authentic Christianity and that no real truth of Christianity is above or beyond reason. The heart of Toland's book is expressed in the principle that "whoever reveals anything, that is, whoever tells us something we did not know before, *his words must be intelligible, and the matter possible.* This rule holds good, let *God* or *Man* be the Revealer."[14]

When Toland asserted that revelational claims must be intelligible in order to be acknowledged as true, he meant they must conform to the "self-evident notions" common to all reasonable human beings. These include logic and basic moral distinctions. When he asserted that revelational claims must be possible, he meant they must not ask us to believe things that clearly are inconceivable. Claims that are unintelligible and impossible are inherently mysterious, and therefore mysteries do not belong in the realm of true religion or authentic Christianity. They require a sacrifice of the intellect and thereby violate the very image of God in humanity, which is the gift of reason. Toland objected most strenuously to basing beliefs on "the illuminating and efficacious operation of the Holy Spirit"—

Calvin's *testimonium internum Spiritus Sancti.* In the end, so he averred, reason alone must be sovereign when it comes to deciding which, if any, claimed special revelations qualify for belief. There cannot be two equal authorities—reason and revelation—for it is reason that judges the truth of revelation. For Toland, then, sovereign reason replaces the witness of the Spirit in Christian authority.

After enthroning natural reason as ultimate, Toland took the next step in *Christianity Not Mysterious* and asserted that true religion is by nature eternal and immutable. Positive religions change over time. Only God's truth abides forever the same. Reason establishes that which is abiding truth. Therefore, the natural religion of reason is the standard by which every positive religion, including Christianity, is judged. Whatever is mysterious (unintelligible, impossible) cannot be part of the natural religion of reason. Therefore it cannot be part of authentic Christianity. By the end of *Christianity Not Mysterious* the reader has the distinct impression that Christianity has become a pale reflection of natural religion—a vague, generic theism without anything distinctive to it. Even Jesus Christ receives little attention in Toland's treatment of religion, except as a religious and social reformer.[15]

Toland's work represents a baby step beyond Locke that quickly turned into a quantum leap. Locke condemned *Christianity Not Mysterious* and disowned its author as his protégé. Toland, however, cannot be blamed for feeling wrongly treated by his mentor. To his own mind he was simply drawing out the natural conclusions of Locke's own methodology in religious thought. Yet it does seem that Toland had crossed a kind of "Caesar's Rubicon" when he departed from previous forms of rationalistic Christianity by insisting that everything valid in New Testament revelation and Christian tradition boils down to what natural reason can know, thus reducing Christianity to natural religion. Apparently, he genuinely believed that his conclusions represented the ultimate outworking of the best impulses of the Protestant Reformation.[16] Many of the educated elite of Europe and especially Great Britain hailed Toland's book as courageous, and many "learned people seized on the possibility that one could be 'religious' and still not believe *everything* that traditional Christianity taught."[17] Of course a strongly negative reaction from traditionalists of all kinds was inevitable. The Irish parliament condemned the infamous book of their native son and the official hangman of Ireland burned it in public ceremony.

*Matthew Tindal.* The second and only other major proponent of Deism in its early, pristine form was Matthew Tindal, whose 1730 book *Christianity as Old as the Creation: Or, The Gospel A Republication of the Religion of Nature* came to be known as "the Deists' Bible." Tindal was an English gentleman born in 1657 who became a fellow (tutor and lecturer) of prestigious All Souls College at Oxford University. He was "certainly the most learned of the Deists"[18] and he called himself a "Christian deist" even though one of his major projects was to demonstrate "the impossibility of reconciling the petty and arbitrary God of Revelation [Scripture] with the impartial and magnanimous God of Natural Religion."[19] Tindal's view of Christianity took the trajectory set by Locke and Toland to its ultimate conclusion: true Christianity is nothing more than a rational ethical system set against a vaguely theistic background. "It consists in observing the rules that reason discovers. The whole of religion, according to [Tindal] consists in performing all the duties of morality."[20] This is a religion that has no real need of any special revelation, grace or Savior. It needs only belief in a vaguely personal, transcendent and immanent supreme Being knowable by natural reason alone as a prop and support for objective, universal morality. Tindal did not reject as necessarily false all claims of special revelations and miracles, but he made them dependent on natural religion, including natural morality. Their only valid function is to confirm in special ways what is generally knowable without them.

Tindal died a controversial but respected hero of rational religion in 1733, only three short years after publication of his one major work. *Christianity as Old as the Creation* became the norm for Deism and profoundly influenced leading American thinkers such as Benjamin Franklin and Thomas Jefferson. Under its influence Jefferson, the architect of the United States, created his own Bible, which consisted of the New Testament excised of all reports and teachings deemed contrary to reason. What remained was those teachings of Jesus and the apostles that the third president of the republic believed to be consistent with natural religion. Tindal's influence could also be seen in several of the leading pamphleteers of the revolutions of the late eighteenth century. Thomas Paine, a leading advocate of democratic revolutions and separation of church and state, wrote *The Age of Reason* in 1794 and took the next step beyond Toland and Tindal to an anti-Christian natural religion. Unfortunately, many North Americans came to define Deism solely in terms of Paine's virulent anti-Christian polemics. A little over one hundred years later, United States president Theodore Roosevelt labeled Paine "that filthy little atheist." The impression stuck in the minds of many North Americans that all Deists had been and were closet atheists or at least ardent opponents of Christianity.

## Common Notions of Deism

What were the common ideas adumbrated by Deism's precursors and promoted by its proponents? In a somewhat harsh but not incorrect or uncharitable statement of Deism's core, noted British philosopher of religion Ian Ramsey explained that

> the Deists, of whom Toland and Tindal are the best-known representatives, had argued for the reasonableness of Christianity only by taking away altogether its distinctiveness. The Christian faith was credible only where it was reasonable, and it was reasonable only where it repeated those beliefs and moral maxims which could be reached by anyone if they had the ability and time to work out independently a philosophical viewpoint. Once again the reasonableness of Christianity was defended only at the cost of diluting beyond recognition the Christian religion.[21]

The Deists, building on the foundation partially laid by Locke and other Enlightenment religious thinkers, all aimed at developing and defending three main ideas. First, that authentic Christianity is completely consistent with reasonable, universally accessible natural religion and morality, and insofar as a belief or moral rule could not be shown consistent with that, it should not be believed or followed. Even though they were loath to attack the doctrine of the Trinity overtly, the Deists clearly considered it incompatible with natural religion and therefore virtually ignored it. The same is true of virtually every other distinctively Christian doctrine.

While it is deplorable, one has to wonder whether this Procrustean distortion[22] of Christianity by the Deists is worse in kind or only in degree from that practiced by certain early and medieval Christian thinkers who went beyond using Greek philosophical categories as tools of interpretation and contextualization of the gospel to accommodating biblical teachings to fit them. The Gnostics, of course, were guilty of that and are almost universally vilified for it in Christian history by orthodox thinkers. Less commonly acknowledged—especially by modern proponents of Protestant orthodoxy—is a tendency by certain church fathers in the same direction. Without in any way equating Augustine's use of Neo-Platonism with Deism's use of Enlightenment rationalism, one might be justified in comparing them. Augustine's God, though trinitarian, is made captive to the Greek philosophical theology of divine simplicity, immutability and impassibility, and turns out to be more like a great cosmic emperor than a loving, compassionate heavenly Father. Anselm denied that God experiences feelings of compassion at all. The portrait of the God of traditional Christian theism would seem to be painted with both biblical and Hellenistic colors. Those who rightly criticize Deism for subverting biblical teachings by overwhelming them with Enlightenment philosophical and natural religion ought to consider the extent to which classical Christian doctrines of God have been unduly influenced by Greek philosophical categories of metaphysical perfection.[23]

A second idea common to Deism is that true religion, including true Christianity, is primarily about social and individual morality. Deists tended to reduce valid religion to a set of basic beliefs about God, immortality of the soul and rewards and punishments for behavior that were universally accessible to reason and primarily of value only as supports for virtue in this life. Deists were not much interested in metaphysical or theological speculation. If beliefs could not be shown to have some practical value for humanity's progress toward total reformation of life, they tended to be actively uninterested in them. They were all convinced, however, that some kind of belief in God and immortality of souls as well as judgment after death was necessary for the progressive reformation of life. Religious beliefs, then, became merely utilitarian supports for ethics in most Deists' minds.

The third and final common notion of Deism is that intelligent, enlightened people ought to be skeptical toward all claims of supernatural revelations and miracles. While the eighteenth-century Deists such as Toland and Tindal did not deny these, they clearly relegated them to a lesser status than universal truths of reason and reduced the supernatural element in religion almost to a vanishing point. Later, more radical Deists rejected miracles altogether and opted for a purely naturalistic, demythologized Christianity stripped of everything miraculous. The worldview of Deism was largely shaped by Newtonian physics and its universe ruled by rigid natural laws. It was a "world machine" with little room for divine intervention. To the extent Deists acknowledged miracles, they remained a foreign element in their system of thought waiting to be eradicated.

### The Legacy of Deism

The original ideal of the leading Deists was the transformation of Christianity into a universal natural religion of pure reason. As shocking as it seems to some people, the Deists did not think of their version of Christianity as a different religion. They saw it as the next step in the progress of Christianity away from medieval superstition and blind subservience to arbitrary authority inaugurated by Erasmus and Luther. However, the powers of the religious denominations of the eighteenth century by and large rejected Deism even when they sometimes secretly sympathized with some of its ideals.

Once it became clear to Deists that the Church of England might take the step away from Reformed theology to Arminianism—a move in the right direction—but *not* into natural religion, some of them began organizing a new denomination. Some who came together to form the new Deist church were disillusioned Anglicans and some were progressive Congregationalists. A few were disenchanted Baptists. In 1774 the first Unitarian congregation was formed in London as Essex Chapel. The first North American Unitarian church was King's Chapel, Boston, founded in 1785 out of a previously existing Episcopalian (Anglican) church. Throughout the 1790s numerous Congregational churches in both England and the United States (mostly in New England) became Unitarian with a theology strongly influenced by Deism. A new denomination was officially formed as the American Unitarian Association in 1825 and organized along strictly congregational lines without creed or doctrine. Harvard Divinity School became its official seminary, and although the denomination remained relatively small in numbers, it became one of the most influential religious groups in modern North America, with many United States presidents and congressional representatives claiming it as their spiritual home.

Most Deists did not join the Unitarian churches but either remained independent religious seekers without denominational affiliation or continued to attend established Christian churches while quietly dissenting from traditional Christian doctrines and practices. Deism quietly filtered into the fabric of North American religious and political life, and the God of Deism and natural religion became the "God" of civil religion in the United States ("In God We Trust"). An interesting duality has set into the religious life of the United States such that most Christian denominations and the grassroots Christian spirituality of most people are strongly pietistic in flavor, while the public religion of politicians and government officials is marked by Deism. The very same people who speak publicly in cool, rational tones about God's blessing on America without any mention of Jesus Christ or sin or salvation often revel in experiential religion in their private lives and churches. One late-twentieth-century United States president of strongly pietistic, evangelical leanings attempted to inject some of that language into his public life and was almost universally criticized for it. On the other hand, another presidential candidate of the 1980s may have lost the election in part for lack of any evidence of belief in God or spirituality.[24] The ethos of the United States is deeply influenced by both Deism and Pietism. A politician who is not at least a Deist is rejected. A politician who is too publicly pietistic is criticized.

Deism's legacy may also be seen in the rise of liberal Protestant theology in the nineteenth century. The founders and leading proponents of liberal theology in Europe and North America were not Deists. In fact, the "father of liberal theology," Friedrich Schleiermacher, claimed to be a Pietist "of a higher order" rather than a Deist or rationalist. Nevertheless, as liberal Protestant theology evolved throughout the nineteenth century, it echoed many of the common notions of Deism, and in one of its leading popularizers, the noted German church historian Adolf von Harnack, liberal theology turned out to look very much like the Deism of John Toland. That is where we go next in our narrative of Christian theology: the rise of liberal Protestant thought and various reactions and responses to it.

# PART IX

# The Overall Plot Divides

## *Liberals & Conservatives Respond to Modernity*

*In 1901, the first year of the twentieth century, two significant theological books* appeared in English announcing what the title of one book called *Reconstruction in Theology.*[1] The other volume's more prosaic title was *What Is Christianity?*[2] The authors were the president of Oberlin College in Ohio and the world's leading church historian at the University of Berlin respectively. Together the two books and the lectures they contained triumphantly proclaimed a new kind of Christian theology for the new century: liberal Protestant theology. Of course, it was not new in 1901. The authors and others like them were simply popularizing for preachers and theology teachers what they took to be a *fait accompli*—the rise of a thoroughly modern type of Protestant Christian reflection throughout the nineteenth century. Their books communicated to audiences throughout Europe and North America two basic tenets of this new, modern type of theology: (1) the necessity of reconstructing traditional Christian thought in the light of modern culture, philosophy and science; and (2) the necessity of discovering Christianity's true essence apart from the layers of traditional dogma that were no longer relevant or even possible to believe in light of modern thought. To many academic theologians of 1901, liberal theology seemed the inevitable wave of the future. It would sweep away hundreds of years of dry and dusty orthodoxy and authoritarian traditionalism as well as the embarrassments of theology's continual defeats in conflicts with modern science. It would show that authentic Christianity and valid theology do not conflict with the new modern spirit of the age, but work hand in hand with it toward a better world for all humanity.

The liberal Protestant theologians' triumphalist vision was premature. While this new type of theology was a force to be reckoned with in Protestant theology, it would not go unchallenged. Already in 1901 Protestant orthodox theologians of Europe and North America were gathering strength to fight it off. Soon there would emerge from among them a coalition of theologians, pastors and educated lay Christians to mount a theological battle against what they called "modernism" in theology. This new, intense form of orthodox traditionalism would come to be known as "fundamentalism." Rooted in Protestant orthodoxy and energized with a militant spirit of antimodernism (especially in theology), the fundamentalists mounted a campaign to drive liberal and modernist influences out of the Protestant denominations. They accused liberal theology of being a different religion from Christianity—a barely disguised unitarianism that was more rationalist and humanist than gospel-centered. A leading theologian of the fundamentalist reaction was J. Gresham Machen (1881-1937), a conservative Presbyterian committed to the Westminster Confession of Faith and to the timeless truths discovered and enshrined by Protestant orthodox divines of the sixteenth and seventeenth centuries. Added to those would often be a strong emphasis on the inerrancy and literal truth of the biblical record and the falseness of modern, skeptical, evolutionary science and philosophy. Machen's battle cry was sounded in *Christianity and Liberalism*,[3] published at the height of fundamentalism's strength, in which he sought to expose liberal theology as a false gospel and alternative religion to true Christianity.

Fundamentalism was not the only response to liberal Protestant theology. Much more damaging, perhaps, was the critical opposition by the so-called neo-orthodox theologians, many of whom had been trained in seminary and university under leading liberal theologians such as Adolf Harnack, author of *What Is Christianity?* The neo-orthodox theologians were Protestants who harked back to the Reformation, especially Luther, more than to Protestant orthodoxy or Puritanism. They were willing to adjust some aspects of Christianity to modern thought, but they believed liberal Protestant theology had accommodated too radically to modernity. A leading North American neo-orthodox thinker, H. Richard Niebuhr of Yale Divinity School, declared that in liberal theology, "a God without wrath brought men without sin into a kingdom without judgment through the ministrations of a Christ without a cross."[4] In Europe, Swiss theologian Karl Barth (1886-1968) led the neo-orthodox revolt against liberal Protestant theology and developed the most influential theology of the twentieth century. To many observers of modern theology, Barth stands as a great reformer alongside Luther because, like the sixteenth-century German, the twentieth-century Swiss author almost single-handedly routed the opposition and restored a semblance of the Christian gospel in a time of crisis.

The final decades of the twentieth century witnessed a sudden and surprising pluralization process in Christian theology. That is, numerous new "special interest" theologies sprang up in a vacuum of dominating theological voices. The last of the century's theological giants died in the early 1970s and no one appeared to replace them. Contemporary Christian theology is marked by profound variety and diversity: evangelical theology, a new Roman Catholic theology, process theology, liberation theology and eschatological theology may all be taught in the same seminary or divinity school. Some people find this situation deeply troubling, while others find it exciting and liberating. We will end this telling of the unfinished story of Christian theology by describing this pluralistic situation and the different responses to it.

## The Twentieth-Century Divide Over Modernity

One way of reading and telling the story of Protestant theology after the Reformation is to delineate two great watersheds or continental divides. The first is between monergism and synergism. People often refer to this divide as Calvinism versus Arminianism. However, many Protestant monergists do not identify with Calvin or even Reformed theology. Some Lutheran thinkers, for example, are monergistic as was Luther himself, without adopting full-blown Calvinist speculation about predestination (divine decrees) or even meticulous providence. Likewise, many evangelical synergists do not identify with Arminius or Arminianism. Some Lutheran theologians look back to Luther's successor Philipp Melanchthon as a model of evangelical synergism. Many Anglicans follow Richard Hooker's brand of synergism and, of course, Anabaptists claim Balthasar Hubmaier and Menno Simons as evangelical synergists well before Arminius. Most Protestant scholastic and orthodox thinkers, however, have been monergists in the classical Augustinian-Calvinist mold. For many of them it is the one and only truly Protestant mode of thinking about the God-human relationship in salvation as in history. Protestant synergists of various kinds protest that exclusivism and claim for evangelical synergism a role in the Protestant heritage going back to its beginnings. This divide is illustrated in the story of John Wesley's falling out with George Whitefield over predestination. Many Protestant leaders and thinkers have tried to bridge the gulf between those like Wesley who espouse human free will together with divine grace and those like Whitefield who insist that salvation is only a free gift if God does everything and the human person is entirely passive. Few have been able truly to combine the two perspectives, however, and from time to time the controversy reerupts, demonstrating that it remains a rift in the bedrock of Protestant thought.

The second great divide within Protestant theology began two hundred years after Arminius openly opposed Calvinist monergism in the Reformed Church of the Netherlands. This time the issue was even more basic—proper authority for Christian belief. For hundreds of years Protestants had held firmly to the principle of *sola scriptura* even while using reason, tradition and experience as tools of biblical interpretation. However, many Protestant thinkers, especially within the broad and deep Protestant orthodox tradition of Protestant scholasticism, had come to treat certain doctrinal statements of church history as unquestionable standards of theological correctness. The Nicene Creed was accepted by nearly all Protestants up until the Unitarian churches openly rejected it in the late eighteenth century under the influence of Deism. For that defection other Protestants rejected Unitarianism as a heretical sect or even a cult. The Westminster Confession of Faith and the two Westminster catechisms had become for many in the Reformed Protestant tradition veritable additions to Scripture in terms of authority. Most Protestant theologians of all denominations recognized as beyond serious questioning implicit belief in a transcendent, personal God who acts supernaturally at times (as in Christ's bodily resurrection) and whose grace is above nature. In other words, Protestant thinkers all held firmly to a certain basic Christian worldview that was increasingly under pressure from Enlightenment philosophy and science throughout the eighteenth century.

Enter the religious rationalists, Deists, skeptics and other Enlightenment thinkers of Europe and North America, most of whom claimed to be Protestant Christians even if of a "higher order." For them, modernity—a barely definable new *Zeitgeist* (spirit of the age)—became a touchstone of truth alongside of, if not above, Scripture and tradition. For them, reason itself became virtually synonymous with Enlightenment thought, which constituted modernity, and it could not be sacrificed even for the sake of preserving Christian tradition. For those thinkers deeply impressed with the irreversible and positive advances of modern science and philosophy, two options seemed open if they wanted to remain Christians. First, they could openly develop their own modern forms of Protestant Christianity as alternatives to Protestant orthodoxy. Unitarianism was such a project, and it publicly rejected classical Christian and Protestant standards of belief such as Nicaea and Chalcedon and the Westminster Confession and catechisms. These Protestant "free thinkers" quickly wandered further and further away from classical Christianity into a variety of experiments with philosophy of religion and mystical spirituality. Ralph Waldo Emerson's Transcendentalism was one such experiment that was barely Christian if at all. In many ways it resembled a syncretistic blend of Christianity and Hinduism.

The other option for those who wished to remain Protestant Christians while becoming thoroughly modern and even giving maximal acknowledgment to the claims of modernity was to stay within the mainstream Protestant denominations and their offshoots and attempt to transform them by reconstructing their theologies in the light of modern knowledge. In other words, these liberal Protestant thinkers would not go the separatist route of Unitarianism, which rejected classical doctrines because they conflicted with the best of modernity, but would simply reinterpret classical Protestant doctrines and the entire Christian worldview so that its "true essence" would be shown to be compatible with modernity. This was the project of classical liberal Protestant theology—to discover a "true essence of Christianity" distinct from whatever conflicted with modernity and reconstruct Protestant theology around that core. Conservatives fairly quickly jumped to the defense of the entire body of traditional Christian and Protestant beliefs and hardened its categories against the perceived pernicious influence of modernist theology. A new continental divide opened up within Protestant theology—between those who saw reconstruction of doctrine in the light of modernity as not only inevitable but necessary, and those who defended traditional doctrinal systems against reconstruction as a "do-or-die" project for Christianity.

# CHAPTER 32

# Liberal Theology Accommodates to Modern Culture

Like *Pietism, Puritanism and Deism, liberalism is a much misunderstood* category and often misused label. People often think of liberal theology as denial of something instead of as a distinct and positive approach to theological methodology. In other words, it is equated simply with denial of the virgin birth of Jesus or of his bodily resurrection or both. It may be identified with denial of biblical inspiration and rejection of dogmas such as the Trinity and deity of Christ. No doubt some—perhaps many—liberal Protestant thinkers of the nineteenth and twentieth centuries have denied these items of classical Protestant orthodoxy. Most have questioned at least some of them. But in order to get at the heart of liberal Protestant thought, we need to ask *why* these theologians questioned traditional beliefs. To be fair to them, we must acknowledge that in their own minds, at least, they were not so much rejecting tradition as reinterpreting or reconstructing it. Furthermore, the classical liberal thinkers disagreed among themselves about the specifics of doctrine. The movement was not so much an attempt to reject some beliefs as to transform Christian thinking in light of the new, modern cultural context.

This then might serve as a preliminary working definition of classical liberal Protestant theology. What all of its precursors and proponents had in common was maximal acknowledgment of the claims of modernity within Christian theology.[1] Liberal theologians were convinced that human culture had taken a quantum leap forward with the Enlightenment and that the very existence of Christianity as more than a privatized folk religion depended on updating it to square with the best of Enlightenment's "modernity project." In other words, Christian theology had to become modern or die out as a public religion with universal appeal and influence. If it did not adjust to the new modern situation, liberal theologians were persuaded, it would become a superstitious and esoteric spirituality for the backward and uneducated few—just like astrology. As one leading popularizer of liberal theology put it in doctrinal sermons to his American Protestant congregation in 1913, "This generation needs to have the highest and best thought of the day, on these great themes of the religious life"[2] because when doctrinal "subjects are presented in the form in which they were presented fifty years ago they fail to produce conviction in the minds of men; they cannot be believed."[3] That is because, Washington Gladden explained, modern philosophy, science and biblical scholarship have provided new information that the formulators of Christianity's past creeds and doctrines simply did not have, and it makes a world of difference. Those young Christian men and women who are trained in churches only in traditional doctrines without those being corrected in the light of new, modern knowledge will inevitably lose faith in Christianity when they are turned out into the modern world and encounter that new knowledge.

Liberal theologians did not agree among themselves on how best to reconstruct Christian beliefs in the light of modernity, but they agreed on the necessity of that ongoing project as the fundamental task of modern theology. While none of the classical liberal Protestant thinkers of the nineteenth century were willing to place modernity explicitly on a par with Scripture, all of them saw modern thought as a necessary tool of interpretation and most of them gave it a guiding and even controlling authority in determining the essence of Christian truth. That is what made them "liberal theologians." Some were more radical in their conclusions, discarding entirely any literal belief in the supernatural or miraculous. Few went that far. More often classical liberal Protestant theologians of the nineteenth and early twentieth centuries simply downplayed or neglected the supernatural. The same is true with classical dogmas such as the Trinity and the deity of Christ. Some rejected them completely, while more chose to neglect or reinterpret them. Each in his own way attempted to construct a new Christian theology that would be completely compatible with what was conceived to be the best of modernity in philosophy, science and biblical scholarship. There was no one set of conclusions at which all liberal theologians arrived.

**Modernity: The Cultural Context for Liberal Theology**

What is modernity? Some commentators describe it as a cultural mood—a set of perspectives and attitudes—that lasted only from about 1650 to about 1950. It was roughly synonymous with the Enlightenment and its cultural afterglow. It is supposedly being superseded by something called "postmodernity" since the 1960s. One way of approaching a description of modernity is by comparing it to Hellenistic culture in the Roman Empire during the early centuries of Christianity. In the first episodes of this story of Christian theology we saw how Christian thinkers of the second through the fourth, and even into the fifth, centuries contextualized the Christian gospel and worldview within that culture in varying ways. We saw also that there was no single "Hellenistic view" of reality. There were common features of Hellenistic culture that were shaped by pre-Christian Greek philosophers such as Socrates, Plato, Aristotle and their heirs. Modernity represents a similar situation. It never was a monolithic set of beliefs about the world. Rather, modern thought was constituted by certain pervasive cultural themes that together formed a cultural mood shaped by the Enlightenment.

Modernity's common and pervasive themes arose out of Enlightenment philosophy and science. We have already noted some of them in the story of Deism (chapter thirty-one). To recapitulate and extend briefly: Enlightenment-modern thought tended to focus on the omnicompetence of reason and its authority over tradition or faith, the uniformity of nature rather than supernatural control and interventions, and inevitable progress of humanity through education, reason and science. For Enlightenment thinkers, religion's main role in modernity would be moral education of humanity rather than metaphysical speculation or indoctrination in dogmas about things beyond rational investigation. The *Zeitgeist* (spirit of the age) of the Enlightenment and modernity generally was anthropocentric—human-centered. Enlightenment essayist Alexander Pope gave this advice to Enlightenment people: "Know then thyself. Seek not God to scan. The proper study of mankind is man." He also expressed the Enlightenment fascination with science and natural laws when he wrote, "Nature and nature's laws lay wrapped in night. God said 'Let Newton be!' and all was light."

Perhaps the greatest Enlightenment thinker of all was the great German philosopher Immanuel Kant, who was born in Königsberg, Prussia, in 1724 and died there in 1804 without ever having left the city. He is often judged to have been both the apex and greatest critic of the Enlightenment because he expressed and embodied many of its crucial themes while at the same time limiting reason to a narrower sphere than earlier Enlightenment thinkers allowed. Kant wrote a famous essay titled *What Is Enlightenment?* in which he summed it up in the imperative *sapere aude!*—"think for yourself." For him this applied in religion as in any other realm of culture. For Kant, religion had one main purpose: to provide moral foundations and education for society. In his most influential book on religion, *Religion Within the Limits of Reason Alone,* the great German philosopher relegated religion to the ethical realm.[4] So much for both natural theology and revealed theology. For Kant, authentic religion including valid Christianity was simply living a life in accordance with rationally discernible duty. This was his version of natural religion, and it had a tremendous affect on Enlightenment thinkers of the early nineteenth century seeking a thoroughly modern religion. Kant's religion could not possibly fall into conflict with science because it had nothing to do with speculative beliefs about the nature of the world or history and did not depend on any supernatural revelations or miracles. And yet it did retain belief in God, the immortal existence of souls, and rewards and punishments after death.

Not all Enlightenment philosophers were satisfied with Kant's almost naturalistic philosophy of religion. To another great German philosopher of the early nineteenth century, it seemed to reduce God to a prop, as it were, for human moral and ethical endeavor. Georg Wilhelm Friedrich Hegel (1770-1831) attempted to reintroduce a strong concept of God as central to modern philosophy without requiring belief in anything that would conflict with modern science or require blind faith in authority or supernatural revelation. In his *Lectures on the Philosophy of Religion* Hegel explained "God" as an immanent World Spirit *(Geist)* underlying and evolving together with nature and history.[5] For Hegel, belief in this God was both rational and fully compatible with the best of modern culture even though it was metaphysical and speculative contrary to Kant's dicta limiting philosophy of religion to ethics. Hegel's God was fully immanent in the world. One of the philosopher's maxims was "Without the world God would not be God." God and the world go and grow together. Humanity and human culture are God coming to self-consciousness, and God is what humanity may become at its best.

In a modern age searching for a religious perspective fully compatible with Enlightenment reason and science, both Kant's and Hegel's religious views were readily accepted, widely discussed and deeply influential. Neither one required belief in dogmas or miracles deemed incompatible with the spirit of the age, which was rationalistic and naturalistic. But both provided ways of regarding God that avoided atheism or sheer agnosticism. Like Plato and his pupil Aristotle in ancient Athens and Hellenistic culture afterward, Kant and Hegel provided two distinct philosophical viewpoints for modernity that many thought could be combined in creative ways. For many educated despisers of traditional religion in the nineteenth century, Kant's emphasis on religion as ethics without dogma and Hegel's concept of God as immanent within history and culture could be made twin pillars of a new philosophical theology that would not conflict with science. Just as many educated pagans of the Roman Empire like Celsus embraced a kind of vague, generic Greek religious philosophy that combined aspects of several specific philosophies, so many educated modern people of Europe and (later) North America in the nineteenth century came to accept a vague, generic Enlightenment religious philosophy influenced by Deism, Kant and Hegel. This modern way of being religious sought above all to avoid conflicts with science because science always seemed to win them. It also sought to redefine religion entirely in nonmetaphysical and nonspeculative ways as living a life of ethical duty and moral courage. From Hegel it took an immanentist idea of God as an impersonal, universal, spiritual force marching ever upward and onward toward the end of history in a state of utopian cultural perfection. Every cultural advance was interpreted as a triumph of the human spirit and a moment in the history of God's own self-realization through humanity within history.

**The Father of Modern Liberal Theology: Friedrich Schleiermacher**

The vague philosophical religion of nineteenth-century Enlightenment thought seemed a far cry from classical Christianity even though both Kant and Hegel and most of their followers claimed to be Christians in at least a cultural sense. That is, they belonged to the state church and occasionally participated in its rituals while rejecting its dogmas. So pervasive was this modern religiousness among the cultural elite of Europe that it seemed a generation would be lost to the church unless it could adjust its preaching and teaching to their worldview. Until the first decade of the nineteenth century, the Protestant theologians of Europe and North America had by and large insisted on a firm resistance to modernity wherever it conflicted with orthodoxy. They may have read and been somewhat influenced by Kant and later Hegel, but the Protestant orthodox theologians of the faculties of theology resisted any accommodation to their Enlightenment philosophies. Then came Friedrich Schleiermacher, who was the first professional Protestant theologian to call for sweeping changes in Protestant orthodoxy to encounter and come to terms with the *Zeitgeist* of modernity. The result was the birth of liberal Protestant theology.

Friedrich Daniel Ernst Schleiermacher was born in Prussia in 1768. His father was a devout Pietist Christian with strong orthodox beliefs. He sent young Friedrich to a boarding school operated by Pietists and later to a Pietist seminary. While pursuing higher studies at the University of Halle, also founded by Pietists, young Schleiermacher drank deeply at the wells of Enlightenment thought and especially the philosophy of Kant and began expressing doubts about the truth of some orthodox doctrines in letters to his father. This led to a rift between them that eventually was healed, but Schleiermacher always struggled with his father's Christianity. In a letter to his sister years later, he expressed his own consciousness of always remaining a Pietist of a "higher order." Schleiermacher became a minister of the Reformed Church and served as a chaplain at a hospital in Berlin and then as professor of theology and university preacher at the University of Halle. In 1806 he moved back to Berlin when Halle was closed by Napoleon. There he pastored the large and influential Trinity Church and helped found the University of Berlin. He became the dean of its faculty of theology and gained a reputation as a national hero, powerful preacher and great intellectual throughout Germany. When he died in 1834, the people of Berlin lined the streets in mourning as the funeral procession went by.

Schleiermacher wrote many books during his career, but two stand out as most influential in the formation of the new liberal Protestant school of theology. In 1799, while participating heavily in the salon culture of Berlin, the young minister and hospital chaplain wondered how to reach Christianity's "cultured despisers" with the gospel and persuade them of the truth of Christianity as a positive religion based on divine revelation. The current cultural fad at the time was Romanticism—an emotional reaction to an overemphasis on objective reason in the eighteenth-century Enlightenment. The Romantics reveled in "feelings," by which they meant not irrational emotions but deep, human longings and appreciation for beauty in nature. The Romantic movement gave rise to new flowerings of the arts in the midst of a culture that tended to value hard, scientific data and intellectual philosophies. Goethe in literature and Beethoven in music were all the rage. Schleiermacher wanted to find a point of contact for Christianity in his circle of friends, most of whom were quite skeptical of traditional religion. For them he wrote what has become a classic volume of modern, liberal Christian apologetics: *On Religion: Addresses in Response to Its Cultured Critics.* In a sense this book laid the foundation for liberal theology to come. In it the author explained that the essence of religion lies not in rational proofs of the existence of God, supernaturally revealed dogmas or churchly rituals and formalities, but in a "fundamental, distinct, and integrative element of human life and culture"[6]—the feeling *(Gefühl)* of being utterly dependent on something infinite that manifests itself in and through finite things.

Schleiermacher removed authoritative, objective revelation from the center of religion and replaced it with *Gefühl*—an untranslatable German word. The closest English translation would be "deep, inner awareness." It is often translated "feeling," but that conveys a wrong impression. For Schleiermacher, both religion in general and Christianity as a positive religion are mainly about a universal human faculty and experience that he called *Gefühl.* It is the distinctly human awareness of something infinite beyond the self on which the self is dependent for everything. Christianity has its own unique form of *Gefühl,* which Schleiermacher believed to be its highest form, but every human being has this experiential awareness as his or her "religious a priori." It is universal and an intrinsic part of human nature itself, according to Schleiermacher. This appealed to the Romantics as well as to Enlightenment people looking for a religious spirituality without blind faith in churchly dogmas that required a sacrifice of the intellect. Schleiermacher had explained to them how they could be more religious without giving up any of what they saw as the Enlightenment enhancement of their true humanity. The path was to discover and foster that universal human religiousness within themselves that Schleiermacher sometimes simply referred to as "piety" and discover their link with the infinite that was already there within themselves.

In *On Religion* Schleiermacher laid the foundation on which he built a specifically Christian theological edifice in his greatest work, *The Christian Faith.* This systematic theology first appeared in 1821 and then was updated and revised by Schleiermacher in 1830. In this mammoth work the Berlin pastor and theology professor presented a system of Christian doctrine for modern times. Most scholars of modern theology would agree with the commentator who wrote that "nothing on such a scale, and so systematic, had appeared in Protestantism since John Calvin's *Institutes of the Christian Religion* nearly three centuries earlier."[7] Schleiermacher's intent in *The Christian Faith* was to present a specifically Christian theology that would provide an alternative to the vague religiousness of Kant and Hegel while taking fully into account the advances of modern thought and avoiding conflicts with them. It was an updating of Protestant orthodoxy even if most Protestant orthodox theologians reacted harshly and repudiated it.

By the time he wrote *The Christian Faith,* Schleiermacher had come to refer to *Gefühl* as "God-consciousness," and he argued that there is both a universal God-consciousness in humanity and specific religious forms of it in the positive religions. According to Schleiermacher, Christian theology is not so much reflection on supernatural, divine revelation as it is the attempt to set forth the Christian religious affections in speech.[8] The key Christian religious affection is the feeling of being totally dependent upon the redemptive work of Jesus Christ for one's relationship with God. This is the "essence of Christianity"—a deep awareness of being dependent upon God (God-consciousness) and upon Jesus Christ as one's link to God. This *Gefühl* formed the authoritative source and norm for Schleiermacher's theology, and even Scripture itself would be not only interpreted but judged by it. The author was confident that for the most part both Scripture and Christian tradition would hold up well under critical scrutiny using experience as the touchstone, but he was more than willing to revise any particular doctrine in its light if necessary. No doctrine, however traditional, would be sacrosanct. Only those that were compatible with God-consciousness and its particular Christian expression would be allowed by Schleiermacher.

Without any doubt Schleiermacher held Scripture and the Great Tradition of church teaching in high regard. But he also held religious experience as higher in authority. The Bible, he averred, is not an absolute authority but a record of the religious experiences of the earliest Christian communities and therefore provides a model for contemporary attempts to interpret the significance of Jesus Christ for specific historical circumstances. It is neither supernaturally inspired nor infallible. Schleiermacher tended to relegate the Old Testament to an irrelevant status as it seemed to him to lack the normative dignity of the New Testament. Even the New Testament, however, could be wrong if at any point it conflicted with human religious experience generally or its specifically Christian form. The German liberal theologian proceeded to reconstruct the doctrine of God by affirming that "all attributes which we ascribe to God are to be taken as denoting not something special in God, but only something special in the manner in which the feeling of absolute dependence is to be related to Him."[9] In other words, talk about God is always talk about human experience of God. Such statements describe not God-in-himself but a certain mode of experiencing God.

Schleiermacher believed that the doctrine of the Trinity does not comport well with the experience of God-consciousness, and so he reduced discussion of it to an appendix to his theology. He did not reject or deny it, but admitted to doubts about it and stated that it is virtually useless for Christian theology because it is not an utterance concerning the religious consciousness. He argued that Christian God-consciousness requires believers to regard absolutely everything that happens in nature and history as the activity of God, and therefore theology must abandon the distinction between the natural and the supernatural. Without completely denying special acts of God that some might properly call miracles, Schleiermacher stated,

> On the whole . . . as regards the miraculous, the general interests of science, more particularly of natural science, and the interests of religion seem to meet at the same point, i.e., that we should abandon the idea of the absolutely supernatural because no single instance of it can be known by us, and we are nowhere required to recognize it.[10]

Thus for Schleiermacher and liberal Protestant theology generally, science and Christianity in principle cannot conflict. The former deals with proximate causes only, whereas the latter deals with the ultimate cause of everything. In the end, however, Schleiermacher did seem to discourage or forbid belief in special divine interventions. That he never denied the bodily resurrection of Jesus or his empty tomb may indicate a reluctance on his part to carry through his antisupernatural sentiment to its bitter end.

Nowhere does Schleiermacher's theological liberalism show more clearly than in his Christology. He rejected the traditional doctrine of the two natures of Jesus Christ and replaced it with a Christology based entirely on Jesus' experience of God-consciousness. Jesus Christ, he taught, is completely like the rest of humanity in nature. The only difference is that, unlike other humans, "from the outset he has an absolutely potent God-consciousness."[11] From his birth on, he lived in full awareness of his dependence on God and never sinfully violated that relationship of dependence by asserting his autonomy over against God, his heavenly Father. Schleiermacher expressed his functional Christology (as opposed to an ontological Christology) when he wrote that "the Redeemer, then, is like all men in virtue of the identity of human nature, but distinguished from them all by the constant potency of His God-consciousness, which was a veritable existence of God in Him."[12] According to Schleiermacher, because of this potency of God-consciousness, Jesus Christ was the Savior of humanity because he was able to communicate it in some measure to others through the community he founded known as the church. Schleiermacher denied both the satisfaction and substitution theories of the atonement in favor of something closer to Abelard's moral influence model. Through his life and death, he averred, Jesus Christ draws believers into the power of his own God-consciousness and imparts it to them in some measure. Clearly, Schleiermacher's Christology treats Jesus as an "exalted human being" rather than as God incarnate in any traditional sense. It is more adoptionistic than incarnational.

Schleiermacher's intention was to provide a theology that was both thoroughly modern and thoroughly Christian. It required no beliefs essentially contrary to modern thought and discarded none essentially necessary to Christianity. Or so he thought. Critics were not confident that he had managed to pull it off. On the left, deists and followers of Kant and Hegel found Schleiermacher's project far too Christian even if it treated Christianity as a subset of universal religiousness. By making a human being in history the Savior of humanity, Schleiermacher fell into the "scandal of particularity," whereas the great Enlightenment German philosopher G. E. Lessing had declared that universal truths could not be founded on particular historical events. On the right, Christian critics thought Schleiermacher had too radically reinterpreted Christian belief and subverted it to modern culture. A frequent charge was that he had made it entirely subjective by defining theology as reflection on experience rather than on objective, historical revelation in Scripture.

**Albrecht Ritschl and the Search for Christianity's Essence**

If any one theologian's name is most closely connected with classical liberal Protestant theology, it is Albrecht Ritschl's. During the last two decades of the nineteenth century and first two decades of the twentieth century, liberal theology was frequently called "Ritschlianism." Albrecht Ritschl lived a remarkably uneventful life from 1822 until 1889. He taught systematic theology for the last twenty-five years of his life at Göttingen University in Germany and became a world-famous interpreter of Protestant theology for the modern age. His magnum opus was his three-volume treatise *The Christian Doctrine of Justification and Reconciliation*, which was published gradually from 1870 to 1874. Its English translator and editor, Scottish theologian H. R. Mackintosh, said of it, "Not since Schleiermacher published his *Christliche Glaube [The Christian Faith]* in 1821 has any dogmatic treatise left its mark so deeply upon theological thought in Germany and throughout the world."[13] An entire generation of Protestant theologians was trained in Ritschl's theology.

Ritschl was concerned, among other things, to disentangle Christianity from science. By "science," he meant not only the natural sciences but any objective discipline whose stock-in-trade is "facts." The Göttingen theologian was convinced that theology and religion in general must be distinguished from science—a far cry from the medieval project of establishing theology as the "queen of the sciences." Two strategies would accomplish this all-important task of disengaging theology from science. First, Ritschl believed and argued that religious propositions, including Christian doctrines, must be understood as completely different from scientific ones. Science deals with *facts* and speaks the language of assertions of facts. Religion deals with *values* and speaks the language of judgments of value. The two must be distinguished from each other. To use twentieth-century philosophical jargon, they are completely different "language games." The second and closely related step in disentangling religion from modern science would be discovery of Christianity's true essence as completely compatible with the modern worldview. Together, these two methodological strategies for transforming and reconstructing Christian theology form the heart of Ritschlianism, which is the heart of classical liberal Protestant theology.

Under the influence of Immanuel Kant's philosophy, Ritschl believed that he had found the way to create a thoroughly modern Protestant theology. He delineated a distinction between two kinds of propositions or truth claims: judgments of fact and judgments of value. The former are statements about objective reality that are in some way testable. They are theoretical and morally neutral. The person making a judgment of a fact does not have to commit to anything personally or morally in order to be quite accurate. An example of such a judgment of fact would be "the world is round." A value judgment, on the other hand, is person-involving and demands commitment. One is never neutral when making a value judgment. An example of such a statement would be "God is love." These two assertions are of entirely different orders, according to Ritschl.

The key to Ritschl's liberalism lies in the fact that he relegated all purely religious assertions, including the statements that make up Christian theology, to the realm of value judgments. While admitting that it is impossible to entirely disentangle the two orders of speech, Ritschl saw the clearing away of all confusion and conflict with science as the key to making theology modern. Theology is not interested in the same kinds of things that interest science. Science is interested in constructing a system of facts that accurately and objectively describe the physical world. Theology seeks to construct a system of value judgments based solely on the effects God has on people's lives and the worth of those effects for people's highest good. Theology has no interest in scientific knowledge. It has some interest in historical knowledge, but only insofar as necessary to establish what values Jesus and his disciples taught.

When Ritschl turned to determining Christianity's true essence, he had already decided it cannot be some objective scientific or metaphysical truth that is open to all. Such could always fall before the onslaughts of modern research. The essence must be a value judgment or set of them. Ritschl believed that he had found that essence in Jesus' ideal of the "kingdom of God." But that ideal, according to Ritschl, has nothing to do with supernatural comings or goings, or earthly or heavenly miracles, or judgments, or heavens or hells. The kingdom of God is an ideal unity of humanity organized according to love within human history.[14] Such a kingdom is both God's and humanity's highest good and theology's sole interest.

Like Kant before him, Ritschl almost reduced Christianity to moralism. That is, for him the core of Christianity was a way of life that has little to do with anything supernatural, miraculous or dogmatic. One is being "Christian" by working to establish God's kingdom on earth in meaningful, reasonable and practical ways. For Ritschl, Christianity was not an otherworldly religion but a religion of world transformation through ethical action inspired by love. Theology was not a metaphysical system of quasi-scientific statements about objective reality but a set of value judgments to which one commits oneself as a means of building God's kingdom.

An example of this transformation of religious and theological statements is Ritschl's interpretation of Jesus' divinity. Like Schleiermacher, Ritschl rejected the classical two-natures Christology of Chalcedon. When Christians affirm Jesus as God, he explained, they are making a value judgment about Jesus' life's worth for both God and humanity. He was called to and perfectly fulfilled a "vocation" given to him by God the Father to be the perfect embodiment of the kingdom of God among humans. Christians confess Jesus to be "God" because his life vocation made possible partial achievement of God's kingdom within history. But, Ritschl argued, Jesus did not preexist his earthly, human life in some heavenly realm except in the mind of God.

Like Schleiermacher's theology, Ritschl's cannot conflict with science—even in the broadest sense of that term. With liberal Protestantism, theology lost its scientific status. It became more closely linked with spirituality and morality. Some would say it became subsumed under them. The advantage was that no longer would Christians have to fear the latest findings of science, be they about the solar system, as in the famous conflict between Galileo and the Catholic church, or about origins of the species, as in the conflict between Darwin and conservative Christian theologians. The liberals reconstructed Christian theology around its newly discovered "essence" (whatever that might be) in such a way that its essence could not be touched by new scientific findings. The disadvantage, of course, was a nearly complete subjectivizing of Christian theology. Now it would be about experience, whether Schleiermacher's God-consciousness or Ritschl's moral experience of the kingdom of God as humanity's highest good. With Ritschl, theology no longer dealt in facts but only in values. Traditional beliefs that might conflict with modernity such as the virgin birth, Jesus' nature, miracles and second coming, and realms of angels and demons and heaven and hell were all gradually relegated to the dust bin of ancient theology through neglect or radical reinterpretation. On the other hand, at least now no one would be burned at the stake like Servetus in Geneva for questioning orthodox doctrines. Quite the contrary. Once liberal Protestant theologians controlled seminaries and divinity schools, scholars who insisted on teaching orthodox doctrines as facts would often be excluded as old-fashioned obscurantists.

### Liberal Theology's Common Themes

Earlier in this chapter we identified an essence of liberal Protestant theology:

maximal acknowledgment of the claims of modernity within a Christian framework. In other words, the liberal Protestant thinkers like Schleiermacher and Ritschl were not interested in being deists, Unitarians, free thinkers or independent spiritual seekers. They were men of the church who preached, led in the sacraments and taught systematic theology. They held the Bible in high regard, even if they denied its verbal inspiration and inerrancy. They aimed to be Christ-centered and to preserve the belief that in some sense Jesus Christ is the world's Savior. They believed in a personal, involved God of love who is self-revealing and did not limit theology to what autonomous human reason can discover. On the other hand, they started out their theological projects with the presupposition that one must not choose between being Christian and being modern. One must be both in equal measure. That would mean that just as Christian truth confronts and transforms modernity (e.g., Jesus is Lord), so modernity confronts and transforms traditional Christianity (e.g., the dogma of Jesus' two natures is no longer tenable within a modern worldview).

Beyond acknowledging modernity as an authoritative source and norm for Christian theology, liberal Protestant thinkers from Schleiermacher on held to three main themes that conditioned their theological reflections: the immanence of God, the moralization of dogma, and the universal salvation of humanity. Hegel's influence overshadowed liberal theology's doctrine of God. Nearly all liberal Protestant thinkers of the late nineteenth and early twentieth centuries emphasized continuity between God and nature in a way that often smacked of pantheism or at least panentheism (mutuality between God and the world). At its best, liberal theology stopped short of reducing God to a universal World Spirit and affirmed God's personal nature. But always the imagery of humanity and nature as somehow extensions of God arose in the background if not the foreground of liberal thinking. The idea of God's "wholly otherness"—an infinite qualitative difference between God and the world—as proclaimed by antiliberal philosophers and theologians such as the Dane Søren Kierkegaard was anathema to liberal theologians. A favorite metaphor for the God-human relationship among some liberal thinkers was that of a bay and a large body of water. The bay is distinct from the ocean or sea but made of the same "stuff." So humanity is spiritually an extension of God while certainly not all of God.

The second common theme was the moralization of dogma. Under the influence of Kant, liberal Protestant thinkers insisted on reinterpreting all doctrines and dogmas of Christianity in ethical and moral terms, and those that could not be so reinterpreted were neglected if not discarded entirely. The deity of Christ could be moralized as an expression of his moral influence. He brought the kingdom of God into human social history as an ideal. But to many liberals the Trinity could not be so moralized. Its significance for community eluded them, so they neglected it altogether.

The third common theme was the universal salvation of humanity. Almost entirely missing from liberal Protestantism was any acknowledgment of radical sin and evil or of God's judgment, wrath and hell. The latter were reinterpreted as states of consciousness when humans are alienated from God and God's kingdom by their own decisions and actions. It is not that God judges them so much as they judge themselves.

**The Legacy of Liberal Protestant Theology**

One of liberal Protestant theology's great interpreters and popularizers was Adolf Harnack (1851-1930), who wrote *What Is Christianity?* Harnack was a leading German intellectual who taught church history and historical theology at the University of Berlin. In many ways he was Schleiermacher's and Ritschl's successor as leader of the liberal movement in theology. He was a German-government insider who wrote Kaiser Wilhelm's speech declaring war on France and Great Britain in 1914. After the war he was offered the position of ambassador to the United States by the German government but turned the position down. A major government building in Berlin is named after him. His most influential scholarly work was the multivolume *History of Dogma,* in which he attempted to demonstrate the Hellenization of early Christian thought and launched the "de-Hellenization" project of rediscovering the simple gospel of Jesus Christ by stripping away the alleged layers of Greek speculative philosophy from creeds and formulas of faith. Almost every aspiring young theologian and church historian of Germany sat under Harnack for at least one year.

In *What Is Christianity?* the great German professor of theology summed up the supposedly simple essence of Christianity in three great ideas introduced by Jesus, whose message, Harnack claimed, was not about himself but only about God the Father. The first basic principle of authentic Christianity, Harnack claimed, is the kingdom of God and its coming.[15] This has nothing whatever to do with supernatural events of the future but only with "the rule of God in the hearts of individuals." Harnack's second of three basic ideas of the New Testament gospel is God the Father and the infinite value of the human soul. According to Harnack, Jesus made no distinction between God's fatherhood of believers and his fatherhood of unbelievers. God is humanity's Father, and every human soul is of infinite value and worth to God, which makes us all brothers and sisters. This is sometimes expressed as the fatherhood of God and the brotherhood of man. Finally, according to Harnack, Jesus introduced the higher righteousness and the commandment of love. By "higher righteousness," he meant a righteousness centered on love rather than mere legalistic keeping of the law. According to Harnack, these three basic religious ideas together form the "kernel" of authentic Christianity and everything else is the "dry husk" to be stripped away and discarded.

Harnack's influence reached across the Atlantic Ocean to North America and helped develop a school of liberal thought known as the Social Gospel, whose leading proponent was Baptist theologian Walter Rauschenbusch. Rauschenbusch was born into the family of a German Baptist pastor and professor of theology in New York in 1861. He died just at the end of World War I in 1918 after a distinguished career following in his father's footsteps. He taught theology and church history for many years in the German-speaking division of Rochester Theological Seminary in Rochester, New York.[16] But Rauschenbusch's first love was what was known as the Social Gospel, and together with Ohio pastor Washington Gladden and others, he helped develop and promote it largely on the foundation of Ritschlian theology. Harnack's message of Jesus' "simple gospel" of the kingdom of God within history also influenced the prophets of the social gospel.

Rauschenbusch's most important book was his last: *A Theology for the Social Gospel,* published in 1917. While carefully avoiding any open denial of fundamental doctrinal tenets of Protestantism, the liberal Baptist professor completely reoriented theology away from dogmas about supernatural realities toward social ethics. The key categories of this theology were the "Kingdom of Evil" and the "Kingdom of God" and the "salvation of super-personal beings." By the latter, Rauschenbusch meant the great structures of social life that take on a life of their own much greater and more powerful than the individuals who live in them. A modern corporation, for example, is a "super-personal being," as is a modern nation-state. According to Rauschenbusch, Christ came not only to save individuals but even more to save super-personal beings:

> The salvation of the super-personal beings is by coming under the law of Christ. The fundamental step of repentance and conversion for professions and organizations is to give up monopoly power and the incomes derived from legalized extortion, and to come under the law of service, content with a fair income for honest work. The corresponding step in the case of governments and political oligarchies, both in monarchies and in capitalistic semi-democracies, is to submit to real democracy. Therewith they step out of the Kingdom of Evil into the Kingdom of God.[17]

Harnack's and Rauschenbusch's theologies are examples of liberal theology's Kantian "moralizing of dogma." Muted are the great themes of doctrine developed over hundreds of years. Christianity is virtually reduced to a few simple religious statements and a socialist political and economic program. The heyday of this kind of liberal Protestant theology was the decade of the 1920s, especially in the United States. The horror of the First World War took much of the wind out of its sails in Europe before that. Even in the United States, liberal theology underwent dramatic changes in response to the great world wars, the holocaust and neo-orthodoxy's challenge. Varieties of new forms of liberal theology arose to renew its vitality and keep it viable for changing times. But in spite of its ups and downs, classical liberal theology left an enduring and powerful legacy on mainstream Protestant theology. That legacy may be seen whenever and wherever theologians express disdain for doctrine and individual Christian experience of God and emphasize in their place ethical education and social activism. It may especially be seen whenever "modern thought and experience" is elevated as the primary norm for theology and wherever God is reduced to a spiritual force immanent within all things. A major contemporary form of liberal theology that stands in the tradition of Hegel and Schleiermacher is "process theology." Standing in the tradition of Kant and Ritschl is a rich variety of liberation and political theologies.

Classical liberal Protestant theology swept triumphantly through the seminaries and mainstream denominations of Europe and North America with such transformative power and influence that many traditional Protestant thinkers and leaders were caught off guard. But a strong reaction to such a radical reforming movement was bound to set in, and it appeared in most intense form under the label "fundamentalism" in the early decades of the twentieth century.

# CHAPTER 33

# Conservative Theology Hardens Traditional Categories

O*nce the full impact of liberal Protestant theology was felt, a stern reaction* erupted from theologians committed to forms of Protestant orthodoxy. Around 1910 the great Dutch theologian and statesman Abraham Kuyper (1837-1920) declared,

> There is no doubt . . . that Christianity is imperilled by great and serious dangers. Two life systems are wrestling with one another, in mortal combat. Modernism is bound to build a world of its own from the data of the natural man, and to construct man himself from the data of nature; while, on the other hand, all those who reverently bend the knee to Christ and worship Him as the Son of the living God, and God himself, are bent upon saving the "Christian Heritage." This is the struggle in Europe, this is the struggle in America, and this also, is the struggle for principles in which my own country is engaged, and in which I myself have been spending all my energy for nearly forty years.[1]

Many other Protestant thinkers and leaders felt the same way: that liberal theology was threatening to destroy authentic Christianity and even the "Christian heritage" in Western culture.

Out of Protestant orthodoxy arose a militant theology of reaction against liberal theology and modern thought in general that came to be called fundamentalism. While seeking simply to preserve classical Protestant theology and defeat liberal accommodation to modern thought, fundamentalism ended up developing a new form of Protestant theology that was rationalistic, separatistic and absolutistic. That is, full-blown fundamentalist theology tended to develop absolute systems of internally coherent doctrinal propositions that must either be accepted entirely without question or rejected totally. Anyone who questioned even one point of a fundamentalist Protestant doctrinal system could be accused of heresy if not apostasy. This was characteristic of extreme fundamentalism's overreaction to liberal theology's doctrinal relativism.

### *Fundamentalism*—A Contested Term and Category

We have already noted how many theological labels and categories are imprecise and often stretched, misused and abused. The same is true of *fundamentalism* and *fundamentalist.* What began as a label for a theological movement defending Protestant orthodoxy against the "acids of modernity" and dissolution by liberal theology is frequently used as a term of derision and ridicule toward any fanatical, militant form of religion. Scholars of religion have spent thousands of hours and dollars attempting to pin down the essence of fundamentalism because of that term's almost universal misuse in the mass media and by people in the street.[2] Here the term will be used in its historical-theological sense. Every attempt will be made to avoid using the label as journalists often do—to describe and marginalize ardent, passionate religious belief. Many people—Christian and non-Christian—are strong, passionate believers in religion and spirituality without being fundamentalists. True fundamentalism is a particular twentieth-century form of Protestant orthodoxy largely defined by its reaction against liberal and modernist theologies such as we discussed in the last chapter.[3]

If the essence of liberal Protestant theology was maximal acknowledgment of the claims of modernity within Christian thought, the essence of fundamentalist theology may be described as maximal acknowledgment of the claims of Protestant orthodoxy against modernity and liberal theology. Its core attitude and approach is what has been called "maximal conservatism" in Christian theology. Its passion is to defend the verbal inspiration and absolute infallibility (inerrancy) of the Bible as well as all traditional doctrines of Protestant orthodox theology perceived as under attack by modern thought and liberal theology. Over the decades from about 1910 to 1960, this fundamentalist project became increasingly intense and militantly separatistic as different fundamentalist leaders disagreed among themselves about the "fundamentals of the faith" and degrees of separation from secular and modernistic religion. In the beginning of the movement the fundamentals of the faith needing a defense were fairly few and obvious. By the 1940s and 1950s many acknowledged fundamentalist leaders had added premillennialism (belief in a literal one-thousand-year reign of Christ on earth after the second coming) and young-earth creationism (belief that God created all of nature and everything in it less than ten thousand years ago in a literal week of twenty-four-hour days) to the list of essential doctrines.

Historically and theologically, it is wrong to label anything before the rise to dominance of liberal Protestant theology fundamentalism. The latter movement is a twentieth-century reaction against the former. It is tied to it as its counterpoint. Without liberal theology there would be Protestant orthodoxy, but not fundamentalism per se. In addition, it is historically and theologically wrong to label as "fundamentalist" anyone who believes strongly and passionately in religious doctrines or promotes them through evangelism. Finally, it is a false stereotype that depicts all fundamentalists as uneducated, socially and economically disadvantaged persons on the fringes of modern society. Many fundamentalists are educated, affluent people, and that's always been the case.

Historically and theologically, then, fundamentalists are those Protestant Christians who defend entire, detailed systems of very conservative doctrines against perceived modernist, liberal encroachments and dilutions, and they often call for and practice separation from Christians who are guilty of participating in or condoning modernism in theology. More often than not, fundamentalists insist on belief in the supernatural, verbal inspiration of the Bible, absolute biblical inerrancy with regard to historical and natural as well as theological matters, a literalistic biblical hermeneutic, and strong opposition to any and all deviations from these principles or fundamental beliefs of conservative Protestantism. One late-twentieth-century fundamentalist historian of the movement defines it this way: "Historic fundamentalism is the literal exposition of all the affirmations and attitudes of the Bible and the militant exposure of all non-Biblical affirmations and attitudes."[4]

### Backgrounds and Precursors of Fundamentalism

At several points in the story of Christian theology we have briefly encountered Protestant orthodoxy—a very broad and general movement that is almost facetiously referred to as a "hardening of the categories" of Protestant theology after the first generation of reformers. The hallmarks of Protestant orthodoxy were a return to and application of a scholastic method of theology in Protestant thought and a strong emphasis on Scripture as verbally inspired, propositionally infallible and even inerrant. An excellent, if somewhat extreme, example of Protestant orthodox theology is the influential Italian-Swiss Reformed systematic theologian Francis Turretin (1623-1687), whose three-volume *Institutiones theologiae elenchticae* represents "the most systematic and thorough treatise on doctrinal theology in the Reformed camp after Calvin's *Institutes.*"[5] Modern historical theologian Justo González explains that Turretin was a "typical exponent of Protestant orthodoxy . . . in his scholastic style and methodology" because "here again we find the endless and subtle distinctions, the rigid outlines, the strict systematization, and the propositional approach that had been characteristic of late medieval scholasticism. Therefore, there is ample reason to call Turretin and his contemporaries 'Protestant scholastics.' "[6] Turretin emphatically affirmed the verbal inspiration of all of Scripture in a fairly extreme form that came close to viewing it as a process of dictation by the Holy Spirit. One of the great amusements of the story of Christian theology is Turretin's claim that even the vowel points of the Hebrew text of the Old Testament were divinely inspired and therefore inerrant! Already in Turretin's time scholars knew that the original text of the Hebrew Scriptures contained no vowel points. They were added by Jewish scholars known as the Masoretes beginning in the sixth century. In order to safeguard the Bible from ambiguity regarding its exact content and meaning, the Protestant scholastic theologian argued that the Masoretic text of the Old Testament is inspired and inerrant and needs no correction from older Hebrew manuscripts.[7]

Turretin's scholastic Protestant orthodoxy formed the foundation for theological study and ministerial training at the influential Princeton Theological Seminary, where most American Presbyterian ministers matriculated in the nineteenth century. Turretin's Latin systematic theology was required reading there until late in that century, and for many professors and students it provided not only one possible view of correct theology but the one and only true view of Protestant doctrine. A dynasty of theological scholarship, known as the "Princeton school of theology," grew up around Turretin's teaching. It was exemplified by Archibald Alexander, the father-and-son team of conservative Presbyterian theologians Charles Hodge and Archibald Alexander Hodge, and their successor, Benjamin Breckinridge Warfield. During its theological reign at Princeton from 1812 to 1921, the Alexander-Hodge-Warfield dynasty of Princeton theology translated Turretin-type Protestant scholasticism and orthodoxy into a nineteenth-century American context and laid the theological and doctrinal foundation upon which fundamentalism would build in the next century.[8]

Of the four Princeton precursors of fundamentalism, the greatest was without doubt Charles Hodge, who was born in New England in 1797 into a very conservative Presbyterian family in which the Westminster Confession and Shorter Catechism were revered second only to the Bible itself. Hodge studied for the Presbyterian ministry under Archibald Alexander at Princeton Seminary, and his main textbook was Turretin's systematic theology. After seminary the newly ordained Presbyterian minister furthered his education at various universities in Europe. He sat in Schleiermacher's lectures at Berlin and soaked in Hegel at Tübingen. These encounters convinced him of the weaknesses of the new, liberal approach to Protestant theology and the strength of his own heritage in Protestant orthodoxy. In his search for a suitable philosophical foundation for his own theology, Hodge discovered the Scottish commonsense realism of Thomas Reid (1710-1796), which advanced the empiricism of John Locke in a nonidealistic and nonskeptical direction, in contrast to his more influential fellow Scotsman David Hume (1711-1776). Reid held that "all normal human beings are endowed by God with various faculties. These faculties permitted observations and ideas about the world on which human beings may rely. Persons needed only to gather and classify evidence and carefully generalize these 'facts.' "[9] Hodge accepted Reid's view of knowledge and rejected the prevailing and more skeptical views of Hume and Kant as well as the more speculative and rationalistic view of Hegel. Reid's Scottish commonsense realism became the "orthodox" philosophy of Princeton theology through Hodge, and later fundamentalists adopted it as well.

Hodge applied Reid's epistemology to systematic theology and attempted to revive the tradition of theology as a rational science on its foundation. In his massive three-volume work *Systematic Theology* (1871-1873) Hodge explained theology's proper method as gathering and organizing the data of divine revelation from Scripture just as modern natural science gathers and organizes the data of nature: "The Bible is to the theologian what nature is to the man of science. It is his store-house of facts; and his method of ascertaining what the Bible teaches, is the same as that which the natural philosopher adopts to ascertain what nature teaches."[10] Hodge presented a tightly coherent system of conservative Reformed theology based on a verbally inspired, infallible Bible, which he treated as a collection of divinely revealed propositions (truth statements) just waiting to be organized by rational human beings led and illumined by the Holy Spirit.

Although he denied that the human authors of Scripture were mere "machines" who wrote mechanically under divine inspiration, Hodge insisted that inspiration and infallibility extend to the very words and not merely to the ideas of the Bible. He elevated the divine aspect of Scripture and denigrated the human when he wrote that "it is enough to impress any mind with awe, when it contemplates the Sacred Scriptures filled with the highest truths, speaking with authority in the name of God, and so miraculously free from the soiling touch of human fingers."[11] On the other hand, Hodge refused to take seriously objections to Scripture's supernatural, verbal inspiration and inerrancy based on a few discrepancies that cannot be cleared up. He implicitly admitted their existence, but claimed that "they furnish no rational ground for denying [Scripture's] infallibility" and "a Christian may be allowed to tread such objections under his feet."[12] Without any doubt, then, Hodge presented one of the highest and most absolute views of the sole authority of Scripture in the history of Christian theology. Against what he perceived to be liberal Protestant theology's diminution of that authority in favor of experience and reason, Hodge inflated the doctrine of Scripture to a role of prominence unparalleled before his time.

Hodge's concepts of theology and the doctrine of Scripture constitute him as a precursor of twentieth-century fundamentalism, as does his polemical reaction against liberal Protestant theology. Ritschl's contribution was yet to come, so Hodge's critique of liberal theology focused almost exclusively on Schleiermacher, whose thought he deplored as a pernicious and debilitating influence on Christianity. He accused Schleiermacher's theology of subjectivism that empties Christianity of its doctrinal content and reduces it to a mystical intuition. Against Schleiermacher Hodge declared,

> Christianity has always been regarded as a system of doctrine. Those who believe these doctrines are Christians; those who reject them, are, in the judgment of the Church, infidels or heretics. If our faith be formal or speculative, so is our Christianity; if it be spiritual and living, so is our religion. But no mistake can be greater than to divorce religion from truth, and make Christianity a spirit or a life distinct from the doctrines which the Scriptures present as the objects of faith.[13]

So harsh is Hodge's criticism of Schleiermacher and his theology that it amounts to condemnation. It drove him to treat Christianity primarily as assent to a system of supernaturally revealed truths virtually devoid of any ambiguity or need of correction.

Hodge's actual doctrinal system is an expression of classical Protestant orthodoxy and is presented in such a manner that any significant disagreement with it in part or whole is tantamount to heresy if not apostasy. In the doctrine of God, Hodge emphasized God's transcendent majesty and sovereignty. God is absolutely immutable and sovereignly controls all of nature and history. With regard to election, Hodge supported a strongly Calvinistic interpretation, although he opted for infralapsarianism over supralapsarianism. Arminianism is condemned as a concession to humanism and treated as a steppingstone to theological liberalism. Overall, Hodge's theology is a repristination of seventeenth- and eighteenth-century Protestant scholasticism. The Princeton professor is alleged to have remarked toward the end of his career that he was pleased to say that during his tenure no new ideas had been developed or taught there. The entire thrust of Hodge's and the other Princeton theologians' approach to theology was to secure and defend what they saw as the "truth once and for all delivered" in Protestant orthodoxy and to avoid theological innovation or experimentation.

Hodge's successor as professor of didactic and polemic theology at Princeton Seminary was Benjamin Breckinridge Warfield, a Princeton graduate and student of Hodge's. Warfield continued and extended his mentor's strong emphasis on divine inspiration and inerrancy of Scripture as the cornerstone doctrines of orthodox theology. During his tenure at Princeton (1887-1921), the Northern Presbyterian denomination experienced a sustained divisive controversy over the nature of Scripture and the newer methods of biblical scholarship known as "higher criticism." The latter attempted to investigate Scripture using purportedly objective literary and historical methods and often resulted in conclusions that questioned traditional views of authorship, date and composition of biblical books. There was no question where Warfield stood—firmly against higher criticism and any lessening of Princeton theology's high view of Scripture. In numerous articles and several books Hodge's successor reiterated and defended that doctrine and argued that anything less than full belief in the complete inerrancy of the original autographs of Scripture (the nonexistent original manuscripts) would result in a slippery slide of theology into liberalism and sheer relativism, for, Warfield argued, "we cannot modify the doctrine of plenary inspiration in any of its essential elements without undermining our confidence in the authority of the apostles as teachers of doctrine,"[14] and inerrancy is a necessary ramification of inspiration.

It comes as a surprise to many people that neither Hodge nor Warfield found Darwin's theory of evolution particularly threatening to Protestant orthodoxy. In fact, Warfield studied biology in his undergraduate education and always considered himself a believer in evolution. Of course, together with all other conservatives they opposed naturalistic evolution and considered evolution—if true—a means God used in creation.[15] In certain ways the theologians of the Princeton school did not anticipate fundamentalism. In other ways they not only anticipated it but laid the foundation for it. The major ways in which they foreshadowed it and paved the way toward it were their identification of Christianity with correct doctrine, their strong emphasis on revelation as objective, propositional truths delivered through supernatural inspiration in an inerrant Bible and their polemical responses to liberal Protestant theology and higher-critical methods of biblical scholarship. Unlike many of the self-avowed fundamentalists of a later generation, however, they were highly educated intellectuals with broad and deep acquaintance with culture and awareness of philosophy, languages and historical theology. They were also men of the church who saw themselves as standing in the Great Tradition of catholic-orthodox Christianity throughout the ages. Later fundamentalists would largely disavow much of that tradition in favor of a view of apostasy immediately after the apostolic era and rediscovery of the true gospel only in their own preaching and teaching.

### The Fundamentalist Movement

As a distinct movement of Protestant Christianity, fundamentalism began around 1910. Scholars debate endlessly the exact time and nature of its birth and even the origin of the label "fundamentalism." Nearly all agree, however, that the publication of a series of booklets called *The Fundamentals* beginning in 1910 was a crucial catalyst and a possible source of the movement's name. Inspired by the great revivals of evangelist Dwight Lyman Moody (1837-1899), dismayed and appalled by the growing influence of liberal theology, and energized by the resurgent Protestant orthodoxy of Warfield and others, two wealthy Christian businessmen sponsored the publication and free distribution of twelve collections of essays by leading conservative Protestant scholars. *The Fundamentals* were sent free of charge to thousands of pastors, denominational leaders, professors and even YMCA directors all over the United States. The first volume contained defenses of the virgin birth by Scottish theologian James Orr and of the deity of Christ by Warfield, as well as a critique of higher criticism of the Bible by a Canadian Anglican canon.[16]

*The Fundamentals* tapped into a reservoir of conservative Protestant anxiety and helped to galvanize a conservative response to liberal theology and the increasingly popular and influential social gospel. Throughout the following decade several groups of antiliberal Christians formulated lists of fundamentals of the faith. Often these lists of essential doctrines were conditioned by liberalism in that they placed at the heart of Christian belief doctrines perceived as threatened by that theology. Even more to the point, some of the lists included beliefs never before considered essential Christian doctrines by any significant group of Christians. An example is belief in the premillennial return of Christ. Along with biblical inerrancy; the Trinity; the virgin birth of Christ; the fall of humans into sin; Christ's substitutionary atonement, bodily resurrection and ascension; the belief that Christ would return visibly and bodily to rule and reign on earth for one thousand years before the final resurrection and judgment was elevated from an opinion held by some Christians to a "fundamental of the faith" by the World's Christian Fundamentals Association founded by leading fundamentalist minister W. B. Riley (1861-1947) in 1919. Even some other very conservative Protestants were shocked by this because Protestant orthodoxy generally and Princeton theology in particular never held to premillennialism. One may be forgiven for suspecting that Riley and certain other fundamentalists were simply elevating to essential status pet doctrines that they knew no one with even moderately liberal or progressive views could or ever would affirm. Already emerging from within fundamentalism as early as 1919, then, was a tendency within the movement toward sectarian divisiveness and the use of shibboleths (tricky tests) to determine whether Christians were perfectly sound and pure in doctrine.

The first group of any size or significance to label its members "fundamentalists" was the Fundamentalist Fellowship founded in 1920 by the editor of a leading conservative Baptist magazine known as the *Watchman-Examiner.* Curtis Lee Laws was at first more moderate than W. B. Riley and tried to maintain fundamentalism as a movement within the broader church for the preservation and defense of true fundamentals of the faith. Throughout the decades of the 1920s and 1930s, however, moderate fundamentalists and more militant fundamentalists grew closer together as they perceived their common enemy—liberal theology—growing in strength. In fact, liberal Protestant theology of the classical Ritschlian type was waning during these decades and being replaced by neo-orthodoxy and a chastened form of liberalism. Nevertheless, fundamentalists tended to see all but their own movement as "liberal," and even neo-orthodoxy was labeled a "new modernism" by some of them because most of its proponents rejected the inerrancy of the Bible.

During the heyday of early fundamentalism in the 1920s, the leading scholarly theologian embraced by the movement who embraced it in return was J. Gresham Machen (1881-1937). Machen studied under Warfield at Princeton Seminary and taught New Testament there from 1906 to 1929. After Warfield's death in 1921, the mantle of leadership of the Princeton school of theology fell upon Machen's shoulders, and he engaged in theological and ecclesiastical battles against what he perceived as the rising tide of liberal theology in his own Presbyterian denomination and in American mainstream Protestantism generally. Machen was a genuine scholar who studied New Testament and theology at German universities before beginning his career at Princeton. Even his liberal theological opponents could not fault his scholarship or dismiss him as a raving obscurantist, as many of them tended to do with other fundamentalists. Machen's book *Christianity and Liberalism* was published in 1923 and created a furor.[17] In it the Princeton theologian argued that liberal Protestant theology represented a different religion from Christianity and that its proponents ought to be honest enough to admit that. He asserted, "If a condition could be conceived in which all the preaching of the Church should be controlled by the liberalism which in many quarters has already become preponderant, then, we believe, Christianity would at last have perished from the earth and the gospel would have sounded forth for the last time."[18] But Machen went beyond merely *asserting* that polemical thesis to *arguing* for it with strong arguments based on his thorough knowledge of biblical studies—including modern higher-critical methods—and the history of Christian theology.

One reason that Machen's book created such a stir was that a leading secular commentator, Walter Lippmann, agreed with its basic argument and called upon liberal Protestants such as the influential New York minister Harry Emerson Fosdick (1878-1969) to respond to it. Fundamentalists looked upon Machen as a hero and regarded his book and its reception by Lippmann as a great triumph. Machen allowed the fundamentalists to embrace him as their scholarly spokesman even though he did not completely fit their mold. While an ardent defender of Protestant orthodoxy and biblical inerrancy, he was not sympathetic with 1920s fundamentalism's increasingly narrow antievolution and premillennial views. He agreed with Hodge and Warfield about evolution and completely rejected premillennialism in favor of a traditional Reformed amillennial view of the kingdom of God[19] at a time when many leading spokesmen for the movement were singling out Darwin and evolution as the great enemies of the true faith and including premillennialism as one of Christianity's fundamentals. Machen's prestige among fundamentalists increased as he gradually separated from the mainstream of Presbyterianism under tremendous pressure from its more liberal hierarchy. In 1929 he was forced out of his own denomination for "insubordination" at an infamous ecclesiastical trial where he was not allowed even to defend himself. After that he was considered a martyr even by fundamentalists who disagreed with his particular views on evolution and the end times.

A turning point for fundamentalism came in 1925 during the famous "Scopes monkey trial" in Dayton, Tennessee, which has been immortalized by the Broadway play *Inherit the Wind* and two movies based on it. One of the emerging leaders of fundamentalism was Nebraska politician and statesman William Jennings Bryan (1860-1925), a former candidate for president and President Wilson's secretary of state. After his political career ended, the folk hero of prairie populism became a leading spokesman for fundamentalism and tireless campaigner against "godless evolution." In 1925 the newly founded American Civil Liberties Union (ACLU) manipulated the arrest of a high-school biology teacher named John Scopes for allegedly teaching evolution against Tennessee state law. Scopes was not sure he had taught evolution, but he agreed that the state law was unconstitutional and the entire purpose of his arrest and trial was to test that in court. Fundamentalists by and large supported such laws and arranged for Bryan to be the visiting celebrity prosecutor of the case. The ACLU hired famous Chicago trial lawyer and agnostic Clarence Darrow to defend Scopes. The trial turned into a media circus as the first-ever live coast-to-coast broadcast on radio. Nationally famous antifundamentalist journalist H. L. Mencken reported the trial blow by blow in his newspaper columns. The trial's result was the conviction of Scopes but also the humiliation of fundamentalism. Bryan's answers to Darrow's questions on the witness stand were embarrassingly naive, and Darrow and Mencken together made Bryan and the forces of fundamentalism arrayed against evolution look like obscurantist fools bent on turning back the cultural clock to premodern and prescientific days. Five days after the trial, Bryan died in humiliation, and eventually the antievolution laws were struck down by higher courts.[20]

Before 1925 fundamentalism was a cultural and theological force to be reckoned with. It had a serious chance of turning back the tide of liberal theology and returning at least some of the mainstream Protestant denominations to Protestant orthodoxy. Many scholars, however, believe that by allowing antievolutionism to become its rallying point, and by adding relatively minor views such as premillennialism to its theological agenda, and by insisting on absolute inerrancy combined with a literalistic hermeneutic, fundamentalism doomed itself to theological obscurity. Be that as it may, there is no doubt that after 1925 and especially after Machen's departure from the Presbyterian Church and Princeton in 1929 to found a rival denomination and seminary, fundamentalism went into a lengthy period of retreat. Fundamentalist leaders bickered among themselves not only about strategy but also about minor doctrinal matters and fine points of lifestyle, church polity and degrees of separation. Emerging as major voices within the movement were men like John R. Rice, Bob Jones and Carl McIntire, who insisted on the practice of "biblical separation"—the refusal to fellowship or cooperate with other conservative Christians who fellowshiped or cooperated with nonfundamentalist Christians. During the 1940s and 1950s, when young evangelist Billy Graham was a rising star, these and other extreme fundamentalists—his own mentors—rejected him and his revivals because of Graham's friendly relations with nonfundamentalist Protestant ministers and Roman Catholics.[21]

Some scholars of twentieth-century American Christianity would argue that Rice, Jones, McIntire and other separatistic and hyperconservative fundamentalists represent a departure from true fundamentalism, which is best represented by Machen and the scholarly authors of the essays contained in *The Fundamentals,* most of whom were simply following traditional Protestant orthodoxy. The fact of the matter is that by the 1950s and 1960s the narrow, separatistic factions of conservative American Protestantism led by Rice, Jones and McIntire were almost the only ones calling themselves "fundamentalists." The more moderate defenders of Protestant orthodoxy and heirs of orthodox Pietism adopted the label "evangelical" to describe their movement. A definitive break within conservative theology took place in the early 1940s when Carl McIntire, a self-proclaimed "Bible Presbyterian" of New Jersey who accused other conservative Protestants of defecting from true fundamentalism, formed the American Council of Christian Churches (ACCC) as an umbrella organization for pure, separated fundamentalist churches and denominations. The following year, the rival National Association of Evangelicals (NAE) was founded by Boston conservative minister Harold John Ockenga and other evangelical Protestants who were fed up with the hairsplitting negativism and separationist mentality of the leading fundamentalists. The NAE went on to embrace a large segment of conservative American Protestant Christianity, from Pentecostals to Baptists to Christian Reformed, whereas the ACCC dropped into obscurity.

The basic beliefs of most evangelicals were the same as those of most leaders of early fundamentalism. McIntire and Ockenga, for example, did not quarrel over the essentials of Christian doctrine. The points of conflict between the two parties—which overlapped one another considerably—had to do with attitudes toward nonconservative Christians and Roman Catholics and toward culture, education, science and biblical interpretation. Whereas most self-identified fundamentalists came to reject any fellowship with Roman Catholics and even moderate nonconservatives, evangelicals became more and more willing to dialog and cooperate with them in sociopolitical and even evangelistic endeavors. Whereas leading fundamentalists insisted on the most literal interpretation of scriptural passages dealing with origins and end times (Genesis and Revelation), evangelicals allowed more latitude of interpretation. The statements of faith of the ACCC and the NAE reveal the differences. The ACCC's is much longer and more detailed. Little room is left for opinion or interpretation. All true Christians will think exactly alike on virtually every point of doctrine, lifestyle, sociopolitical thought and virtually everything else. The NAE's statement of faith is a basic affirmation of conservative Protestant doctrine that says little or nothing about specifics over which conservative Protestants have traditionally disagreed.[22]

### Common Features of Fundamentalism in Theology

As the preceding historical sketch of the fundamentalist movement indicates, pinning down its common features is bound to be a difficult enterprise. All depends on which phase of fundamentalism is under consideration and which fundamentalist leaders are being considered as paradigmatic for the entire movement. Here I will discuss the movement's common features in two phases, using 1925 as the watershed. I will also make a distinction between moderate and extreme fundamentalism. Before 1925 fundamentalism was virtually synonymous with a reassertion and defense of Protestant orthodoxy as interpreted by Princeton theology and people under its influence. Machen's *Christianity and Liberalism* and the essays in *The Fundamentals* best represent that relatively moderate first phase. After 1925 the movement has no single outstanding theologian and becomes increasingly focused on side issues of Protestant orthodoxy such as campaigns against evolution, communism and ecumenism, and for dispensationalism (a particular brand of premillennial eschatology) and separationism. In other words, in its second phase an extreme fundamentalism emerged and succeeded in capturing the movement and its label.

Early fundamentalism (pre-1925) was marked by belief that the ills of modern theology stem from defections from strong belief in supernatural, verbal inspiration and inerrancy of the Bible. Under the influence of Warfield and Machen, fundamentalists traced the disease of modernism right back to this single infection and blamed Schleiermacher for introducing it into Protestant theology. Conveniently ignored was the fact that in spite of strong affirmation of *sola scriptura,* many early Protestant Reformers as well as the Pietists did not teach anything like verbal inspiration or meticulous inerrancy of Scripture.[23] According to later fundamentalists, it took the rise of liberal Protestant theology to clarify the necessity of these doctrines, which were implicit and latent within classical Protestant theology all along. There was no need to highlight and emphasize these crucial doctrines until liberals openly challenged Scripture's authority. Once liberal theology became a force to be reckoned with, fundamentalists averred, verbal, plenary inspiration and meticulous inerrancy became necessary safeguards against a total loss of biblical authority.

This point brings out early fundamentalism's second major common theme: militant opposition to liberal, modernist Protestant theology in all its forms. *Militant* does not mean "terrorist" or "violent," of course. It only means "stringent, vocal and unrelenting" and also "without compromise." Machen expressed this attitude clearly when he wrote in *Christianity and Liberalism,*

> If we are to be truly Christians, then, it does make a vast difference what our teachings are, and it is by no means aside from the point to set forth the teachings of Christianity in contrast with the teachings of the chief modern rival of Christianity.

> The chief modern rival of Christianity is "liberalism." An examination of the teachings of liberalism in comparison with those of Christianity will show that at every point the two movements are in direct opposition. That examination will now be undertaken.[24]

The third and final common feature of early fundamentalism was the identification of authentic Christianity with a coherent system of doctrinal propositions called Protestant orthodoxy. Early fundamentalists did not deny that personal experience of repentance and conversion is important. But because of the threat they saw in liberal theology, they tended to emphasize assent to unrevisable doctrinal propositions as the essential and timeless core of Christianity. Whereas the motto of many pietists had become "If your heart is warm, give me your hand," fundamentalists would say, "If your beliefs are correct, give me your hand." They distrusted religious experience and affections because liberals could claim to have them, and there was no objective test for orthopathy. Orthodoxy, on the other hand, could be measured. Since no liberal theologian would affirm belief in the literal virgin birth, the substitutionary atonement, the literal second coming of Christ and so on, fundamentalists tended to focus on these as doctrinal tests of authentic Christianity. Those who were not sure these sufficed to root out liberalism first added premillennialism and then belief in a literal week of creation that occurred just a few thousand years before Christ. Other points of doctrine quite extraneous to classical Protestant orthodoxy were also added.

At least one common feature was added during fundamentalism's second phase (post-1925). In addition to belief in strict inerrancy of the Bible, antiliberal activism and strong affirmation of Protestant orthodoxy, many later fundamentalists insisted on biblical separationism. This is the belief that genuine Christians ought to have as little as possible to do with "false Christians" and their organizations (churches, ministries, societies). This separation even includes persons who call themselves "fundamentalist" or "evangelical" but engage in fellowship, dialogue or cooperation with doctrinally impure Christians, because "it is clear that the Bible commands separation from those who aid and encourage any kind of compromise with infidelity."[25] Fundamentalists such as McIntire, Rice and Jones debated the exact nature and extent of separation and came to somewhat differing conclusions, which led to mutual rejection. Some insisted on "secondary separation," by which they meant "a severance of relations even with other fundamentalists who were not militant enough in their own separation."[26]

**The Legacy of Fundamentalism**

Fundamentalism has been and is a powerful force in American Christianity in spite of repeated announcements of its demise. That is especially true if one characterizes fundamentalism as encompassing all Protestant Christians who seek to defend traditional tenets and viewpoints of Protestant orthodoxy against modernism in all its forms, and who insist that authentic biblical Christianity includes belief in the supernatural verbal inspiration and inerrancy of Scripture and a literalistic hermeneutic. If one narrows the definition to include only those who practice some form of "biblical separation" as well, then the movement's influence has weakened and declined over the decades since 1925. This is the distinction between moderate and extreme fundamentalism mentioned earlier. While the former seems to be gaining strength, the latter seems to be stagnant and even in retreat.

Without any doubt fundamentalism's main appeal has been at the level of grassroots Christianity. Literally thousands of pastors and congregations and hundreds of national ministries of various kinds are fundamentalist to some degree. Almost every city of any size has large, active fundamentalist congregations, flourishing fundamentalist bookstores and often relatively small but established fundamentalist Bible colleges or institutes. More often than not, in the last decades of the twentieth century these churches and institutions dropped the word *fundamentalist* from their names and from their advertising. Many of them began backing away from strict separationism and entered into conservative social political activism together with other conservative Protestants and occasionally with Roman Catholics, especially in prolife campaigns. Many such militantly conservative churches and institutions began preferring the label "conservative evangelical" during the 1980s—much to the chagrin of more irenic evangelicals who emerged from fundamentalism in the 1940s under the influence of moderates such as Ockenga.

In the 1990s only those conservative Protestants who still practice "biblical separation" from other Christians continued to identify themselves as fundamentalists. The true heirs of Machen, *The Fundamentals* and the early fundamentalist movement are numerous, influential and quickly becoming part of the mainstream of American Christianity. More often than not they call themselves conservative evangelicals. While they have virtually no influence in the hierarchies of the mainstream Protestant denominations,[27] they exercise tremendous influence on American social, political and religious life through their own institutions such as Liberty University founded by fundamentalist media evangelist Jerry Falwell and the Focus on the Family ministry of conservative-evangelical psychologist, author and radio speaker James Dobson. Very few professional theologians of standing and stature in Europe, Britain or North America call themselves fundamentalists, but the spirit of early fundamentalism lives on wherever theologians consider the true essence of Christianity to be a system of detailed and precise unrevisable doctrinal propositions (Protestant orthodoxy), see their primary mission as defending that true Christian faith against liberal theology and higher criticism, and teach that strict biblical inerrancy is the cornerstone doctrine of evangelical Christianity. In other words, fundamentalism lives on to some extent wherever theological "maximal conservatism" holds sway.

Fundamentalism is one major theological response to liberal Protestant theology. Another twentieth-century response has been variously called "dialectical theology," "neo-orthodoxy" or simply "Barthianism." Karl Barth of Switzerland and neo-orthodoxy's other main formulators and promoters rejected both liberal Protestantism and fundamentalism and attempted to return to pure Reformation theology within a modern context. Some observers and interpreters of twentieth-century Protestant thought say that it offers three main options, with considerable variety in each one: liberal theology, orthodox-fundamentalist theology and neo-orthodoxy.[28] We turn now to the story of the third option.

# CHAPTER 34

# Neo-Orthodoxy Transcends the Divide

L*ike every other theological movement discussed in recent chapters, neo-*orthodoxy is notoriously difficult to describe precisely. Not all of its adherents like the label. Many prefer simply "New Reformation Theology" or "dialectical theology." The movement's founder and prophet, Karl Barth, simply wished to recover a "theology of the Word of God." Nevertheless, as vague and imprecise as the category may be, this new form of Protestant theology clearly exists as a major force within modern theology and is conventionally known in North America, at least, as "neo-orthodoxy." Its movers and shapers were disillusioned with both traditional Protestant orthodoxy and liberal Protestant theology but strongly disagreed with fundamentalism about the Bible. Some of them referred to the Bible as fundamentalism's "paper pope" because of the typical fundamentalist doctrine of scriptural inerrancy. All of the neo-orthodox leaders embraced higher-critical methods of biblical study in some measure and rejected a literalistic hermeneutic. On the other hand, they believed that liberal Protestant theology had accommodated far too much to the modernist spirit of the age and thereby lost the gospel in its search for Christianity's true essence.

Neo-orthodox theologians such as Karl Barth and his Swiss colleague Emil Brunner and their American counterparts Reinhold and H. Richard Niebuhr, who are brothers, wished to recover the great Protestant themes of human depravity, grace above nature, salvation by faith alone and especially the transcendence and sovereignty of God. For them, God is "wholly other" and knowable only through his own Word, which is not identical with the words or even the propositions of Scripture. For neo-orthodox thinkers, "God's Word" is God's speech to humanity in the history of Jesus Christ. The Bible may *become* God's Word, but it is never merely identical with it. God's Word, like God himself, is above any object or even history as a whole. It is sovereignly unpredictable and comes to humans in time and space from beyond. Neo-orthodoxy rejects liberal theology's natural theology and rational or experiential approach to knowledge of God. God is known only through God's Word, and God's Word can often only be expressed in paradoxes. God's Word is transcendent—even to the Bible. The Bible is an *instrument* of God's Word. It *becomes* God's Word whenever God chooses to use it to bring humans into saving encounter with himself. But it is not a set of divinely revealed propositions.

The essence of neo-orthodoxy lies in its unique concept of divine revelation. Revelation proper is God's Word as God's special self-disclosure in events and above all in Jesus Christ. God reveals *himself,* not propositional statements. God reveals himself *specially,* not in vague, universal human experiences (Schleiermacher's *Gefühl)* or nature or universal history. For neo-orthodox Protestant theologians, God's revelation comes as an invasion into human history and experience and is never identical with the results of "man's search for God" or even the words and propositions of Scripture. "Man's search for God" through natural religion, world religions, spiritualities and philosophies is at best an indicator of human fallenness and need of transcendent revelation and grace. Holy Scripture, the Bible, is at best the unique instrument and channel of God's Word and at worst a magical talisman or "paper pope." For most people it is simply another great book of history and wisdom. It is not always God's Word. It becomes God's Word when God chooses to speak through it to demand decision for or against God as Lord.

Neo-orthodoxy's view of authority for Christian belief and practice is quite different from those of either liberal Protestantism or conservative Protestant orthodoxy. And it has come in for harsh criticism from both of those alternatives. Liberal theologians such as Harnack were horrified by neo-orthodoxy and accused it of being an irrational retreat from the modern age into supernaturalism and dogmatism. For the Liberals, the neo-orthodox emphasis on God's transcendence was "otherworldly," and their belief that humans are unable to know God apart from God's Word was obscurantist. One liberal theological wag described neo-orthodoxy as "fundamentalism with good manners" and "fundamentalism in a suit and a tie." In other words, liberal theologians suspected that Barth and his neo-orthodox colleagues were little more than fundamentalist theologians with degrees from major European universities. They also considered them traitors and turncoats because most of them had begun their careers within liberal theology.

Fundamentalists were as suspicious and hostile to neo-orthodoxy as were liberal theologians. Because the leading neo-orthodox theologians rejected the fundamentalist doctrine of Scripture and its literalistic hermeneutic, fundamentalists considered them even more dangerous than out-and-out liberals. A leading fundamentalist theologian labeled neo-orthodoxy "The New Modernism" in a 1946 book of that title.[1] Even into the later decades of the twentieth century many conservative evangelicals (moderate fundamentalists) were continuing the harsh attack on Barth and other neo-orthodox theologians.[2] In every case the conservative reaction focused on the neo-orthodox view of divine revelation and authority for Christian belief. Because it insisted on a real distinction between "God's Word" and the words of the Bible, neo-orthodoxy is accused of being a Trojan horse for liberalism.

In spite of harsh criticisms from the theological left and right, neo-orthodoxy managed to survive, flourish and even force transformations within the liberal and conservative Protestant theologies. It pushed liberalism to take sin and evil as well as God's transcendence more seriously. In a more effective manner than Machen, Barth and other neo-orthodox theologians exposed liberal Protestantism's drift toward modernistic humanism and away from anything recognizable as historic, classical Christianity. Barth's trenchant critique of liberal theology's cultural accommodation had its effect, and liberal theology went on the defensive first in European and then in American theological circles. Many liberal theologians converted to neo-orthodoxy or at least seriously modified their liberalism under its pressure. Similarly, large numbers of conservative Protestant theologians have found neo-orthodoxy a refuge and haven from what they came to see as fundamentalism's extreme propositionalism, biblical literalism and obscurantist wholesale rejection of modernity. Even those conservative proponents of Protestant orthodoxy who did not jump onto the neo-orthodox bandwagon were challenged by it and often modified their scholasticism and biblicism in its light.

### The Precursor of Neo-Orthodoxy: Søren Kierkegaard

Liberal Protestant theology borrowed heavily from Enlightenment philosophy and especially Kant's critical idealism and moral objectivism. It was foreshadowed by Locke's rationalism and Deism's natural religion and influenced heavily by Hegel's religious philosophy of Absolute Spirit. Fundamentalist and conservative evangelical theology stood on the foundation laid by the Princeton theologians Hodge and Warfield and looked to Thomas Reid's commonsense realism as their common philosophical framework. Neo-orthodoxy attempted to rediscover a pure theology of the Word of God free of any dominating philosophical influence. In the early episodes of the story of Christian theology the same struggle over philosophy's role in theology divided great church fathers like Clement of Alexandria and Tertullian of Carthage. Then as now it seems philosophy cannot be avoided altogether in theological reflection. Neo-orthodoxy was profoundly influenced from the very beginning by an eccentric and little-known Danish philosopher and cultural critic who also played the role of amateur theologian. His name was Søren Kierkegaard.

Kierkegaard has come to be known as "the melancholy Dane" because of his dark, brooding, pessimistic and sometimes cynical writings. Few thinkers, however, have had as great an impact on an entire culture. Kierkegaard lived a reclusive and lonely life in his home city of Copenhagen, Denmark, from 1813 to 1855. His father was a melancholy Pietist Lutheran who expressed fear to his young son that he may have brought a curse on the entire family by some sin of his youth. Perhaps because of an internalized fear of his father's alleged curse, young Kierkegaard broke off his engagement to Regine Olson without explanation and never married. He had few friends and seemed at times to go out of his way to offend and alienate people. Kierkegaard became a well-known writer in Denmark during his own lifetime, but his influence outside of his homeland was minimal until long after his death. Eventually books such as *Fear and Trembling, Philosophical Fragments, Concluding Unscientific Postscript to Philosophical Fragments* and *Either-Or* were translated into German and English, and the general view of life expressed in them came to be labeled "existentialism." After World War I existentialism became a popular philosophy in Europe, and from there made its way to America. Although Kierkegaard was himself a devout Christian and regarded his philosophy as consistent with authentic Christianity, later existentialists developed secular and even atheistic forms of that philosophy.

Kierkegaard perceived himself as a prophet to cultural Christianity, which he considered not authentically Christian at all. In his view the state church of Denmark (Lutheran) had capitulated entirely to the *Zeitgeist* of modernity. An underlying theme running throughout the Danish philosopher's religious writings is opposition to the prevailing belief in smooth continuity between the divine and the human. This religion of continuity was based largely on Hegel's philosophy of religion but was also influenced by Enlightenment rationalism (natural religion) and Romanticism. Hegel's philosophy of religion stressed the immanence of God in human cultural history such that God—an impersonal Absolute Spirit—comes to self-realization or self-actualization in and through humanity's development toward a utopian civilization. According to Hegel and his many theological followers in the early nineteenth century, Christendom and the Prussian state together formed the pinnacle of the march of Absolute Spirit (God) through history. The "end of history" was supposed to have arrived in them, and eventually all human culture and civilization would see the beauty and perfection of that synthesis of all truth and value and emulate it. God would then be "all in all," and the kingdom of God would have arrived. For Hegel and his followers, the path to this cultural perfection was one of reason overcoming conflicts. Truth itself was considered a process of increasing coherence ending in a perfect system of rational ideas concretely embodied in a benevolent state and rational church working hand in hand for the common good.

Hegel's religious and cultural philosophy had a profound impact in Denmark through the Lutheran bishop H. L. Martensen. Kierkegaard was appalled at what he considered a complete subversion of authentic biblical-prophetic Christianity to cultural Christendom. In one of his last writings, *Attack upon Christendom* (1855), the melancholy Dane wrote sarcastically about the great bishop and the state church: "In the magnificent cathedral the Honorable and Right Reverend *Geheime-General-Ober-Hof-Prädikant,* the elect favorite of the fashionable world, appears before an elect company and preaches *with emotion* upon the text he himself elected: 'God hath elected the base things of the world, and the things that are despised.' And nobody laughs."[3] According to Kierkegaard, true Christianity was supposed to be (and always is) a great risk taken by a few "knights of faith" and was never respectable to the cultural elite. In *Attack upon Christendom* he argued that in a society where everyone is a "Christian," true Christianity no longer exists. In fact, he went so far as to accuse the cultural elite (Hegel and his religious followers) of engaging in a conspiracy to destroy authentic Christianity. They realized it would be impractical to wipe it out, so they conspired to destroy it by embracing it within their own false Christianity called "Christendom."

Decades later, Barth and the other neo-orthodox Protestants of Europe discovered Kierkegaard's attack upon cultural Christianity and the Hegelian theology of continuity between God and humanity, kingdom of God and culture, and used it within their own prophetic reform of Protestant theology. The true kingdom of God, they all asserted, is eschatological and not historical-cultural. It is not a human possibility (contrary to liberal theology and especially the Social Gospel) but a divine ideal set in judgment over against all human achievements. As one leading neo-orthodox theologian declared of the kingdom of God, it is "always coming but never arriving" within history by human effort. Kierkegaard's critique of Hegelian immanentism (God as immanent within the historical evolution of culture) and the cultural Christianity built on it foreshadowed and paved the way for neo-orthodoxy's emphasis on God's transcendence and the purely eschatological nature of God's kingdom.

Hegel sought to develop a perfectly coherent and objective world philosophy through reason alone. For him, the "real" (being) was the rational and the rational was the real. The human mind and reality are connected in such a way that at its very best human intellect can grasp and fully understand whatever is true and real. Hegel's philosophy left little room for special, supernatural revelation or personal faith. Christianity is the "absolute religion" simply because it represents in images what rational, objective philosophy knows apart from them. Philosophy is a perfect system of abstract ideas about reality. One of these ideas is the unity of the divine and human. Christianity represents this abstract truth concretely by means of the image of the incarnation. Hegel believed that truth is the synthesis of seemingly opposite ideas—"thesis" and "antithesis." Even in religion, paradoxes—seemingly opposite but necessary truths—are capable of being relieved rationally. The ultimate idea of reason is the unity of the infinite and the finite—of God and creation—and rational philosophy expresses this idea abstractly while Christianity expresses it concretely as an image and a doctrine: Jesus Christ as the God-man.

Kierkegaard was appalled and disgusted with Hegel's abstract, speculative and objective philosophy. He believed that it was a substitute for true Christianity and, if it should prevail, Christianity would no longer exist. For him, Christianity is not a philosophy and existence is not open to complete rational understanding. Truth—especially about God and God's relationship with the world—is not rational, objective correspondence between thought and reality. Because of the "infinite qualitative difference" between God and humans, and because humans are fallen as well as finite, truth itself in its depths must be embraced in passionate inwardness through decision—a "leap of faith"—which cannot be reduced to a logical syllogism or system of ideas rationally accepted. In other words, knowing God truly necessarily involves faith, and faith necessarily involves risk.[4]

Knowing God is a matter of ultimate concern—unlike knowing the names of the planets in the solar system—and in matters of ultimate concern truth cannot be found by remaining in the position of an observer. Because God is personal, holy and transcendent, and because humans are finite, dependent and sinful, God can be known only as one leaves the objective position of observer and becomes a participant in a relationship with God through passionate inwardness. That is the "leap of faith"—the risk—that alone can bring one into true knowledge of and relationship with God. Apart from that leap of faith, a person can have an ethical religion but not true Christianity.

Neo-orthodoxy found an ally in Kierkegaard when Barth and his cohorts set out to present an alternative to both liberal theology and Protestant orthodoxy. Both had swamped faith in a morass of rational and moralistic ideas. The neo-orthodox thinkers sought to reassert the necessity of faith for authentic Christianity. Barth was opposed to the identification of Christianity with a coherent system of doctrines, whether based on reason or revelation or some combination of both. For him, Christianity—as opposed to religion—is a relationship between the holy God who speaks from beyond the world and the finite, sinful human who bows before mysteries that reason cannot anticipate, let alone understand. Kierkegaard's assertion of "truth as subjectivity" provided a philosophical foundation for neo-orthodoxy's rediscovery of a theology of God's Word that places faith in the supreme position and reason as a mere tool or instrument. Barth and other neo-orthodox theologians also wished to affirm the paradoxical nature of the basic truths of God's Word. For them, as opposed to most liberal and conservative theologians, Christian belief cannot be a synthesis of opposites. Even the logical law of noncontradiction (*A* is not not-*A*) cannot be ultimate within Christian theology because God's thoughts are beyond human thoughts and God's ways transcend human ways. Here as elsewhere Kierkegaard anticipated neo-orthodoxy and the dialectical theologians looked back to him as an ally.

Kierkegaard defined *truth* (especially about God and human existence) as "an objective uncertainty held fast in an appropriation-process of the most passionate inwardness."[5] That is simply a longer version of "truth is subjectivity." What kind of ideas emerge from this process resulting in objective uncertainty? Paradoxes. "When subjectivity, inwardness, is the truth, the truth objectively defined becomes a paradox."[6] The incarnation, for example, is for Kierkegaard an "absolute paradox" that can only be revealed and grasped by faith. Hegel's attempt to include it as a logical idea within a universal, coherent, rational system of all truth violates it, tames it and turns it into something it is not—a symbolic representation of an abstract philosophical concept. For Kierkegaard, the truth that Jesus Christ was both truly God and truly human and yet one person is a logical contradiction and not a symbol of Hegel's metaphysical unity of divine and human being; nor is it a mere doctrine. It is a transforming truth of divine revelation that demands decision for or against Jesus Christ as Lord.

In these and many other ways Kierkegaard adumbrated neo-orthodoxy. His was an antiphilosophical philosophy, and the neo-orthodox theologians were seeking to free theology from captivity to philosophies of all kinds. Only Kierkegaard's existential philosophy could be theology's ally and conversation partner. That is not to say that Barth or any other neo-orthodox thinker followed Kierkegaard slavishly. Far from it. Kierkegaard's Christian philosophy was far too individualistic for Barth, the author of *Church Dogmatics.* Nevertheless, without Kierkegaard's philosophy, which was being rediscovered by European thinkers after World War I, neo-orthodoxy may not have been as powerful a force as it became by standing on his shoulders and shouting out to church and culture that Christianity is neither a religion among the religions nor the pinnacle of human religious feelings or a system of morals or doctrines. Instead, Christianity offers a gospel that transcends all human religion, culture and systems of thought. In 1922 Barth paid tribute to Kierkegaard's influence on his own theology in his preface to the second edition of his groundbreaking commentary on Romans, *Der Romerbrief (The Epistle to the Romans):*

> If I have a system, it is limited to a recognition of what Kierkegaard called the "infinite qualitative distinction" between time and eternity, and to my regarding this as possessing a negative as well as a positive significance: "God is in heaven, and thou art on earth." The relation between such a God and such a man, and the relation between such a man and such a God, is for me the theme of the Bible and the essence of philosophy.[7]

**The Founder of Neo-Orthodoxy: Karl Barth**

When historians of Christian theology look back on the twentieth century and scan it for one great representative thinker, there is no doubt who that will be: the Swiss Protestant church father and reformer Karl Barth. Barth almost single-handedly turned the tide of European Protestant theology. In that he is comparable to Luther. Protestant theology in Europe and North America was quickly devolving into the thinly veiled humanism of classical liberal theology. Fundamentalism was quickly disintegrating into a squabbling camp of sectarian ultraconservatives more concerned about fighting evolution and enforcing premillennialism than creatively and critically engaging the culture. Barth emerged out of a childhood in Protestant orthodoxy and an education in liberal theology and created a new form of Protestant theology for the new century. His idea was to rediscover the gospel apart from all human systems—whether liberal or orthodox—and make it the basis of a Christian theology that transcends the divide between liberalism and conservatism, which he saw as equally captivated by modernity. Liberal theology was captive to modernity by accommodation to it. It had enthroned modern categories of thought as supreme and allowed divine revelation to be judged by it. Conservative theology, especially fundamentalism, was captive to modernity by reacting to it. It had become so obsessed with rejecting everything "modern" and "liberal" that it became imprisoned by them. Barth wished to relativize modernity, not reject it. To him modernity was, like every culture, a passing fad that would eventually fade away while the Word of God (Jesus Christ, the gospel message) stands forever.

Karl Barth was born in 1886 in Basel, Switzerland. His father was a professor of theology at a Reformed seminary who moved to the University of Berne when Karl was a small child. The young Barth grew up in that capital city of Switzerland and resolved to become a theologian at the time of his confirmation—he was only sixteen years old. He studied theology under some of the leading liberal Protestant thinkers of Europe, including Adolf Harnack, and became a minister of the Reformed church, first in Geneva and then in the small town of Safenwil on Switzerland's border with Germany. According to his later memoirs, Barth found that the liberal theology of his education did not translate into meaningful preaching that connected with the lives of the average people of the parish. He became disillusioned with liberal Protestantism when his own theological mentors such as Harnack and other German professors publicly supported the Kaiser's war policy in 1914. The young pastor delved into that perennial source of theological renewal—the apostle Paul's epistle to the Romans—and published *Der Romerbrief* in 1919. In that theological commentary Barth set forth the basic precepts for the neo-orthodox program of dialectical theology, or the "theology of the Word of God." The basic thesis is expressed in a separately published essay titled "The Strange New World Within the Bible": "It is not the right human thoughts about God which form the content of the Bible, but the right divine thoughts about men."[8]

Barth was invited to teach theology in Germany after World War I. First he taught at Göttingen, where Ritschl's influence was still dominant. Then he moved to the University of Münster and then the University of Bonn. While teaching at Bonn, he began his great life's project of writing a complete system of theology based on God's Word with the title *Church Dogmatics*. When he died in 1968, it was unfinished at thirteen massive volumes. Barth intended to write a systematic theology completely free of any overpowering philosophical influences and based purely on exegesis of God's Word in Jesus Christ as witnessed to in Scripture. Unlike most other systems of theology—whether liberal or conservative, Protestant or Catholic—*Church Dogmatics* has no prologomena, or foundational section on natural theology or rational evidences for belief in God and Holy Scripture. Instead, Barth launched directly into an exposition of the Word of God in Jesus Christ, the church and Scripture—that is, of special revelation. His basic axiom is "the possibility of knowledge of God lies in God's Word and nowhere else."[9] Since Barth considered Jesus Christ to be God's Word in person and therefore identical with God's Word, he asserted that "the eternal God is to be known in Jesus Christ and not elsewhere."[10] Barth eschewed natural theology, philosophical defenses of divine revelation, rational apologetics and any other possible foundation for Christian knowledge of God outside of the self-authenticating gospel of Jesus Christ itself.

While teaching at Bonn, Barth began aiding the anti-Nazi church in Germany, and he refused to pledge loyalty to Hitler and the Nazi party. He was expelled from Germany by the National Socialist government and took a position as professor of theology at the University of Basel. He remained there until his retirement and death. From Switzerland, Barth supported the Christian opposition to Hitler. One of his former German students, Dietrich Bonhoeffer (1906-1945), became a leading Protestant theologian in Berlin and eventually participated in the underground plot to kill Hitler. For that Bonhoffer was arrested, imprisoned and hanged. Barth was convinced that Nazism was a quasi-religion that represented the ultimate outcome of natural religion and natural theology.

Throughout his career Barth tirelessly waged theological war against any and every theological attempt to ground Christian belief in something other than God's Word, because to do so is to make something other than Jesus Christ lord and master. Hundreds of students came to Basel to study with Barth, and during the 1940s and 1950s he became the dominating force in Protestant theology throughout the world. Liberals and conservatives had to reckon with Barth, who knew exactly how to expose their theologies as culturally conditioned.

Barth was something of an enigma in modern theology, and he remains so today. To liberals he was the bane of their existence—an archconservative with world-class intellectual credentials. To conservatives and especially fundamentalists, he was a wolf in sheep's clothing—a liberal masquerading as a Bible-believing, Jesus-loving Christian. Neither side could make much sense of him, and in their writings they often distorted his theology out of recognition. One story from near the end of Barth's career reveals much about his personal Christian life. In the early 1960s he made his only trip to the United States and stopped at the University of Chicago's Rockefeller Chapel, an enormous Gothic cathedral, for a panel conversation with several American theologians. During the question-and-answer time after the panel discussion, a young student stood and asked a question that drew a gasp from the audience: "Professor Barth, could you please summarize your entire life's work in a few words?" Barth is said to have paused only momentarily and then replied, "Yes. In the words of a song my mother taught me when I was a child: 'Jesus loves me, this I know, for the Bible tells me so.' "

Barth's theology is impossible to summarize in a few paragraphs. Here we will focus attention on a few of his major themes and compare and contrast them with liberal theology and conservative, fundamentalist theology. Barth self-consciously rejected any attempt to bridge those two twentieth-century approaches. Instead, he saw the possibility of transcending both of them and their conflict through pure reflection on the Word of God. First, then, we will discuss Barth's concept of divine revelation as God himself in his Word. Then we will continue to explore his ideas about God as he who loves in freedom, and salvation as God's gracious "Yes!" to humanity in Jesus Christ. While not every neo-orthodox theologian would agree with Barth's entire program in Protestant theology, his is the best example of neo-orthodoxy, and the entire movement stems from it. Other neo-orthodox theologians, such as Barth's fellow Swiss professor Emil Brunner and American Reinhold Niebuhr, offered their own amendments and contributions, but none achieved the stature or influence of Barth.

One of the most hotly contested concepts in modern Christian theology is divine revelation. Where does God reveal himself? How does God reveal himself? Liberal theologians tended to emphasize a general revelation of God in human religious experience or in universal history, and they treated special revelation as the highest representation of what can be known about God generally. The effect was to diminish the Christian gospel's distinctiveness and turn it more or less into a philosophy of religion or a moral and ethical agenda. Conservative and especially fundamentalist theologians tended to identify revelation with the propositional content of the Bible. They acknowledged the reality of the general revelation of God in nature, but they looked to special revelation in Scripture for Christian knowledge of God. The effect was to overintellectualize the gospel as a doctrinal system to be learned and believed.

Karl Barth rejected both approaches to understanding divine revelation and began his entire mature theology with the basic principle that divine revelation is God communicating himself to humanity in his speech. *Deus dixit*—God speaks. God speaks himself. God's Word *is* God himself communicating not something—like information or an experience—but himself. In its most proper sense, then, divine revelation is the event of God's self-communication, and that can only be in Jesus Christ and the prehistory and posthistory of his incarnation.

For Barth, then, Jesus Christ is God's Word. The gospel is Jesus Christ. Jesus Christ is God's revelation. When Barth identified divine revelation with Jesus Christ, he was not referring to Jesus' teachings or example. He was referring to the person of Jesus Christ in time and eternity. To know Jesus Christ (with or without knowing his human name) is to know God, and one cannot know God without knowing Jesus Christ (with or without knowing his human name). Barth did not say that it is impossible to know God without knowing about the Jewish Messiah, who was born in Palestine and died there in about A.D. 30. He was and is the Lord, but his human life on earth does not exhaust his divine-human reality. Barth's view of divine revelation is that Jesus Christ, the Son of God, is God's perfect and complete self-expression, and whatever other authentic revelations of God there may be center around him as promise, hope and memory.

Barth's view of revelation is intensely particularistic and actualistic. It revels in the "scandal of particularity" that Enlightenment thinkers and liberal theologians tried to avoid. Barth went almost to an opposite extreme. Revelation proper is not some universal, generic principle waiting to be discovered through mental or mystical endeavors. It is Jesus Christ, and Christ is not merely a historical figure—an example, a representation, a prophet. He is a specific person who has always existed as the Father's Son and self-expression.[11]

For Barth, the Bible was not God's Word in the same sense that Jesus Christ is. Jesus Christ is God's Word because he is God himself in action and communication. He shares in God's very being. The Bible is one form of God's Word, and a secondary form at that. It is the God-ordained witness to God's Word in the person of Jesus Christ, and it *becomes* God's Word whenever God chooses to use it to encounter and confront people with the gospel of Jesus Christ: "The Bible is God's Word to the extent that God causes it to be His Word, to the extent that He speaks through it."[12]

Barth opposed the orthodox Protestant view of the Bible found in Turretin and Hodge and others who insisted on the Bible as primary revelation in propositional form. He rejected propositional revelation—the idea that when God wishes to communicate to humans, he communicates information in truth statements. He especially rejected the idea of biblical inerrancy. The Bible for Barth was human through and through. It is a book of human testimony to Jesus Christ, and in spite of all its humanness it is unique because God uses it. According to Barth, the statements of the Bible can be wrong at any point. That does not matter. God has always used fallible and even sinful witnesses, and the Bible is just such a witness. In spite of strong rejection of the orthodox Protestant doctrine of verbal inspiration and especially of inerrancy, Barth held the Bible in high esteem. His denials were not meant to demean the Bible but only to elevate Jesus Christ above it. Jesus is Lord! Scripture is not. It is a witness to the Lord.

It is important to recognize a distinction between Barth's doctrine of Scripture and his treatment of it. In the doctrine the Bible is treated as merely a witness to Jesus Christ and a fallible one at that. At best it is a form of divine revelation—not identical with revelation itself. But when he turned to explicating other doctrines,

Barth treated the Bible *as if* it were verbally inspired and at least infallible in terms of its teaching about God and salvation. In his *Church Dogmatics* the Bible is the source, while Jesus Christ is the norm, but without the Bible we would know nothing about Jesus Christ or the history of God's activity before him and after him. The Bible is the narrative of the history of God's self-revelation in Jesus, and as that it cannot be dispensed with. No human philosophy can be placed above it. And yet, unlike fundamentalists, Barth was completely disinterested in debating the fine points of apparent discrepancies within Scripture or its literalness and absolute accuracy in historical detail. All of that attention to the minutiae of Scripture detracts from the lordship of Jesus Christ, which is the heart of Scripture. So while on the one hand Barth disagreed with the orthodox Protestant doctrine of Scripture, on the other hand he agreed with the Protestant principle of *sola scriptura* because Scripture is the only source of knowledge of Jesus Christ, and it is the only book God uses as an instrument of his Word to encounter human beings and call them to decision about Jesus' lordship.

Barth recognized a third form of divine revelation: the proclamation of the church. The church's proclamation is tertiary—third in priority after Jesus Christ and Scripture. But it can be a means of divine revelation. In and through the preaching and teaching of the church, God sometimes speaks and draws people into encounter with himself. That is not to say that every sermon or service of worship or catechism class is an event of God's Word. It may or may not be. That is Barth's "actualism"—the idea that God reveals himself in acts of self-disclosure. God's Word—divine revelation—is never an object to be possessed. It cannot be manipulated or owned. It happens. It has happened in Jesus Christ. It happens through Scripture. It may happen in the church's proclamation and teaching. Jesus Christ is Lord of Scripture and the church. Scripture is the authority in the church because it is the primary witness to Jesus Christ. The church is the context for divine-human encounter in which Scripture is expounded and Jesus proclaimed. All of this is divine revelation. But it all centers upon Jesus Christ.

Barth had no use whatever for natural theology and even discounted general revelation in nature, history and human experience (e.g., conscience or spirituality). His concept of divine revelation is radically particularistic and in that differs fundamentally from liberal Protestant theology. He was not interested in looking for universal points of contact for the Christian message in human experience, and he rejected apologetics and proofs of the existence of God. For him, the gospel was its own proof. "The possibility of God's Word lies in God's Word and nowhere else."[13] The best apologetic is proclamation. On the other hand, he was not the least interested in the orthodox Protestant or fundamentalist identification of divine revelation with the Bible. The Bible *is*. Revelation *happens*. Jesus is *Lord*. The Bible is the primary witness to his lordship. Its inspiration lies in God's use of it as a special instrument and witness.

In his doctrine of God, Barth attempted to balance God's transcendence and immanence by defining God as "He who loves in freedom."[14] Of course Barth rejected any attempt to actually "define" God in the literal sense of pinning down God's essence. God is mystery and beyond finite comprehension. On the other hand, Barth equally rejected any attempt to deny valid knowledge of God. If revelation means anything, it must mean that God has actually shown himself as he truly is. God's revelation and God's being cannot be separated. In this the twentieth-century Swiss theologian disagreed with Luther. Barth left no room in his theology for some "hidden God" behind Jesus Christ, as if God might actually be other than he appears to be in his own Word. If God reveals himself as loving, gracious and merciful in Jesus Christ, then God actually *is* loving, gracious and merciful. He cannot be cruel, hateful and evil. God's Word is God himself, but that does not mean the human mind can circumscribe God and exhaust the mystery of his being in thought. Barth's doctrine of God is dialectical. Like Kierkegaard before him, Barth believed that if God is God, finite thought cannot "think God's thoughts after him" (a popular definition of *theology* in rationalism) but must think about God and speak about God in paradoxical ways.

For Barth, the ultimate paradox in the Christian doctrine of God is that God is both absolutely loving and absolutely free within both his own eternal trinitarian being and in his relationship with creation. God reveals himself as "he who loves freely" in time and eternity. That does not mean that humans can fully understand the depths and riches of either God's love or God's freedom, but it does mean that we have been given insight into them in Jesus Christ. Barth described God's attributes under the rubric of freedom and love. Reflection on God's revelation leads to a delineation of certain attributes or characteristics—"perfections"—of God's freedom such as eternity (lordship over time) and immutability (faithfulness to himself). The perfections of God's freedom show him to be Lord over all. Nothing outside of God conditions God. God is absolutely free in all his relationships *ad extra* (toward creation). Equally important and true in God's revelation, however, is that God's absolute freedom does not mean that he cannot bind himself to creatures in love. God's very essence is love within the community of three *Seinsweisen* (modes of being)—Father, Son and Holy Spirit. This love overflows freely in creation and redemption so that humans are taken up into it through Jesus Christ. The perfections of God's love include mercy and grace.

The paradox of God lies for Barth in the truth drawn directly from divine revelation that God actualizes himself in his relation with the world (à la Hegel) and also is absolutely free in that self-actualizing relationship. "God is not swallowed up in the relation and attitude of Himself to the world and us as actualized in His revelation,"[15] and yet his relationship with the world is not something merely contingent and exterior to his own being. God's being is being-in-act, not a static essence aloof from God's dynamic relationship with the world. God's love for the world means that he is truly involved and that the world affects God. Barth broke radically from classical Christian theism insofar as he saw it infected by static Greek categories of being. And yet, on the basis of divine revelation, Barth insisted that even in his loving, suffering, thoroughly involved relationship with the world, God remains ever the Lord of that relationship.

Thus in the final analysis Barth said that God is fully actualized in his own trinitarian being from all eternity. The world adds nothing essential to him, otherwise, "if we are not careful at this point we inevitably rob God of His deity."[16] On the other hand, God freely chooses from all eternity to have this relationship with the world in which he actualizes his already fully self-actualized being in and through the covenant he makes with humanity in Jesus Christ. God's love for the world is eternal but not necessary.[17]

Liberal theology had leaned more and more in the direction of immanentism under the influence of Hegel and post-Hegelian philosophy. Many liberal theologians neglected God's transcendence and freedom and emphasized God's loving relationship with the world in a way that implied God is a prisoner in that relationship. Hegel declared, "Without the world God is not God." Barth's response is "God could be God without the world but chooses not to be such a God." Protestant orthodoxy had emphasized God's transcendence and sovereignty so strongly that God's relationship with the world appeared something merely external to God. For classical Christian theism—and Protestant orthodoxy tended to harden those categories—the world adds absolutely nothing to God. God is *actus purus*—pure actuality. Nothing in God is potential. God's perfection is static. Barth's response is "God chooses not to be perfect without the world." In Jesus Christ, God opens his own life up to a genuine relationship with the world such that it affects him internally and not merely in some external way. Barth's doctrine of God may be paradoxical, but Barth's defense would be that such paradoxes are part of the mystery of God reflected on. He saw both liberal and conservative Protestant theologies as forms of rationalism in that they sought perfect coherence. For Barth, if God is God, then finite thought cannot arrive at a perfectly coherent synthesis of truth about God. It must simply follow divine revelation wherever it leads and be satisfied if it leads into deadends of thought where seemingly opposed truths must be equally embraced.

A third important contribution of Barth's theology lies in the doctrine of salvation. Liberal theology was almost universally universalistic. That is, from Schleiermacher on, almost all liberal Protestant theologians affirmed an ultimate reconciliation of God with all creatures. The tendency was to reject God's wrath as a primitive notion that Jesus came to dispel by showing God's fatherhood, which was interpreted sentimentally by most liberals. Hell, damnation, and eternal punishment were relegated to the stockpile of outmoded relics of medieval theology. Even those liberal theologians who stood in the Reformed tradition rejected double predestination and the entire doctrine of election in favor of a sentimental idea of God's universal fatherhood of all creatures. Fundamentalism tended to go to an opposite extreme, at least in its preaching. Hell was portrayed in vivid and starkly realistic terms and the "eternal suffering of the wicked" in literal flames became an item of absolute dogma for many conservative Protestant ministers and theologians. The notes of grace, mercy and hope were muted, and universalism was vilified as one of the worst heresies of all.

Barth wanted to transcend this polarization within the Christian doctrine of salvation. On the basis of divine revelation he affirmed the reality of God's judgment and wrath. On the basis of divine revelation he also affirmed the greater reality of God's grace and mercy. As a Reformed theologian in the tradition of Calvin and Zwingli, he affirmed the sovereignty of God in election and rejected synergism. In fact, Barth was a supralapsarian! He believed that God's decree to elect and reject precedes his decrees to create and allow the fall into sin.[18] God's entire purpose in creation is salvation, and election is an intrinsic part of salvation by grace alone. But Barth called his doctrine of salvation and election "purified supralapsarianism," by which he meant that God's entire purpose in election is love, and although he allows evil from the very beginning, he negates it through Jesus Christ. God does not will and foreordain a portion of his creation to be eternally lost for some abstract self-glorification. Rather, God wills, foreordains and decrees to allow sin and evil and their total negation in Jesus Christ and his cross and resurrection.

God's "no" is not spoken against humanity—not even a portion of humanity—but only against himself in Jesus Christ. God does speak a "no" and a "yes" in double predestination. But for Barth "double predestination" does not refer to a dual determination of humans but to Jesus Christ, who is the one "elect *and* reprobate man." "In the election of Jesus Christ which is the eternal will of God, God has ascribed to man . . . election, salvation and life; and to Himself He has ascribed . . . reprobation, perdition and death."[19] For Barth, "predestination means that from all eternity God has determined upon man's acquittal at His own cost."[20] That cost is "the way of the Son of God into a far country" and his death on the cross at sinners' hands.

Does Barth's doctrine of salvation imply universalism? Is it a twentieth-century form of Origen's *apokatastasis* (ultimate reconciliation)? It would seem so. Yet Barth refused to affirm that, and the best interpreters of Barth's theology disagree about it. When asked whether he taught universalism, Barth responded, "Neither do I teach it nor do I not teach it." The inner logic of his doctrine of election, however, would seem to imply universal salvation. Barth wrote that "on the basis of this decree of His [God's decree of election] the only truly rejected man is His own Son"[21] and "by permitting the life of a rejected man to be the life of His own Son, God has made such a life objectively impossible for all others."[22] However, Barth was a dialectical theologian and therefore cannot be pinned down to a fully rational position. In the final analysis he left open the possibility that the final "count" of the elect may not correspond entirely with the world of all humans who ever live while at the same time forbidding any limitation of final salvation to less than that number. God's freedom and love require that the possibilities be left open.

Barth's neo-orthodox vision of Christian theology reveals a certain irony. The Swiss theologian rejected Hegel's rationalistic philosophy of religion as a prison of ideas about God and the world that attempts to domesticate God and rob him of his deity. On the other hand, his own theology represents a kind of Hegelian synthesis—an *Aufhebung* (transcending two opposites in a higher unity)—of liberal theology's thesis and fundamentalism's antithesis. Barth rejected both liberal theology and Protestant orthodoxy as one-sided extremes and sought to transcend them in a higher unity that preserves the truth in each while canceling out their errors. In the final analysis Barth's theology is quite conservative compared to classical liberal Protestant theology such as that of his own professor Adolf Harnack. Yet it was vehemently rejected as a "new modernism" by fundamentalists. Perhaps because it pointed a way out of the impasse between the warring twentieth-century camps of Protestant theology, Barth's theology was widely accepted, and even where rejected, it left an impact in its wake.

### Neo-Orthodoxy's Common Themes and Legacy

While Barth was the founder and main formulator of neo-orthodoxy, other Protestant and a few Catholic theologians joined in his reformation of modern theology, adding their own twists to it. Emil Brunner (1889-1966) taught at Zurich, Switzerland, at the same time that Barth taught at Basel. While they were early comrades in the new dialectical theology of neo-orthodoxy, the two Swiss theologians had a classic falling-out and hardly spoke to one another for decades. Brunner criticized Barth's total rejection of natural theology and neglect of general revelation. He urged recognition of a natural "point of contact" for the gospel in human nature. Barth reacted angrily with a treatise simply titled *Nein! (No!)* and hardened his own position against any possibility for God's Word outside of God's Word itself. Brunner also criticized Barth's doctrine of election as unavoidably universalistic. Brunner's own positive contribution to neo-orthodoxy appeared in many books, including his programmatic *Truth as Encounter* (1938 and 1954) and *Revelation and Reason* (1941). His own systematic theology was much briefer than Barth's and appeared in three volumes from 1946 to 1960 under the common title *Dogmatics.* Brunner emphasized a more experiential aspect of Christianity. Whereas Barth emphasized the objective Word of God and God's eternal decision for human salvation, Brunner emphasized the divine-human encounter and the moment of decision each human person must make for or against Jesus as Lord. Without any doubt Brunner was more influenced by Pietism than was Barth.

The leading American neo-orthodox theologian was Reinhold Niebuhr (1893-1971), who taught for many years at New York's Union Theological Seminary. Niebuhr was less of a systematic theologian than a Christian social ethicist, but he wrote much on the doctrines of humanity, including his magnum opus, *The Nature and Destiny of Man* (1941-1943). A school of Christian ethics known as "Christian realism" grew out of and around Niebuhr's theology. Deeply influenced by Kierkegaard and Barth, it emphasized the inevitably tragic and sinful situation of human existence before a holy and transcendent God and focused on the lesser of evils as the greatest good achievable in human history. Niebuhr was concerned to counter the Social Gospel's naive optimism regarding the possibility of God's kingdom within history. For him, justice was the closest approximation to love under the conditions of sin. Christians ought to settle for justice rather than insist on a society ordered according to perfect love, because perfect love is an "impossible ideal" within human history. God's kingdom is radically eschatological and not a human historical possibility. Niebuhr became America's most influential theological voice during the post-World War II era and his face graced the cover of *Time* magazine on its twenty-fifth anniversary issue.

What do all neo-orthodox theologians have in common? Some would say, "Not much!" At the very least, however, they all oppose both liberal Protestant theology and fundamentalism. They seek a thoroughly modern form of Protestant theology that is consistent with the New Testament gospel and the great themes of the

Reformers Luther, Zwingli and Calvin. All the neo-orthodox thinkers (with the possible exception of Niebuhr) are thoroughly Christocentric. That is, they see Jesus Christ as the revelation of God in person and seek to center everything in their theological reflections on him. To the dialectical theologians, Jesus Christ is more than a prophet of history and more even than a fully God-conscious man. He is God's Son breaking into the world of nature and history from beyond. Whether they would use the term *supernatural* or not, all the neo-orthodox theologians affirm a supernatural source of Jesus Christ and human salvation. They would agree that since Jesus Christ is God's Word and God's Son, he must be the heart of Christianity. No doctrine or idea may speculate around or beyond or behind him. He is the center of every truly Christian system of thought.

All of the neo-orthodox theologians reject natural theology and embrace God's Word as source and norm for Christian theology. They all refuse to identify "God's Word" with the words and propositions of Scripture while holding the Bible in high regard as the special witness to and instrument of God's Word, which is itself always event. In neo-orthodoxy the Bible is neither merely a great book of human religious wisdom (as in much liberal theology) nor "that manuscript from heaven." It is a thoroughly human book with all the marks and characteristics of the human authors. It is historical, fallible and culturally conditioned at every point. On the other hand, it is the unique channel of God's Word and becomes God's Word in the moment that God chooses to use it to bring people into encounter with himself. One analogy that accurately depicts the neo-orthodox view of the Bible is the light and the light bulb. The Word of God is the light, and the Bible is the filament and glass of the light bulb. The light (Word of God) shines through the light bulb (Bible), and the light bulb (Bible) is in some sense necessary to the light (Word of God).

Finally, all of the neo-orthodox theologians emphasize what Kierkegaard called the infinite qualitative difference between time and eternity. That includes the "wholly otherness" of God and God's kingdom. It implies also the paradoxical nature of human formulations about God arising out of reflection on God's Word. No human social order or organization, including the church, can be identified with God's kingdom. No ideology or philosophy, including theological systems, can be identified with God's own truth. God stands in judgment over and above everything that bears the smear and smudge of human touch. At best they can be broken lights of God and God's Word. And yet, according to the neo-orthodox theologians, there can be broken lights of God's Word within history. Because God has acted and spoken in Jesus Christ and left a witness to him in the Bible and the church, all is not lost. Now and again a breakthrough of social progress can approximate God's kingdom in history, and a new idea can become an echo of God's truth within the world of human thought. But if and when these things happen, the proper response is humility and gratitude, but never pride. Humanity can never place God in its debt by some achievement. It is all of God and God's grace.

Neo-orthodoxy's legacy is still being measured. Today the movement initiated by Barth and continued by Brunner, Niebuhr and others is alive and well and being carried on by their students and disciples. Many self-identified progressive evangelicals who reject fundamentalism and liberal theology have drunk deeply at neo-orthodox wells. Among them are Bernard Ramm (1916-1992) and Donald Bloesch (b. 1928). Their reception of neo-orthodoxy is critical but appreciative. Most evangelicals find neo-orthodoxy's doctrine of Scripture inadequate and affirm verbal inspiration if not inerrancy, but some such as Ramm and Bloesch affirm the neo-orthodox distinction between God's Word and the human words and propositions of the Bible. Even some Roman Catholic theologians have embraced aspects of Barth's theology and Niebuhr's Christian realism. Among Barth's most enthusiastic disciples stands Catholic theologian Hans Küng (b. 1928), who argued in *Justification: The Doctrine of Karl Barth and a Catholic Reflection* (1957) that Barth's doctrine of salvation is in fundamental agreement with that of the Catholic church and vice versa. Other schools of modern and postmodern theology that have been deeply influenced by Barth and neo-orthodoxy include narrative theology and postliberal theology. Even the few remaining classical liberal Protestant theologians express a debt of gratitude to Barth, Brunner and Niebuhr for reminding everyone of God's transcendence and human sinfulness. Most liberal theologians after World War II are "chastened liberals" in that they read the neo-orthodox thinkers and have adjusted their anthropocentric (human-centered) optimism in light of neo-orthodox critiques of liberal thought. Barth's reminder that "you cannot speak of God by speaking of man in a loud voice" has been taken to heart by most liberal theologians. The few who rejected the maxim became known as "radicals" and "secular theologians" in the 1960s.

Throughout much of the twentieth century there seemed to be only three viable options for Christian theology: liberal Protestant theology, fundamentalism and neo-orthodoxy. That was especially true from the 1920s to the 1950s. During the 1960s some new options appeared. Some died out quickly, such as the notorious movement of Christian atheism spawned by the death-of-God movement. Others took root and became permanent parts of the theological landscape and added their own twists and turns to the plot of theology's story. The final chapter in our story of Christian theology will deal briefly with some of these relatively new characters.

# CHAPTER 35

# Contemporary Theology Struggles with Diversity

A*nyone who has ever read a nineteenth-century Russian novel has probably* experienced the same confusion that most people feel when they first encounter the story of contemporary theology. Who are these characters and what are their exact roles in the plot? What has happened to the plot? Is there one plot? Post-World War II Christian theology is diverse as never before. Especially during the culturally revolutionary 1960s, the story of Christian theology took so many dizzying twists and turns and went in so many new directions that even experts find it difficult to draw it all together into one coherent story. What makes it all "Christian"? Where is the thread that is supposed to tie it all together as one story line? Perhaps we are still too close to the present stage of the story to see where that thread is. Hopefully later observers and interpreters will be able to discern it and explain this chapter of the story better than we can.

One great dream for twentieth-century Christianity that captivated the minds and hearts of many liberal theologians on its threshhold was ecumenical unity. They believed, in typically optimistic fashion, that the twentieth century would become "the Christian century" through a gradually emerging consensus of Christians worldwide. That consensus would look something like Harnack's simple religion of Jesus—a warm, ethical religion centered on the universal "fatherhood of God and brotherhood of man." World events and the negative voices of fundamentalists and neo-orthodox thinkers dispelled that dream. Of course, fundamentalism had its own vision for Christian unity that looked to the past and the revival of an imaginary Christian doctrinal consensus imposed on everyone. When that vision died in the aftermath of the 1925 Scopes trial, fundamentalists by and large gave up on any wider Christian unity and narrowed authentic Christianity to those already unified around "the fundamentals" as they interpreted them. Neo-orthodox thinkers kept alive a dream of Christian unity, but insisted that it could not come through an imposed, legalistic formula of doctrinal orthodoxy or through a lowest-common-denominator ecumenism that abandoned orthodoxy altogether. It would have to come through a renewal of the Reformation theology of God's Word. Neo-liberals and fundamentalists refused to get on Barth's bandwagon, however, and in the 1950s the situation seemed hopelessly deadlocked.

Gradually the dream of Christian unity as uniformity faded away, and Christian theologians settled for a new paradigm of unity. Instead of picturing Christian unity as a group of children following a pied piper, they began to explore the possibility of unity as a symphony orchestra with each musician and instrument adding its own unique sound to a multifaceted composition. Could there be unity without uniformity? How diverse can the parts be and still produce a symphony? These questions are unanswered. The present situation of Christian theology sounds very much like the warming up of an orchestra before it begins the concert. To switch metaphors, it is very much like the middle of a Russian novel with so many seemingly unrelated plots and actors that the reader has no idea how it can all come together and form one coherent story.

Some readers will no doubt see the tremendous diversity of contemporary Christian theology as negative and be tempted to dismiss the story as a sham, perhaps even a hoax. For them, theology must be unified in order to be authentically Christian. Perhaps they need to be reminded that for almost one thousand years Christian theology was more or less unified by coercion. Dissent was suppressed by threat of excommunication, torture and even death. Apart from that, there has never been perfect unity of belief among Christians. Diversity can be healthy, but it takes a mature person to handle it. Hope must rest in God, the ultimate author of the story, to bring it to its final denouement. In the meantime, we should look for those voices in Christian theology that prophetically speak the needed words of exhortation and correction and point the ways toward renewal and vitality among God's people.

Other readers will no doubt celebrate the diversity of contemporary Christian theology and resist any attempt to discover or even encourage unity as a new totalitarianism. To them all metanarratives (overarching stories) are necessarily totalizing. Metanarratives silence the stories of the weak and marginalized and impose those of the strong and powerful. For such readers theology's contemporary diversity—even if it represents a blooming, buzzing confusion—is liberating and exciting. Perhaps they need to be reminded that anything that is consistent with everything is strictly meaningless. If no metanarrative—even a nontotalizing one—can be discovered within the seemingly incommensurate stories of contemporary theology, then Christianity itself is lost. A theology that claims to be Christian must have something in common with the gospel of Jesus Christ, the apostolic witness to him in the New Testament, and the Great Tradition of the Christian church throughout its history. There has to be a center, a unifying thread of discernible truth that connects a theological movement with others. The instrument and its part in the composition must somehow mesh with the others or it does not belong in the orchestra.

Each of the theological movements included here claims to be Christian and attempts to translate the gospel of the early church and the Great Tradition of the Christian heritage into the present cultural context. Some of them do it more radically than others. Only the future will tell which ones are viable and lasting contributions to the ongoing story of Christian theology and which ones will drop away from the story into oblivion. These five movements are included here because, of all the options, they seem the most durable and influential. They are the "live options" of contemporary theology. In each case only a thumbnail sketch will be presented and only a few representative theologians of the movement will be briefly described. Each movement is described, analyzed and critically evaluated in more detail in volumes that deal specifically with contemporary theology.[1]

**Evangelical Theology**

The adjective *evangelical* is used in many different ways in the story of Christian theology. It simply means "of the good news" or "gospel-based." European Protestants—Lutheran and Reformed—use it as a synonym for "Protestant" as contrasted with "Roman Catholic" and even "Eastern Orthodox." Some Protestant denominations in North America include the term in their names simply to designate that they are based on the gospel, the good news of Jesus Christ, and that they are rooted in the great Protestant Reformation of the sixteenth century. The Evangelical Lutheran Church of America (ELCA) is the largest Lutheran denomination in the United States and was formed by the merger of two previous Lutheran synods or denominations in 1988. The word *evangelical* in the name of the new church is meant to convey the sense that it is Protestant and that it affirms the good news of the gospel. Another historical and contemporary use of the term *evangelical* comes from British history and the various factions within the Church of England. In the eighteenth century, especially, the evangelicals within that national church were those who wished to emphasize its Protestant aspects and resist what they saw as increasing power of Catholicizing elements. The English evangelicals also often rejected baptismal regeneration and high sacramentalism in favor of conversional piety. The Wesleys' Methodist movement began as an "evangelical renewal movement" within the Church of England.

In the United States the term *evangelical* has been used in various ways. In the eighteenth century it was adopted by many Protestant Christians to differentiate between those who supported the Great Awakening revivals led by George Whitefield and Jonathan Edwards and those who opposed them. The evangelicals supported revivals, and that use of the term stuck in North America. Another use of the label arose in the context of the growing conflict between liberal theology and Protestant orthodoxy. Those theologians and ministers who opposed liberalism and supported the early fundamentalist reaction against it were often called evangelicals. In the 1890s, however, some moderate liberals of New England labeled their movement "evangelical liberalism." Without any doubt the great theologian of the social gospel Walter Rauschenbusch, considered himself an "evangelical liberal." Gradually, however, the two terms fell into opposition in the popular mind and even among most theologians.

Already mentioned in our chapter on fundamentalism is the split within that movement in the 1940s and 1950s over "biblical separation" and "secondary separation." As fundamentalists became more and more sectarian and narrow, many conservative Protestants wanted to distance themselves from that movement while remaining theologically orthodox. Several issues divided those conservative Protestants who wished to be called evangelicals and those who were fundamentalists. Their areas of agreement were significant as well. Both fundamentalists and the new evangelicals emphasized the supernatural inspiration of the Bible and the major doctrinal achievements of the early Christian church such as the Nicene Creed and Protestant orthodoxy. Both closely related movements emphasized conversional piety as a hallmark of authentic Christianity and rejected baptismal regeneration as well as universalism. The new evangelicals rejected what they saw as fundamentalism's divisiveness over relatively minor doctrinal and moral issues and wished to develop and nurture a broader coalition of conservative, conversional Protestant Christianity. For them, biblical inspiration implied scriptural infallibility but not necessarily absolute technical accuracy of every detail recorded in the biblical literature. Nor did it require a literalistic hermeneutic, especially with regard to origins and the end times. The new evangelicals insisted on God as Creator of everything *(creatio ex nihilo)* and the second coming of Jesus Christ in the future, but they allowed great variation of interpretation regarding the details of these doctrines.

Besides differences over the doctrine of Scripture and biblical hermeneutics, the new evangelicals and fundamentalists fell into severe disagreement over biblical separation. The latter insisted on firm rejection of cooperation or dialogue with liberals and harshly criticized Billy Graham for allowing not only moderately liberal ministers but also Pentecostals and Roman Catholics to help in his evangelistic endeavors. Most of the leading fundamentalists rejected the growing Pentecostal movement with its emphasis on what they considered "counterfeit miracles," and they regarded Roman Catholicism as apostate and dangerous. The new evangelicals coalesced around Billy Graham and his various ministries. Gradually, throughout the 1950s and 1960s a relatively diverse movement of postfundamentalist evangelicalism began developing its own distinctive theology that represented a blend of Protestant orthodoxy and pietism with an element of revivalism thrown in for good measure. Due to the perceived need to provide an alternative to both narrow, sectarian fundamentalism and liberal Protestant theology, the new evangelicals overlooked their own differences. Some leaned closer to Protestant orthodoxy and looked askance at pietism and especially revivalism as too experiential and not sufficiently focused on the doctrinal content of Christianity. Others leaned closer to pietism and revivalism, and while valuing sound biblical doctrines, emphasized more the experiential side of authentic Christianity.

This shaky evangelical coalition carried within it seeds of tension between these two distinct but compatible Protestant theologies. At the far ends of the evangelical spectrum, some conservatives whose main agenda was to promote a Protestant orthodoxy of the old Princeton theology criticized experiential evangelicals whose main interests were in evangelism, conversion and spirituality. The conservative evangelicals feared that this focus on Christian experience could lead their coalition partners into liberalism. Experientialist evangelicals—equally committed to biblical authority and historic Christian doctrines—criticized their suspicious orthodox coalition partners for failing to shed entirely the fundamentalist mentality and for one-sidedly emphasizing the doctrinal content of Christianity to the neglect of experience of the living God. Tensions developed and grew between these two wings of the post-World War II evangelical coalition so that by the late 1980s and early 1990s they were sparring with one another over which one represented true evangelicalism. One wing of the movement has been labeled the Puritan-Princeton paradigm of evangelicalism, while the other may be labeled the Pietist-Pentecostal paradigm.[2]

The first paradigm looks to Jonathan Edwards and Charles Hodge as the great evangelical theologians and sees the Westminster Confession of Faith as a prime doctrinal standard for all evangelicals. The focus in that paradigm is on correct doctrine, including biblical inspiration and inerrancy, as the enduring essence of evangelical Christianity. The second paradigm looks to Pietists Spener, Francke and Zinzendorf and to revivalist theologians John Wesley and Charles Finney (1792-1875) as the great precursors of modern evangelicalism. The focus in that paradigm is on authentic experience, including especially regeneration and sanctification, as the enduring essence of evangelical Christianity. The first paradigm tends to regard monergism as the norm for evangelical doctrine, whereas the second paradigm at least allows synergism as an equally valid option for evangelical theology.

What do the various versions of evangelical theology have in common? Adherents of the two paradigms share commitment to a basic historic Christian worldview, including belief in God's transcendence and supernatural activity, the Bible as divinely inspired and infallible in matters of faith and practice, Jesus Christ as crucified and risen Savior and Lord of the world, conversion as the only authentic initiation into salvation, and evangelism through communication of the gospel to all people. They also reject liberal theology and fundamentalism to varying degrees. Evangelicals have been ambivalent about Karl Barth and neo-orthodoxy. Those closest to the fundamentalist roots of the movement sternly reject them, while those furthest away from fundamentalism see them as friends and allies.

Many evangelical theologians have arisen within the movement in its post-World War II history, but none is better known or more influential than Carl F. H. Henry (b. 1913), a Baptist theologian who was chosen by Billy Graham to give intellectual and theological shape to the new movement as it struggled to define itself over against fundamentalism and liberal theology. Henry was a prolific author and powerful teacher and speaker. He emerged as the leading spokesperson for postfundamentalist evangelicalism in the 1950s and 1960s, but his star faded in the 1980s and 1990s as he retreated more and more toward a narrow, almost fundamentalistic mentality. A new spokesperson for moderate evangelicalism emerged in the 1970s and 1980s who intended to hold the two impulses of Protestant orthodoxy and pietism together in a "theology of Word and Spirit."[3] Donald G. Bloesch (b. 1928) taught theology for many years at Dubuque University School of Theology in Iowa. Throughout his career he called for evangelicals to recognize their common ground and set aside petty squabbles over details of the doctrines of Scripture. He labeled his own approach "progressive evangelicalism" because it was open to higher criticism of the Bible so long as it did not work from a naturalistic bias.

The Iowa theologian also sought to incorporate the strengths of various strands of the historic Christian tradition into his theology without allowing it to become an eclectic hodgepodge of conflicting themes. For him, the gospel message of the cross and resurrection of Jesus Christ is the heart and soul of evangelical theology. Wherever men and women of the church have enhanced it through their theologies, he is more than willing to draw upon them, whether they are Eastern Orthodox, Roman Catholic or Protestant.

**Roman Catholic Theology**

Until the mid-twentieth century the only ecumenical council of the Roman Catholic Church after Trent was the First Vatican Council (Vatican I) in the 1870s. Vatican I was a conservative, almost reactionary council in that it rejected innovative proposals of modernists in the church and tightened the control of tradition over biblical and theological scholarship. For almost a century Catholic theology stagnated as pope after pope insisted on strong traditionalism centered on the teachings of Thomas Aquinas. In 1961 the elderly Pope John XXIII called for the twenty-first ecumenical council to meet at the Vatican in Rome. The Second Vatican Council (Vatican II) met from 1962 to 1965 and revolutionized the Roman Catholic Church. While it did not promulgate any new dogmas or radically alter doctrine, the council "threw open the windows of the church and let the fresh breezes blow through it." Hard-core traditionalists thought the breezes were stiff winds of modernism. Progressives interpreted the breezes bringing change into the church as the refreshing wind of the Holy Spirit. In any case, Vatican II radically altered the life of the Roman Catholic Church so that it was no longer isolated from modern philosophy, science, Protestantism and world religions. The mass would henceforth be said in the vernacular (the language of the laity); the laypeople would be given greater say in the day-to-day operations of Catholic churches; lists of banned books were abolished and Catholic scholars given freedom to publish exploratory works without prior restraint from the Catholic hierarchy.

Perhaps the most significant change in Catholic theology brought about by Vatican II was the affirmation of the supremacy of Scripture. Although the council's decree on Scripture and tradition stopped short of affirming *sola scriptura,* it did seriously qualify the "two sources of authority" doctrine so abhorrent to the Protestant Reformers of the sixteenth century. In practice, at least, Vatican II opened the Roman Catholic Church and its scholarship to a new era of biblical teaching and study. The Bible took on a new role and value as ultimate source and standard of truth. Protestants who watched the council carefully stood back in amazement at the changes taking place. Some Protestants, including Karl Barth, were invited to the council as observers and even advisers to the bishops and Catholic theologians debating and writing its decrees. After the council, ecumenical contacts between leading Catholic and Protestant thinkers continued so that in the 1990s even conservative evangelical Protestants and moderate Roman Catholic theologians were regularly engaging in dialogue and reaching agreement on vast areas of Christian belief and ethics.[4]

The most influential post-Vatican II Roman Catholic theologian was Karl Rahner, who was born in Austria in 1904. He died there in 1984 after a career of teaching and writing Catholic theology paralleled in history only by Thomas Aquinas himself. His collected works, *Theological Investigations,* fill twenty volumes. Over 3,500 books and articles were published by Rahner during his lifetime. Toward the end of his life and career, he published a single-volume systematic summary of his life's teaching entitled *Foundations of Christian Faith* (1978). No other Catholic thinker in the modern world so deeply influenced Roman Catholic theology. Rahner was the Catholic counterpart to Karl Barth in terms of influence and impact. He was *the* Catholic theologian of the twentieth century and perhaps of the modern era itself.

Unfortunately, Rahner's theological reflections are extremely difficult to understand. He borrowed heavily from philosophy and used its terminology often without explanation. His main aim was to demonstrate the intellectual viability of the Christian revelation and witness within the modern cultural context. In order to do that, he developed a theological anthropology (doctrine of humanity) that serves as a "fundamental theology" or philosophical-apologetical theology that "comprises the scientific substantiation of the fact of the revelation of God in Jesus Christ."[5] This is meant to replace or add to the traditional Thomistic natural theology. Rahner attempted to demonstrate through a scholarly exploration of human nature and existence that human beings are by nature "open to God" and find their personal fulfillment only in a relationship to God through Jesus Christ as absolute Savior. Space does not permit even a cursory description of Rahner's method or conclusions. Suffice it to say that he believed it was possible to show not only that atheism is ultimately impossible but that all human thought finds its ultimate source and horizon in God and all human spiritual longings and aspirations find their ultimate fulfillment in Jesus Christ.

Two of Rahner's most controversial concepts are the "supernatural existential" and "anonymous Christianity." According to the Austrian theologian, human beings are by nature open to God's self-revelation in Jesus Christ. Beyond nature, however, lies the supernatural revelation and redemption, and human beings are universally gifted by God with a capacity to receive grace. In fact, every human has an element of grace within—a supernatural existential—that constitutes a possibility of salvation. Anyone who follows and builds on this inward grace will find full salvation regardless of whether that person ever hears the explicit message of Jesus Christ. Those who follow it and develop it in a life lived according to God's will—whether as baptized Christians or not—are "anonymous Christians." Rahner leaned in the direction of universal salvation such that in order to be eternally damned to hell a person had to explicitly reject God's offer of saving grace. Even those who reject it could be saved if their rejection is based on a false understanding of the gospel—so long as they live the kind of life that God has revealed as pleasing to him: a life of love and mercy toward others.

Rahner's doctrines of God, Jesus Christ and salvation were within the boundaries of the Catholic tradition even if they were often cast in highly abstract philosophical language. He affirmed the doctrine of the Trinity and coined a phrase that has become known in contemporary theology as "Rahner's Rule": the economic Trinity is the immanent Trinity, and the immanent Trinity is the economic Trinity.[6] In other words, Rahner taught both Catholic and Protestant theologians to avoid dividing the trinitarian life of God in eternity (immanent Trinity) from the trinitarian activity of God in history (economic Trinity). According to Rahner, God is who he is among us. Father, Son and Holy Spirit do not constitute some heavenly circle of fellowship untouched by the concrete, historical events of Jesus and acts of the Holy Spirit. The Trinity is God's openness to humanity, just as humanity is by nature open to God. That does not mean a Hegelian pantheistic synthesis of divinity and humanity, but it does mean an alteration in classical Christian theism such that God is affected by what happens in history because he chooses to be affected by it.

The combined influences of Vatican II and Karl Rahner's theological reflections caused the boundaries between Catholic theology, modern philosophy and Protestant theology to become more elastic and flexible. Priests and theologians trained in Catholic universities and seminaries since the 1960s live in a different thought world from those trained prior to the council and without Rahner's broadening influence. They tend to be much more open to modern thought generally and to critical revision of Catholic tradition specifically. They often affirm the whole church as the whole people of God so that Protestants are included in the true church of Jesus Christ. Ecumenical dialogue with Protestants and even non-Christian religions is more common and accepted in Catholic circles. Many Catholic priests and theologians have become so liberal that in the 1980s and 1990s the Vatican became suspicious and began a series of investigations of Catholic theologians that resulted in several progressives being silenced or even forced out of the church. Most observers, however, believe the tightening of the authority of the Vatican and of tradition under Pope John Paul II is a temporary reaction. Many look forward to a day when Catholics and Protestants will enjoy full communion and fellowship and when Catholic thinkers will enjoy all the freedoms most Protestants take for granted.

**Process Theology**

Throughout the story of Christian theology we have seen that philosophy and theology are seemingly inseparable conversation partners. In the second through the fifth centuries Christian thinkers used Hellenistic categories and thought forms to explicate and communicate the biblical message to educated pagans of the Roman Empire. Origen and Augustine both borrowed heavily from Platonism and at times seemed to allow it to overpower and control their formulations of Christian doctrine. In medieval theology Thomas Aquinas turned to the newly discovered Aristotelian philosophy as theology's "handmaid," and yet many critics charge that his own version of classical Christian theism ended up being shaped by that pagan philosophy. Liberal theologians have been among those in modern theology who often find philosophy a valuable and equal partner in the theological enterprise. One form of current theology that is both liberal and positive toward some philosophy in theology is process theology.

Process theology represents an attempt on the part of some contemporary Christian thinkers to reconstruct the doctrine of God and all of Christian theology to be more in tune with modern beliefs about the nature of the world. Process thinkers begin with the working assumption that Christian theology must be revised and updated in every new culture in light of its peculiar concerns, issues and questions. Even more, they believe that a viable Christian theology cannot fly in the face of the culture's most basic assumptions about reality. One of the basic assumptions of Hellenistic culture was that perfection of being is static. That is, change is evidence of imperfection. The ultimately real—the divine—must be absolutely simple (noncomposite) and immutable (changeless). Otherwise it would be imperfect. Process theologians insist that modern thought cannot agree with that view of being and perfection. Intelligent, thinking modern men and women simply know that this is flawed metaphysics. Change is no longer regarded as evidence of imperfection. In fact, according to modern thought, to be is to change. Everything is related to everything else. Being itself is relational. And relationship means openness to being affected by others within the network of influential relationships. Nature works that way, as do humans. Being is social and being social means being dynamic.

Process theologians are convinced that a new philosophy is needed to help modern Christian thought shed its outdated metaphysic of timeless and changeless perfection and reconstruct theology so that it is viable in a modern world that places becoming above being. They discovered that new philosophy in the thought of British mathematician Alfred North Whitehead (1861-1947). Whitehead turned from mathematics to speculative philosophy when he left his native England to teach at Harvard University in 1924. According to some observers, he produced the most impressive metaphysical system of the twentieth century by reconceptualizing reality itself as a network of interrelated moments of energy called "actual occasions." Instead of conceiving reality in terms of objects, whether physical or spiritual or both, Whitehead reconceived all of reality as occasions, or drops of experience. Reality is a series of happenings rather than a great chain of being. To be real is to "happen" in relation to other happenings and to "experience" within a network of experiencing entities.

Whitehead found room in his philosophy for God as a great cosmic organizing principle. God creates the world by unifying it insofar as possible. However, in Whitehead's philosophy of religion God is neither omnipotent nor timeless. God contains the world and is contained in it. In a manner reminiscent of Hegel's "without the world God is not God," Whitehead affirmed that "it is as true to say that the world creates God as that God creates the world." God is superior to the world at any given moment but is always capable of becoming superior to himself as well. In fact, in every given moment God is becoming superior to himself. God evolves with the world and under its influence.

A key concept of Whitehead's philosophy is the "dipolarity," or "bipolarity," of every actual entity. (*Actual entity* is another term for the basic building blocks of reality otherwise known as "actual occasions.") Nothing but actual entities are real. Every one—including God—has two aspects or poles: physical and mental. God's two poles may also be described as "primordial" and "consequent." In his primordial pole—God's basic, stable character containing ideals yet to be achieved—God does not change. It is abstract and potential rather than concrete and actual. God's consequent pole is his lived reality—his actual experience—and it is constantly changing as God "feels" the world. Just as the condition of the world affects God and even constitutes God's concrete existence, so God affects the world. God feeds into it the ideals of his primordial nature and attempts to lure or persuade the world's actual occasions to achieve them in order to enhance harmony, beauty and enjoyment. But God cannot coerce any actual entity to achieve its "ideal subjective aim." He can only try to persuade it. Every actual entity has some degree of free will and self-determination and may comply with

God's ideal or resist it. Evil is the result of resistance to God's ideals by actual entities and it causes God to suffer. God is enriched and impoverished by the world's responses to his persuasive influence.

Whitehead was not a Christian in any traditional sense of the word. His own religion was a natural religion dictated by his philosophy. But many liberal Christian thinkers found something valuable in his philosophy for reconstructing Christian doctrine in light of modern knowledge. Those who sought to correlate Christian theology with Whitehead's philosophy became known as process theologians, and by the 1970s their tribe was increasing. Entire mainstream Protestant seminaries and divinity schools of universities in the United States and Canada adopted process theology as their main emphasis and approach. The United Methodist-related Claremont Graduate School of Theology (California) became a center of process theology. Located there are the Center for Process Studies and the editorial offices of the journal *Process Studies.* The most articulate Protestant promoter of process theology throughout the 1960s and into the 1990s was John Cobb Jr. (b. 1925), a United Methodist minister and son of missionaries. The Claremont professor of theology published several books applying Whitehead's philosophy to Christian theology, including *A Christian Natural Theology* (1965), *God and the World* (1965) and *Christ in a Pluralistic Age* (1975). In every book Cobb emphasized the mutual relationship of interdependence between God and the world.

All process theologians including John Cobb wish to move Christian theology away from classical Christian theism as it was developed in the early and medieval church. Instead of God's transcendence, they emphasize God's immanence. Rather than God's absoluteness, they stress God's personal nature. Divine love, including vulnerability and suffering, takes precedence over power and sovereignty. Second, Cobb and the other process theologians reject monergism and any depiction of God's work in the world as coercive. God never forces any actual entity—and humans are made up of actual occasions—to do anything. God always works only through persuasion. God calls the world to its own fulfillment in the perfect wholeness and harmony of his kingdom, but free creatures decide whether and how to respond. Traditional theology said, "Man proposes but God disposes"; process theology says, "God proposes but man disposes." Finally, process theology is naturalistic in that it rejects the whole idea of supernatural interventions by divine power in the natural order. While that does not rule out special persuasive acts of God, it does rule out absolute miracles and inexplicable signs and wonders. God works directly on each actual entity by providing it with its ideal initial aim and luring it toward his vision for what it should become, but God never interrupts the natural order of events or forces anything to happen against nature or free will. God cannot even know the future in complete detail with absolute certainty because it will only be "filled in" by free decisions of actual entities that do not yet exist.

Process theology is a uniquely twentieth-century form of liberal Protestant theology. Some Roman Catholic thinkers have also accepted aspects of it. Its appeal seems to lie in the solution it offers to the problem of evil and innocent suffering. World War II and the holocausts that accompanied it radically challenged many theologians' ideas about God and suffering. Where was God when six to nine million Jews were being gassed and burned by the Nazis? The horrors of twentieth-century war and genocide seemed to many contemporary theologians to require radical revision of traditional Augustinian notions of God's power and sovereignty. If God could have stopped the mass killings of innocent men, women and children, they reason, he should have. Therefore, it must be the case that he could not stop them. Process theologians found solace and refuge in Whitehead's concept of God as "the fellow sufferer who understands" and who cannot coerce actual entities or societies of them to do good rather than evil.

Many of process theology's critics suggest that it went too far in the opposite direction from Augustinian monergism. The Whiteheadian God of Cobb's process theology would seem to be incapable of most of the things Christian theology traditionally attributes to God's creative and redemptive activity. The process God did not create the world in the beginning. The world is God's "body" and God is the world's "soul," or "mind," and the two are always inseparable and interdependent. Furthermore, according to process theology there is no guarantee or even reason to believe that God will ever finally overcome the intransigence of resistance to his vision of good. For all we know the future is just more of the same. The debate over whether process theology can even be considered "Christian" raged in theological circles during the 1970s and 1980s without any final agreement. It continues to be taught as a viable version of Christian theology in many liberal, mainstream Protestant seminaries while at the same time being condemned as heresy by many conservative theologians.

### Liberation Theologies

Throughout the 1970s groups of socially, economically and politically oppressed Christians in North and South America began to develop theologies of liberation. North American black theologians focused their attention on the problem of racism and interpreted salvation as including the liberation of African Americans from racial prejudice and exclusion. Some of the leading black theologians of the 1970s went so far as to suggest that God is black and that salvation in the modern North American context means "becoming black with God." These enigmatic statements should not be taken too literally. The point James Cone and others were making is that God is on the side of the oppressed and downtrodden, and people seeking salvation cannot remain neutral in the situation of racial division and oppression. In Latin America both Catholic and Protestant theologians began reflecting theologically on that continent's situation of extreme poverty and economic injustice, and interpreted salvation as including abolition of structural poverty and unjust political orders. Throughout the 1980s North American feminist theologians focused their attention more and more on the problem of sexism and patriarchy in both church and society. They interpreted salvation as including equality of men and women and even radical readjustment of not only male domination but all political-social hierarchies.

All three major forms of liberation theology share certain common features in spite of their differences over which social injustices are primary. African-American theologians such as James Cone of Union Theological Seminary in New York identify racism as the primary social sin in North America. Feminist theologians such as Rosemary Ruether of Garrett-Evangelical Theological Seminary in Evanston, Illinois, identify sexism and patriarchy (male domination) as the primary social sins. Gustavo Gutiérrez of Peru identifies structural poverty as Latin America's primary social evil. All agree, however, that theology is neither universally applicable nor socially and politically neutral. Theology must be contextualized anew in each and every social-cultural situation and made concrete and committed to justice within that specific situation.

Liberation theologians of all kinds reject a universal theology that is for all people everywhere. Each oppressed group must have the freedom to reflect critically on Scripture and the contemporary situation in which they live and to decide for itself how best to interpret and live out the gospel message. For liberation theologies of all kinds, theology is concrete, committed reflection on praxis in the light of God's Word. *Praxis* means "liberating activity" and is what happens in any situation of oppression when people begin to free themselves and seek equality and justice. The theologians' task is to help the people in their struggle for liberation by linking it together with God's Word. A leading Latin American liberation theologian has described this view of theology succinctly:

> Theology, as here conceived, is not an effort to give a correct understanding of God's attributes or actions but an effort to articulate the action of faith, the shape of praxis conceived and realized in obedience. As philosophy in Marx's famous *dictum,* theology has to stop explaining the world and start transforming it. *Orthopraxis,* rather than orthodoxy, becomes the criterion for theology.[7]

A second point of agreement among liberation theologians is that God has a preferential option for the oppressed, and the oppressed have special insight into God's will in any given social situation. This does not mean that African Americans or women or the poor have an automatically favorable relationship with God that gives them an advantage in being saved. Liberation theologians tend to think of "salvation" mainly in historical and social ways rather than individualistically. In this they have much in common with the older Social Gospel movement. However, they do believe that in the prophetic-biblical message God takes sides with his oppressed people and actively seeks to liberate them from all bondage, slavery and inequality. Thus when there is a situation where one group is being oppressed by another such that its people are being hindered from the fulfillment of their potential, God sides with the oppressed group in its active struggle to liberate itself and to achieve full humanity for its members.

Third and finally, all liberation theologians agree that Christian mission necessarily includes active participation by the Christian church in liberation of oppressed people. The church is called by God to identify with the oppressed and marginalized people rather than with the rich, the powerful and the privileged. Too often, liberationists claim, Christian churches and denominations have aligned themselves with the small, privileged classes and groups in society and thus have indirectly contributed to injustice and inequality.

In Latin America liberation theologians have called on the Catholic bishops to shed their alliances and friendships with the oligarchs of power who control most of the wealth and use force to keep the majority of people in permanent poverty. At the behest of liberation theologians the Latin American bishops agreed, and they endorsed the basic principles of liberation theology at two major conferences in 1968 and 1979 (CELAM II and CELAM III). Powerful bishops and archbishops of Latin American countries put tremendous pressure on military dictators to radically change the social arrangements in their countries. In some cases, such as in Nicaragua, the bishops endorsed revolutions against the ruling families. In El Salvador liberationist bishop Oscar Romero was assassinated by a death squad and became a martyr of liberation theology.

The three main liberation theologians have already been mentioned. James Cone (b. 1938) is often considered the father of African-American theology. In the late 1960s and early 1970s he became closely associated with the Black Power movements of Malcolm X and other African Americans who were dissatisfied with Martin Luther King Jr.'s pacifist approach to combating racism. Cone wrote two groundbreaking and highly controversial theological volumes that justify radical activism: *Black Theology and Black Power* (1969) and *A Black Theology of Liberation*

(1970). He argued that God is black and that black power is "Christ's central message to twentieth-century America,"[8] and he seemed to condone if not actually advocate race war if that is what it takes to abolish racism in the United States. Cone became Charles H. Briggs Professor of Systematic Theology at the prestigious and liberal Union Theological Seminary in the 1970s. He continued to develop black theology based on African-American experience of oppression and liberation in numerous books and articles. Critics consider him a dangerously radical and divisive voice in contemporary Christian theology, while sympathizers see him as a prophet like Amos in the Old Testament.

The father of Latin American liberation theology is Gustavo Gutiérrez (b. 1928), who lives in Lima, Peru, and whose book *A Theology of Liberation* (1971) is still that movement's basic text. Gutiérrez is a Catholic theologian with wide ecumenical contacts. He travels frequently to North America and Europe to spread the message of liberation theology and to engage in frank discussions with theologians of affluent countries. He has identified the root causes of Latin American political and economic injustice in North American and European manipulation and interference through his "dependency theory." According to the Peruvian theologian, Latin American economic dependency on North American and European economies and governments is purposely structured to benefit those already affluent societies and keep southern-hemisphere societies and cultures underprivileged. Like many other liberation theologians, most of whom look to him as their spokesman and leader, Gutiérrez sees salvation as the overthrow of those forces that keep Latin America majorities poor and the subsequent establishment of economic democracies that are basically socialistic if not communistic in nature. He looks to the economic and political theories of Karl Marx for inspiration and guidance while rejecting Marx's atheism and materialism.

The leading voice in feminist theology is Rosemary Ruether (b. 1936), author of one of the movement's major texts, *Sexism and God-Talk* (1983). Together with other feminist Christians, Ruether, a Catholic theologian who teaches at a Methodist seminary, argues that patriarchy is a basic evil that needs to be abolished in order for salvation to be accomplished. By *patriarchy* she means not just male domination—although that is the literal meaning of the term—but also the entire hierarchical structure of society put in place by both men and women in which father figures control everything. Even God ought not to be conceived as an all-controlling being above everyone else. According to Ruether, God ought to be called "God/dess" and conceived as the "matrix of being" that connects everyone and everything together in a web of equality and interrelatedness. Because women are closer to being attuned to such a vision of society, Ruether advocates the establishment of "Women-Churches" as alternative communities to male-dominated denominations and congregations. Such Women-Churches will be safe places for feminists (including males with feminized consciousnesses) to explore the new paradigm of feminist theology in teaching and liturgy centered entirely on women's experiences.

Liberation theologies have sparked great controversy in contemporary theology. Some critics reject entirely their political orientation and accuse them of dividing the body of Christ between men and women, rich and poor, whites and blacks. Sympathetic observers often find much value in liberationists' prophetic messages about making theology concrete in relation to overcoming injustice and oppression. Liberationists themselves are not particularly interested in responding to critics and have little use for objective observers' comments. Their attitude is that theology is for and from oppressed people and ought not to concern itself with pleasing others. To many feminists, feminist theology is not about seeking dialogue with, let alone approval from, men. It is about seeking radical equality between men and women at every level of society, including churches. If that is threatening to men, it only shows that patriarchy is highly resistant to change. Similarly, Latin American liberation theology is less concerned with gaining acceptance and approval from North American and European theologians and church leaders than with transforming Latin American societies. And James Cone clearly does not care about white criticism of black theology. The principle that "God is black" is meant to support African-American consciousness, and if it offends some whites, that is a side benefit.

**Eschatological Theology**

One of the most influential new theologies stemming from Europe in the post-World War II era is eschatological theology closely associated with the writings of two German professors: Jürgen Moltmann and Wolfhart Pannenberg. Both were born in the late 1920s and lived through the horrors of World War II and retired from stellar careers as professors at German universities in the early 1990s. Throughout the late 1960s into the 1980s they were often identified as the two most influential contemporary world-class Protestant theologians. While their theologies are very different in several ways, together they stimulated a new interest in and appreciation for eschatological realism in mainstream Christian theology. For much of the nineteenth and twentieth centuries, belief in a real kingdom of God on earth was relegated to mythology by liberal and some neo-orthodox theologians. While Ritschl and the Social Gospel theologians talked much about the kingdom of God, they meant a human social order rather than a literal advent of Jesus Christ and the rule and reign of God in the future. Fundamentalist theologians delved into all kinds of speculation about eschatology and often insisted on dispensational premillennialism—a very specific view of the end times that often included greater attention to the so-called great tribulation and the antichrist than to Jesus Christ's lordship over the earth. This fundamentalist obsession with the end times drove many moderate, liberal and neo-orthodox Christians away from paying any attention at all to Christ's second coming or events of the future.

Moltmann and Pannenberg sought to recover a realistic approach to biblical eschatology completely apart from fundamentalism. Neither German professor had any roots in conservative Protestantism. Both were raised in homes devoid of religious influence and converted to Christianity as young adults in the aftermath of the devastation of Germany in 1945. Moltmann became a Christian while in a prisoner of war camp in Great Britain. Pannenberg had an intellectual conversion to Christianity while a university student in Berlin. For a while they taught together at a state-church seminary and then went their separate ways. Moltmann joined the Reformed Church and taught for many years at the prestigious Tübingen University, and Pannenberg became a Lutheran and retired from a career at the University of Munich. Both taught at North American universities and seminaries during sabbaticals and both became fluent in English. Most of their writings were translated into English, and they gained great reputations in North America as leading moderate Protestant theologians—bridges between liberalism and conservatism. They consider their own basic approaches to theology "critically orthodox" in that they respect the Great Tradition of Christian doctrine of the early church and Reformation, but they reject knee-jerk confessionalism and maximal conservatism.

Jürgen Moltmann came to fame with the publication of his programmatic book *Theology of Hope* in 1964. In it he emphasized revelation as promise (rather than experience or proposition) and salvation as God's historical work from the future. He placed the kingdom of God at the center of his theological reflections but avoided the liberal identification of God's kingdom with a human society. Instead the German theologian argued that only God can and will bring about his kingdom and that God is to be understood as the "power of the future" breaking into history and pulling it forward into the new age of peace and justice that can only be anticipated from within history. While strictly avoiding eschatological literalism, Moltmann left no doubt that he believed the church must recover a sense of God's eschatological lordship. For him, history must end in God, and Jesus Christ's resurrection is the guarantee of that. It is the historical prolepsis (concrete anticipation) of the kingdom of God when all the dead will be raised and God's promises of a new heaven and earth fulfilled. Especially novel was Moltmann's identification of God with the power or "pull" of the future. In later volumes such as *The Crucified God* (1974) and *The Trinity and the Kingdom* (1981) he left no doubt that he also considered God triune and personal, but he continued to identify God's being with futurity rather than with temporal origins of nature and history.

Wolfhart Pannenberg broke through to fame with the publication of his Christology, *Jesus—God and Man* (1964). There he affirmed the rational verifiability of the historical event of the bodily resurrection of Jesus Christ—something dismissed as impossible or mythological by most German theologians of the modern era. In concert with Moltmann, Pannenberg interpreted the resurrection of Jesus as an eschatological event—the prolepsis of the future kingdom of God when God will finally reveal his deity and lordship and be "all in all." In later writings such as *Theology and the Kingdom of God* (1969) and *The Idea of God and Human Freedom* (1973) the German Lutheran thinker expressed fairly radical ideas about God's futurity and even claimed that "God does not yet exist." Such statements must not be misinterpreted. For Pannenberg, God exists fully in and for himself in all eternity, but for the world God exists in the future and presently only as the power of his future lordship breaking into history from ahead of time. The same could be said of Moltmann's eschatological doctrine of God. For the two eschatological theologians, God does not need the world to become who he is, and yet at the same time he chooses to relate to the world in such a way that he goes through a history together with it. Pannenberg makes explicit that God actualizes himself in and through world history without becoming dependent on it. In our finite, human experience, however, God appears to be "not yet" in that his lordship is eschatological.

The attraction of eschatological theology for many young Protestant thinkers in the 1970s and 1980s lay in its alternative to both classical Christian theism with its all-controlling and static God and process theology's impotent and developing God. Eschatological theology seemed to be a new paradigm for thinking about the God-world relationship. That paradigm is centered on a divine self-limitation in which God freely chooses to allow the world of nature and history to affect him without losing his lordship in it. God's being is not swallowed up in his relationship with the world. But once God has created the world and given it its freedom, he must work with it without dominating it. That is eschatological theology's solution to the problem of evil: Evils such as the Holocaust happen because the world is not yet God's kingdom. God gives human history its own freedom and struggles with it and in it from his own powerful futurity through both the lure of love and powerful prolepsis. God sends Jesus Christ and the Holy Spirit into the world from the future to demonstrate his love and release spiritual forces of anticipation into the stream of human history. In the end God will come to the world and cancel out all sin and evil and make it his home.

Critics from a variety of viewpoints have objected to eschatological theology. Those with a more liberal orientation, such as process theologians, see it as too supernaturalistic and ask why God does not intervene from the future to stop evils such as the Holocaust if he can. They also find eschatological theology's embrace of the historical resurrection of Jesus Christ and of the reality of God's triunity in eternity mythological. To them, its critical orthodoxy is not critical enough. Conservative theologians—especially fundamentalists—view eschatological theology as too critical and not sufficiently orthodox. Neither Moltmann nor Pannenberg endorses biblical inerrancy or a literalistic interpretation of origins or the end times. They also lean heavily toward universalism, although both stop short of endorsing it completely.

**Cacophony or Choir?**

This chapter opened with comments concerning the diversity and pluralism of contemporary theology. It has ignored some of the more radical theological movements that can hardly be taken seriously as "Christian" at all (for example, death-of-God theology), and yet the basic problems should be clear to any discerning reader. Lacking from the scene of turn-of-the-millennium Christian theology is any overarching metanarrative that could serve to reunify it. Many will inevitably view the present situation as a cacophony of voices and either hold their hands over their ears in disgust or embrace the noise as joyful liberation from imposed uniformity. Some will see the present situation as at best hopeful. Diverse voices, when brought together in harmony, can make a chorus out of cacophony and a choir out of confusion. Only the future will reveal whether Christian theology will remain radically pluralistic or rediscover a common chord that will unite diverse voices without obliterating them.

# CONCLUSION
# The Unfinished Story & Its Future

The story of Christian theology began with diversity, tension and the search for unity of belief. Throughout the Christian churches of the Roman Empire great thinkers stepped forward to confront the difficult challenges posed by cultists posing as Christians and by pagan critics ridiculing Christian teachings. Their projects of developing intelligible answers to questions and excluding false answers led to the standardization of certain beliefs that could not be explicitly found in Christian sources. For example, nowhere in Scripture or in the apostles' teachings does the concept of *creatio ex nihilo* (creation out of nothing) appear. Nor can one find the idea of God's triunity explicitly expressed. Certainly the fully developed idea of the incarnation as a hypostatic union of two natures is at best implied in Christian sources that are considered divine revelation. These and many other orthodox doctrines were not so much revealed as developed through reflection on divine revelation. That does not take anything away from their truth. It is only to say that they represent the second-order language of the church. The first-order language is the language of revelation. Developing this second-order language of doctrine and enforcing it within the church became a necessary project to preserve Christianity from dissolving into the meaninglessness of being compatible with anything and everything.

That project of developing, preserving and defending orthodoxy was perceived by the early church fathers and the sixteenth-century Reformers and their heirs as necessary for the sake of salvation. Doctrines were never understood as ends in themselves—ideas to be studied and believed for their own sakes. Rather, at their best the church fathers and Reformers saw the theological task as a survival project. Without doctrines there would be no way to keep the gospel of Jesus Christ distinct and clear. Without a vision of the truth, proclamation of the gospel would be impossible. And without gospel proclamation, salvation would be unlikely. That is the line of reasoning that lay behind the great fathers' and Reformers' sometimes seemingly esoteric teachings.

Sometimes, of course, doctrines and systems of ideas did become ends in themselves, and salvation was wrongly equated with mere intellectual assent to them. Whenever that misunderstanding of the gospel became prevalent, new characters stepped onto the page of the story of theology to reform the church and return it to a balance between orthodoxy and experience of God, with the latter having priority and the former serving a protective function. Occasionally, as we have seen, people calling themselves Christians rejected doctrine and orthodoxy altogether and tried to identify authentic Christianity with unintelligible experience of God. The Great Tradition of the church has fought both extremes and always tried to make clear that Christianity is neither primarily a philosophy to be understood intellectually nor an indescribable mystical experience without cognitive content. A nonconceptual experience of God is meaningless; theologically correct belief without a corresponding experience of God is empty. Orthodoxy and orthopathy must go hand in hand. But the tensions between them have plagued the Christian church for two thousand years. The transitional contemporary age is no exception. If anything, the tension is greater at the turn of the millennium than ever before.

The story of Christian theology is not finished. Perhaps it never will come to a final conclusion. Even in God's kingdom there will no doubt be more to learn. Some have envisioned heaven as endless school without the pain of quizzes and exams. In any case, Christians are still in the historical school of theology, and its story with all the conflicts and tensions and twists and turns of plot continues. As we learned from the final chapter of the story thus far, the contemporary age is a transitional one. One reason for that uncertainty lies in the radical pluralism that plagues theology. For all the interest and "spice" that pluralism adds to the story, it cannot continue without some rediscovery of a central focus holding all the diverse theologies together as Christian. Many observers would argue quite rightly that the worldwide church of Jesus Christ is overdue for a new reformation. This time that reformation will need to be a reassertion of basic, or mere, Christianity that strikes a healthy balance between experiencing God and knowing about God intellectually. A new reformer of the universal church is needed—a great spiritual thinker like Irenaeus, Augustine, Thomas Aquinas, Luther, Calvin, Edwards, Wesley or Barth must step forward to provide a new unifying vision of Christian theology that is solidly based on divine revelation, consistent with the Great Tradition of the church and spiritually reinvigorating.

Is it possible that the twenty-first-century reformation of the church will begin somewhere in the Two-Thirds World and spread from there to North America and Europe? I think it is likely. The majority of Christians now reside outside of those continents, and the most vigorous spiritual movements also are taking place in cultures of the so-called Third World. The younger Christian churches of Asia, Africa and Latin America may provide the theological prophet for the next century and perhaps the next millennium. Perhaps the European and North American wells of spiritual and theological renewal have run dry and need to be refreshed from new sources. For over three centuries Western theology has been obsessed with issues and problems posed by modernity so that all of its major branches have become prisoners of that *Zeitgeist,* or cultural ethos. Both liberal and conservative Christian thinkers have tied their ideas about God and salvation too closely to it. A vision of Christian theology unfettered by now-outmoded modern thought forms may have to arise from a non-Western Christian source if the story of Christian theology is to move on into the twenty-first century and third millennium with new vigor and vitality.

Whatever the future of the story of Christian theology brings forth, it is bound to be interesting. It always has been. And there are as-yet unresolved issues for theological reformers to work on. The major one, of course, is the old debate between monergists and synergists over God's relationship with the world. New light from God's Word on that issue is badly needed as the extremes of process theology and resurgent Augustinian-Calvinism polarize Christian thought as never before. While I am neither a prophet nor the son of a prophet, I predict (with fear and trembling) that this issue will be the all-consuming one in Christian theology in the twenty-first century and that new insights and suggestions for resolving it will come from non-Western Christian thinkers. All the options of Western (European and North American) thought seem to have been proposed and have led only to reactions rather than resolutions. If this particular problem of theology is ever to be solved—even in part—the crucial insights will almost certainly need to come from outside of Western culture, with its dualistic mindset that insists on seeing divine and human agencies as in competition with one another.

As Christians we can confidently and joyfully sing with the old gospel hymn, "This is my story!" In spite of all its many troubling aspects and unresolved problems, it is the story of God's work in the world through people dedicated to God's kingdom and Christ's lordship. It is a story of the gradual growth of tradition—a firm foundation of basic Christian beliefs that guide and regulate Christian discipleship. It is also the story of amazing reforms within that tradition that continually called God's people back to the sources of divine revelation and forward to new light breaking forth from it. If the story continues to unfold with great coherence and surprise—two necessary ingredients of any good story—it will be because Christians continue to value the twin principles of tradition and reform by drawing on deep wells continually being refreshed by new springs.

# Notes

### Introduction: Christian Theology as Story

[1]J. G. Sikes, *Peter Abailard* (New York: Russell & Russell, 1965), p. 179.

[2]The development of a Christian canon (limited collection) of inspired Scriptures—what modern Christians call the Bible of the Old and New Testaments—was a painfully slow and lengthy process. The unified church of the Christian Roman Empire (catholic and orthodox church) finally and formally identified a definite list of Christian writings consisting of sixty-six books (Genesis through Revelation) in 392 at a local council of bishops in Hippo, North Africa. This story will be told in detail in chapter 8, "Christianity Gets Its Act Together."

[3]Gregory of Nyssa, *On the Deity of the Son and of the Holy Spirit,* quoted in Harold O. J. Brown, *Heresies: The Image of Christ in the Mirror of Heresy and Orthodoxy from the Apostles to the Present* (Garden City, N.Y.: Doubleday, 1984), p. 104.

[4]Here *doctrine* is being used in a fairly special, technical sense for this category of Christian beliefs. Elsewhere (somewhat confusingly, I admit) I use it in the more common sense of any Christian belief officially taught by someone as a true interpretation of the Bible or of the Great Tradition of the church. For more explication of this entire rubric of "dogma, doctrine, opinion," see Stanley J. Grenz and Roger E. Olson, *Who Needs Theology? An Invitation to the Study of God* (Downers Grove, Ill.: InterVarsity Press, 1996), pp. 73-77.

[5]In this book (as elsewhere for the most part) *church father* designates a particular role as does *Reformer.* Both are technical labels for persons who shaped the theologies of Christianity in general or in particular branches and traditions within Christianity. The label "church father" is not an example of patriarchal preference for men. There simply were no female theologians in the early church. There were women martyrs and mystics, but no women until the nineteenth or even twentieth centuries contributed influentially to the doctrinal formulations of any of the major branches of Christianity. I know of no serious scholar—male or female—who debates that. Therefore, the label "church father" may stand without apology.

[6]During the 1980s a popular phrase for describing President Ronald Reagan's economic policies was "the trickle-down theory." It meant that if the wealthy people of America increased in wealth due to tax cuts, all of society—including the poor—would ultimately benefit. The wealth would "trickle down" through economic growth in the whole economy through job expansion, etc.

### Introduction to Part I: The Opening Act: *Conflicting Christian Visions in the Second Century*

[1]Of course even Jesus and his disciples and apostles could be considered "theologians" in some sense. Insofar as theology is simply any reflection on God and salvation, everyone is a theologian! However, here the term is used to mean something narrower and more specific—reflection on the God of Jesus Christ and on Christ himself as well as on his work and message. In a sense, Jesus Christ and his disciples engaged mainly in the ministry of proclaiming the gospel, while theology takes up the ministry of explaining it.

[2]The definition of *apostle* is debatable. It may belong to a large class of terms generally labeled "essentially contested concepts." That is, for some concepts and terms there is no scholarly consensus as to their exact meaning. One popular theory about early Christian apostles is that they were those men and possibly a few women who were eyewitnesses of the resurrection of

Jesus Christ. This is what gave them special authority in the early churches. Some support for such a view of apostleship may be found in Paul's defense of his own apostleship. He based it on the fact that Christ appeared to him also—even though at a later time and in a different manner than he appeared to Peter and the other apostles (1 Cor 9:1; 15:5-11). It is probable, however, that there was no single qualification for genuine apostleship. It is certain that by the end of the century (100), the impression of nearly all Christians throughout the Roman Empire was that all of the apostles had died. The crisis of authority this created is self-evident. Whatever else they were, the apostles were personal links to Jesus and his teaching, death, resurrection and ascension. They were the founders of the churches and the living authorities for faith and practice. Once they were gone, a different way of settling controversies had to be found.

[3]Modern biblical scholarship has seriously challenged the genuine Johannine authorship of all the writings attributed to Jesus' beloved disciple. The literature on this controversy is vast. Here John's authorship of at least the Gospel of John and the Apocalypse (Revelation) is assumed. A strong case can also be made for his authorship of the three epistles attributed to him that found their way into the New Testament.

**Chapter 1: Critics & Cultists Cause Confusion**

[1]Church father Irenaeus of Lyons reported that he heard this from his own Christian teacher, Polycarp, who was one of John's disciples in Ephesus in the late first century. See Irenaeus, *Against Heresies* 3.3.4 *ANF* 1.

[2]George Trevelyan, *A Vision of the Aquarian Age: The Emerging Spiritual World View* (Walpole, N.H.: Stillpoint, 1984), pp. 1-2.

[3]It is highly unlikely that the second-century Christian Gnostics believed in reincarnation, although it is possible that some of them were influenced by emissaries from India and came to believe in transmigration of souls. Certainly all of the Gnostics believed in a spiritual progression after death that involved a kind of spiritual travel "upward" and back to their true spiritual home in union with God.

[4]Elizabeth Clare Prophet, with Erin L. Prophet, *Reincarnation: The Missing Link in Christianity* (Corwin Springs, Mont.: Summit University Press, 1997).

[5]These alleged sayings of Montanus were recorded by church historian Eusebius and may be found in almost any standard work about second-century Christianity. See Marjorie Strachey, *The Fathers Without Theology* (New York: George Braziller, 1958), p. 169.

[6]Michael G. Maudlin, "Seers in the Heartland: Hot on the Trail of the Kansas City Prophets," *Christianity Today* 35, no. 1 (1991): 18-22.

[7]Fortunately one does not have to peruse Origen's refutation in order to get the contents of Celsus's work. It has been collected, edited and translated for modern readers: Celsus, *On the True Doctrine: A Discourse Against the Christians,* trans. R. Joseph Hoffmann (New York: Oxford University Press, 1987).

[8]Ibid., p. 116.

[9]Ibid., p. 78.

[10]Giovanni Filoramo, *A History of Gnosticism,* trans. Anthony Alcock (Cambridge, U.K.: Basil Blackwell, 1991), p. 2.

[11]Ibid., pp. 52-53.

[12]The five family resemblances are adapted from Stuart G. Hall, *Doctrine and Practice in the Early Church* (Grand Rapids, Mich.: Eerdmans, 1991), pp. 41-44. Hall lists and describes seven family resemblances of Gnostics. I have reduced it to five and revised them somewhat.

[13]Some of the Gnostics' Gospels, including the much-discussed *Gospel of Thomas,* may be found in modern language in Ron Cameron, ed., *The Other Gospels: Noncanonical Gospel Texts* (Philadelphia: Westminster Press, 1982).

[14]The terms *orthodox* and *catholic* will be used frequently in the early chapters of this book simply to designate the early Christian church in its theological correctness and unity. When spelled

without capital letters, they do not signify "Eastern Orthodoxy" or "Roman Catholicism."
[15]Filoramo, *History of Gnosticism,* p. 4.

**Chapter 2: The Apostolic Fathers Explain the Way**

[1]Justo González, *A History of Christian Thought,* vol. 1, *From the Beginnings to the Council of Chalcedon,* rev. ed. (Nashville: Abingdon, 1987), p. 96.
[2]Clement *To the Corinthians* 21:6 Lightfoot, Harmer and Holmes.
[3]Ibid., 44.6.
[4]Ibid., 63.1.
[5]Ibid., 25.
[6]*The Didache* or *The Teaching of the Twelve Apostles* Lightfoot, Harmer and Holmes.
[7]Ibid.
[8]Ibid.
[9]Ignatius *To the Romans* 4 Lightfoot, Harmer and Holmes.
[10]Ibid., p. 81.
[11]Ignatius *To the Magnesians* 7 Lightfoot, Harmer and Holmes.
[12]Ignatius *To the Ephesians* 6 Lightfoot, Harmer and Holmes.
[13]Ignatius *To the Trallians* 10 Lightfoot, Harmer and Holmes.
[14]Ignatius *To the Ephesians* 19.
[15]Ibid., 20.
[16]Ignatius *To Polycarp* 2 Lightfoot, Harmer and Holmes.
[17]*The Epistle of Barnabas* 10 Lightfoot, Harmer and Holmes.
[18]Ibid., 21.
[19]*The Apostolic Fathers,* trans. J. B. Lightfoot and J. R. Harmer, ed. and trans. Michael W. Holmes, 2d ed. (Grand Rapids, Mich.: Baker, 1989), p. 189.
[20]*The Shepherd of Hermas* 31 Lightfoot, Harmer and Holmes.
[21]Ibid., 32.
[22]Ibid., 26.
[23]Ibid., 59.

**Chapter 3: The Apologists Defend the Faith**

[1]Tertullian *Prescription Against Heretics* 7 *ANF* 3.
[2]This generic Greek-Hellenistic philosophy of the Roman Empire in the second century is well described and explained in Christopher Stead, *Philosophy in Christian Antiquity* (Cambridge, U.K.: Cambridge University Press, 1994).
[3]Robert M. Grant, *Gods and the One God* (Philadelphia: Westminster Press, 1986), p. 84.
[4]Robert M. Grant, *Greek Apologists of the Second Century* (Philadelphia: Westminster Press, 1988), p. 11.
[5]Ibid., p. 110.
[6]Ibid., p. 50.
[7]Justin *The First Apology* 2 *ANF* 1.
[8]Ibid., 68.
[9]Justin *The Second Apology* 15 *ANF* 1.
[10]Justin *Dialogue with Trypho, a Jew* 128 *ANF* 1.
[11]Ibid., 68.
[12]Justin *Second Apology* 13.
[13]Athenagoras *A Plea for the Christians* 10 *ANF* 2.
[14]Ibid., 24.
[15]Marcus Dods, "Introductory Note to Theophilus of Antioch," in *ANF,* 2:88.
[16]Theophilus *To Autolycus II* 10 *ANF* 2.
[17]Ibid.

[18]Grant, *Gods and the One God*, p. 87.

**Chapter 4: Irenaeus Exposes Heresies**

[1]R. A. Norris, *God and the World in Early Christian Theology: A Study in Justin Martyr, Irenaeus, Tertullian and Origen* (New York: Seabury Press, 1965), p. 72.
[2]Irenaeus *Against Heresies* 1.11 (selections) *ANF* 1.
[3]Ibid.
[4]Irenaeus *Against Heresies* 3.17.7.
[5]Gustaf Wingren, *Man and the Incarnation: A Study in the Biblical Theology of Irenaeus*, trans. Ross Mackenzie (Philadelphia: Muhlenberg, 1959), pp. 95-96.
[6]Norris, *God and the World*, p. 94.

**Introduction to Part II: The Plot Thickens: *Third-Century Tensions & Transformations***

[1]H. Kraft, *Early Christian Thinkers: An Introduction to Clement of Alexandria and Origen* (New York: Association Press, 1964), p. 9.
[2]The term *Great Church* here refers to the undivided church of both East and West (Greek and Latin) in the Roman Empire during the first few centuries of Christianity. It is the universal church whose bishops claimed to be the apostles' true heirs. It is an abstract concept and does not refer to a particular building or specific congregation. This family of congregations and their leaders (elders, bishops) laid claim to being "orthodox" (theologically correct), "apostolic" (descending through teachings and ordination from the apostles themselves) and "catholic" (united throughout the world). Later the term *Great Church* also came to designate the great cathedral in the heart of Constantinople (Byzantium), known also as the Hagia Sophia. The two uses of the term should not be confused here.

**Chapter 5: North African Thinkers Examine Philosophy**

[1]Hans von Campenhausen, *The Fathers of the Greek Church*, trans. Stanley Godman (New York: Pantheon, 1959), p. 34.
[2]Clement of Alexandria *The Instructor (Paedagogus)* 1.13 *ANF* 2.
[3]Clement of Alexandria *The Stromata (Miscellanies)* 1.1 *ANF* 2.
[4]H. Kraft, *Early Christian Thinkers: An Introduction to Clement of Alexandria and Origen* (New York: Association Press, 1964), p. 33.
[5]Clement *Stromata* 1:1.
[6]Ibid., 1.20.
[7]Ibid., 1.22.
[8]Clement *Instructor* 1.2.
[9]Ibid., 1.2.
[10]For definitions and descriptions of these two modern approaches to Christian theology, see Stanley J. Grenz and Roger E. Olson, *20th-Century Theology: God & the World in a Transitional Age* (Downers Grove, Ill.: InterVarsity Press, 1992).
[11]Timothy David Barnes, *Tertullian: A Historical and Literary Study* (Oxford, U.K.: Clarendon, 1971), p. 142.
[12]Tertullian, quoted in Justo González, *A History of Christian Thought*, vol. 1, *From the Beginnings to the Council of Chalcedon*, rev. ed. (Nashville: Abingdon, 1992), p. 178.
[13]González, *History of Christian Thought*, 1:178.
[14]Tertullian *Apology* 21 *ANF* 3.
[15]Tertullian *Prescription Against Heretics* 7 *ANF* 3.
[16]Ibid., 13.
[17]Tertullian *On the Flesh of Christ* 5 *ANF* 3.
[18]González, *History of Christian Thought*, 1:175.
[19]Tertullian *On Baptism* *ANF* 3.

[20]Tertullian *Against Praxeas* 1 *ANF* 3.
[21]Tertullian *Against Praxeas* 2.
[22]Ibid., 8.
[23]Ibid., 30.
[24]Clement's "true gnostic" was intended to be different from and an alternative to a follower of the kind of Gnosticism that flourished as a heresy in second-century Egypt.

**Chapter 6: Origen of Alexandria Leaves a Troubling Legacy**
[1]Henri Crouzel, *Origen,* trans. A. S. Worrall (San Francisco: Harper & Row, 1989), p. 14.
[2]Ibid., p. 37.
[3]Ibid., pp. 27-28.
[4]Origen *Against Celsus* 68 *ANF* 4.
[5]Ibid., 6.18.
[6]Crouzel, *Origen,* p. 158.
[7]Origen *Against Celsus* 68.
[8]Origen *De Principiis* 3.1 *ANF* 4.
[9]Crouzel, *Origen,* pp. 257ff.
[10]Origen *De Principiis* 3.6.
[11]Origen *Against Celsus* 4.72.
[12]For example, Origen believed in the creation of the world out of nothing *(creatio ex nihilo),* against the preponderance of Greek thought, and in the resurrection of bodies, which was also anathema to most educated Greeks.
[13]Origen *De Principiis* 1.
[14]Ibid.
[15]Origen *Against Celsus* 4.14.
[16]Origen *De Principiis* 1.
[17]Origen, quoted in Crouzel, *Origen,* p. 187.
[18]Origen *De Principiis* 1.
[19]Origen, quoted in Crouzel, *Origen,* p. 203.
[20]Origen *De Principiis* 2.
[21]Origen *Against Celsus* 7.16.
[22]Crouzel, *Origen,* pp. 171, 174.

**Chapter 7: Cyprian of Carthage Promotes Unity**
[1]Hans von Campenhausen, *The Fathers of the Latin Church,* trans. Manfred Hoffman (Stanford, Calif.: Stanford University Press, 1964), p. 37.
[2]Pontius the Deacon *The Life and Passion of Cyprian, Bishop and Martyr* 1.3 *ANF* 5.
[3]Cyprian *Epistle 1, To Donatus* 3; 4 *ANF* 5.
[4]Cyprian *Epistle 58, To Fidus, On the Baptism of Infants* 5 *ANF* 5.
[5]Cyprian *Epistle 71, To Jubaianus, Concerning the Baptism of Heretics* 5 *ANF* 5.
[6]Ibid., 7.
[7]Cyprian *Treatise 1: On the Unity of the Church* 2 *ANF* 5.
[8]Cyprian *Epistle 6, To "Confessors"* 2 *ANF* 5.
[9]Justo González, *A History of Christian Thought,* vol. 1, *From the Beginnings to the Council of Chalcedon,* rev. ed. (Nashville: Abingdon, 1992), p. 242.
[10]Cyprian *On the Unity of the Church* 23.
[11]Ibid., 7; 6.
[12]Cyprian *Epistle 26, Cyprian to the Lapsed* 1 *ANF* 5.
[13]González, *History of Christian Thought,* 1:244.
[14]Ibid., p. 245.
[15]Hans Leitzmann, *A History of the Early Church,* vol. 2, *The Founding of the Church Universal*

(Cleveland and New York: World, 1950), p. 57.

[16]Hans von Campenhausen, *Ecclesiastical Authority and Spiritual Power in the Church of the First Three Centuries,* trans. J. A. Baker (Stanford, Calif.: Stanford University Press, 1969), p. 290.

**Chapter 8: Christianity Gets Its Act Together**

[1]W. H. C. Frend, *The Rise of Christianity* (Philadelphia: Fortress, 1984), pp. 401-2.

[2]Ibid., pp. 405-7.

[3]Ibid., p. 403.

[4]Ibid., p. 405.

[5]Ibid., p. 407.

[6]This is known as the "Vincentian Canon" after its author, Vincent of Leríns, a fifth- to sixth-century theologian of France.

[7]Gerald Bray, *Creeds, Councils & Christ* (Leicester, U.K., and Downers Grove, Ill.: Inter-Varsity Press, 1984), pp. 204-5. The italicized words indicate changes from an earlier form of the creed in the Book of Common Prayer of the Church of England.

[8]Ibid., p. 101.

[9]Of course later the so-called apocrypha of thirteen or fourteen intertestamental books that were in the Septuagint were included in the Christian Bible by the Western, Latin (Roman Catholic) churches. The Eastern, Greek churches came over time to respect them as secondary sources of historical information and inspiration while rejecting them as having the same authority as the other books of the Old and New Testaments. During the Protestant Reformation, most of the Reformers followed the Eastern churches' pattern and eventually dropped the apocrypha altogether because those books became identified too closely with Roman Catholic theology.

[10]Hans von Campenhausen, *The Formation of the Christian Bible,* trans., J. A. Baker (Philadelphia: Fortress, 1972), p. 148.

[11]Ibid., p. 254.

[12]Ibid., p. 327.

**Chapter 9: Alexandrians Argue About the Son of God**

[1]Frances Young, *From Nicea to Chalcedon* (Philadelphia: Fortress, 1983), p. 59.

[2]Robert C. Gregg and Dennis E. Groh, *Early Arianism: A View of Salvation* (Philadelphia: Fortress, 1981), p. 8.

[3]Ibid., p. 9.

[4]Bernard Lonergan, *The Way to Nicea,* trans. Conn O'Donovan (Philadelphia: Westminster Press, 1976), pp. 70-71.

[5]Athanasius *Deposition of Arius* 6 *NPNF* 4.

[6]The Watchtower Bible and Tract Society, or Jehovah's Witnesses, teach that Jesus Christ is the incarnation of the archangel Michael, who is God's first and greatest creature and through whom God created the world and by whom God provided sacrifice for sin. Arius and his followers in the fourth century did not so identify the Logos or Son of God. However, the basic structure of their belief about the Son of God is nearly identical to the Jehovah's Witnesses': the Son of God is a great creature and not of the same nature as God the Father, who alone is truly and fully "God." For more on the Jehovah's Witnesses' teaching, see their publication *Should You Believe in the Trinity?* (Watchtower Bible and Tract Society of Pennsylvania, 1989) and the evangelical response by Robert Bowman, *Why You Should Believe in the Trinity* (Grand Rapids, Mich.: Baker, 1989).

[7]Athanasius *Deposition of Arius* 2.

**Chapter 10: The Church Responds at the Council of Nicaea**

[1]Justo González, *A History of Christian Thought,* vol. 1, *From the Beginnings to the Council of Chalcedon,* rev. ed. (Nashville: Abingdon, 1992), pp. 266-67.

[2]Ibid., p. 267.
[3]Ibid., pp. 267-68.
[4]Ibid., p. 271.

**Chapter 11: Athanasius Stubbornly Keeps the Faith**

[1]Justo González, *A History of Christian Thought,* vol. 1, *From the Beginnings to the Council of Chalcedon,* rev. ed. (Nashville: Abingdon, 1992), p. 291.
[2]W. H. C. Frend, *The Rise of Christianity* (Philadelphia: Fortress Press, 1984), p. 524.
[3]Frances Young, *From Nicea to Chalcedon* (Philadelphia: Fortress, 1983), pp. 82-83.
[4]Harold O. J. Brown in *Heresies: The Image of Christ in the Mirror of Heresy and Orthodoxy from the Apostles to the Present* (Garden City, N.Y.: Doubleday, 1984), p. 119.
[5]Alvyn Pettersen, *Athanasius* (Harrisburg, Penn.: Morehouse, 1995), p. 188.
[6]Ibid., p. 175.
[7]Ibid., p. 18.
[8]Young, *From Nicea to Chalcedon,* p. 72.
[9]Athanasius *Four Discourses Against the Arians* 1.14 *NPNF2* 4.
[10]Ibid., 1.25.
[11]Ibid., 2.35.
[12]Athanasius *On the Incarnation of the Word* 17.4 *NPNF2* 4.
[13]Athanasius *Against the Arians* 2.67.
[14]Athanasius *On the Incarnation of the Word* 54.3.
[15]Ibid., 8.2 and 4.
[16]Young, *From Nicea to Chalcedon,* pp. 74-75.
[17]Pettersen, *Athanasius,* p. 157.
[18]Athanasius *Against the Arians* 2.81.
[19]Pettersen, *Athanasius,* p. 187.

**Chapter 12: The Cappadocian Fathers Settle the Issue**

[1]Gregory of Nyssa, *On the Deity of the Son and of the Holy Spirit,* quoted in Harold O. J. Brown in *Heresies: The Image of Christ in the Mirror of Heresy and Orthodoxy from the Apostles to the Present* (Garden City, N.Y.: Doubleday, 1984), p. 104.
[2]Justo González, *A History of Christian Thought,* vol. 1, *From the Beginnings to the Council of Chalcedon,* rev. ed. (Nashville: Abingdon, 1992), p. 300.
[3]Ibid., p. 322.
[4]Ibid., p. 324.
[5]Anthony Meredith, *The Cappadocians* (Crestwood, N.Y.: St. Vladimir's Seminary Press, 1995), p. 103.
[6]*Binity* is perhaps not found in any dictionary, but it helpfully describes the pneumatomachian doctrine of the Godhead as consisting only of Father and Son.
[7]Frances Young, *From Nicea to Chalcedon* (Philadelphia: Fortress, 1983), p. 114.
[8]Editor's introduction to *The Select Orations of Saint Gregory of Nazianzen: The "Theological Orations," NPNF2* 7, p. 280.
[9]Young, *From Nicea to Chalcedon,* p. 95.
[10]Basil *Letter 38, To His Brother Gregory* 7 *NPNF2* 8.
[11]Basil *De Spiritu Sancto: On the Spirit* 10.24 *NPNF2* 8.
[12]Ibid.
[13]Ibid., 15.36.
[14]Ibid., 10.25.
[15]Basil *Letter 8, To the Caesareans* 2 *NPNF2* 8.
[16]Basil *Letter 38, To His Brother Gregory* 3.
[17]Ibid., 5.

[18]As already noted, some scholars believe that Basil's priority in terms of influence among the three Cappadocian fathers is not clear and would argue for a greater interdependence among the three. However, it is traditional in historical theology to treat Basil the Great as the "first among equals" of the three friends. While his genius may not have been as great as his brother's, he was significantly older and was probably Gregory of Nyssa's mentor and inspirer. Gregory of Nazianzus does not seem to have been as original a thinker as either of the other two.

[19]Gregory of Nazianzus *Fourth Theological Oration* 4 *NPNF2* 7.

[20]Gregory of Nazianzus *Fifth Theological Oration* 11 *NPNF2* 7.

[21]Ibid., 8.

[22]González, *History of Christian Thought,* 1:316.

[23]Gregory of Nazianzus *Third Theological Oration* 19 *NPNF2* 7.

[24]Gregory *Letter 101,* quoted in Meredith, *Cappadocians,* p. 44.

[25]Gregory *Fourth Theological Oration* 21.

[26]Gregory of Nyssa *On "Not Three Gods": To Ablabius NPNF2* 5.

[27]Ibid.

[28]Ibid.

[29]Ibid.

[30]Meredith, *Cappadocians,* p. 44.

[31]Gerald Bray, *Creeds, Councils & Christ* (Leicester, U.K., and Downers Grove, Ill.: Inter-Varsity Press, 1984), pp. 206-7. The words in italics are meant to indicate changes from one English translation of the creed to a newer one.

**Chapter 13: The Schools of Antioch & Alexandria Clash over Christ**

[1]R. V. Sellers, *The Council of Chalcedon: A Historical and Doctrinal Survey* (London: SPCK, 1961), p. 136.

[2]Justo González, *A History of Christian Thought,* vol. 1, *From the Beginnings to the Council of Chalcedon,* rev. ed. (Nashville: Abingdon, 1992), p. 340.

[3]Sellers, *Council of Chalcedon,* p. xv.

[4]H. Maurice Relton, *A Study in Christology: The Problem of the Relation of the Two Natures in the Person of Christ* (New York: Macmillan, 1934), p. 11.

[5]Gregory of Nazianzus *Epistle 101 NPNF2* 7.

[6]Theodore of Mopsuestia, *Commentary of Theodore of Mopsuestia on the Nicene Creed,* ed. A. Mingana (Cambridge, U.K.: Heffer, 1932), p. 82.

**Chapter 14: Nestorius & Cyril Bring the Controversy to a Head**

[1]Justo González, *A History of Christian Thought,* vol. 1, *From the Beginnings to the Council of Chalcedon,* rev. ed. (Nashville: Abingdon, 1992), p. 361.

[2]Aloys Grillmeier, S.J., *Christ in Christian Tradition,* vol. 1, *From the Apostolic Age to Chalcedon (451),* 2d, rev. ed., trans. John Bowden (Atlanta, Ga.: John Knox Press, 1975), p. 462.

[3]Ibid., p. 576.

[4]Ibid., p. 477.

[5]Ibid., p. 486.

[6]Ibid.

[7]Ibid., p. 479.

**Chapter 15: Chalcedon Protects the Mystery**

[1]R. V. Sellers, *The Council of Chalcedon: A Historical and Doctrinal Survey* (London: SPCK, 1961), p. 29.

[2]Ibid., p. 33.

[3]Justo González, *A History of Christian Thought,* vol. 1, *From the Beginnings to the Council of*

*Chalcedon,* rev. ed. (Nashville: Abingdon, 1992), p. 371.
[4]Sellers, *Council of Chalcedon,* p. 87.
[5]Ibid., p. 103.
[6]Ibid., p. 109.
[7]Gerald Bray, *Creeds, Councils & Christ,* (Leicester, U.K., and Downers Grove, Ill.: Inter-Varsity Press, 1984), p. 162.
[8]H. Maurice Relton, *A Study in Christology: The Problem of the Relation of the Two Natures in the Person of Christ* (New York: Macmillan, 1934), p. 36.
[9]Ibid., p. 53.

**Chapter 16: Fallout from the Conflict Continues**
[1]H. Maurice Relton, *A Study in Christology: The Problem of the Relation of the Two Natures in the Person of Christ* (New York: Macmillan, 1934), p. 66.
[2]Frances Young, *From Nicea to Chalcedon* (Philadelphia: Fortress, 1983), p. 178.
[3]R. V. Sellers, *The Council of Chalcedon: A Historical and Doctrinal Survey* (London: SPCK, 1961), p. 254.
[4]Relton, *Study in Christology,* p. 66.
[5]Ibid., p. 67.
[6]Justo González, *A History of Christian Thought,* vol. 2, *From Augustine to the Eve of the Reformation,* rev. ed. (Nashville, Tenn.: Abingdon, 1987), p. 78.
[7]John Meyendorff, *Christ in Eastern Christian Thought* (Crestwood, N.Y.: St. Vladimir's Seminary Press, 1987), p. 38.
[8]Ibid.
[9]Severus, quoted in González, *History of Christian Thought,* 2:77-78.
[10]Timothy Aelurus, quoted in Sellers, *Council of Chalcedon,* p. 260.
[11]Sellers, *Council of Chalcedon,* p. 316.
[12]Ibid.
[13]Relton, *Study in Christology,* p. 77.
[14]Ibid.
[15]González, *History of Christian Thought,* 2:97.
[16]Ibid., pp. 97-98.
[17]Sellers, *Council of Chalcedon,* p. 320.
[18]González, *History of Christian Thought,* 2:86.
[19]Sellers, *Council of Chalcedon,* p. 341.
[20]González, *History of Christian Thought,* 2:91

**Chapter 17: Augustine Confesses God's Glory & Human Depravity**
[1]Justo González, *A History of Christian Thought,* vol. 2, *From Augustine to the Eve of the Reformation,* rev. ed. (Nashville, Tenn.: Abingdon, 1987), p. 15.
[2]T. Kermit Scott, *Augustine: His Thought in Context* (Mahwah, N.J.: Paulist, 1995), p. 153.
[3]Ibid., p. 13.
[4]Augustine *The Confessions* 8.12.
[5]Scott, *Augustine,* p. 153.
[6]Gerald Bonner, *St. Augustine of Hippo: Life and Controversies* (Norwich: Canterbury, 1986), p. 157.
[7]Augustine *Concerning the Nature of Good* 4.
[8]Ibid., 36.
[9]Bonner, *St. Augustine of Hippo,* p. 204.
[10]Ibid., p. 284.
[11]Ibid., p. 287.
[12]Ibid., p. 290.

[13]Ibid., p. 292.
[14]Augustine *The Enchiridion: On Faith, Hope and Love* 52.
[15]Augustine *On Nature and Grace* 9.
[16]Augustine, quoted in Bonner, *St. Augustine of Hippo,* p. 317.
[17]B. R. Rees, *Pelagius: A Reluctant Heretic* (Woodbridge and Rochester: Boydell, 1988).
[18]Pelagius, quoted in Rees, *Pelagius: A Reluctant Heretic,* p. 91.
[19]Ibid.
[20]Ibid., p. 93.
[21]Augustine *The Enchiridion* 26.
[22]Augustine *On the Grace of Christ and On Original Sin* 44.
[23]Augustine *On the Spirit and the Letter* 5.
[24]Scott, *Augustine,* p. 162.
[25]Augustine *On Grace and Free Will* 41.
[26]Scott, *Augustine,* p. 181.
[27]Augustine *On Grace and Free Will* 28.
[28]Augustine *On Nature and Grace* 2.
[29]Augustine *On Grace and Free Will* 45.
[30]Ibid.
[31]Scott, *Augustine,* p. 224.
[32]Augustine *The Enchiridion* 96.
[33]Scott, *Augustine,* p. 227.

**Chapter 18: The Western Church Becomes Roman Catholic**
[1]Edgar C. S. Gibson, "Prolegomena" to *The Works of John Cassian, NPNF2* 11, p. 189.
[2]Ibid., p. 191.
[3]John Cassian *Conference 13, The Third Conference of Abbot Chaeremon* 11 *NPNF2* 11.
[4]Ibid.
[5]Cassian *Conference 18, Third Conference* 8 *NPNF2* 11.
[6]Ibid., 16.
[7]Ibid., 17.
[8]If this description of the official Roman Catholic theology of salvation as pronounced at the Synod of Orange in 529 seems somewhat confused and confusing, that may be because the statements of the synod and later interpretations within Catholic theology are somewhat inconsistent with each other. For example, the teaching of the Synod of Orange on predestination includes the following:

> According to Catholic faith we also believe that after grace has been received through baptism, all the baptized, if they are willing to labor faithfully, can and ought to accomplish with Christ's help and cooperation what pertains to the salvation of their souls. We do not believe that some are predestined to evil by the divine power; and, furthermore, if there are those who wish to believe in such an enormity, with great abhorrence we anathematize them. We also believe and profess for our salvation that in every good work it is not that we make a beginning and afterwards are helped through God's mercy, but rather, that without any previous good merits on our part, God himself first inspires us with faith in him and love of him so that we may faithfully seek the sacrament of baptism, and so that after baptism, with his help, we may be able to accomplish what is pleasing to him. (*The Church Teaches: Documents of the Church in English Translation,* [St. Louis & London: Herder, 1955], p. 228)

On the one hand, the synod affirmed faith as a gift of God rather than a free decision of the human person in response to grace—an idea that would seem to involve belief in predestination—and on the other hand, it affirmed the necessity of grace-assisted meritorious works for full salvation. This is an unstable combination of monergism and synergism and has led to tensions within Catholic theology ever since. Apparently, it is legitimate for a Roman Catholic to believe in a moderate monergism (without any hint of predestination to evil) or in a moderate synergism (without any hint of human initiative or meritorious work for salvation apart from assisting grace).

[9]Judith Herron, *The Formation of Christendom* (Princeton, N.J.: Princeton University Press, 1987), p. 150.

[10]Justo González, *A History of Christian Thought*, vol. 2, *From Augustine to the Eve of the Reformation*, rev. ed. (Nashville, Tenn.: Abingdon, 1987), p. 71.

[11]Gregory, quoted in Carole Straw, *Gregory the Great: Perfection in Imperfection* (Berkeley: University of California Press, 1988), p. 140.

[12]Ibid.

[13]Ibid., p. 159.

[14]Gregory *The Book of Pastoral Rule of Saint Gregory the Great* 27 *NPNF2* 12.

**Chapter 19: The Eastern Church Becomes Eastern Orthodox**

[1]John Meyendorff, *Byzantine Theology: Historical Trends and Doctrinal Themes* (New York: Fordham University Press, 1974), pp. 25-26.

[2]Ibid., p. 115.

[3]The Roman Catholic Church recognizes twenty-one ecumenical councils so far, with the most recent one being Vatican II in 1962-1965. There will surely be more ecumenical councils of the Roman Church. The Eastern church stopped recognizing councils as "ecumenical" with the seventh, and there is even some debate among Eastern Orthodox Christians as to the exact nature of that one. In general, however, Eastern Orthodox tradition is not open to more ecumenical councils. All truly important issues of theology are settled.

[4]Meyendorff, *Byzantine Theology*, p. 116.

[5]Ibid., p. 128.

[6]J. N. D. Kelly, *Golden Mouth: The Story of John Chrysostom—Ascetic, Preacher, Bishop* (Ithaca, N.Y.: Cornell University Press, 1995), p. 94.

[7]Ibid., pp. 135-36.

[8]Ibid., p. 130.

[9]Maximus, quoted in *The Byzantine Fathers of the Sixth to Eighth Century*, vol. 9, *The Collected Works of Georges Florovsky*, ed. Richard S. Haugh, trans. Raymond Miller, Anne-Marie Döllinger-Labriolle and Helmut Wilhelm Schmiedel (Vaduz, Liechtenstein: Büchervertriebsanstalt, 1987), p. 211.

[10]John Meyendorff, *Christ in Eastern Christian Thought* (Crestwood, N.Y.: St. Vladimir's Seminary Press, 1987), p. 132.

[11]Maximus, quoted in *Byzantine Fathers*, 9:220.

[12]Ibid., p. 223.

[13]Ibid., p. 216.

[14]Lars Thunberg, *Man and the Cosmos: The Vision of St. Maximus the Confessor* (Crestwood, N.Y.: St. Vladimir's Seminary Press, 1985), p. 71.

[15]*Byzantine Fathers*, 9:206.

[16]Meyendorff, *Christ in Eastern Christian Thought*, p. 149.

[17]Justo González, *A History of Christian Thought*, vol. 2, *From Augustine to the Eve of the Reformation*, rev. ed. (Nashville, Tenn.: Abingdon, 1987), p. 200.

[18]*Byzantine Fathers*, 9:254.

[19]John of Damascus, quoted in Meyendorff, *Byzantine Theology*, pp. 45-46.

[20]"The Decree of the Holy, Great, Ecumenical Synod, the Second of Nice," *The Seven Ecumenical Councils of the Undivided Church NPNF2* 14.

**Chapter 20: The Great Schism Creates Two Traditions Out of One**

[1]The term *Great Schism* is used twice for two entirely distinct events in the history of Christianity.

Here it designates the split between Eastern Orthodoxy and Roman Catholicism that is still unhealed. Later on it is used again to designate a split in the Roman Catholic Church between two and then three popes during the Middle Ages. It is important not to confuse these two entirely distinct events even though the same term is traditionally used for both.

[2]Jaroslav Pelikan, *The Christian Tradition: A History of the Development of Doctrine,* vol. 2, *The Spirit of Eastern Christendom (600-1700)* (Chicago: University of Chicago Press, 1974), p. 179.

[3]John Meyendorff, *Byzantine Theology: Historical Trends and Doctrinal Themes* (New York: Fordham University Press, 1974), p. 98.

[4]Ibid., p. 91.

[5]Ibid., pp. 91-92.

[6]Pelikan, *Christian Tradition,* 2:171.

**Introduction to Part VI: The Saga of the Queen of the Sciences: *Scholastics Revive & Enthrone Theology***

[1]B. B. Price, *Medieval Thought: An Introduction* (Oxford: Blackwell, 1992), p. 120.

[2]Ibid., p. 130.

[3]Ibid., p. 121.

[4]Ibid., p. 142.

**Chapter 21: Anselm & Abelard Speculate About God's Ways**

[1]Justo González, *A History of Christian Thought,* vol. 2, *From Augustine to the Eve of the Reformation,* rev. ed. (Nashville, Tenn.: Abingdon, 1987), p. 167.

[2]Joseph M. Colleran, "Introduction: St. Anselm's Life," in Anselm of Canterbury, *Why God Became Man and The Virgin Conception and Original Sin,* trans. Joseph M. Colleran (Albany, N.Y.: Magi, 1969), p. 21.

[3]Ibid., p. 17.

[4]Ibid., p. 15.

[5]*St. Anselm: Basic Writings (Proslogium, Monologium, Cur Deus homo, and the Fool by Gaunilon),* 2d ed., trans. S. N. Deane, intro., Charles Hartshorne (LaSalle, Ill.: Open Court, 1962), pp. 6-7.

[6]Jasper Hopkins, *A Companion to the Study of St. Anselm* (Minneapolis: University of Minnesota, 1972), p. 66.

[7]*St. Anselm: Basic Writings,* pp. 42-43.

[8]Ibid., p. 7.

[9]Ibid., p. 8.

[10]Ibid., pp. 13-14.

[11]Carol Straw, *Gregory the Great: Perfection in Imperfection* (Berkeley: University of California Press, 1988), p. 155.

[12]Colleran, "Introduction," pp. 34-35.

[13]Anselm of Canterbury, *Why God Became Man and The Virgin Conception and Original Sin,* trans. Joseph M. Colleran (Albany, N.Y.: Magi, 1969), p. 55.

[14]González, *History of Christian Thought,* 2:167.

[15]Ibid., p. 170.

[16]Leif Grave, *Peter Abelard: Philosophy and Christianity in the Middle Ages,* trans. Frederick and Christine Crowley (New York: Harcourt, Brace & Word, 1964), p. 151.

[17]Ibid., p. 157.

[18]Peter Abelard, quoted in J. G. Sikes, *Peter Abailard* (New York: Russell & Russell, 1965), p. 208.

[19]Ibid., pp. 210-11.

[20]Ibid., p. 210.

## Chapter 22: Thomas Aquinas Summarizes Christian Truth

[1]Philotheus Boehm, introduction to William of Ockham, *Philosophical Writings: A Selection* (Indianapolis: Bobbs-Merrill, 1957), pp. xvi-xvii.
[2]Brian Davies, *The Thought of Thomas Aquinas* (Oxford: Clarendon, 1992), p. 2.
[3]Ibid., p. 5.
[4]Ibid., p. 8.
[5]Thomas Aquinas *The Summa Theologica* part 1, question 1.
[6]Aquinas *Summa Theologica* part 7, question 93.
[7]Aquinas's "five ways" of demonstrating God's existence by reason alone may be found in Aquinas, *Summa Theologica* part 1 question 2.
[8]Aquinas *Summa Theologica* part 1, question 2.
[9]Ibid.
[10]Ibid.
[11]Ibid.
[12]Ibid.
[13]Ibid.
[14]Davies, *Thought of Thomas Aquinas,* p. 39.
[15]Aquinas *Summa Theologica* part 1, question 9.
[16]Justo González, *A History of Christian Thought,* vol. 2, *From Augustine to the Eve of the Reformation,* rev. ed. (Nashville: Abingdon, 1987), p. 265.
[17]Ibid., p. 267.
[18]Aquinas *Summa Theologica* part 1, question 4.
[19]Aquinas *Summa Theologica* part 1, question 9.
[20]Thomas Aquinas, quoted in Davies, *Thought of Thomas Aquinas,* p. 75.
[21]Ibid., p. 77.
[22]Ibid., p. 157.
[23]Davies, *Thought of Thomas Aquinas,* p. 64.
[24]Aquinas *Summa Theologica* part 1, question 13.
[25]Davies, *Thought of Thomas Aquinas,* p. 67.
[26]*Thomism* is a label for Thomas Aquinas's basic theological approach and his fundamental doctrinal perspectives.
[27]Davies, *Thought of Thomas Aquinas,* p. 262.
[28]Ibid., p. 264.
[29]Ibid., pp. 338-39.
[30]Aquinas *Summa Theologica* part 1, question 83.
[31]Davies, *Thought of Thomas Aquinas,* p. 185.

## Chapter 23: Nominalists, Reformers & Humanists Challenge the Scholastic Synthesis

[1]Meyrick H. Carré, *Realists and Nominalists* (London: Oxford University Press, 1946), p. 103.
[2]Ibid., p. 107.
[3]Ibid., p. 112.
[4]William of Ockham is not as obscure a figure of history as some might suppose. Like many of the characters of the story of Christian theology, Ockham appears in modern literature and media as well as in books of historical theology. Two popular late-twentieth-century novels and the movies based on them serve as cases in point. In Italian novelist Umberto Eco's 1983 novel *The Name of the Rose* the main character (played by actor Sean Connery in the movie) is loosely based on Ockham. Astronomer and writer Carl Sagan mentioned Ockham and his "razor" in his 1985 novel *Contact* (made into a feature movie in 1997). Many people consider William of Ockham to have been the first "modern man" because of his revolutionary ideas about knowledge, politics and philosophy. By profession, however,

he was a Christian theologian.
[5]Carré, *Realists and Nominalists,* p. 104.
[6]Ibid., p. 107.
[7]Ibid.
[8]Ibid., p. 117. For Ockham's own treatment of universals, see William of Ockham, *Philosophical Writings: A Selection,* trans. Philotheus Boehm (Indianapolis: Bobbs-Merrill, 1957), pp. 35-44.
[9]For an excellent discussion of Ockham's view of faith, reason and natural theology, see Boehner,'s introduction to Ockham, *Philosophical Writings,* pp. xlv-xlvi.
[10]Carré, *Realists and Nominalists,* pp. 121.
[11]Boehner's introduction to Ockham, *Philosophical Writings,* pp. xlviii-xlix.
[12]Justo González, *A History of Christian Thought,* vol. 2, *From Augustine to the Eve of the Reformation,* rev. ed. (Nashville: Abingdon, 1987), p. 319.
[13]Carré, *Realists and Nominalists,* pp. 116.
[14]B. B. Price, *Medieval Thought: An Introduction* (Oxford: Blackwell, 1992), p. 153.
[15]Ibid., p. 153.
[16]John Wycliffe, quoted in John Stacey, *John Wyclif and Reform* (Philadelphia: Westminster Press, 1964), p. 21.
[17]Ibid., p. 42.
[18]Stacey, *John Wyclif,* p. 52.
[19]Wycliffe, quoted in Stacey, *John Wyclif,* p. 107.
[20]Matthew Spinka, ed., *Advocates of Reform: From Wyclif to Erasmus,* The Library of Christian Classics 14 (Philadelphia: Westminster Press, 1953), p. 49.
[21]Ibid., p. 26.
[22]Stacey, *John Wyclif*, p. 156.
[23]Johan Huizinga, *Erasmus and the Age of Reformation* (New York: Harper, 1957), p. 116.
[24]Stefan Zweig, *Erasmus of Rotterdam,* trans. Eden Paul and Cedar Paul (New York: Viking, 1956), pp. 7-8.
[25]Erasmus, quoted in Spinka, *Advocates of Reform,* p. 338.
[26]Spinka, *Advocates of Reform,* p. 288.
[27]Zweig, *Erasmus of Rotterdam,* p. 102.
[28]Ibid., p. 187.
[29]E. Gordon Rupp and Philip S. Watson, eds., *Luther and Erasmus: Free Will and Salvation* (Philadelphia: Westminster Press, 1964), p. 51.
[30]Ibid., p. 140.
[31]John P. Dolan, ed., *The Essential Erasmus* (New York: New American Library, 1964), p. 377.
[32]Ibid., p. 378.
[33]Ibid., p. 364.
[34]Ibid., p. 369.
[35]Ibid., p. 379.
[36]Ibid.

**Introduction to Part VII: A New Twist in the Narrative: *The Western Church Reforms and Divides***

[1]John Dillenberger, ed., *Martin Luther: Selections From His Writings* (Garden City, N.Y.: Doubleday, 1961), p. xviii.

**Chapter 24: Luther Rediscovers the Gospel & Divides the Church**

[1]David C. Steinmetz, *Luther in Context* (Bloomington, Ind.: Indiana University Press, 1986), p. 5.
[2]Heiko Oberman, *Luther: Man Between God and the Devil,* trans. Eileen Walliser-Scharzbart (New York: Doubleday, 1992), p. 120.

[3]Martin Luther, "Preface to the Complete Edition of Luther's Latin Writings," in *Martin Luther: Selections From His Writings,* ed. John Dillenberger (Garden City, N.Y.: Doubleday, 1961), p. 11.
[4]Martin Luther, "The Ninety-Five Theses," in *Martin Luther: Selections From His Writings,* p. 498.
[5]Oberman, *Luther,* p. 203.
[6]Martin Luther, "Confession Concerning Christ's Supper," in *Martin Luther's Basic Theological Writings,* ed. Timothy Lull (Minneapolis: Fortress, 1989), p. 389.
[7]Oberman, *Luther,* p. 79.
[8]Steinmetz, *Luther in Context,* p. 41.
[9]Paul Althaus, *The Theology of Martin Luther,* trans. Robert C. Shultz (Philadelphia: Fortress, 1966), p. 121.
[10]Oberman, *Luther,* p. 154.
[11]Martin Luther, "The Heidelberg Disputation," in *Martin Luther's Basic Theological Writings,* p. 31.
[12]Althaus, *Theology of Martin Luther,* p. 26.
[13]Ibid., p. 27.
[14]Ibid., p. 30.
[15]Martin Luther, quoted in Timothy George, *Theology of the Reformers* (Nashville: Broadman, 1988), p. 77.
[16]Ibid., p. 79.
[17]Martin Luther, *"De Servo Arbitrio* (On the Bondage of the Will)," in *Luther and Erasmus: Free Will and Salvation,* ed. E. Gordon Rupp and trans. Philip S. Watson (Philadelphia: Westminster Press, 1969), p. 236-37.
[18]Althaus, *Theology of Martin Luther,* p. 23.
[19]Oberman, *Luther,* p. 160.
[20]Althaus, *Theology of Martin Luther,* p. 11.
[21]Martin Luther, "Concerning Rebaptism," in *Martin Luther's Basic Theological Writings,* p. 346.
[22]Martin Luther, "Prefaces to the New Testament," in *Martin Luther's Basic Theological Writings,* p. 115.
[23]Martin Luther, quoted in Althaus, *The Theology of Martin Luther,* p. 75 n.8.
[24]Ibid., p. 81.
[25]Luther, "Prefaces to the New Testament," p. 117.
[26]Althaus, *Theology of Martin Luther,* p. 38.
[27]Ibid., p. 165.
[28]Ibid., p. 166.
[29]Ibid., pp. 24-40.
[30]Ibid., p. 225.
[31]Ibid., p. 149.
[32]Oberman, *Luther,* p. 184.
[33]Martin Luther, "Two Kinds of Righteousness in Christ," in *Martin Luther's Basic Theological Writings,* p. 156.
[34]Martin Luther, "A Commentary on St. Paul's Epistle to the Galatians," in *Martin Luther: Selections From His Writings,* p. 130.
[35]Althaus, *Theology of Martin Luther,* p. 44.
[36]Martin Luther, "The Freedom of a Christian," in *Martin Luther: Selections From His Writings,* p. 64.
[37]Althaus, *Theology of Martin Luther,* p. 345.
[38]Ibid., p. 356.
[39]Oberman, *Luther,* p. 227.
[40]Luther, "Concerning Rebaptism," p. 353.
[41]Althaus, *Theology of Martin Luther,* p. 399.

[42]Oberman, *Luther,* p. 244.
[43]Ibid., p. 237.
[44]Martin Luther, "The Sacrament of the Body and Blood—Against the Fanatics," in *Martin Luther's Basic Theological Writings,* p. 321.

**Chapter 25: Zwingli & Calvin Organize Protestant Thought**

[1]Paying money to a prince or bishop to gain a ministerial position—technically known as "simony"—was a common practice in Europe before and during Zwingli's lifetime. It was abolished by both Catholics and Protestants during the reformations of the sixteenth century.
[2]Ulrich Gäbler, *Huldrych Zwingli: His Life and Work,* trans. Ruth C. L. Gritsch (Philadelphia: Fortress, 1986), p. 40.
[3]Ulrich Zwingli, *Commentary on True and False Religion,* eds. Samuel Macauley Jackson and Clarence Nevin Heller (Durham, N.C.: Labyrinth, 1981).
[4]See Jacques Courvoisier, *Zwingli: A Reformed Theologian* (Richmond, Va.: John Knox Press, 1963), pp. 27-37.
[5]Ulrich Zwingli, "On the Providence of God" in *On Providence and Other Essays,* eds. Samuel Jackson and William John Hinke (Durham, N.C.: Labyrinth, 1983), p. 130.
[6]Ibid., p. 134.
[7]Ibid., p. 137.
[8]Ibid., p. 157.
[9]Gäbler, *Huldrych Zwingli,* pp. 146-47.
[10]Ibid., pp. 138.
[11]Zwingli, "On the Providence of God," p. 227.
[12]Ibid., pp. 186-87.
[13]Ibid., p. 182.
[14]Ibid., p. 183.
[15]Ulrich Zwingli, quoted in Courvoisier, *Zwingli,* p. 64.
[16]Ulrich Zwingli, "A Short and Clear Exposition of the Christian Faith," *On Providence and Other Essays,* p. 240.
[17]Gäbler, *Huldrych Zwingli,* p. 145.
[18]Ulrich Zwingli, "An Account of the Faith of Zwingli," *On Providence and Other Essays,* pp. 47-48.
[19]Ibid., pp. 42-43.
[20]For material from Zwingli, see Zwingli, "A Short and Clear Exposition of the Christian Faith," *On Providence and Other Essays,* pp. 248-50.
[21]Ibid., p. 252.
[22]Courvoisier, *Zwingli,* p. 75.
[23]T. H. L. Parker, *John Calvin: A Biography* (Philadelphia: Westminster Press, 1975), p. 50.
[24]Ibid., p. 53.
[25]John Calvin *Institutes of the Christian Religion* 1.16.9 Battles.
[26]Ibid.
[27]Ibid., 3.23.8.
[28]Timothy George, *Theology of the Reformers* (Nashville: Broadman, 1988), p. 232.
[29]Calvin *Institutes* 3.24.17.
[30]Ibid.
[31]Ibid., 3.23.10.
[32]Ibid., 4.17.12.
[33]Ibid., 4.17.10.
[34]Ibid., 4.17.33.

**Chapter 26: Anabaptists Go Back to the Roots of Christianity**

[1]This delineation of the two types of sixteenth-century Protestant Reformers is drawn loosely

from George H. Williams, *The Radical Reformation* (Philadelphia: Westminster Press, 1962), pp. xxiii-xxxi.

[2]Most of the historical material about the Anabaptist movement comes from William R. Estep, *The Anabaptist Story* (Grand Rapids, Mich.: Eerdmans, 1963).

[3]Ibid., p. 11.

[4]Ibid., p. 15.

[5]Ibid., p. 11.

[6]A fascinating study of the magisterial Reformers' views of the Anabaptists is Leonard Verduin, *The Reformers and Their Stepchildren* (Grand Rapids, Mich.: Eerdmans, 1964). Verduin demonstrates quite convincingly that the magisterial Reformers (Luther, Zwingli, Calvin, et al.) and the civil rulers (magistrates) of mainline sixteenth-century Protestantism failed to understand the radical Reformers and attacked them quite unfairly. For the most part they were neither revolutionaries nor heretics and there was sufficient evidence at the time to know this. Verduin's volume is a strong indictment of those magisterial Protestant Reformers for their willful ignorance and malicious mistreatment of their religious "stepchildren," the Anabaptists.

[7]Ibid., p. 63.

[8]Balthasar Hubmaier, "On Heretics and Those Who Burn Them," in *Balthasar Hubmaier: Theologian of Anabaptism,* ed. H. Wayne Pipkin and John H. Yoder (Scottdale, Penn.: Herald Press, 1989), p. 62.

[9]Balthasar Hubmaier, "Dialogue with Zwingli's Baptism Book," in *Balthasar Hubmaier: Theologian of Anabaptism,* p. 175.

[10]The description of Hubmaier's view of Christian initiation is taken largely from the last chapter of "On the Christian Baptism of Believers," titled "The Order of Christian Justification," pp. 143-49.

[11]Hubmaier, "On the Christian Baptism of Believers," p. 117.

[12]Ibid., p. 98.

[13]Ibid., p. 146.

[14]Balthasar Hubmaier, "A Christian Catechism," in *Balthasar Hubmaier: Theologian of Anabaptism,* p. 349.

[15]Balthasar Hubmaier, "Freedom of the Will 1," in *Balthasar Hubmaier: Theologian of Anabaptism,* p. 440.

[16]Balthasar Hubmaier, "Freedom of the Will 2," in *Balthasar Hubmaier: Theologian of Anabaptism,* p. 454.

[17]Ibid., p. 477.

[18]Ibid., pp. 465-66.

[19]Timothy George, *Theology of the Reformers* (Nashville: Broadman, 1988), p. 255.

[20]Menno Simons, quoted in ibid., p. 261.

[21]George, *Theology of the Reformers,* p. 263.

[22]Menno Simons, "Foundation of Christian Doctrine," *The Complete Writings of Menno Simons,* ed. J. C. Wenger, trans. Leonard Verduin (Scottdale, Penn.: Herald, 1956), p. 131.

[23]Ibid., p. 112.

[24]Ibid., pp. 133-34.

[25]George, *Theology of the Reformers,* p. 269.

[26]Menno Simons, "Foundation of Christian Doctrine," p. 175.

[27]Ibid., p. 200.

[28]For Menno's own words, see his "The Incarnation of Our Lord" in *Complete Writings,* pp. 783-834. For discussion, see George, *Theology of the Reformers,* pp. 280-85.

[29]George, *Theology of the Reformers,* p. 284.

**Chapter 27: Rome & Canterbury Go Separate but Parallel Ways**

[1]I thank my colleague Cornelis (Neil) Lettinga for the labels "prayer-book men" and "hot

gospelers" and for the information and insights offered in his Johns Hopkins University doctoral dissertation, "Covenant Theology and the Transformation of Anglicanism" (1987).

[2]Lionel S. Thornton, *Richard Hooker: A Study of His Theology* (London: SPCK, 1924), p. 7. The "Temple" was a prestigious church on the Thames River in the center of London. It was built by the crusading order the Knights Templar in the twelfth century. Two excellent books on this "odd couple" of the London Temple are S. J. Knox, *Walter Travers: Paragon of Elizabethan Puritanism* (London: Methuen, 1962); and Nigel Atkinson, *Richard Hooker and the Authority of Scripture, Tradition and Reason: Reformed Theologian of the Church of England?* (Carlisle, Cumbria, U.K.: Paternoster, 1997).

[3]Much progress toward mutual understanding and acceptance between Catholics and Protestants took place at the Second Vatican Council, the twenty-first ecumenical council of the Catholic Church, in the early 1960s. Throughout the 1970s and 1980s and into the last decade of the twentieth century Catholic and Protestant theologians engaged in vigorous and fruitful ecumenical dialogues. The Roman Catholic hierarchy has not officially lifted Trent's anathemas against Luther and his followers as of the writing of this volume, but for many Catholics they are little more than relics of a polemical era long past. Many Catholic and Protestant thinkers and leaders agree to ignore them.

[4]British historical theologian Philip Edgcumbe Hughes has made the case for the authentically Protestant flavor of the English (including Anglican) Reformation quite successfully in *Theology of the English Reformers* (Grand Rapids, Mich.: Eerdmans, 1965).

[5]G. W. Bromiley, *Thomas Cranmer Theologian* (New York: Oxford University Press, 1956), p. 98.

[6]Ibid., p. 9.

[7]Thomas Cranmer, quoted in Hughes, *Theology of the English Reformers,* p. 16.

[8]Ibid., p. 20.

[9]Bromiley, *Thomas Cranmer Theologian,* p. 25.

[10]Philip Edgcumbe Hughes, *Faith and Works: Cranmer and Hooker on Justification* (Wilton, Conn.: Morehouse-Barlow, 1982), p. 33.

[11]Thomas Cranmer, "A Homily of the Salvation of Mankind by Only Christ Our Savior from Sin and Death Everlasting," in Hughes, *Faith and Works,* p. 51.

[12]Ibid., p. 57.

[13]An excellent treatment of the English Protestant-Anglican doctrine of ministry (including Cranmer's) may be found in Hughes, *Theology of the English Reformers,* pp. 162-88.

[14]Ibid., p. 164.

[15]Justo González, *A History of Christian Thought,* vol. 3, *From the Protestant Reformation to the Twentieth Century,* rev. ed. (Nashville, Tenn.: Abingdon Press, 1987), p. 194.

[16]For a discussion of Hooker's mentality and general approach to metaphysics, see Thornton, *Richard Hooker,* pp. 25-40, especially chapter 3. For discussion of his view of Scripture and other authorities, see chapter 4 of the same book (pp. 41-53). Thornton, a twentieth-century Anglican, is perhaps overly sympathetic to Hooker and too critical of his Puritan opponents, but his insights into the mind of the Master of the Temple and author of *Laws of Ecclesiastical Polity* are unsurpassed in modern literature.

[17]Ibid., p. 36.

[18]Ibid., p. 50.

[19]Richard Hooker, "A Learned Discourse of Justification, Works and How the Foundation of Faith is Overthrown" in Hughes, *Faith and Works,* pp. 61-109.

[20]Thornton, *Richard Hooker,* p. 68.

[21]Ibid., p. 96.

[22]Ibid., p. 92.

[23]Ibid., pp. 74, 77.

[24]John H. Leith, ed., *Creeds of the Churches,* rev. ed. (Richmond, Va.: John Knox Press, 1973),

pp. 266-81.
[25]González, *History of Christian Thought,* 3:195.
[26]Henri Daniel-Rops, *The Catholic Reformation,* trans. John Warrington (New York: E. P. Dutton, 1962), p. 94.
[27]Ibid.
[28]Ibid., p. 99.
[29]Ibid., p. 95 n. 1.
[30]*The Church Teaches: Documents of the Church in English Translation,* trans. John F. Clarkson, S.J., et al. (St. Louis, Mo.: Herder, 1961), p. 45.
[31]Ibid., pp. 231-32.
[32]Ibid., p. 233.
[33]Ibid., p. 234.
[34]Ibid., p. 243.
[35]Ibid.
[36]Ibid., p. 246.
[37]Ibid., pp. 330-31.

**Chapter 28: Arminians Attempt to Reform Reformed Theology**

[1]Most of the biographical information about Jacob Arminius is taken from Carl Bangs, *Arminius: A Study in the Dutch Reformation* (Grand Rapids, Mich.: Zondervan, 1985).
[2]Charles M. Cameron, "Arminius—Hero or Heretic?" *Evangelical Quarterly* 64, no. 3 (1992): 213.
[3]Richard A. Muller, *God, Creation and Providence in the Thought of Jacob Arminius* (Grand Rapids, Mich.: Baker, 1991), p. 269.
[4]Ibid., p. 3.
[5]Ibid., p. ix.
[6]Ibid., p. 31.
[7]Ibid., p. 32.
[8]Robert Schnucker, "Theodore Beza," in *The New International Dictionary of the Christian Church,* ed. J. D. Douglas (Grand Rapids, Mich.: Zondervan, 1974), p. 126.
[9]Justo González, *A History of Christian Thought,* vol. 3, *From the Protestant Reformation to the Twentieth Century,* rev. ed. (Nashville: Abingdon, 1987), pp. 270-78.
[10]Bangs, *Arminius,* p. 96.
[11]Ibid., p. 19.
[12]Ibid., p. 144.
[13]Ibid., p. 195.
[14]Ibid., p. 248.
[15]Ibid., p. 282.
[16]Ibid., p. 331.
[17]W. Harrison, *Arminianism* (London: Duckworth, 1937), p. 84.
[18]Ibid., pp. 81-82.
[19]All quotations from Arminius's treatises will be from *The Works of James Arminius,* London Edition, trans. James Nichols and William Nichols (Grand Rapids, Mich.: Baker, 1986).
[20]Arminius, "Certain Articles to be Diligently Examined and Weighed," *Works of James Arminius,* 2:706.
[21]Alan P. F. Sell, *The Great Debate: Calvinism, Arminianism and Salvation* (Grand Rapids, Mich.: Baker, 1983), p. 12.
[22]Arminius, "A Declaration of the Sentiments of Arminius," in *Works of James Arminius,* 1:695.
[23]Ibid., p. 700.
[24]Ibid., p. 614.
[25]Ibid., p. 630.

[26]Ibid., pp. 650-51.
[27]Ibid., p. 313.
[28]Ibid., pp. 653-54.
[29]Arminius, "Certain Articles to be Diligently Examined and Weighed," 2:716.
[30]Arminius, "Examination of Dr. Perkins's Pamphlet," in *Works of James Arminius,* 3:284. Muller rightly makes much of Arminius's belief in divine self-limitation within the covenant as a basic difference between him and Reformed theologians of his day. See Muller, *God, Creation and Providence,* pp. 235-45.
[31]Skevington Wood, "The Declaration of Sentiments: The Theological Testament of Arminius," *Evangelical Quarterly* 65, no. 2 (1993): 219.
[32]Arminius, "A Declaration of Sentiments," 1:279.
[33]Arminius, "A Letter Addressed to Hippolytus A Collibus," in *Works of James Arminius,* 2:701.
[34]Ibid., pp. 700-701.
[35]See Muller, *God, Creation and Providence,* p. 281.
[36]Bangs, *Arminius,* pp. 348-49.

**Chapter 29: Pietists Seek to Renew Lutheran Theology**
[1]Ernest Stoeffler, *The Rise of Evangelical Pietism* (Leiden: Brill, 1971), p.1.
[2]Dale W. Brown, *Understanding Pietism* (Grand Rapids, Mich.: Eerdmans, 1978), p. 7.
[3]Ibid., p. 83.
[4]Stoeffler, *Rise of Evangelical Pietism,* p. 13.
[5]Ted A. Campbell, *The Religion of the Heart: A Study of European Religious Life in the Seventeenth and Eighteenth Centuries* (Columbia: University of South Carolina Press, 1991), p. 71.
[6]Justo González, *A History of Christian Thought,* vol. 3, *From the Protestant Reformation to the Twentieth Century,* rev. ed. (Nashville: Abingdon, 1987), p. 300.
[7]James Stein, *Philipp Jakob Spener: Pietist Patriarch* (Chicago: Covenant Press, 1986), p. 21.
[8]Stoeffler, *Rise of Evangelical Pietism,* pp. 17-18.
[9]Philipp Spener, quoted in Brown, *Understanding Pietism,* p. 85.
[10]Johann Arndt, *True Christianity* in *Pietism,* Christian Classics, ed. Thomas Halbrooks (Nashville: Broadman, 1981), p. 165.
[11]Ibid., p. 166.
[12]Stoeffler, *Rise of Evangelical Pietism,* p. 211.
[13]Campbell, *Religion of the Heart,* p. 79.
[14]The information about Spener's life here is largely derived from the biography by Stein, *Philipp Jakob Spener,* p. 21.
[15]Philip Jacob Spener, *Pia Desideria,* trans. Theodore G. Tappert (Philadelphia: Fortress, 1964), pp. 36-37.
[16]Ibid., p. 67.
[17]Ibid., p. 108.
[18]Ibid., pp. 116-17.
[19]Campbell, *Religion of the Heart,* p. 86.
[20]The main modern English-language biography of Francke is Gary R. Sattler, *God's Glory, Neighbor's Good* (Chicago: Covenant Press, 1982).
[21]Ernest Stoeffler, *German Pietism During the Eighteenth Century* (Leiden: Brill, 1973), p. 4.
[22]August Hermann Francke, "From the *Autobiography,*" in *Pietists: Selected Writings,* The Classics of Western Spirituality, ed. Peter C. Erb (New York: Paulist, 1983), p. 105.
[23]Stoeffler, *German Pietism,* p. 31.
[24]George W. Forell, introduction to Nikolaus Ludwig von Zinzendorf, *Nine Public Lectures on Important Subjects,* trans. and ed. George W. Forell (Iowa City: University of Iowa Press, 1973), p. vii.
[25]Stoeffler, *German Pietism,* p. 141.

[26]Count Zinzendorf, quoted in Stoeffler, *German Pietism,* p. 143.
[27]Stoeffler, *German Pietism,* p. 144.
[28]Zinzendorf, *Nine Public Lectures,* p. 31.
[29]Ibid., pp. 50-51.
[30]Brown, *Understanding Pietism,* pp. 48-50.
[31]Ibid., p. 50.
[32]Two Baptist denominations in North America are rooted in German and Scandinavian pietism rather than in English Puritan Congregationalism. They are the Baptist General Conference (Swedish) and the North American Baptist Convention (German). The Evangelical Free Church of America and the Evangelical Covenant Church of America are both rooted in Scandinavian pietism and originally gave parents choice between infant baptism and believers' baptism after conversion.
[33]Stoeffler, *Rise of Evangelical Pietism,* p. 242.
[34]Brown, *Understanding Pietism,* p. 43.
[35]Stoeffler, *German Pietism,* p. 19.
[36]Ibid., p. 21.
[37]Ibid., p. 153.
[38]August Hermann Francke, *On Christian Perfection,* in *Pietists: Selected Writings,* p. 114.
[39]Ibid., p. 115.
[40]See the transcript of the Wesley-Zinzendorf debate in Forell's introduction to Zinzendorf, *Nine Public Lectures,* pp. xvii-xix.
[41]Stoeffler, *German Pietism,* p. 7.

**Chapter 30: Puritans & Methodists Struggle to Revive English Theology**

[1]Wheaton College professor Leland Ryken's book *Worldly Saints: The Puritans As They Really Were* (Grand Rapids, Mich.: Academie/Zondervan, 1986) should be made required reading for every school teacher and journalist who speaks or writes about the Puritans. It corrects many of the misconceptions and distorted images of the Puritans and the Puritan movement that plague almost all popular, nonscholarly treatments of them.
[2]Edmund S. Morgan, *Visible Saints: The History of a Puritan Idea* (New York: New York University Press, 1963), p. 82.
[3]Ibid., p. 128.
[4]John von Rohr, *The Covenant of Grace in Puritan Thought* (Atlanta: Scholars Press, 1986), p. 8.
[5]Ibid., p. 10.
[6]Ibid., p. 15.
[7]John E. Smith, *Jonathan Edwards: Puritan, Preacher, Philosopher* (Notre Dame: Notre Dame University Press, 1992), p. 1.
[8]Robert W. Jenson, *America's Theologian: A Recommendation of Jonathan Edwards* (New York: Oxford University Press, 1988).
[9]Among many other contemporary evangelical scholars, Wheaton College professor Mark Noll points back to Jonathan Edwards as this kind of landmark in his book *The Scandal of the Evangelical Mind* (Grand Rapids, Mich.: Eerdmans, 1994).
[10]Jonathan Edwards, "Dissertation Concerning the End for Which God Created the World" in *Jonathan Edwards: Representative Selections,* rev. ed., ed. Clarence H. Faust and Thomas H. Johnson (New York: Hill and Wang, 1962), p. 340.
[11]Jonathan Edwards, "Doctrine of Original Sin," in *Jonathan Edwards: Representative Selections,* p. 334.
[12]Smith, *Jonathan Edwards,* p. 60.
[13]Jonathan Edwards, "Freedom of the Will," in *Jonathan Edwards: Representative Selections,* p. 286.

[14]Edwards, "Doctrine of Original Sin," p. 338.
[15]Edwards, "Religious Affections," in *Jonathan Edwards: Representative Selections,* p. 209.
[16]Alan P. F. Sell, *The Great Debate: Calvinism, Arminianism and Salvation* (Grand Rapids, Mich.: Baker, 1983), p. 6.
[17]A fascinating biography of Wesley written in the form of an autobiography is Robert G. Tuttle Jr., *John Wesley: His Life and Theology* (Grand Rapids, Mich.: Zondervan, 1978). A more detailed historical treatment of the Methodist movement in England during the eighteenth century, including Wesley's life and thought, is Henry D. Rack, *Reasonable Enthusiast: John Wesley and the Rise of Methodism,* 2d ed. (Nashville: Abingdon, 1992).
[18]The exact number of children in the family varies according to different sources. Apparently a total of nineteen children were born to Samuel and Susanna Wesley, but only ten survived to adulthood. Most historians settle on sixteen as the number of siblings, including John. Some of them died as children. Apparently three were either stillborn or died shortly after birth and are not counted as among John's siblings.
[19]From Wesley's *Journal* as quoted in Tuttle, *John Wesley,* p. 195.
[20]See quotes and commentary in Thomas C. Oden, *John Wesley's Scriptural Christianity: A Plain Exposition of His Teaching on Christian Doctrine* (Grand Rapids, Mich.: Zondervan, 1994), pp. 258-59.
[21]Just when evangelical Christians in Britain and North America think the great theological debate among them over monergism and synergism is passé, it breaks out again. As this book is being written, the old controversy between evangelical Arminians like Wesley and evangelical Calvinists like Edwards and Whitefield is threatening to break out anew as evidenced in the formation of Reformed renewal movements such as Christians United for Reformation (C.U.R.E.) and the Alliance of Confessing Evangelicals. Both groups of evangelical theologians, pastors and evangelists see Arminian theology as a bane on evangelicalism's existence and seek to elevate monergism in the Augustinian-Calvinist-Puritan tradition as the norm for evangelical orthodoxy.
[22]One of the best recent expositions and interpretations of the Wesleyan quadrilateral is Donald A. Thorsen, *The Wesleyan Quadrilateral: Scripture, Tradition, Reason and Experience as a Model of Evangelical Theology* (Grand Rapids, Mich.: Zondervan, 1990).
[23]Oden, *John Wesley's Scriptural Christianity,* p. 56.
[24]For an excellent summary and critical interpretation of Wesley's soteriology, see Kenneth J. Collins, *The Scripture Way of Salvation: The Heart of John Wesley's Theology* (Nashville: Abingdon, 1997), especially chapter 4: "Regeneration by Grace Through Faith," pp. 101-30.
[25]John Wesley, *A Plain Account of Christian Perfection* (London: Epworth, 1952), pp. 112-13.
[26]John Wesley, quoted from "Remarks on a Defence of Aspasio Vindicated" in Collins, *The Scripture Way of Salvation,* p. 95. Collins's entire chapter 3, "Justification by Grace Through Faith" (pp. 69-100), constitutes a convincing argument that Wesley never varied or wavered on this matter from shortly after his "conversion" to his death.

**Chapter 31: Deists Try to Transform Protestant Theology**

[1]G. Hefelbower, *The Relation of John Locke to English Deism* (Chicago: University of Chicago Press, 1918), p. 117.
[2]James M. Byrne, *Religion and the Enlightenment: From Descartes to Kant* (Louisville, Ky.: Westminster John Knox, 1996), pp. 5-10.
[3]Peter Gay refers to Lord Herbert as "the father of deism" and a "precursor of deism" in his introductory notes to the reading selection from Lord Herbert's *De veritate,* in *Deism: An Anthology* (Princeton, N.J.: Van Nostrand, 1968), p. 29. Gay also expresses something of the ambiguous status of Locke in relation to deism in his general introduction to the anthology where he writes that Locke helped to make deism inevitable even though he was not himself a deist (p. 26).
[4]From Lord Herbert, *De veritate,* in Gay, *Deism: An Anthology,* pp. 32-38.

[5]Ibid., p. 40.

[6]Ibid., p. 31.

[7]Byrne, *Religion and the Enlightenment,* p. 105.

[8]The precise relationship of Locke to Deism is and has been a matter of much debate in the history of modern philosophy and theology. I believe that the matter was virtually settled in 1918 by S. G. Hefelbower, *The Relation of John Locke to English Deism.* There the author surveys a variety of options for describing that relationship and ends up demonstrating quite convincingly that "Locke and English Deism are related as co-ordinate parts of the larger progressive movement of the age" (p. v.) and that while Locke clearly influenced and even made possible the rise of deism, he was unsympathetic with its more radical conclusions.

[9]Hefelbower, *Relation of John Locke to English Deism,* p. 100.

[10]I. T. Ramsey, editor's introduction to John Locke, *The Reasonableness of Christianity, with "A Discourse of Miracles" and part of "A Third Letter Concerning Toleration,"* ed. I. T. Ramsey (London: Black, 1958), p. 8.

[11]Locke, *A Discourse of Miracles,* p. 84.

[12]Byrne, *Religion and the Enlightenment,* p. 107.

[13]Ibid., p. 108.

[14]John Toland, *Christianity Not Mysterious,* in Gay, *Deism, An Anthology,* p. 61.

[15]For discussion of Toland's views on Christian dogmas such as the Trinity and two natures of Christ, see Robert E. Sullivan, "The Task of Criticism," chap. 4 in *John Toland and the Deist Controversy: A Study in Adaptations* (Cambridge, Mass.: Harvard University Press, 1982), pp. 109-40.

[16]Ibid., pp. 121ff.

[17]Byrne, *Religion and the Enlightenment,* p. 109.

[18]Ernest Campbell Mossner, *Bishop Butler and the Age of Reason: A Study in the History of Thought* (New York: Macmillan, 1936), p. 75.

[19]Ibid., p. 77.

[20]Hefelbower, *Relation of John Locke to English Deism,* pp. 138-39.

[21]I. T. Ramsey, editor's introduction to John Locke, *The Reasonableness of Christianity,* p. 19.

[22]Procrustes was the evil innkeeper of ancient Greek legend who crept into guests' rooms at night and forced their bodies to fit his beds by amputation or stretching. "Procrustes bed" is a metaphor for a system of thought used as an implicit and presupposed standard that everything else must fit. A "Procrustean distortion" is the process of forcing a positive religion or philosophy to fit another scheme of thought such as natural religion by distorting it out of all recognition.

[23]For more discussion of the point made in this paragraph, see the excellent book on the biblical concept of God and how it has been subverted in much Christian doctrine by Greek as well as modern categories of thought written by South African Reformed theologian Adriö König, *Here Am I: A Believer's Reflections on God* (Grand Rapids, Mich.: Eerdmans, 1982).

[24]Jimmy Carter and Michael Dukakis respectively.

**Introduction to Part IX: The Overall Plot Divides: *Liberals & Conservatives Respond to Modernity.***

[1]Henry Churchill King, *Reconstruction in Theology* (New York: Hodder & Stoughton, 1901).

[2]Adolf von Harnack, *What Is Christianity?* (New York: Putnam's, 1901).

[3]J. Gresham Machen, *Christianity and Liberalism* (Grand Rapids, Mich.: Eerdmans, 1985).

[4]H. Richard Niebuhr, *The Kingdom of God in America* (New York: Harper & Row, 1959), p. 193.

**Chapter 32: Liberal Theology Accommodates to Modern Culture**

[1]The phrase "maximal acknowledgment of the claims of modernity" was coined by Claude Welch, *Protestant Theology in the Nineteenth Century,* vol. 1, *1799-1870* (New Haven, Conn.: Yale

University Press, 1972), p. 142. Many books by liberal and conservative theologians have attempted to dissect the movement and discern its core or essence. Three that focus on liberal Protestant theology in North America and that have especially influenced this writer's interpretation of that movement are Kenneth Cauthen, *The Impact of American Religious Liberalism*, 2d ed. (Lanham, Md.: University Press of America, 1983); William R. Hutchison, *The Modernist Impulse in American Protestantism* (Oxford: Oxford University Press, 1982); and Donald E. Miller, *The Case for Liberal Christianity* (San Francisco: Harper & Row, 1981).

[2]Welch, *Protestant Theology*, 1:142.

[3]Washington Gladden, *Present Day Theology*, 2d ed. (Columbus, Ohio: McClelland, 1913), pp. 3-4.

[4]Immanuel Kant, *Religion Within the Limits of Reason Alone*, trans. Theodore M. Greene and Hoyt H. Hudson (New York: Harper Torchbooks, 1960).

[5]W. F. Hegel, *Lectures on the Philosophy of Religion*, ed. E. B. Speirs, trans. E. B. Speirs and J. Burden Sanderson, (New York: Humanities Press, 1962).

[6]Terrence N. Tice, introduction to Friedrich Schleiermacher, *On Religion: Addresses in Response to Its Cultured Critics*, trans. Terrence N. Tice (Richmond, Va.: John Knox Press, 1969), p. 12.

[7]Keith W. Clements, *Friedrich Schleiermacher: Pioneer of Modern Theology* (London: Collins, 1987), p. 7.

[8]Friedrich Schleiermacher, *The Christian Faith*, ed. H. R. Mackintosh and J. S. Stewart, 2d ed. (Philadelphia: Fortress, 1928), p. 76.

[9]Ibid., p. 194.

[10]Ibid., p. 183.

[11]Ibid., p. 367.

[12]Ibid., p. 385.

[13]R. Mackintosh, introduction to Albrecht Ritschl, *The Christian Doctrine of Justification and Reconciliation*, trans. H. R. Mackintosh and A. B. Macaulay (Edinburgh, U.K.: Clark, 1900), p. v.

[14]Ritschl, *Christian Doctrine of Justification*, pp. 334-35.

[15]These principles may be found stated in Adolf von Harnack, *What Is Christianity?* (New York: Putnam's, 1901), p. 55, and interpreted on following pages.

[16]The German division of Rochester Theological Seminary was a semi-autonomous department of that Baptist divinity school that separated and moved to Sioux Falls, South Dakota, in the 1940s. It is now known as North American Baptist Seminary and claims Rauschenbusch as its own.

[17]Walter Rauschenbusch, *A Theology for the Social Gospel* (New York: Macmillan, 1918), p. 117.

**Chapter 33: Conservative Theology Hardens Traditional Categories**

[1]Abraham Kuyper, quoted in Alan P. R. Sell, *Theology in Turmoil: The Roots, Course and Significance of the Conservative-Liberal Debate in Modern Theology* (Grand Rapids, Mich.: Baker, 1986), p. 108.

[2]A major scholarly study of fundamentalism that focuses on its sociological aspects and tends to use the label very broadly is the series of five volumes by Martin E. Marty and R. Scott Appleby, ed., *The Fundamentalism Project* (Chicago: University of Chicago Press, 1991-1995).

[3]The most accurate and insightful scholarly accounts of Protestant fundamentalism are those written by historian George Marsden. See his two excellent volumes: *Fundamentalism and American Culture: The Shaping of Twentieth-Century Evangelicalism, 1870-1925* (New York: Oxford University Press, 1980); and *Understanding Fundamentalism and Evangelicalism* (Grand Rapids, Mich.: Eerdmans, 1991).

[4]George W. Dollar, *A History of Fundamentalism in America* (Greenville, S.C.: Bob Jones University Press, 1973), n.p.

[5]Justo González, *A History of Christian Thought*, vol. 3, *From the Protestant Reformation to the*

*Twentieth Century,* rev. ed. (Nashville: Abingdon, 1987), p. 276.

[6]Ibid., p. 278.

[7]Francis Turretin, *The Doctrine of Scripture: Locus 2 of "Institutio theologiae elencticae,"* ed. and trans. John W. Beardslee III (Grand Rapids, Mich.: Baker, 1981), pp. 135-46.

[8]For information about and readings from the four figures of the Princeton theology dynasty, see the excellent compilation Mark A. Noll, ed., *The Princeton Theology 1812-1921: Scripture, Science and Theological Method from Archibald Alexander to Benjamin Breckinridge Warfield* (Grand Rapids, Mich.: Baker, 1983).

[9]James H. Smylie, "Defining Orthodoxy: Charles Hodge (1797-1878)" in *Makers of Christian Theology in America,* eds. Mark G. Toulouse and James O. Duke (Nashville: Abingdon, 1997), p. 154.

[10]Charles Hodge, *Systematic Theology,* 3 vols. (Grand Rapids, Mich.: Eerdmans, 1973), 1:10.

[11]Ibid., 1:170.

[12]Ibid.

[13]Ibid., 1:179.

[14]Benjamin Breckinridge Warfield, *The Inspiration and Authority of the Bible,* ed. Samuel G. Craig (Philadelphia: Presbyterian & Reformed, 1948), p. 181.

[15]See selections on "Science" from both Hodges and Warfield in Noll, *The Princeton Theology,* pp. 135-52; 233-37; 289-98.

[16]*The Fundamentals: A Testimony to the Truth,* vol. 1 (Chicago: Testimony, 1910).

[17]J. Gresham Machen, *Christianity and Liberalism* (Grand Rapids, Mich.: Eerdmans, 1985).

[18]Ibid., p. 8.

[19]A fascinating account of Machen's relationship with fundamentalism is contained in D. G. Hart, *Defending the Faith: J. Gresham Machen and the Crisis of Conservative Protestantism in Modern America* (Baltimore: Johns Hopkins University Press, 1994). Hart points out the ironies of that relationship.

[20]People who know of the Scopes trial only through the play (or the movies) *Inherit the Wind* know little about it. The true story is told in any historical book about the trial, and many have been written. An excellent collection of scholarly historical treatments of the event is contained in chapter six of Willard B. Gatewood Jr., ed., *Controversy in the Twenties: Fundamentalism, Modernism and Evolution* (Nashville: Vanderbilt University Press, 1969), pp. 331-67. While it is true that the trial represented a defeat for fundamentalism in the court of public opinion, that was in part because of H. L. Mencken's biased reporting, which has sadly become the basis of much misrepresentation of Bryan and other opponents of evolution.

[21]See Billy Graham, *Just As I Am: The Autobiography of Billy Graham* (New York: HarperCollins, 1997). On pages 302-3 the evangelist describes his early associations with Bob Jones, John R. Rice and Carl McIntire and his own painful rejection by them.

[22]While liberal theologians and most secular religious scholars use the term *fundamentalism* to label *all* twentieth-century conservative Protestants—especially all who affirm the inerrancy of the Bible—many conservative Protestants in the United States and Great Britain insist on a distinction between those who are fundamentalists and those who are postfundamentalist evangelicals. The latter generally agree with early fundamentalism (Machen, *The Fundamentals*) on basic doctrines and the dangers of liberal theology while rejecting later, extreme fundamentalism's ethos of separationism and literalistic biblical hermeneutic. Excellent sources on this distinction are George Marsden, *Reforming Fundamentalism: Fuller Seminary and the New Evangelicalism* (Grand Rapids, Mich.: Eerdmans, 1987); and Joel Carpenter, *Revive Us Again: The Reawakening of American Fundamentalism* (New York: Oxford University Press, 1997).

[23]Jack Rogers and Donald McKim, *The Authority and Interpretation of the Bible: An Historical Approach* (San Francisco: Harper & Row, 1979).

[24]Machen, *Christianity and Liberalism,* p. 53.

[25]Dollar, *History of Fundamentalism,* p. 281.

[26]Mark Taylor Dalhouse, *Bob Jones University and the Shaping of Twentieth Century Separatism, 1926-1991* (Ph.D. dissertation, Miami University, 1991).

[27]Eight denominations are generally identified by sociologists of religion as constituting the Protestant "mainstream" in the United States: the Episcopal Church, the Presbyterian Church (U.S.A.), the Evangelical Lutheran Church in America, the United Methodist Church, the United Church of Christ, the American Baptist Churches/U.S.A., the Reformed Church in America, the Christian Church/Disciples of Christ. These eight denominations are most often identified as "mainstream" simply because of their social histories as influential religious organizations in United States political and economic life. For the most part the leadership of these denominations is dominated by forms of liberal, neo-liberal or neo-orthodox theology. Fundamentalists have by and large abandoned them and are now excluded from their core leadership.

[28]In 1959 Presbyterian publisher Westminster Press of Philadelphia published a three-volume set by three authors. Each volume was to present as succinctly as possible the basic ideas of one of these three main options in twentieth-century Protestant theology. The authors and volumes are L. Harold De Wolf, *The Case for Theology in Liberal Perspective,* Edward John Carnell, *The Case for Orthodox Theology;* and William Hordern, *The Case for a New Reformation Theology* (neo-orthodox). Ironically, Carnell's volume, which was supposed to present the case for conservative Protestant theology, set forth a case against fundamentalism that offended even some moderate evangelicals.

**Chapter 34: Neo-Orthodoxy Transcends the Divide**

[1]Cornelius Van Til, *The New Modernism* (Philipsburg, N.J.: Presbyterian & Reformed, 1946).

[2]Two influential conservative-evangelical theologians, sometimes considered moderate fundamentalists, who relentlessly blamed Karl Barth and neo-orthodoxy in general for all kinds of twentieth-century Protestant theological ills were Francis Schaeffer (1912-1984) and Carl F. H. Henry (b. 1913). As late as 1990 the latter, often considered the "dean of conservative evangelical theologians," blamed Barth for a pervasive irrationalism in contemporary theology and even linked him with the relativistic "deconstructionist" theology. See Carl F. H. Henry, *Toward a Recovery of Christian Belief* (Wheaton, Ill.: Crossway, 1990), pp. 32-39.

[3]Robert Bretall, ed., *A Kierkegaard Anthology* (Princeton, N.J.: Princeton University Press, 1951), p. 448.

[4]See Søren Kierkegaard, *Concluding Unscientific Postscript to the "Philosophical Fragments"* in *A Kierkegaard Anthology* (Princeton, N.J.: Princeton University Press, 1951), p. 215.

[5]Ibid., p. 215.

[6]Ibid., p. 215.

[7]Karl Barth, *The Epistle to the Romans,* trans. Edwyn C. Hoskyns (London: Oxford University Press, 1933), p. 1.

[8]Karl Barth, *The Word of God and the Word of Man,* trans. Douglas Horton (Boston: Pilgrim, 1928), p. 43.

[9]Karl Barth, *Church Dogmatics* I/1, *The Doctrine of the Word of God,* part 1, trans. G. W. Bromiley (Edinburgh, U.K.: T & T Clark, 1975), p. 222.

[10]Barth, *Church Dogmatics* II/2, *The Doctrine of God,* part 2, trans. G. W. Bromiley, et al. (Edinburgh, U.K.: T & T Clark, 1957), pp. 191-92.

[11]This explanation of Barth's view of divine revelation is based especially on Barth's first volume of *Church Dogmatics, The Doctrine of the Word of God,* part I/1.

[12]Ibid., p. 241.

[13]Ibid., p. 222.

[14]Barth's doctrine of God's being and attributes and his exposition of God as "He who loves in freedom" is found primarily in *Church Dogmatics* II/1, *The Doctrine of God,* part 1.

[15]Ibid., p. 260.

[16]Ibid., p. 281.
[17]Ibid., p. 280.
[18]This interpretation of Barth's doctrine of salvation is drawn mainly from *Church Dogmatics* II/2, *The Doctrine of God,* part 2.
[19]Ibid., p. 163.
[20]Ibid., p. 167.
[21]Ibid., p. 319.
[22]Ibid., p. 346.

**Chapter 35: Contemporary Theology Struggles with Diversity**

[1]See, for example, Stanley J. Grenz and Roger E. Olson, *20th-Century Theology: God and the World in a Transitional Age* (Downers Grove, Ill.: InterVarsity Press, 1992).
[2]This distinction and terminology are adopted and adapted from a discussion between two leading historians of the evangelical movement: George Marsden and Donald W. Dayton. Their articles and responses by a variety of evangelical thinkers may be found in *Christian Scholar's Review* 23, no. 1 (1993).
[3]At the time of this writing Bloesch's seven-volume systematic theology with the overarching title *Christian Foundations* is being published one volume at a time by InterVarsity Press. The first volume, containing Bloesch's theological method, is *A Theology of Word and Spirit: Authority and Method in Theology* (Downers Grove, Ill.: InterVarsity Press, 1992).
[4]The document "Evangelicals and Catholics Together" was first promulgated in 1994. An updated version may be found under the title "The Gift of Salvation" in *Christianity Today* (December 8, 1997), pp. 34-38. This version is signed by eighteen leading evangelical theologians and fifteen well-known Catholic theologians.
[5]Karl Rahner, *Hearers of the Word,* trans. Michael Richards (New York: Herder & Herder, 1969), p. 17.
[6]Karl Rahner, *The Trinity,* trans. Joseph Donceel (New York: Seabury Press, 1974), p. 22. The term "Rahner's Rule" was coined by Ted Peters, "Trinity Talk, part I," *Dialog* 26 (1987): 46.
[7]José Míguez Bonino, *Doing Theology in a Revolutionary Situation* (Philadelphia: Fortress, 1975), p. 81.
[8]James H. Cone, *Black Theology and Black Power* (New York: Seabury Press, 1969), p. 1.

## Name Index

## Subject Index